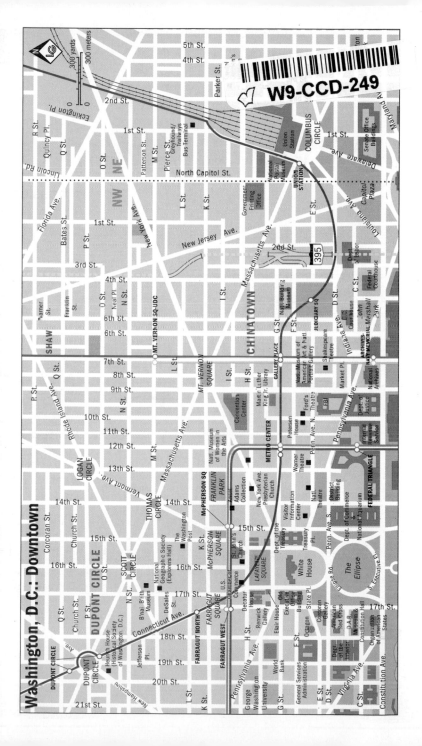
Washington, D.C.: Downtown

W9-CCD-249

300 yards
300 meters

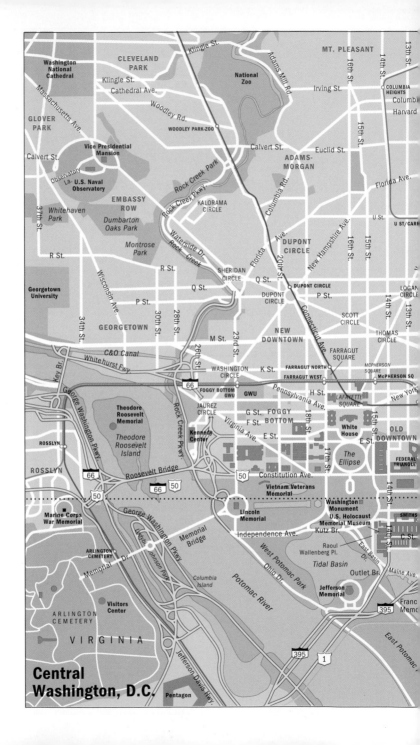

Central
Washington, D.C.

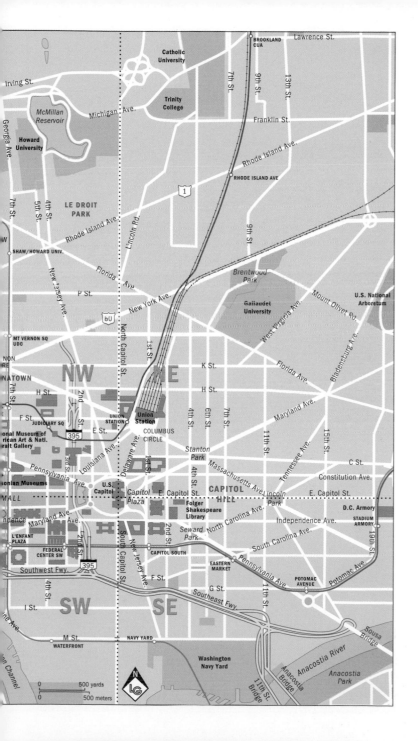

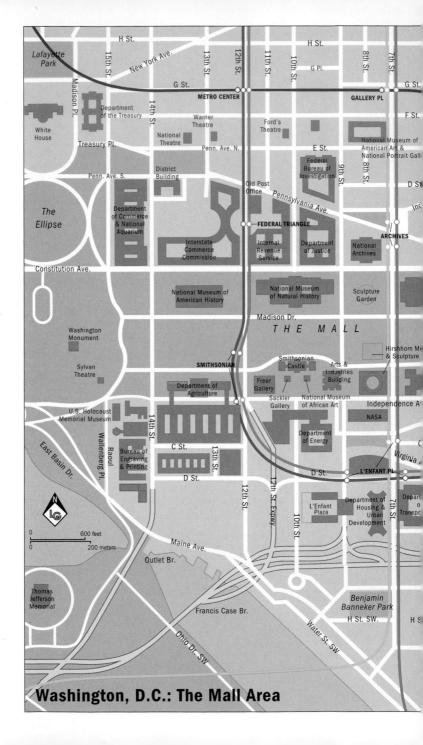

Washington, D.C.: The Mall Area

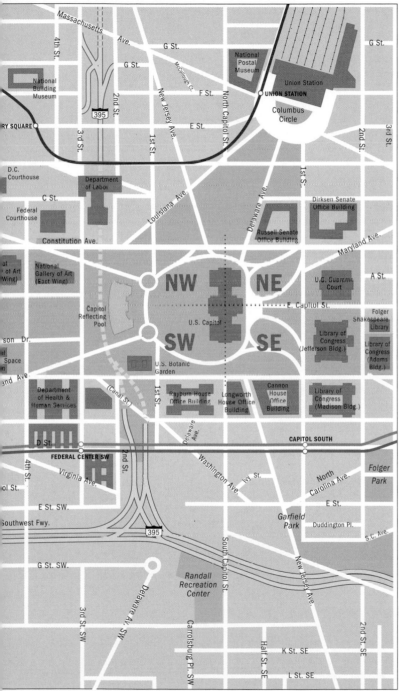

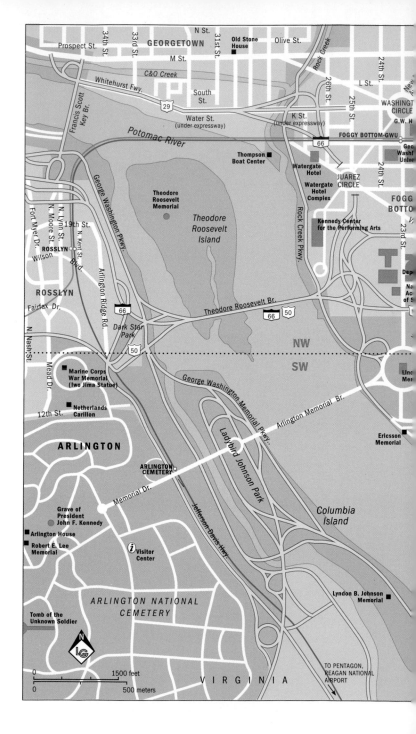

Washington, D.C.:
White House Area, Foggy Bottom, and Nearby Arlington

Washington, D.C. Metro

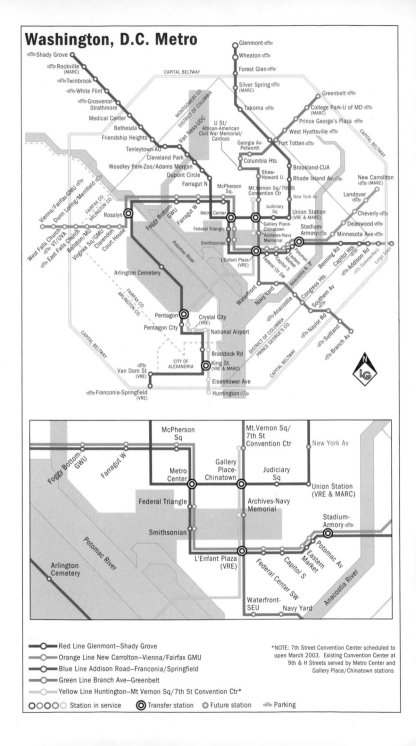

Red Line Glenmont–Shady Grove
Orange Line New Carrolton–Vienna/Fairfax GMU
Blue Line Addison Road–Franconia/Springfield
Green Line Branch Ave–Greenbelt
Yellow Line Huntington–Mt Vernon Sq/7th St Convention Ctr*

○○○○○ Station in service ◎ Transfer station ○ Future station 🚗 Parking

*NOTE: 7th Street Convention Center scheduled to open March 2003. Existing Convention Center at 9th & H Streets served by Metro Center and Gallery Place/Chinatown stations

LET'S GO

■ THE RESOURCE FOR THE INDEPENDENT TRAVELER

"The guides are aimed not only at young budget travelers but at the independent traveler; a sort of streetwise cookbook for traveling alone."

—*The New York Times*

"Unbeatable; good sight-seeing advice; up-to-date info on restaurants, hotels, and inns; a commitment to money-saving travel; and a wry style that brightens nearly every page."

—*The Washington Post*

"Lighthearted and sophisticated, informative and fun to read. [Let's Go] helps the novice traveler navigate like a knowledgeable old hand."

—*Atlanta Journal-Constitution*

"A world-wise traveling companion—always ready with friendly advice and helpful hints, all sprinkled with a bit of wit."

—*The Philadelphia Inquirer*

■ THE BEST TRAVEL BARGAINS IN YOUR PRICE RANGE

"All the dirt, dirt cheap."

—*People*

"Anything you need to know about budget traveling is detailed in this book."

—*The Chicago Sun-Times*

"Let's Go follows the creed that you don't have to toss your life's savings to the wind to travel—unless you want to."

—*The Salt Lake Tribune*

■ REAL ADVICE FOR REAL EXPERIENCES

"The writers seem to have experienced every rooster-packed bus and lunar-surfaced mattress about which they write."

—*The New York Times*

"A guide should tell you what to expect from a destination. Here Let's Go shines."

—*The Chicago Tribune*

"[Let's Go's] devoted updaters really walk the walk (and thumb the ride, and trek the trail). Learn how to fish, haggle, find work—anywhere."

—*Food & Wine*

LET'S GO PUBLICATIONS

TRAVEL GUIDES

Alaska 1st edition **NEW TITLE**
Australia 2004
Austria & Switzerland 2004
Brazil 1st edition **NEW TITLE**
Britain & Ireland 2004
California 2004
Central America 8th edition
Chile 1st edition
China 4th edition
Costa Rica 1st edition
Eastern Europe 2004
Egypt 2nd edition
Europe 2004
France 2004
Germany 2004
Greece 2004
Hawaii 2004
India & Nepal 8th edition
Ireland 2004
Israel 4th edition
Italy 2004
Japan 1st edition **NEW TITLE**
Mexico 20th edition
Middle East 4th edition
New Zealand 6th edition
Pacific Northwest 1st edition **NEW TITLE**
Peru, Ecuador & Bolivia 3rd edition
Puerto Rico 1st edition **NEW TITLE**
South Africa 5th edition
Southeast Asia 8th edition
Southwest USA 3rd edition
Spain & Portugal 2004
Thailand 1st edition
Turkey 5th edition
USA 2004
Western Europe 2004

CITY GUIDES

Amsterdam 3rd edition
Barcelona 3rd edition
Boston 4th edition
London 2004
New York City 2004
Paris 2004
Rome 12th edition
San Francisco 4th edition
Washington, D.C. 13th editi

MAP GUIDES

Amsterdam
Berlin
Boston
Chicago
Dublin
Florence
Hong Kong
London
Los Angeles
Madrid
New Orleans
New York City
Paris
Prague
Rome
San Francisco
Seattle
Sydney
Venice
Washington, D.C.

COMING SOON:
Road Trip USA

LET'S GO

WASHINGTON, D.C.

DUNIA DICKEY EDITOR
MEGAN MORAN-GATES ASSOCIATE EDITOR

RESEARCHER-WRITERS
DAVID DODMAN
JENNIFER JUE-STEUCK
BRADLEY OLSON

EVAN HUDSON MAP EDITOR
NITIN SHAH MANAGING EDITOR

ST. MARTIN'S PRESS ❧ NEW YORK

HELPING LET'S GO If you want to share your discoveries, suggestions, or corrections, please drop us a line. We read every piece of correspondence, whether a postcard, a 10-page email, or a coconut. **Address mail to:**

> Let's Go: Washington, D.C.
> 67 Mount Auburn Street
> Cambridge, MA 02138
> USA

Visit Let's Go at **http://www.letsgo.com,** or send email to:

> **feedback@letsgo.com**
> **Subject: "Let's Go: Washington, D.C."**

In addition to the invaluable travel advice our readers share with us, many are kind enough to offer their services as researchers or editors. Unfortunately, our charter enables us to employ only currently enrolled Harvard students.

Maps by David Lindroth copyright © 2004 by St. Martin's Press.

Distributed outside the USA and Canada by Macmillan.

Let's Go: Washington, D.C. Copyright © 2004 by Let's Go, Inc. All rights reserved. Printed in the United States of America. No part of this book may be used or reproduced in any manner whatsoever without written permission except in the case of brief quotations embodied in critical articles or reviews. Let's Go is available for purchase in bulk by institutions and authorized resellers. For information, address St. Martin's Press, 175 Fifth Avenue, New York, NY 10010, USA.

ISBN: 0-312-32001-9

First edition
10 9 8 7 6 5 4 3 2 1

Let's Go: Washington, D.C. is written by Let's Go Publications, 67 Mount Auburn Street, Cambridge, MA 02138, USA.

Let's Go® and the LG logo are trademarks of Let's Go, Inc.
Printed in the USA.

ADVERTISING DISCLAIMER All advertisements appearing in Let's Go publications are sold by an independent agency not affiliated with the editorial production of the guides. Advertisers are never given preferential treatment, and the guides are researched, written, and published independent of advertising. Advertisements do not imply endorsement of products or services by Let's Go, and Let's Go does not vouch for the accuracy of information provided in advertisements.
  If you are interested in purchasing advertising space in a Let's Go publication, contact: Let's Go Advertising Sales, 67 Mount Auburn St., Cambridge, MA 02138, USA.

HOW TO USE THIS BOOK

COVERAGE LAYOUT. Certain chapters in this guide are organized alphabetically by neighborhood—**Food & Drink, Nightlife,** and **Accommodations.** Within each neighborhood, listings are organized in order of quality, from best to worst. **Sights** are organized by neighborhood rather than in alphabetical order; sights are grouped into either Political Washington & Northwest, Beyond Northwest, Virginia, or Parks & Trails In & Around D.C. In neighborhoods where the sights can be seen in a logical geographical progression, they are organized in that order. Otherwise, sights are oganized by quality, from best to worst. **Museums** are split into two categories: on and off the Mall. Within each category, they are organized alphabetically. **Entertainment** is organized according to type of entertainment (music, film, theater), and listings within each category are in alphabetical order. **Shopping** is in alphabetical order by type, and listings within each category are also in alphabetical order. **Daytripping** destinations are organized in an approximate geographical loop around D.C.; accommodations, restaurants, sights, entertainment, and nightlife are organized in order of quality, from best to worst.

TRANSPORTATION INFO. For transportation info like finding flights to D.C., see **Planning Your Trip.** For tranportation info within D.C. (getting from the airports, public transportation), see **Once In D.C.** Within bus and train listings, the information in parentheses is ordered by "(duration, departure time, and price)."

SOLO TRAVELERS. Unless otherwise stated, this book assumes that the reader is a solo traveler. However, accommodations listings list prices for singles or doubles, but group rates are only listed occasionally. If you are using this book to plan a tour of D.C. for a group, we recommend calling establishments directly to find out group rates and make advance reservations.

SCHOLARLY ARTICLES. This book contains four fabulous scholarly articles on various topics. For **Adams Morgan's Global Origins** by Dinaw Mengetsu, see p. 32; for **Home Rule for D.C.,** by Asher Price and contribution from Brad Olson, see p. 34; for Nathan Glazer's **☒The Mall and its Future,** see p. 50; for Zachary Schrag's extended feature, **Tales from the Underground,** see p. 71; for Alex Krieger's **☒Anacostia and Planning in D.C.,** see p. 93.

PRICE DIVERSITY. Establishments in this book are organized in order of quality, and we give the thumbs-up (☒) to the best establishments, sights, and activities. Since the best does not always mean the cheapest price, we have incorporated a system of price ranges in the guide. Price diversity icons are designated by the ❶❷❸❹❺ symbols. The table below lists how prices fall within in each bracket.

	❶	❷	❸	❹	❺
ACCOM.	$1-50	$51-75	$76-100	$101-125	$126 and up
FOOD	$1-6	$7-12	$13-18	$19-24	$25 and up

For an extended explanation of these price ranges, see **next page**.

PHONE CODES AND TELEPHONE NUMBERS. Phone numbers are preceded by the ☎ icon. Unless otherwise noted, the area code is ☎202. In **Daytripping,** the area code is listed on the same line as the city or town name. See p. 24 for a chart of local area codes.

A NOTE TO OUR READERS The information for this book was gathered by *Let's Go* researchers from May through August of 2003. Each listing is based on one researcher's opinion, formed during his or her visit at a particular time. Those traveling at other times may have different experiences since prices, dates, hours, and conditions are always subject to change. You are urged to check the facts presented in this book beforehand to avoid inconvenience and surprises.

PRICE RANGES>> D.C.

Our researchers list establishments in order of value from best to worst; our favorites are denoted by the Let's Go thumbs-up (👍). Since the best value is not always the cheapest price, we have incorporated a system of price ranges for quick reference. Our price ranges are based on a rough expectation of what you will spend. For **accommodations,** we base our price range off the cheapest price for which a single traveler can stay for one night. For **restaurants** and other dining establishments, we estimate the average price of an entree in the restaurant. The table below tells you what you will *typically* find in D.C. at the corresponding price range; keep in mind that a particularly expensive ice cream stand may still only be marked a ❷, depending on what you will spend.

ACCOMMODATIONS	RANGE	WHAT YOU'RE *LIKELY* TO FIND
❶	$1-50	Dorm rooms or dorm-style rooms. Expect bunk beds and a communal bath; you may have to provide or rent towels and sheets.
❷	$51-75	Upper-end hostels or small hotels, guesthouses, and B&Bs. You may have a private bathroom, or there may be a sink in your room and communal shower in the hall.
❸	$76-100	Guesthouses, B&Bs, and hotels. A small room with a private bath. Should have decent amenities, such as phone and TV. Breakfast may be included.
❹	$101-125	Similar to 3, but may have more amenities or be in a more touristed area.
❺	$126 and above	Large hotels or upscale chains. If it's a 5 and it doesn't have the perks you want, you've paid too much.
FOOD		
❶	$1-6	Mostly sandwich shops and lunch takeout spots. Rarely ever a sit-down meal.
❷	$7-12	Some sandwiches and take-out options, but also quite a few ethnic restaurants in and around D.C.
❸	$13-18	Entrees are more expensive, but chances are, you're paying mostly for decor and ambience.
❹	$19-24	As in 3, the higher prices are probably related to better service, but in these restaurants, the food will tend to be a little fancier or more elaborate.
❺	$25 and above	If you're not getting delicious food with great service in a well-appointed space, you're paying for nothing more than hype.

CONTENTS

⊞ discover d.c. 1

d.c. overview 2-3
orientation 4
d.c. inner neighborhoods 4
d.c. outer neighborhoods 5

top 15 reasons to visit d.c. 10
suggested itineraries 11
walking tours 14

more free in d.c. 14
calendar of events 15

⊏ once in d.c. 21

getting into d.c. 21
d.c. area airports 22
getting around d.c. 23
embassies & consulates in
d.c. 27

tourist office 27
keeping in touch 27
the media 29
protocol 30
safety 30

money matters 31
health 31

⊞ life & times 33

history 33
architecture 41
visual arts 41

music 42
literature 43
theater 43

print media 43

◉ sights 45

political washington & north
west 45
georgetown university 76
beyond northwest 91

virginia 96
**arlington national ceme-
tery 98**

parks & trails in & around d.c.
108
rock creek park overview 109

🏛 museums 115

on the mall 115

off the mall 124

⊡ food & drink 133

by cuisine 133

by neighborhood 136

⊠ nightlife 163

by neighborhood 164

gay bars and clubs 180

♫ entertainment 183

music 183
theater & dance 187
comedy 189

billiards 189
literary life 190
film 190

sports & recreation 191

bold denotes a map

◘ shopping 197

⋔ accommodations 207

hostels 207
guest houses & hotels 208

campgrounds 219
long-term housing 219

⬔ daytripping 223

baltimore 223
daytripping area 224
metropolitan washington &
environs 226
downtown baltimore 230
annapolis 246
annapolis 247
the eastern shore 253

on the atlantic 256
lewes 257
rehoboth beach 260
ocean city 263
virginia beach 267
virginia beach 268
norfolk 272
norfolk 273

williamsburg 277
williamsburg 279
jamestown 284
richmond 284
downtown richmond 286
charlottesville 291
wine & hunt country 295

⋈ planning your trip 301

when to go 301
embassies & consulates 301
money 304
health 307

insurance 308
packing 308
accommodations 309
getting to d.c. 311

specific concerns 314
other resources 316

⬚ alternatives to tourism 319

volunteering 320

studying 324

working 325

⬓ service directory 331
taxi zones 336

⬔ index 337

⬚ map appendix

d.c. inner and outer neighborhoods 352
capitol hill 353
the mall 354
gallery district 354
17th & p st. 354
dupont circle 355
federal triangle & china
  town 356
farragut 357

foggy bottom 358
georgetown 359
adams morgan 360
shaw/u district 361
south of the mall 362
takoma park 362
northeast overview 363
upper northwest overview
  364

bethesda 365
southeast & anacostia
  366
arlington & alexandria
  367
wilson & clarendon blvd.
  368
old town alexandria 369

ABOUT LET'S GO

GUIDES FOR THE INDEPENDENT TRAVELER

Budget travel is more than a vacation. At *Let's Go*, we see every trip as the chance of a lifetime. If your dream is to grab a knapsack and a machete and forge through the jungles of Brazil, we can take you there. Or, if you'd rather enjoy the Riviera sun at a beachside cafe, we'll set you a table. If you know what you're doing, you can have any experience you want—whether it's camping among lions or sampling Tuscan desserts—without maxing out your credit card. We'll show you just how far your coins can go, and prove that the greatest limitation on your adventure is not your wallet, but your imagination. That said, we understand that you may want the occasional indulgence after a week of hostels and kebab stands, so we've added "Big Splurges" to let you know which establishments are worth those extra euros, as well as price ranges to help you quickly determine whether an accommodation or restaurant will break the bank. While we may have diversified, our emphasis will always be on finding the best values for your budget, giving you all the info you need to spend six days in London or six months in Tasmania.

BEYOND THE TOURIST EXPERIENCE

We write for travelers who know there's more to a vacation than riding double-deckers with tourists. Our researchers give you the heads-up on both world renowned and lesser-known attractions, on the best local eats and the hottest nightclub beats. In our travels, we talk to everybody; we provide a snapshot of real life in the places you visit with our sidebars on topics like regional cuisine, local festivals, and hot political issues. We've opened our pages to respected writers and scholars to show you their take on a given destination, and turned to lifelong residents to learn the little things that make their city worth calling home. And we've even given you Alternatives to Tourism—ideas for how to give back to local communities through responsible travel and volunteering.

OVER FORTY YEARS OF WISDOM

When we started, way back in 1960, Let's Go consisted of a small group of well-traveled friends who compiled their budget travel tips into a 20-page packet for students on charter flights to Europe. Since then, we've expanded to suit all kinds of travelers, now publishing guides to six continents, including our newest guides: *Let's Go: Japan* and *Let's Go: Brazil*. Our guides are still annually researched and written entirely by students on shoe-string budgets, adventurous travelers who know that train strikes, stolen luggage, food poisoning, and marriage proposals are all part of a day's work. Even as you read this, work on next year's editions is well underway. Whether you're reading one of our new titles, like *Let's Go: Puerto Rico* or *Let's Go Adventure Guide: Alaska*, or our original best-seller, *Let's Go: Europe*, you'll find the same spirit of adventure that has made *Let's Go* the guide of choice for travelers the world over since 1960.

GETTING IN TOUCH

The best discoveries are often those you make yourself; on the road, when you find something worth sharing, please drop us a line. We're Let's Go Publications, 67 Mt. Auburn St., Cambridge, MA 02138, USA (feedback@letsgo.com).

For more info, visit our website: www.letsgo.com.

RESEARCHER-WRITERS

David Dodman *Alexandria, Arlington, Foggy Bottom, Arlington, The Mall, Adams Morgan, Northeast, Upper Northwest*

A rising junior at Harvard College from New Jersey, Dave took to D.C. with determination and a meticulous eye for detail. Thorough to a fault, he constantly went the extra mile to find information on upcoming exhibitions. Dave's favorite neighborhood in D.C. is the Upper Northwest. At Harvard, Dave is a music major and enjoys singing and globe-trotting with the Harvard Glee Club.

Jennifer Jue-Steuck *Daytripping*

Hailing from Laguna Beach, California, Jennifer brought a mix of West Coast chill and New York chic to her fabulous daytripping coverage. With an impeccable sense of style, Jennifer adeptly added St. Michaels, Chincoteague, Charlottesville, Leesburg, and Middleburg to our Daytrips section. Jennifer studied film-making at NYU's Tisch School of the Arts, received a Master's in Education from Harvard, and is now in a PhD program in Anthropology at Columbia.

Bradley Olson *Bethesda, Capitol Hill, Dupont, Federal Triangle, Southeast, All Nightlife, 16th St. Walking Tour*

A recent Harvard grad from Wisconsin, Brad took D.C.'s nightlife by storm. Brad's low-key, laid-back style made all his hard work and quality research seem effortless. Aside from the blur of bars, clubs, and restaurants Brad covered, he particularly enjoyed exploring the Capitol, where he finagled his way onto a children's tour through his Senator's office. A government major at Harvard, Brad was drawn to D.C.'s politically charged atmosphere. He now lives in Chicago where he is an Associate Consultant at Bain & Co.

CONTRIBUTING WRITERS

Nathan Glazer, Harvard University professor emeritus of sociology and education, writes on urban issues, ethnicity, race relations—among his books are *Beyond the Melting Pot* (1970), *The Limits of Social Policy* (1988), and *We Are All Multiculturalists Now* (1997). He also writes on architecture and urban design, and with Mark Lilla, he edited the volume *The Public Face of Architecture* (1987). He is currently co-editing a book on the National Mall, past, present, and future.

Alex Krieger, FAIA, is a founding principal of Chan Krieger & Associates and a tenured professor at the Harvard University Graduate School of Design, where he serves as Chairman of the Department of Urban Planning & Design. He was one of the founding members of the Boston Civic Design Commission, is an advisor to the Boston Redevelopment Authority on various downtown planning and design projects, and as a former director of the National Endowment for the Arts' Mayor's Institute on City Design, he is a frequent advisor to mayors and their staffs.

Dinaw Mengestu lived in Adams Morgan for several years. He has written for the Princeton Review and SparkNotes, and is currently writing his master's thesis.

Asher Price is the assistent to the editor at *The New Republic.*

Zachary Schrag was the editor of *Let's Go: Paris 1993* and a Researcher-Writer for *USA, California, and Hawaii 1991, Europe 1992,* and *Britain & Ireland 1992.* He wrote his dissertation on the Metro, has been published in *Washington History,* and is now teaching history at the City Univesity of New York.

ACKNOWLEDGMENTS

LET'S GO

Dunia Dickey: Thanks first to my fabulous bookteam. Brad, Dave, and Jennifer, you did an amazing job. Nitin, Megan, Ankur, Scrobins, and Evan—this book would not have made it without you (you know it's true). Mike, thanks for indexing me in your book. Prod, I am helpless in the face of technology without you. Thanks too to all the managing editors who helped me out in the wee hours. Special thanks to Nathan Glazer and Alex Krieger for their excellent scholarly articles. Thanks to my family for living near D.C. (and far from Moscow) and letting me come home once in a while. And supplying the whole of Northern Virginia's feline population. Becky and Sasha—the three of us will soon meet for brunch at "Wilson's." Alex—your role in helping me explore D.C. nightlife was essential to my understanding of the city. Elena—thanks for all your pampering; I highly recommend *Let's Go: London 2004* next. Jill, Emily, Abbey, and Nora—thanks for your support this summer and for dragging me out of the office kicking and screaming. Tabby—rooming with you was great fun (and thanks for the *Buffy*).

Megan Moran-Gates: Dunia, thanks for making it all come together. Your work ethic, persistence, and positive attitude were truly inspiring. Scrobins, thanks for the unrelenting support, cookies, and laughs. To the rest of the pod: the absurd discussions, constant distractions, and tomfoolery were much appreciated. Special thanks to Chez Renard for good times and a rent-free summer. As always, Mom, Dad, Taylor, Adri, and Rob: thanks for your love and friendship.

Evan Hudson: My thanks go out to Cynthia, Randolph, and Ryan for their patience and unfailing support.

Editor Dunia Dickey
Associate Editor Megan Moran-Gates
Managing Editor Nitin Shah
Map Editor Evan Hudson
Photographer Luke Marion
Typesetter Dusty Lewis

Publishing Director
Julie A. Stephens
Editor-in-Chief
Jeffrey Dubner
Production Manager
Dusty Lewis
Cartography Manager
Nathaniel Brooks
Design Manager
Caleb Beyers
Editorial Managers
Lauren Bonner, Ariel Fox,
Matthew K. Hudson, Emma Nothmann,
Joanna Shawn Brigid O'Leary,
Sarah Robinson
Financial Manager
Suzanne Siu
Marketing & Publicity Managers
Megan Brumagim, Nitin Shah
Personnel Manager
Jesse Reid Andrews
Researcher Manager
Jennifer O'Brien
Web Manager
Jesse Tov
Web Content Director
Abigail Burger
Production Associates
Thomas Bechtold, Jeffrey Hoffman Yip
IT Directors
Travis Good, E. Peyton Sherwood
Financial Assistant
R. Kirkie Maswoswe
Associate Web Manager
Robert Dubbin
Office Coordinators
Abigail Burger, Angelina L. Fryer,
Liz Glynn
Director of Advertising Sales
Daniel Ramsey
Senior Advertising Associates
Sara Barnett, Daniella Boston
Advertising Artwork Editor
Julia Davidson
President
Abhishek Gupta
General Manager
Robert B. Rombauer
Assistant General Manager
Anne E. Chisholm

INSIDE

orientation **4**

top 15 reasons to visit d.c. **10**

suggested itineraries **11**

walking tours **14**

more free in d.c. **14**

calendar of events **15**

Discover D.C.

This is a city where romance means wonks in love discussing policy late into the night.
  —*The New York Times*

For outsiders, comprehending D.C. as anything more than a passionless hub of politics and pomposity often presents a serious challenge. Its residents and other D.C. enthusiasts, though, love the city because they know its true nature: a thriving international city filled with cultural offerings on par with the finest in the world. While the city's biggest draws may be its museums and marbled monuments, a richer visit to D.C. includes time spent away from the tourist-saturated landmarks of Capitol Hill.

Political Washington is a whirlwind of endless press conferences and power lunches, potent memorials and presidential intrigues. Lobbyists and journalists hover around senators, creating the masterful mix of rhetoric, policy, and spin that keeps the country running smoothly. And the hallways of Capitol Hill are always abuzz with congressional strategizing and hand-shaking, the likes of which you won't see on CNN or C-SPAN.

Outside the federal enclave, Washington's neighborhoods flaunt cultural delights. Dupont Circle showcases easels of the masters beside those of budding artists, Adams Morgan embraces a banquet of multi-ethnic offerings, and Bethesda rightly claims the most diversity in culinary establishments. High culture bows and pirouettes on the Kennedy Center stage almost every night as local and big-name rock groups deafen their young audiences in the "New U" St. corridor. Political powerhouse, thriving metropolis, and intern party town, D.C. packs more punch per square mile than any other city.

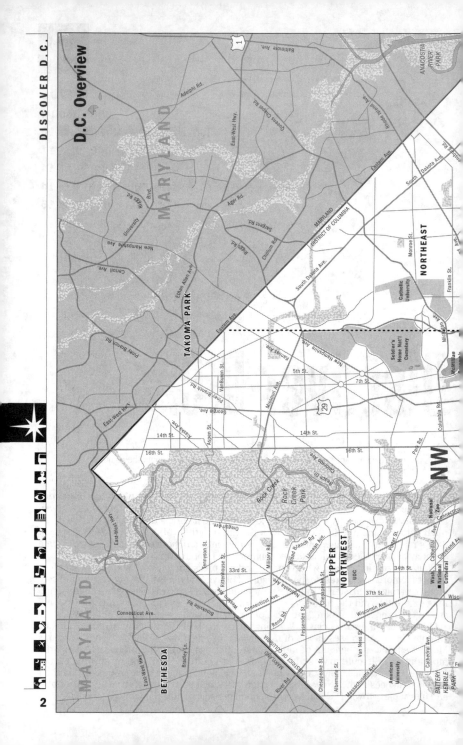

D.C. Overview

MARYLAND

MARYLAND

DISTRICT OF COLUMBIA

Baltimore Ave.

Adelphi Rd.

East-West Hwy.

Queens Chapel Rd.

Riggs Rd.

University Blvd.

New Hampshire Ave.

Carroll Ave.

Ager Rd.

Sargent Rd.

Riggs Rd.

Chillum Rd.

Ethan Allen Ave.

TAKOMA PARK

Eastern Ave.

Piney Branch Rd.

East-West Hwy.

East-West Hwy.

BETHESDA

Connecticut Ave.

Bradley Ln.

Brookville Rd.

Wisconsin Ave.

Tennyson St.

Rittenhouse St.

33rd St.

Military Rd.

Oregon Ave.

Western Ave.

River Rd.

Reno Rd.

Fessenden St.

Connecticut Ave.

Nebraska Ave.

Chesapeake St.

Albemart St.

Chesapeake St.

Van Ness St.

Massachusetts Ave.

American University

Cathedral Ave.

37th St.

34th St.

Wisconsin Ave.

UDC

UPPER NORTHWEST

Wash. National Cathedral

Wisc

BATTERY KEMBLE PARK

Fe

NW

NORTHWEST

Rock Creek Park

Rock Creek

Beach Dr.

16th St.

14th St.

16th St.

Park Rd.

Columbia Rd.

Porter St.

National Zoo

Cathedral Ave.

Connecticut

Cleveland Ave.

29

7th St.

5th St.

Missouri Ave.

Kansas Ave.

New Hampshire Ave.

Georgia Ave.

Piney Branch Rd.

Van Buren St.

Alaska Ave.

Aspen St.

14th St.

Soldier's Home Nat'l Cemetery

Catholic University

NORTHEAST

Monroe St.

Franklin St.

South Dakota Ave.

South Dakota Ave.

Eastern Ave.

Michigan Ave.

Michigan

Rhode Island Ave.

ANACOSTIA RIVER PARK

1

2

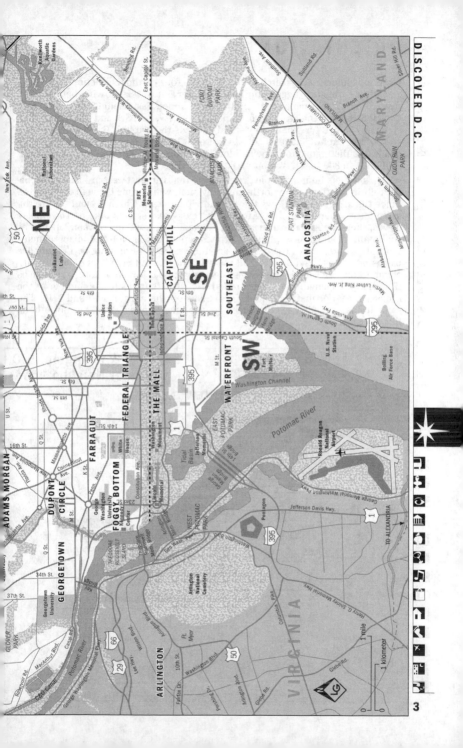

3

ORIENTATION

Diamond-shaped D.C. stretches its tips in the four cardinal directions. The **Potomac River** forms the jagged southwest border, its waters flowing between the district and Arlington, Virginia. **North Capitol Street, East Capitol Street,** and **South Capitol Street** cut the city into four quadrants: NW, NE, SE, and SW. These divisions are named for where they stand vis-à-vis the Capitol. **The Mall,** stretching west of the Capitol, makes a "West Capitol St." unnecessary. The suffixes of the quadrants distinguish otherwise identical addresses. For instance, you might find both an 800 G St. NW *and* an 800 G St. NE.

D.C.'s streets lie in a simple grid. Streets that run **east-west** are labeled **alphabetically** in relation to the north-south division, which runs through the Capitol. Since the street plan follows the Roman alphabet, in which "I" and "J" are the same letter, there is no J St. After W St., east-west streets take on **two-syllable names,** then **three-syllable names,** then the names of **trees and flowers.** The names run in alphabetical order, but sometimes repeat or skip a letter; discrepancies multiply as you shift farther from downtown. Streets running **north-south** are **numbered** (1st St., 2nd St., etc.) all the way out to 52nd St. NW and 63rd St. NE. Numbered and lettered streets sometimes disappear for a block, then resume as if nothing happened. Addresses on lettered streets indicate the number of the cross street. For instance, 1100 D St. SE is on the corner of D and 11th. The same holds for addresses on some avenues, like Pennsylvania, but not others, like Massachusetts or Wisconsin.

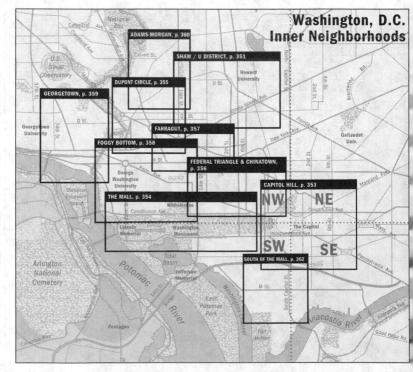

Washington, D.C. Inner Neighborhoods

Avenues named for states radiate outward from the Capitol **(Pennsylvania, New Jersey, Delaware, Maryland)** and the White House **(New York, Connecticut, Vermont),** and criss-cross downtown **(Massachusetts, New Hampshire, Virginia).** Downtown avenues meet at circles and squares, notably **Dupont Circle, Washington Circle,** and **Scott Circle.**

NEIGHBORHOODS

POLITICALLY SPEAKING

CAPITOL HILL. Postcard-perfect and pristine white, Capitol Hill holds the democratic dream with the **Capitol** building, the **Supreme Court,** and the **Library of Congress.**

THE MALL. The **Smithsonian Museums** and the **National Gallery of Art** flank this long grassy strip. Monuments and memorials fill the Mall's west end; cherry trees bud and blossom along the brink of the **Jefferson Memorial's Tidal Basin.**

FOGGY BOTTOM. The **State Department, Kennedy Center,** and the infamous **Watergate Complex** make Foggy Bottom their stomping grounds, but this area's blockbuster is the **White House** at 1600 Pennsylvania Ave.

FEDERAL TRIANGLE. This area is home to a growing commercial and banking district. The new **Ronald Reagan Building and International Trade Center** shares the wide avenues with federal agencies like the **FBI** and the **IRS.**

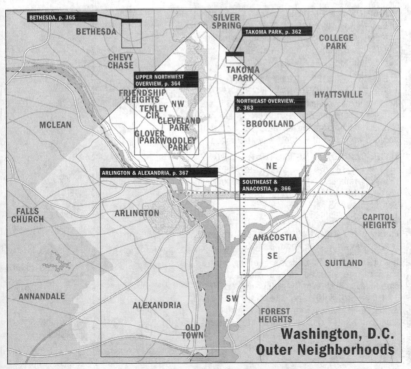

Washington, D.C.
Outer Neighborhoods

Time: 4-5 hours (6-8 with a show).

Distance: 2 miles.

Time of Day: Early afternoon thru evening.

Starting Point: 16th and Harvard St. NW, near Metro: Columbia Heights.

Finish Point: 16th and P St. NW, near Metro: Dupont Circle.

1 EMBASSY ROW, JR. Massachusetts Ave. may be known as Embassy Row, but this area houses the embassies of Spain (1B), Poland (1D), Lithuania (1F), and Ecuador (1C), as well as the Cuba Interests Section of the Swiss Embassy (1E) and the Mexican Embassy's Cultural Institute (1A).

2 MERIDIAN INTERNATIONAL CENTER. 1630 Crescent Pl. NW (☎667-6800). Housed in two historic homes designed by famed architect John Russell Pope, the Center offers cultural programs and rotation exhibits of international art. See **Sights**, p. 85.

3 MERIDIAN HILL PARK. Take a midday break at this beautiful 12-acre park that resembles an Italian garden. Highlights include the James Buchanan Memorial and the cascading fountain. See **Sights**, p. 85.

4 SCOTTISH RITE FREEMASONRY TEMPLE. 1733 16th St. NW (☎232-3579). Another legacy of architect John Russell Pope, this grand and imposing structure offers visitors a peek inside the ultra-secret fraternal order to which 14 presidents have belonged.

5 THE CARNEGIE INSTITUTION. 1530 P St. NW (☎387-6400). See where federal research dollars go at the headquarters of this cutting-edge scientific research institution. See **Sights**, p. 84.

6 DINNER... Housed at 1633 P St. NW, **Cafe Luna** (☎387-4005) offers excellent low-fat, veggie-heavy fare. See **Food**, p. 146.

7 ...AND A SHOW. End the evening with a show at one of three neighborhood theater companies. Both **Woolly Mammoth** (☎393-3939; see p. 189) and **Theatre J** (☎777-3229; see p. 189) perform at the Jewish Community Center (7B), and **The Foundry Players** (☎332-2453; see p. 187) puts on three shows each year at the Foundry United Methodist Church (7A).

WALKING TOUR

6

GEORGETOWN HISTORIC HOMES & GARDENS

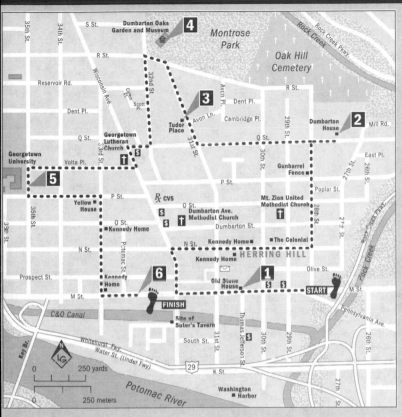

1 OLD STONE HOUSE. 3051 M St. (☎426-6851). Open W-Su noon-5pm. Garden open W-Su 10am-5pm. the oldest house in Georgetown. After a walk through its gardens, turn right onto M St., a window shopper's heaven.

2 DUMBARTON OAKS MANSION. 1703 32nd St. (☎339-6401). The 30min. guided tour provides a fascinating glimpse into high living in the 18th century.

Time: 3 hours.

Distance: 2 miles.

Time of Day: A not-so-lazy afternoon.

Starting Point: Pennsylvania Avenue and M Street in east Georgetown.

Finish Point: Clyde's of Georgetown.

3 TUDOR PLACE. 1644 31st St. (☎965-0400). The estate, which remained in the same family for more than two centuries, contains countless numbers of precious antiques collected over the family's history. A stroll through the beautiful gardens is a must.

4 DUMBARTON OAKS GARDEN & MUSEUM. At 31st and R St. (☎339-6401). View a collection of Byzantine art, as well as pre-Columbian artifacts, in a pristine mansion setting.

5 GEORGETOWN UNIVERSITY. 37th and O St. (☎687-1457). Marvel at the picturesque lawns and stone courtyards on the campus of this world-class college.

6 CLYDE'S. 3236 M St. NW (☎333-9180). End your Georgetown odyssey with good, old-fashioned American chow at this restaurant, the best of the of Georgetown saloons.

WALKING TOUR

7

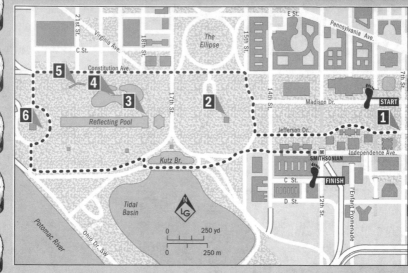

1 HIRSHHORN SCULPTURE GAR-DEN. At this hour, the Garden won't be open, but surely you can make out the glistening edges of Maillol and Matisse's figures. Pick the least and most lifelike shapes and then try to name the sculptors.

2 WASHINGTON MONUMENT.
The great American phallus is doubly impressive at night, illuminated from above by the moon and below by massive

Time: 1 hour.

Length: 1 mile.

Time of Day: After dark, whenever the moon is out.

Starting Point: Walk from Capitol Hill, Foggy Bottom, or the Smithsonian.

Finish Point: Smithsonian Metro.

spotlights. Fifty American flags fly in a circle at its base. Be sure to turn northward for a stunning view of the White House, the South Lawn, and the Ellipse. The massive fountain and towering columns are often impressive enough to make visitors forget that the White house is still a residence, not just a figurehead or museum.

3 REFLECTING POOL. The mirror of all the nation's glory is calm at night. Admire the glimmering image of the Washington Monument, or if you're bold enough, dip your toes for a mid-walk refresher. Full-on Forrest Gump runs down the length of the pool are discouraged, except for steeplechase champions with no fear of mounted park police.

4 CONSTITUTION GARDENS. Beside a perfectly placid pond, this is the ultimate lovers' trysting ground. Look for slumbering ducklings and play hide-and-seek among the trees, or steal off for a kiss or two on the shaded island before heading west again.

5 VIETNAM VETERANS MEMORIAL. A wall of marble testifies to the losses in a divisive time. Admire the reflections off the smooth, black surface and run your hands of the near-countless names for a reminder of the nation's loss. If you have paper and a pencil, make a rubbing of a name that resonates with you.

6 LINCOLN MEMORIAL. Abraham Lincoln sits proudly atop this marble pedestal, perhaps the most classically beautiful of all the monuments, overlooking the Potomac. Lincoln's most famous quotes line the walls here, inspiring recollections of high school history classes and thoughts of bygone eras when presidents wrote their own speeches. Breathe in the midnight air and survey the land before returning to the Metro and heading home.

WALKING TOUR

FARRAGUT. It's a wonderful (corporate) life in glass-walled Farragut, where government agencies, lobbying firms, and lawyers make their office space their home.

POLITICS ASIDE

ADAMS MORGAN. A hub of 20-something nightlife, good food, live music, and a real cross-section of D.C.'s multi-ethnic heritage. Did we mention Ethiopian food?

CHINATOWN. More of a block than a neighborhood, this slice of the Federal Triangle area offers the most authentic Chinese cuisine in the District.

SOUTH OF THE MALL. A strong seafood aroma saturates this stretch of Potomac waterfront. Crustacean-mongers pile into the **Wharf Seafood Market,** while riverboat cruises rev their engines at the marina's docks.

GEORGETOWN. Even if you don't have money to spend, window shopping along **M Street** and **Wisconsin Avenue** will up your sartorial IQ considerably. The neighborhood has the feel of a college-town with **Georgetown University** nearby and enough nightlife to keep college students adequately bibulous and entertained.

DUPONT CIRCLE. If you're hip, glamorous, and like good food and cutting edge art, then Dupont Circle is made for you. Art sophisticates jet in for the **R Street galleries,** while diplomats and ambassadors from all parts of the world live and work along **Embassy Row. 18th Street** has the hottest in mainstream clubs, while 17th St. caters to D.C.'s ever-expanding **gay scene.**

UPPER NORTHWEST. With exclusive private schools, mansions, and the **Washington National Cathedral,** this neighborhood first appears to be just wealthy and residential. But watch out for major attractions like **American University** and the **National Zoo,** not to mention the world-class **Kreeger Museum.**

SHAW/U DISTRICT. Historically African-American in the years before desegregation, today the "New" **U Street** rocks out nightly—and deafens passersby—as its **clubs** and **lounges** blast punk, trance, and house music until the sun rises.

"TOTO, WE'RE NOT IN KANSAS ANYMORE": VENTURING & ADVENTURING OUTSIDE NW

SOUTHEAST. The **Navy Yard,** stocked with old torpedoes and a fascinating museum, will excite anyone who admires American defensive might. Southeast also hosts the rowdiest **concerts** and the wildest **raves** in the entire District.

ANACOSTIA. Besides the **Frederick Douglass Home,** Anacostia is home to D.C.'s poorest housing projects and its **highest crime rates.** *Let's Go* does not recommend exploring Anacostia.

NORTHEAST. Northeast's **National Arboretum, Kenilworth Aquatic Gardens,** and the salsa dance clubs of **Mt. Pleasant** provide a welcome break from traditional sightseeing. Though on the upswing, the Northeast area still struggles with **crime.**

DESTINATION: SUBURBIA

BETHESDA. Home to over 100 restaurants of every genre of cuisine imaginable, Bethesda is a place for eating, more eating, and a bit of bookstore coffee-sipping. Outside its central dining and shopping area, Bethesda is exclusively residential.

ARLINGTON COUNTY. Across the Potomac from the District, **Arlington National Cemetery's** vast green hills hold the remains of America's distinguished military veterans. This county also houses the **Pentagon,** the Defense Department's headquarters, as well as the bustling nightlife in and around **Clarendon** and **Courthouse.**

LET'S GO PICKS

Best place to get sloshed with sophistication: Order obscure Eastern European beers to your heart's desire at **Brickskeller.**

Best place to get sloshed without sophistication: $1 jello shots at **Millie & Al's.** Rinse. Repeat.

Best (read: worst) place to get caught using a fake ID: Anywhere in **Georgetown.**

Best place to check your mate: Playing chess at **Dupont Circle.**

Best place to get trampled by schoolchildren: Try the **Air and Space Museum,** the **Natural History Museum,** or if worse comes to worst, the **National Zoo.**

Best after-midnight dessert: **Afterwords Café,** followed closely by **Tryst.**

Best place to whisper sweet nothings: The **Bishop's Garden** at the **National Cathedral.**

Best place to get engaged: Two Quail. To ensure success, first head to **Tiffany & Co.,** 5500 Wisconsin Ave. (☎301-657-8777), in Chevy Chase.

ALEXANDRIA. Preserved homes and shops line King St. in **Old Town Alexandria,** where you can see the town that early America's political elite called home. Make sure to take in views of D.C.'s monuments from this side of the Potomac.

FAIRFAX COUNTY. Across the Potomac, prosperous Fairfax County features **Great Falls National Park** as well as **Mount Vernon,** George Washington's plantation home, and historical **Manassas Battlefield Park.**

TOP 15 REASONS TO VISIT D.C.

15. MCI Center (p. 73). This 20,000-seat arena is home to the NBA's Washington Wizards, the NHL's Washington Capitals, the WNBA's Washington Mystics, the NLL's Washington Power, and the NCAA's Georgetown Hoyas.

14. National Zoo (p. 89). The two giant pandas, Mei Xiang and Tian Tian, are huge draws, along with the baby African elephant and the Sumatran tiger cub, Berani. Check out the Reptile Discovery Center, the Great Ape House, and the glassed-in rainforest exhibit.

13. Mount Vernon (p. 102). Home and plantation of the nation's first president, Mount Vernon lathers on the charm of old-school Southern comfort. At the Mount Vernon Museum, ogle such carefully preserved relics as George Washington's toothbrush.

12. National Archives (p. 70). Pack rats will think that they've died and gone to heaven. Some junk treasures include a portrait of Nixon painted on a grain of rice and JFK's doodles during the Cuban Missile Crisis. You'll also find such national treasures as the Declaration of Independence, the Constitution, and the Bill of Rights.

11. Vietnam Veterans Memorial (p. 57). The polished black stone wall contains the names of the 58,209 Americans who died or are still missing in Vietnam. Visitors leave flowers and offerings, or take rubbings of the names from the Memorial.

10. Embassy Row (p. 84). Traipse down this grand avenue, lined with embassies and diplomatic mansions, and pick out and identify foreign countries by the flags fluttering overhead. The Indonesian Embassy and the Islamic Center are particularly striking.

9. Arlington National Cemetery (p. 97). 612 acres of rolling green hills hold the bodies of Purple Heart and Silver Star veterans, from five-star generals to unidentified soldiers. Visit the Tomb of the Unknowns and the Kennedy gravesites.

8. Washington National Cathedral (p. 87). Seat of D.C.'s Episcopal diocese, home to a top-ranked high school, and the product of 100 years of work by thousands of artisans, the Cathedral and its campus are literally a city on a hill, looking down resplendent on downtown from the highest point in the city.

7. US Holocaust Memorial Museum (p. 127). A vivid and chilling reminder of the atrocities the Jews were forced to undergo during the Nazi terror of World War II.

6. Kennedy Center (p. 69). Home to the spectacular National Symphony Orchestra, the Washington Opera, and the Washington Ballet. The Millennium Stage concert series holds free performances daily at 6pm.

5. National Gallery of Art (p. 122). Da Vinci. Renoir. Fra Angelico. Vermeer. Rembrandt. Rubens. Dali. Calder. Picasso. Matisse. Miró. Man Ray. Giacometti. Rothko. Magritte. The best in the world, at the refreshing price of $0. The six-acre sculpture garden is also a delight.

4. Jefferson Memorial and the Tidal Basin (p. 59). Rimmed by cherry trees, this shrine to TJ overlooks the man-made Tidal Basin. Tool around the pond in a rented paddleboat.

3. White House (p. 62). Home and headquarters of the President. Although tours have been suspended indefinitely, you can still sneak a peek at the Rose Garden made famous by Jackie O.

2. Smithsonian Museums (p. 115). So much and so free. Our favorites: the Wright brothers' biplane at the National Air and Space Museum, the Hope Diamond at the National Museum of Natural History, and Dorothy's red ruby slippers at the National Museum of American History. Art lovers will delight in the Freer Gallery, the Hirshhorn Museum and Sculpture Garden, and the African Art and Sackler Complex.

1. The Capitol (p. 46). The epicenter of American democracy, accessible to the public. Inside, check out the House and Senate Chambers, Statuary Hall, and the crypt containing Washington's empty tomb. Out front, the US Botanical Gardens brim with exotic flora.

SUGGESTED ITINERARIES

Those new to the city should check out our day-by-day breakdown of must-see places—from the cultural to the culinary, with some stops for your credit card in between. For those interested in a specific region or activity, we've also included several walking tours and insider's city features, ranging from monument sightseeing to pub crawls and gallery walks. Don't let these suggestions limit you—D.C. is ripe for exploration as long as you're careful.

LET'S GO PICKS

Best place to exploit the fact that you plan to vote in the next election: Your **Congressman's** office.

Best shoes: Judy Garland's **Red Ruby Slippers** from *The Wizard of Oz*, at the **National Museum of American History.** For your own pair, try **Wild Women Wear Red.**

Best eggs: Drool over the largest collection of **Fabergé Eggs** this side of Russia at the **Hillwood Museum.**

Sexiest new thing: Frank Gehry's ultra-modern, sleek design for the **Corcoran Gallery's** planned expansion.

Best daytrip: Middleburg, Virginia. Bring your riding boots and plenty of plastic (read: $$$).

Best weekend trip: Stop in port-side **Annapolis, Maryland** on your way to **St. Michaels** on Maryland's **Eastern Shore**—a short ride from the beaches at **Lewes** and **Rehoboth, Delaware,** and **Ocean City, Maryland.** Then spend a lazy Sunday afternoon petting the wild ponies in **Chincoteague, Virginia.**

THREE DAYS

DAY ONE: CAPITOL HILL & THE MONUMENTS

Kick off your Washington pilgrimage with a sweep of **Capitol Hill.** Start your morning at the **Capitol** (p. 46) building, perhaps eavesdropping on a committee hearing if you're curious. On your way out, stroll briskly through the **US Botanic Gardens** (p. 51). Then, stomp on over to either the **Supreme Court** (p. 49) or the **Library of Congress** (p. 49) to marvel at more marble. A bit further north, window-shop briefly at **Union Station** (p. 52) before pausing for lunch at its international fast food court. Take the Metro from Union Station to the Smithsonian stop. From there, hit up the monuments in the afternoon. Begin with the **Washington Monument** (p. 53) and its famous **Reflecting Pool** (p. 56), and the leafy **Constitution Gardens** (p. 56) nearby. From there, go west to the **Vietnam Veterans Memorial** (p. 57), and then south to the **Lincoln Memorial** (p. 57), the **Korean War Veterans Memorial** (p. 58), and the **Franklin Delano Roosevelt Memorial** (p. 59). Cool off in the shade of cherry trees lining the **Tidal Basin** (p. 60) by the **Jefferson Memorial.** For dinner on the cheap, feast on all-you-can-eat pasta at **Il Radicchio** (p. 144) on Pennsylvania Ave.

DAY TWO: THE MALL & WATERFRONT

Get to the **Mall** (p. 53) early for a whirlwind museum tour. Start with the **National Gallery of Art** (p. 122) and its **sculpture garden.** Next, work your way down Madison Dr. to either the **National Museum of Natural History** (p. 117) or the **National Museum of American History** (p. 116). In the afternoon, take your pick between the **Freer Gallery** (p. 121), the **Sackler** (p. 120), or the **National Museum of African Art** (p. 120). The **Hirshhorn Museum and Sculpture Garden** (p. 119) or the **National Air and Space Museum** (p. 118) shouldn't be missed. After you're thoroughly spent, head south to the **Waterfront** (p. 61) for a fresh crab and lobster dinner at the **Wharf Seafood Market** (p. 158) In the summer, roam the fairs by the **Gangplank Marina** (p. 61) or board a river cruise for dancing, dining, and drinks.

DAY THREE: FOGGY BOTTOM & GEORGETOWN

Putz around **Foggy Bottom** at smaller sites such as the **Renwick Gallery** (p. 131), **St. John's Church** (p. 64), the **American Red Cross** (p. 66), the **Corcoran Gallery** (p. 125), or the **Daughters of the American Revolution** (p. 66). Be sure to drop in and roam around at the massive **Kennedy Center** (p. 69). As you're walking out, catch a glimpse of the notorious **Watergate Complex** (p. 69), a product of the 1960s concrete building binge. For lunch, head over to Georgetown for quiche and cream-puffs at **Cafe La Ruche** (p. 154). Amble along the **C&O Canal** (p. 112) or board a **canal boat** for a floating tour. Shop the afternoon away at the **Shops at Georgetown Park** (p. 203) and along **M Street** and **Wisconsin Avenue,** schmooze with comely coeds at **Georgetown University** (p. 79), or visit the **Old Stone House** (p. 79). Before dusk, head up to the **Dumbarton Oaks Estate** (p. 80) for a tour of the mansion and the gorgeous garden. For dinner and entertainment, check out **Blues Alley** (p. 186) for cool jazz with Creole cuisine or any of Georgetown's tasty M St. restaurants.

FIVE DAYS

In addition to the previous three days, round out your itinerary with these regions:

DAY FOUR: FEDERAL TRIANGLE

Spend the morning visiting either the **National Archives** (p. 70), the **FBI** (p. 71), **Ford's Theater** (p. 72). Grab a polish sausage or fried dough from a street vendor and eat near the fountains of the **Navy Memorial.** Complete the afternoon at the **National Build-**

ing **Museum** (p. 129) and the new **International Spy Museum** (p. 127). Dine along **H Street** in nearby Chinatown (p. 71) for spicy Asian fare. After dinner, go to the nearby **14th Street Theater District** (p. 187) to catch a Mamet play. Alternatively, go clubbing at hot new nightspot **Home** (p. 174).

DAY FIVE: ROCK CREEK PARK & DUPONT CIRCLE

Spend the morning hiking around **Rock Creek Park** (p. 108). Hop on the Metro to **Dupont Circle** (p. 81) and grab a Japanese Bento box lunch at **Teaism** (p. 148). Walk past the circle down **Embassy Row** and visit the **Phillips Collection** (p. 130) and the **R** and **21st Street galleries** (p. 82). Choose from the multitude of ethnic eateries around the Circle and groove the night away at the über-hip **Eighteenth Street Lounge** (p. 171).

Center of Town

SEVEN DAYS

In addition to the above, tack on these neighborhoods to explore:

DAY SIX: UPPER NORTHWEST & SOUTHEAST

Spend the morning in Upper Northwest with the wild things at the **National Zoo** (p. 89). Head to the **National Cathedral** (p. 87) and lunch at **Cactus Cantina** (p. 161) or **2 Amys** (p. 161) before you browse around the shops in Friendship Heights. Then, Metro down to Southeast for a tour of **Barracks Row** and the **Navy Yard** (p. 91). Once there, climb aboard the former torpedo-laden destroyer, the **USS Barry**. Dine in **Eastern Market** (p. 91)—may we suggest crabcakes, an indigenous D.C. specialty?—before heading out to an all-night dance party at **Nation** (p. 185).

National Zoo

DAY SEVEN: ARLINGTON, ALEXANDRIA, & FAIRFAX

Catch the sunrise at **Arlington National Cemetery** (p. 97). Next, board the Metro to visit the **Pentagon** (p. 101), the pinnacle of WWII and Cold War military bureaucracy and the world's largest office building. From there, take the Metro to the King St. stop in **Old Town Alexandria** (p. 104). Visit **historic homes** and the shops along **Washington** and **King St.** Mid-day, feast on Old Town's best burgers at **Five Guys** (p. 138). Learn all about Old Town on a 45min. **Potomac Riverboat Tour** (p. 106) along the **Alexandria Waterfront.** Complete your

Inside the Library of Congress

China Gilded Archway

Dupont Circle

C&O Canal

day by touring **Mount Vernon** (p. 102), plantation home of **George Washington,** a short bus ride away from the Huntington Metro.

WALKING TOURS

Each tour (see pp. 6-8) offers a different slice of D.C. life. Learn some history while you eat and drink, and then walk off the calories as you follow these tours along with their accompanying maps for a whirlwind D.C. immersion. Each map lays out a path to take and describes the tour, both stop-by-stop and in a global perspective, with total time, distance, and suggested time of day for walking it.

MORE FREE IN D.C.

Here are 20 deliciously irreverent suggestions for your exploring pleasure:

1. Attend a live broadcast of **CNN's Crossfire** debate at **George Washington University.** See **Free Summer Lovin',** p. 185.

2. Sing *The Star Spangled Banner,* the US national anthem, in front of the flag that inspired Francis Scott Key to reword an **old English drinking song**, at the National Museum of American History (p. 116).

3. Find your roots at the National Archives (p. 70); if you don't have American roots, learn how to **do your own genealogy.**

4. In-line skate in front of the **White House** (p. 62). Don't worry about cars; concrete barricades seal off this famous stretch of road from traffic. Venture out on your own, or join the **Washington Area Roadskaters** (p. 193) for a skate around the city.

5. Compete in the monthly **3km race** at the Tidal Basin (p. 60).

6. Watch **millions of freshly-minted dollars** roll off the presses. You'll be rolling in money, but you won't have to spend a cent at the **Bureau of Engraving and Printing** (p. 61).

7. Play **chess** in Dupont Circle (p. 81), or just watch the rook-and-knight action along with the hordes of **daredevil bike messengers.**

8. Dip your feet in the Kennedy Center's **fountains** (p. 69) while overlooking the Potomac's waterfront **rowing and boating** scene. Take in views of Georgetown and the National Cathedral from the **rooftop terrace,** then head to a free 6pm **concert** at the **Millennium Stage.**

9. Ring in **spring** at the US National Arboretum's **Garden Fair** (p. 95) or check out the Kenilworth Aquatic Gardens's annual **Waterlily Festival** in mid-summer (p. 95).

10. Observe the stars at an **Exploring the Sky** telescope viewing in **Rock Creek Park** (p. 108), or attend an outdoor **poetry reading** in summer at the **Joaquin Miller Cabin** (p. 110).

11. Attend a lunchtime **live jazz** concert in **Farragut Square** (p. 74), or listen to **jazz bands** and other groups perform **Sunset Serenades** at the **National Zoo** (p. 89).

12. In June, reconnect with the Bard at a free outdoor Shakespeare production at the **Carter Barron Amphitheatre** (p. 110) in **Rock Creek Park.**

13. Watch the changing of the guard at the **Tomb of the Unknowns** in **Arlington National Cemetery** (p. 97), or be inspired by the weekly **Marine Corps Sunset Parades** at the **Iwo Jima Memorial** (p. 99) on Tuesday nights.

14. Take an **embassy tour** (p. 84). Occasionally, you will get **free food.**

15. Visit a politician. If you make an appointment during lunch, you might get fed (p. 45).

16. Hit a **parade** in D.C. Pennsylvania Avenue comes alive with the sound of marching bands from **St. Patrick's Day** (March 17th) to **Bastille Day** (July 14th).

17. Fly a **kite** on the Mall. If you don't own a kite, consider hunting for a Sunday **polo match** on the nearby field; these matches are rare but always worth watching (p. 53).

18. Scout out the best **Happy Hour** deals on weeknights (see **Bibulousness Plan,** p. 175).

19. Watch performances and sample regional food at the **Smithsonian Folklife Festival** (www.folklife.si.edu) on the Mall. In **June and July 2004,** the annual festival will highlight **Mid-Atlantic maritime culture.**

20. See a **free movie** on the Washington Monument lawn on summer Mondays at dusk during the **Screen on the Green** festivities (see **Free Summer Lovin',** p. 185).

CALENDAR OF EVENTS

NATIONAL HOLIDAYS IN 2004

DATE	HOLIDAY	DATE	HOLIDAY
January 1	New Year's Day	September 6	Labor Day
January 19	Martin Luther King Day	October 11	Columbus Day
February 16	Presidents Day	November 11	Veterans Day
May 31	Memorial Day	November 25	Thanksgiving Day
July 4	Independence Day	December 25	Christmas Day

MONTH BY MONTH

JANUARY

Martin Luther King's Birthday (☎ 619-7222), observed Jan. 19. Wreaths laid, "I Have a Dream" speech recited at the Lincoln Memorial. Choirs, speakers, etc. Free.

Robert E. Lee's Birthday (☎ 703-557-0613), Jan. 19th at Arlington National Cemetery. 19th century music, sampler of Civil War-era food, displays of restored artwork. Free.

Chinese New Year Parade (☎ 638-1041), late Jan., sometimes early Feb. Metro: Gallery Place. Firecrackers, lion dances, drums, and dragons. Free.

FEBRUARY

Black History Month Celebration (☎ 357-2700), at the Smithsonian Institute. Month-long special exhibits and activities on African-American history and culture.

Abraham Lincoln's Birthday (☎ 619-7222), observed Feb. 12. Laying down of wreaths and recitation of the Gettysburg address at the Lincoln Memorial. Free.

NO WORK ALL PLAY

July 4th, D.C.-Style

Washington celebrates Independence Day like no other. Here's the lowdown:

The day starts with the **Independence Day Parade** beginning at 11:45am and running along Constitution Ave. between 7th and 17th St. NW.

Throughout the day, the **Navy Band** and guest celebrities (usually country music singers) provide **live entertainment** at the Sylvan Theater at the Washington Monument and on the West Lawn of the Capitol. Meanwhile, the **Smithsonian Folklife Festival** on the National Mall features the culture of a particular US region (2004 will celebrate Mid-Atlantic maritime culture) together with the traditions and practices of other nations in a world-renowned festival. (See www.folklife.si.edu.)

The highlight of the day is the **Fireworks on the Mall,** a grand 20min. pyrotechnic show that begins at 9:10pm, set to the tune of the **National Symphony Orchestra,** (orchestra begins at 8pm). The best places to view the fireworks are the Capitol, the Lincoln, Jefferson, or FDR memorials, or anywhere along the Mall from 14th St. to the Capitol. Contact ☎ 619-7222 or visit www.nps.gov/nama/events/july4/july4.htm.

George Washington's Birthday Parade (☎ 800-388-9119), Feb. 16 at 1pm, through Old Town Alexandria. Pageantry and excitement. Free.

Mount Vernon Open House (☎ 703-780-2000), 3rd M in Feb (Feb. 16, 2004). Free admission to Mount Vernon, fife and drums on the green, and the obligatory wreath-laying.

MARCH

St. Patrick's Day Parade, Mar. 17, Constitution Ave. NW from 7th to 17th St. A celebration of all things green. Dancers, bands, bagpipes, and floats. Free.

Smithsonian Kite Festival (☎ 202-357-2700), late March on the Mall. Watch kite designers compete for prizes on the Washington Monument grounds. Call for exact date.

Washington Flower and Garden Show (☎ 703-823-7960), Mar. 25-28. Explore and admire the gardens, waterfalls, bridges, and statuaries crammed into the Convention Center, 801 Mt. Vernon Pl. NW. $10, under 12 $6.

D.C. Spring Antiques Fair (☎ 547-9215), D.C. Armory, 2001 E. Capitol St. SE. The most popular show of its kind, featuring a 3-day display of rugs, porcelain, sterling, and furniture. Perfect place to connect with foreign dealers who'll ship to you. Admission $6.

Environmental Film Festival (☎ 342-2564), Mar. 18-28 at the National Museum of Natural History. Films on everything from mites to elephants as well as global environmental issues.

APRIL

National Cherry Blossom Festival (☎ 547-1500), Mar. 27-Apr. 12, all over town. Parade, fireworks, fashion show, ball, concerts, and Japanese Lantern Lighting Ceremony.

Filmfest DC (☎ 628-3456), Apr. 21-May 2, at local movie theaters and museums. International screenings, discussion panels, and concerts. Features highbrow independent film often seen at the Sundance or Cannes film festivals. Admission $8.50 per film.

White House Spring Garden Tours (☎ 456-2200), mid-Apr. at the White House Gardens. Free music, flowers, and festivities highlight the blooming gardens.

Shakespeare's Birthday (☎ 544-4600), Apr. 25 at the Folger Shakespeare Library, 201 E. Capitol St. SE. Music, theater, food, and kids' events. Free.

American College Theater Festival (☎ 416-8000), Apr. 12-18 at the Kennedy Center. A jury chooses the best college shows from around the country. All shows are free.

White House Easter Egg Roll (☎ 456-2200), late Apr. on the White House South Lawn. For kids 3-6 years old. Famous morning egg roll brings out the president and the press.

MAY

Department of Defense/Joint Services Open House (☎ 301-568-5995 or 301-981-4424), mid-May, at Andrews Air Force Base, Camp Springs, MD. Fabulous air aerobatics.

National Symphony Orchestra Memorial Day Weekend Concert (☎ 467-4600), May 30 at 8pm on the West Lawn of the Capitol. Free.

Memorial Day Ceremonies at Arlington Cemetery (☎ 703-607-8000), May 31. Wreaths at JFK's tomb and the Tomb of the Unknowns. Services in Memorial Amphitheater.

Memorial Day Ceremonies at the Vietnam Veterans Memorial (☎ 619-7222), May 31. Wreath-laying, speeches, bands, and a keynote address.

Memorial Day Jazz Festival (☎ 703-838-4844), May 31 noon-8pm, in Old Town Alexandria. Local big bands swing all afternoon. Free.

Virginia Gold Cup (☎ 540-347-2621), same day as the Kentucky Derby, at The Plains, Virginia's premier steeplechase, 5089 Old Tavern Rd. $60 per car in advance.

JUNE

Dance Africa D.C. (☎ 269-1600), 1st week of June at Dance Place. Traditional dance, food.

Dupont-Kalorama Museum Walk Day (☎ 667-0441), first weekend in June. 10 museums north of Dupont Circle seek publicity. Music, tours, food, crafts, etc. Free.

Carnival Extravaganza (☎ 829-1477), first week of June at Emery Park, corner of Georgia and Missouri Ave. NW. Large Caribbean population celebrates with costumes, dancing, and songs. Free.

Capital Pride, alongside the Gay Pride Festival (early June). Parade from 23rd and P St. NW, clubbing, pageants, bachelor auction, and comedy. Free.

Red Cross Waterfront Festival (☎ 703-549-8300), early June at Oronoco Bay Park in Old Town, Alexandria. Ethnic food, canoe rides, and fireworks set to the tune of rock and reggae. Admission $5-8.

National Capital Barbecue Battle (☎ 301-860-0630), late June, Pennsylvania Ave. from 9th to 13th St. Live music and the best BBQ outside of Houston and Memphis. Admission $7.

Smithsonian Folklife Festival (☎ 357-2700), June 23-27 and June 30-July 4, on the Mall. Huge Smithsonian fair demonstrates the crafts, customs, food, and music of D.C. Free.

JULY

Independence Day Celebration (☎ 619-7222), July 4, on the Mall between Independence and Constitution Ave. NW. Parade, colonial military maneuvers, concerts at the Sylvan Theatre, National Symphony Orchestra performances on the West Capitol steps.

Bastille Day (☎ 296-7200), early July, 12th St. and Pennsylvania Ave. NW. Live entertainment, food, and music mark the French Independence Day. Free.

Virginia Scottish Games (☎ 703-912-1943), late July, in Alexandria, VA, on the grounds of Episcopal High School. 2-day annual Scottish festival is one of America's largest. Admission $10-15.

Hispanic Festival (☎ 835-1555), in late July at the Washington Monument. Food, music, and dance from 40 Latin American nations. Free.

AUGUST

Georgia Ave. Day (☎ 667-6669), late Aug. At the intersection of East Ave. NW. America's largest business corridor comes alive with parades, carnival rides, live music, a 5k race, and ethnic food from Africa and the American South. Free.

National Frisbee Festival (301-645-5043), late Aug. Watch world-champions flip discs on the Mall. Talented frisbee-catching dogs are also amusing to watch. Free.

National Army Band's 1812 Overture Performance (☎208-1631), mid-Aug. at the Sylvan Theatre. Performance of this classical piece with firepower from the Salute Gun Platoon of the 3rd US Infantry.

D.C. Blues Festival (☎828-3028), late Aug. at the Carter-Barron Amphitheater near Rock Creek Park. Blues, folk, twang, wail, and moan. Free.

SEPTEMBER

Kennedy Center Open House (☎467-4600), early Sept. A one-day medley of classical, jazz, folk, and ethnic music, dance, drama, and film from D.C. performers. Free.

Adams Morgan Day (☎321-0938), early Sept., on 18th St. between Florida Ave. and Columbia Rd. Live music on 3 stages, stuff for sale, and a kaleidoscope of ethnic food. Free.

Kalorama House and Embassy Tour (☎387-4062), Sept. 12. Begin at the Woodrow Wilson House (2340 S St. NW) for an exclusive look at normally-closed ambassadors' residences. Tickets $18 in advance, $20 same day.

Oktoberfest (☎703-787-6601), 2nd to last weekend in Sept. Reston Town Center, Market St. Four days of beer, polka, and sauerbraten—not to be missed. Free, but meal purchase required.

St. Sophia Greek Festival (☎333-4730), late Sept. or Oct., Massachusetts Ave. NW at the corner of 36th St. Enjoy live Greek music, cathedral tours, arts and crafts, and authentic Greek food. Free.

OCTOBER

Taste of D.C. Festival (☎724-5347), Columbus Day weekend. Top restaurants line Freedom Plaza for public tastings, concerts, arts and crafts, and games. Admission free, but food sampling starts at $4.

White House Fall Garden Tours (☎456-2200), mid-Oct. Like the spring garden tours.

Jewish Film Festival (☎777-3248), late Oct. to early Nov. at the D.C. Jewish Community Center Cecile Goldman Theatre in Dupont Circle. Documentaries, discussion forums, screenings. Tickets $9.

Reel Affirmations (☎986-1119), usually mid-Oct. Screenings at the Lincoln and Cecile Goldman Theatres. Gay and lesbian film festival, complete with frequent Absolut Martini parties. Tickets $30 per day, $20 in advance.

Marine Corps Marathon (☎800-786-8763), last weekend of Oct. This world-famous marathon draws elite runners to a course that snakes past D.C.'s most famous landmarks.

Theodore Roosevelt's Birthday (☎703-289-2530), Oct. 27, Theodore Roosevelt Island, George Washington Memorial Parkway in Arlington. Birthday cake, TR look-alikes, and hiking in the urban wilderness. Free.

Vienna Halloween Parade (☎703-255-6300), Oct. 31, from Branch to Maple Ave. in Vienna, VA. Purportedly the region's oldest and largest parade of its kind.

NOVEMBER

Civil War Living History Day (☎703-838-4848), Nov. 10, at the Fort Ward Museum, 4301 W. Braddock Rd., in Alexandria. Reenactment of Civil War camp life, including artillery drill.

Veteran's Day Ceremonies (☎703-619-7222), Nov. 11, around Arlington Cemetery. Solemn ceremony with military bands.

Alexandria Antiques Show (☎410-435-2292), 2nd or 3rd weekend in Nov., 625 1st St., Old Town Alexandria. Admire formal furniture, oil paintings, and European pieces. Admission $8.

DECEMBER

Kennedy Center Holiday Celebration (☎467-4600), throughout Dec. Free concerts include choral, chamber, "Tubachristmas," and a sing-along to Handel's *Messiah*.

Kwanzaa Celebration (☎357-2700), at the Smithsonian Institute. Music, song, dance, games, lectures, and storytelling. Free.

National Christmas Tree Lighting/Pageant of Peace (☎619-7222), mid-Dec. to Jan. 1, on the Ellipse south of the White House. Christmas trees, menorahs, music, yule logs.

Washington National Cathedral Christmas Celebration and Services (☎537-6247), Dec. 24-25 at the Cathedral. Christmas service and music.

Don't be left out...

Get your travel on.
The International
Student Identity Card

$22 **is all it takes**
to save hundreds.

Accepted worldwide for awesome discounts!

The International Student Identity Card (ISIC) is a great
way to take advantage of discounts and benefits such
as airfare, accommodations, transportation, attractions,
theme parks, hotels, theaters, car rentals and more!

visit www.ISICus.com to find out about discounts
and the benefits of carrying your ISIC.

Call or visit STA Travel online to find the nearest
issuing office and purchase your card today:

www.ISICus.com   (800) 474.8214

enough already...
Get a room.

Book your next hotel with the people who know what you want.

» hostels
» budget hotels
» hip hotels
» airport transfers
» city tours
» adventure packages
» and more!

(800) 777.0112
www.statravel.com/hotels

STA TRAVEL

WE'VE BEEN THERE.

Exciting things are happening at www.statravel.com

INSIDE

getting into d.c. **21**
getting around d.c. **23**
embassies & consulates **27**
tourist office **27**
keeping in touch **27**
the media **29**
protocol **30**
safety **30**
money matters **31**
health **31**

Once in D.C.

GETTING INTO D.C.

TO AND FROM THE AIRPORTS

RONALD REAGAN NATIONAL AIRPORT

To get from the airport: Driving from **National Airport** to downtown is easy. Take **George Washington (GW) Pkwy. North** and then take the **Theodore Roosevelt Bridge** across the Potomac; you'll find yourself on **Constitution Avenue** with the Mall on your right.

To get to the airport: From downtown, take either the **Roosevelt Bridge** or **I-395 South** to **GW Pkwy. South.** Then take the airport exit. Signs for the airport will guide you to the proper terminal. The ride takes 15-20min. without traffic. **Metrorail's** Blue and Yellow Lines stop just outside the airport, and are within easy walking distance and accessible via the airport shuttle (www.wmata.com/metrorail). The **SuperShuttle** (☎800-258-3826; www.supershuttle.com) bus runs between National and the city; the typical cost of a trip to downtown is about $10 per person. **Cabs** cost $10-15 for a ride to downtown.

DULLES INTERNATIONAL AIRPORT

To get from the airport: Driving to downtown Washington from Dulles usually takes about 40min.—but more during rush hour. Take **Rte. 267 East** (the **Dulles Tollroad**) to **I-66 East,** which will take you to **Constitution Avenue** in downtown D.C.

To get to the airport: To reach the airport, take **I-66 West** to **Exit 67.** Follow signs to the airport, which is 16 mi. from Exit 67. Taxis between Dulles from downtown cost around $44-50 one-way (☎703-661-6655). **Metrobus** is the cheapest option; it runs from Dulles to the

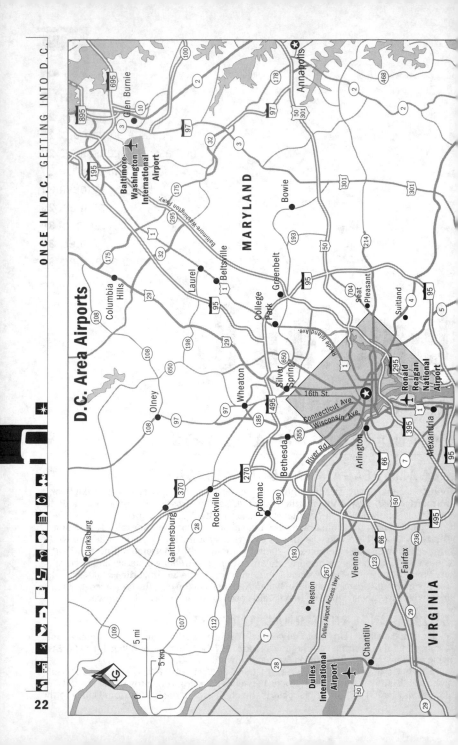

D.C. Area Airports

MARYLAND

VIRGINIA

Baltimore-Washington International Airport

Dulles International Airport

Ronald Reagan National Airport

Annapolis

Glen Burnie
Columbia Hills
Clarksburg
Gaithersburg
Rockville
Potomac
Olney
Wheaton
Silver Spring
Bethesda
Laurel
Beltsville
College Park
Greenbelt
Bowie
Seat Pleasant
Suitland
Arlington
Alexandria
Reston
Vienna
Fairfax
Chantilly

16th St.
Connecticut Ave
Wisconsin Ave
River Rd.
Rhode Island Ave.
Baltimore-Washington Pkwy.
Dulles Airport Access Hwy.

5 mi
5 km
N

L'Enfant Plaza Metro (D & 7th St. SW), stopping at the **Rosslyn Metro** on the way (☎637-7000; www.wmata.com/metrobus; 1hr.; 18 times per day 6:28am-11:40pm from Dulles, 5:33am-10:37pm from L'Enfant Plaza; $2.50). The **Washington Flyer Coach Service** (☎888-927-4359; www.washfly.com) leaves frequently to **Metro: West Falls Church.** It runs every 30min. departing from the airport at 15 and 45min. past the hr. M-F 5:45am-10:15pm, Sa-Su 7:45am-10:15pm; departing from the Metro every 30min. M-F 6:15am-10:45pm, Sa-Su 8:15am-10:45pm ($8, round-trip $14, discounts for groups of 3 or more, seniors 55+, and international students). **SuperShuttle** (☎800-258-3826; www.supershuttle.com) runs buses to downtown daily; the average cost of a trip downtown is about $21, $11 for each additional person.

BALTIMORE-WASHINGTON INTERNATIONAL

BWI lies 10 mi. south of Baltimore.

To get from the airport: To reach D.C., Take **I-195 West** to the **Baltimore/Washington Parkway (BW Parkway), I-295 South,** which will take you to **New York Avenue** in downtown D.C. To reach Baltimore, take **I-195 West** to the **BW Pkwy. North.**

To get to the airport: From D.C., take the **BW Parkway I-295 North** to **I-195 East**, or take the **Capital Beltway (I-495)** to **I-95 North** and take **Exit 47A;** follow airport signs for both. From Baltimore, take **I-295 South (BW Parkway)** to **I-195 East;** follow signs for the airport. Without traffic, driving time is about 50min. from D.C. The **MARC** (☎800-543-9808; www.mtamaryland.com) is the cheapest way to get to D.C. ($6 to **Union Station;** M-F only). **Amtrak** (☎800-872-7245; www.amtrak.com) provides train service from BWI to **Union Station** in D.C. (40min., 10 per day, $9-38). **SuperShuttle** (☎800 258 3826; www.supershuttle.com) buses also run to D.C. (average cost of transportation to downtown D.C. about $31, each additional person $11).

TO & FROM THE TRAIN STATION

Union Station (☎371-9411; www.unionstationdc.com), 50 Massachusetts Ave., NE, is easily accessible by metro. The **Union Station Metro,** on the red line, connects directly to the train station. Union Station is within 10min. walking distance of the Capitol and 15-20min. from the National Mall.

TO & FROM THE BUS STATION

The **Greyhound Bus Station,** 1005 1st. St. NE (☎289-5154), at L St, lies several blocks north of Union Station. Walk down 1st St. to reach **Metro: Union Station.**

GETTING AROUND D.C.
BY PUBLIC TRANSPORTATION

BY METRORAIL

Metrorail (**Metro** for short), the Washington subway system, along with **Metrobus,** which celebrated its 30th anniversary in 2003, forms the backbone of the D.C. public transportation system. The Metro stations, sterile and relentlessly beige with high, curved ceilings, reflect a 70s architectural aesthetic. The Metro cars are quiet, carpeted, air-conditioned, and clean. Between the brown-capped Metro cops and the stations themselves, which leave no place to hide, the system has remained nearly crime-free. The **Wheaton Station** has the world's second-longest escalator, which at 230 ft. takes 5min. to ride up. Metro system route maps and rail and bus passes are sold at the sales office at the **Metro Center Line Exit,** 12th and F St. (☎636-3425. Open M-F 7:30am-6:30pm). For general Metro info call ☎637-7000 or go to www.wmata.com.

HOURS & FARES

The Metro runs Monday to Thursday 5:30am-midnight, Friday 5:30am-3am, Saturday 7am-3am, and Sunday 7am-midnight. Parking is available at some Metro lots and is free on weekends. The Metro operates on a computerized "farecard" system; your fares are

based on the distance you travel and the time of day you are traveling. Peak hours are Monday through Friday 5:30-9:30am and 3-7pm, when fares range from $1.20 to $3.60; at all other times, fares range from $1.20 to $2.20. To get your ticket, purchase a card from the vending machines in the station in front of the turnstiles. Be sure to note the appropriate rate: rush hour or regular. You can credit your farecard with any amount from $1.10 to $45, but the machines give at most $4.95 in change. Note that you must use your ticket in an electronic turnstile to enter and leave the Metro; **save your ticket during the ride.** If you don't have enough money to cover the fare on your card, you can add money to it at your destination. Exact-fare cards are eaten up by the exit turnstiles; cards with money left on them are returned. If you plan to connect with a bus after you ride, get a transfer pass from machines on the train platform before you board a train.

SPECIAL PASSES

If you plan to ride the subway several times, buy a **One-Day Pass** ($6). This is undoubtedly the most economical choice for a day's sightseeing. The pass offers unlimited Metro usage M-F 9:30am to closing or all day Sa-Su. Also available are seven-day **Short Trip Passes** ($20), which are valid for seven consecutive days of Metro trips up to $2 between 5:30-9am and 3-7pm; **Fast Passes** ($30) offer seven days of unlimited Metro travel. Passes are available at the main office and other Metro sales offices, some grocery stores and banks, and online at www.wmata.com. If you're staying in D.C. for an extended period of time, consider purchasing a **SmarTrip** card, a plastic farecard that costs $5, can be recharged, and can hold up to $200 in value; this card can be replaced if lost; purchase online at www.wmata.com or at a metro sales office or other retail location. Call ☎ 962-1488 for information about advance fare purchases for groups. Up to two children four years old or younger ride free with each paying passenger. Qualified **senior citizens** and **persons with disabilities** use $3 or $10 specially encoded farecards and pay half the peak fare, not to exceed $1.80, regardless of the time of day. You must obtain an Metro ID card to buy the $3 and $10 farecards, and you must have your Metro ID card with you when using the system. The special farecards are available at all Metro sales offices, at other retail locations, and online. Call ☎ 637-7000 for more information; disabled persons can call ☎ 962-1245. Elevators are available. The **Lost and Found,** 8405 Colesville Rd., Silver Spring, MD (☎ 962-1195) is open M, W, F 7am-3:30pm and Tu, Th 9:30am-6:30pm.

METRO IN GEORGETOWN

As Zachary Schrag explains in his article on the history of Metrorail (see p. 74), a host of historical reasons stopped Metro from installing a station in the popular Georgetown area. Rosslyn, Foggy Bottom, and Dupont Circle are the closest stops, each a considerable walk from Georgetown. Fortunately, proponents of commerce in the area operate shuttle buses called the **Georgetown Metro Connection.** Big blue buses ferry shoppers and partiers along two routes: M St. to Rosslyn and Dupont Circle; and along Wisconsin Ave. to Foggy Bottom. The shuttles run every 10min. along both streets and cost $1 one-way ($0.35 with Metro transfer; monthly passes $20; call ☎ 703-525-1995 to purchase monthly pass; www.georgetowndc.com/shuttle.php).

BY METROBUS

The extensive **Metrobus** (same address, phone, and website as metrorail; some buses run 24hr.) system reliably serves **Georgetown, downtown,** and the **suburbs.** Downtown, the bus stops every few blocks. Regular fare in D.C. is $1.20 (exact change required); express buses, usually in the suburbs, cost $2.50. Seniors and disabled persons are entitled to discounts. Up to two children four years or younger ride free when accompanied by a paying passenger. Schedules and route maps for buses operating near Metrorail are available in those stations. A comprehensive bus map is available from the main Metro office and at www.wmata.com/metrobus/maps. Alexandria (**DASH;** ☎ 703-370-3274; www.dashbus.com), Montgomery County (**Ride-On;** ☎ 240-777-7433; www.dpwt.com), and Fairfax County (**Fairfax Connector;** ☎ 703-339-7200;

www.co.fairfax.va.us/comm/trans/connector) have their own, smaller bus systems; these routes are included in Metro maps. **Metro Information** (☎ 637-7000) describes the exact buses and trains needed to reach any destination.

ROUTES

Bus routes with a letter followed by a number (like D4, S2) or with a two-digit number make stops in D.C. and Maryland, or sometimes (like the J buses) only in Maryland. Some routes (like the 30-series buses) run only in D.C. If the number precedes the letter (18L, 5D), the route runs in Virginia. Most Virginia routes connect through the Pentagon Metro stop. The following list gives some useful bus routes for tourists.

30-series (30, 32, 34, 35, 36) goes downtown up Pennsylvania Ave. NW to Georgetown and then up Wisconsin to Upper Northwest.

42 goes from Metro Center to Farragut and then up Connecticut Ave., through Dupont Circle to Columbia Rd., on which it passes through Adams Morgan.

D2 goes from Glover Park in far NW to Dupont Circle.

L2 runs from McPherson Sq. in downtown up Connecticut Ave. to Chevy Chase.

N2 and **N4** run from Farragut and Dupont Circle up Massachusetts Ave., past Embassy Row to American University and Friendship Heights.

BY TAXI

Washington taxi fares are based on a map that splits the city into **eight zones** and a number of subzones. Zone prices are fixed, and the basic cost of your cab ride is determined by the zones in which you begin and end—but not the route in between. Prices between subzones within a particular zone vary only slightly.

A zone map and fare chart are posted in every legal cab (see **Service Directory,** p. 331). To ensure honesty in billing, ask your driver to calculate your fare in advance. If you take a cab within a single zone, your fare will be $5. Special charges include a $1 surcharge during **rush hour** (M-F 7-9:30am and 4-6:30pm). Each **additional passenger** incurs a $1.50 charge. After the first piece of luggage, **baggage** costs $0.50 or $2 for "trunk-sized" suitcases. If you call a taxi service to request a cab, there is an added $1.50 charge. Taxi rides to, from, and within Maryland and Virginia are calculated based on mileage rather than by zones, and vary based on local rules. The interstate fee is $2.65 for the first ½ mi. and $0.80 for each additional ½ mi. (also $1 extra for rush hour, $1.50 dispatch fee, and $1.25 for trunk-sized luggage). During the day, the Metro makes taxis mostly unnecessary. A cab ride from the club district in Adams Morgan to Metro Center should cost $6.90 for one person.

If you can't hail a taxi, either because it's too late or because of the neighborhood, call **Yellow Cab** (☎ 544-1212). Call the **Transit Commission** (☎ 331-1671) for price quotes on trips to Maryland and Virginia. If you think you're being overcharged or have a complaint, get a receipt, write down the cab number, and call the **D.C. Taxicab Commission** (☎ 645-6018), which will help you lodge a formal complaint.

BY CAR

Driving in D.C. is unnecessary and invites needless traffic and parking woes. *Let's Go* recommends using the Metro instead.

TRAFFIC

Rush-hour traffic creates massive delays M-F 7-9:30am and 4-6:30pm. Lunchtime is also a jam, and Friday afternoon a nightmare. For better access to downtown sights at these times, take the Metro or the bus.

PARKING

Expect to pay $10 or more for garage parking. The most widespread provider is **Colonial Parking,** which operates under the name **Landmark Parking** in D.C. (☎ 888-672-7536 or 628-1950) and runs lots all over the city. Finding on-street parking during the day is almost impossible, especially near the Smithsonian. During afternoon rush hour

(M-F 4-6:30pm), most downtown spaces are illegal. Nighttime parking is scarce in Georgetown, and essentially nonexistent in Dupont Circle and Adams Morgan. Luckily, the Metro now runs until 3am F-Sa, so it's possible to take the Metro back after a late night out on the town and avoid both parking worries and D.C. taxi zone ripoffs.

TICKETS

To pay a D.C. **traffic ticket,** go to the Department of Motor Vehicles' (DMV) **Bureau of Traffic Adjudication,** 65 K St. NE (☎727-5000; open M-F 8:15am-6:45pm; Metro: Union Station). Hearings close at 2pm each weekday. Pay with cash or credit card (MC/V). Otherwise, make a check payable to the D.C. Treasurer and send it to the Bureau of Traffic Adjudication, Washington, D.C. 20002. Towing will cost you $75 plus a $10 daily storage fee. Check out www.dmv.washingtondc.gov for further details about traffic tickets, towing, and other things that won't happen to you if you take our advice and take the Metro.

CAR RENTAL

Renting for local trips is reasonably cost-efficient, especially if several people share the burden. Renting is often cheapest in **Arlington, Virginia,** near Reagan National Airport. When dealing with any car rental company, make certain the price includes insurance against theft and collision. **American Express** automatically insures any car rented with its card. Although rental charges run $18-55 per day for an economy car, plus $0.10-0.30 per mi., most companies have special deals—especially on weekends. If you have a credit card, you can avoid leaving a cash deposit. Most companies charge those aged 21-24 an extra $10-20 per day and will not rent to anyone under 21. Policies and prices vary by agency. See p. 331 for car rental listings.

BY CITY TOUR

If you'd like to see the city in a more organized manner than by just wandering around, consider the *Let's Go* walking tours (see **Discover D.C.**, p. 14) Check out the excellent **Cultural Tourism D.C.** website (www.culturaltourismdc.org) for more ideas on walking tours you can follow yourself. But if you're tired of walking, tours on wheels might be just the thing for your weary, monument-trekking feet.

BUS AND TROLLEY TOURS

Tourmobile Sight-Seeing, 1000 Ohio Dr. SW (☎888-868-7707, 554-7950, or 554-5100; www.tourmobile.com), runs its blue-and-white buses mid-Apr. to mid-Sept. 9:30am-6:30pm, mid-Sept. to mid-Apr. 8:30am-4:30pm. For the standard 18-sight loop, get on at any stop marked by blue-and-white signs and buy tickets from the driver. $18, children 3-11 $8. Special routes travel to the Frederick Douglass home (a 2½hr. loop leaving at noon; $7, children $3.50) and to Mount Vernon (daily 10am, noon, and 2pm; $25, children $12; price includes admission). These tours leave from the Washington Monument, Lincoln Memorial, and Arlington Cemetery; purchase tickets from Tourmobile kiosks up to 1hr. prior to departure.

Discover Downtown D.C., MCI Center, 601 F St. NW (☎639-0908), leaves from the MCI Center and winds through Old Downtown for 1½hr., stopping at some well-known and a few fairly obscure sights. $7.50, children and seniors $5; tours leave Sa 10:30am and Su 1pm.

Capitol Entertainment Services (☎636-9203; www.washington-dc-tours.com) runs standard tours of major sights, but specializes in a 3hr. **African American History Tour** through Lincoln Park, Anacostia, and the Frederick Douglass home. Tours begin from area hotels during the summer. Call for winter group tours. $22, children 3-11 $15.

WALKING & BIKING TOURS

Anthony S. Pitch (☎301-294-9514; www.dcsightseeing.com). These nationally recognized walking tours (including one on Lincoln's assassination) guide you on a stroll around Adams Morgan, Lafayette Square, Georgetown, or Political Washington. $10-15; Su 11am-1pm.

Bike the Sites, Inc., 3417 Quesada St. NW (☎966-8662; www.bikethesites.com), offers tours complete with bicycles, helmets, equipment, water, and snacks. Tours lead 2-15 people to major hotels or Metro stations. Designed for a variety of skill levels. Call ahead as prices, start times, and locations vary seasonally. $40 for a 3hr. capital sites tour to $85 for a day-long Mount Vernon ride, or have a guide custom-tailor a tour to your specifications.

Tour D.C. (☎301-588-8999) leads 1½hr. walking tours through historic Georgetown every Th and Sa at 10:30am. Book these popular tours well in advance, as they almost always sell out completely. $12, special group rates and times available.

ODDBALL TOURS

D.C. Ducks, 1323 Pennsylvania Ave. NW (☎832-9800; www.dcducks.com), provides an entertaining land-and-water tour of the monuments and Mall sights. Kids ogle when the van (actually a renovated amphibious military vehicle) transforms into a boat. Tours leave from Union Station Apr.-Oct. every hr. daily 10am-3pm. $23-26, children 4-12 $12.

Scandal Tours (☎783-1212; www.gnpcomedy.com/scandaltours.html), a comedy show on wheels, hires actors to impersonate disgraced politicians as they steer tourists from one place of infamy to the next. In good weather, the 1¼ hr. tour whizzes past Gary Hart's townhouse, Watergate, and the Vista Hotel, where former mayor Marion Barry was caught smoking crack. Tours depart from the 12th St. entrance of the Old Post Office (opposite Metro: Federal Triangle). Apr.-Sept. Sa at 1pm. Reservations required. $27.

EMBASSIES & CONSULATES IN D.C.

Australia, 1601 Massachusetts Ave., 20036 (☎797-3000; fax 797-3168).
Canada, 501 Pennsylvania Ave., 20001 (☎682-1740; fax 683-7726).
Ireland, 2234 Massachusetts Ave., 20008 (☎462-3939; fax 232-5993).
New Zealand, 37 Observatory Cir., 20008 (☎328-4800; 667-5227).
South Africa, 3051 Massachusetts Ave., 20008 (☎232-4400; fax 265-1607).
UK, 3100 Massachusetts Ave., 20008 (☎588-6500; 588-7878).

TOURIST OFFICE

The D.C. Visitor Information Center, 1300 Pennsylvania Ave. NW (☎328-4748 or toll-free 866-324-7386; www.dcvisit.com), on the ground fl. of the Ronald Reagan Building, is the official tourist site of the D.C. Chamber of Commerce. It offers free brochures, hotel reservations, and help with ticket purchases. (In summer open M-F 8:30am-5:30pm, Sa 9am-4pm; in winter M-F 9am-4:30pm.)

KEEPING IN TOUCH
BY MAIL

SENDING MAIL FROM D.C.

Airmail letters under 1 oz. between North America and the world cost $0.80. Envelopes should be marked "airmail" or "par avion" to avoid having letters sent by sea. **Aerogrammes,** printed sheets that fold into envelopes and travel via airmail, are available at post offices and cost about $0.70 apiece. It helps to mark "airmail" if possible, though "par avion" is universally understood. Most post offices will charge exorbitant fees or simply refuse to send aerogrammes with enclosures.

If regular airmail is too slow, **Federal Express** (☎800-247-4747) can get a letter from D.C. to Sydney in two days for a whopping $30. By **US Express Mail,** a letter from D.C. arrives within four days and costs $15. **Surface mail** is by far the cheapest and slowest way to send mail. It takes one to three months to cross the Atlantic and two to four to cross the Pacific—appropriate for sending large quantities of items you won't need to see for a while. When ordering books and materials from abroad, always include one or two **International Reply Coupons (IRCs)**—a way of providing the postage to cover delivery. IRCs are available at your local post office for $1.05.

RECEIVING MAIL IN D.C.

There are several ways to arrange pickup of letters sent to you by friends, relatives, and lovers while you are abroad. Mail can be sent to D.C. through **General Delivery.** Unfortunately, all mail sent General Delivery in D.C. goes to the sorting facility on **Brentwood Road NE** (p. 334), miles from everywhere and not served by Metrorail (the closest stop is Rhode Island Ave.). If you must receive mail at Brentwood, bring a passport or other ID. **American Express** travel offices will hold mail up to 30 days for cardholders with advance notice. Some offices offer these services to non-members; call ahead. (☎ 800-528-4800; http://travel.americanexpress.com.)

TELEPHONES

AREA CODES

Unless otherwise noted, phone numbers in this book have a **202** area code. To call within D.C., you do not need dial this area code. Maryland and Virginia use **10-digit dialing,** so dial the area code with every call, even local calls. When calling D.C.'s contiguous suburbs from within D.C., do not dial 1 before the area code when calling the US from abroad.

AREA CODES		COUNTRY CODES	
Arlington and Alexandria, VA	703	Australia	61
Annapolis, MD	410	Canada	1
Baltimore, MD	410	Ireland	353
Charlottesville, VA	434	New Zealand	64
Fairfax County, VA	703, 540	South Africa	13
Fredericksburg and Middleburg, VA	540	United Kingdom	44
Williamsburg & Historic Plantations, VA	757	United States	1
Richmond, VA	804		
Virginia Beach, VA	757		
Washington, D.C.	202		

To call direct from home, dial:

1. The **international access code** of your home country. International access codes include: Australia 0011; Ireland 00; New Zealand 00; South Africa 09; UK 00. Country codes and city codes are sometimes listed with a zero in front (e.g. 033), but after dialing the international access code, drop successive zeros .

2. 1 (US and Canada's country code).

3. The area code (see chart below).

4. The local number.

CALLING ABROAD FROM THE US

To call another country direct from the US, dial:

1. 011 (international access code for the US).

2. Country code for the country you want to call: Australia 61; Ireland 353; New Zealand 64; South Africa 27; UK 44.

3. City/area code. If the first digit is a zero, omit it.

4. Local number.

CALLING WITHIN THE US

The simplest way to call within the country is to use a **coin-operated phone.** Most cost $0.25 or $0.35 for a local call, but it is expensive to use coins for long-distance or international calls. You can also buy **prepaid phone cards,** which carry a certain amount of phone time depending on the card's denomination. The time is measured in minutes or talk units (e.g. one unit/one minute), and the card usually has a toll-free access telephone number and a personal identification number (PIN). To make a phone call, you dial the access number, enter your PIN, and at the voice prompt, enter the phone number of the party you're trying to reach.

THE MEDIA

D.C. is a veritable ant farm of journalists. Eager reporters scurry all over the city, meet mysterious "sources close to the president," dredge up dirt wherever they can get it, and constantly try to tap into new veins of inside information. The powers that be never disappoint them—something spectacular (or sordid) is always brewing, and someone is always willing to leak it.

IN PRINT

The Washington Post (www.washingtonpost.com), D.C.'s major newspaper, contains comprehensive national, and international coverage. Founded in 1877, it floundered until 1933, when financier **Eugene Meyer** purchased it at a bankruptcy sale. His daughter **Katherine Graham** assumed control of the paper in 1963, leading the paper through its Watergate glory days. The *Post* is still one of the most influential papers in the country, covering everything from world crises to D.C. art and fashion.

    The Washingtonian is D.C.'s big magazine, billing itself as the publication "Washington lives by." It caters mainly to an older, more highbrow audience, but its annual "Cheap Eats" issue is a budget diner's bible. Reliable political gossip, fluffy features, and a sprawling real estate/classified section round out its hefty page count.

    The smaller, intellectual **Washington Monthly** (www.washingtonmonthly.com) likes to boast that it broke famous stories, like Mayor Barry's corruption, National Security Council misdeeds, and design flaws in the space shuttle, years before better-known pages got hold of them. If it's Congress you're interested in, read **Roll Call** (www.rollcall.com), which prints gossip and news for members of the House, the Senate, and their lucky staffers twice a week.

    The Washington **CityPaper** (www.washingtoncitypaper.org) is a thick, free, "alternative" weekly distributed on Thursdays to vending machines and stores around town. *CityPaper* provides excellent local investigative reporting, features, and comprehensive listings of the arts in D.C., especially regarding theater and popular music. The paper occasionally offers special coupons for clubs. *CityPaper* also has a Classifieds section, including apartments and personals.

NEIGHBORHOOD PAPERS

Away from the bright lights of national news, Washington's communities run their own papers. The daily **Washington Afro-American** covers black D.C. in a friendly, earnest way, with attention to individual citizens' achievements. The free, weekly **Washington Blade** (www.washblade.com), stacked in various stores (especially around Dupont Circle), is the gay and lesbian community's paper, with articles, listings, and an events calendar. **Washington Jewish Weekly** offers community news, editorials, kosher dining information, and a synagogue directory; look for it in vending machines all over town.

PHONE FACTS

Emergency: ☎911 (toll-free). Fire, police, ambulance.

Operator: ☎0 (toll-free).

Collect or Reverse-charge calls: ☎0 (toll-free).

Local Directory Assistance: ☎411 (toll-free; sometimes there's a connection fee).

National Directory Assistance: ☎1 + area code + 555-1212 (from a pay phone).

Numbers with the area code **800** or **888** are toll-free and can be dialed from a pay phone without depositing coins; numbers with the area code **900** generally charge a hefty rate per minute.

The Capitol Hill neighborhood cleans up weekly with **Hill Rag,** an area paper distributed all over downtown. The **In Towner** (www.intowner.com) covers local issues (zoning and crime, for example) for Dupont Circle, Adams Morgan, and points east (Scott and Logan Circles) and west (Cleveland Park). Another local favorite is **The Common Denominator** (www.thecommondenominator.com), a weekly paper covering all local news, available at most CVS pharmacies. Event listings congregate in **Go, Where,** and **On Tap,** free magazines distributed at hotels and libraries.

ON TELEVISION

Political junkies can get their fix 24hr. a day from the **Cable Satellite Public Affairs Network** (C-SPAN), which, along with its two sister stations, broadcasts "live gavel-to-gavel" coverage of all full congressional proceedings and other Washington events. National political programs like *Crossfire*, *Meet The Press*, *Hardball*, and the *McLaughlin Group* are filmed in D.C. Check the *Post* for complete TV listings.

PROTOCOL

TIPPING & BARGAINING

It's customary to tip cab drivers and waiters about 15-18%; exceptionally good waiters—or those who work at exceptionally good restaurants—are often tipped 20% of the pre-tax tab. Bartenders usually expect between $1 and $2 per drink. Bargaining is generally frowned upon and fruitless in the US, unless you're buying from a flea-market vendor.

TAXES

The prices quoted throughout *Let's Go: Washington, D.C.* are the amounts before sales tax has been added. Sales tax in D.C. is 6%. Hotel tax is 14.5%. Restaurant, car rental, and liquor taxes are all 10%. Parking in commercial lots (as opposed to Metro lots) incurs a 12% tax. The D.C. government sometimes grants sales-tax holiday weeks during traditionally slow periods at the end of the summer.

DRUGS & ALCOHOL

You must be 21 to purchase **alcoholic beverages** legally in D.C. Popular drinking spots, as well as upscale liquor stores, are likely to check your ID, especially in Georgetown, where recent crackdowns on fake IDs have resulted in hundreds of arrests. Bars and clubs can serve alcohol until 3am. Only beer and wine are sold on Sunday.

SAFETY

D.C.'s reputation as a nexus of muggings, drive-by shootings, and worse precedes it. Just as with any other urban area, always exercise caution. Rule number one: know which areas to avoid. The majority of crime occurs in places that do not get many visitors, primarily the **Northeast** and **Southeast** neighborhoods, and **east of 14th Street NW.** Avoid walking through these regions, and if you must, exercise extreme caution.

PERSONAL SAFETY

BLENDING IN & EXPLORING

Tourists are vulnerable to crime because they often carry large amounts of cash and are not as street-savvy as locals. Extra vigilance is always wise, but there is no need for panic when exploring D.C. Find out about unsafe areas from the D.C. tourist office, from the manager of your hotel or hostel, or from a local whom you trust. This book attempts to warn of unsafe areas, but remember that D.C. neighborhoods can change drastically between blocks.

SELF DEFENSE

A good self-defense course will give you concrete ways to react to different types of aggression. **Impact, Prepare,** and **Model Mugging** can refer you to local self-defense courses in the US (☎800-345-5425).

FINANCIAL SECURITY

PROTECTING YOUR VALUABLES

To prevent theft, don't keep all your valuables in one place. **Photocopies** of important documents allow you to recover them in case they are lost or filched.

Don't put a wallet with money in your back pocket. Avoid carrying large sums of cash, and keep some money separate from the rest in case of emergency. Record your traveler's check numbers, and never sign them until you are ready to cash them.

PICKPOCKETS

In D.C.'s massive city crowds and especially on public transportation, **pickpockets** are amazingly deft at their craft. Rush hour is no excuse for strangers to press up against you on the Metro—hold your bags tightly and move toward free space.

MONEY MATTERS

If you will be in D.C. for a lengthy period of time (say, for an entire summer), it may pay off to open a local checking account. Popular D.C. banks are **Allfirst** (☎800-441-8455), **Citibank** (☎800-926-1067), **First Union Bank** (☎800-398-3862), and **SunTrust** (☎301-206-6000). Locals recommend SunTrust, with its banks and cash machines all over the area. To open a checking account, you'll need a Social Security number, local address, and minimum deposit (for the cheapest accounts, it's usually around $100-200). Non-US citizens will find it nearly impossible to open a checking account; consider opening a savings account instead. Call the bank about its requirements for foreign account holders; usually, a Social Security number is mandatory.

HEALTH

MEDICAL CARE & HEALTH INSURANCE

Should you require medical attention while in D.C., clinics and emergency rooms are the best places to be treated. Both accept walk-ins and spare you the hassle of having to choose a doctor and go through an initial screening. For foreign visitors, arrange health insurance before you arrive in the US, as it is notoriously difficult to procure. Both clinics and emergency rooms in public hospitals will treat the uninsured, but **private-sector health insurance** is important to procure. For a list of hospitals and pharmacies, see the **Service Directory,** p. 331.

INSIDE

history **33**
architecture **41**
visual arts **41**
music **42**
literature **43**
theater **43**
print media **43**

Life & Times

HISTORY

IN THE BEGINNING

When Americans won their independence in 1781, their new government needed a home. But the location of this shrine to democracy created intense debate among the nation's founders. Northerners and southerners both wanted the capital city—America's symbolic center—within their own turf. Rivals **Alexander Hamilton** and **Thomas Jefferson** finalized plans to found Washington, D.C., during a 1790 dinner in Manhattan. The dinner deal was essentially a compromise on **debt assumption.** Hamilton argued that Congress should pay for state war debts, which the South opposed and the North favored. Jefferson agreed to debt assumption in exchange for a southern capital. The two parties decided to build the capital along the **Potomac River,** bordering Virginia and Maryland. **President George Washington** had the power to select a site along the Potomac and eventually picked an undeveloped area next to the small city of Georgetown, MD. Virginia and Maryland each agreed to donate land contiguous to Georgetown to create the District of Columbia. By February of 1791, **Andrew Ellicott,** the US Geographer General, had etched boundaries for the 100-square-mile district. Washington hired 36-year-old French engineer **Pierre L'Enfant** to design a nexus of grand avenues centered around a majestic Capitol building.

But L'Enfant's brash behavior outstripped his talent; when L'Enfant tore down a wealthy resident's porch because it stood in the way of New Jersey Ave., not even George Washington's influence could save him. He was fired and replaced by his associates, Elli-

33

from the
road

POLITICS
AND THE
CITY

In college, I preferred sleep to class and Happy Hour to study hour. That said, I read the newspaper daily, I interned for a senator, and I do have in my possession a degree in government—from Harvard, no less. I have even been known to stop momentarily on C-SPAN while flipping through channels (please don't tell anyone).

That said, I was still ill-prepared for the major role politics play in daily life in the District. Surely, this is due to the sizable percentage of D.C.-area residents who work for the federal government or government-funded enterprises. However rational the explanation, it still comes as a shock when every friendly conversation somehow shifts to politics.

Example #1: I meet two young women at a bar who happen to be from my hometown. We chat over a beer or two until one of them lets slip that she's "obsessed with the Supreme Court." Said chat turns into a heated debate over judicial activism (the extent to which the Supreme Court makes, rather than interprets, laws).

cott and African-American astronomer **Benjamin Banneker.** Despite exhaustive construction efforts, when Congress moved to the city in 1800, Washington only contained a meager 84 brick houses, 151 wooden houses, and 3210 people.

Toward the end of the **War of 1812,** D.C. fell to ashes in August 1814, when British troops set Washington ablaze and sacked the White House. The city's most important documents and works of art were salvaged by **First Lady Dolly Madison,** when she fled the burning city. Mrs. Madison is credited with the rescue of the famous **Gilbert Stuart** portrait of George Washington that hangs in the White House today.

D.C.'s location as the gateway to the South made it the logical first stop for **slave traders,** whose shackled captives awaited sale in the crowded pens on the Mall and near the White House. Elected officials decided crude and undeveloped D.C. was no place for families: politicians left their families at home and lived in boarding houses. The free black section of D.C. grew quickly. By 1850, Washington had 2000 slaves, 8000 free blacks, and 30,000 whites. Enterprising free black residents established 15 schools in Georgetown and Washington City before the beginning of the Civil War in 1861.

During the 1830s and 40s, many British travelers published their Washington journals—describing the city's unpaved streets, half-erected buildings, and horrifying slave traffic. **Charles Dickens,** a visitor in 1842, said that D.C., the "City of Magnificent Distances," should be renamed the "City of Magnificent Intentions." It had the fragile makings of a great city but was still little more than a muddy ghost-town.

THE CIVIL WAR TO WWI

In 1861, the Civil War turned the capital into the Union's most valued possession as the army erected a system of 68 forts around the city. **Abraham Lincoln** had an area in the Treasury Building converted into a bunker, and Congress ordered government agencies to house soldiers in their offices. Lincoln directed that work continue on the Capitol dome. "It is a sign," he reasoned, "that the Union shall go on." D.C. survived the Civil War relatively unscathed and was only attacked once, in 1864; the Confederates were thwarted by Union general **Ulysses S. Grant.**

The Civil War fueled a period of explosive growth for Washington. By the war's end, the population had increased by 50,000 to 125,000. The Civil War and Reconstruction sent tens of thousands of former slaves north for a better life. After Lincoln's assassination in 1865, the postwar Republican ascent spelled better times for blacks. The five years after 1868 were called the **Golden Age of Black Washington,** with new, enforced civil rights laws, black senators and Congressmen, a black public school system, an African-American at the helm of Georgetown University, and the founding of Dunbar High School and Howard University. President Grant appointed former slave and abolitionist **Frederick Douglass** as the District's recorder of deeds.

After the war, **Alexander "Boss" Shepherd** of the Board of Public Works, protected by Grant, embarked on an ambitious city improvement program. He paved the city's roads, installed streetlights and sidewalks, built sewers, tore down decrepit buildings, and financed the construction of grand new facades. Modernized at last, D.C. was mired in debt. In 1874, Congress fired Shepherd for overspending by $22 million.

The city's landscape developed under **Senator James McMillan,** chairman of the Senate's district committee during **President Theodore Roosevelt's** administration. Rotund **President William Howard Taft** set the maximum height for buildings within the city limits at 110 feet, so the Washington Monument could tower above the others. Taft's wife made her own contribution to the cityscape, securing the donation of the now-famous **cherry blossom trees** from Japan. For more on the Mall, see **The Mall and its Future,** p. 54.

Meanwhile, D.C.'s blacks were losing economic power. As employment discrimination flared, most had to work in service positions. Georgia-born **Woodrow Wilson** supported a segregation so thorough even young poet **Langston Hughes** could not find a job at the **Library of Congress.** The early 20th century brought segregation in public facilities; at the 1922 dedication of the Lincoln Memorial, world-famous educator **Booker T. Washington** was made to sit in a "colored" section. Black Washington in these years was virtually an autonomous city, with its own movie houses, theaters, shops, social clubs, and political leaders. But even black Washington was segregated along economic lines. Middle-class blacks in **LeDroit Park** had little to do with those who lived in the impoverished alley dwellings of Southeast and Southwest D.C.

FDR AND WWII

After the stock market **crash of 1929, President Herbert Hoover** reacted to the **Great Depression** with platitudes instead of money. The **Bonus Army** of unemployed veterans marched to the

Example #2: I am riding the Capitol subway when the intern to my right grabs my arm and excitedly points out Senator Rick Santorum, a Pennsylvania Republican now infamous for his anti-homosexual remarks. I explain that unless he is doing something worthy of blackmail, I couldn't care less. Honestly, could you even pick Rick Santorum out of a lineup? Unless you live in Pennsylvania or the District of Columbia, I bet not.

Politicians here are like celebrities in Los Angeles. They are always surrounded by an entourage, sometimes including paparazzi. People are always pointing and staring when they're around, and critiquing every aspect of their private lives when they're not.

The lesson? If you want to fit in here, do your homework. Dig out your old high school civics book. Make the Drudge Report (www.drudgereport.com) your home page. Better yet, flip on C-SPAN.

—Brad Olson

There's a saying in Adams Morgan: you can always tell what country's in trouble by finding the new restaurant in the neighborhood. Like most sayings, it isn't exactly accurate, but walking up 18th Street, past the rows of Ethiopian, Ghanaian, Salvadorian, Sudanese, Vietnamese, Indian, and Thai restaurants, it's easy to understand where it came from. Adams Morgan, as it stands today, is a product of immigration, and there are few streets in America that so perfectly reflect the changing political maps of the world.

18th Street, and Adams Morgan as a whole, is a relatively recent incarnation. The neighborhood was created out of the turmoil and wars that plagued Central America and parts of Africa during the 1980s. This was when the "evil empire" could have referred to both the Star Wars trilogy and the Soviet Union; when El Salvador, and much of Central America, felt the not-so-benevolent hand of American Cold War foreign policy; when Ethiopia, under a new communist dictatorship, was the world's poster-child for famine.

Adams Morgan was different back then, even if much of Washington has managed to remain stoically the same. D.C. was the murder capital of the country, and both the city and its mayor were having a hard time just saying no. Originally conceived in the 19th century as a wealthy suburb within Washington, Adams Morgan's tree-lined streets and oversized brick houses had fallen into a slump fueled by the city's high crime rate and dwindling population. The neighborhood was a mere shadow of its present self, a blend of young urban bohemianism and a solid working class population made up almost exclusively of Latin American and Caribbean immigrants. Beginning around 1980, though, the neighborhood started to change radically as a new influx of immigrants began to restore and rebuild the community. Between 1980 and 1990, the El Salvadorian population of Washington, D.C., increased by 584%, the Ethiopian population by 248%. Thousands of others from Africa, Asia, and the Caribbean also followed suit. For the new immigrant, Adams Morgan became a portal to a country and culture left behind.

The restaurants and stores that line 18th Street and Columbia Road are the most visible marks of Adams Morgan's cultural diversity. There are dozens of them, one after another, as if the neighborhood was built with solely this purpose in mind. They are the places you hear and see first, and everyone who lives here has a favorite (the pupuseria on Columbia Road, Meskerem restaurant on 18th Street). Neighborhoods are built in layers, though, and underlying the brick facade of 18th Street's restaurants are the quiet ways communities preserve, support, and engage one another. The local non-profits and cultural organizations, both formal and informal, are what have sustained the new immigrants, and in turn, Adams Morgan as well. A flyer taped to a light pole advertises Spanish language classes open to the community at large. Neighborhood residents volunteer as ESL teachers at a local non-profit that offers language classes for hundreds of immigrants from all over the world.

Adams Morgan has another side, however, one that splits the neighborhood between day and night. Walking around Adams Morgan in the afternoon, you can plainly see the dozens of ethnic stores and local non-profits that have given the neighborhood its reputation. At the bottom of 18th street, a small cluster of Ethiopian markets offer everything from incense to stacks of injera wrapped in plastic. Up the road, a small botanica has its window filled with Santeria icons: a tall black Virgin Mary surrounded by saints. Next door, a narrow staircase leads to a makeshift photo and ID shop used for passports and temporary identification. Across the street, a spread of purple, pink, and red saris hang from the window. But come nightfall, the red neon lights of the bars turn on, the skinny sidewalks fill up, the streets become jammed with suburban license plates, and the neighborhood gives itself over to a techno-80s-hip-hop-jazz-reggae scene that can either quicken your pulse or leave you exhausted. At the end of the night, most of the neighborhood will empty out once again, and the simple and quiet day-to-day motions that have kept Adams Morgan culturally vibrant and alive will continue.

Dinaw Mengetsu lived in Adams Morgan for several years. He has written for SparkNotes and the Princeton Review, and is drafting a novel for his masters thesis.

Mall to demand new benefits, but Hoover answered only with the National Guard. In 1932, newly elected **President Franklin Delano Roosevelt** arrived in D.C. accompanied by a herd of determined, idealistic liberals.

World War II solidified the big-city feel of D.C. Government agencies seized hotels for office space, and civilians poured into D.C. as clerical jobs opened up daily. This era saw the construction of the Federal Triangle, the government buildings between Pennsylvania and Constitution Ave.

Black Washington was changing, too, but slowly. The city's segregation came to national attention when the Daughters of the American Revolution barred black soprano **Marian Anderson** from singing at Constitution Hall. Anderson sang instead on Easter Sunday, 1939, on the steps of the **Lincoln Memorial** to a crowd of 75,000. The Supreme Court's 1953 **"Lost Laws"** ruling that civil rights laws from 1872 could still be enforced, desegregated most of the city. Paradoxically, integration destroyed many black-owned businesses, and the black commercial districts north of Massachusetts Ave. began to deteriorate, foreshadowing the area's decline.

FROM THE COLD WAR TO TODAY

The post-war era ushered in tremendous prosperity for the country, and D.C.'s growth continued. During the baby-boom era, the District grew until it spilled past its borders, with the area's population doubling between 1950 and 1970. Overflow population moved to the suburbs of Bethesda, Chevy Chase, and Potomac, MD, which soon became the favored retreats for the area's upper-middle class. This so-called "white flight" robbed D.C. of a large portion of its tax base and sent many flourishing businesses packing. Only quite recently have formerly impoverished areas like Shaw/U Street and Adams Morgan returned to vogue as residential communities and centers of commerce and nightlife.

The presidential administration has a defining influence on the character of the city. For three short years in the 60s, **John F. Kennedy** and his glamorous wife **Jacqueline** enchanted the press and brought a cultural savvy to the capital. D.C. saw protests galore during the rocky term of Kennedy's Texan successor, **Lyndon B. Johnson,** whose civil rights and Vietnam War policies brought applause and controversy to the city, respectively. **Richard Nixon** stepped down from office in 1974 after the *Washington Post's* Woodward and Bernstein exposed the **Watergate Scandal.** Home to **President Bill Clinton** from 1992 to 2000, the city in 2001 saw its most prestigious address change hands to Republican **George W. Bush,** former **President Bush's** son and Governor of Texas. Since taking office, Bush has had to contend with the terrorist attacks of September 11, 2001, war in Iraq, corporate fraud scandals, and a poor economy. The Bush administration has brought with it Texas license plates and Mexican, Tex-Mex, and Southern restaurants to the city's diverse culinary landscape.

POLITICAL D.C.

The capital represents the synthesis of the federal system—at once state, country, and city. Granted home rule by Congress in 1973, D.C. has its own court system as well as a department of motor vehicles, licensing organizations, unemployment agencies, food and drug inspections, and its own lottery. However, the administration and management of the city is controlled by the federal government. Though its three electoral votes ensure a say in presidential contests, D.C. has no voting power in Congress despite having a representative in the House. D.C.'s non-voting Congresswoman, Eleanor Holmes Norton, leads the D.C. statehood movement. For more on D.C. representation and voting, see p. 38.

D.C. has had an interesting and sometimes entertaining history of mayors. The winning mayoral candidate in 1973, **Walter E. Washington,** represented the black middle class. He was replaced in 1978 by **Marion Barry,** a prominent civil rights leader. Barry replaced two-thirds of the city government's staff and initiated pro-

The Ongoing Saga of "Taxation Without Representation"

Baseball and democracy are about as American as, well, apple pie. But they are both curiously absent from the nation's capital. Major League Baseball's Senators carpetbagged out of town 33 years ago, never to be heard from again. And while we can report that democracy functions fabulously within the Capitol itself, the people of its precincts have nary a vote on matters of national interest.

Washingtonians are, simply put, disenfranchised. Though 572,898 people live in the District (as of 2002), they have no voting representative in the Senate or Congress. They can, of course, choose a mayor and city council. D.C. only gained the right to vote in presidential elections in 1964 and did not receive a representative in the House until 1971. In a presidential election, the district represents 3 electoral college votes. But when it comes to true representation on a federal level, city residents have no voting voice; their lone delegate to Congress has no actual voting power.

And that's only half the story. Despite the dearth of voting rights, Washingtonians absorb all the burdens of federal participation; in other words, they pay taxes. Residents of the District pay more federal income taxes per capita—about $5000—than residents in 49 of the 50 states.

While the issue of representation is a perennial topic in the Capitol, it has lately come to a head. The recent economic upswing in the District—coupled with 2000's Florida balloting disaster—have given residents the sense that they deserve genuine voting rights.

A recent, indicative *Washington Post* poll showed that 86% of D.C. residents favor congressional voting representation. "For too long, D.C. residents have been invited to dinner, but not allowed to eat," Council Chairman Linda Cropp told the *Post*. "D.C. residents are hungry for democracy. D.C. residents are starving for voting representation in Congress."

To make things more complicated, Congressional voting rights are intimately tied up with statehood. Washington, D.C. would essentially have to become the 51st state before its voting rights were recognized. And becoming a state is no easy matter. In 1993 the House considered a bill that would have granted Washington statehood; the legislation garnered only 153 votes, 151 of them cast by Democrats.

After Virginia and Maryland ceded land for the creation of the federal seat in the late 18th century, early residents managed to vote for Congressional representatives from the two states. But soon both states decided to turn responsibility for the district—and representation—over to Congress.

When the city sputtered economically in the late 19th century, Congress dissolved the city's elected bodies and appointed a panel to govern the city. (In 1995 Congress would take similar action: it appointed a five-member financial control board to oversee an ineffective DC government.)

A House District Committee was eventually formed to administer city governance. The Committee, chaired in the 1950s and 1960s by white South Carolina Dixiecrat John McMillan, was notorious for killing bills designed to grant voting rights for District residents. A local "Free DC" movement—as much about civil rights as about political rights—began to flourish in response.

In 1964 Congress finally gave Washingtonians the right to vote for president. And the defeat (led by McMillan) of a 1965 bill intended to grant home rule set off a boycott of businesses unsympathetic to Free DC (spearheaded by none other than Marion Barry).

In 1967 the District was allowed an appointed mayor and city council, an elected school board in 1968, and, a nonvoting delegate to Congress in 1971.

In 1972 D.C. activists actually journeyed to South Carolina and successfully campaigned against McMillan in the primary. With McMillan gone from the District Committee, President Nixon signed a home rule charter in 1973, allowing residents to elect their own city officials. The same charter denied federal voting rights and maintained Congress's control of city spending.

(Continued on next page.)

Things remained quiet until 1978. That year saw both houses of Congress passing a constitutional amendment calling for full voting representation. But in the subsequent seven-year ratification effort just 16 of a necessary 38 state legislatures approved the measure.

In the spring of 2002, Senator Joseph Lieberman and long-time District Congressional delegate Eleanor Holmes Norton introduced "Taxation Without Representation" legislation. The proposed act demanded two votes in the Senate and one in Congress or an exemption from federal income taxes for District residents.

Recent plans to rescue Washington from representation and taxation limbo range from recasting the city as a commonwealth to reincorporating much of the District into Maryland (and gaining attendant voting rights in that state). The city even filed suit in 1998 for full voting rights. (The judges recognized "the inequity of the situation" but said that such rights could not be granted unless the District became a state.)

Conventional wisdom says that the District will not get federal voting rights anytime soon. For one thing, Republicans are wary of granting any expansion of powers to the reliably Democratic city. When Lieberman, as chairman of the Senate Governmental Affairs Committee, called for a hearing in May 2002 to review the matter, zero Republican committee members showed up.

It comes as a shock, then, that a Republican congressman from Virginia is proposing a bill that will give the District's representative a vote. The bill, authored by Rep. Thomas M. Davis III (R-Va), would propose adding a seat each for D.C. and largely-Republican Utah, which lost a seat in the House in the last redistricting, thus retaining the current party balance. "It's hard to make a straight-faced argument that the capital of the free world shouldn't have a vote in Congress," he said. Davis, chairman of the Committee on Government Reform, is currently researching the best way to introduce such a bill.

While most District activists are lauding Davis's proposal as a landmark step toward full representation, not everyone is as thrilled. "I don't support this," said Democratic non-voting Congresswoman Eleanor Holmes Norton. "But I think it's important for Tom Davis to be encouraged so we can get to full Congressional voting rights."

District government has scheduled an informal presidential primary for January 13, 2004, in order to precede even New Hampshire and to highlight the capital's lack of representation. Even the DMV has gotten involved in the cause. In an act of protest, the slogan on District license plates that once read "Celebrate & Discover" now reads "Taxation Without Representation." President Bill Clinton had the new plates affixed to the presidential limo just before he left office, but not surprisingly, when President George W. Bush, who is not a supporter of D.C. statehood, took office in 2001, special inaugural plates took their place.

In the meantime, District residents will pursue another favorite pastime fit for the nation's capital: the quest a home baseball team (see **Williams at Bat,** p. 194).

Asher Price is the assistant to the editor at The New Republic *in Washington, D.C. Brad Olson, a Researcher-Writer for* Let's Go: D.C. 2004, *contributed to this article.*

Hirshorn Museum, Rodin

Sculpture Garden at National Gallery

Woodlawn Plantation

grams that turned Washington into a mini-welfare state. By the end of his third term, D.C. employed 48,000 workers. By the mid-80s, however, the shine had worn off the Barry administration. Corruption was as rampant as crack cocaine. The grand finale came when Barry himself was caught by the FBI on videotape using crack in January 1990. He was charged with possessing cocaine and sentenced to 6 months in prison. Political outsider **Sharon Pratt Kelly** campaigned with a broom in her hand and was elected mayor the following November. However, her promises of security and stability proved hollow, and she was defeated in 1994 by a Barry fresh from detox. This election made D.C. the nation's laughingstock. Barry inherited a deficit of around $700 million, but he didn't have to worry about it for long. A month after he took over, Congress created a **Financial Control Board** with total control over D.C. spending. During the first year of Congressional fiscal control, D.C. ran a surplus of $186 million. Legislation in June 1997 took away most of Barry's remaining power, prompting the Mayor to protest "the rape of democracy." His cries fell on deaf ears; the Financial Control Board retained control over D.C. until the city's budget remained balanced, a feat finally achieved under **Anthony Williams,** the former Chief Financial Officer of D.C., who took office on January 2, 1999. His platform contained five goals: improving customer service, cleaning up the city, expanding employment, bringing in more businesses, and nurturing strong communities. In his most recent reelection campaign, a large portion of the nearly 10,000 signatures Williams's campaign staff collected to ensure his presence in the November 2002 Democratic primary were found to be forged, and the D.C. elections board banned him from the election. Williams ran and won as a write-in candidate. He spent 2003 urging the D.C. Council to approve his $339 million package to build a baseball stadium in downtown D.C.; in June, he finally decided to hold off until Major League Baseball decides to move a team to D.C. For more on the controversy surrounding baseball in the area, see **Williams at Bat,** p. 194.

D.C. BY DAY AND NIGHT

During business hours, commuters pour into the Northwest section of the city, but after dark the power lunches end and the city quiets down. White flight has plagued the city, its population dropping from 638,432 in 1980 to 572,898 in 2002. The suburbs have absorbed much of the post-workday spending, with larger homes, better schools, and big malls flanking the mostly white areas. Fairfax County, Virginia and Montgomery County, Maryland are the two richest counties in the nation. Cities of strip malls, such as Rockville, Maryland, have also grown. A better economy and reduced crime rates have renewed appreciation for the city's private schools and cultural offerings and have lured citizens back to Georgetown and Dupont Circle.

ARCHITECTURE

Early D.C. architects knew their mission was to design what they saw as the greatest capital since Ancient Rome. Their federal style, composed of marble columns, pediments, and friezes, echo the Classical world. Even creating the early city was a democratic process, as plans for many buildings, including those for the Capitol and the White House, were selected in anonymous competitions entered mostly by amateur architects. By the mid-1800s, however, professional architects took over. The outstanding designer of the period was **Benjamin Latrobe,** who designed two models of sophistication, **St. John's Church** and **Decatur House.**

D.C.'s architecture turned **Victorian** and excessive in the 1870s under **Boss Shepherd,** who authorized A. B. Mullet's State, War, and Navy Building (now the **Old Executive Office Building,** see p. 64). The building's gingerbread windows delight tourists today, but severe Neoclassicists of the early 1900s hated the building and repeatedly tried to get it demolished. The Library of Congress's **Jefferson Building** (see p. 49), the magnificent Pension building (now the **National Building Museum,** see p. 129), and the **Old Post Office** (see p. 72) are dignified examples of the Victorian style.

The budget-inspired freeze on building that followed Boss Shepherd's fall from power thawed around the turn of the century, when **Daniel Burnham** brought the **Beaux Arts** style to Washington. The McMillan Commission funded Burnham's **Union Station** (see p. 52). The Commission also proposed the **Lincoln Memorial** (see p. 57), which heralded a return to a bigger and sparser variety of Neoclassicism. **John Russell Pope,** the undisputed master of 30s and 40s Greco-Roman building, designed the domed **West Building** of the **National Gallery of Art** (see p. 122).

When the dust of World War II cleared, D.C. began striving to blend International Modernism's clean lines and brutal simplicity with the classical feel of existing construction; some buildings, like the **Kennedy Center** (see p. 69), do this fairly successfully, signaling the beginning of postmodern architecture's influence in the late 80s. The **Canadian Embassy** (see p. 84) is one of the best postmodern buildings in D.C.; Frank Gehry's plans for an expansion of the **Corcoran Gallery** (see p. 66) will add a unique and dramatic twist to D.C.'s architectural landscape.

VISUAL ARTS

MEMORIALS

Inspired by the desire to commemorate, planners and various interest groups have filled D.C. with public art in nearly every stretch of the city. The public memorial, its own art form, half sculpture and half architecture, may have reached its apex in Washington. D.C.'s memorials reach their highest concentration west of the Mall (see p. 53). The memorials near Foggy Bottom showcase a variety of architectural styles from Robert Mill's 1836 design for the classical obelisk now known as the **Washington Monument** (see p. 53) to Maya Ying Lin's minimalist granite creation, the **Vietnam Veterans Memorial** (see p. 57). Don't miss the **Adams Memorial,** by far one of the most beautiful in the city, located far from the rest of the memorials in Rock Creek Cemetery, and the **Franklin Delano Roosevelt Memorial,** built in the late 1990s (see p. 59). Most public statues showcase historical figures and date either from the 1870s or the years directly following WWII. D.C.'s traffic circles are home to many statues, among them General Winfield Scott in Scott Circle, Benito Juarez on Virginia Ave. NW, and the statue of Robert Emmet near Dupont Circle.

OUTDOOR ART

D.C. is home to an assortment of public gardens filled with art. Along the Mall, the **Hirshhorn Sculpture Garden,** the **National Gallery Sculpture Garden,** and the **Smithsonian Castle Garden** offer some of the finest outdoor sculpture. The city's biggest universities, **Georgetown, George Washington,** and **Howard University,** are decorated with famous sculptures, from GWU's famous hippos to Howard's assortment of sculptures of African-American leaders. Public art is often found in unexpected places, especially in abandoned lots around **U Street** and the booming **Gallery Place** art scene.

MUSEUM COLLECTIONS

Sadly, in the midst of the attention placed on politics, D.C.'s tremendous offerings in visual art are all too often overlooked. Washington boasts world-class museums and the best collection of **Raphaels** and **Vermeers** in the **National Gallery of Art's West Wing.** The **Hirshhorn Museum's** collection features contemporary art and D.C.'s best collection of 20th-century sculpture. Away from the Mall, check out the **Corcoran Gallery** and the **Renwick.** Collector **Duncan Phillips's** museum, now known as the **Phillips Collection,** was showing off modern art when New York's Museum of Modern Art was still just a dream. D.C. had no famous native painters until the 1960s, when **Kenneth Noland's** spartan abstracts, **Gene Davis's** parallel trips, and the experimental works of critical darling **Morris Louis** were said to form the **Washington Color School.** For more information on Washington's museums, see **Museums,** p. 115.

MUSIC

John Philip Sousa, who led the **Marine Corps Marching Band** from the 1880s to the 1900s, was the first D.C. citizen to become successful in the music world. Sousa taught the band to play, then initiated the bevy of **military brass** concert parades that stomp and honk by the Mall to this day. Later, things began to swing: the **Howard Theater** and other jazz venues cultivated a string of Washington artists, most notably the immortal band leader, jazz composer, and pianist **Duke Ellington.** One of America's most prolific composers, Ellington is an epic figure in the history of jazz, from **ragtime** and **big-band swing** in the 20s and 30s to experimental in the 1960s and 70s. Jazz songstresses from D.C. include **Roberta Flack** and **Shirley Horne.**

D.C. is famous for **go-go,** born in Washington's African-American community in the late 1960s. Go-go is a genre of raw, rhythmic dance music that blends funk rhythms, African percussion, and instrumental skill with hypnotic rap music. According to legend, the father of go-go, **Chuck Brown,** got his first guitar in prison in exchange for five packs of cigarettes. After his release in 1962, he put together the **Soul Searchers,** whose *Bustin' Loose* became a national hit. Keep your ears open for the go-go groove at clubs around town and at festivals like **Malcolm X Day, Marvin Gaye Day,** or **Adams Morgan Day** (see **Calendar of Events,** p. 15).

D.C. **rock 'n' roll** didn't get off the ground until punk touched down in the early 80s. Bands like local boy and legendary punkster **Henry Rollins's Black Flag** led the trend of hardcore and straight-edged punk in the early 1980s. In 1985, they proclaimed the **Revolution Summer of '85.** The **9:30 Club** and **The Black Cat** host big and small acts nightly (see **Rock and Pop,** p. 184, for more live music venues). Today, **Fugazi** is one of the few remaining hardcore acts.

As it entered the 21st century, D.C. shed antiquated punk, ska, and swing music for trance, house, and ultra-lounge. A burgeoning D.C. lounge scene, led by the DJ-owned **Eighteenth Street Lounge,** produced a boom in D.C.-based indie DJ and dub-artist releases. As for mainstream musicians, D.C. continues to breed R&B stars, including sex-symbol **Ginuwine.** Also, Baltimore's **WHFS** (99.1 FM) is still one of the nation's foremost alternative-rock forums, hosting the massive **HFStival** concert each May, which brings the country's biggest modern-rock names to D.C.'s RFK stadium.

LITERATURE

The earliest writer to settle in the capital was poet **Walt Whitman,** who lived in D.C. from 1862 to 1873. He originally came to find and care for his wounded brother; he stayed to volunteer as a Union Army nurse. During his time in Washington, he also published two editions of his watershed book, *Leaves of Grass*, shocking the literary world with his spontaneous and whimsical verses.

Literature emanated from the African-American community in the early 20th century, when the famous Harlem Renaissance established a D.C. outpost around U St. **Langston Hughes** and **Jean Toomer** emulated Ballad-poet **Paul Dunbar**'s move to D.C. Other poets made strange pilgrimages to see *Cantos* verse-maker **Ezra Pound,** who was confined in St. Elizabeth's for criminal insanity. Literary hawks and doves converged on D.C. for the **1968 March on the Pentagon,** led by novelist **Norman Mailer** and by **Robert Lowell,** whose poem *July in Washington* may be the best ever written about the city. Since World War II, the **Library of Congress** has attracted important poets for the two-year position as Poet Laureate, a post currently held by **Louise Elizabeth Gluck**.

Katharine Graham's *Personal History* and **Meg Greenfield's** *Washington* are two excellent memoirs that reveal a slice of the city's history, character, and heart.

THEATER

D.C.'s most famous theater may be **Ford's Theatre,** the site of President Lincoln's assassination. But D.C.'s theater scene is only second to New York City's and its claim as the nation's capital attracts the best of the international theater companies. From 1964 to 1973, Washington was the only city in the country outside New York with two professional resident theater companies. The **Arena Stage** was the first professional resident theater in D.C., followed shortly by the now-defunct **Washington Theater Club.** The Washington Theater Club imported famous actors like Gene Hackman and Billy Dee Williams to premiere new works by aspiring playwrights: plays like **Harold Pinter's** *The Birthday Party* and works by **Eugene Ionesco** and **Lanford Wilson** were produced on the club's stage sometimes years before they arrived in New York. For a listing of D.C. theaters, see **Theater and Dance,** p. 187.

The construction of the **John F. Kennedy Center for the Performing Arts** (see p. 188) in 1971 provided a much-needed cultural center. Today, the Kennedy Center is home to the Washington Ballet (see p. 187), the Washington Opera (see p. 186), the American College Theater Festival (see **Calendar of Events,** p. 15), and scores of other productions. The **Washington Shakespeare Company** enchants the city, especially with its free outdoor performances in the summer. The dance scene in Washington has also grown over the past two decades, particularly since the arrival of hyperactive and creative **Septime Webre,** who assumed the post of Artistic Director of the Washington Ballet in 1999 (see **Theater and Dance,** p. 187).

PRINT MEDIA

The biggest business in D.C. is politics, and an entire industry has developed to tell the public about the wheelings and dealings of politicos. Journalists swarm the city, anxious for a big scoop that will inform the nation of corruption and scandal. The **Washington Post** has the widest circulation in the D.C. area. For $0.35 ($1.50 Su), the *Post* delivers superb reporting on national and international politics and provides comprehensive coverage of all D.C. happenings. The **Washington Times** is the conservative answer to the *Post*'s liberal slant, one of many a Republican's pet peeves. For more comprehensive listings of the city's art and entertainment goings-on as well as the area's most cynical reporting on D.C. politics, look to the weekly **Washington CityPaper.** The **Washington Blade,** another weekly paper, is the voice of D.C.'s gay community and often features events catering to gay audiences. **On Tap** (www.ontaponline.com) focuses exclusively on D.C.'s nightlife.

INSIDE

political washington & northwest **45**

beyond northwest **91**

virginia **96**

parks & trails in & around d.c. **108**

Sights

Washington's colors don't truly emerge in the whites and grays that form the buildings along the Mall. Although you shouldn't miss the classic sights of **Political Washington,** be sure to seek out the rest of the city's color spectrum in its diverse neighborhoods, where D.C.'s ethnic restaurants, nightclubs, and galleries roost. Even the less-traveled areas **beyond the Northwest Quadrant** reward cautious, streetwise visitors with a dose of D.C. reality. To get away from it all, lose yourself in one of D.C.'s **parks and trails.** For a complete breakdown of neighborhoods, see **Discover,** p. 5.

POLITICAL WASHINGTON & NORTHWEST

CAPITOL HILL

◪ Highlights: *Capitol, Supreme Court, Library of Congress.* **Museums:** *National Postal Museum, Children's Museum, Sewall-Belmont House.* **Food and Drink:** *p. 143.* **Nearby:** *Mall, Old Downtown, South of the Mall.* **Metro:** *Capitol South, Eastern Market, Federal Center, or Union Station.* **See also:** *Southeast Capitol Hill, p. 91.*

YOU ARE HERE

SEE MAP P. 353

Capitol Hill is the heart of American government, Washington's principal tourist attraction, and one of democracy's most potent symbols. Prepare to spend at least a day here exploring the halls of power, but **be cautious in this area at night.** The Hill's approximate boundaries are 3rd St. NW and SW to the west, H St. NE to the north, Lincoln Park to the east, and the SE-SW Freeway to the south. Most major sights, including the **Library of Congress,** the **Folger Shakespeare Library,** and the **Supreme Court,** cluster close to the **Capitol** itself. At dusk, night owls head for the bars and restaurants that line **Pennsylvania Ave.** between 2nd and 4th St. SE.

THE CAPITOL

⚐ Metro: *Capitol South or Union Station.* **Contact:** *Tourist information ☎ 225-6827, Senate offices 224-3121, House offices 225-3121; www.aoc.gov.* **Hours:** *Generally M-Sa 9am-4:30pm; closing time occasionally extended until 8pm depending on the time of year, call for details. Closed Thanksgiving, Christmas, and New Year's Day.* **Tours:** *Access by 30min. guided tour only. Tickets required. Same-day tickets can be acquired at the kiosk at Garfield Circle on the West Front, across from the Botanic Gardens. Kiosk is open from 9am until all tickets are distributed; get there about 45-60min. before opening time to guarantee yourself a ticket. Tickets not available in advance.* **Admission:** *Free.* **Viewing the proceedings:** *Americans must get a pass from their senator or representative. Passes can easily be obtained at the House or Senate office buildings with proof of residence and are valid for an entire 2-year session of Congress. Foreign nationals may get passes valid for a single day at either the House or Senate appointment desks on the crypt level. Visitors are often disappointed to find that Congress is not meeting during their visit; call ahead to check. Pages and interns are allowed to take visitors with them to closed areas of the building.* **Accessibility:** *Handicapped accessible. Call ☎ 224-4048, TDD 224-4049).*

The US Capitol may be an endless source of political cynicism, but the structure's scale and style still evoke the glory of the republican ideal. In the spirit of all things Congressional, the Capitol was built by committee. A design by amateur architect **William Thornton** was selected in an anonymous competition in 1793. Thornton resigned in 1800 amid politicking among the project's architects, and **Benjamin Latrobe** took over in 1803. The Brits, on a destructive 1814 tear through Washington, burned down the whole complex, using books from the Library of Congress as kindling. **Charles Bulfinch** replaced Latrobe as Congress's interior designer in 1818, finishing the Capitol's central section with a dome made of copper-plated wood. By 1850, the building could no longer contain the expanding Congress, so President Fillmore hired **Thomas U. Walter** to expand the edifice. Assisted by **Montgomery Meigs,** Walter oversaw the 1860s construction of the Rotunda, the building's massive iron dome. **2005** will bring the opening of the underground **Capitol Visitors Center,** which will better accommodate the 18,000 visitors who pass through the Capitol each day.

THE EXTERIOR

The three-tiered **East Front** stands opposite the Supreme Court and the Library of Congress Jefferson Building. From Jackson (1829) to Carter (1977), most US presidents took their inaugural oath on the East Front. Reagan's 1981 inauguration ceremony was the first administered on the **West Front,** whose grand entrance overlooks the National Mall. At night the West Front makes for a romantic stroll. It is generally deserted but is patrolled by the Capitol Police.

The **Senate** and **House of Representatives** are located in the north and south wings, respectively; a US flag over either wing denotes that the corresponding body is in session. At the apex of the dome stands Thomas Crawford's statue *Freedom;* a full-size, plaster model in the basement of the Russell Senate Office Building lets you get a close-up view of the statue without uncomfortable neck craning.

Outside the East Front, at 1st St. NW, the 1922 **Grant Memorial** is encircled by driveways and barricades. A weary General Ulysses S. Grant contemplates war in a sea of equine chaos. Near the entrance, note the trio of female statues representing America, Hope, and Justice. The East Portico displays Randolph Rogers's huge bronze **Columbus Doors,** which mimic Ghiberti's Gates of Paradise in Florence.

THE ROTUNDA

Inside the doors, the 180 ft. high, 96 ft. wide Rotunda stretches and yawns. A frieze of condensed history encircles the collar of the dome. The frieze was largely executed by **Constantino Brumidi,** but was finished by others after Brumidi fell off his scaffold in 1877 and died three months later; the face of one of his successors is painted on a tree (look behind the two rows of soldiers over the door to the corridor leading south toward the House Chamber). Brumidi's face is also thought to be among the many depicted on the frieze (look at the face of the baby in the woman's arms a few over from Christopher Columbus). In the overhead **Apotheosis of George Washington,**

George occupies the center of a giant allegory, as Liberty, Victory, the 13 states, and countless virtues look on.

Eight enormous paintings from the early years of the United States hang below the fresco at ground level. Among them is John Trumbull's **The Declaration of Independence,** featured on the rare $2 bill. A sculpture by Adelaide Johnson was recently moved nearby after protests over the lack of sculptures of women in the Capitol. It depicts the heads of women suffragists **Elizabeth Cady Stanton, Susan B. Anthony,** and **Lucretia Mott** emerging from a large white block of marble. The uncut marble jutting up behind the heads is for a bust of the first woman president.

Statesmen from Lincoln to JFK have lain in state in the Rotunda center for a day prior to burial, but only those to be buried in the Tomb of the Unknowns are required by law to do so. In his much-publicized "Living Will," President **Richard Nixon** opted to forego this highest of national honors. **Andrew Jackson** was the target of an assassination attempt when he was viewing a body lying in state. The would-be assassin's bullets just missed him; luck-seekers still rub the feet of a bronze Jackson located in the Rotunda.

The Capitol

OLD HOUSE CHAMBER (STATUARY HALL)

Just south of the Rotunda, still on the second level, is the Old House Chamber, the meeting place of the House of Representatives until 1857. **John Quincy Adams** (the only president to serve in Congress after being president) was the first to realize that the room was a rather effective echo chamber. Legend has it that Adams used to lie on his desk "sleeping" and listen to his political adversaries converse across the room; Adams later had a stroke at the same desk.

The Supreme Court

The growing House was eventually forced to move down the hall to the current House Chamber. Since then, raising the floor by 12 ft. has eliminated the acoustic idiosyncrasies of the room; only one disturbingly clear whisper tunnel remains (look for the plaque on the floor denoting the former location of Adams' desk). After the House moved, a joint resolution of Congress renamed the chamber Statuary Hall and asked each state for statues of two famous natives. Actually, there are only 97 statues, 38 of which reside in Statuary Hall. Nevada, New Mexico, and North Dakota sent only one each. The statues quickly became too much weight for the floor to bear, and the figures were dispersed throughout the building. A recent law allows states to change their submissions to the collection; in 2003, Kansas' statue of former Governor George Washington Glick was sent back to the

Washington Monument

Sunflower State to make way for President Dwight D. Eisenhower. And in an effort to complete the unfinished collection, North Dakota, Nevada, and New Mexico will each soon submit their second statues. These figures are, respectively: Sacagawea, Lewis and Clark's female Native American guide; Sarah Winnemucca, who founded Nevada's first public school for Native Americans; and Pope, who led a Native American rebellion against Spanish settlers in 1680.

OLD SENATE CHAMBER

North of the Rotunda is the Old Senate Chamber, former stomping ground of such renowned blabbermouths as **Daniel Webster, John C. Calhoun,** and **Henry Clay.** In a rare instance of government thrift, much of the furniture here was moved to the Capitol with the senators in 1859. The chamber was restored in 1976 for the American bicentennial celebration to look as it did when it was last occupied.

THE CRYPT

The designers of the Capitol had planned to bury George and Martha Washington in a tomb below the crypt. The architects commissioned a statue of **George Washington** to sit above the tomb, but the Washingtons' descendants thwarted the plans when they refused to allow the couple's bodies to be exhumed from Mount Vernon. The statue of Washington eventually found its way to the Smithsonian National Museum of American History (see **Museums**, p. 116). An enormous bust of **Abraham Lincoln** now keeps watch over Washington's empty tomb. Lincoln's head has no left ear—the sculptor (Gutzon Borlgun, who later sculpted Mount Rushmore) claimed that the absent feature is representative of Lincoln's unfinished life.

The crypt also contains the **compass stone,** originally the exact center of Washington, D.C.; it is from this point of origin that the District's quadrants (NW, NE, SW, SE) are drawn. The stone ceased to be the center of the city in 1847 when Arlington was given back to Virginia. On the House side of the crypt rests Hawaii's statue honoring **Father Damien,** who contracted leprosy on an island colony he founded for the state's lepers. Since clothes irritated his skin, a cage was built to hold his clothes away from his body. The statue, located on the ground floor on the House side, shows the cylindrical shape the cage gave him. Nearby are Colorado's statue of Apollo XIII astronaut **Jack Swigert** and Wyoming's statue of **Chief Washakie,** two of the newest in the collection and the only ones in color.

OLD SUPREME COURT CHAMBER

Also on the crypt level is the Old Supreme Court Chamber, where the justices supreme met from 1819 to 1860. The Chamber has a somewhat sinister history: in 1806, the ceiling gruesomely crushed one of Latrobe's assistants, effectively ending an ongoing argument Latrobe had been having over what kind of support was necessary for the Capitol's walls. Latrobe's cat disappeared at the same time, and ghost stories of the Demon Cat have haunted the Capitol ever since. After the Court's departure, the Chamber was used as a library, the headquarters of the Joint Committee on Atomic Energy, and a storeroom before it was restored to its original grandeur in 1975.

HOUSE AND SENATE CHAMBERS

To reach the galleries of the House and Senate chambers, climb up from the crypt levels on the respective sides of the Capitol. Visitors must check all bags and electronic equipment and then go through metal detectors before being allowed in the galleries. Unless a contentious bill is up for debate, the House and Senate Chambers can prove boring, with only a handful of elected officials listening halfheartedly to one of their colleagues. Many proceedings in Congress take place solely for the record, making for hours of sleep-inducing C-SPAN. The House Chamber hosts official Washington every January for the president's State of the Union Address.

The real business of Congress is conducted in committee hearings all over the Capitol and in the House and Senate office buildings. Most hearings are open to the public. The *Washington Post's* "Today in Congress" box in the paper's A-section lists hearings and their assigned rooms. Especially interesting and controversial hearings can get very crowded; the few seats are usually reserved for lobbyists. Potential visitors should show up early and keep their fingers crossed.

THE SUPREME COURT

⚑ Location: *11st St. NE, visitor entrance on Maryland Ave.* **Metro:** *Capitol South or Union Station.* **Contact:** *☎ 479-3000; www.supremecourtus.gov.* **Hours:** *Court open M-F 9am-4:30pm.* **Tours:** *The court is in session Oct.-June, and hears 1hr. oral arguments Oct.-Apr. M-W 10am-noon and occasionally 1-3pm for about 2 weeks of each month. Arguments open to the public on a first come, first-seated basis. Seating begins at 9:30am. Everyone is cleared out of the courtroom and the Great Hall during the lunch break (noon-1pm); lines form again if there is a 1pm session. The "3min. line" shuffles visitors through the courtroom for a glimpse. Check the Post or the court website for case listings. When the court is not sitting, visitors can attend 30min. lectures on the court in the courtroom (hourly every 30min. 9:30am-3:30pm).* **Admission:** *Free.*

Even though they're not looking for votes, the nine appointed justices of the nation's highest court graciously open their courtroom to the touristing masses. From 1800 to 1935, the justices met in the Capitol, first in any empty office they could find and later in the room now known as the **Old Supreme Court Chamber.** This chamber was so poorly illuminated that when some justices complained that a newly arrived statue of Justice depicted the abstract female without the traditional blindfold, Chief Justice **John Marshall** replied that it was fine—she couldn't possibly see anything in the room anyway. In 1935, the Court decided to take the nation's separation of powers literally and moved into its current location.

The grand staircase leading to the entrance on 1st St. is flanked by James Earle Fraser's sculptures *Contemplation of Justice* and *Authority of Law*. Nearby, nine impressive figures strike a pose in the pediment (three former chief justices; three classical Greek virtues; one former senator; Cass Gilbert, the building's architect; and Robert Aitken, the pediment's sculptor). The entrance leads to the impressive Great Hall, which features busts of all former chief justices. Straight ahead, behind the red curtain, is the **Chamber,** where the Court meets to hear cases. The lower level features exhibits on the Court and its history, a cafeteria, and a gift shop. Although the Supreme Court is known as "the highest court in the land," the highest court in this building is actually the basketball court directly above the courtroom, constructed by clerks to shoot hoops when the Court is not in session.

THE LIBRARY OF CONGRESS

⚑ Location: *101 Independence Ave. SE, Visitors Center entrance on 1st St. SE between E. Capitol St. and Independence Ave.* **Metro:** *Capitol South.* **Contact:** *Operator ☎ 707-5000, exhibition information 707-4604, treasures exhibit 707-3834, research 707-6400, TTY 707-6200; www.loc.gov.* **Hours:** *Great Hall open M-Sa 8:30am-5:30pm, but areas of interest not fully accessible until 10am. Visitors Center in the Jefferson Building open M-Sa 10am-5:30pm. Treasures Gallery open M-Sa 10am-5pm.* **Tours:** *Leave from the Visitors Center M-Sa 10:30, 11:30am, 1:30, 2:30, and 3:30pm (no 3:30pm tour on Sa). Tours in Spanish available, call ahead for times.* **Research:** *Researchers should enter the Madison Building on the Independence Ave. side and go to room LM140 to pick up a reader registration card (photo ID required). The Main Reading Room is open M and W-Th 8:30am-9:30pm, Tu and F-Sa 8:30am-5pm.*

With over 126 million objects stored on 532 miles of shelves, the Library of Congress is the largest library in the world. The original library was founded in 1800, when Congress began to assemble mostly law and history books for members' personal use. The British torched them all in 1814 (using some, legend has it, as kindling when they set the Capitol on fire). After the war, Congress bought Thomas Jefferson's personal collection of 6487 volumes to replace those that were lost. A fire in 1851 wiped out two-thirds of Jefferson's collection, at which point the surviving volumes were moved to a fire-proof iron room in the Capitol. The collection mushroomed after an 1870 copyright law guaranteed the library two free copies of

Kenilworth Aquatic Gardens

Jefferson Memorial

Ford's Theater

every book registered in the US. Today the library holds 28 million books and other printed materials in 460 languages.

The **Jefferson Building,** whose green copper dome and gold-leafed flame seals a spectacular octagonal reading room, is one of the most beautiful edifices in the city. Visitors can wander the Great Hall and peer into the reading room on their own, but the guided tours are excellent. The Visitors Center provides maps and screens a jazzy 12-minute film, narrated by James Earl Jones, which runs continuously beginning at 10am. In the second floor **Treasures Gallery,** a rotating exhibit, "Treasures of the Library of Congress," showcases the library's holdings. The famous Gutenberg Bible, one of the three volumes comprising the original 1455 edition, is in a protective case in the Great Hall.

The octagonal **Main Reading Room** has 250 desks, spread out under a spectacular dome whose apex hovers 160 ft. above the floor; visitors can peer in on researchers from a sound-proof gallery. On the top of the dome, Edwin Bashfield's painting *Human Understanding* depicts the major civilizations of history and their primary contributions to mankind; America is represented by a depiction of Abraham Lincoln's head on a body of Rodin's *Thinker* with wings grafted to its back. The dome's windows feature the seals of each state in the Union. At the gallery level, sculptures represent major academic disciplines flanked by statues of individuals who have distinguished themselves in that field. On the ceiling of the hall are mosaics honoring Americans who have excelled in a variety of professions. Three medallions representing Medicine, Law, and Theology—considered to be the three most educated professions at the time of the library's construction—are at the center.

Outside the Jefferson Building, the **Neptune Fountain** bubbles in the plaza. Wildly twisting horses flank the central figure of Neptune, turtles spit water at Nereids (high-class mermaids), Tritons (mermen) recline half-hidden in water, and twisting snakes spit water at tourists in this homage to Rome's Trevi Fountain.

When the Italian Renaissance Jefferson Building, the heart of today's library complex, opened in 1897, it was praised as a suitably grand home for one of the grandest collection of books in the world. In 1939, the library constructed the Art Deco **John Adams Building** (across 2nd St. from the Jefferson) to accommodate the growing collection, and added the enormous, marble **James Madison Building** in 1980. The Madison's 34.5 acres of floor space are packed almost exclusively with books, but the lobby hosts a small rotating exhibit.

The best way to see the library is to do research there, and tourists have been known to feign scholarly interests to gain access to the library's inner reaches. The huge collection, including the rarest items, is open to anyone over high school age with a legitimate research purpose. The stacks are closed—the librarians bring the books to you. The collection is non-circulating.

Uncoming exhibitions of note include *The Dream of Flight*, celebrating the centennial of the Wright Brothers' first flight (Sept. 25, 2003-Apr. 24, 2004) and *Churchill and the Great Republic*, focusing on Sir Winston Churchill's lifelong links with North America (Jan. 22-June 26, 2004).

FOLGER SHAKESPEARE LIBRARY

🚩 *Location: 201 E. Capitol St. SE, next to the Adams Building at the Library of Congress. **Contact:** Operator ☎ 544-4600, box office ☎ 544-7077; www.folger.edu. **Hours:** Exhibits open M-Sa 10am-4pm. Highlight tours M-F 11am, Sa 11am and 1pm. Garden tours Apr.-Oct. the 3rd Sa of each month at 10 and 11am. Library open for researchers M-F 8:45am-4:45pm. The restricted portions of the library are open to the public on the Su closest to Apr. 23, Shakespeare's birthday. **Admission:** Free. **Events:** Performances and concerts in the Elizabethan Theater; call or visit website for details.*

Dedicated in 1932 as a "gift to the American people" by industrialist Henry Clay Folger and his wife Emily, the Folger Shakespeare Library houses the world's largest collection of Shakespeareana—over 310,000 books and manuscripts. Although research areas are open to scholars and graduate students, they are unfortunately only accessible to the general public one April Sunday a year in celebration of Shakespeare's birthday. However, visitors can go inside the building and see the Great Hall exhibition gallery, a re-created gallery with oak panels and carved Elizabethan doorways. Exhibitions usually feature drawings from the library's collection. The Library's theater hosts performances of the Bard's plays (*Comedy of Errors*, Apr. 14 - May 16, 2004) as well as the Folger Consort, the ensemble in residence (see p. 186). During the day, you can peek at the theater, which imitates Elizabethan "innyard" theaters like Blackfriars, where Shakespeare's company performed. Outside, on the 3rd St. side of the building, tourists can stop for a quiet read in the cozy Elizabethan "knot" garden, named because the different plants—chosen based on their popularity in Shakespeare's day—are arranged in intertwining patterns.

US BOTANIC GARDENS

🚩 *Location: 100 Maryland Ave. SW, at 1st St. **Metro:** Federal Center SW. **Contact:** ☎ 225-8333; www.usbg.gov. **Hours:** daily 10am-5pm. **Admission:** Free.*

In front of the Capitol, exotic foliage from all continents and climates vegetates inside and outside the US Botanic Gardens. After an extensive renovation project, which closed the building to the public from 1997 to 2001, the garden's 20,000 plants are now on full display for visitors. Included as part of the renovation project is the creation of a new outdoor **National Garden**, which is tenatively scheduled to be completed in 2005. Until then, visitors will have to do with **Bartholdi Park,** across the street at 1st and Independence Ave. SW. The park has exhibits from the botanical gardens that will remain open to the public. Bartholdi, who designed the Statue of Liberty, is also responsible for the 40-ton cast-iron fountain that is the park's centerpiece. Purchased by Congress in 1877, the green fountain's wild turtles heartily spew water, while live ducks express bewilderment.

HOUSE & SENATE OFFICE BUILDINGS

🚩 *Location: On Constitution and Independence Ave. **Metro:** Capitol South for the House, Union Station or Capitol South for the Senate. **Contact:** Senate offices ☎ 224-3121; www.senate.gov. House offices ☎ 225-3121; www.house.gov. **Hours:** M-F 8am-6pm.*

Flanking the Capitol are the House **(Cannon, Longworth, and Rayburn)** and Senate **(Dirksen, Hart, and Russell)** office buildings. Although the Capitol is the site for all formal meetings of the House and Senate, the real work of legislating is done here, where congressmen have their offices. Visitors should consult the directories posted near all entrances and elevators to find their congressman's office, which give passes to the House and Senate galleries with proof of residence in your state or district. You can ride the underground subway to the Capitol from any of the buildings.

Notice the gigantic sculpture by **Alexander Calder,** *Mountains and Clouds,* in the Hart Senate Office Building (the actual buildings are uninteresting for visitors). Calder's sculpture occupies all nine stories of the building's atrium and may be viewed in its natural light from the ground floor or from the building's various open balconies. The stable black "mountains," sculpted from sheet metal, weigh 39 tons; the mobile "clouds," made from aircraft aluminum, weigh 4300 lb., and a computer controls the mobile's rotation.

SEWALL-BELMONT HOUSE

🔏 *Location:* 144 Constitution Ave. NE, at the corner of Constitution and 2nd St. *Metro:* Union Station. *Contact:* ☎ 546-1210; www.sewallbelmont.org. *Tours:* 1hr. tours begin on the hr. Tu-F 10am-2pm, Sa noon-3pm, and by appointment. *Admission:* Free.

Nestled beside the Hart building is the Sewall-Belmont House, which was built in 1798 by **Robert Sewall** but incorporates parts of a house dating back to 1680. The British set the house ablaze in 1814 but restorations returned it to tip-top shape. In 1929, the **National Woman's Party** bought the building for its headquarters, a function the house still serves today. The house showcases a small museum on the women's movement open by tour only.

STANTON PARK

🔏 *Location:* 3 blocks SE of Union Station down Massachusetts Ave. NE.

Stanton Park offers lots of shady benches and a playground. The assorted mix of white-collar lunchers, homeless loungers, and children frolicking in the playground here will give you an instant sense of Capitol Hill's diversity. The park's visual anchor is an impressive equestrian statue of **Nathaniel Greene, Esq.,** a Revolutionary War Major General.

UNION STATION

🔏 *Location:* 50 Massachusetts Ave. NE. Walk NE on Delaware Ave. from the Capitol or take the Metro to Union Station. *Contact:* ☎ 371-9441; www.unionstationdc.com. *Hours:* Shops open M-Sa 10am-9pm, Su 10am-6pm.

Two blocks north of the Capitol grounds, Union Station draws nearly three times as many visitors each day—70,000—as the Capitol itself. Most are there to use the Metro or hop on an Amtrak train, but many come to admire Daniel Burnham's monumental Beaux Arts design, which cost $25 million to erect from 1905 to 1908. The station has welcomed visitors with over 100, a nine-screen movie theater, and a glitzy food court since its 1988 renovation. Statues of Roman legionnaires populate the Main and East Halls. They were originally sculpted as nudes, but later, shield accessories were added as "modesty panels" so as not to offend the public. The train concourse itself is so expansive that the Washington Monument could fit in it if the monument were lying on its side. A sculpture of Christopher Columbus stands in the circle outside the station. Across the street, Union Station plaza runs from the station to the Capitol.

Union Station also occasionally hosts functional art exhibits, like a recent display of artistically-interpreted Yugo cars. In December, the station erects a massive Christmas tree, complete with gifts and a sprawling toy train display.

TAFT MEMORIAL

⛊ Location: *Northwest of the Capitol, on 1st St. between Constitution and Louisiana Ave. NW.*
This 1958 statue of Ohio Senator **Robert A. Taft** (son of President Taft) assiduously defends a large concrete obelisk. Twenty-seven bells set into the obelisk briefly ring like church chimes every 15min. The statue marks the beginning of **Union Station Plaza**, a park running from the Capitol to the Station.

THE MALL

⛊ Highlights: *Smithsonian (see p. 115), National Gallery of Art (see p. 122).*
Nearby: *Memorials, Old Downtown, South of the Mall.* **Contact:** *☎ 485-9880;* *www.nps.gov/nama/index.htm.* **Metro:** *Smithsonian, L'Enfant Plaza, or Archives-Navy Memorial stops.*

This long grassy strip, replete with memorials, monuments, and museums, is bounded by the Lincoln Memorial to the west and the Smithsonian Museums and the US Capitol to the east. To the south, cherry trees blossom along the brink of the Jefferson Memorial's Tidal Basin. The White House constitutes the northern border.

America's national backyard, the Mall was a railway yard and vacant lot until the early 20th century. Museum construction lasted from 1911 to the late 80s, while the majority of the memorials were built post-World War II, including the **National World War II Memorial** itself, which is due to open to the public in mid-2004 (see p. 58). Today's Mall is a hub of activity, home to the **Smithsonian Institute** and memorials ranging from battle scenes to Classical architecture. Hundreds of people use the Mall's grassy lawn to sunbathe, play soccer or baseball, and fly squadrons of kites, while die-hard runners pound the gravel paths throughout the year, carefully avoiding the flocks of noisy schoolchildren and map-wielding tourist groups that descend upon the popular monuments and museums.

The Mall and the banks of the Tidal Basin are the best places to welcome spring, when hundreds of cherry blossoms burst into life. These delicate flowers only last a week or two, so be sure to look for "blossom" updates on local news programs during early spring; see Tidal Basin, p. 60, for more on the annual **Cherry Blossom Festival**. The portions of the Smithsonian Institute on the Mall constitute the world's largest museum complex, which will be further enlarged when the latest Smithsonian museum, the **National Museum of the American Indian,** opens in 2004 (see p. 116). Nearby lies a close cousin, the National Gallery of Art, which is technically separate from the Smithsonian.

THE MONUMENTS

WASHINGTON MONUMENT

⛊ Location: *Just west of the Smithsonian museums, between 15th and 17th St.* **Metro:** *Smithsonian.* **Contact:** *☎ 426-6841; www.nps.gov/wash/index.htm.* **Hours:** *Labor Day-Mar. daily 9am-4:45pm., Apr.-Labor Day daily 8am-11:45pm.* **Tours:** *Tours every 30min. from 9am-4:30pm (last tour leaves at 4:30). Ticket required.* **Admission:** *Free. Obtain same-day timed tickets (limited availability, first-come, first-served) at the ticket kiosk at the intersection of 15th St. and Madison Dr. (kiosk open from 8am); limit 6 per person. Purchase advance tickets through the National Park Reservation Service (☎ 800-967-2283; http://reservations.nps.gov) before 3pm the day before you wish to visit the monument ($1.50 per ticket plus one-time $0.50 handling fee). Arrive 30min. before appointed time.* **Accessibility:** *Handicapped accessible.*

The world's tallest building until the construction of the Eiffel Tower in 1889, the Washington Monument, at 555 ft. tall and 90,854 tons, is the largest free-standing obelisk of its kind and a gargantuan, phallic shrine to America's first president. No

The National Mall, stretching from the Capitol to the Lincoln Memorial, is the defining space of ceremonial and public Washington. The main sights, museums, and monuments are clustered there, every visitor goes there, and many do not venture far from it. The space has always been there, but what it should be was not quite clear. In L'Enfant's 1791 plan, he envisaged something like the Champs Elysées in Paris—people promenading along a wide avenue banked by theaters, restaurants, and stores. In the 19th century, what was generally proposed, and sometimes built, were romantic gardens in the English style, with clumps of trees, patches of meadow, and curving roads, something akin to Central Park in New York. What the Mall finally became and what we see today was the vision proposed in 1902 by the McMillan Commission, composed of four of the leading figures in American architecture and design of the time, Daniel Burnham, Charles McKim, Frederick Law Olmstead Jr., and Augustus Saint Gaudens.

They had an imperial, indeed a Roman, vision of what Washington, capital of a newly imperial nation, should be. Once can see McKim's taste in Columbia University in New York and the Boston Public Library. Burnham's style is visible in Washington's Union Station, which he designed after his Commission made its proposal for the new Mall, partly in order to move a railway station then on it to a grand new terminal off the Mall. Union Station was the first building that expressed what the McMillan commissioners thought was suitable for the new Washington.

The key figure in defining what the Mall would become may well have been Olmstead, son of the great Frederick Law Olmstead who designed New York's Central Park and the Emerald Necklace of parks in Boston. At Harvard, Frederick Law Olmstead, Jr. shaped the development of landscape architecture in the United States. It is possibly because of him that the Mall is not a ceremonial avenue, but rather a vast expanse of grass, bordered by trees, edged by monumental buildings. The Capitol and the Washington Monument were already in place: the Commission proposed the extension of the Mall westward beyond the Washington Monument to a new great memorial to Lincoln. They envisaged museums and ceremonial buildings in Roman style along

the northern and southern borders. The Commission proposed that the north-south axis running across the Mall from the White House through the Washington Monument should be extended south, and another monument should be built there—and so the Jefferson Memorial came to be.

Few plans for city rebuilding on this large a scale have been as completely fulfilled as the proposal for the National Mall. But halfway through the course of realizing it, something very radical happened in how we think about architecture and design, as well as how we think about our history as a nation. The classical tradition, which had pretty much defined what great public building should be for 2500 years, was suddenly upended by the rise of modernism. Our history suddenly changed shape, and we had to think not only of Washington, Jefferson, and Lincoln, but also of the fate of the American Indian, slavery, and even of the Holocaust.

So the imperial building project began with the domed Natural History Museum and climaxed with the great domed National Gallery of Art. But then there came what the architectural historian Richard Guy Wilson called "the shootout on the Mall," when John Russell Pope, who had designed the sublime National Gallery, was given the Commission to design the Jefferson Memorial—and of course came up with another great domed structure. The world of modernism, architects and critics alike, exploded and protested: this is not the way Jefferson should be memorialized. Pope's design was built in the end, but it was the last classical building to grace the Mall and its environs. Then came the flat-rooted Museum of American History, the equally flat-roofed National Air and Space Museum, the huge donut of the Hirshhorn Museum, and perhaps most striking of all, the riot of triangles which is the eastern addition to the sober National Gallery. But that will all be upstaged when Frank Ghery's design to expand the Corcoran Gallery with enormous billowing metal forms à la Bilbao is built.

Our ideas of what we should celebrate and memorialize in our history have also changed. And so a huge Museum of the American Indian (see **A Native Space,** p. 116) is currently rising on the last space on the Mall available for a museum. We will have to shoehorn in a museum as large for African American history, which has already been approved by Congress. And where will the museum—can one doubt there will be demand for one?—for Hispanic Americans? If Native Americans and African Americans are represented on the Mall, can Hispanics be denied? One can think of other claimants. Will the disabled be satisfied with the statue of Roosevelt on a wheelchair which now fronts the Franklin D. Roosevelt Memorial? What shall we do with the Adamses? A monument to them will undoubtedly be built. After all, they are the only two non-slaveholding presidents among the first half-dozen, and such a monument offers the possibility of including with John and John Quincy the formidable Abigail, thus somewhat lessening the Mall's patriarchal aura.

The last great shootout on the Mall was over the World War II Memorial (see **WWII, 2004,** p. 58), now being built west of the Washington Monument. Here the battle was not only over design—because after the long reign of modernism on the Mall something like a classical monument was proposed—but also voer whether anything that large should break the great vista that runs from the Capitol to the Lincoln Memorial. But WWII was indeed the good war, and the greatest enterprise in warfare in American history. If the Civil War is celebrated in the expansive Grant Memorial spread out below the east front of the Capitol, if we have found space on the Mall for the Vietnam and the Korean War Memorials, how can we deny a larger, more central space to the World War II Memorial? How do we say—can we ever say—the Mall is finished, and no more?

The Mall might have been different. Think of the Champs Elysées, or the Tuileries, edged by restaurants, hotels, shops, apartments, and playgrounds, providing along with the tourists a flow of local residents to enliven and animate the scene. Washington developed differently—beyond the museums, on the north and south sides of the Mall, only government buildings are to be found. Daniel Patrick Moynihan, former Harvard professor and longtime Senator, hoped to enliven Pennsylvania Ave. with the theaters, apartments, and shops that would bring people downtown and onto the Mall, but his hope was only weakly realized. J. Edgar Hoover insisted on plunking his enormous FBI building right in the middle of Pennsylvania Ave., depriving a huge part of it of any possible life.

Despite all this, the Mall can feel very alive—particularly during the summer months when the Smithsonian Folklife Festival (see p. 14) fills the grassy expanse with musicians, performers, temporary theaters, exotic refreshment stands, perhaps pony or yak rides, festival structures, all celebrating some distant or nearby culture. People are brought together among the monuments and museums in a democratic confusion, and the surprising scene tells us what a grand, distinctively American space has been created on the Mall.

Nathan Glazer, Harvard Univeristy professor emeritus of sociology and education, writes on urban issues, ethnicity, race relations—among his books are Beyond the Melting Pot *(1970),* The Limits of Social Policy *(1988), and* We Are All Multiculturalists Now *(1997). He also writes on architecture and urban design, and with Mark Lilla, he edited the volume* The Public Face of Architecture *(1987). He is currently co-editing a book on the National Mall, past, present, and future.*

cement holds the loose granite blocks together, but the monument is incredibly stable, capable of withstanding a tornado blowing at 145mph. A healthy sway of an eighth of an inch in 30mph winds helps to maintain stability. The monument tilts about 3 in. to the north on hot sunny days, as the stones on the sunlit side expand and those on the shaded side contract.

Architect L'Enfant's original plan for D.C. called for an equestrian statue of Washington to be placed in the center of the Mall. After lengthy Congressional bickering, prominent Washingtonians formed the **Washington National Monument Society,** a private organization dedicated to the construction of the monument, in 1833. The society accepted a design by Treasury Building architect **Robert Mills** that called for a variation of the present obelisk with a one-story, 30-column temple around the base. Construction began on July 4, 1848, but the project soon ran out of money. Alabama, strapped for cash, sent a stone in lieu of a monetary contribution, which started a trend mimicked by over 100 nations, states, towns and individuals—from the Cherokee Nation to the American residents of Fu-Chow Fu, China. When the Vatican sent a block of marble in 1854, the Know-Nothings, a political party opposed to Southern European immigration, protested by stealing "the Pope's stone." During the Civil War, the half-finished monument was nicknamed the Beef Depot Monument, in honor of the cattle that Army quartermasters herded on the grounds. Notice the different hue of the stones about a third of the way up from the monument's base: postwar builders, having exhausted the stone supply in the original quarry, began to mine rock at another location. When problems with the structure's foundation called for a change in Mill's original plan, Victorian devotees, decrying the monument's lack of decoration, sent in hundreds of more complicated alternative designs, with one of the more interesting plans combining Renaissance and Hindu architectural styles. Under the direction of Thomas Lincoln Casey, who assumed command of the project in 1878, the monument was finally completed. Today, a 70-second elevator ride brings visitors 500 ft. up to a gallery with spectacular views of D.C.; visitors can see the structure's "memorial stones" on the ride back to the ground.

After a recent multi-million dollar restoration, the monument reopened its doors to the public for the 2000 July 4th celebration. Countering over 100 years of rain, sleet, and snow, the overhaul included a complete restoration of exterior masonry, a redesigned observation level, and an expanded interpretive exhibit area.

REFLECTING POOL

Location: *Between the Washington Monument and Lincoln Memorial.*

The Reflecting Pool reflects the famed obelisk in seven million gallons of water. Modeled after similar pools at **Versailles** and the **Taj Mahal,** the Reflecting Pool's design minimizes wind ripples and sharpens the watery visage of the monument. Swarms of people surround the 2000 ft. by 160 ft. pool at civil rights marches, war protests, and the yearly July 4th fireworks display.

The area near the Pool is also the future home of the **National World War II Memorial**, currently slated to be finished in time for Memorial Day weekend of 2004. A majestic and striking acknowledgement of the sacrifices of WWII veterans, the Memorial will be located opposite the Lincoln Memorial near the end of the Reflecting Pool. For more information, see **WWII, 2004,** p. 58.

CONSTITUTION GARDENS

Location: *Walking from the Washington Monument toward the Lincoln Memorial, the Gardens lie along the winding paths to the right of the Reflecting Pool.*

The romantic Constitution Gardens were created in the 1970s to beautify the area between the Washington Monument and the Lincoln Memorial. Trees and paths surround a lake, whose serene waters make for impressive reflections of the Washington Monument. At the center of the lake lies a willow-draped island commemorating the 56 signers of the **Declaration of Independence.** To reach the island, take the small wooden footbridge from the lake shore farthest from the Reflecting Pool.

VIETNAM VETERANS MEMORIAL

🚩 Location: *Between the Reflecting Pool and Constitution Ave. and adjacent to the Lincoln Memorial. Face the Washington Monument and Reflecting Pool from in front of the Lincoln Memorial; the Vietnam Veterans Memorial is down a trail to the left.* **Metro:** *Foggy Bottom or Smithsonian.* **Contact:** *☎ 426-6841; www.nps.gov/vive/index.htm.* **Hours:** *24hr. Park rangers on staff daily 8am-11:45pm.* **Events:** *On Father's Day, children and grandchildren of veterans wash the wall.* **Tours:** *Guided tours (from rangers) are available upon request.* **Accessibility:** *Handicapped accessible. Wheelchairs available for use.*

The reflective black granite wall offers somber contemplation and remembrance of one of the darker periods of American history: the Vietnam War. A public competition selected the design for the memorial in 1981. **Maya Ying Lin,** a Yale College senior who originally received a "B" when she submitted her memorial concept to a professor at Yale, beat the other 1421 entrants, including her professor, with the monument dedicated in 1982. She described her design as a "rift in the earth—a long, polished black stone wall, emerging from and receding into the earth...to be understood as one moves into and out of it." The walls bear the names of the 58,209 Americans who died or are still missing in Vietnam in chronological order of their deaths. A diamond adjacent to each name denotes that the death was confirmed, while a cross signals that the person remains unaccounted for.

When Maya Lin's design for the memorial was chosen, many veterans, citizens, and politicians criticized the design for its lack of pomp and circumstance. Less artistic minds prevailed in the negotiations and a compromise was reached in which an alternate memorial would be erected alongside Lin's design. Noted sculptor **Frederick Hart** was commissioned to design a sculpture of troops emerging from an unknown battlefield. To this day, however, the powerful Lin memorial overshadows the **Three Servicemen** sculpture. Nonetheless, the argument led to an upsurge in special interest groups desiring their own memorials. To this end, a **Vietnam Women's Memorial** was also commissioned and stands in a small alcove adjacent to the "men's" memorial. Sculpted by **Glenna Goodacre** in 1993, the memorial depicts three women around a wounded soldier. Eight yellowwood trees surround the statues, honoring the eight servicewomen killed in action in Vietnam.

Brilliant flowers, haunting pictures, poems, toys, and other memorabilia line the wall and compose makeshift shrines to the deceased. Veterans, friends, and families come to leave these personal offerings and trace the names of the deceased. Rangers collect the offerings daily and move them to a government warehouse. A small sample is on view at the **National Museum of American History** (p. 116). Park rangers stationed at the west end of the memorial (the end nearest the Lincoln Memorial) answer questions and provide a printout with the full name, date of birth, date of death, and location on the memorial of the fallen or missing soldiers. Directories are available at either side of the memorial. Rangers provide paper for rubbings.

A poignant supplement to the Memorial itself can be found online at www.thevirtualwall.org. **The Virtual Wall** offers individual webpages for each fallen soldier, including such information as his or her hometown, dates of birth and death, military division, and the location of the name on the wall itself. Each page also contains personal "remembrances"—memories and recollections about the individual left by a family member or friend. Names can be found through The Virtual Wall's extensive search engine, and a listing of names on the site's homepage (updated daily) commemorates and honors those who died on the particular date of visit.

LINCOLN MEMORIAL

🚩 Location: *Adjacent to the Vietnam Memorial, near the Reflecting Pool and opposite the Washington Monument at 23rd St.* **Metro:** *Smithsonian or Foggy Bottom-GWU.* **Contact:** *☎ 426-6841; www.nps.gov/linc.* **Hours:** *24hr. Park rangers on staff daily 8am-11:45pm.* **Tours:** *Guided tours (from rangers) are available upon request.*

Modeled after the Parthenon, the commanding Lincoln Memorial looms over the reflecting pool in dramatic stone splendor. Though the nation demanded a memorial to Lincoln, the 16th US president, almost immediately after his assassination in 1865,

in recent
news

WWII, 2004

The **National World War II Memorial,** to be dedicated to much fanfare on May 29, 2004, will be the only structure along the central axis of the Mall to honor a 20th-century event. Located directly between the Reflecting Pool and the Washington Monument, the new memorial will be a place of commemoration of war victories and sacrifices.

The construction of the monument is itself a type of victory. Though legislation for a WWII memorial was first proposed in 1987 (and again in 1989 and 1991), it was not until 1993 that the American Battle Momuments Commission received the go-ahead to proceed with a monument in the D.C. area. It would take another 2 years to select the Rainbow Pool as the future sight. Funding campaigns for the project and considerations for the monument's design continued through 2000, and though groundbreaking finally took place that November, a 2001 lawsuit voicing objections over the structure's design threatened to delay it still further. The memorial is expected to be completed in March 2004.

For more info, call ☎800-639-4992 or check out www.wwiimemorial.com.
—David Dodman

the resentment still lingering from Reconstruction prevented its realization until 50 years later. The grandiose memorial was designed by American architect **Henry Bacon,** whose plans came to fruition with the beginning of the monument's construction in 1914. President Warren G. Harding dedicated the memorial upon its completion in 1922. **Daniel Chester French** was chosen to design the sculpture of Lincoln, which depicts him seated, keeping a stern watch over the city; French wanted the former President's face to "show the burdens of war in his rugged features." The **Picirrili Brothers'** stonecutting firm, which did the actual sculpting, couldn't find a block of marble big enough for Lincoln; instead, they joined 28 blocks so tightly that visitors can barely see the seams. During World War II, an anti-aircraft shell hit the memorial during a misfire, knocking out a chunk of marble near the "Maryland" engraving on the front right of the upper level.

Lincoln's stirring Gettysburg Address appears on the wall to the left of the statue as you enter. His second inaugural address, given 63 days prior to his assassination, appears on the right. Look for the word "future," not too subtly corrected from the erroneously carved "euture." Looming above Lincoln's famous words are **Jules Guerin's** allegorical, gold-detailed canvas murals, representating the ideals for which Lincoln's life and presidency stood. The effect of the symbolism is largely lost, however, as the murals are unfortunately faded and yellowed. Thirty-six simple Doric columns, each 44 ft. high, surround the building and commemorate the states in the Union when Lincoln was assassinated; their names are inscribed into a frieze directly above. The names of the 48 states in existence when the memorial was dedicated wrap around its roof.

Take the elevator down from the statuary or turn right after you walk down the steps to enter the exhibit area. Excerpts from some of Lincoln's famous speeches and writings are etched into a series of dark grey stone slabs that surround the room. The small museum also includes an intriguing display of the various considered—and ultimately rejected—ideas for the Memorial, as well as a video presentation on the use of the site for demonstrations and protests (including Martin Luther King, Jr.'s "I Have a Dream" speech).

KOREAN WAR VETERANS MEMORIAL

🔊 *Location: Between the Reflecting Pool and Independence Ave. and adjacent to the Lincoln Memorial. Facing the Washington Monument and Reflecting Pool from in front of the Lincoln Memorial; the Korean War Veterans*

Memorial is down a trail to the right. **Metro:** *Foggy Bottom-GWU or Smithsonian.* **Contact:** ☎ *426-6841; www.nps.gov/kowa.* **Hours:** *24hr. Rangers daily 8am-11:45pm.* **Tours:** *Guided tours (from rangers) are available upon request.*

Composed of 19 larger-than-life stainless-steel statues, the Korean War Veterans Memorial honors the 54,000 American soldiers who died in the Korean conflict from 1950 to 1953. Rather late in the making, the memorial was dedicated on July 27, 1995, 42 years after the armistice was signed. The $18 million tribute received 60% of its funding from Korean War veterans and made no use of federal money.

The statues, sculpted by World War II veteran **Frank Gaylord,** depict a platoon on patrol with monstrous rain ponchos and roughly cut, grizzled faces. The patrol forms a triangle which intersects a circle of trees, flowers, and a central fountain. A black granite wall emerges from the fountain, representing the Korean peninsula protruding into the Pacific Ocean. Etched on the wall closest to the center of the fountain are the words "Freedom is not free," a chilling reminder of the costs of liberty and of the hardships American forces endured in the war. The remainder of the wall is covered with over 2000 hazy, etched images of troops, tanks, helicopters, and nurses, invoking the Korean conflict's common nickname, the "Forgotten War." Visit at night for a particularly haunting view; the gray statues are illuminated by small white lights and reflect eerily on the smooth, black facade.

FRANKLIN DELANO ROOSEVELT MEMORIAL

🏶 **Location:** *West Potomac Park. Walking from the Korean War Memorial, head across Independence Ave. toward the right-hand bank of the Tidal Basin.* **Metro:** *A long walk from Smithsonian.* **Contact:** ☎ *426-6841; www.nps.gov/frde/index.htm* **Hours:** *24hr. Rangers on site daily 8am-11:45pm.* **Tours:** *Guided tours (from rangers) are available upon request.*

The Franklin Delano Roosevelt Memorial deviates from the grand tributes to early presidents surrounding it, replacing their imposing marble statuary with sculpted gardens, cascading fountains, and thematic alcoves.

Congress established the **FDR Memorial Commission** in 1955, dropped a controversial 1960 memorial plan, selected the current design in 1974, and then was mired in controversy over funding and design issues for the following two decades. The 90s saw a heated debate regarding to what degree the memorial would show the President's physical disability, which he cleverly hid from the public thanks to a tacit agreement with a then-cooperative press. The $52 million memorial, finally opened in May of 1997, features a statue of Roosevelt seated, covered in his Navy cape, a pose based on a famous image of FDR at the 1945 Yalta conference. His wheelchair is not immediately visible, but a close look at the back of the chair reveals a small wheel peeking out from behind his cloak, a discreet nod to the reality of his condition. Insufficient for those who wanted Roosevelt's disability more clearly displayed, however, this statue was followed with a second, 1999 rendition of FDR—this time without a cape, sitting in his wheelchair; it can be found at the main entrance.

The memorial is divided into a series of four thematically organized sections depicting the four terms of Roosevelt's presidency. The first and second rooms focus on the New Deal, Roosevelt's revolutionary scheme of social programs designed to lift America out of the Great Depression. They feature bronze sculptures of a breadline, a rural couple, and a man listening to one of the President's trademark "fireside chats," as well as several quotes from Roosevelt (etched into the rock) describing the creation of the Civilian Conservation Corps and the Tennessee Valley Authority. The third and fourth rooms focus on FDR's response to World War II and include a statue of his wife, Eleanor, the first US delegate to the United Nations. Note the roughness on the stone wall faces in the third room, a subtle symbol of the hardships of war.

JEFFERSON MEMORIAL

🏶 **Location:** *Across the Tidal Basin from the Washington Monument. From the FDR Memorial, follow the path over the bridge to East Potomac Park. Or from the Smithsonian/L'Enfant metro stop area, walk towards the Washington Monument along Independence Ave. Make a left onto 15th St. and then another left onto the lakeside trail at the Tidal Basin. Continue around the lake to the*

Memorial. **Metro:** *A long walk from L'Enfant Plaza or Smithsonian.* **Contact:** ☎ 426-6841; www.nps.gov/thje/. **Hours:** 24hr. Park rangers on site daily 8am- 11:45pm. **Tours:** Guided tours (from rangers) are available upon request.

Dedicated in 1943, the Jefferson Memorial is the coolest of D.C.'s memorials due to the cross-breezes off the Potomac. A 19 ft. hollow bronze statue of **Thomas Jefferson** stands enshrined in a domed, open-air rotunda, encircled by massive Ionic columns that throw shafts of light and shadow across the memorial floor in the late evening. The building sits on the shore of the picturesque **Tidal Basin** and offers an excellent perspective for gazing over the surrounding area. A break in the trees of the opposing Tidal Basin shore allows for a straight-shot view of the White House.

Jefferson himself designed a number of Neoclassical buildings during his life, including the Virginia state capitol, his home, Monticello, and the quadrangle and library at the University of Virginia. The memorial's design by **National Gallery of Art** architect **John Russell Pope** pays homage to Jefferson's designs. Corn and tobacco, Virginia's cash crops, are visible under his coat as reminders of Jefferson's agrarian ideal. The interior walls quote from Jefferson's writings: the *Declaration of Independence*, the Virginia Statute of Religious Freedom, his *Notes on Virginia*, and an 1815 letter. The carved squares on the dome grow smaller near the top, creating the illusion that the ceiling is higher than 30 ft.

TIDAL BASIN

⚑ Location: *By the Jefferson Memorial.*

The Tidal Basin is a lovely man-made lake as polluted as it is popular. Despite the unsavory waters, the shady paths along the lake provide visitors with a tranquil escape from the overpopulated memorials. Sea-faring types can brave the waters in rented paddleboats (see **Entertainment**, p. 192).

The Japanese **cherry blossom trees** along the Tidal Basin's rim are surrounded by tourists during the two weeks in late March or early April when most of the trees are in bloom. When President Taft transformed the Potomac River from swampland into a river with a vista in 1909, his wife suggested adding a grove of cherry trees, the blossoms of which she had admired during a recent visit to Japan. The original trees, sent in 1909 from Japan as a symbol of trans-Pacific friendship, arrived bearing insects and fungi and were immediately destroyed by the Department of Agriculture. The current trees, received in 1912, represent Japan's more successful second try.

After Japanese bombers attacked Pearl Harbor in 1941, irate Washingtonians took buzz-saws to several of the trees. However, these landmarks regained favor so quickly that a group of women threatened to chain themselves to the trees in order to prevent them from being cleared to make room for the Jefferson Memorial; more trees were planted along the southern side of the Tidal Basin as a compromise.

The Arakawa River grove, which supplied the D.C. specimens, began to decline in the early 1950s, and the National Park Service helped restore the grove by sending budwood from those trees' Washingtonian descendants back to Japan. The gift of cherry trees was renewed by Japan in 1965, and American dogwood trees sent in 1973 bloom today in downtown Tokyo.

This horticulturally-driven international friendship is epitomzed in the annual **Cherry Blossom Festival**, when the D.C. area is graced with not only the lovely flowerings of the trees but also a variety of special events—many of them celebrating the culture of Japan. The annual parade, held along Constitution Ave., is the biggest yearly spectator event in the city and features marching bands from around the the world—as well as the "United States Cherry Blossom Festival Queen." Also of note is the **Sakura Matsuri,** the Japanese street festival (held on 12th St. NW and Pennsylvania Ave.) at which Japanese musical drumming performances and sushi and sake tastings are offered. The **2004** festival will take place from March 27 to April 12 (with the Sakura Matsuri on April 3). For more information, see the official website at www.nationalcherryblossomfestival.org.

SOUTH OF THE MALL

🛐 **Highlights:** *The Bureau of Engraving and Printing.* **Museums:** *Holocaust Memorial Museum, Navy Museum, Marine Corps Historical Museum.* **Food and Drink:** *p. 157.* **Nearby:** *The Mall, Monuments, Potomac River Parks, Capitol Hill.*

SEE
MAP
YOU ARE   P.362
HERE   U.S. Capitol
Building

NEAR THE SMITHSONIAN

BUREAU OF ENGRAVING & PRINTING

🛐 **Location:** *14th and C St. SW.* **Metro:** *Smithsonian.* **Contact:** *☎ 847-2808; www.moneyfactory.com.* **Hours and Tours:** *Ticket booth opens M-F at 8am to distribute tickets for same-day tours 9am-2pm. May-Aug ticket booth reopens M-F at 3:30pm to distribute tickets for 4-6:45pm same-day tours. Booth closes when all tickets are distributed. Obtain timed tickets but expect to wait. Oct-Feb: no ticket required.* **Admission:** *Free.*

The buck starts here, arguably the birthplace of the good and bad of modern capitalism. The Bureau of Engraving and Printing, the largest producer of currency, stamps, and security documents in the world, offers guided tours of the presses that print $696 million in money and stamps each day. Although often punctuated by long waits, the tour proves highly entertaining, mesmerizing its visitors with the sight of millions of freshly-minted dollars being stacked before their eyes.

VOICE OF AMERICA

🛐 **Location:** *330 Independence Ave. SW. Enter on C St. between 3rd and 4th St.* **Metro:** *Federal Center SW.* **Contact:** *☎ 619-3919; www.voa.gov.* **Tours:** *45min. tours M-F except holidays, 10:30am, 1:30, and 2:30pm. Reservations required; no more than 20 people per tour.* **Accessibility:** *Wheelchair accessible.* **Admission:** *Free.*

The year 2002 marked the 60th anniversary of VOA, a live television, radio, and Internet broadcast heard virtually everywhere except the US. Over 94 million people worldwide tune in to hear US news broadcast in 55 languages. Since 1942, the VOA has been willing to tell the good and the bad about America to the rest of the world. Guided tours take visitors into vital areas of the building at a rapid pace. The biggest allure of the broadcasts today are its live phone-in interviews with American leaders.

THE WATERFRONT

George Washington chose the precise location for Washington, D.C. with an eye to its suitability as a port. Although shipping on the Potomac may have been possible in the 18th century, its narrow stretches and windy bends keep today's large ships out of the area. The waterfront district is home to recreational boaters, a thriving seafood wharf, and excellent views of the Washington Channel, Potomac River, and East Potomac Park. The area extends roughly from Water St. and the 12th St. Expwy. along Maine Ave. and the parallel, smaller Water St. SW, to Fort McNair at the mouth of the Washington Channel and the Anacostia River.

The Waterfront promises few standout tourist spectacles, but it's worth a walkthrough. To hit all of the smaller sites and enjoy some intimate time with the fishier side of the Potomac, follow these directions: exit Waterfront Metro and walk away from the strip mall down 4th St. for about five minutes. Turn right onto P St. and walk straight toward the water. On the left stands the 18-foot **Titanic Memorial,** sculpted in 1931 by Gertrude Vanderbilt Whitney to honor the men who "gave their lives that women and children might be saved." Turn right and walk along the pedestrian pathway, one of the cleanest, most beautiful, and least populated walking, jogging, and biking spots in D.C.; on the left is the Washington Channel. Capital Yacht Club, the Washington Marina, and Gangplank Marina house the many yachts, houseboats, and sailboats bobbing in the water.

Events like recipe exchanges and "Boater of the Month" ceremonies take place for members at many of these private clubs. If you're interested in lunch or dinner boat cruises ($37-120), contact **Spirit Cruises** (☎ 554-8000; www.spiritcruises.com) or **Odyssey Cruises** (☎ 488-6000; www.odysseycruises.com) for more information. Continue strolling along the pathway until it dead-ends into the **Wharf Seafood Market.** In operation since 1794, the wharf is the oldest open-air seafood market in the US. Here, aproned vendors sell impressively fresh seafood year-round (see **Food and Drink,** p. 159). Buy raw seafood to cook yourself or venture to a nearby shack to feast on freshly cooked shrimp, fish, or crab. For the nearest **Metro,** cross the street alongside the seafood market and climb the dirt path along the hill to the I-395 bridge. Walk halfway across the bridge. At the top of the bridge you'll see a post office off to the right. Across the street lies a green railing leading to steps below ground. Go down those steps and take a right after entering through the glass doors. Follow signs through the L'Enfant shops to the Metro.

FOGGY BOTTOM

🛈 Highlights: *White House, Kennedy Center.* **Museums:** *Corcoran, Renwick.* **Food and Drink:** *p. 152.* **Nearby:** *The Mall, Farragut, Dupont Circle, Georgetown. Metro: runs along the northern edge neighborhood; Foggy Bottom-GWU provides access to western half and Washington Circle, Farragut West is near* **White House** *in the east. 30-series buses also run along edge of neighborhood.*

The misty swamp air that once pervaded downtown D.C. gave this neighborhood its name long before heavy industry and fog-like pollutants made the moniker even more appropriate in the early 1900s. During WWII, the **State Department** took up quarters here at 23rd and C St. NW. Foggy Bottom extends from 15th St. NW west to the Potomac River, and from M St. south to Constitution Ave.

Near the Mall, government departments and national organizations like the **Daughters of the American Revolution** and the **American Red Cross** form a scenic continuum of gardens, columns, and statues. Above F St., the neighborhood is dominated by **George Washington University,** hotels, townhouses, and the mirrored buildings of the **World Bank,** located at 19th and G St.

Before the Civil War, when most of Washington remained undeveloped, the White House anchored its own neighborhood: socialites and Cabinet secretaries lived around Lafayette Square, across from the President's House, or slightly farther up 16th St. Since WWII, development has turned the White House from a center into a boundary: the blocks it occupies separate Farragut to the north, Federal Triangle to the east, Foggy Bottom to the west, and the Mall to the south.

THE WHITE HOUSE

🛈 Location: *1600 Pennsylvania Ave. NW; Visitors Center along Pennsylvania Ave., between 14th and 15th St., in the Department of Commerce building.* **Metro:** *McPherson Sq., Vermont Ave. exit.* **Contact:** *Visitors center 24-hr. info line ☎ 456-7041, TDD 456-2121; www.whitehouse.gov.* **Hours:** *Visitors center open daily 7:30am-4pm.* **Tours:** *Self-guided group tours for parties of 10 or more people can be arranged through one's Member of Congress. Submit requests at least one month in advance. Tours run Tu-Sa 7:30-11:30am.*

In 1792, after Pierre L'Enfant had been decommissioned, Thomas Jefferson proposed a contest to design the president's residence. President George Washington judged the anonymous competition, choosing **James Hoban's** more regal plan over Jefferson's own modest design. John Adams was the first chief executive to live in the White House, although the building was still unfinished at the time of his occupancy; in fact, the Adamses hung laundry to dry in what is now the **East Room.** Jefferson made the building habitable and was the first to build additions.

The British burned down the house, along with much of D.C., in 1814; First Lady **Dolly Madison** interrupted her dinner to flee the flames, taking with her one of **Gilbert Stuart's** famous portraits of Washington (a version of which now hangs in the neighboring **Corcoran Gallery of Art).** The building was rebuilt shortly thereafter, and since then technical alterations and advances have been a regular, almost yearly, event. The White House was made handicapped-accessible and had a swimming pool installed in 1933 to adapt to the needs of **Franklin D. Roosevelt,** who suffered from polio. However, despite remodeling in 1902 and 1948, the central third of the mansion still looks more or less like Hoban planned it. Today, whenever the president is in town, an American flag flies over the house. The president's personal staff works in the West Wing, while the first lady's staff shares the East Wing with other essential offices. The Oval Office is the official headquarters of the president and the site of many televised speeches, but his working office is in a small room next door, perhaps more famous as the room in which hyper-scandalized President Bill Clinton conducted his liaisons with intern Monica Lewinsky.

Before tours were suspended following September 11, 2001, visitors started on the ground of the East Wing and covered the next two floors; the top two floors are entirely private. The two middle floors contain the state rooms, which are used 250 times a year for events and press conferences. The **China Room** is filled with presidential place-settings from across the decades; not every president is represented because new china is only ordered every 17 years. Upstairs, the **East Room** has been used for the wakes of those presidents who died in office. It also held boxing during Theodore Roosevelt's administration and hosted Susan Ford's senior prom.

Three colorful rooms lie between the East Room and the State Dining Room: the **Green Room,** whose decor was once thought by ladies of Andrew Jackson's administration to impart an unflattering tone to the skin; the **Blue Room;** and the **Red Room.** Dolly Madison held Wednesday-night socials here—all it took to be admitted was "proper attire." **The State Dining Room** is used for entertaining large groups of guests. It also served as a trophy room for Teddy Roosevelt, who was an avid hunter.

The surrounding grounds developed in the same fitful manner as the house: John Adams was the first to plant seedlings, and his son John Quincy Adams fenced off the grounds. One hundred and twenty years later, Jacqueline Kennedy made the **Rose Garden** famous; journalists later called Gerald Ford's stay-at-home re-election effort the "Rose Garden Campaign." An obsolete bomb shelter under the Treasury building, built during WWII, connects to the White House by a tunnel under the East Lawn; aides in the know use it as quick exit to 15th St. NW. Big lawns, fences, long driveways, and closed gates discourage terrorists, though four or so assailants or unruly protesters manage to jump over the fences each year.

More peaceful occurrences on the White House grounds include the **Easter Egg Roll,** a tradition started by President Rutherford B. Hayes in 1878. Every year on Easter Monday (the day after Easter), the South Lawn is opened to military service members and their families and hosts a variety of special events, including readings of childrens' books by prominent White House employees and officials. The Roll has inspired annual contributions of masterfully decorated Easter eggs by artists from each of the 50 states, as well as D.C. itself.

ELLIPSE

Location: *South of the White House.*

This grassy area was once used to raise cattle, but its function nowadays is a bit more glamorous. Since Christmas Eve of 1923, when President Calvin Coolidge helped to light a Christmas tree on the Ellipse, every Commander-in-Chief has participated in the annual tree-lighting ceremony. After decades of being held on the White House grounds, the event moved to the Ellipse for good in 1954, when it gained the title "Christmas Pageant of Peace" as well as series of smaller trees (a "Pathway of Peace") representing the 50 states and the District of Columbia. The current **National Christmas Tree,** a 40ft., live Colorado blue spruce from York, Pennsylvania, was installed here in 1978. It can be seen year-round, directly across the street from the White House South Lawn. Nearby **George Washington University** (see p. 68) has also held commencement ceremonies on the Ellipse.

EISENHOWER EXECUTIVE OFFICE BUILDING (OLD EXECUTIVE OFFICE BUILDING)

🖩 Location: *1600 Pennsylvania Ave. NW, directly adjacent to the White House, at the intersection with 17th St.* **Metro:** *Farragut West.* **Contact:** *☎ 395-5895 (M-F 8am-5pm), TDD 395-9103; www.whitehouse.gov/history/eeobtour.* **Tours:** *Guided tours and all tourist access to the building have been suspended indefinitely.*

The Dwight D. Eisenhower Office Building is an explosion of architectural superfluity. Alfred B. Mullett, who designed the building in 1870, was later denied payment for his work by the government and committed suicide in 1890 after a court case ruled that he would not receive his $150,000 payment due to a legal technicality. Trendsetting when it was erected in 1888, the building's frills regularly waver in and out of fashion. President Truman called it "the greatest monstrosity in America," and the Old Executive barely escaped demolition in the latter half of the 20th century.

Today the building houses the bulk of the White House staff, the Vice President's office, the National Security Council, and a few lucky interns. Even though in-person tours have been suspended, an online tour through the White House website offers pictures and descriptions of the building's various rooms, including the Vice President's Office.

LAFAYETTE PARK

🖩 Location: *Across Pennsylvania Ave. from the north side of the White House.* **Metro:** *Farragut North, Farragut West or McPherson Sq.*

Statues of prominent military leaders, American allies in the Revolutionary War, guard the park's four corners of the park; they serve as reminders that the US could not have won its independence without help from foreign armies. In 1891, a statue of the Marquis de Lafayette joined Jackson at the southeast corner of the park, near 15th St. and Pennsylvania Ave. A half-dressed woman, perhaps representing France, hands him his sword; an old joke has the lady saying, "Give me my clothes, and I'll give you back your sword." Lafayette's compatriot Rochambeau, Polish Brigadier Thaddeus Kosciuszko, and Prussian Baron Von Steuben defend the southwest, northeast, and northwest corners of the park, respectively.

Lafayette's close proximity to the President's home is reflected in Clark Mills's statue of Andrew Jackson, the first equestrian statue in America, which stands in the center of the park. Legend has it that Mills bought a thoroughbred and trained it to rear on demand to be a model for the unprecedented work.

Lafayette Park's location makes it a prime spot for protests; a 24hr. anti-nuclear "White House Peace Vigil" has been held here continuously since 1981. Green and yellow billboards feature pictures of war atrocities, while a series of bumper stickers and hand-painted phrases proclaim slogans such as "You can't hug a child with nuclear arms" and "Chernobyl is everywhere!"

ST. JOHN'S CHURCH

🖩 Location: *At 16th and H St. NW on the north end of Lafayette Park.* **Metro:** *Farragut North or Farragut West.* **Contact:** *☎ 347-8766; www.stjohns-dc.org.* **Hours:** *July-Aug. M-Th 9am-5pm, F 9am-3pm; Sept.-June M-Th 9am-5pm, F 9am-4pm.* **Tours:** *Following services on the first Su of each month.* **Services:** *June-Aug. Su 8 and 10:30am, Spanish service 1pm; Sept.-May 8, 9, 11am, Spanish service 1pm.*

One of the architects responsible for the restoration of the US after the War of 1812, Benjamin Latrobe also created St. John's Church. St. John's forms a subtle cross whose arms have the triangular pediment of a Greek temple with Latrobe's signature half-moon windows. A registered national historic landmark since 1961, it is also known as the Church of Presidents: each president since Madison has dropped in at least once, all sitting in the same row denoted by a small brass plaque marked "President's Pew" and featuring custom-made kneelers, each bearing the name of a different Commander-in-Chief. The Church's storied history includes Lincoln's visit during the Civil War and LBJ's entrance to mourn the loss of JFK. George W. Bush attends the 8am service when he is in town. Church sermons usually include prayers for the president.

DECATUR HOUSE

⚐ Location: *1610 H St. NW; standing on H St. with the White House and Lafayette Park to your back, the house is one block to the left.* **Metro:** *Farragut North or Farragut West.* **Contact:** *☎ 842-0920; www.decaturhouse.org.* **Hours:** *Tu-W and F-Sa 10am-5pm (last tour 4:15pm), Th 10am-8pm, Su noon-4pm.* **Tours:** *Free guided tours given every hr. at 15min. past the hr. Tours can also be arranged for larger groups and vary in price depending on the size of the group.* **Events:** *The museum offers a selection of educational events and lectures.* **Admission:** *Free.*

At the northwest corner of Lafayette Park lies Decatur House, designed and built in 1818 by Benjamin Latrobe for **Stephen Decatur,** the Navy's youngest captain. A dashing military hero who defeated the Barbary pirates and captured the top British frigate during the War of 1812, Decatur spent only one year in the house before experiencing an untimely death in a duel. During the 1830s and 40s, hotelier **John Gadsby** entertained Washington's elite in the ballrooms; in 1871, the house was purchased by **Edward Beale,** best remembered for carrying official news of the California Gold Rush to Washington in a frontiersman's disguise. Other notable inhabitants of the House include **Edward Livingston**, **Henry Clay**, and President **Martin Van Buren.**

Today the house serves as a museum and is in the process of a $4 million renovation aimed at restoring the building to its original condition and appearance. The structure is one of only three remaining private American homes designed by Latrobe, who also helped design the White House, the Capitol building, and several projects with fellow architect and statesman **Thomas Jefferson.** The museum also features rotating temporary exhibits. **2004** will bring *"The Making of an American Hero: Stephen Decatur and the Burning of Philadelphia"* from mid-February to mid-May, while *"The Grand Tour: The Marquis de Lafayette's Return to America"* will run from June to early October.

THE OCTAGON

⚐ Location: *1799 New York Ave. NW.* **Metro:** *Farragut West.* **Contact:** *☎ 638-3221; www.archfoundation.org/octagon.* **Hours:** *Tu-Su 10am-4pm.* **Tours:** *Free 45min. tours by request.* **Admission:** *$5, students and seniors $3.*

No relation to the Pentagon, the Octagon was designed by William Thornton in 1799 as a house for wealthy Virginia landowner John Tayloe III. Thornton's design, which more closely resembles a hexagon, was a clever solution to cope with the awkward triangular lot upon which it was built.

First used as a winter home by the Tayloe family, the small house was able to hold not only all of the 15 Tayloe children (and the family slaves) but also receptions for Washington's elite—including the President. Legend has it that tunnels lead from the Octagon to the White House and the Potomac, though guides assert that this is untrue. The Madisons did manage to flee here quickly when British troops torched the White House in 1814, and for a short period the building became the official presidential residence. The Tayloes were kind enough to let the first family stay for a few hundred dollars per month, and Madison even signed the famed Treaty of Ghent on the desk which still sits in the second floor study. The building was used as a tenement house in the post-Civil War years and at one time housed ten families simultaneously. Today the house serves as a small museum highlighting Tayloe family pieces and period furniture, as well as rotating exhibitions.

The most interesting feature of the Octagon, however, is certainly the building itself. Architectural elements added for symmetry and order, like fancy doors that open into small closets and doors that lead to hidden passageways and back stairs, and the unusual burn marks along the handrails (a result of the system of ropes used to pull heavy buckets of coal and laundry from one floor to the next) have contributed to the ghost stories surrounding the house. Even more provocative are the repeated reports of modern-day visitors smelling lavender—said to have been former resident Dolly Madison's favorite scent.

AMERICAN RED CROSS

◪ Location: *Visitors Center 1730 E St. NW (entrance between 17th and 18th St.).* **Metro:** *Farragut West and Farragut North.* **Contact:** ☎ *639-3300, 639-3038 for tours info; www.redcross.org/museum.* **Hours:** *Building open M-F 8:30am-4pm.* **Tours:** *Tu and F at 9am.* **Admission:** *Free; suggested donation $2 per person, $5 per family.* **Accessibility:** *Wheelchair access from 17th St.*

The Red Cross museum features exhibits on the history of the service, which is a subgroup of the international movement founded in 1863 by Swiss Jean-Henri Dunant, who was inspired while he passed by a bloody battlefield in Solferino, Italy. Dunant received the Nobel Peace Prize for his efforts in 1901. Old posters, many from WWI and WWII, detail the rise of the organization. Special attention is given to Clara Barton, who convinced Congress to allow the US to join the Red Cross in 1882. Display cases in the entrance hall exhibit a series of books written by or about Barton. Also on display are uniforms created for the movie *In Love and War*, which tells the story of American journalist and novelist Ernest Hemingway's affair with a Red Cross nurse. Particularly worthwhile is "Images of Hope," an exhibit displaying accounts of those who experienced and survived (or helped others to survive) the September 11th terrorist attacks; included is the Red Cross cap and vest worn by New York City Mayor **Rudolph Giuliani** during his visits to the disaster site.

DAUGHTERS OF THE AMERICAN REVOLUTION CONSTITUTION HALL

◪ Location: *1776 D St. NW, between 17th and 18th streets; the visitors entrance is along D St.* **Metro:** *Farragut West; walk down 17th St., making a right onto D St.* **Contact:** ☎ *628-1776, 879-3241 for group tour info, 879-3229 for the DAR library; www.dar.org/museum.* **Hours:** *Museum open M-F 9:30am-4pm, Sa 9am-4pm; library open M-F 8:30am-4pm, Sa 9am-5pm.* **Tours:** *Tours of the DAR period rooms M-F 10am-2:30pm and Sa 9am-4:30pm every 30min.; group visits to the library should be pre-arranged by phone or by emailing library@dar.org.* **Admission:** *Free, although a small fee is charged for non-members to use the DAR library.*

The museum and library of the Daughters of the American Revolution (DAR) exude patriotic reverence with seemingly every plaque and kiosk display. The organization's headquarters, a national historic landmark since 1985, features a series of seventeen restored period rooms that display furniture, paintings, and historical artifacts specific to a particular state during the 19th century. Each room, named for its corresponding state, contains a binder providing detailed descriptions of virtually every item displayed. Highlights include the **Maryland** room, in which the wallpaper consists of large, colorful murals depicting scenes from the French Revolution of 1830. The **Massachusetts** room is a model of the Lexington parlor in which American patriots **John Hancock** and **Samuel Adams** heard the famous warning of **Paul Revere's** "midnight ride" that the British were coming. Don't miss the DAR **Library,** a completely white, illuminated space featuring a series of detailed wall moldings and was originally the meeting hall for the **Daughters of the American Revolution Congress.**

ORGANIZATION OF AMERICAN STATES (OAS)

◪ Location: *Main hall at 17th St. and Constitution Ave. NW, across the street from the west corner of the Ellipse. Museum at 201 18th St. NW, near the intersection of Virginia and Constitution Ave.* **Metro:** *Farragut West.* **Contact:** ☎ *458-3000, museum 458-6016, 458-6031 for tours and special events information; www.oas.org.* **Hours:** *OAS open M-F 9am-5pm; museum Tu-Su 10am-5pm.* **Tours:** *Group tours of the museum available by advance reservation only Tu-F 10am-4pm.* **Admission:** *Free.* **Events:** *lectures, special tours, and films.*

The Organization of American States building is a terracotta marriage of North and South American architectural styles. Busts of famous Latin American and American leaders line its corridors, the cavernous **Hall of Americas** displays crystal chandeliers and flags of member nations, and upstairs formal sessions are held in the spectacular OAS meeting rooms (closed when meetings are in session). The entrance atrium, illuminated by the glass ceiling windows overhead, features a small indoor garden of tropical greenery and palm trees, including the "Peace Tree" planted by President **William Howard Taft** in 1910. Note the photo of the tree's planting near the main hall

66

entrance; Taft is standing next to **Andrew Carnegie,** who donated most of the money for the building's construction. Behind the OAS building, the Aztec Garden leads to the **Art Museum of the Americas** (main entrance on 18th St.). Established in 1976, the museum displays temporary exhibits of 20th-century art from its extensive collection of Central American, South American, and Caribbean works.

DEPARTMENT OF THE INTERIOR

🖪 Location: *1849 C St. NW, between 18th and 19th St.* **Metro:** *Farragut West.* **Contact:** *☎ 208-4743; www.doi.gov.* **Hours:** *Museum open M-F 8:30am-4:30pm and 1-4pm on the third Sa of each month.* **Tours:** *Call in advance to schedule free tours and to obtain entrance to the museum. Advance notice of 2 weeks is requested. New Deal murals and building tours by appointment only.* **Admission:** *Free.*

Franklin Roosevelt laid the cornerstone for the building in 1936, using the same trowel George Washington had used to lay the Capitol's cornerstone in 1793. This was the first government building to have escalators, a gymnasium, and central A/C. Today the government agency doubles as a museum, with over 117 million objects and documents in their possession. Intricately detailed dioramas present the Department's mission, which revolves around the development and conservation of national and cultural resources as well as the maintenance of trust responsibilities to Native American lands. Many dioramas and hand-painted wall maps of the museum date from its opening years in the 1930s, including displays, images, and artifacts depicting the settlement of the West and relations with Native Americans. Among a series of black-and-white photographs of late-19th century American Indians is a shot of **Chief Sitting Bull.** Four paintings by William Henry Jackson depict the landscapes explored on geological surveys undertaken by the Department of the Interior in the 1860s and 70s; check out the Hayden Survey, which explored land that would later become **Yellowstone National Park.** The large model of the city of Washington, D.C., circa 1939 is worth a look. May to June **2004** will bring "For the Birds," an exhibit celebrating International Migratory Bird Day and features selected sculptures by Susan Leibovitz Steinman and Andree Singer Thompson.

NATIONAL ACADEMY OF SCIENCES

🖪 Location: *2100 C St. NW, between 21st and 22nd St.* **Metro:** *Foggy Bottom-GWU or Farragut West.* **Contact:** *☎ 334-2000; www.nationalacademies.org/nas.* **Hours:** *M-F 7:30am-5:30pm.* **Admission:** *Free.*

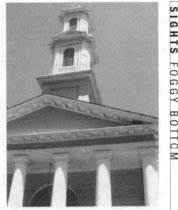
St. John's Church

Shiniest House in Georgetown

Georgetown University

Founded with the approval of President **Abraham Lincoln** in 1863, the National Academy of Sciences is a non-profit, private association of 2300 scientists, including more than 180 winners of the coveted **Nobel Prize.** The Academy's building along C St. (its more impressive façade faces Constitution Ave.) was dedicated in April 1924. Though not a museum, the Academy's building is open to the public and houses several small galleries with temporary exhibitions. Its most visually impressive feature is the building's **Great Hall,** which features a fantastic gold-tiled dome decorated with friezes depicting the four classical elements (earth, air, fire, and water) and also various scientific fields (including Anthropology, Geology, Physics, and Mathematics). A pair of carved doors leading to the main, domed hall from the (now closed) Constitution Ave. entrance contain representations of the 12 astrological symbols. A version of Foucault's Pendulum dangles from the dome's center. Around the atrium hall are a handful of large paintings and photographs showing celestial objects and natural phenomena, such as a large satellite image of Hurricane Andrew bearing down on the southeastern United States in 1992.

Outside the building at the corner of 22nd St. NW and Constitution Ave., a surprisingly friendly looking 21 ft. statue of physicist **Albert Einstein** sits on a large semicircular bench around a 28 ft. field of emerald pearl granite studded with metal chips that represent 55% of the entire sky: galaxies, planets, sun, moon, and stars. The statue is by **Robert Berks,** who also did the bust of President John F. Kennedy that sits in the Grand Foyer of the nearby **Kennedy Center.** The map shows the position of these celestial bodies at the time the statue was dedicated: noon, April 22, 1979. In Einstein's hand is a paper inscribed with equations relating to three of his most significant scientific discoveries (the photoelectric effect, the theory of general relativity, and the equivalence of energy and matter); look for the famous $E=mc^2$.

STATE DEPARTMENT

🚩 *Location: 2201 C St. NW, between 21st and 23rd St.; visitors entrance along 23rd St. **Metro:** Foggy Bottom-GWU. **Contact:** ☎ 647-3241, TDD 736-4474; www.state.gov. **Hours:** Daily 9am-4pm. **Tours:** M-F at 9:30, 10:30am, and 2:45pm by appointment; tours are the only means for visitors to enter the building. Call for reservations. **Admission:** Free.*

The State Department, established in 1787 by Congress for matters of diplomatic relations, is the nation's oldest cabinet agency. The current building in Foggy Bottom was constructed in 1960 and is the department's headquarters and "worldwide communications hub." Shortly after its opening, Secretary of State Dean Rusk redecorated the State Department's unflattering avocado-green interior with Chippendale chairs and Boston highboys. While the decor is still an exercise in grotesquerie, many *objets d'art* and pieces of Americana are on display, including a portrait of Thomas Jefferson in a toga, a highboy capped by a bust of John Locke, and the desk at which Jefferson penned the Declaration of Independence.

GEORGE WASHINGTON UNIVERSITY

🚩 *Location: Visitors Center at 801 22nd St. NW, near the intersection with H St. From the metro, walk along I (as in "Eye") St. to 22nd St. and make a right; the Visitors Center will be on the left, with the main entrance from H St. **Metro:** Foggy Bottom-GWU. **Contact:** ☎ 994-6602; www.gwu.edu. **Hours:** During the academic year M-F 9am-5pm, Sa 9am-4pm; closed Sa from the end of May through July. **Tours:** M-F 10am and 2pm, Sa 10am and 1pm.*

Founded in 1821 as the Columbian College in the District of Columbia, the school was renamed George Washington University in 1904. Although George Washington had hoped to establish a college in the District, the founding of the university had little to do with Washington himself. Ministers established the college under guidance of President Monroe with the hope of educating religious leaders.

Jacqueline Kennedy's alma mater stretches north of F St. in Foggy Bottom. The visitors desk in the Academic Center gives away brochures, campus newspapers, and *The Big To Do,* an entertainment calendar. Dance, theater, and music flourish at GWU's **Lisner Auditorium** (see p. 185), and the GWU Colonials play basketball from November to March. CNN's **Crossfire** is televised M-F 4:30-5pm at GWU's Jack Morton Auditorium and is free and open to the public. (805 21st St. NW. Call ☎994-8266 or email cnn@gwu.edu for free tickets. Doors open 3:30-4:10pm). The campus is sprinkled with rose bushes, statues, and red bricks engraved with the names of GWU graduates. Also notable is a copy of a statue of George Washington by **Jean-Antoine Houdon,** whose work can be seen in the **National Gallery of Art** (see p. 122). The statue stands guard over the university quad along H St. between 20th and 21st streets.

THE WATERGATE COMPLEX

⊠ Location: *Near the intersection of G St. and Virginia Ave., near 25th St. and New Hampshire Ave. From the metro stop, walk away from Washington Circle on 23rd St., making a right onto G St.* **Metro:** *Foggy Bottom-GWU.*

Composed of black-and-white half-cylinders with curving, toothy-looking balconies, this ugly concrete monstrosity of a complex contains law and business offices and condominiums of the rich, as well as the luxury Swissôtel. The Watergate's office space housed the Democratic National Committee's headquarters when President Nixon ordered them burgled in 1972. Across the street at the Howard Johnson (now a GWU dorm), chief burglar (now Washington radio talk show host) G. Gordon Liddy watched the burglary from a room that cost him only $50, including breakfast and valet parking. The ground floor hosts a few restaurants for the area's interns in an open-air seating area, and a D.C. branch of the Austin restaurant Jeffrey's, which opened when its biggest fan, President George W. Bush, took office in 2001.

THE KENNEDY CENTER

⊠ Location: *2700 F St. NW. The Center rises above Rock Creek Pkwy. just off 25th St. at the end of New Hampshire Ave. NW.* **Metro:** *Foggy Bottom-GWU, then walk away from downtown on H St. and turn left onto New Hampshire Ave. Shuttles run to and from the Metro every 15min.* **Contact:** *☎467-4600 or 800-444-1324, TTY 416-8524; www.kennedy-center.org.* **Hours:** *Daily 10am-midnight.* **Tours:** *Free tours given on demand and leave from the level A gift shop, M-F 10am-5pm, Sa-Su 10am-1pm (call ☎416-8340).* **Accessibility:** *All theaters are handicapped accessible.* **Performance Information:** *See p. 186.*

Completed in the late 1960s, the John F. Kennedy Center for the Performing Arts is a living monument to the assassinated president. The $78 million edifice boasts four major stages, a film theater, sumptuous red carpets, mirrors, crystal chandeliers, and 3700 tons of marble. Many pieces of freestanding art and

Hippo Hooray

According to local legend, the Potomac River was once inhabited by hippopotamuses. George Washington loved to watch them cavort in the shallows from his porch on Mount Vernon, and his children tried to rub the hippopotamuses' noses for luck.

Is it coincidence that his false teeth were made in part from hippo ivory or that the National Zoo was well known for its success at breeding pygmy hippopotami? You decide. In any case, there hasn't been a hippo sighting in the D.C. area for quite a while, but George Washington University honors the great "river horse" with a 4 ft. bronze hippo statue at the corner of H and 21st St.

The inscription reads: "Art for wisdom, Science for joy, Politics for beauty, and a Hippo for hope."

many of the furnishings were donated by various nations in memory of JFK. Art scattered about the center ranges from blast-damaged sheet metal to tapestries depicting the Creation.

Visitors enter through the flag-lined **Hall of States** or **Hall of Nations,** both of which lead to the **Grand Foyer,** one of the largest rooms in the world. The foyer boasts a 7 ft. bronze bust of JFK by **Robert Berks,** 18 chandeliers shaped like cubical grape clusters (each weighing 1 ton) and a series of interactive displays at which visitors can learn about Kennedy's presidency. The foyer is used to access the **Concert Hall,** the **Opera House,** and the **Eisenhower Theater.** The stage in the Concert Hall was a gift from over 692 high school, college, and community organizations from the US, Britain, and Japan. In return, the stage frequently hosts youth ensembles, and serves as a home to the **National Symphony Orchestra.** The President's box includes a reception room and a banner with his seal that hangs from the balcony when he is attending a performance. The **Millennium Stage** in the foyer puts on a free concert for the public at 6pm every day, featuring many prominent musicians; a live broadcast of each concert can be viewed online at www.kennedy-center.org/millennium. The Roof Terrace Restaurant is expensive, but walks along the outdoor roof terrace are free. The view of the Potomac, Georgetown, the Mall monuments, and the **National Cathedral** (see p. 87) make the roof one of the most romantic spots in the city.

FEDERAL TRIANGLE

◪ Highlights: *National Archives, MCI Center, FBI Building.* **Food and Drink:** *p. 150.* **Museums:** *National Building Museum, National Museum of Women in the Arts, International Spy Museum.* **Nearby:** *White House, North Mall, Farragut.* **Metro:** *Metro Center, Gallery Place-Chinatown, Judiciary Square, Archives-Navy Memorial, or Federal Triangle.*

The Federal Triangle area is an example of D.C.'s mutable neighborhood boundaries. The area north of the Mall bounded by Constitution Ave., 2nd St., New York Ave., and 15th St. NW has been called Old Downtown and Penn Quarter. New presidents traverse Pennsylvania Ave. during the Inaugural Parade, giving it its nickname: **The Street of Presidents.** But the history of this area has not always been so positive: it has been plagued by cyclical decline and renewal. While Pennsylvania Ave. remained largely residential until the 1820s, Federal Triangle became the city's red-light district after **Union General Joseph Hooker** restricted prostitution in the city to this area. Construction of the Federal Triangle government building complex after the turn of the 20th century finally restored the avenue's good reputation, placing it once again in the very center of national government. This period of urban revitalization was short-lived: in 1968, riots centered in the former commercial areas of the neighborhood cemented its reputation as one of the most dangerous and seedy sections of the city. To counter this image, Congress created the Pennsylvania Ave. Development Corporation in 1972 to encourage private enterprise in Federal Triangle. The next decade saw a series of large construction projects infuse the area with new life. Within the past few years, two new additions—the **MCI Center** sports complex and the **Ronald Reagan Building and International Trade Center**—have brought even more commercial energy to the neighborhood. In March 2003, the city opened the doors to the 2.3 million sq. ft. **New Washington Convention Center** on Mt. Vernon Place between 7th and 9th St. NW; the old center, just west of Chinatown, is expected to reemerge in coming years as a mixed-use venue. Despite the urban renewal, **walking through parts of Federal Triangle and areas north may be unsafe at night.**

NATIONAL ARCHIVES

◪ Location: *700 Pennsylvania Ave. NW, between 7th and 9th St. JFK Archives are at 8601 Adelphi Rd., College Park, MD.* **Metro:** *Archives-Navy Memorial.* **Contact:** *☎ 501-5000, research 501-5400, JFK Archives 301-713-6400, TTY 501-5404; www.nara.gov.* **Hours:** *Apr.-Labor Day daily*

*10am-9pm; Sept.-Mar. 10am-5:30pm. Research hours M and W 8:45am-5pm, Tu and Th-F 8:45am-9pm, Sa 8:45am-4:45pm. **Tours:** 1hr. M-F 10:15am and 1:15pm. Call ☎501-5205 at least 4 weeks in advance for tour reservations. No reservation required to view Rotunda. US citizens can arrange tours through their Congressional representatives. **Admission:** Free.*

If the federal government has an attic, this is it. The National Archives is home to everything the government thinks is worth saving ("permanently valuable" is how they like to put it). This select collection amounts to only 2-5% of the documents generated by the government every year. The numbers are still staggering: 16 million pictures and posters, 18 million maps, and billions of pages of text. The collection includes all sorts of unusual objects—wacky contributions from the Nixon years include a tiny portrait of Tricky Dick painted on a grain of rice and a red wig worn by Watergate burglar Howard Hunt. The building's long-tiered steps, stone friezes, fluted columns, and mammoth bronze doors (1 ft. thick and 40 ft. high) are indicative of architect John Russell Pope's work and can also be seen in his design of the National Gallery (see **Museums,** p. 122).

The three cornerstones of American legal tradition—the **Declaration of Independence,** the **Constitution,** and the **Bill of Rights**—draw crowds up to the hundreds; expect to wait over an hour at peak times. These "Charters of Freedom" are exhibited in the Rotunda (enter on Constitution Ave.) and are displayed in humidity-controlled, helium-filled cases made of glass and bronze. The refractive property of the glass, and the protective filters that shield the documents from harmful light, give them a greenish tinge. Every night the cases sink 22 ft. into a 55-ton steel and concrete basement vault, insuring their contents against theft and nuclear attack.

Largely ignored by tourists is a copy of the **Magna Carta.** Originally signed and issued in 1215, the document detailed King John I's guarantee of rights to his angry British noblemen. On display is one of four extant copies of the 1297 version. Eccentric billionaire and former presidential hopeful H. Ross Perot purchased the famous document in 1984 and loaned it to the Archives indefinitely. The guided tour gives a more in-depth look at some interesting lesser-known holdings such as **President John F. Kennedy's** doodles during the Cuban Missile Crisis and a wall of unlabeled presidential baby pictures. Scholars can access the research room here and at Archives II, a monstrous two-million cubic foot warehouse in Maryland. Conspiracy theorists will be interested in the John F. Kennedy Assassination Records Collection at the College Park location—it can also be accessed through the website.

FEDERAL BUREAU OF INVESTIGATION (FBI)

The J. Edgar Hoover Building, 935 Pennsylvania Ave. NW, closed to visitors in August 2002 for extensive renovations. Tours will not resume until fall 2004. For information on the reopening, call ☎324-3447 or visit www.fbi.gov.

CHINATOWN

🚇 Location: *Centered at H St. between 6th and 7th Sts. NW.*

After the Chinese Exclusion Act of 1882 restricted immigration and barred Chinese aliens from most jobs, the persecuted immigrants lived and worked near 4th St. and Pennsylvania Ave. NW. Two rival *tongs* (merchants' associations) formed to offer protection to Chinese-owned businesses. When government buildings displaced the old Chinatown, the *tongs* led the move to today's neighborhood.

Washington's Chinatown is one of the nation's smallest, and it has been fighting decline for years. Despite the grand entrance provided by the Friendship Archway at 7th and H St. (built by the city in 1986 in an attempt to revitalize the area), Chinatown has been essentially reduced to one block of grocery stores and restaurants. The national chain stores (CVS) and restaurants (Hooters) along 7th St. may have secondary signage in traditional Chinese characters, but their presence is steadily marginalizing what was once a larger and more vibrant neighborhood. Chinatown now sits in the shadow of the massive, ultra-modern MCI Center. Though the arena's designers tried to blend the building into Chinatown by including Chinese elements in its architecture, its central location and sheer mass rendered this effort futile.

Despite these challenges, a string of excellent restaurants (see **Food and Drink,** p. 145) and Chinese grocers can still be found on the 600 block of H St. and on the 700 block of 6th St. The streets in this area swarm around noon with the professional lunch crowd from downtown, but **be careful in the surrounding area at night.**

OLD POST OFFICE

🚩 *Location:* 1100 Pennsylvania Ave. NW, at 11th St. *Metro:* Federal Triangle. *Contact:* ☎ 289-4224; www.oldpostofficedc.com. *Hours:* Tower open mid-Apr. to mid-Sept. M-Sa 9am-7:45pm, Su 10am-5:45pm; off-season M-F 9am-4:45pm, Sa-Su 10am-5:45pm. Tower closes during inclement weather and Washington Ringing Society rehearsals Th 6:30-9:30pm. Shops open M-Sa 10am-7pm, Su noon-6pm. *Admission:* Free.

Once criticized as "a cross between a cathedral and a cotton mill," the Old Post Office remains a delightful rebuke to its sleeker contemporary neighbors. Having hosted such tenants as the Departments of Defense, the Smithsonian Institute, and the FBI, the first few floors of the building now house **The Pavilion,** which consists of a stage with local entertainment and a touristy collection of shops and eateries. High above, the **tower** allows visitors to perch 270 ft. above downtown with unobstructed views of the Capitol, the White House, and the Lincoln Memorial without the wait or tiny windows of the Washington Monument.

FORD'S THEATRE

🚩 *Location:* 511 10th St. NW, between E and F Sts. *Metro:* Metro Center. *Contact:* ☎ 426-6924, TDD 426-1749; www.nps.gov/foth. *Hours:* Daily 9am-5pm. 15min. talks at 9:15, 10:15, 11:15am, 2:15, 3:15, 4:15pm, except during matinees. Call for details. *Admission:* Free.

Except for the sets of the constantly changing short run productions (see **Entertainment,** p. 187), the poorly lit theater looks much as it did on April 14, 1865, when actor **John Wilkes Booth** sneaked into **Abraham Lincoln's** box, shot him in the head with a Derringer pistol, then leapt clumsily to the stage breaking a bone in his left leg and shouted "Sic semper tyrannis," or "thus always to tyrants," the state motto of Virginia. This declaration was symbolic of Booth's plan to rid the South of Lincoln's influence. National Park Rangers describe the events with animated gusto during a 15 min. talk in the theater. Downstairs, artifacts related to the assassination are displayed. Every president since 1868 has taken his chances and seen a play at the theater at least once a year. Of course, they avoid the unlucky box and sit front row center. Lines to see the theater can be very long, so plan on going in the morning.

PETERSEN HOUSE

🚩 *Location:* 516 10th St. NW, between E and F Sts. *Metro:* Metro Center. *Contact:* ☎ 426-6830; www.nps.gov/foth. *Hours:* Daily 9am-5pm. *Admission:* Free.

The mortally wounded Lincoln was carried across the street to the Petersen House, where he died the next morning in a bed too small for his massive frame. The tiny room where he passed away (rumored to be the size of the log cabin where the entire Lincoln family lived when Abe was a boy) is an impeccable historic reconstruction, with the original interior structure and moldings. The intimacy of the room gives visitors the unnerving impression that they are strangers at a wake. Lines are long, so arrive early.

NAVY MEMORIAL & NAVAL HERITAGE CENTER

🚩 *Location:* Across from the National Archives. *Metro:* Archives-Navy Memorial. *Contact:* ☎ 737-2300; www.lonesailor.org. *Hours:* Memorial open 24hr. Visitors Center open Mar.-Oct. M-Sa 9:30am-5pm; Nov.-Feb. Tu-Sa 9:30am-4pm. *Events:* A film of naval interest shown daily; call for info. *Admission:* Free.

The Navy Memorial is a popular outdoor rest and lunch spot. The memorial's cascading fountains and naval flags suggest the deck of a ship. An engraving of the naval hymn and Bleifeld's statue *The Lone Sailor* create a contemplative mood.

Don't skip over the bronze sculptures featuring depictions of important moments (and ships) in naval history which encircle the memorial. In the summer, the Navy Band hosts weekly concerts at the memorial (Tu 8pm), and the Navy Ceremonial Guard performs a drill (Tu 1pm), but call ahead. At the rear of the memorial on the northern side, the **Naval Heritage Center** is a hidden treasure. Exhibits include magnificent paintings from the Navy Art Collection, the Navy Log (a video record of Navy veterans), the Naval Heritage Library, and interactive video kiosks. The Presidents' Room shows portraits of presidents who have served.

NEW YORK AVENUE PRESBYTERIAN CHURCH

🚹 *Location:* 1313 New York Ave. NW, at the intersection of H St. *Metro:* Metro Center. *Contact:* ☎ 393-3700; www.nyapc.org. *Tours:* Summer 11am; Fall-Spring 10:45am, noon. Visitors also welcome Tu-Th 9am-6pm, F 9am-5pm, Sa 9am-1pm. Groups of 10 or more should call in advance.

This church, which celebrated its 200th anniversary in 2003, has served as the place of worship for presidents Lincoln, Buchanan, and Johnson. Visit the sanctuary and sit in the second-row pew where Abraham Lincoln took in Sunday services; this pew, along with the organ, are the only remaining artifacts from the original church. Then head downstairs to the Lincoln Parlor to view a rough draft of the Emancipation Proclamation, featured alongside portraits of the Civil War-era pastor and Lincoln himself. The couch below the display is no ordinary piece of furniture—Lincoln sat there while writing the draft.

NATIONAL LAW ENFORCEMENT OFFICERS MEMORIAL

🚹 *Location:* At the Judiciary Sq. Visitors Center at 605 E St. NW, near the corner of 6th and E St. *Metro:* Judiciary Sq. *Contact:* ☎ 737-3400; www.nleomf.com. *Hours:* Memorial open 24hr.; Visitors Center open M-F 9am-5pm, Sa 10am-5pm, Su noon-5pm. *Admission:* Free.

Dedicated by President George Bush in October 1991, this memorial honoring law enforcement officers killed on the job since 1794 displays the influence of Michelangelo's Piazza del Campidoglio in Rome and Maya Ying Lin's Vietnam Veterans Memorial in D.C. (see p. 57). Over 16,000 names of slain officers are engraved in the marble walls along opposing curved and tree-lined "pathways of remembrance," which are flanked by 14,000 daffodils in early April. Every year on May 13 at 8pm, new names are added to the memorial during a candlelight vigil. The **Visitors Center** details the history of the memorial and the officers it honors.

MARTIN LUTHER KING, JR. LIBRARY

🚹 *Location:* 901 G St. NW, entrance on G St. between 9th and 10th. *Metro:* Metro Center. *Contact:* ☎ 727-0321; www.dclibrary.org. *Hours:* M-Th 9:30am-9pm, F-Sa 9:30am-5:30pm, Su 1-5pm; closed Su in summer. *Events:* The library hosts concerts, lectures, readings, and book signings.

Opened in 1972, the flagship of D.C.'s library system is a brick, steel, and bronze building representing the Bauhaus style of famed architect Ludwig Mies van der Rohe. Note painter Don Miller's mural of Dr. King. The third fl. of the library houses a non-circulating Black Studies Room and the Washingtonian Room, filled with resources detailing every fact you ever and never wanted to know about the city.

MCI CENTER

🚹 *Location:* 601 F St. NW. *Metro:* Gallery Place-Chinatown. *Contact:* ☎ 628-3200; www.mcicenter.com.

This 20,000-seat arena opened in 1997 as D.C.'s premier sports venue. It hosts the NBA's Washington Wizards, the NHL's Washington Capitals, the WNBA's Washington Mystics, and the NCAA's Georgetown Hoyas, as well as most major concerts that come through town (see **Entertainment,** p. 194).

CANADIAN EMBASSY

🚹 *Location:* 501 Pennsylvania Ave. NW, between 6th St. and Constitution Ave. *Metro:* Judiciary Sq. or Archives-Navy Memorial. *Contact:* ☎ 682-1740; www.canadianembassy.org. *Hours:* M-F 9am-5pm. *Admission:* Free.

in recent news

Tales from the Underground

To most visitors, Washington's 103-mile rapid transit system may seem to be nothing more than a convenience provided for the benefit of tourists. But over the last three decades, the Metro has had a much greater role in the life of the city.

To understand the Metro's impact, try walking from Union Station to the National Building Museum at Judiciary Square, scarcely half a mile to the west. As you walk along F Street, you will find your way blocked by a vast trench, one city block wide, between 2nd and 3rd St.

In that trench is the stub end of I-395, an expressway cutting through the heart of the city. According to plans made in 1955, this highway was to be just one part of a larger system of freeways through Washington. These roads would have lacerated downtown, the U Street and Dupont Circle neighborhoods, Cleveland Park, and such near-in suburbs as Bethesda and Takoma Park.

Fortunately for Washington, activists from several parts of the city rose to demand a transit system instead. Some took to the streets, some filed suit, and some joined the Kennedy

(continued on next page)

The embassy is a stunning blend of neoclassical and modern architecture designed by Canadian architect Arthur Erickson. Its smooth, unpolished Canadian marble and blue-tinted windows interject architectural vitality into the gloomy conglomeration of federal buildings that make up this section of downtown. Worth a quick stop, the **Rotunda of Provinces** is majestically serene, with twelve 50 ft. aluminum columns (representing Canada's 12 provinces) towering over a cascading fountain (representing Niagara Falls). Bill Reid's sculpture, *The Spirit of Haida Gwaii*, depicts a canoe filled with legendary figures from early Haida (aboriginal nation) mythology.

FARRAGUT

⚐ Highlights: National Geographic Society, Washington Post. **Museums:** The Bethune Museum and Archives, B'nai B'rith Klutznick Museum. **Food and Drink:** p. 149. **Nearby:** White House, Foggy Bottom, Dupont Circle. **Metro:** Farragut North, Farragut West, or McPherson Sq.

Farragut is the epicenter of corporate Washington. The 13-story height limit prevents New York-style claustrophobia in this glass-walled business district, but white-collar joggers, businessmen in expensive ties, and honking taxicabs reveal its corporate soul. A few scenic circles, residential areas, and small museums lie amid the clamor. Farragut is bounded roughly by N, I, and 13th St. NW on the north, south, and east, respectively, and by 21st St. on the west.

Picnickers enjoy the summer sounds of occasional street musicians in **Farragut Square,** adjoining the Farragut North and Farragut West Metro Stations. A statue of Civil War Admiral David Farragut stares off into the distance, spyglass in hand. Farragut, who coined the phrase "Full speed ahead!" during the 1864 Battle of Mobile Bay, Alabama, is now patron to a regular crowd of homeless people and corporate suits who lounge and lunch in the park. On Thursdays from June through August, Farragut Square hosts **Farragut Sounds in the Square,** a series of free jazz concerts beginning at noon (call ☎ 463-3400 or check out www.gtbid.com for more info). Nearby **McPherson Square** commemorates Gen. James McPherson, who commanded the Union Army during Sherman's march through Georgia.

THE WASHINGTON POST

⚐ Location: 1150 15th St. NW. **Metro:** Farragut North or McPherson Square. **Contact:** ☎ 334-7969; www.washingtonpost.com. **Tours:** 1hr. tours (M 10, 11am, 1, 2, 3pm) given only by advance reservation to groups of 10-30, in which the entire group consists of members of one club or organization. Reservations must be made in writing 2-4 weeks in advance; requests must include a list of the names of all tour visitors. No children under 11. **Admission:** Free.

The domineering tan building at 1150 15th St. houses *The Washington Post*, one of the most influential newspapers in the world. This paper was responsible for uncovering the Watergate Scandal and the Pentagon Papers. If you can land a spot on the popular tour, you'll see the *Post*'s hectic newsroom, a small museum, and a short video giving an overview of the paper. Guides detail the complicated, time-consuming printing process of yore and explain how the paper is printed today. Before or after the tour, visitors should note the lobby, where four light boards display information about the various departments of the *Post*. Those who can't get a tour will need to make do with the *Post*'s exterior and entrance area, where an old Linotype machine and displayed reproductions of historic front pages await the curious.

NATIONAL GEOGRAPHIC SOCIETY

🔲 Location: On the corner of M and 17th St. NW; main visitors entrance on 17th St. **Metro:** Farragut North or Farragut West. **Contact:** ☎857-7588, group tours 857-7689, Grosvenor Auditorium 857-7700; www.nationalgeographic.com. **Hours:** M-Sa 9am-5pm, Su 10am-5pm. **Admission:** Free. **Accessibility:** Handicapped accessible.

Video clips, interactive computer booths, and life-size displays fill **Explorer's Hall**, an educational museum on the first floor of the National Geographic Society's headquarters. A trickling fountain near the main entrance simulates a melting iceberg, while a three-dimensional, topographical model of the **Grand Canyon** hangs overhead in the hallway near the elevators. In spring and fall (late Sept.-Dec. and Feb.-May), the **Gilbert H. Grosvenor Auditorium** hosts lectures, films, and performances; call or pick up a schedule at the front desk for the latest info. Exhibitions, ranging from animal paintings to model ships, change every few months.

Explorer's Hall's southern half (facing away from M St.) is home to the **Window Walk,** a series of displays of three-dimensional maps and giant models of artifacts. A map of the Chesapeake Bay and Appalachian Ridge shows a satellite view of D.C. and its environs (visible near the map's center).

GEORGETOWN

🔲 Highlights: Shops and eateries along M St. and Wisconsin Ave., Dumbarton Oaks Estate, C&O Canal. **Museums:** Dumbarton Oaks. **Food and Drink:** p. 153. **Nightlife:** p. 176. **Nearby:** Upper Northwest, Adams Morgan, Dupont Circle, Foggy Bottom.

YOU ARE HERE
U.S. Capitol Building
SEE MAP P. 359

and Johnson administrations to fight from within. Eventually, they succeeded in persuading Congress to block the planned highways and to pay instead for the more radical regional rail system.

The Metro caused the most distress, however, among historians and residents of the wealthy Georgetown area. While many Washingtonians suspect the residents' clout was enough to keep a Metro stop out of their backyards, the planning committee actually decided to route Metro around Georgetown because of the structural risk to the neighborhood's priceless 18th-century buildings.

The transit authority broke ground in 1969, the first trains ran (from Rhode Island Avenue to Farragut North) in 1976, and the 103-mile system was completed in 2001. But Metro is still growing, with a Blue Line extension and a new Red Line station under construction. A new line from West Falls Church to the Reston area, with stops in Tysons Corner, will begin construction in 2005.

See www.chnm.gmu.edu/metro for more of the story.

–Zachary Schrag

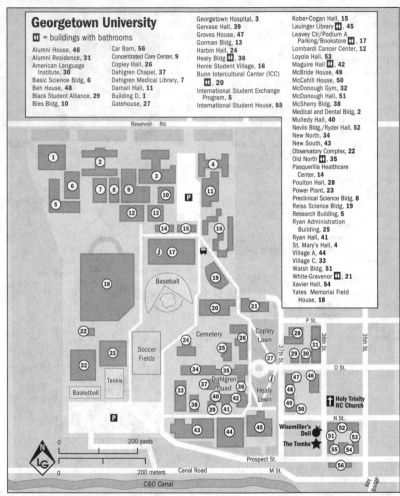

Georgetown University

🚻 = buildings with bathrooms

Alumni House, **46**
Alumni Residence, **31**
American Language
Institute, **30**
Basic Science Bldg, **6**
Beh House, **48**
Black Student Alliance, **29**
Bles Bldg, **10**

Car Barn, **56**
Concentrated Care Center, **9**
Copley Hall, **26**
Dahlgren Chapel, **37**
Dahlgren Medical Library, **7**
Darnall Hall, **11**
Building D, **1**
Gatehouse, **27**

Georgetown Hospital, **3**
Gervase Hall, **39**
Groves House, **47**
Gorman Bldg, **13**
Harbin Hall, **24**
Healy Bldg 🚻, **36**
Henle Student Village, **16**
Bunn Intercultural Center (ICC)
🚻, **20**
International Student Exchange
Program, **5**
International Student House, **55**

Kober-Cogan Hall, **15**
Lauinger Library 🚻, **45**
Leavey Ctr/Podium A
Parking/Bookstore 🚻, **17**
Lombardi Cancer Center, **12**
Loyola Hall, **53**
Maguire Hall 🚻, **42**
McBride House, **49**
McCahill House, **50**
McDonough Gym, **32**
McDonough Hall, **51**
McSherry Bldg, **38**
Medical and Dental Bldg, **2**
Mulledy Hall, **40**
Nevils Bldg./Ryder Hall, **52**
New North, **34**
New South, **43**
Observatory Complex, **22**
Old North 🚻, **35**
Pasquerilla Healthcare
Center, **14**
Poulton Hall, **28**
Power Plant, **23**
Preclinical Science Bldg, **8**
Reiss Science Bldg, **19**
Research Building, **5**
Ryan Administration
Building, **25**
Ryan Hall, **41**
St. Mary's Hall, **4**
Village A, **44**
Village C, **33**
Walsh Bldg, **51**
White-Gravenor 🚻, **21**
Xavier Hall, **54**
Yates Memorial Field
House, **18**

Reservoir Rd.

Baseball

Cemetery
Copley
Lawn
Dahlgren
Quad
Healy
Lawn

Soccer
Fields

Tennis

Basketball

200 yards

200 meters   Canal Road

P St.
O St.
N St.
Prospect St.
M St.

36th St.
35th St.
37th St.

Holy Trinity
RC Church

Wisemiller's
Deli

The Tombs

C&O Canal

Key
Bridge

Georgetown's quiet historical homes are balanced by raucous bars. The tree-lined streets of boxy, brick rowhouses are home to politicos like former Secretary of State Madeleine Albright, a world-class university, and blocks and blocks of shopping, dining, and drinking. Both high-income and high-status, Georgetown attracts a strange blend of students, twenty-something singles, and tourists. But Georgetown is not merely a party town. In the lush gardens of **Dumbarton Oaks** and the **Tudor Place Estate,** the history along the **C&O Canal** and in the **Old Stone House,** and the serene architecture of its residential, tree-lined streets, Georgetown has a great deal of (often free) wonders to offer that are not related to Happy Hours or weekend sales.

HISTORY OF GEORGETOWN
In the late 17th century, George Gordon and Ninean Beall, both of Scottish descent, came to own much of the land in the Georgetown area. In the early 1700s, immigrants fleeing Scotland's social unrest flocked to the lands owned by Gordon and George Beall (Ninean's heir) and eventually forced those estates to relinquish some

of their property. This became "Georgetown," although it is unknown whether the town was named for the two Georges who reluctantly gave up their land or for England's King George II.

Located on the Potomac, at the border of Virginia and Maryland, the town immediately thrived as a center of trade for tobacco and African slaves. In the 1750s, Georgetown's bustle attracted **George Washington,** who would later select a parcel of land adjacent to the city for the site of the nation's capital, Washington City. From 1780 to 1830, while Washington City was still a minimally developed swamp, Georgetown became the fashionable and civilized residence of many government officials and foreign ambassadors. Visitors can still distinguish the smaller rowhouses below Dumbarton St., built for the workers and African-Americans, from the larger, aristocratic houses of upper Georgetown.

In 1871 an act of Congress took away the region's self-government, absorbing it into Washington. The late 19th and early 20th centuries saw Georgetown become less rich and fashionable, as more blue-collar workers and minorities moved into the city. Georgetown's fate seemed sealed with the death of the Chesapeake and Ohio Canal, which was deemed too shallow for modern steamships and struggled against competition from the Baltimore and Ohio Railroad.

During the New Deal and World War II, the size of the federal work force in Washington ballooned. The influx of academics-turned-bureaucrats renewed Georgetown at a ferocious pace. In order to form wealthier, more commercially viable communities, a federal agency expelled poor African-American families from Georgetown, and real estate developers bought out longtime homeowners. Once remodeled and spiffed up, the properties were then sold to the new army of white-collar civil servants, creating modern, upscale Georgetown.

Today, only a privileged few can afford the inflated real estate prices in Georgetown. **John F. Kennedy** lived here as a US Senator (at 3260 N St.), as did **Senator John Warner** and his then-wife **Liz Taylor.** Hollywood has also found the area compelling, using it as a backdrop for films like *True Lies, The Exorcist,* and *Minority Report.* Drawn to the energy of college students and interns, tourists have helped transform Georgetown from a collection of staid federal-style buildings and rowhouses into a booming shopping, dining, and drinking district. Visitors with an interest in Georgetown's past will be happy to know that

Rock Creek Park

Arlington National Cemetery

Iwo Jima

77

despite the noxious presence of touristy chain stores and restaurants, historical sights abound. Places like the **Dumbarton Oaks Mansion and Garden, Mount Zion Methodist Church, Tudor Place, Dumbarton House,** and the **C&O Canal** are all worth a visit. Unfortunately, many of Georgetown's other historic homes are closed to the public.

ORIENTATION

Wisconsin Ave. and **M St.** are the main thoroughfares of Georgetown, and their intersection (Washington's oldest) marks the center of this consumer-driven universe. Address numbers on Wisconsin Ave. start below M St. and go up as the avenue goes north (in this area, uphill). Numbered streets run perpendicular to M St., increasing east to west. For most of its Georgetown length, K St., which turns into Water St., is directly under the Whitehurst Fwy. and thus hard to find on maps. Because Rock Creek Park cuts through the city on one side of Georgetown, M St., Pennsylvania Ave., P St., and Q St. are the only routes to Georgetown for pedestrians coming from downtown or Dupont Circle. West of Key Bridge, M St. becomes Canal Rd. (leading to Bethesda, MD) as neon and brick abruptly yield to the trees of Glover Park.

Although it is possible to walk to Georgetown from the Rosslyn, Dupont Circle, and Foggy Bottom-GWU Metro stops, the easiest method of transportation are the privately operated **Georgetown Metro Connection** shuttles. The blue buses run frequently from all three Metro stops, shuttling passengers into the heart of Georgetown along M St. and Wisconsin Ave. for $1 ($0.35 with Metro transfer). If you can't find a shuttle, try the Metrobus from Dupont Circle. Take the red line to the Metro stop there and exit from the Q St. entrance. Turn left on 20th St. and walk two blocks to the corner of 20th and P St. From there catch the G2 bus to Georgetown.

Walking to Georgetown is easiest from Foggy Bottom. From the Metro, proceed along 23rd St. to Washington Circle, bearing left onto Pennsylvania Ave., which leads directly into M St. in Georgetown.

Finding **parking** is difficult, and you may waste the whole day trying to find a spot. Try 35th St. near the university (particularly in the summer), the northern sections near R and S St., or Georgetown's eastern edge near 29th St. Garages like **Georgetown Parking** (1044 Wisconsin Ave., ☎333-1898) are reasonable ($8 per day) and conveniently located near the center of town.

⬛DUMBARTON OAKS ESTATE

🔲 *Location: Mansion entrance at 1703 32nd St. NW between R and S St. Garden entrance at 31st and R St. Contact: ☎339-6401, tour info 339-6409; DumbartonOaks@doaks.org; www.doaks.org. Hours: Mansion open Tu-Su 2-5pm. Garden open Apr.-Oct. Tu-Su 2-6pm, Nov.-Mar. 2-5pm. Tours: Docent-led garden tours are usually given daily at 2:10pm, weather permitting; call ahead to confirm tour time. Tours meet at information booth near R St. entrance. Admission: For mansion, there is a suggested donation of $1. For garden $5, seniors and children 2-12 $3; Nov.-Mar. free.*

The **Dumbarton Oaks Mansion,** now a museum, should not be confused with the entirely separate Dumbarton House (see below). This estate is part of the remains of the original **Rock of Dumbarton** property, upon which Georgetown was founded. The mansion has switched names and architectural styles frequently since its 1801 construction. Dumbarton's collection focuses on Byzantine art, but also includes a fascinating collection of pre-Columbian artifacts. See **Museums,** p. 126.

The ten stunning acres of the **Dumbarton Oaks Gardens** have a separate entrance. Each season reveals different facets of the garden, from the spring explosion of flowers such as the bearded iris, foxglove, and southern magnolia, to the winter bare "bones" of arched tree limbs. A self-guided tour map can be picked up at the main information booth (near the garden's entrance) and leads visitors through the landscaped paths here. Warning: no picnicking or pets allowed.

Immediately to the east of Dumbarton Oaks is **Lover's Lane,** officially recognized as such in 1900. The beautiful canopied path winds behind the tennis courts of Dumbarton Oaks Park and heads north to where it connects to Rock Creek Park, beginning a two-mile trail that leads through the park (see p. 86) up to the National Zoo. This path is **very unsafe at night** and should be avoided after dark. Concerts from the Dumbarton Oaks Friends of Music are held every winter (☎339-6436 for info).

C&O CANAL

🛈 Location: Visitors center at 1057 Thomas Jefferson St. NW, south of M St. on the towpath. **Contact:** ☎653-5190; www.nps.gov/choh. **Hours:** Bookstore and Visitors Center open W-Su 9am-5pm. Boats leave mid-June to early Sept. W 11am, 1:30, and 3pm; Th-Su 11am, 1:30, 3 and 5pm. Sept.-Nov. and Apr.-June W-F 11am and 3pm; Sa-Su 11am, 1:30, 3 and 5pm. As hours for boats change frequently, visitors are encouraged to call ahead (or check the website) to get the latest information. **Tours:** A variety of free, local-area walking tours, each with its own unique theme or region, are offered June-Aug. Sa-Su 12:15pm; call ahead to obtain the latest schedule information. **Admission (for boat tour):** $8, seniors $6, children $5. Admission to the Visitors Center itself is free. **Accessibility:** Visitors Center and boat ride are wheelchair accessible.

For decades, George Washington advocated construction of a canal in Georgetown. Expanding on Washington's ideas, in 1828 **President John Quincy Adams** began construction of the Chesapeake & Ohio (C&O) Canal. Today the canal and adjacent towpath, which run parallel to M St., two blocks south, exist merely as a historic landmark administered by the National Park Service. As a a reminder of the canal's original function, the canal boat **Georgetown** takes tourists through the locks of the canal, pulled from the towpath by mules. Board the one-hour ride at the Visitors Center. Information on fishing, ranger-led hiking, biking, tours, and upcoming events is also available at the Visitors Center.

2004 marks the 50th anniversary of the 1954 towpath hike, led by Supreme Court Justice **William O. Douglas.** The hike was instrumental in saving the canal from proposed development projects that would have destroyed it. (See **Parks,** p. 108.)

THE OLD STONE HOUSE

🛈 Location: 3051 M St. **Contact:** ☎426-6851; www.nps.gov/rocr. **Hours:** House open W-Su noon-5pm. Garden open W-Su noon-5pm. **Tours:** By appointment only. **Admission:** Free. **Events:** A variety of free public programs are offered Sa-Su and include tours and special events in Rock Creek Park; call 895-6239 or see the website for the latest schedule.

Built in 1766, the Old Stone House is generally accepted to be the oldest standing building in Washington. Its past includes periods as a paint store, a clock shop, a tailor's shop, and the offices of a used car dealership. The US government bought the property in 1953 for a mere $90,000, opening the Old Stone House to the public in 1960. Displayed within are cooking, baking, candle-making, and fabric-spinning tools meant to represent those that the original family here would have owned and used. Much of the exterior stone work is original to the house's 18th-century construction. Unfortunately for taller visitors, the curators have also preserved the original low ceilings and door frames. In back, lovely gardens make this a nice place to stop and literally smell the roses in late spring.

GEORGETOWN UNIVERSITY

🛈 Location: 37th and O St. **Contact:** ☎687-1457 for the information center; www.georgetown.edu. **Tours:** Campus tours (☎687-3600) begin at the Office of Undergraduate Admissions, White-Gravenor Hall, Rm. 103. Call the admissions office for the latest guided tour information. **Transportation:** Shuttle bus (☎687-4417) stops outside Leavey Center. Shuttle runs every 15min. to nearby Metro stops, including Rosslyn and Dupont Circle. $1, Georgetown students free.

Archbishop John Carroll was fully aware of Georgetown's lively nature when he chose to found his university there instead of on then-rural **Capitol Hill.** The first building was constructed in 1788, and the university opened in 1789, becoming the United

States' first Catholic institution for higher learning. Today, approximately 50% of Georgetown's 6000 undergraduates are Catholic, and a Jesuit brother resides in every dorm, although students of many creeds attend.

Georgetown boasts a long list of rich and powerful graduates, such as Supreme Court Justice **Antonin Scalia;** the late New York Archbishop, **Cardinal John O'Connor;** television journalist and author **Maria Shriver;** and former top dog **Bill Clinton** himself. The popular men's basketball team, which launched the careers of **Patrick Ewing, Alonzo Mourning,** and **Allen Iverson,** is a perennial NCAA tournament contender. They now play at the **MCI Center** (see p. 73). Buy tickets through TicketMaster (☎432-7328) for these games; buy other sporting event tickets through the campus ticket office (☎687-4692).

Through the main gate (at 37th and O St.) lie the prominent Gothic curlicues of **Healy Hall,** named after Father Patrick Healy, an African-American priest and president of Georgetown University in the 1870s. Look for the hands of the clock mounted on Healy Hall's tower—if they're there. Most years, seniors attempt to steal them and ship them to the president of the university—or, rumor has it, to destinations as far as the Vatican. Tighter security near the clock tower has stymied some theft attempts. But undergraduates still find channels for mischievous delight; students can sometimes be seen "swimming" in the shallow fountain in front of nearby **Dahlgren Chapel.** Healy and Copley Lawns host major social gatherings in warm weather, including the amusement-park festivities of "Georgetown Day" (held on the last day of classes each spring) as well as the annual commencement ceremonies.

TUDOR PLACE ESTATE

⛿ Location: *1644 31st St.* **Contact:** *☎965-0400; www.tudorplace.com.* **Hours:** *House open by tour only. Gardens open Tu-Sa 10am-4pm, Su noon-4pm.* **Tours:** *45min. tours of the house Tu-F 10, 11:30am, 1, 2:30pm; Sa every hr. 10am-3pm.* **Admission:** *Suggested donation for garden $2; tour $6, seniors $5, students and under 12 $3. Reservations for groups of 10 or more.*

Martha Custis Peter used the $8000 willed to her by her step-grandfather **George Washington** to build Tudor Place, the Neoclassical mansion designed by William Thornton. During the Civil War, Mrs. Peter's daughters used to signal to their cousins, **Robert E. Lee** and siblings, by waving petticoats like flags out of the upstairs window. A Confederate supporter to the end, Martha's daughter Britannia Peter cleverly rented the estate to Union officers in order to preserve the building during the Civil War. The building would have been turned into a Union hospital if Mrs. Peter had not returned from Richmond to save the property after abandoning it due to a Civil War battle near the area. Six subsequent generations of the Peter family ensured that the house and estate remained intact. These efforts kept the Tudor Place in the family for nearly 180 years. The Peters' obsessive collecting over this lengthy span allows today's visitors a glimpse of American life over two centuries. Tucked away in a garage opposite the main entrance is a beautifully restored **1919 Pierce-Arrow 48-B5 Roadster,** once owned by the Peter family. Its shiny maroon finish, large headlights, and excellent condition make it a must-see.

DUMBARTON HOUSE

⛿ Location: *2715 Q St., between 27th and 28th St.* **Contact:** *☎337-2288; www.dumbartonhouse.org.* **Hours:** *Gardens and grounds open Tu-Sa 10am-2pm. House open by guided tour only.* **Tours:** *Tu-Sa 10:15, 11:15am, 12:15, 1:15pm. Reservations required for groups of 10 or more.* **Admission:** *$5, students with ID and school groups free.*

Not to be confused with the entirely separate Dumbarton Oaks Mansion, Dumbarton House was completed circa 1800. Its first inhabitant, Joseph Nourse, Registrar of the Treasury to the first six presidents, did not move in until 1804. In 1813, the house passed to Charles Carroll (who later founded Rochester, NY) and hosted **Dolly Madison** when she fled the British in 1814. Although most of the furniture is not original to the building, it still gives a sense of how wealthy families in the early 19th century lived. Of special interest is a 1789 painting of the **Benjamin**

Stoddert children by Charles Willson Peale, one of the forefathers of American portraiture; Stoddert himself was a prominent resident of Georgetown and the Secretary of the Navy under President **John Adams.**

The house originally blocked and interrupted the path of Q St. until it was moved (to its current location) in 1915. It was later purchased by the **National Society of Colonial Dames of America** in 1928, underwent a restoration to its early federal period appearance, and was opened to the public in 1932. Today the house is the headquarters of the Colonial Dames.

MOUNT ZION UNITED METHODIST CHURCH

Location: 1334 29th St. *Contact:* ☎ 234-0148. *Hours:* Services June-Sept. Su 10am, Sept.-June Su 11am. The church and its office are typically open M, W, F 10am-3pm. Call ahead for tours. *Admission:* Free.

Washington's oldest African-American congregation, the Mount Zion Methodist Church was founded in 1816 by 125 African-Americans who angrily broke away from the segregated **Montgomery Street Methodist** congregation—today known as the **Dumbarton Avenue Methodist Church**. The current church building, listed on the National Register of Historic Places, was constructed between 1880 and 1884; its carved balcony, cast-iron pillars, and pressed tin roof display the skill of early black artisans. Look for its gorgeous pastel-colored stained-glass windows.

HERRING HILL

The area above M St., around 28th and 30th St.

Herring Hill was named after the hordes of fish that haunted nearby waterways, providing a staple in the local diet into the 19th century. This was an African-American neighborhood until the 1940s and 50s, when blacks were forced out by federal agencies and real estate developers in an attempt to create wealthy white communities. The building at 1239 30th St., between N and Olive St., a private residence known as Spite House, is the **skinniest house** in Georgetown. A converted alley, about 11 ft. wide, the building has room for only one window and one door across the width of its façade.

DUPONT CIRCLE

Highlights: Galleries, Embassy Row, Nightlife. *Museums:* Phillips Collection. *Food and Drink:* p. 146. *Nightlife:* p. 171. *Nearby:* Georgetown, Adams Morgan, Farragut, Foggy Bottom. Use Metro: Dupont Circle to access the area.

Once a rural backwater, Dupont Circle became one of Washington's most heavily-moneyed neighborhoods after the Civil War when Nevada Senator William Morris Stewart and a group of wealthy California miners moved in. After the Depression of 1929 wiped out the wealth of many Dupont residents, embassies began to acquire elegant townhouses along Massachusetts Ave. Later, as politicians left for Georgetown and Upper Northwest, Dupont emerged as the primary destination for Washington's large and active gay community, which now has a very strong presence in the neighborhood. With crowded restaurants, raucous bars and clubs, a boisterous art scene, and streets full of beautiful people expressing themselves fully, Dupont is both loud and proud.

Dupont's main drag is its section of **Connecticut Ave.,** lined with an array of restaurants, bookstores, and small boutiques. Upscale galleries cluster around **21st St.** and **R St.,** just a few blocks away from the Phillips Collection, one of the finest art museums in the city. The area along 17th and 18th St. east of Connecticut Ave. remains quieter than the main streets around Dupont, but is slowly becoming more developed as restaurants, cafes, shops, and bars spring up. The neighborhood is bounded by **16th St., 22nd St., M St.,** and **T St. NW.** Side streets west and northeast of Connect-

the insider's
CITY

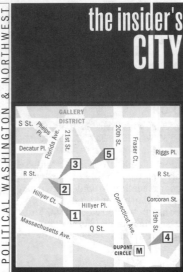

DUPONT GALLERIES

D.C.'s art community thrives outside the starchy confines of the Smithsonian, especially at the radically progressive and highly respected galleries around Dupont Circle.

1 Start at the high-end **Foundry Gallery** to see the most established artists. (☎387-0203)

2 Latin American art is at its best in the **Fondo del Sol Visual Arts Center.** (☎483-2777)

3 Stop into the basement **Studio Gallery** for surprising bargains on top-quality art. (☎232-8734)

4 For a visit to the absolute fringe of modern art, try the high-concept **Gallery 10 Ltd.** (☎232-3326)

5 Finish this whirlwind exhibit tour with soothing teas and lunches from Teaism. (☎667-3827)

icut Ave. often have parking spaces. During the day, Massachusetts Ave. might have parking. At night, park as far west as you can and make sure your car has absolutely nothing of value in it; break-ins are common.

DUPONT CIRCLE

▶ *Location: The intersection of Massachusetts Ave., Connecticut Ave., New Hampshire Ave., P St., and 19th St. NW.*

The heart of the neighborhood is Dupont Circle itself, a small park inside a traffic circle that joins the incoming spokes of five avenues and streets. Named in honor of Rear Admiral **Samuel F. Dupont's** service to the Union during the Civil War, the Circle was graced with a statue of the war hero by Congress in 1882. Although Dupont's millionaire descendants moved his statue from the center of this park to Delaware in 1921, the family commissioned Daniel Chester French, now known for his 19 ft. sculpture of Lincoln at the Lincoln Memorial, to create a stately replacement. Today, a fountain supported by three semi-nude women (representing the three arts of ocean navigation: sea, stars, and wind) graces the circle, watching over the chess players, lunching office workers, and spandex-clad bike messengers who populate the park. Blocked staircases on either side of the circle, across the street, stand as vestigial reminders of Dupont Down Under, a failed subterranean mini-mall built in the early 1990s. The circle is safe during the day, but **exercise caution at night and walk around, rather than through, the park.**

GALLERIES OF DUPONT

Many visitors are startled to discover that Washington, D.C. is home to a thriving arts community, with numerous galleries and art spaces. Dupont Circle has fostered the city's gallery scene since its heyday in the 1980s, when everyone who was anyone was an amateur art collector. Today, over 30 galleries displaying everything from contemporary photographs to tribal crafts reside in the Dupont Circle area; the oldest and best-known galleries lie on **R St.** between Florida and Connecticut Ave. NW.

Twenty-four galleries have organized themselves into **The Galleries of Dupont Circle.** Together they hold a joint open house the first Friday of each month from 6 to 8pm (www.artgalleriesdc.com), complete with free wine at each venue. These "First Fridays" are the best way to discover D.C.'s local art scene. Six times a year, the organization also publishes the **Gallery Guide,** which provides a list of local galleries, current shows, and an area map. You can explore the galleries almost any afternoon of the week, although many galleries are traditionally closed Mondays and have variable hours (or are closed) in August; call ahead. Most galleries will also schedule appointments outside of regular hours.

The following are some of the area's more interesting galleries; refer to the *Gallery Guide* for detailed information on each gallery. The **Washington Printmakers Gallery**, 1732 Connecticut Ave. NW, 2nd fl., is the only D.C. gallery devoted exclusively to prints. (☎332-7757; www.washingtonprintmakers.com. Open Tu-Th noon-6pm, F noon-9pm, Sa-Su noon-5pm.) The **Kathleen Ewing Gallery**, 1609 Connecticut Ave. NW, is Dupont's place for photography. (☎328-0955; www.kathleenewinggallery.com. Open W-Sa 12-5pm.) Along R St., **Gallery K**, 2010 R St. NW (☎234-0339; www.galleryk.com; open Tu-Sa 11am-6pm), **Marsha Mateyka Gallery**, 2012 R St. NW (☎328-0088; www.marshamateykagallery.com; open W-Sa 11am-5pm), **Robert Brown Gallery**, 2030 R St. NW (☎483-4383; www.robertbrowngallery.com; open Tu-Sa noon-6pm), and **Anton Gallery**, 2108 R St. NW (☎328-0828; www.antongallery.com; open Tu-Sa noon-5pm) are all quality galleries showing some of the most well-known regional and national artists. Each of these galleries has its own focus, but all lean toward the contemporary abstract art common to the works of many living artists. Anton and Marsha Mateyka Galleries both frequently showcase work by a number of women artists, and Robert Brown Gallery often shows Chinese antiquities.

Some of the cooperative galleries, comprised of groups of artists themselves, are hodgepodges of top-notch and mediocre work. Browse through **Studio Gallery**, 2108 R St. NW (☎232-8734; www.studiogallerydc.com; open W-Sa 11am-5pm, Su 1-5pm) and the **Foundry Gallery**, 9 Hillyer Ct. NW, which are both on the upscale end of art co-ops and often show the work of nationally recognized visiting artists. (☎387-0203; www.foundry-gallery.org. Open Tu-Sa 11am-5pm, Su 1-5pm.) **Gallery 10 Ltd.**, 1519 Connecticut Ave. NW, stretches the limits of modern art, leaving sales as a second priority. (☎232-3326. Open W-Sa 11am-5pm.)

The **Pensler Gallery**, 2029 Q St. NW, a more upscale venue, began with a grad student selling paintings out of his car and has become one of Washington's leading private galleries for early 20th century American art. (☎328-9190. Open by appointment.) **St. Luke's Gallery**, 1715 Q St. NW, digs further into history, specializing in 16th- to 18th-century Dutch and Italian paintings. (☎328-2424. Open Tu-Sa 11am-6pm.) **Fondo del Sol Visual Arts Center**, 2112 R St. NW, is a bilingual, alternative museum devoted to the culture and art of Latin America, and hosts daily video programs and occasional special programs. (☎483-2777. Open W-Sa 12:30pm-6pm. Suggested donation $3, students $1, children free.)

Other specialized galleries include **Affrica**, 2010½ R St. NW, which features traditional African art from masks to textiles (☎745-7272; www.affrica.com. Open Tu 2-6pm, W-Sa noon-6pm) and the **Burdick Gallery**, 2114 R St. NW, a collection of Inuit sculpture and art. (☎986-5682; www.burdickgallery.com. Open Tu-F noon-6pm, Sa 11am-5pm.)

THE SCOTTISH RITE FREEMASONRY TEMPLE

⁊ Location: *1733 16th St. NW.* **Contact:** ☎ *232-3579; www.srmason-sj.org.* **Hours:** *M-F 8am-4pm.* **Tours:** *1¾hr. tours available anytime during open hours.* **Admission:** *Free.*

Fourteen presidents, from George Washington to Gerald Ford, have been Masons, members of a fraternal order devoted to the promotion of good citizenship which, given its list of past members, has had undeniable power in US politics. Completed in 1915, the temple of the Scottish Rite Masons is flanked by 33 ft. columns and guarded by two sphinxes with eyes open ("Power") and half-open ("Wisdom"). Inside the temple, the outstanding architecture alone is worth the lengthy tour. Based on John Russell Pope's design, which copies the ancient mausoleum at **Halicarnassus** in Turkey, the temple is incredible in its exacting details. Tour guides are thorough and accommodating. If you are pressed for time, ask for a short version of the tour—say, 30min.—to see the grand, Gotham-City-style meeting rooms, hear the king of spooky organs play, and marvel at the Hall of Masonic Heroes.

THE CARNEGIE INSTITUTION

🛈 Location: *1530 P St. NW, at 16th St.* **Metro:** Dupont Circle. **Contact:** ☎ 387-6400; www.carnegieinstitution.org. **Hours:** *M-F 8:45am-5pm.* **Admission:** *Free.* **Events:** *Frequent scholarly lectures open to the public; call or visit website for details.*

Founded in 1912 by industrialist and philanthropist Andrew Carnegie, The Carnegie Institution performs groundbreaking research in life, planetary, and space sciences. Exhibits featuring current research topics are open to the public, and the Institution also offers a special program for D.C.-area elementary school children on Saturdays.

EMBASSY ROW

The stretch of Massachusetts Ave. between Dupont and Observatory Circles is also called Embassy Row. Before the 1930s, Washington socialites lined the avenue with their extravagant edifices. Status-conscious diplomats later found the mansions perfect for their prestigious purposes, and embassies moved in by the dozen. You can identify an embassy by the national coat of arms or flag out front, and small plaques near the door name the country. Major nations have designed their own compounds (Great Britain and Japan) and some have moved away from downtown for more space (France and Germany), but smaller countries still occupy the townhouses. Many embassies used to host public tours and cultural events, but heightened security since the attacks of September 11, 2001 has resulted in nearly all embassies closing their doors to the public.

The ornate **Indonesian Embassy,** 1020 Massachusetts Ave., once belonged to the Walsh family, whose daughter Evelyn Walsh McLean was the last private owner of the infamous **Hope Diamond** (now housed at the National Museum of Natural History, see p. 117). The building's swirling curves, two symmetrically rounded bay windows, and iron grating are exquisite. Call in advance for tours. (☎ 775-5200. Open M-F 9am-5pm.) Other embassies of note, although closed to tourists, include the **Brazilian Embassy,** 3006 Massachusetts Ave. (☎ 745-2700; www.brasilemb.org), designed by John Russell Pope, who also designed the National Gallery and the National Archives, and the **British Embassy,** 3100 Massachusetts Ave. (☎ 462-1340; www.britainusa.com), which has a working red box telephone booth just inside its gates.

ISLAMIC CENTER

🛈 Location: *2551 Massachusetts Ave. NW, near Belmont Rd. NW.* **Contact:** ☎ 332-8343. **Hours:** *Daily 10am-5pm; prayers 5 times daily.* **Admission:** *Free.*

Flags line the entrance to this brilliant white marble mosque, whose stunning tile and intricate geometric designs stretch to the tips of its spired ceilings. Ambassadors of several Islamic nations (Egypt, Iran, Turkey, and Afghanistan) founded the mosque after World War II, and President George W. Bush spoke here just days after the attacks of September 11, 2001, saying "Islam is peace." Visitors may enter the tranquil mosque, but note that shorts are not allowed and women must cover their heads and wear sleeved shirts.

SHERIDAN CIRCLE

🛈 Location: *23rd St. NW and Massachusetts Ave.*

Sheridan Circle features an equestrian statue of **General Philip Sheridan,** the Northern cavalry leader who forced the Southern surrender at Appomatox during the Civil War. His famous words are often misquoted in letter but not in spirit as "the only good Indian is a dead Indian." A small, raised plaque on the sidewalk of the Q St. side of the circle commemorates exiled Chilean diplomat **Orlando Letelier,** who was killed near the circle in 1976 by a car bomb along with his aide Ronni Moffitt. Letelier represented the Marxist government of Salvador Allende, which dictator Pinochet overthrew with CIA help in the same year. Conspiracy theories abound that the car bomb was planted by the CIA, or at least with prior CIA knowledge.

WOODROW WILSON HOUSE

⚑ Location: *2340 S St. NW.* **Contact:** ☎*387-4062.* **Hours:** *Tu-Su 10am-4pm.* **Admission:** *$5, students $2.50, seniors $4, under 7 free.* **Accessibility:** *Wheelchair accessible.*

The Woodrow Wilson House preserves the memory of Wilson in the fragile and embittered years after he lost the White House in 1920. Wilson, partially paralyzed after a stroke, lived out the last two years of his life here and is still the only president to retire to the District of Columbia after his tenure. As a tribute to his second wife, Edith Bowling, Wilson lavishly decorated the house with gifts bestowed upon him by foreign dignitaries and adoring admirers. A 25 min. video precedes the 1hr. tour given by well-informed guides, so plan to spend a bit of time here. The gardens have been landscaped to reflect how the Wilsons' garden once looked.

MERIDIAN INTERNATIONAL CENTER

⚑ Location: *1630 Crescent Pl. NW, just off 16th St.* **Metro:** *Metrobus S1, S2, or S4.* **Contact:** ☎*667-6800; www.meridian.org.* **Gallery Hours:** *W-Su 2-5pm.* **Admission:** *Free.* **Tours:** *By appointment.* **Events:** *Rotating exhibitions, concerts, and programs. Call or visit website for details.*

Dedicated to promoting greater cultural awareness through the arts, exchange programs, and community outreach, the non-profit Meridian Center is based in two adjacent homes, both designed by John Russell Pope. **Meridian House,** built in 1919, was the home of Irwin Boyle Laughlin, Ambassador to Spain and Greece, before the Center acquired it in 1960. **White-Meyer House,** built in 1912, first belonged to Henry White, Ambassador to Italy and France, and later to Eugene Meyer, owner of the *Washington Post.* Under both owners, the house saw its share of political visitors, from Henry Cabot Lodge to President John F. Kennedy. Of particular note to visitors are the Center's **rotating art exhibitions,** housed in White-Meyer House. The staff works with embassies and museums to bring in international art, which it then complements with concerts, lectures, and readings that feature the country of origin.

MERIDIAN HILL PARK

⚑ Location: *Bounded by 15th, 16th, Euclid, and W St. NW.*

Once the grounds of John Quincy Adams' post-presidential mansion and a campground for Union troops, Meridian Hill Park (also known as Malcolm X Park) was reintroduced as a formal park in 1936. Based on the famed gardens of Renaissance Italy, the Park includes a 13-level cascading fountain, a human-sized chessboard, and statues of President James Buchanan, Dante, and Joan of Arc (the only equestrian statue of a woman in the District). By the 1970s, the park had become one of the city's most dangerous areas, but in 1990, a neighborhood group began patrolling the park, resulting in a 95% reduction in crime. Although the area is now much safer, **Let's Go does not recommend visiting the park after dark.**

ADAMS MORGAN

⚑ Highlights: *Dining, nightlife, shopping.* **Food and Drink:** *p. 136.* **Nightlife:** *p. 164* **Nearby:** *Rock Creek Park, Shaw, Dupont Circle, Upper Northwest (Woodley Park).*

Adams Morgan brims with multicultural hipness. The neighborhood's name came from residents' organizations which planned to integrate the neighborhood by mixing students from the largely white Adams School and the predominantly black Morgan School. Immigrants from Mexico, El Salvador, and Ethiopia add to the diversity in Adams Morgan, sealing its reputation for international restaurants, bars, and clubs. Slick dance, world beat, and do-it-yourself punk venues start up, change names, and collapse yearly here. A wreath of fantastic ethnic restaurants circles Columbia Rd., 18th St., and Calvert St., while quirky second-hand stores, swank boutiques, and small *bodegas* line 18th St. south of Columbia Rd.

ORIENTATION

Florida Ave. NW divides Adams Morgan from Dupont Circle to the south; Rock Creek Park lines its western side. Adams Morgan's eastern edge, near 16th St., is peppered with churches and embassies but has unsafe areas to its south and east. Harvard St. forms a vague northern boundary and separates Adams Morgan from Mount Pleasant, a heavily Hispanic and slightly less prosperous neighborhood. Although Adams Morgan is generally one of the safer areas in the city, **use caution here at night,** especially around the parks and the eastern and southern edges.

Though the region has no direct Metro stop, the new **U-Street Link Shuttle** offers transportation through Adams Morgan from the Woodley Park-Zoo/Adams Morgan Metro stop at one end of the route to U St. NW at the other ($0.25, every 15min., Su-Th 6pm-midnight, F 6pm-3am, Sa 10am-3am). The neighborhood suffers from a **lack of parking,** especially at night. To reach Adams Morgan **on foot** from the Woodley Park Metro, turn right immediately upon exiting the Metro onto Connecticut Ave. Walk one block to the intersection with Calvert St. and make a left, crossing the Duke Ellington Memorial Bridge. Walk down Calvert St. for about seven minutes until you reach the five-pronged intersection of Columbia Rd. and 18th St. The entire walk takes about 15 minutes.

UPPER NORTHWEST

⚑ Highlights: *National Zoo, National Cathedral.* **Museums:** *Kreeger, Doll's House, Hillwood.* **Food and Drink:** *p. 158.* **Nearby:** *Rock Creek Park, Adams Morgan, Dupont Circle, Georgetown.* **Metro:** *The Metro serves the area with stops at each of its major neighborhoods: Woodley Park-Zoo, Cleveland Park, Van Ness-UDC, Tenleytown-AU, and Friendship Heights.*

In Upper Northwest's hills and angular streets, one finds shopping and dining options similar to those in Georgetown, its southern neighbor. Nestled into the trees of Rock Creek Park, visitors descend upon the National Zoo, operated by the same Smithsonian Institution that dominates the National Mall. And towering above it all is the National Cathedral, a massive Gothic edifice that exudes a majestic beauty equaling any of the monuments located further south.

Located west of Rock Creek Park and north of Georgetown between downtown D.C. and Maryland, the neighborhood's small communities are linked by the parallel north-south axes of **Wisconsin** and **Connecticut Ave.**

GETTING THERE & GETTING AROUND

The L1, L2, and L4 Metrobuses shuttle up and down Connecticut Ave., linking Chevy Chase, MD, with Dupont Circle and Farragut; the Van Ness-UDC, Cleveland Park, and Woodley Park-Zoo Metro stations are all stops along the bus route. The N2, N3, N4, N6, and N7 buses from Dupont Circle run up Massachusetts Ave. to the National Cathedral, with most heading onward to Friendship Heights and Tenleytown-AU. The #30, 32, 34, 35, or 36 buses can shuttle you all the way up Wisconsin Ave. from Georgetown; at the District line in Friendship Heights, a central Metrobus terminal allows travelers to change buses to travel into Maryland. Other buses, including the 90-, H-, M-, D-, and W-series, criss-cross the remaining less-traveled routes in the area. Metro stations are located at Woodley Park, Cleveland Park, Van Ness (on Connecticut Ave.), Tenley Circle (Tenleytown), and Friendship Heights. The neighborhoods are easy to navigate. Most of the cross streets fit into D.C.'s alphabetical scheme: letters, then two-syllable names, then three-syllable names.

FOXHALL ROAD TO GLOVER PARK

The money trail in D.C. almost inevitably leads to the far west section of Upper Northwest, particularly along **Foxhall Rd.** One of the most impressive testaments to this wealth is the **Kreeger Museum** (p. 128), 2401 Foxfall Rd., several miles from any public transportation. **Glover Park,** a more subdued extension of upscale, brick-laden Georgetown, lies east of Foxhall Rd.

US NAVAL OBSERVATORY

🔟 *Location: 3450 Massachusetts Ave. Enter the South Gate on Observatory Circle across from the New Zealand Embassy. Parking is available outside the gate on Observatory Circle, near the British Embassy. **Contact:** Recorded information ☎ 762-1467, group reservations ☎ 762-1438 or online at www.usno.navy.mil. **Tours:** Open for 1½hr. guided tours every other M night (except federal holidays) at 8:30pm, only by reservation, by phone or via Internet. Tour reservations must be made at least 4-6 weeks before the tour date. Arrive at 8pm, as all tour participants must submit to a screening; photo ID also required. **Accessibility:** no handicapped access.*

Visitors must remain for the entire tour, which has three parts: a 30min. video presentation about the mission and history of the U.S. Naval Observatory, a gander at celestial objects through a 12 in. refracting telescope if the night is clear, and a look at the atomic clock which keeps official US time. Note. the tour involves walking over rough grounds and is therefore not wheelchair accessible. This site, rarely ever visited due to complicated hours and distance from main tourist attractions, is actually one of D.C.'s most fascinating. Learn about official clocks, timepieces, the discovery of longitude and the importance of monitoring the sky and sea.

OBSERVATORY CIRCLE

The looming Vice Presidential Mansion lies within Observatory Circle and is best viewed from the intersection of Massachusetts Ave. and 34th St., though high fences and dense foliage effectively conceal it. There are no tours of this residence.

Across from the Observatory sits the green glass and copper **Finnish Embassy,** which looks as if it's been gift-wrapped in a chain-link fence. The embassy of the **Vatican** next door marks the end of the stretch of Massachusetts Ave. known as **Embassy Row,** which begins southeast of Dupont Circle (see p. 84).

▩ WASHINGTON NATIONAL CATHEDRAL

🔟 *Location: Massachusetts and Wisconsin Ave. NW. Take Massachusetts Ave. north from downtown and turn right on Wisconsin Ave. **Metro:** From Tenleytown station, take a 30-series bus toward Georgetown; from Cleveland Park station, walk 15min. uphill on Ordway, turn left at 36th St., and walk south 5 blocks. **Contact:** ☎ 537 6200, recording 364-6616; www.cathedral.org/cathedral. **Hours:** Mid-May-Labor Day M-F 10am-8pm, Sa*

National Archives

Voice of America

Basilica of National Shrine

*10am-4:30pm, Su 8am-7:30pm; Labor Day-mid-May M-Sa 10am-4:30pm, Su 8am-7:30pm. Su 11am service takes place in the nave. Shops open 9:30am-5pm year-round. **Tours:** Guided highlights tour offered year-round every 15min. M-Sa 10-11:45am and 12:45-3:15pm, Su 12:30-3:15pm; includes crypt and Observation Gallery ($3 suggested donation, $1 for children). ☎ 537-6207; tours@cathedral.org. Self-guided audio tours available during same hours $5; National Cathedral Association (NCA) discount available. Other more specialized tours include a garden tour (Apr.-Oct., W 10:30am, meet at Herb Cottage) and the behind the scenes tour (Jul.-Feb., M-Sa 10:30am and 1:30pm), which allows visitors access the north tower, an overview of the cathedral's vaulting, and the south roof ($10). **Admission:** Free. **Accessibility:** Wheelchair ramp is around the building's front facade on the left. **Events:** Check the website for the latest calendar or call ☎ 537-2221 for recorded schedule information. **Festivals:** The grounds here host annual festivals, such as the Flower Mart (on the first F and Sa in May) and Open House (last Sa of Sept.).*

Quietly tucked away in the far northwest corner of the city is one of Washington's gems, the Cathedral Church of Saint Peter and Saint Paul, commonly referred to as the Washington National Cathedral. The cathedral shares its serene grounds with the campuses of the prestigious St. Albans School, the National Cathedral School, and the elementary-level Beauvoir School. Construction of the cathedral has spanned three centuries. First proposed in 1791, it was not approved until 1893, when construction began. Though the first service was held here in 1912, it was only completed in 1990; the last stained glass window was installed as recently as 2001. The sixth largest cathedral in the world, it is built entirely of stone in Gothic tradition in the shape of a Latin cross. Artisans hovered on scaffolding more than 100 ft. above the floor while they sculpted with soaring ceiling.

The cathedral was constructed with two intentions: to attract dignitaries and to serve as a burial ground for the nation's most important citizens. Successful on one count, the cathedral managed to attract **Rev. Martin Luther King, Jr.,** every US president since Theodore Roosevelt, and more recently, the **Dalai Lama** of Tibet. The only real notable politicos buried on the property are **President Woodrow Wilson** and former Secretary of State Cordell Hull, who both died during the brief moment when burial in the cathedral was in vogue. Blind- and deaf-education pioneer **Helen Keller** and her teacher, Anne Sullivan Macy, are also buried in the crypt. Immediately to Wilson's right is the cathedral's most unusual stained-glass window, a blue and red spacescape with an actual moon rock embedded in the center. Look closely, and you'll see that one gargoyle on the left tower depicts **Darth Vader.** The crypt level harbors the **Bethlehem Chapel,** the **Chapel of St. Joseph of Arimathea,** and the **Resurrection Chapel.** The **Chapel of the Good Shepherd** is also located on this level and is open for private prayer from 6am until 10pm daily. The **Cathedral Center for Prayer and Pilgrimage** can also be found in the crypt. (Open M-Sa 10am-4pm and Su 1-4pm.)

To access the chapel at night, enter from the North Rd. side, nearest the intersection of Wisconsin Ave. and Woodley Rd. An elevator, located near the main doors of the west entrance, takes you to the top floor of the **Pilgrim Observation Gallery,** which offers a spectacular view of Washington from one of its highest vantage points. From here, visitors can see not only the nearby Mall monuments but also the city's more distant neighborhoods and landmarks, including the **Basilica of the National Shrine of the Immaculate Conception,** the Cathedral's only rival in beauty, size, and splendor (see p. 94). The **Bishop's Garden,** near the South Transept and facing Wisconsin Ave., is filled with herbs and roses (open daily until dusk). Though the garden is technically closed at night, people often take midnight strolls nonetheless. The lights illuminating the fountain cast shadows against the cathedral, creating a romantic atmosphere.

On **May 29th, 2004**, the National Cathedral will host a special Saturday morning service for the dedication of the new **National World War II Memorial** (see p. 58).

TENLEY CIRCLE & FRIENDSHIP HEIGHTS

Tenley Circle is the residential neighborhood north of Glover Park on Wisconsin Ave., which extends through condominium complexes and apartment buildings to its northern border along Fessenden St. **American University** fans out from **Ward Circle**

between Massachusetts Ave. and Nebraska Ave. and offers many affordable performing arts events and free film screenings. Above Fessenden St. on Wisconsin Ave. is **Friendship Heights,** straddling the border between D.C. and Maryland along Western Ave. Primarily the land of upscale stores (Neiman Marcus, Tiffany, etc.; see **Shopping,** p. 202), Friendship Heights is also home to the **Washington Dolls' House and Toy Museum** (see p. 131) as well as its own residential area.

CLEVELAND PARK & WOODLEY PARK

Running north along Connecticut Ave., between 34th St. and Rock Creek Park, are the neighborhoods of Woodley Park and Cleveland Park. In **Cleveland Park,** at 3133 Connecticut Ave., are the **Kennedy-Warren Apartments.** The three structures of this block-long building were among the city's most prominent homes in the 1930s. The Egyptian roof adornments and mildly Art Deco exterior panels, as well as the gardens out front, still testify to the apartments' aristocratic stature. Cleveland Park, especially surrounding the Metro stop, contains a collection of neighborhood restaurants and bars, some of which attract Washingtonians from other areas. **Grover Cleveland** planned to build a summer cottage in this area to which he could retreat incognito; in grateful recognition, the neighborhood immediately blew his cover and named itself in his honor. **Hillwood,** 4155 Linnaean Ave. (☎ 686-5807), just off Connecticut Ave., was the mansion of General Foods heiress Marjorie Meriweather Post. Now a museum (see p. 127), the house contains her extensive collection of Russian decorative arts and jewelry, including the largest collection of Fabergé eggs outside Russia. Just as beautiful, the adjacent gardens blossom with begonias.

Directly south along Connecticut Avenue is **Woodley Park,** Cleveland Park's sister neighborhood, whose many cafes and restaurants are all packed into a single block between Woodley Rd. (which leads west to the **Washington National Cathedral**) and Calvert St. Woodley Park is bordered on the south and east by the winding paths of **Rock Creek Park,** while its western reaches are largely residential, abutting the **US Naval Observatory, Embassy Row,** and the grounds of the Cathedral.

Roughly halfway between the Woodley Park and Cleveland Park Metro stops is the entrance to the **National Zoo** (see below), operated by the **Smithsonian Institution.**

NATIONAL ZOO

⚑ Location: 3001 Connecticut Ave. NW. **Metro:** A few blocks uphill from Calvert St. NW and the Woodley Park-Zoo Metro. **Contact:** ☎ 673-4800; www.si.edu/natzoo. **Hours:** Grounds open May 1-Sept. 15 daily 6am-8pm; Sept. 16-Apr. 30 6am-6pm. Buildings open May 1-Sept. 15 daily 10am-6pm; Sept. 16-Apr. 30 10am-4:30pm. Closed Dec. 25. **Admission:** Free. **Events:** Free "Sunset Serenade" concerts July to mid-Aug. every Th 6pm on Lion-Tiger Hill, featuring jazz bands and other local groups. Feeding schedules available at information desk; audio tours available. **Accessibility:** Wheelchair accessible. Free handicapped parking in lots B and D. Wheelchairs available.

Founded in 1889 and designed by Frederick Law Olmsted, designer of both New York City's Central Park and Boston's "Emerald Necklace" parks, the National Zoo is one of D.C.'s least crowded sights. More than just a home for exotic animals, the zoo is heavily involved in species preservation and worldwide ecological research and thus technically known as a "biopark." By providing marsh dwellers with patches of wetland and larger animals with spacious outdoor ranges, landscapers have taken great care to ensure that the zoo replicates the animals' natural habitats. Recent additions include the tiger cub Berani, born September 2001, the elephant Kandula, and the lowland gorilla Kojo, both born in November 2001. In a recent giraffe exchange with a Boston zoo, the two-year-old Malaika has taken the place of Jana.

Walking paths criss-cross the zoo. All are segments of either the blue-flagged **Valley Trail** or the red-flagged **Olmsted Walk.** The more level Olmsted Walk explores land-animal houses. On the Valley Trail, the **Amazonia** building showcases the flora and fauna of the rainforest. Farther along the trail, at the **Seals and Sea Lions** exhibit, visitors can watch zookeepers brush the animals' teeth with seafood-flavored toothpaste.

Near the main entrance, the **Cheetah Conservation Station** chronicles the cheetahs' disappearance from the wild. The zoo's biggest attraction is undoubtedly Mei Xiang and Tian Tian, two **giant pandas** acquired in January 2001 from China. The pandas are available for viewing 9am-6pm daily.

Visit the zoo early in the morning or late in the afternoon, when the majority of the animals are most active, and when the unruly hordes school children visiting on field trips—an exhibit in and of themselves—have departed. Watch out for another unwelcome exhibit: local foxes visiting the zoo for lunch. In 2003, foxes were responsible for a number of bird killings, including that of a bald eagle who ironically succumbed on July 4 to wounds allegedly sustained from a *foxus hungrius*.

SHAW/U DISTRICT

◤ Highlights: *Nightlife, shopping, eateries.* **Museums:** *African-American Civil War Memorial and Museum.* **Food and Drink:** *p. 156.* **Nightlife:** *p. 178.* **Nearby:** *Adams Morgan, Northeast, Federal Triangle.* **Metro:** *U Street-Cardozo, Shaw-Howard U.*

Shaw was once the address of choice for important African-American politicians (presidential advisor Mary McLeod), poets (Jean Toomer and Langston Hughes), musicians (Duke Ellington), journalists, and lawyers. In the early 20th century, these leaders developed the "Black Broadway" along U St. as music lovers of every color crowded into local theaters until the desegregation of the 50s lured much of the black middle class away from Shaw. Today, one still can experience a community life centered around the arts, from open mike poetry nights at the famous **Bohemian Caverns** to plays and concerts at historic **Lincoln Theatre.**

U St. crams a healthy cross-section of D.C. nightlife into just a few blocks (see **Nightlife,** p. 178 and **Entertainment,** p. 184). Make sure to also stop by earlier in the day to check out the women's boutiques (1500 block of U St.), trendy home furnishing shops (14th St. between S and T St.), and plenty of spectacular dining options. Venerable neighborhood institutions like **Ben's Chili Bowl** and the **Florida Avenue Grill** (see **Food and Drink,** p. 156) offer possibly the best country or Southern-style cooking outside of the Deep South. The best way to see many of U Street's historical sights and sample its cultural highlights is through one of the Friday evening **walking tours** led by **Sisterspace and Books** (see p. 200). Though results from the area's overall development and renewal are evident, **be careful after dark.** Greater Shaw runs roughly between 13th and 1st St. and between P St. and Florida Ave. NW.

AFRICAN-AMERICAN CIVIL WAR MEMORIAL & MUSEUM

◤ Location: *Memorial at 10th and U St. Museum at 1200 U St. NW, at 12th St.* **Metro:** *U St.-Cardozo, Memorial exit.* **Contact:** *☎ 667-2667; www.afroamcivilwar.org.* **Hours:** *Museum open M-F 10am-5pm, Sa 10am-2pm.* **Tours:** *By appointment.* **Admission:** *Free.*

A recent addition to Washington's memorials, this monument, occupying a space which was once Union barracks for blacks, honors the 209,145 black soldiers who fought for the Union Army during the Civil War. Its centerpiece is an 11 ft. tall bronze statue entitled *The Spirit of Freedom,* which depicts black troops bearing their rifles and the families left behind upon their heroic departure. The statue is circled by plates of gray steel, which bear the names of all of the African-American soldiers who fought in the Civil War. The small accompanying museum, two blocks down U St., details African-Americans' roles during the Civil War and the progression from the Civil War to the Civil Rights Movement almost a century later.

THE LINCOLN THEATRE

◤ Location: *1215 U St. NW, between 12th and 13th St.* **Metro:** *U St.-Cardozo.* **Contact:** *☎ 328-6000; www.thelincolntheatre.org.* **Tours:** *Available by appointment.*

Opened in 1922, the Lincoln Theatre long served as the flagship of "Black Broadway," hosting such illustrious entertainers as Duke Ellington, Pearl Bailey, Louis Armstrong, and Ella Fitzgerald. After desegregation, many longtime Shaw residents left the area, and the theater fell into disrepair and closed in 1979. Coinciding with the neighborhood's resurgence, the Lincoln's distinctive plush Spanish interior and 1250 seats were restored and reupholstered in the early 1990s. The theater provides a venue for concerts, theater, and film productions. See **Entertainment,** p. 188.

HOWARD UNIVERSITY

🚩 *Location: 500 Howard Pl. NW. **Metro:** Shaw-Howard U. From the Metro, walk 15 min. north (toward S St.) on 7th St., which becomes Georgia Ave. **Contact:** ☎806-6100, for tours 806-2900; www.howard.edu. **Tours:** 2hr. tours M-F 9am-3pm by appointment only; call recruitment ☎806-2900 or information ☎800-822-6363.*

America's most historically important black university was founded in 1867 to educate newly freed slaves in the fields of religion, medicine, and law. Named for General **Oliver Otis Howard,** head of the Freedmen's Bureau after the Civil War, the private university now has over 10,000 students, most of whom are African-American. Late Supreme Court Justice Thurgood Marshall, ex-New York City Mayor David Dinkins, and novelist Toni Morrison are only a few of Howard's famous alums. Noted sociologist E. Franklin Frazier, Phylicia Rashad (Claire Huxtable of *The Cosby Show*) and rapper P. Diddy also have graced the 89-acre campus.

The **Founders Library,** the main branch of the library system, is open to the public. Free Internet access is available on the second floor of the central building. The library's **Moorland-Spingarn Research Center** maintains the largest collection of black literature in the US. The National Center for African-American Heritage and Culture is the largest African-American studies institution in the nation. **Be careful walking on 7th St. and Georgia Ave. at night.**

DUKE ELLINGTON MURAL

🚩 *Location: 13th and U St. NW.*

The appealing bright colors of G. Byron Peck's impressive mural featuring Shaw's most famous resident uplift the surrounding neighborhood. Commissioned by local businesses in 1997, the mural was created by Peck with help from student painters from the neighborhood he hired to assist him. The mural of the legendary musician greets those exiting the U St.-Cardozo Metro Stop at 13th St.

BEYOND NORTHWEST

SOUTHEAST CAPITOL HILL

🚩 *Highlights: Museums: Navy Museum, Marine Corps Historical Museum. Nearby: Capitol Hill, Anacostia, Waterfront.*

The Southeast quadrant isn't so much a neighborhood as a man-made geographical fact, a perfect right triangle bounded by **East Capitol St., South Capitol St.,** and the **District line.** Clubs and concerts in Southeast are the rowdiest and most exciting in the District, while the **Washington Navy Yard** is an oasis of well-landscaped grounds and several public museums (see **Museums,** p. 129). Unfortunately, the area can be dangerous: **stay extremely cautious and do not walk alone in this area, especially at night.**

BARRACKS ROW

The Eastern Market Metro stop takes you close to the Navy Yard, a stretch sometimes known as "Barracks Row." The Metro escalator dumps visitors into a littered, unkempt, grassy plot, and the walk down 8th St. SE passes fast-food restaurants,

in recent news

GOT CARS?

While the traditional car thief sells stolen auto parts to "chop shops," auto theft for sport has emerged in the high-crime Anacostia area of the District. The surprise? The thieves are children.

"Ten. That's about as young as I've locked them up. I'll see them sitting behind the steering wheel of a car on a stack of phone books while another one is down there working the pedals," said veteran Metro Police investigator Kevin Rachlin.

Approximately two-thirds of all cars stolen in the District are taken for joy rides, and most of these thieves are under 18. Police and neighbors report that kids regularly steal cars and parade down neighborhood streets showing off their work. Once they're through with the car, the junior thieves either crash or abandon the cars.

Some Anacostia residents are taking the issue into their own hands. When one resident spots stolen cars abandoned or crashed by youths, he searches out identification in the car and calls the owner. Another local woman is trying to organize youth activities to get kids off the streets.

—Brad Olson

and boarded-up storefronts. The disorder and general disrepair on 8th St. is abruptly interrupted by the uniformity, nobility, and basic cleanliness of the **Marine Barracks** (☎ 433-2258), at 8th and I St. SE. The barracks house the Eighth and Eye Marines, the Commandant of the Marine Corps, and The President's Own, the Marine Corps marching band. No official tour exists, and the area is restricted to military personnel. The only sure way to see the grounds is to attend one of the Friday Evening Parades. Barracks Row is usually safe during the day (Marines keep watch over some of the blocks), **but don't walk alone here at night.**

ANACOSTIA

🔲 *Highlights: Douglass Home. Nearby: Southeast Capitol Hill.*

Ironically enough, Anacostia began as Washington's first suburb when white developers founded the area know as **Uniontown** in the 1850s to escape the growing working-class presence on Capitol Hill. After the Civil War, the Freedmen's Bureau sold one-acre plots in the neighborhood for $200-300 to freed slaves, who founded the **Barry's Farm** community. Blue-collar African-Americans who took up residence in the neighborhood worked in the city by day and built their houses in Anacostia by firelight at night. While this kind of conscious self-improvement built a strong sense of community for the neighborhood, the area's isolation from the rest of the city led to its virtual abandonment by city administration. Over time, housing, education and employment opportunities for residents deteriorated and drugs took over.

While community residents today struggle to overcome drug-related violence, progress is slow and costly, and **Anacostia remains extremely dangerous.** The neighborhood is dominated by dilapidated low-rise apartment buildings, littered streets, and boarded-up storefronts, as a drive down **Martin Luther King, Jr. Ave. SE** will reveal. Bus rides provide a convenient and safer way to visit the neighborhood. **If you prefer exploring on foot, take appropriate precautions, like traveling in groups.** Look north from the parking lot of **Our Lady of Perpetual Help Church,** 1600 Morris Rd. SE (☎ 678-4999), for a spectacular view of downtown, the Washington Monument, the Lincoln Memorial, and the Capitol. Although *The Washingtonian* called this lot the best vantage point for gazing at the monuments, don't roam the area alone. See **Anacostia and Planning in D.C., next page.**

I t began in 1791 with Pierre L'Enfant, or rather with his patron George Washington, who commissioned the French Revolutionary War veteran to produce a plan for a capital worthy of the nation's ideals and its nascent territorial ambitions. L'Enfant rose to the challenge, drafting a unique layout of streets and public spaces, and designating locations for future edifices and monuments for the fledgling government. There have been few such initial visions for a city that have had equal impact on that city's growth across two centuries and counting.

Still, L'Enfant's role has in some respects been over-celebrated. His direct involvement with the capital was brief. Having shown considerable obstinacy in dealing with major area landowners—Washington's neighbors, colleagues, and rivals—he was relieved of his responsibilities within a year. Andrew Ellicott, who had surveyed the area in preparation for L'Enfant's work, translated L'Enfant's vision into the official plan with assistance from Benjamin Banneker, a free black man self-educated in astronomy and mathematics.

Jefferson, Secretary of State at the time, meddled often in L'Enfant's work. The famous street pattern consisting of a superimposition of diagonal avenues onto a regular grid of streets (infamous to any visitor trying to maintain one's sense of direction) was in part Jefferson's doing. L'Enfant dreamed grandly of outdoing Versailles with its grand boulevards radiating from the king's palace and of matching the spatial splendor of other great Baroque gardens designed by his near contemporary, Le Nôtre. But Jefferson's conviction that the grid embodied democracy forced L'Enfant (against his own sensibilities) to create that unique combination of street systems.

Brilliant plan notwithstanding, the city grew very slowly during much of the 19th century, requiring neither exact adherence to the L'Enfant vision nor the resolution of compromises between the plan's intent and specific growth pressures. Not until the capital's centennial approached, amidst the City Beautiful Era's enthusiasm for civic enhancement and corresponding to a rapid expansion of the federal government, did a new round of planning commence. The McMillan Commission famously created the current out-lines of the Mall during this time (see **The Mall and its Future,** p. 54).

Despite such a robust planning tradition, not all of the District's areas prospered. While L'Enfant's plan stretched from the Potomac to the Anacostia rivers, its geometric hierarchy clearly privileged the former. Similarly, the McMillan Commission, with its emphasis on completing the Mall, did not thoroughly address the environs of the capital's second river. One reason for this continuing geographic bias was the initial rationale for locating the nation's capital along the Potomac. To Washington, Jefferson, and Madison, the Potomac offered the best access to the Ohio River Valley, and thus they imagined it as a gateway to the nation's future heartland. The city's destiny, like that of the nation overall, was assumed to lie westward up the banks of the Potomac, not along the "Eastern Branch," as the mouth of the Anacostia was labeled on early maps. The area evolved into working-class neighborhoods and the center of African-American life. Soon after the Civil War, African Americans already made up half the city's population, but their future in Washington was to resemble the future of black populations in most other large American cities.

For much of the 20th century, Washington was a city of dual identities, the proud symbol of a nation and the typically blighted American city, marred by ghettoes and sundered by highways, largely through its poorer neighborhoods. Even great plans require periodic reinterpretation: although neither L'Enfant nor the McMillan Commission ultimately foresaw the Anacostia's potential to direct the city's growth a century or two hence, this is certainly the present generation's challenge.

Ongoing plans for Washington focus on Anacostia's revitalization. In 1998 the National Capital Planning Commission published its *Legacy Plan*, which described growth potential along the Anacostia, S. Capital St., and throughout SE. The District government has advanced its own long-range framework plan for the Anacostia. Washington's current planners are intent on capturing some of the growth that Washington's suburbs have enjoyed for decades and channeling it to the center. Their plans will no doubt continue D.C.'s tradition of planning excellence far into the 21st century.

Alex Krieger, FAIA, is a founding principal of Chan Krieger & Associates and a tenured professor at the Harvard University Graduate School of Design, where he serves as Chairman of the Department of Urban Planning & Design.

FREDERICK DOUGLASS HOME

◪ Location: *1411 W St. SE. Take the B-2 bus (Mt. Ranier) from Howard Rd. near the Anacostia Metro station.* **Contact:** *☎ 426-5960, TDD 426-5961; www.nps.gov/frdo.* **Hours:** *Daily mid-Apr. to mid-Oct. 9am-5pm; mid-Oct. to mid-Apr. 9am-4pm.* **Tours:** *17min. video and 30min. walking tour daily 9, 10, 11am and 1, 2, 3pm, with a 4pm tour in the summer; make reservations early.* **Admission:** *Guided tour $3, seniors $1.50, kids 6 and under free. No charge for Visitors Center and video.* **Accessibility:** *Only the 1st fl. of the home is wheelchair accessible.*

Frederick Douglass taught himself to read and write as a slave, escaped from slavery in 1838, published *The North Star* newspaper and a best-selling autobiography in the 1840s, served as the US Marshal for D.C. from 1877 to 1881, and was the US Minister to Haiti from 1889 to 1891. Over the course of his life, the great abolitionist and orator also spoke up as a champion for world peace, Irish home rule, women's rights, political activism, and human rights. The **Douglass Home** honors the great "Sage of Anacostia," who broke a whites-only covenant when he bought the building in 1877 and named it **Cedar Hill.** The house remains as Douglass furnished it.

NORTHEAST

◪ Highlights: *National Arboretum, Kenilworth Aquatic Gardens, Basilica of the National Shrine.* **Nearby:** *Capitol Hill, Shaw.*

Northeast Washington is formed by **North Capitol St., East Capitol St.,** and **Eastern Ave.** and covers over a quarter of the District's land area, containing several distinct neighborhoods. Much of the area, however, has been overwhelmed by the crack epidemic, especially the areas near the Prince George's County line and east of the Anacostia River. **Catholic University** forms one safe enclave north of Michigan Ave. off N. Capitol St., while the **National Arboretum** and **Kenilworth Gardens** form another at the far eastern edge of D.C. Tourists should avoid walking through this quadrant, and should drive or take the Metro between sights. **Exercise extreme caution if you choose to visit this area.**

ORIENTATION

North Capitol St. forms the western boundary of this quadrant of the District, while its counterpart, **East Capitol St.,** forms the southern end. Four roads run roughly parallel through Northeast on a southwest-northeast diagonal: **Maryland Ave., New York Ave., Rhode Island Ave.,** and **Michigan Ave. Florida Ave.** runs from upper NW to lower NE, and is one way to avoid some of the congestion on other roads. **13th St.,** which becomes **Brentwood Rd.** south of Rhode Island Ave., slices through the middle-class Brookland neighborhood. **South Dakota Ave.** parallels the District line, while **Eastern Ave.** follows the line itself. Northeast sights are spread out all over the quadrant. Use the Union Station, Rhode Island Ave., Brookland-CUA, Ft. Totten (all on the red line), Minnesota Ave., or Deanwood Metros (both on the orange line) to access the area.

▨ BASILICA OF THE NATIONAL SHRINE OF THE IMMACULATE CONCEPTION & THE CATHOLIC UNIVERSITY OF AMERICA (CUA)

◪ CUA Location: *620 Michigan Ave. NE, between Harewood and John McCormack Rd. The Visitors Center is just off Michigan Ave.* **Shrine Location:** *400 Michigan Ave. NE, near the corner of Michigan Ave. and Harewood Rd.* **Metro:** *Brookland-CUA.* **CUA Contact:** *☎ 319-6000; www.cua.edu.* **Shrine Contact:** *☎ 526-8300; www.nationalshrine.com.* **Shrine Hours:** *Apr.-Oct. daily 7am-7pm; Nov.-Mar. 7am-6pm.* **Mass:** *Su mass 7:30, 9, 10:30am, noon, 1:30 (Spanish), 4:30pm; weekday (M-Sa) mass 7am, 7:30, 8, 8:30am, 12:10, 5:15pm.* **CUA Visitors Center Hours:** *M-F 9am-5pm, Sa 10am-3pm.* **CUA Tours:** *30min. admissions info. sessions, followed by 45min. campus tours: late May-early Sept. M-F 10:30am; early Sept.-late May, M-F 10:30am and 2pm.* **Shrine Tours:** *1hr. tours M-Sa every hr. 9-11am and 1-3pm, Su 1:30-4pm.* **Admission:** *Free.* **Accessibility:** *Wheelchair accessible.*

Completed in 1959, the Basilica is the eighth-largest church in the world and the largest Catholic church in the Western hemisphere. The shrine's striking architecture combines elements from all Christendom and beyond. Romanesque arches support stark Byzantine facades and a blue-and-gold onion dome that looks imported direct from Kiev, while the massive bell tower beside the main entrance resembles an Islamic minaret. The interior is covered with golden mosaics portraying highlights of Christian scripture, from the Creation to the Last Judgment. A huge mosaic of Christ clad in fiery red robes presides over the sanctuary, while natural light filters in from the huge circular dome over the altar and pews. Between the upper church and the lower crypt level, over 60 chapels dedicated to the Virgin Mary and to a number of famous (and some not-so-famous) saints envelop worshipers with detailed, awe-inspiring artistry and serenity.

GALLAUDET UNIVERSITY

🚻 *Location:* 800 Florida Ave. NE, at 8th St. NE. *Metro:* Union Station. Take the D4 bus to K St. and 8th, then walk two blocks north. Though Gallaudet is relatively close to Union Station metro stop, visitors should take the bus whenever possible. For the safest route from Union Station, follow Massachusetts Ave. to Maryland Ave. (at Stanton Park); bear left onto Maryland and make another left at Florida Ave.; Gallaudet lies at the intersection of Florida and West Virginia Ave. The main gate entrance is just beyond the intersection. Walkers should avoid taking H St. eastward to 3rd St. NE. *Contact:* ☎ 651-5000; www.gallaudet.edu. *Hours:* Visitors Center open M-F 9am-4pm. *Tours:* 1hr. tours 10am and 2pm are conducted in American Sign Language (ASL); if a voice interpreter is needed, call ☎ 651-5050 or email visitors.center@gallaudet.edu.

Established in 1864, Gallaudet University is still the world's only university for the deaf. In 1988, Gallaudet students made national news by demanding—and subsequently getting—a deaf president, Dr. I. King Jordan. This beautiful 99-acre campus, with fine examples of Victorian Gothic and Queen Anne style architecture, has a student body of 2200. A stroll through the grounds will take you to a statue of the founder, **Edward M. Gallaudet,** as well as the sizeable athletic fields, where the Gallaudet Buffaloes roam.

NATIONAL ARBORETUM

🚻 *Location:* 3501 New York Ave. NE. Main entrance at 24th and R St. NE. If possible, drive to the arboretum; **the surrounding area is dangerous.** If walking during the week, take the Metro to Stadium-Armory, take the B2 bus to 1600 Bladensburg Rd. (by R St.), and walk east down R St. about 300 yd. to the entrance gate on R St. It's best to go on the weekend, when the X6 bus takes you from Union Station straight to the Visitors Center. *Contact:* ☎ 245-2726; www.usna.usda.gov. *Hours:* Daily 8am-5pm. Bonsai collection and Penjing Museum open daily 10am-3:30pm. *Tours:* 40min. narrated tram tour mid-Apr. to mid-Oct. Sa-Su 10:30, 11:30am, 1, 2, 3, 4pm. $4, seniors $3, ages 4-16 $2, under 4 free. Special (free) group tours, including a walking tour, should be pre-arranged and registered 3 weeks in advance. Groups may also reserve their own tram tour; call ahead for details and reservations. *Events:* Classes on painting, Japanese flower arranging, flower sales, Bonsai demonstrations, and hikes. Many are free. *Admission:* Free. Leashed pets allowed.

Stroll through the arboretum's 9½ mi. of paved roads and 446 acres of botanical wildlife, or picnic in the National Grove of State Trees, where all 50 state trees are represented. The Bonsai collection is exquisite, boasting miniature trees and a 350-year-old white pine. Surrounding the Visitors Center is a water lily pond where visitors can feed the hungry carp. Other highlights include the Asian Collections and the Azalea Hillside, atop which one can see the Capitol.

KENILWORTH AQUATIC GARDENS

🚻 *Location:* 1550 Anacostia Ave., at Anacostia Ave. and Douglas St. NE. *Directions:* From Metro: Deanwood, take the Polk St. exit, walk west over the bridge and head straight down Douglas St. Entrance on Anacostia Ave. between Quarles and Douglas St. Drivers should take New York Ave. NE out of the city and take the first Kenilworth Ave. exit just after crossing the District line, taking the exit for Eastern Ave.

immediately afterwards; turn right on Quarles St., and left on Anacostia Ave. **Contact:** ☎ *426-6905;* *www.nps.gov/kepa/index.htm.* **Hours:** *Daily 7am-4pm. Visitors Center 8am-4pm.* **Tours:** *Available upon request with 2 weeks' advance notice. Occasional evening and dawn walks; call for schedule.*

Across the Anacostia River from the National Arboretum, the Kenilworth Aquatic Gardens breed and raise aquatic plants and flowers. The garden's sanctuary consists of thousands of lilies, lotuses, and hyacinths on 12 acres of marshy plots. Summer mornings are the best time to visit, when the lilies and tropical plants reach their luscious peak. The last patch of natural marsh on the Anacostia River lies next to the gardens. A 1 mi. river trail leads past the marsh to an outlook over the Anacostia. The patient and quiet can see turtles, frogs, waterfowl, muskrats, raccoons, opossums, and occasional flocks of migrating birds. Look for migrating waterfowl in the spring and fall. Rough trails lead around the the 20 ponds. The annual **Waterlily Festival,** held on the third Saturday of July, brings special tours, events for children, and a day's worth of activities relating to the environment to the Kenilworth gardens. The Visitors Center offers pamphlets and brochures, an exhibit the garden's history, and an aquarium exhibit. If at all possible, come by car and **exercise caution: the gardens are located in an extremely dangerous area.**

TAKOMA PARK

Covering an area that includes both Northwest D.C. and Montgomery County, Maryland, Takoma Park declared itself a nuclear-free zone during the mid-80s, joining Berkeley, CA, and Madison, WI, as the bastions of peace and love. Lately though, Takoma's rebellious counterculture has been compromised by increasing migration from downtown into the suburbs. Luckily, a few offbeat shops remain. Every Saturday from April to December, Takoma Park hosts a **Farmer's Market** at the corner of Laurel Ave. and Carroll Ave. from 10am to 2pm. For Takoma Park's commercial heart, head up Carroll St. from Metro: Takoma to where Carroll St. becomes Carroll Ave. on the left and Laurel Ave. on the right.

VIRGINIA

ARLINGTON COUNTY

🚩 *Highlights:* Arlington National Cemetery, the Pentagon. *Food and Drink:* p. *139.* *Nearby:* Foggy Bottom, Fairfax, Alexandria.

Arlington County was incorporated into Virginia in 1846 after the struggling District of Columbia decided it did not want to deal with administrative hassles found in the rolling countryside across the river. Though physically divided, the city and the county remained inexorably linked. An extensive ring of Union forts was built across Arlington during the Civil War, but the area appealed to interests on both sides of the Mason-Dixon line in later years, serving as a gateway for commerce to the South in the early 20th century. Today the county is tied to the District by four major bridges, two Metro lines, and broad expanses of federally-owned land.

Arlington's western reaches contain sprinklings of shopping malls, restaurants, and bars within often semi-suburban areas (such as near the **Ballston, Virginia Square-GMU, Clarendon,** or **Courthouse** Metro stops). Arlington's more urbanized area near the **Rosslyn** stop draws greater tourist interest, a reflection of its proximity to Georgetown (just across Francis Scott Key Bridge over the Potomac River), massive **Arlington National Cemetery,** and **The Pentagon.** Locals are sometimes drawn to the **Farmer's Markets** held at a variety of locales around the county: the plaza adjacent to the Clarendon Metro exit (W 3-7pm); at the Arlington Courthouse (Sa 9am-1pm); and along the streets near the Rosslyn Metro stop, especially N. Lynn St. (Th 11am-4pm). The

Clarendon and Courthouse Farmer's Markets run from Apr.-Oct., while their Rosslyn counterpart offers goods from mid-May-mid-October.

ORIENTATION

Arlington is virtually impossible to navigate; even natives get lost in the maze of streets. However, the network of cross-county routes, highways, and boulevards can provide a general guide. **I-395** and **Columbia Pk.** (Rte. 244) run roughly east-west in south Arlington; **Arlington Blvd.** (Rte. 50), **Fairfax Dr., Wilson Blvd.,** and I-66 run in the same general east-west direction in central Arlington; and **Lee Highwway** is the north Arlington equivalent. From east to west, **Washington Blvd.** (Rte. 27/237), **Glebe Rd.** (Rte. 120), and **George Mason Dr.** are the major north-south conduits. Fortunately, the Metro and Metrobus can take you to most of the county. Check with the Metro (☎202-637-7000) before you make the trip. The Metro's Orange Line shuttles visitors to most of Arlington's bars and ethnic restaurants. The Blue Line will take you to sights like the Pentagon and the Cemetery. If you discover you're really lost, check street signs for "N" (north of Rte. 50, or Arlington Blvd.) or "S" (south of it).

The **Arlington Visitors Center,** 735 S. 18th St., will happily provide armloads of brochures and maps, directions to local sights, and answers to all your questions. From the Pentagon City Metro, walk south on S. 18th St. (toward Crystal City); the entrance is behind the fire station. (☎800-677-6267 or 703-228-5720; www.co.arlington.va.us. Open daily 9am-5pm.)

🖼 ARLINGTON NATIONAL CEMETERY

🚇 Metro: Arlington Cemetery. **By car:** From downtown Washington, take Independence or Constitution Ave. and turn left onto 23rd St. to cross the Arlington Memorial Bridge. Stay in the left lane as you enter the circle and follow it into the cemetery directly in front. **Contact:** ☎703-607-8000, ext. 0; www.arlingtoncemetery.org. **Hours:** Apr.-Sept. daily 8am-7pm; Oct.-May daily 8am-5pm. **Tours:** Tourmobile (☎202-554-5100) drives through the cemetery 8:30am-4:30pm daily; buses run every 15min. from the Visitors Center (sometimes every 10min. Jun.-Aug.). $6, ages 3-11 $3, seniors who reached the Cemetery by Metro free (but otherwise regular adult fee). **Info:** Visitors Center dispenses maps of the grounds and will locate specific gravesites upon request. Temporary passes to drive into the cemetery can be obtained here, but only if visiting a family member's grave. **Admission:** Free. Parking $1.25 per hr. for the 1st 3hr. and $2.50 each additional hr.

The largest military cemetery in the US, Arlington holds 285,000 veterans and their dependents within 624 acres of rolling hills.

Folger Shakespeare Library

MCI Center

Lee-Fendall House

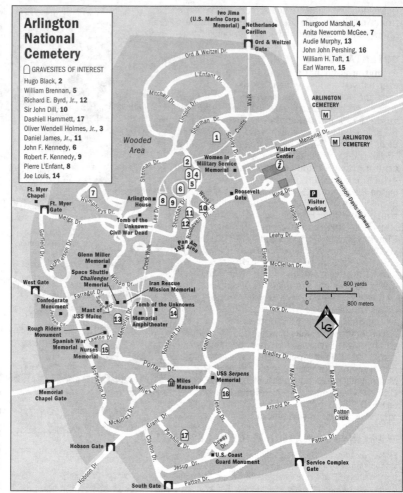

Arlington National Cemetery

GRAVESITES OF INTEREST

Hugo Black, **2**
William Brennan, **5**
Richard E. Byrd, Jr., **12**
Sir John Dill, **10**
Dashiell Hammett, **17**
Oliver Wendell Holmes, Jr., **3**
Daniel James, Jr., **11**
John F. Kennedy, **6**
Robert F. Kennedy, **9**
Pierre L'Enfant, **8**
Joe Louis, **14**

Thurgood Marshall, **4**
Anita Newcomb McGee, **7**
Audie Murphy, **13**
John John Pershing, **16**
William H. Taft, **1**
Earl Warren, **15**

Simple white tombstones note the name, birth date, rank, and war in which each soldier fought. With its current rate of 24 funerals per day, caretakers expect the cemetery to reach its capacity around 2025, at which point the cemetery will be rededicated as a memorial.

Visitors flock to the **Kennedy Gravesites,** located off Sheridan Dr. a short walk from the Visitors Center. (From the center, walk along Roosevelt Drive away from the main entrance, turn right onto Weeks Dr., and follow it to Sheridan.) President **John F. Kennedy** is buried next to his wife, **Jacqueline Kennedy Onassis.** Patrick and an unnamed daughter, children who died shortly after birth, are buried here as well. JFK supposedly once stood near Arlington House (see below), and, seeing the spectacular view of Washington, declared, "I could stay here forever." An **Eternal Flame,** lit by his widow at his funeral, flickers above his memorial stone. The modest grave of JFK's brother, **Senator Robert F. Kennedy,** lies a few feet away. The statesman wished for only a plain cross to mark his final resting place. His grave is the only wooden cross in the cemetery.

Just uphill of the Kennedys' gravesites is the newly restored **Arlington House,** once owned by **Robert E. Lee.** The famed general abandoned his estate when he moved to Richmond to join the Confederacy, and the Union government immediately seized the property. Major General Montgomery Meigs, who hated Lee for joining the Confederacy, began burying Union troops in places like Mrs. Lee's rose garden, ensuring that the family could never reclaim their estate. Lee's home is now a museum of antebellum life (open daily 9:30am-4:30pm), and provides one of the best views of D.C. from across the Potomac.

Arlington is also the final resting place for former President and Supreme Court Justice **William Howard Taft.** His simple grave is hidden among the trees on Custis Walk, a short distance from both the Kennedy gravesites. Taft is one of several justices to be buried in Arlington, a list including Thurgood Marshall, the first African American justice; Chief Justice Earl Warren, who played a crucial role in *Brown v. Board of Education*; and Oliver Wendell Holmes, who was also a Civil War veteran.

Pierre L'Enfant, originally buried within the District, was reinterred at Arlington along with soldiers from the Revolutionary War and the War of 1812. His distinctive grave on the hillside in front of Arlington House overlooks the city he designed. Farther down the hill among the plain headstones lies General of the Armies **John J. Pershing,** commander of US forces during WWI, who asked to be buried among his men. Arlington also holds the bodies of **Joe Louis,** history's longest-lasting world heavyweight boxing champion; actor and decorated soldier **Lee Marvin;** Arctic explorers **Robert E. Peary** and **Richard Byrd;** and legendary populist attorney and presidential candidate **William Jennings Bryan.**

The nation's **Tomb of the Unknowns** honors unidentified servicemen who died fighting for the US. The famous inscription reads, "Here rests in honored glory an American soldier known but to God." The Tomb of the Unknowns was known as the **Tomb of the Unknown Soldier** until 1998, when the remains of the fallen veteran were positively identified as those of **Michael Joseph Blassie,** a First Lieutenant in the Vietnam War who has since been reinterred in Missouri. The tomb is guarded 24 hours a day by silent sentries from the Army's Third Infantry. Don't miss the ritualized **changing of the guard,** when each guard takes 21 steps and then turns to face the tomb for 21 seconds to symbolize the 21-gun salute. (Oct.-Mar. every hr. 8am 4pm, Apr.-Sept. every 30min. 8am-6pm.)

Memorial Day each year brings a small American flag to each of the cemetery's gravesites, as well as a series of dedication and memorial services throughout the park. Perhaps most notable is the annual ceremony at the Tomb of the Unknowns, where the President lays a memorial wreath and makes a speech commemorating the day. Visitors to the cemetery for Memorial Day services are strongly encouraged to arrive early. Shuttles around the cemetery grounds are free until the President's service is over at the Tomb of the Unknowns.

The newest addition to the cemetery is the impressive **Women in Military Service for America Memorial** (☎ 800-222-2294; www.womeninmilitaryservicefo-ramericamemorial.com). The nation's first major memorial honoring servicewomen, the memorial is set inside the broad facade capping the end of Memorial Dr. A skylit exhibit gallery traces the history of US servicewomen through photographs, artifacts, a computer database, and an informative video on the history of women in the military. Future memorial additions to the cemetery will include several commemorating recent disasters and tragedies. A memorial recognizing the **September 11th Attacks** is planned for cemetary section 64 (in the southeast corner of the grounds), while a memorial dedicated to the crew of the lost space shuttle **Columbia** is in the works for section 46. The *Columbia* memorial will be located directly adjacent to the current **Challenger** memorial (also in section 46, across Memorial Dr. from the Tomb of the Unknowns), dedicated to astronauts killed in the 1986 shuttle disaster.

IWO JIMA MEMORIAL

🚶 *Directions: Walking from the cemetery continue down Custis Walk from Arlington House and exit through Weitzel Gate. Follow the path for 20min. If driving, go to the junction between Arlington Blvd. and Ridge Rd. **Metro:** Rosslyn. From the Rosslyn stop, walk 10 min. south on Ft. Myer Dr. until you reach the memorial.*

Also known as the Marine Corps War Memorial, the Iwo Jima Memorial is a monumental sculpture based on Joe Rosenthal's Pulitzer Prize-winning photograph of six Marines straining to raise the US flag on Iwo Jima's Mount Suribachi. Iwo Jima saw 6321 US soldiers die in battle in February 1945. Admiral Nimitz's comment on the battle, "Uncommon valor was a common virtue," adorns the statue's base. The US flag is real, but the "flagpole" is a lead pipe—just as in the photo. The memorial, dedicated in 1954, offers a nice view where one can see the Lincoln Memorial, Washington Memorial, and the Capitol all at once. The **Marine Corps Marathon** begins here each year, and the **Marine Corps Tuesday Evening Sunset Parades** (☎ 703-289-2500) are held at the memorial every Tuesday at 7pm. Parking is extremely limited, so consider parking at the Arlington Cemetery and taking the free shuttle from the Visitors Center to the memorial. The shuttle starts running at 6pm and continues after the performances are over.

ROOSEVELT ISLAND

⚐ Location: *In the Potomac River between the Little River and the Georgetown Channel. From D.C., cross the Roosevelt Bridge, take a right onto the George Washington Parkway northbound, and exit into the Roosevelt Island lot; if you see Key Bridge, you've missed it.* **Metro:** *Rosslyn. From the station, walk straight (away from the station) for 1 block and then turn left on N. Lynn St., cross Lee Hwy., make a right onto the Mount Vernon Trail, and follow the trail as it passes over George Washington Parkway and through a small parking lot, leading to the Roosevelt Island footbridge. Alternatively, cross Key Bridge from Georgetown and make a left onto the Mount Vernon Trail.* **Contact:** *☎ 703-289-2500; www.nps.gov/gwmp.* **Hours:** *Daily dawn to dusk.* **Tours:** *Rangers give nature and history tours in summer if called 7 days in advance at ☎ 703-285-2600.* **Restrictions:** *Bicycles and camping prohibited. Pets must be leashed.*

Originally used as a fishing village by local Native Americans, the 88.5 acre island was home to the mansion estate of 1790s resident John Mason, a "picnic resort" during the 19th century, and a training ground for the Union Army (including some of its African-American regiments) during the Civil War. To commemorate the popular hunter, conservationist, and president, the **Theodore Roosevelt Memorial Association** purchased this property in 1932. A later act of Congress officially named it Roosevelt Island, and the development of the land into a "woodland sanctuary" was spearheaded by the New-Deal-era **Civilian Conservation Corps** and landscape architect **Frederick Law Olmsted, Jr.**, whose father had planned the design of such national landmarks such as the **National Zoo**, New York City's Central Park, and Boston's Emerald Necklace park system.

Now a wilderness preserve, Roosevelt Island sits in the **Potomac River** just west of Foggy Bottom, a mere 15 minutes walking from downtown. The island still maintains an ecologically vibrant sampling of swamp, marsh, and forest habitats that hosts such critters as turtles, muskrats, cottontails, foxes, and redwing blackbirds, despite its location close to the city and most of D.C.'s major highways. Visitors are welcome to disappear into the thick forest on the island, but not to partake of Teddy's favorite pastime, hunting. The soft gravel paths and cooler temperature of the forest make the island popular among joggers.

Secluded in the center of the island is the impressive and underappreciated **Theodore Roosevelt Memorial,** designed by architect Eric Gugler and dedicated in 1967. Surrounding the 17 ft. bronze statue of Roosevelt (created by artist Paul Manship) is an elliptical plaza area with two large fountains; tall stone obelisks surrounding the statue bear Roosevelt's own words, conveying his ideas on nature, manhood, youth, and the state. The entire plaza itself is ringed by serene reflecting pools, over which footbridges connect to paths leading to the outer reaches of the island.

While animal-watchers flourish here, picnickers are better off at the nearby **Lady Bird Johnson Park,** or the **Potomac Parks** on the other side of the river, which have more open spaces. If visiting in the summer, don't forget your bug spray, as the stagnant moisture here makes a great breeding ground for mosquitoes. Rocky beaches reward those who find them with views of the Kennedy Center and environs. On weekends, local fishermen cast their lines from here into the murky waters of the Potomac. Even harder to find than these beaches, though, are the restrooms, hidden in the **comfort station** on the southwest corner of the island near Roosevelt Bridge.

FREEDOM PARK

⚐ *Location: 1101 Wilson Blvd. **Metro:** Rosslyn. From station, walk 2 blocks down Wilson Blvd.; the park is just after the intersection with Lynn St.*

On a raised walkway a couple blocks from the Rosslyn Metro, Freedom Park wraps around the building that used to be home to the Newseum (closed until 2006, when it will reopen in downtown D.C.). The Park consists of a few outdoor exhibits of symbols of freedom. For example, a section of the Berlin Wall, along with one of its watchtowers, has been preserved and put on display accompanied by several signs explaining its history. The park also has replicas of the fallen and beheaded Lenin Statue, Martin Luther King Jr.'s Birmingham jail cell door, a ballot box from South Square's Goddess of Democracy, and the Freedom statue that sits atop the Capitol. Each exhibit has an explanation and a thought-provoking quote or two.

NETHERLANDS CARILLON

⚐ *Location: Near the Iwo Jima Memorial. **Contact:** ☎ 703-289-2550. **Hours:** Bells play June-Aug. Sa 6-8pm; May and Sept. Sa 2-4pm. Briefing 30min. before each performance. **Admission:** Free.*

To show their appreciation for the Allied Forces' work in WWII, The Netherlands gave the US a carillon, a rectangular 127-foot tower that houses a set of 50 bells made in Dutch foundries as a gift for the Allied liberation of The Netherlands from the Nazis on May 5, 1945. If you stop by on a Saturday afternoon, you can climb the tower to meet the guest Carillonneur. The entrance to the tower is flanked by two bronze panthers and surrounded by an impressive array of tulips.

PENTAGON

⚐ *Location: The Pentagon sits inside a triangle formed by 3 highways: Rte. 110, Rte. 27, and I-395. By car, take the 14th St. Bridge from D.C. to I-395. Once on I-395, the Pentagon exit is about a quarter-mile into Virginia. Visitor parking available but limited; enter through the South Parking Entrance, or try the parking lot next to Macy's in Pentagon City and walk across the street and through the tunnel in the Visitor's Parking lot. **Metro:** Pentagon (not Pentagon City). **Hours:** Not open to the public. **Tours:** No tours available to the general public; group tours for schools, educational organizations, and other select groups available by contacting ☎ 703-695-1776.*

On July 17, 1941, the then-War Department gave its planners one weekend to design a building that would hold all the capital's military offices. On Monday morning, the architects returned with a blueprint for the familiar five-sided behemoth, and a work force of 13,000 immediately set to work 24 hours a day for 16 months to create the steel-reinforced concrete edifice. The statistics on this, the world's largest office building, are mind-boggling: five concentric and ten radial hallways totalling 17½ miles, 7754 windows, 131 stairways, and four zip codes of its own. Yet due to remarkable planning it takes no more than seven minutes to walk between any two points. Due to the attack on the Pentagon on September 11th, 2001, the tours have been indefinitely suspended to everyone except schoolchildren on field trips. The wall that took the impact of the hijacked airplane has been completely restored, and the interior offices were back up and running by September 11th, 2002.

FAIRFAX COUNTY

⚐ *Highlights: Mount Vernon Plantation, battlefields. **Museums:** Stabler-Leadbeater Apothecary Museum. **Nearby:** Virginia Plantations, Arlington Country.*

Fairfax County is home to dozens of historical attractions that take visitors back to the 18th-century charm of porticoes, porches, and well-pruned presidential gardens. When Philadelphia was still the nation's capital, aristocratic planters like **President George Washington**

SEE MAP P. 367

U.S. Capitol Building

YOU ARE HERE

and Virginia Declaration of Rights author **George Mason** lived on lavish Fairfax County estates. A horde of high-tech workers and investors have not left the county untouched, however. Although the city touts itself as "The Gateway to History," most gates in Fairfax surround affluent housing subdivisons. Historical parks, buildings, and avenues are interwoven amongst the burgeoning development. Of all the sights here, Mount Vernon and Manassas Battlefield are most worth the trip.

GETTING AROUND

In order to really explore Fairfax's dispersed attractions, a car may be the only option. While the Metro's Blue and Yellow Lines serve the southeastern portion of Fairfax and the Orange Line transports daily commuters from the northern stretch of the county, the central part of Fairfax remains inaccessible by rail. Metrobuses and Fairfax Connector Buses (☎ 703-339-7200 or www.fairfaxconnector.com for fare, route, and scheduling information) pick up some of the slack in the central areas of the county. Service is slow—check departure times beforehand.

Providing some welcome scenery for jaded commuters, the picturesque **George Washington Parkway** winds southward along the gorgeous bluffs of the Potomac River from the northwest tip of the Capital Beltway toward Alexandria (where it becomes Washington St.). A 14 mi. **bicycle trail** follows the road from D.C. to Mt. Vernon. Duke St. in Alexandria travels west to become the Little River Turnpike (Rte. 236). Lee Hwy. (Rte. 29) and Arlington Blvd. (Rte. 50) run east-west from Arlington through Falls Church to the Manassas National Battlefield Park. In northern Fairfax County, the Georgetown Pike (Rte. 193) is a winding cross-river extension of MacArthur Blvd. in NW Washington. The Dulles Access Rd. connects I-66 and the Capital Beltway to **Dulles International Airport.** Visitors to Fairfax should use the toll road for local traffic parallel to the Dulles Access Rd., or face a steep fine for traveling anywhere but the airport.

POTOMAC PLANTATIONS

MOUNT VERNON

Address: P.O. Box 110, Mt. Vernon, VA 22121. *Driving Directions:* Take the George Washington Pkwy. south from D.C. (which becomes Washington St. in Alexandria) to the entrance. *Public Transportation:* From Metro: Huntington, take the Fairfax Connector 101 bus ($0.50); buses run every hr. only before rush hour, so be sure to check a schedule ahead of time (☎ 703-339-7200; www.fairfaxconnector.com). The Potomac Spirit (☎ 866-211-3811; www.cruisetomountvernon.com) and the Potomac Riverboat Company (☎ 703-548-9000) run to and from Mount Vernon. *Contact:* ☎ 703-780-2000; www.mountvernon.org. *Hours:* Apr.-Aug. daily 8am-5pm, grounds close 5:30pm; Mar. and Sept.-Oct. daily 9am-5pm, Nov.-Feb. daily 9am-4pm. *Tours:* Mansion Tour, A Slave Life Tour, and other seasonal guided tours included in price of admission. Anecdote-filled 40min. audio tour of the grounds $4. River sightseeing aboard the Potomac Spirit Cruise Ship Tu-Su 10:30, 11:30am, 12:30, 2, 3pm. Adults $8, ages 6-11 $4, 5 and under free. Meet at wharf. *Admission:* $11, over 62 with ID $10.50, ages 6-11 $5, 5 and under free. $15 annual admission. *Accessibility:* Mostly wheelchair accessible. Shuttle and manual wheelchairs available. *Events:* Ceremonial wreath-laying at the Washington tomb daily 10am in summer. Free admission on George Washington's birthday, Feb. 22. Call ahead or check website for seasonal events.

From 1754 to 1799, Mount Vernon served as George Washington's beloved abode. Even while completing his official duties as president, Washington found time to dedicate his leisure time to beautifying the mansion's interior and administering the corps of slaves that ran the farm. Washington's descendants continued to live at Mount Vernon until 1858, when the Mount Vernon Ladies' Association purchased it for $200,000; the not-for-profit organization still owns and operates the estate today. Mount Vernon maintains 30-40% of Washington's original furnishings, which are now on display in the house.

THE MANSION. This 1700s Georgian masterpiece—the most visited historic house in America—is actually a clapboard house constructed by splattering sand on smooth wood before it was painted. Outside on the piazza Washington designed, rocking chairs offer the ultimate Southern comfort: a cool breeze and the stunning Potomac. In the entrance hall, the key to the Bastille given to Washington in 1790 by the Marquis de Lafayette, a close friend of the family, is enclosed in a glass case. The exhibit in the Washingtons' second-floor bedroom vividly describes the agony of the president's death in 1799 from an abscessed tonsil. Visitors will need to exercise some patience if they are to tour the Mount Vernon home; lines can be lengthy.

THE GROUNDS. Often overshadowed by the more renowned mansion, the sprawling grounds of Mount Vernon encompass nearly 8000 acres of picturesque land. Down the road, George and Martha Washington's tomb, a marble mausoleum housing a pair of stone sarcophagi labeled "Washington" and "Martha, consort of Washington," contrasts sharply with the older, unassuming tomb. Nearby is the unmarked area believed to have been the slave burial ground. In his time, Washington was the biggest slave owner in Northern Virginia, but in his will he freed all 400 of them. Tours of slave life at Mount Vernon (Apr.-Oct. daily at 10am, noon, 2, and 4pm) pay homage to Washington's slaves.

THE GRISTMILL. After a five year renovation, George Washington's Gristmill is again open to the public. The 18th century water-powered mill was used to process grain and corn into flour and meal, which Washington sold in Europe. Visitors are guided by a professional miller, who demonstrates the mill in action and explains the archaeological excavation of Washington's distillery next door. *(3 mi. west of Mount Vernon on Rte. 235. Open daily Apr.-Oct. 10am-5pm. $4, ages 6-11 $2, under 6 free.)*

GUNSTON HALL

🏠 *Location: 10709 Gunston Rd., Mason Neck, VA. **Driving Directions:** From DC, take I-95 South to Exit 163. Turn left on to Lorton Rd. and right on to Armistead Rd. At light, turn right on to Rte. 1 South. At 3rd light, turn left on to Gunston Rd. (Rte. 242); Gunston Hall is 3½ mi down on right. **Contact:** ☎ 703-550-9220; www.gunstonhall.org. **Hours:** Daily 9:30am-5pm. **Admission:** $8, seniors 60+ $7, grades 1-12 $4, kindergarten-age or under free. $1 discount coupon available online. **Tours:** Every 30min.; last tour at 4:30pm. Weekend theme tours offered Apr.-Oct.; call or see website for details. **Accessibility:** Limited to restrooms and 1st fl. of house.*

Gunston Hall was the home of **George Mason,** author of the Virginia Declaration of Rights and a key framer of the US Constitution, although he refused to sign the document because, among other reasons, it did not explicitly guarantee individual rights. Mason's concerns were addressed in 1791 when his Virginia Declaration emerged as the basis of the US Bill of Rights.

Construction of Gunston Hall was completed in 1759. The house served as the core of a bustling plantation, center of political activity, and home to Mason and his family. Gunston Hall reflects these multiple uses; the grand first-floor rooms, often used for entertaining political colleagues, feature elegant hand-carved woodwork. Due to a lack of documentation about the estate from Mason's era, planners combed through inventories of similar plantations to furnish the home most accurately.

Of the plantation's remaining 550 acres, 525 remain heavily wooded and uncultivated. Numerous formal gardens surround the areas closest to Gunston Hall; trails lined with tall boxwoods (some believed to have been planted during Mason's residence) are a highlight to visiting green thumbs. Archaeologists are currently working to restore the gardens to Mason's original 1750s layout.

WOODLAWN PLANTATION

🏠 *Location: 9000 Richmond Hwy., Alexandria, VA, at the second intersection of Mt. Vernon Hwy. and Rte. 1 (Richmond Hwy.) if coming from D.C. **Public Transportation:** From Metro: Huntington, take the 9A or 9B Metrobus (marked "Pentagon") directly to the intersection. **Contact:** ☎ 703-780-4000; www.woodlawn1805.org. **Hours:** Both Woodlawn Mansion and Pope-Leighey House open Mar.-Dec. daily 10am-5pm. **Admission:** Each house $7.50, grades K-12 $3. Both houses $13, grades K-12 $5. Tickets sales office at Woodlawn Plantation. **Tours:** Every 30min. at each house; last tour at both houses 4:30pm. **Accessibility:** Wheelchair access limited to ground fl.*

Woodlawn Plantation was a wedding present from George Washington to Nelly Custis, his adopted daughter, and Lawrence Lewis, his nephew and personal secretary. The couple was married by candlelight on Washington's last birthday, February 22, 1799. The dramatically different houses at Woodlawn Plantation demonstrate interesting contrast between early American baroque elegance and modern minimalism.

The **Pope-Leighey House,** transported from its original location in Falls Church, VA, represents Frank Lloyd Wright's simple 1940 vision of houses integrated completely into their surroundings. A sign in the parking lot directs guests to the house, one of Wright's Usonian-style houses, designed for inhabitants of moderate means ("Usonia" was utopian author Samuel Butler's acronym for the United States of North America). Commissioned in 1939, the $7000 house first held the four-member family of Laurent Pope, a Washington newspaper writer. The house was later sold to Robert and Marjorie Leighey for $17,000. When the construction of Interstate Highway 66 threatened to destroy the house in 1963, the house was moved to its present site on the grounds of Woodlawn Plantation. Strategic furniture arrangements (notice the kitchen cabinets open away from the window to prevent shadows on the shelves behind) reflect Wright's meticulous attention to detail.

Take a short walk to the towering, 19th-century **Woodlawn Mansion,** built in 1805 and still the anchor of the 125-acre lot. Most obvious to visitors of the mansion is the array of Washington portraits which hang as testaments to Nelly's benefactor. The 40-minute tour of the exquisitely preserved, five-part Georgian mansion begins in the master bedroom and proceeds to the back portico, where a view of five towering oaks marks the distant, beloved neighbor, Mount Vernon. While descending the stairs, take note of the stitched image of two mourners in front of a grave hung on the wall. If you look at the reflection in the situated mirror, one of the mourners mysteriously disappears and an angel appears above the grave.

OLD TOWN ALEXANDRIA

This American cultural center traces its origins over a century farther back than Washington, D.C. Trading began in the area in 1669, when tobacco merchant John Alexander purchased the site from a Brit for "6000 pounds of Tobacco and Cask," foreshadowing Alexandria's rise as a tobacco trading center. In 1749, tobacco merchants banded together to turn Alexander's land into a city, changing the town's name from Hunting Creek Warehouse to Alexandria. Virginia ceded Alexandria to the federal government in 1789 as part of the land grants that created the District of Columbia. The ungrateful feds gave the city back in 1847, a gesture that provoked, in the words of one resident, "rejoicing and cannon firing."

Alexandria didn't become a tourist attraction until the 1980s, when city residents backed away from proposed high-rises and decided to revitalize Old Town. Capitalizing on original 18th-century architecture and the legacy of historical all-stars like George Washington and Robert E. Lee, the town re-cobbled the streets, rebricked the sidewalks, installed gardens, restored over 1000 original facades, and invited tall ships and contemporary shops. Today, the area is packed with tourists.

A plentiful **Farmer's Market,** 301 King St., in Market Sq. (☎703-370-8723; market open 5-9am) proffers baked goods, produce, crafts, and artwork. Free **lunchtime concerts** take place in Market Sq. once a week during the spring and summer, and **Waterfront Park Concerts** between Prince and King St. take place occasionally on Monday evenings in summer (call ☎703-883-4686 for an events schedule).

ORIENTATION

Old Town is a 20 min. drive from downtown D.C. To find Old Town from the King St. Metro, walk down King St. away from the imposing tower of the **George Washington Masonic National Memorial.** A **DASH bus** also runs from the Metro to Old Town; call ☎703-370-3274 for a schedule. DASH also runs buses throughout the city ($0.85). To reach the area **by car,** take the East King St. exit from the George Washington Pkwy. Non-Alexandria residents may obtain free 24hr.

parking proclamations at the Ramsay House Visitors Center at 221 King St.; just present your license plate number and state identification to receive the pass, which is good at two-hour metered spaces. The neighborhood is accessible by Metro: Braddock or King St. I-395 cuts between Alexandria and Arlington far to the north of Old Town, and the Beltway rushes along to the south. Old Town is accessible by King St. (Rte. 7, which connects to I-395 to the west) and the GW Parkway, which runs along the Potomac north of the region and becomes Washington St. near the heart of Alexandria.

Laid out in a visitor-friendly grid, Old Town Alexandria lies in the square bordered by **Oronoco St.** to the north, the **Potomac River** to the east, **Gibbon St.** to the south, and **Alfred St.** to the west. Block numbers (100, 200, etc.) indicate the number of blocks from the Potomac River (east-west) or from King St. (north-south). King St. presides over an array of ships, art galleries, antique shops, and some of the finest bars and restaurants in the DC area. The **Ramsay House Visitors Center,** 221 King St., cordially offers free maps, literature, and directions to everything in town. (☎ 703-838-4200; www.funside.com. Open daily 9am-5pm.) The house, a 1724 building shipped upriver from Dumfries, VA, to Alexandria, was originally the home of Scottish merchant and Lord Mayor William Ramsay. The building went on to become a site for the manufacture of cigars after the Civil War. During Prohibition, it was the location of "Ma's Place," a speakeasy where many an Alexandrian was introduced to the joys of beer under the proprietor's motherly hospitality.

MASONIC NATIONAL MEMORIAL & ENVIRONS
GEORGE WASHINGTON MASONIC NATIONAL MEMORIAL

🚩 *Location: 101 Callahan Dr., at King St., across from the Amtrak and Metro stations. Metro: King St.; from the Metro, proceed under the overhead rail bridge and along King St.; the Memorial's massive tower is directly uphill. Contact: ☎ 703-683-2007. Hours: Daily 9am-5pm. Tours: The 1st. and 2nd. fl. are open to visitors to explore on their own. To go above the 2nd fl., you must take the free 1hr. tour. The tour can be given only to parties of 2 or more, so bring a friend or hope for company. 9:30, 11am, 1, 2:30, and 4pm. Admission: Free. Accessibility: Wheelchair ramps available. The elevator to the observation deck is wheelchair accessible.*

Looming over western Alexandria, the lofty Masonic National Memorial is an imposing testament to the strength of masonry and the legacy of George Washington. The tour leads up through several lodge rooms, including a masonic library and the **Washington Room,** which displays artifacts such as Washington's Revolutionary War field trunk and a lock of his hair. Downstairs, visitors can peer into mysterious masonic meeting rooms. The **Replica Lodge Room** on the second floor includes a clock that was stopped at the moment of Washington's death, a chair from **Mount Vernon,** and furniture used in the Alexandria masonic lodge when he was its "chartermaster;" he was the only mason to have been a masonic chartermaster and a US president at the same time. At 408 ft., the observation deck provides an amazing view of Alexandria.

LEE-FENDALL HOUSE

🚩 *Location: 614 Oronoco St. Metro: King St.; from the Metro, proceed down King St. to Washington St. and make a left; the house is 4 blocks up on the right. Contact: ☎ 703-549-1789; www.leefendallhouse.org. Hours: Tu-Sa 10am-4pm, Su noon-4pm. Tours: Every hr. 10am-3pm. Admission: Access to the house by tour only. $4, ages 11-17 $2, ages 10 and under free. A separate garden entrance (along N. Washington St.) allows visitors to see the garden area for free.*

Constructed by Phillip Fendall in 1785 on land once owned by man-about-Alexandria "Light Horse" Harry Lee, the Lee-Fendall House was inhabited by 37 different Lees. Renovated in 1850 in Greek Revival style, the home stayed in the Lee family until 1903. Among the Lee family documents on display is an original copy of a New York newspaper with Harry Lee's eulogy of George Washington, in which he used the famous phrase "first in war, first in peace, first in the hearts of his countrymen" to describe the president. A 200-year-old magnolia tree is a fitting centerpiece of the large garden just outside the house.

LYCEUM

Location: *201 S. Washington St., at Prince St. (1 block from King St.).* **Contact:** ☎ *703-838-4994; hwww.alexandriahistory.org.* **Hours:** *M-Sa 10am-5pm, Su 1-5pm.* **Admission:** *Free.*

This brick-and-stucco Greek Revival building constructed in 1839 has been a Civil War military hospital, a private home, and an office building. Following a period of neglect in the earlier part of the 20th century, it was almost demolished in the 1960s; outcry from an actively preservationist citizenry helped save the historic site. Originally a cultural center, the Lyceum has come full circle, offering temporary and permanent exhibitions on Alexandria and Virginia history.

BLACK HISTORY RESOURCE CENTER

Location: *638 N. Alfred St.; entrance on Wythe St.* **Contact:** ☎ *703-838-4356; http://oha.ci.alexandria.va.us/bhrc.* **Hours:** *Tu-Sa 10am-4pm, Su 1-5pm.* **Admission:** *Free.* **Accessibility:** *Wheelchair accessible.*

Housed in the unassuming Robert H. Robinson Library, originally built in 1940 for African-Americans after a sit-in over the segregation of the Alexandrian library system, the center showcases paintings, photographs, and other memorabilia that chronicle African-American history in Alexandria. Pick up the printed walking tour that lists historic sites related to black history. The adjacent **Watson Reading Room** houses a non-circulating collection of books primarily concerning African-American history, literature, and social science.

HEART OF KING STREET

POTOMAC RIVER BOAT TOURS

Location: *Boats depart at the city pier.* **Contact:** ☎ *703-548-9000 or 877-511-2628; www.potomacriverboatco.com.* **Boat Tours:** *3 boat tours of various lengths (40min.-2hr.) and to various destinations (the Alexandria seaport area, Mount Vernon, or the District's monuments) have separate schedules; check the website or the pier ticket office for the latest information; all 3 boat tours run Apr.-Oct.* **Admission:** *Alexandria seaport: $8, seniors $7, ages 2-12 $5. Monuments tour: $16, seniors $15, ages 2-12 $8. Mount Vernon tour: $27, seniors $26, ages 6-10 $15, children 5 and under free. Fare for Mount Vernon boat tour includes admission to Mount Vernon itself.* **Hours:** *Ticket office open Tu-F 10am-9:30pm, Sa 10am-10pm, Su 10am-7:30pm.*

Daily 40min. tours of the Alexandria Waterfront discuss the history of the landmarks along the Potomac River, including the construction of National Airport, what really goes on at the Naval Research Laboratory, and legends like that of the Jones Point lighthouse keeper who managed to cram his family of 17 into a telephone-booth-sized home. Two hour-long cruises depart three times per week upstream under several bridges to the monuments and downstream to Mount Vernon and Revolutionary War forts. Call ahead for hours, especially in September and October.

GADSBY'S TAVERN

Location: *134 N. Royal St., near Cameron St.* **Contact:** ☎ *703-838-4242; www.gadsbystavern.org.* **Hours:** *Apr.-Sept. Tu-Sa 10am-5pm, Su 1-5pm; Oct.-Mar. Tu-Sa 11am-4pm, Su 1-4pm.* **Tours:** *House only accessible by guided tour, which run at 15 and 45min. past the hr.; last tour Apr.-Sept. 4:15pm and Oct.-Mar. 3:15pm.* **Admission:** *$4, ages 11-17 $2, ages 10 and under free. $1 discount for AAA members. Block tickets allowing admission to Gadsby's Tavern, Carlyle House, and the Apothecary $9, children $5. Purchase at 1 of the 3 sites or at Ramsay House Visitors Center.* **Events:** *Period dance lessons, summer candlelight tours (Apr.-Sept., F 30min. tours leaving on the quarter 7-9:15pm; $5, $2 for ages 11-17), social gatherings, and themed balls, such as the annual "Birthnight Ball" on George Washington's birthday in February.*

Formerly a hotbed of political, business, and social life, the restored Gadsby's Tavern takes you back to ye good olde days of hospitality, when as many as four hotel guests slept in one bed. Run by proprietor John Gadsby, the tavern would have had an ideal location in the late 18th century, when Cameron St., rather than King St., was intended to be the main corridor of the Alexandria area. The establishment had a prominent clientele; it not only hosted a "birthnight ball" for **George Washington**, still celebrated here annually, but also served each of the first five U.S. presidents. Today, the guided tour winds through the three floors that were the temporary quarters of notables in American history, including George and Martha Washington, Jefferson, John Adams, Madison, and Lafayette. Occasional temporary exhibitions relating to tavern life are featured in the museum's upstairs ballroom.

STABLER-LEADBEATER APOTHECARY MUSEUM & SHOP

fi Location: *105-107 S. Fairfax St.* **Metro:** *King St..* **Contact:** ☎ *703-836-3713; www.apothecary-museum.org.* **Hours:** *M-Sa 10am-4pm, Su 1-5pm.* **Tours:** *Tours for large groups by advance reservation; no guided tours for small groups or individual visitors.* **Admission:** *$2.50, ages 11-17 $2, ages 10 and under free. Block tickets allowing admission to Gadsby's Tavern, Carlyle House, and Apothecary $9, children $5. Purchase at 1 of the 3 sites or at Ramsay House Visitors Center.*

A pharmacy open from 1792 to 1933, the Stabler-Leadbeater Apothecary closed during the Great Depression. With a little help from restorers, the second-oldest pharmacy in America (and the oldest in Virginia) has been preserved in its 1933 condition. In fact, shelves are lined with several hand-blown bottles, still resting in their original 1933 position. Also on display are hundreds of mortars and pestles, powders, eyeglasses, weights, and scales used by old-time druggists. Martha Washington's letter to the pharmacy requesting castor oil hangs in a glass case.

TORPEDO FACTORY & ALEXANDRIA ARCHAEOLOGY MUSEUM

fi Location: *105 N. Union St., at King St.* **Metro:** *King St.; from the Metro exit, walk 18 blocks (heading toward Old Town) and make a left at Union St.; the Factory is on the right.* **Contact:** ☎ *703-838-4565 for Torpedo Factory; 703-838-4399 for Alexandria Archaeology; www.torpedofactory.org; www.alexandriaarchaeology.org.* **Hours:** *Torpedo Factory open daily 10am-5pm. Alexandria Archaeology open Tu-F 10am-3pm, Sa 10am-5pm, Su 1-5pm.* **Admission:** *Free.*

Exhibiting over 165 local, in-house artists, this ex-factory houses 84 working studios on three floors. Visitors can observe works of nearly every artistic genre as they await completion or sale in workshops. The only relic of the building's role as a World War I munitions factory is a small exhibit featuring a massive green torpedo. On the third floor of the factory, in room 327, the **Alexandria Archaeology Museum** welcomes visitors into the city's working urban archaeology lab.

CARLYLE HOUSE

fi Location: *121 N. Fairfax St.* **Contact:** ☎ *703-549-2997; www.carlylehouse.org.* **Hours:** *Tu-Sa 10am-4:30pm, Su noon-4:30pm.* **Tours:** *House accessible only by 30min. guided tours, which are given every 30min.; last tour 4:30pm.* **Admission:** *$4, students 11-17 and seniors $2, under 11 free. Block tickets allowing admission to Gadsby's Tavern, Carlyle House, and Apothecary $9, children $5. Purchase at 1 of the 3 sites or at Ramsay House Visitors Center.*

Faithfully restored in 1976, the home of prosperous Scottish merchant John Carlyle (c. 1753) is a unique showcase of Alexandria in the 18th century. Tours start in the basement, where the servants once lived, and continue upstairs where visitors will be startled by the surprising vibrance of the 18th-century decor. The garden in the back is a public park, beckoning picnickers.

ATHENAEUM

fi Location: *201 Prince St., at S. Lee St.* **Contact:** ☎ *703-548-0035; www.alexandria-athenaeum.org.* **Hours:** *W-F 11am-3pm, Sa 1-3pm, Su 1-4pm.* **Admission:** *Free. Tickets to the 6 yearly shows $7.*

Alexandria's oldest house, built between 1851 and 1852, holds occasional local and touring art shows and is home to the **Virginia Fine Arts Association** and the **Alexandria Ballet.** The peach-colored Greek Renaissance building stands out against the surrounding colonial architecture with its large, round columns and classical aura. Unless there is a ballet rehearsal, visitors can walk on the beautiful wooden floors in the main hall and browse through the local artists' exhibit.

PARKS & TRAILS IN & AROUND D.C.

ROCK CREEK PARK

⚑ Attractions: *Jogging, hiking, biking, horseback riding, tennis, golf, histori-cal sites.* **Nearby:** *Georgetown, Upper Northwest, Dupont Circle, Adams Morgan.* **Directions:** *Board either the E2, E3, or E4 bus from the Friendship Heights Metro; exit at intersection of Military Rd. and Oregon Ave. and follow forest trail to the right uphill to the Rock Creek Park Nature Center.*

Celebrating its 114th birthday in 2004, Rock Creek is the oldest national park in the US after Sequoia and Yellowstone and it offers city-weary travelers a reprieve from the intensity of D.C. urban life. More like a man-aged forest than a landscaped city park, the 3000-acre park property stretches five miles from the Kennedy Center on the Potomac to D.C.'s border with Maryland, pro-viding over 40 miles of hiking, biking, and horse paths. **Rock Creek Parkway,** which becomes **Beach Dr.** north of Klingle Rd., winds through the park from north to south.

Thanks to the thick canopy of leaves overhead, it's always ten degrees cooler inside the park than outside. Along Rock Creek Pkwy., starting at 24th St. below Cal-vert St., stretches a 1½ mi. **exercise trail,** complete with 18 workout stations where you can push-up, pull-up, and sit-up to your heart's content and benefit (use Metro: Woodley Park). An extensive series of hiking and running trails await the adventur-ous from the Maryland border south through the park, even past the **Kennedy Center** and into Virginia. Cyclists will find plenty of **bicycle trails** criss-crossing the park as well, but remember that bicycles are not allowed on foot or horse paths. Cyclists compete with in-line skaters for control of Beach Dr. from 7am Saturdays until 7pm Sundays, when the park closes its gates to motorized vehicles north of Broad Branch Rd. and south of Joyce Rd. Bingham and Sherrill Dr., both north of Military Rd., are also closed during this period, as are several more stretches of Beach Dr. (one just south of Wise Rd., and a second between the D.C.-Maryland border and Wise Rd.)

Parking is plentiful in lots throughout the park, and sporadic meadows along Beach Dr. are designated as daytime picnic spots. Camping is not allowed (and would be dangerous even if it were). **The park is only open from dawn to dusk and is unsafe at night;** unless you're there for an evening event, it is wise to leave before the sun sets. **In an emergency, call park police** (☎619-7300 or 911).

PARK ATTRACTIONS

Nature Center, 5200 Glover Rd. NW (☎895-6070; www.nps.gov/rocr). Exhibits on local flora and fauna, ranging from chestnut laurels to an impressive stuffed bald eagle. Also offers a planetarium show for ages 4+ (W 4pm, Sa-Su 1 and 4pm). Informal "Exploring the Sky" pro-gram offers telescope viewings (once a month Apr.-Nov.); dates vary, so call in advance. view-ings are held just after sunset at the field immediately south of the intersection of Military and Glover Rd., near the Nature Center. Various "Ranger's Choice" events Sa-Su. Rock Creek Park will celebrate its 114th birthday in late Sept. 2004 (**Rock Creek Park Day,** on the last Sa of the month) with special activities, a children's puppet show, planetarium shows, and guided hikes. Monthly schedules available from the Center. Open W-Su 9am-5pm.

Peirce Mill, (☎282-0927; www.nps.gov/pimi), at the corner of Tilden St. and Beach Dr. Peirce Mill was the last running mill in the District, and its long years of service took a pal-pable toll on the structure when the main shaft of its waterwheel became broken in 1993. Restoration efforts and fundraising are currently underway to bring the mill back into oper-ation, and the site has been closed to the public since May of 2002. The adjacent **Peirce Barn** now receives visitors to the site.

Peirce Barn, 2401 Tilden St. (☎282-0927), directly adjacent to the Peirce Mill. The Barn houses exhibits focusing on the mills of the Rock Creek Valley and the Peirce Estate. Orga-nized hikes in this area of the park start at the Barn, and to the relief of summer visitors, the interior has A/C. Open Sa-Su noon-4pm.

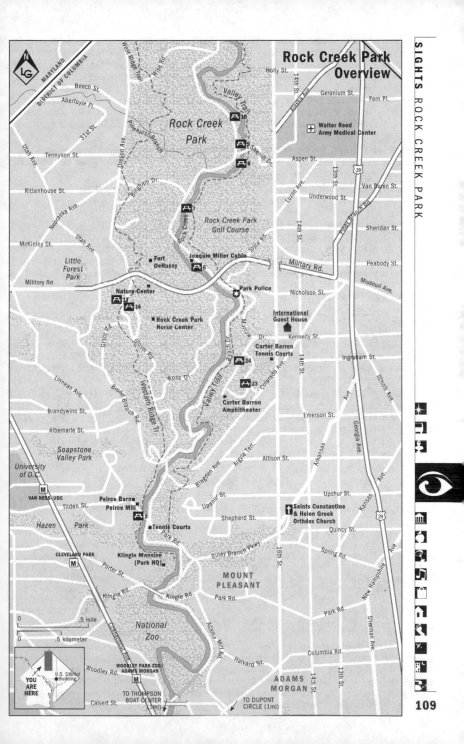

Rock Creek Park
Overview

MARYLAND

DISTRICT OF COLUMBIA

Beech St.
Aberfoyle Pl.
31st St.
Tennyson St.
Rittenhouse St.
Nebraska Ave.
McKinley St.
Utah Ave.
Military Rd.
Utah Ave.

West Ridge Trail
Wise Rd.
Pinehurst Branch
Oregon Ave.
Bingham Dr.

Rock Creek
Park

Holly St.
Valley Trail
14th St.
Alaska Ave.
Geranium St.
Fern Pl.

Walter Reed
Army Medical Center

Aspen St.
Luzon Ave.
Underwood St.
13th St.
Van Buren St.
I-29

Rock Creek Park
Golf Course

Rock Creek

10
9 Sherrill Dr.
8

Sheridan St.

14th St.

Piney Branch Rd.

Little
Forest
Park

Fort
DeRussy

Joaquin Miller Cabin
6

Joyce Rd.

Military Rd.

Peabody St.
Missouri Ave.

Nature Center
13
14

Rock Creek Park
Horse Center

Grant Rd.
Glover Rd.

Park Police

Military Rd.

Nicholson St.

International
Guest House

Morrow Dr.

Dr.   Kennedy St.

Carter Barron
Tennis Courts
24

Colorado Ave.

14th St.

Ingraham St.

Illinois Ave.

Western Ridge Trail
Broad Branch Rd.

Valley Trail
Beach Dr.
Ross Dr.

23

Carter Barron
Amphitheater

Emerson St.

Linnean Ave.

Brandywine St.
Albemarle St.

Soapstone
Valley Park

University
of D.C.

VAN NESS-UDC

Hazen
Park

Tilden St.

CLEVELAND PARK

Peirce Barn
Peirce Mill

Tennis Courts

Klingle Mansion
(Park HQ)

Klingle Rd.

Porter St.

National
Zoo

Bragden Ave.
Argyle Terr.
Allison St.
Upshur St.

Shepherd St.

Piney Branch Pkwy.

Park Rd.

Kingle Rd.
Park Rd.

MOUNT
PLEASANT

Adams Mill Rd.

Connecticut Ave.

Upshur St.

Saints Constantine
& Helen Greek
Orthdox Church

Quincy St.

Georgia Ave.
Arkansas Ave.

Spring Rd.

16th St.

New Hampshire Ave.

Kansas Ave.

Sherman Ave.

I-29

0   .5 mile
0   .5 kilometer

YOU
ARE
HERE

U.S. Capitol
Building

WOODLEY PARK-ZOO/
ADAMS MORGAN

Woodley Rd.

Calvert St.

TO THOMPSON
BOAT CENTER
(1mi)

Harvard St.

Columbia Rd.

TO DUPONT
CIRCLE (1mi)

ADAMS
MORGAN

13th St.

109

Carter Barron Amphitheater, (☎ 895-6000, concert line 426-0486; www.nps.gov/rocr/cbarron), at 16th and Colorado Ave. NW. Outdoor theater offering summertime concerts May-early Sept. and popular, free Shakespeare performances (late May-early June) by members of The Shakespeare Theatre (see p. 188). Concerts include jazz, blues, and Latin music performances. The **National Symphony Orchestra** (see p. 186) has also performed here. Most performances 7:30pm. Some shows $18, others are ticketed but free; pick up tickets at box office on day of show (limit 4 free tickets per adult). Box office open noon-8pm. Advance ticket sales through Ticketmaster (☎ 432-7328; www.ticketmaster.com). Schedule online.

Old Stone House, 3051 M St. NW (☎ 426-6851), in Georgetown. Though this structure is not secluded in the forest, the oldest standing building in the District is still the 3rd major site of Rock Creek Park. See **Georgetown**, p. 79.

Joaquin Miller Cabin Poetry Series (☎ 726-0971), adjacent to the Miller Cabin in the park off Beach Dr. north of the Military Rd. overpass. Miller, an eccentric 19th-century poet who achieved substantial fame among his contemporaries, retreated to writer's seclusion in a cabin (built 1883) à la Thoreau near what is now Meridian Hill Park. When he moved to California, he donated the cabin to the Sierra Club, which gave it to the National Park Service, which then moved it to its present location in Rock Creek Park. Outdoor reading series, sponsored by The Word Works Press and Literary Organization (www.wordworksdc.com), poets selected from an annual poetry competition in Jan.-Mar. Readings (usually 2 artists per night) June-July Tu 7:30pm. Admission is free and does not require a ticket.

RECREATIONAL SPORTS

Carter Barron Tennis Courts, (☎ 426-6837), at 16th and Kennedy St. NW. 10 hard and 15 clay courts. Reservations necessary M-Sa 7-11pm, Sa morning, and in winter. Summer rates $6-12, depending on court surface and time of day. Winter rates $22-30.75 for heated indoor courts. Senior discounts ($17) available to 60+ only in winter. Abundant parking available. Open daily 7am-11pm.

Rock Creek Park Horse Center, 5100 Glover Rd. NW (☎ 362-0118). The only place in the District for riding without required lessons. Must be 12+ for trail rides ($30 for a 1hr. ride) and at least 30 months old and 30 in. tall for weekend pony rides ($20 for a 15min. ride). Trail rides given Tu-Th 3pm and Sa-Su noon, 1:30, and 3pm. There are a few designated equestrian trails. Reservations required (by credit card, at least 24hr. in advance) as rides are popular. 24hr. cancellation policy. Open Tu-F noon-6pm, Sa-Su 9am-5pm. MC/V.

Rock Creek Park Golf Course (☎ 882-7332; www.golfdc.com), at 16th St. and Rittenhouse St. NW. Play golf in luscious Rock Creek. See **Entertainment,** p. 193.

Thompson Boat Center, 2900 Virginia Ave. NW (☎ 333-4861; www.thompsonboatcenter.com), at Rock Creek Pkwy. and Virginia Ave. NW. See **Entertainment,** p. 192.

GREAT FALLS PARK

◪ *Located in McLean, VA. **Directions:** Take the I-495 to Exit 44, then Georgetown Pike (Rte. 193) West 4.3 mi. Soon after passing the Madeira School, turn right at Old Dominion Dr. and drive 1 mi. to the park. **Contact:** ☎ 703-285-2966; www.nps.gov/grfa. **Hours:** Daily 7am-dark. Visitors Center open M-F 10am-5pm, Sa-Su 10am-6pm. **Tours:** Daily ranger talks 12:30 and 3:30pm. 30min. ranger walks Sa-Su 1pm. Call ahead for details. **Admission:** $5 per vehicle, $3 per person without a vehicle. Ticket good for 3 days at both this park and the Great Falls section of C&O Canal Park in Maryland (see p. 112). Under 16 and disabled free. No swimming, wading, alcohol, unleashed pets, or fires allowed.*

Breathtaking views of the Potomac River abound across all 800 acres of Great Falls Park. The park's main attraction is the 16 mi. of hiking trails along the river. The **Visitors Center,** just inside the entrance gate, includes informative exhibits about the park (including a few native snakes on display); free park maps are also available there. The falls' three overlook sites are only a short walk from the center. Kayaking and whitewater rafting are available for experienced boaters on the Potomac. Experienced rock climbers test their mettle on Great Falls' bare granite (climbers must register first at the Visitors Center). No swimming is allowed in the Potomac, and for good reason—the churning river claims an average of seven lives a year in this area alone. **Be careful when hiking near the river.** The park offers excellent catfish and carp fishing, but a Maryland or Virginia fishing license is required to cast your line at any of the three overlook points to the right of the visitors center. Picnic areas with grills available for public use; the snack bar is open Apr.-Oct.

WASHINGTON & OLD DOMINION TRAIL

◪ Runs from Arlington, VA to Purcellville, VA. **Directions:** Access the trail (mile 5) at Metro: East Falls Church. Call or visit website for other access points and parking information. **Contact:** ☎ 703-729-0596; www.nvrpa.org/wod. **Hours:** Open daily during daylight hours.

The Washington & Old Dominion (W&O.D.) trail, popular with runners, walkers, bikers, and rollerbladers, takes its name from the railroad that ran along this route from 1859 to 1968. The 45 mi. paved trail is shadowed for 32.5 mi. by a crushed stone path from Vienna to Purcellville on which horseback riding is allowed. The trail connects with several local parks and other trails, including Mount Vernon Trail. At Vienna, children play around a red caboose that remains from the old W&OD railroad days.

MANASSAS NATIONAL BATTLEFIELD PARK

◪ Located in Manassas, VA, in Prince William County. **Directions:** Take I-66 West to Exit 47B (Rte. 234); the battlefield is on the right. No public transportation. **Contact:** ☎ 703-361-1339; www.nps.gov/mana. **Hours:** Open daily during daylight hours. Visitors Center open daily 8:30am-5pm. **Admission:** $3, under 17 free. Tickets good for 3 days. Seniors 62+ eligible for Golden Age passport ($10), which gives lifetime access to all national parks. Golden Access pass, for the disabled, affords the same benefits. **Tours:** 40min. Henry Hill self-guided walking tour in brochure. 30min. ranger talks given hourly 9am-4pm. **Events:** Battle anniversaries held July 21-22 and Aug. 24-26 with cannon firings and Civil War-era music in a recreated campground. **Accessibility:** Limited.

Upon these undulating green hills, brother fought against brother not once but twice. Marking the battlefield of the First and Second Battles of Manassas, known to the Yankees as the **Battles of Bull Run,** this Virginia landscape witnessed the two-fold slaughter and defeat of the Yankees. On the morning of July 21, 1861, Northern General **Irvin McDowell** rallied his green troops—some only 16 years young— to march to the Confederate lines in the First Battle of Bull Run. The equally untrained Southerners, led by General **Stonewall Jackson,** routed McDowell's untrained soldiers in a chaotic and disorganized fracas. Jackson would earn his nickname that day by stubbornly blockading McDowell's troops at Manassas Junction. Ironically, as the men battled ferociously in what was the first major battle of the Civil War, the event drew hundreds of civilians (including Congressmen) seeking picnic entertainment on the opposite side of Bull Run Creek. While sightseers sipped tea, 900 soldiers were killed and the badly-defeated Union Army retreated to Washington. On August 29 of the following year, the forces gathered for a three-day rematch. Once again, the Southerners, this time under the command of General **Robert E. Lee,** prevailed. After the smoke cleared, over 1700 Union and 1400 Confederate troops lay lifeless here.

The park's recently refurbished **Henry Hill Visitors Center,** located at the park entrance, offers a self-guided walking tour that follows a one-mile trail, stopping at plaques explaining the area's significance to the First Battle of Bull Run. A 16-mile self-guided driving tour covers the areas pertinent to the longer Second Battle. Of particular note are the fording points along the small river, sites of bloody attacks and retreats, and the hilltop artillery placements. The cannons, like ghosts set in the tall grass, eerily pay homage to those who were left behind after the madness ended.

SIGHTS   PARKS & TRAILS IN & AROUND D.C.

C&O CANAL NATIONAL HISTORICAL PARK

⚐ *Follows the Potomac River from Georgetown through West Virginia to Cumberland, MD.* **Billy Goat Trail:** *11710 MacArthur Blvd. (☎ 301-299-3613), in Potomac, MD.* **Directions:** *Take the I-495 to Exit 39, then River Rd. (Rte. 190) North approx. 3½ mi. Turn left on Falls Rd. and continue to MacArthur Blvd.; turn right; street ends at Visitor Center.* **Hours:** *Daily 7am-dark. Georgetown Visitor Center open W-Su 9:30am-5pm. Great Falls Tavern Visitor Center open daily 9am-4:45pm.* **Tours:** *1½hr. themed ranger walks leave from Georgetown Visitor Center Sa-Su 12:15pm. Call ahead for details.* **Admission:** *Free, except at Great Falls entrance: $5 per vehicle, $3 per person without a vehicle. Ticket good for 3 days at both this park and at Great Falls Park in Virginia (see p. 110). Under 16 and disabled persons free. No swimming, wading, unleashed pets, or fires allowed.*

Construction of the **Chesapeake and Ohio Canal** began in 1828 with plans of a 360-mile commercial transportation route along the unnavigable Potomac River from Washington to the Ohio River. By 1850, though, the canal reached only Cumberland, Maryland, and the new Baltimore and Ohio Railroad was running alongside the canal and stealing its business. The C&O Canal Company gave up with only 184.5 miles of the canal completed. The railroad eventually bought the canal, and gave the land to the federal government in lieu of a substantial debt. Conservationists and historians fought a proposal to turn the canal into a roadway, and in 1971, the grounds were designated as a national historical park.

For the brief time when the canal was in use, boats were pulled by mules along 12-foot **towpaths** on each side of the canal. Today, hikers, runners, and bicyclists populate the towpaths, which range from smooth and level to rocky and uneven. (Avoid the towpaths altogether for two days after heavy rain.) Others explore the canal on **mule-drawn boat rides,** which feature tour guides in period costume who tell stories from the old days of the canal. 1hr. roundtrip rides leave from the Georgetown Visitors Center. (May-Oct. W-F 11am, 3pm; Sa-Su 11 am, 1:30, 3pm. Additional rides mid-June-Aug. W-F 1:30pm, Sa-Su 4:30pm. $8, seniors $6, children 4-14 $5.)

Portions of the canal are also open for non-motorized boating, though canoeists and kayakers must portage around each lock. **Swains Lock (Lock 21),** one of the canal's 74 original locks, was operated by the Swain family for years, and a descendant now runs **Swains Boathouse** (☎301-299-9006), which rents bicycles, kayaks, and canoes to visitors. For boating, see **Entertainment,** p. 192. Campgrounds are located along the canal from Swains Lock (mile 16.6) to Evitts Creek (mile 180.1).

In the heyday of the canal, over 100 ferries regularly crossed the Potomac River. Today, only **White's Ferry** remains, carrying cars and pedestrians between Dickerson, MD and Leesburg, VA. Confederate troops used the ferry during the Civil War, and in 1871, Confederate General E.V. White purchased and renamed the operation. (☎301-349-5200. Operates daily 5am-11pm. Cars $3 one-way, bikes $0.50.)

GLEN ECHO PARK

⚐ *Located in Glen Echo, MD.* **Directions:** *From D.C., take Massachusetts Ave. NW through Bethesda, MD until the road ends. Turn left onto Goldsboro Rd., and drive 0.4 mi. until the road ends. Turn right onto MacArthur Blvd. and make the 1st left onto Oxford Rd. The park is on the left.* **Metro:** *Friendship Heights. Take Montgomery County Bus #29.* **Contact:** *☎301-492-6229; www.glenechopark.org.* **Hours:** *Open daily 7am-1am. Park office open daily 9am-5pm.* **Tours:** *1hr. historic tours given by rangers Su 2pm.* **Admission:** *Free. Classes and activities usually require a fee.*

From 1899 to 1968, Glen Echo Park was a popular amusement park featuring a grand ballroom, rides, and a pool holding 3000 people. Today, under the management of the National Park Service, Glen Echo Park is a thriving arts center for children and adults alike. Artists in residence teach **classes** in everything from painting and sculpture to ballroom dancing and tai chi—all in old amusement park buildings. In a throwback to the park's heyday, **evening dances** (F

8:30pm, Sa 9pm, Su 7:30pm; $7-12) draw huge crowds to the Historic Spanish Ballroom to dance to live swing, contra, and big band music. Kids enjoy performances at the **Adventure Theatre** (☎ 301-320-5331; www.adventuretheatre.org) and **The Puppet Co.** (☎ 301-320-6668; www.thepuppetco.org), both based at Glen Echo. Most popular, the amusement park's original **Dentzel Carousel** still runs May-Sept. (W-Th 10am-2pm, F-Su noon-6pm) for just $0.50.

Museums

ON THE MALL

SMITHSONIAN MUSEUMS

⚑ The following information applies to all of the Smithsonian Museums on the Mall, but excludes the National Gallery of Art. Metro: Smithsonian, L'Enfant Plaza, Federal Triangle, or Judiciary Sq. **Contact:** ☎ 357-2700, TTY 357-1729 M-Sa 9am-4pm, 24hr. recorded information ☎ 357-2020; www.si.edu. **Hours:** Museums open daily 10am-5:30pm. Castle open daily 9am-5:30pm. There are special evening hours in the summer, but these vary from year to year. **Tours:** Recorded audio tours available at some museums (usually less than $5). The Museum Bus offers transportation among museums on the Mall and throughout D.C. with 1-day ticket for the 2hr. tour leaving every 15min. from outside the Castle ($16, children $7). Tickets can be bought on the bus. **Admission:** Free. **Accessibility:** Wheelchair accessible. Constitution or Independence Ave. entrances are easier for wheelchairs. **Events:** Frequent lectures and music; call for details. See **Entertainment,** p. 190. **Parking:** Free 3hr. parking on Jefferson and Madison Dr. Metered parking on surrounding streets. Parking is extremely difficult to find in this area.

A visit to the Smithsonian museums asks you to recall everything from biology class to television milestones. Though the Smithsonian displays only a portion of its holdings at any given time, there's still enough in the exhibits to offer more than anyone could see in a few days. The Institute was the brainchild of **James Smithson,** a British chemist who never visited the US but left 105 bags of gold sovereigns—the bulk of his estate—to "found at Washington, under the name of the Smithsonian Institution, an establishment for the increase and diffusion of knowledge among men." But

in recent
news

A NATIVE SPACE

D.C.'s newest museum will focus on the culture and heritage of the area's oldest residents—Native Americans. The museum's location, directly between the Air and Space Museum and the Capitol, on the last available space on the Mall, is symbolic of a reconciliation of sorts between native descendents and the government that displaced their ancestors.

The **National Museum of the American Indian (NMAI)** comes at the end of a long history. American art collector George Gustav Heye amassed a personal collection of nearly 1 million objects of Native American art that became the basis for the New York Museum of the American Indian. More than 3 decades after Heye's death in 1957, a 1989 act of Congress established the NMAI as the latest branch of the Smithsonian and transferred Heye's extensive collection to the Institution.

The NMAI, set to open sometime in 2004, will showcase items ranging from Caribbean artifacts to clothing from the American Plains, from Peruvian textiles to intricate carvings from the Pacific Northwest. For more info, see www.nmai.si.edu.

—David Dodman

Smithson is often given undue credit for his generosity. In all probability, Smithson didn't think his money would actually get to the New World. He gave the money only on the condition that the first beneficiary of his estate, his nephew, would inherit the money unless the nephew died without children. Fortunately for the US, the nephew died heirless within a few years of Smithson's death, and the Institution was officially established in 1846. For the first few decades, the institute focused on research, concentrating on the "increase of knowledge" more than its diffusion. The **Castle**, the large red brick Victorian Gothic building, was built to house both Smithson's zinc collection and the scientists who tended the growing collection of botanical and mineralogical specimens.

The Smithsonian is still a research institution, with facilities scattered from Boston to Nepal. The emphasis changed, however, after the **1876 Centennial Exposition in Philadelphia,** the first world's fair. Countries too poor to pay shipping costs to send their exhibits back donated their displays to the US. Consequently, Congress built the **Arts and Industries Building** to house the displays. Since then, Smithsonian directors have been relentlessly collecting objects of historical importance, as when Smithsonian directors telegraphed Charles Lindbergh for his plane while he was still celebrating his famous transatlantic flight in France. Twenty million tourists visit every year to see Rodin sculptures, dinosaurs, Dorothy's ruby slippers, and the Apollo XI capsule that brought Buzz Aldrin, Neil Armstrong, and Michael Collins back from space.

NATIONAL MUSEUM OF AMERICAN HISTORY

⚑ Location: *14th St. and Constitution Ave.* **Metro:** *Smithsonian or Federal Triangle.* **Contact:** *☎ 357-2700, TTY 357-1729; http://americanhistory.si.edu.* **Tours:** *Museum "highlight" tours are typically given daily at 10:15am and 1pm, but visitors are encouraged to check for times and meeting places at the front desk.* **Events:** *The museum hosts a variety of (mostly free) public events, including musical performances, films, and family programs. Check with the front desk or visit http://americanhistory.si.edu/events for the latest information.*

The National Museum of American History earned the entire institute the nickname "the nation's attic" because of the clutter of old goods from fiber-optic cable to harmonicas that reside here behind Plexiglas. The most unexpected American memorabilia is often the star attraction; the ruby slippers worn by Judy Garland in

The Wizard of Oz have toured and charmed the nation, while others fall under the spell of a Babe Ruth-autographed baseball. When the Smithsonian inherits a quirky artifact of popular culture, like Irving Berlin's piano or the giant glass bucket used in the D.C. Vietnam draft, the article finds its home at the museum, although only between 5-10% of the 140 million objects within the Smithsonian collection is on display at one time. Opened in 1964, the museum was named the National Museum of History and Technology until 1980, and a certain techno-focus remains evident in exhibits like "Information Age" and "Power Machinery." This museum attempts to ensure that even unflattering aspects of the American past are remembered—from the spread of slavery to the Watergate debacle.

The Star-Spangled Banner, the enormous flag that inspired Francis Scott Key to pen the words to America's national anthem on September 14, 1814, is currently undergoing an extensive renovation project that is the focus of an exhibit on the second floor. Visitors can see the enormous flag as it is being restored; displays recount the flag's varied history. (Guided tours of the exhibition Th 11am; the proejct can be followed online at http://americanhistory.si.edu/ssb.)

The American Presidency: A Glorious Burden, an exhibit unveiled in November 2000, features an amazing collection of presidential portraiture, clothing, artifacts, and sound-bites. Hear various presidents take the oath of office as you wind around a wall depicting the figures, photographs, advertisements, and music memorable from each leader's term. Highlights include digital interactive polls asking museum-goers to rate the most effective president and the most crucial role of the office, and the chance to stand behind the presidential podium and read an inaugural speech off a Teleprompter. Also of interest are the ankle and wrist irons used to confine Lincoln's assassin John Wilkes Booth and his nine co-conspirators, and a video of the Kennedy-Nixon Presidential Debate, in which Nixon refused to wear stage makeup and looked pale as death compared to the cool, poised Kennedy.

2004 will bring a new permanent exhibit entitled *America on the Move,* featuring displays on the role of various forms of transportation in the development of the nation. *The Price of Freedom,* an exhibit opening in November 2004, will be dedicated to the contributions and history of the United States Armed Forces.

NATIONAL MUSEUM OF NATURAL HISTORY

M ***Location:*** *10th St. and Constitution Ave.* ***Metro:*** *Smithsonian or Federal Triangle.* ***Contact:*** *☎357-2700; www.mnh.si.edu.* ***Tours:*** *Guided tours meet at rotunda M-Th 10:30am and 1:30pm, F 10:30am. No tours July-Aug.* ***IMAX Theater:*** *Screenings multiple times a day 10:20am-8pm. Tickets $7.50, seniors and children $6; "combo" tickets, good for 1 of 2+ shows per person, are $6 and $5 for seniors and children. Call ☎633-4629 or visit www.smithsonian.org/imax for the latest show information or to buy tickets.*

The National Museum of Natural History contains three crowded floors of rocks, animals, people, and gift shops. When the museum was conceived, "natural history" meant geology and biology; the rarely seen tag "and National Museum of Man" licensed its curators to add anthropology exhibits when the building opened in 1910. This museum's displays, selected from its 124 million possessions, range from not-changed-in-years to redone-last-year. The Hope Diamond and the dinosaurs continue to attract crowds, despite being permanent displays.

On the second floor, the breathtaking gem and jewelry exhibit also draws large crowds. Visitors eagerly line up to see the allegedly cursed **Hope Diamond,** mailed to the Smithsonian in 1958 for $145.29 (insured up to $1 million). At 45.52 carats, this rare blue diamond is less than half its original size when first found in India in the 17th century; nonetheless, it still evokes awe from within its rotating display. The discreet brown wrapper in which it arrived is on display at the **National Postal Museum** (see p. 130). At the rotunda end of the exhibit, the **Moon Rocks and Meteorites** display contains a fragment of rock older than the solar system (4.6 billion years) that a meteorite brought to Earth. Also on the second floor, the Orkin Insect Zoo provides entertaining ways to confront your fear of bugs.

National Air & Space Museum

Hope Diamond

Hirshhorn Museum

The new IMAX Theater screens films such as "Bugs!" and "T-Rex: Back to the Cretaceous." The most recent addition to the museum is the **Behring Hall of Mammals,** opened in November 2003, featuring displays on mammal evolution and adaptation to climactic changes.

NATIONAL AIR & SPACE MUSEUM

Location: *7th St. and Independence Ave.* **Contact:** *☎ 357-2700; www.nasm.edu.* **Tours:** *Free tours daily 10:30am and 1pm from the tour desk in the entrance gallery.* **IMAX:** *Films about every hr. 10:15am-6pm. Tickets $7.50, seniors and children $6. "Double feature" tickets (allowing admission to two IMAX shows on the same day) are $13, $10 for seniors and children; "combo" tickets (good for one IMAX show and the "Infinity Express" planetarium show) are $12, seniors and children $10. Call ☎ 633-4629 or 877-932-4629 daily 10am-5pm; tickets can also be purchased at the theater box office or online at www.smithsonian.org/ imax.* **Planetarium:** *Shows daily 10:30am-5pm, every 30min. Ticket prices are the same as for IMAX shows, with the exception of "double feature" tickets ($11, seniors and children $8), which combine a planetarium show and a lecture on "The Stars Tonight." Stand-alone lecture tickets $5. Tickets are available at the box office on the 2nd fl., near the Spirit of St. Louis, or by phone at ☎ 357-1686.*

The National Air and Space Museum is colossal in its expanse and scope. The individual exhibits themselves soar stories from foundation to rooftop: DC-3s loom over visitors while 80 ft. rockets balance in a pit that reaches from basement to skylight. Seven and a half million visitors come here annually, exceeding the attendance of any other museum.

Air and Space's best exhibits are, well, its biggest: the actual planes and crafts from all eras of flight. The **Wright brothers' biplane** in the entrance gallery looks fragile next to its younger kin, but its wings are made of spruce and ash covered with cloth, making it flexible and strong. **Charles Lindbergh's** transatlantic silver plane, the **Spirit of St. Louis,** hangs next to it. Planes and rockets congregate in the entrance, **Milestones of Flight** (Gallery 100), and **Space Race Hall** (Gallery 114), which includes a full-sized test vehicle for the **Hubble Space Telescope,** refitted to appear exactly as its identical counterpart does in space. Next to the Hubble is the copper-colored **Skylab Orbital Workshop** that would have been sent into space if the original **Skylab** program had continued; it was abandoned in 1974, and the original space station mostly burned up in reentry in 1979.

IMAX movies are shown on a five-story movie screen in the **Lockheed Martin Theater.** Three rotating films are screened, including the perennially popular *To Fly*, an aerial tour of America from balloons to spaceships, as well as *Space Station 3D*. The **Einstein Planetarium** houses a 70 ft. starry dome that is home to a number of productions, including "Infinity Express" and "The Stars Tonight," an exploration of constellations with a museum staff member.

Late 2003 brings several additions to the National Air and Space Museum. A new exhibit entitled "Wright Brothers & The Invention of the Aerial Age" will open at the current Smithsonian site in October, and an entirely new building at **Dulles International Airport** will open its doors to the public in December. The Dulles site will feature the prototype **NASA** space shuttle **Enterprise** and the American bomber plane **Enola Gay,** which made history by dropping the atomic bomb on Hiroshima, Japan. Also on display will be the **Air France Concorde** jet, which was the charter's first plane to offer supersonic, transatlantic service in 1976 and was recently donated to the Smithsonian upon its retirement in 2003.

HIRSHHORN MUSEUM & SCULPTURE GARDEN

If you're convinced that art ended with Picasso, avoid the Hirshhorn Museum and Sculpture Garden—home to the modern, postmodern, and post-postmodern.

MUSEUM

🗹 *Location: Independence Ave. between 7th and 9th St. SW. Contact:* ☎ 633-4674 *for general info, recorded info 633-1618, tour info and scheduling 633-3382; http://hirshhorn.si.edu.* **Hours:** *Museum open daily 10am-5:30pm; all of the Hirshhorn is open Th 10am-8pm from late June to late Aug.; check with the website or call to confirm extended hours. Tours: June-Aug. M-F noon, Sa-Su noon and 2pm; Sept.-May M-F 10:30am and noon, Sa-Su noon and 2pm; tours for groups and school groups, in foreign languages, and for disabled visitors are also available; call for information or to schedule a tour. Events: Many free public programs are available, including films, concerts, and talks by artists and art experts; call or check online for the most up-to-date information.*

Built around immigrant philanthropist Joseph Hirshhorn's gifts, the museum still carries the flavor of personal preference rather than institutional design. Each floor consists of two concentric circles: the outer ring of rooms and paintings holds works by artists such as **Alexander Calder, Willem de Kooning,** and **Georgia O'Keeffe,** while the inner corridor features one of the world's most comprehensive sets of 19th- and 20th-century Western sculpture, including small works by **Rodin** and **Giacometti.** The collection also includes pieces by **Renoir, Degas, Matisse, Gauguin,** and **Picasso,** which are not always on display, as holdings rotate about every six months.

Don't miss **Sam Richardson**'s 1969 *"16 Views of the Northwest Corner of the Northwest Section of that Guy's Land,"* in which a sculptural depiction of a farm landscape is divided along a grid into 16 equal, square sections, each encased in its own clear plastic box. Also worth a look is the room of entirely black and white paintings, including **Ad Reinhardt's** 1956 *"Abstract Painting,"* in which the canvas has been painted solid black. A series of large windows from a 3rd floor room in the outer ring features a striking view of the National Mall, while the lower level houses the amazingly lifelike (and larger-than-life) *"Untitled"* (or *"Big Man"*) by **Ron Mueck.**

2004 will bring to the Hirshhorn temporary exhibitions featuring the works of Scottish artist **Douglas Gordon,** the audio creations of **Janet Cardiff,** and the color photography of **Gabriel Orozco.**

SCULPTURE GARDEN

🗹 *Location: Across Jefferson Dr. Hours: Plaza open daily 7:30am-5:30pm; sculpture garden open daily 7:30am-dusk. Tours: June-Aug. M-Sa 10:30am. May and Sept.-Oct. M-Sa 12:15pm.*

Outdoor sculpture shines in the courtyard plaza of the museum, where aluminum, steel, bronze, and silver creations from the 1880s to the 1960s line the stony pavement. The fountain in the center opening of the museum building is also striking.

Across Jefferson Dr., the sculpture garden, opened in 1974, continues its sunken display of impressive works by **Rodin, Aristide Maillol, Matisse,** and others. The most exuberant item in the outdoor collection is **Mark di Suervo's** 1967 "Are Years What?," (located to the left of the garden with your back to the Hirschorn) which, with its cherry-red-painted steel beams, has a dominating presence over the grounds.

ARTS & INDUSTRIES BUILDING

🚩 *Location:* 900 Jefferson Dr. SW., between the Smithsonian Castle and Haupt Garden and the Hirshhorn Museum. *Contact:* www.si.edu/ai. *Events:* Discovery Theater performances for children.

This large red-brick Victorian building opened in 1881 to celebrate President James A. Garfield's inauguration and became the original home of the National Museum from which the Smithsonian sprang. An exhibit DNA, reproduction, and the future possibilities of genome research, entitled "Genome: The Secret of How Life Works," will be on display through early January **2004** (see http://genome.pfizer.com for more info). Perhaps the most noteworthy aspect of Arts and Industries is its architecture: four main exhibition halls filled with natural light and not divided by any continuous wall. Stop in for a quick look, then head to more interesting museums.

AFRICAN ART & SACKLER GALLERY COMPLEX

Built in 1987, the National Museum of African Art and the Sackler Gallery hide their treasures underground, behind the castle and below the beautifully landscaped, four-acre **Enid A. Haupt Garden.** The garden's main entrance faces Independence Ave. and L'Enfant Plaza, although there are also paths leading from the Mall on either side of the Castle. Both museums have two underground exhibit levels that connect, three stories down, to the **S. Dillon Ripley Center's International Gallery.** The museums access the outside world through paired postmodern pavilions in the Haupt Garden; facing the castle with Independence to your back, the Sackler entrance is on the left and the African entrance on the right. Halls connect the Sackler, the African Art Museum, and the **Freer Gallery.**

NATIONAL MUSEUM OF AFRICAN ART

🚩 *Location:* 950 Independence Ave., SW. *Contact:* ☎ 357-4600 M-F, 357-2700 Sa-Su; www.nmafa.si.edu. *Hours:* Daily 10am-5:30pm; hours are often extended Th in the summer; call for specific details. *Tours:* Daily 11am and 1pm; call to confirm tour times. *Events:* The museum sponsors a series of public programs, including films and activities for children; check the front desk or the website for the latest calendar.

The National Museum of African Art collects, catalogues, and displays artifacts from sub-Saharan Africa, where texture, color, and form regularly play a large role in even the simplest of everyday objects. In addition to its pieces by contemporary African artists, the museum is known in particular for its beautiful collection of metalwork from Benin, some of which is on permanent display in the exhibition entitled "Kerma & Benin: Two Ancient African Cities." A collection of 19th and 20th century tribal art includes many ornate wooden sculptures and masks from various regions of the African continent.

ARTHUR M. SACKLER GALLERY

🚩 *Location:* 1050 Independence Ave. SW. *Contact:* ☎ 633-4880, tours 633-0467, TTY ☎ 786-2374; asiainfo@asia.si.edu; www.asia.si.edu. *Hours:* Daily 10am-5:30pm; hours often extended on certain days in the summer; call for specific details. Visitor's Desk closes daily 4pm. *Tours:* Free tours Th-Tu 12:15pm. *Events:* The Sackler, along with the Freer, sponsors a series of film festivals, musical and storytelling performances, and lectures and talks with experts and artists.

Together with the Freer Gallery, the Arthur M. Sackler Gallery forms the National Museum of Asian Art. The Sackler Gallery showcases Sackler's extensive collection of art from China, Southeast Asia, and Persia. Illuminated manuscripts, Chinese and Japanese paintings from many centuries, carvings and friezes from the Middle East,

Hindu gods, jade miniatures, and other works repose in low light and air-conditioned majesty. The Sackler's permanent displays are noteworthy in and of themselves, especially the stunning vessels carved out of rhinoceros horn—look for the lotus bouquet cup supported by intricately detailed plant stems. The simian and bizarre collide in "Monkeys Grasp for the Moon," a sculpture consisting of representations of the word "monkey" in 20 different languages, including English, Afrikaans, Turkish, Chinese, and even Braille. The words are interconnected along the light-filled, open atrium of the museum and stretch the multiple stories from the bottom basement level to the entrance level ceiling.

The monthly ImaginAsia program leads kids (ages 6-14) through a particular exhibit, after which kids create their own related works of art. The **Sackler Library** (☎ 633-0477; closes at 5pm), on the second level, is open to the public.

2004 brings to the Sackler the temporary exhibitions "Himalayas: An Aesthetic Adventure" (through Jan.), "Love and Yearning: Mystical and Moral Themes in Persian Poetry and Painting" (through Feb.), and "Faith and Form: Selected Calligraphy and Painting from Japanese Religious Traditions" (mid-Mar. to mid-June).

National Gallery of Art

FREER GALLERY

🔲 *Location: Jefferson Dr. and 12th St., SW. Contact:* ☎ *633-4880, tours 633-0467, TTY 786-2374; asiainfo@asia.si.edu; www.asia.si.edu. Hours: Daily 10am-5:30pm; hours are often extended on certain days in the summer; call for specific details. Visitor's desk closes 4pm daily. Tours: Free tours Th-Tu 12:15pm. There are also seasonal and exhibition-based tours given; check with the front desk for the latest schedule. Group tours, tours in foreign languages, and tours for the visually or hearing disabled can be arranged. Email asiatours@asia.si.edu or call the tours number for more info or to schedule a tour. Events: The Freer, along with the Sackler, sponsors a series of public events, including film festivals, musical and storytelling performances, as well as lectures and talks with experts and artists. Check the front desk for the latest calendar.*

Is a chair ever just a chair?

Small compared to other Smithsonian buildings, the Freer Gallery displays both Asian and American art, the outgrowth of railway car manufacturer **Charles L. Freer's** personal holdings. Freer was **James Whistler's** main sponsor and donated his collection with the stipulation that the institution could not add American art, nor could any of the collection travel. The result is a museum whose Asian art exhibits change and grow, and whose static American art collection consists largely of Whistlers.

US Holocaust Museum

121

A sequence of connected galleries surrounds an elegant courtyard and leads visitors past the American art to the Japanese, Korean, Chinese, Buddhist, South Asian, and Islamic works. The Egyptian collection in Gallery 16 consists of pieces which Freer acquired during his visits to Cairo art collectors and dealers; be sure to look for selections from over 1400 glass vessels and fragments, brightly striped in hues of blue, yellow, and green and dating as far back as 1550 BC. The next room (Gallery 17) houses a series of ornate, carved stone reliefs from the Chinese Buddhist cave and cliff temples of Xiangtangshan; traces of what was once bright paint coloring can still be seen on the rock face. Also of note are the monstrous wooden statues guarding either side of the main hall: the Ni-O kings, acquired from alcoves within the entrance of a Sakai temple. Don't miss Whistler's **Peacock Room,** with its walls of deep blue and gold and the ceiling painted to mimic peacock tails. The fully reassembled dining room, which Whistler decorated for an English shipping magnate, is now permanently installed in the Freer Gallery.

Temporary exhibitions in **2004** include "Mr. Whistler's Galleries: The Art of Displaying Art."

NATIONAL GALLERY OF ART

⛿ Location: *Constitution Ave. between 3rd and 9th St.* **Contact:** *☎ 737-4215, TDD 842-6176; www.nga.gov.* **Hours:** *M-Sa 10am-5pm, Su 11am-6pm.* **Tours:** *A variety of free guided tours and foreign-language tours are available; check with the calendar, available at the information desks, for the latest times. Self-guided, audiotape Director's Tours and audio tours for temporary exhibitions $6, students, seniors, and groups $5.* **Admission:** *Free.* **Events:** *In addition to tours, the museum also offers gallery talks, lectures, films, family programs, free classical music concerts, and other events. Schedules are available at the information desks, ☎ 842-6941. Concerts Oct.-June Su 7pm. Most events are free, but seating is limited.* **Accessibility:** *Wheelchair accessible.*

The National Gallery was conceived, proposed, financed, and named by financier **Andrew Mellon,** who realized that other collectors would be more likely to donate to a gallery if it didn't bear his name. His plan succeeded, and the current collection is an impressively encyclopedic summary of the Western tradition. Walking from the West Building to the East offers a chronological tour of European art. The West Building, the gallery's original home, contains masterpieces by such famous folks as Fra Angelico, Leonardo da Vinci, El Greco, Raphael, Rembrandt, Vermeer, and Monet, among many others. The gallery's newer addition, the East Building, is devoted to 20th-century art, with everyone from Magritte and Matisse to Man Ray and Miró, just to mention the "M"s. Together, the two buildings and the neighboring sculpture garden make up North America's most popular art museum, with six million visitors annually.

WEST BUILDING

The traditional bent of this building, opened in 1941, was written into its charter: for its first few decades, the National Gallery only accepted works by artists who had been dead at least 20 years. At last they received an offer of Modernism too good to let go, and the policy was adjusted. The collection is still far from experimental, however. Both entrances to the West Building lead to the domed rotunda, where black marble pillars and a fountain encircle a 16th-century Italian sculpture of the god Mercury. Hallways decorated with sculptures lead right (east) and left (west) from the Mall entrance to the exhibition rooms. Next to the rotunda information desk, the **Micro Gallery** invites museum-goers to look up words in the "talking dictionary" of fine arts terminology or design their own personal tour maps using touch-sensitive screens.

Dutch masters are another main attraction here. Three of the world's 32 **Vermeers** are here; Vermeer, who painted slowly and refused to sell his works, captures perfect moments of silence in his small canvases. **Rembrandt,** arguably the most well-known of the Dutch painters, is represented by a a room full of self-portraits, as well as *The Mill*, a landscape that influenced later British artists. A good number of **Peter Paul Rubens's** works are shown here, including paintings of his second wife and of the affluent and powerful in his day. Keep an eye out for *Daniel in the Lion's Den*, a dramatic Baroque rendition of the Biblical tale, in which life-size lions in various states of sleeping and wakefulness (as well as the bones of less fortunate visitors) encircle the Old Testament prophet, in Gallery 45.

One floor below, visitors can browse through the newly-renovated permanent sculpture gallery, which contains an extensive collection of three-dimensional works from such greats as **Rodin** and **Degas.** Among the collection is Rodin's famous 1880 *"The Thinker,"* as well as his 1889 *"The Burghers of Calais"* and also a 1909 bust of composer Gustav Mahler. The Degas works here represent the world's largest single exhibition of the artist's original sculptures in the entire world.

The nearby **Widener Room** contains wood paneling, wood floors, paintings, and mirrors typical of the 18th century rococo style. The paneling here was at one time installed in the dining room of Mrs. A. Hamilton Rice, whose husband, George D. Widener, died on the Titanic in 1912; this room is named after him. Look above the room's mirrors to find playful works by **Christophe Huet,** in which monkeys replace humans in the depiction of human activities (a form called *"singerie"*).

Salvador Dali's *Last Supper* bridges the ancient and modern, hung in the turn of the stairway between the first floor of the West Building and the underground concourse leading to the East Building. The concourse has a moving sidewalk that takes you to the entrance hall of the East Building.

EAST BUILDING

Completed in 1978, the East Building contains much of the museum's 20th-century collection. **Alexander Calder** designed the 992lb. mobile *Untitled* expressly for this space, which explains why it comes so close to hitting the wall next to the info desk. In fact, Calder originally wanted his moving sculpture to strike the wall each time it completed a revolution, but the museum's designers wisely rejected his plan.

On the entrance level, just to the left of the main entrance, visitors can see the recently opened collection of French impressionist paintings, a selection from the art holdings of the Mellon family. Painters represented here include **Edgar Degas, Henri Matisse, Edouard Manet** and **Claude Monet;** Monet's 1873 *"Ships Riding on the Seine at Rouen"* is particularly striking. Also worth a peek on the entrance level is a temporary exhibition on the 25th anniversary of the

Squished Pennies

This museum is far from the mammoth-sized marble structures on the Mall. **The Squished Penny Museum,** 416 T St. NW (☎986-5644; www.squished.com. Metro: Shaw/U St. By appointment only.) doesn't even have its own building—instead, the entire operation is run out of the quirky curator's living room.

This is not to say that the Squished Penny Museum is not an authentic museum. The collection of over 250 squished pennies are from tourist spots around the country, from The Trees of Mystery in Kalmath, CA to Graceland in Memphis, TN. The current exhibit, The Open Road, includes copper from shops, aquariums, towers, small towns, and zoos.

The museum has one of the original squished pennies, a souvenir from the Columbian Exposition of 1893. The penny is created when a special machine puts it through a pair of hardened steel dies, one or both of which is engraved with a design. The penny is then squished between these dies with 22 tons of pressure, impressing the design upon the coin.

This collection may not be of Smithsonian caliber, but a visit to the Squished Penny Museum is still free.

East Building that will run through June 1, **2004**. The displays here detail the building's history and design and include photographs of its opening ceremonies in 1978. Visitors can also see a 1971 scale model of architect **I.M. Pei's** original design for the structure, whose plan for the courtyard between the East and West Buildings was revised before construction.

The underground (concourse) level houses 20th century art, an extensive collection of modern works featuring the creations of **Mark Rothko, Jackson Pollock,** and many others. **Barnett Newman's** abstract *"The Stations of the Cross,"* depicts the 14 events of Christ's torture and death in a series of 14 canvases painted in varying combinations of tan and grayscale colors. **Andy Warhol's** attraction to pop culture can also be seen here, particularly in the painting *"200 Campbell's Soup Cans,"* in which the title matches exactly what appears on the canvas. Look closely, and notice that each can is a different kind of soup. Warhol's *Self Portrait* hangs in a small alcove on the mezzanine level.

SCULPTURE GARDEN

At the 7th St. and Constitution Ave. NW end of the museum is the six-acre National Gallery of Art **Sculpture Garden,** opened in the spring of 1999. The garden features a Top 40-variety of the famous outdoor sculptors, whose works are arranged around a large circular fountain, where large jets of water converge in its center. The sculpture pieces themselves are often whimsical to the point of a practical joke. **Roy Lichtenstein's** *House I*, whose bright colors seem taken directly out of a comic book, consistantly tricks first-time visitors with its clever optical illusion, while **Hector Guimard's** *Entrance to the Metropolitain* leads nowhere in particular—certainly not to the Parisian metro as any French tourist would expect. Other fun works include the looming *Typewriter Eraser* by husband and wife team **Claes Oldenburg** and **Coosje van Bruggen,** as well as the six stone chairs of **Scott Burton's** *Rock Settee,* the only sculpture in the Gallery's collection to actually invite visitors to sit upon it.

On the more serious side is **Magdalena Abakanowicz's** *Puellae* (or *Girls*), in which a series of bronze, hollow statues of headless girls is meant to be a statement against the evils of totalitarianism. The somewhat disturbing statues can be found hidden in the cool shade of the trees on one side of the garden's fountain.

In addition to all of its sculpture, the garden also hosts the **Jazz in the Garden** program, in which weekly (free) jazz concerts are held on Fridays from Memorial Day to Labor Day. The concerts are given either in front of the garden's fountain or in the Pavilion Cafe; opening hours are extended on these evenings until 9pm.

OFF THE MALL

MARY MCLEOD BETHUNE COUNCIL HOUSE

🚩 *Location: 1318 Vermont Ave. NW, in Farragut. **Metro:** McPherson Square; from the 14th St. exit, proceed along 14th St. past Franklin Sq., bearing right onto Vermont Ave. at Thomas Circle; the museum is 2 blocks down on the left. **Contact:** ☎ 673-2402; www.nps.gov/mamc. **Hours:** M-Sa 9am-5pm, tours given 10am-4pm. **Admission:** Free. **Tours:** 1hr. guided tours for individuals and smaller groups can be given on demand. Tours for large groups (minimum 10 people) must be arranged in advance. **Events:** On July 10, the museum hosts a birthday celebration for Mary McLeod Bethune in Lincoln Park. The Christmas season brings an annual candlelight house tour. Other events include lectures, discussions with historians, and book signings.*

This testament to the participation of black women in American history commemorates the life of educator and pioneer civil rights and women's rights activist **Mary McLeod Bethune.** Born in 1875 and one of 17 children in a family of former slaves, Bethune grew up to become co-founder of the Bethune-Cookman College in Florida, head of the federal government's Division of Negro Affairs, and founder of the **National Council of Negro Women (NCNW).** The museum, located in the NCNW's former headquarters (from 1943-1966) and Bethune's former residence, chronicles her achievements with a 25 min. video and a series of exhibits describing Bethune's life and the NCNW. Also in residence is the extensive **National Archives for Black Women's History,** the largest repository solely dedicated to the collection and preservation of materials relating to African-American women.

B'NAI B'RITH KLUTZNICK NATIONAL JEWISH MUSEUM

Fl Location: *2020 K St. NW, between 20th and 21st St., in Farragut.* **Metro:** *Farragut West, Foggy Bottom-GWU, or Farragut North.* **Contact:** *☎857-6583; www.bbinet.org.* **Hours:** *M-Th noon-3pm, except federal and all Jewish holidays. Museum admission by advance appointment only.* **Admission:** *Suggested donation $3.* **Accessibility:** *Wheelchair accessible.*

A collection of Jewish cultural and ritual objects comprises the bulk of this museum dedicated to the exploration of Jewish life and tradition. Original copies of the correspondence between George Washington and Moses Seixas (the sexton of the Touro Synagogue in Newport, Rhode Island) contain the first written statement of America's commitment to religious and ethnic toleration. **Stars of David** is a new room that offers tribute to Jews in the world of sports; exhibits rotate every few months. The museum continues to add to their collection by Jewish artists from the last 150 years, including Pissarro and Chagall.

CAPITAL CHILDREN'S MUSEUM

Fl Location: *800 3rd St. NE, enter on 3rd St. between H and I St. NE.* **Metro:** *Union Station.* **Contact:** *☎675-4120; www.ccm.org.* **Hours:** *Memorial Day to Labor Day daily 10am-5pm, Labor Day to Memorial Day Tu-Su 10am-5pm.* **Admission:** *$7; AAA $6, seniors $5, children under 2 free. All children must be accompanied by an adult.* **Events:** *Craft activities every Sa-Su noon-3pm; call for details. "Scienterrific Sundays" hands-on experiments.* **Accessibility:** *Wheelchair accessible.*

This huge, interactive museum is the ultimate escape from glass-encased artifacts. Visitors can brew hot chocolate, roll tortillas, and weave ponchos in a two-story mock-up of life in **Mexico,** one of the museum's most popular exhibits. Demonstrations in the chemist-staffed laboratory teach science basics and allow children to perform experiments of their own. Also popular is the bubble laboratory, in which kids can experiment with suds of all sizes.

CORCORAN GALLERY OF ART

Fl Location: *500 17th St. NW, at the corner with New York Ave., in Foggy Bottom.* **Metro:** *Farragut West or Farragut North.* **Contact:** *☎639-1700; www.corcoran.org.* **Hours:** *W and F-M 10am-5pm, Th 10am-9pm.* **Tours:** *Free tours M and W-F noon, Sa-Su 2:30pm.* **Admission:** *$5, seniors $3, students $1, family pass $8, children under 12 free. General admission is free all day M and Th after 5pm. Special exhibits additional.* **Events:** *Visiting artists, lectures, and concerts, including a free jazz series and a weekly Gospel brunch (Su 10:30am-2pm in the Corcoran Cafe).* **Accessibility:** *Wheelchair access at E St. entrance.*

Founded in 1869, the Corcoran is the oldest art museum in the US and is fittingly home to one of the largest collections of American art in the world. Highlights include **Alfred Bierstadt's** powerful, panoramic paintings *The Last of the Buffalo* and *Mount Corcoran,* which was named in an attempt to sell it to the museum. The colonial and pre-Civil War collections include **Gilbert Stuart's** famous portrait of **George Washington** (found on the $1 bill), a silver teapot made by Revolutionary figure **Paul Revere,** and the large painting *The House of Representatives* by **Samuel F. B. Morse,** the same Morse after whom the famous dots-and-dashes code is named. His failure as an artist, including the commercial flop of *The House of Representatives,* led Morse to other interests, including science and, eventually, the telegraph.

Don't miss the **Salon Doré,** an early neoclassical French room, originally found in the Parisian Hotel de Clermont, that was sold en masse to Senator William A. Clark and then given to the museum in 1926. The room features large mirrors, crimson-colored drapes, a ceiling mural, and plenty of gold leaf. In addition, the Corcoran

Gallery K

Dumbarton Oaks

Corcoran Gallery

houses a fine selection of modern and contemporary American art, displaying such greats as de Kooning and Kelly, as well as works from the affiliated Corcoran *College of Art + Design*.

2004 exhibitions include *The Quilts of Gee's Bend*, a display of quiltwork from an isolated artist community in Alabama and "American Falls: Video Installation by Philip Solomon," which will involve a series of video and image projections onto the gallery's Rotunda.

The most exciting project in the Corcoran's near future, however, is a grand renovation and construction project for the gallery itself. An entirely new wing, designed by acclaimed California architect **Frank Gehry,** will more than double the current exhibition space. A striking, shiny outer facade of stainless steel will lead into an open, 130ft. atrium, criss-crossed with suspended, mid-air walkways connecting the three new floors of gallery space.

DUMBARTON OAKS

🏛 **Location:** *1703 32nd St. NW, in Georgetown.* **Contact:** *Recorded info* ☎ *339-6401, tour info 339-6409; DumbartonOaks@doaks.org; www.doaks.org.* **Hours:** *Tu-Su 2-5pm.* **Admission:** *Free; suggested donation $1.* **Note:** *No parking on site.*

Built by **Robert** and **Mildred Bliss** in the Dumbarton Oaks Mansion (see **Sights,** p. 80), this fine museum houses superbly documented exhibits focusing on Byzantine and pre-Columbian art. The **Byzantine Collection** contains mosaics, bronzes, and jewelry, mostly from the Byzantine Empire, but also Coptic (Egyptian Christian) art. One of the foremost Byzantine collections in the world, it showcases exquisite jewelry, ivories, and textiles. The museum also includes later works, such as a 13th-century icon of St. Peter.

Between the Byzantine and pre-Columbian galleries is the **Music Room,** added to the mansion in 1929, where **El Greco's** Mannerist painting *The Visitation* disrupts the otherwise flawless Renaissance decor. The furniture, paintings, tapestries, and sculpture span the 13th to 17th centuries. The painted wooden ceiling is modeled after a similar one in the Salle des Gardes of the Chateau de Cheverny, a 16th-century castle in the Loire Valley in France. Igor Stravinsky's **Dumbarton Oaks Concerto** premiered here for the Blisses' 30th wedding anniversary in 1938; today, the room is used for lectures and concerts. Every year, the Dumbarton Oaks Friends of Music welcomes world-renowned musical artists to perform. The 2003 season marked 25 years of music at Dumbarton. The 2004 season, lasting Oct. 11, 2003-Apr. 3, 2004, includes 9 performances (tickets $28). For concert schedules and ticket information, call ☎ 339-6400 or visit www.dumbartonconcerts.org.

HILLWOOD MUSEUM & GARDENS

🏠 *Location:* 4155 Linnean Ave. NW, in Upper Northwest, 10min. down Tilden St. off Connecticut Ave. *Metro:* Van Ness. Take the L1 or L2 bus down Connecticut Ave. to Tilden St., and follow Tilden toward Rock Creek Park; Linnean Ave. is on the left. *Contact:* ☎ 686-8500; www.hillwoodmuseum.org. *Hours:* By reservation only, Tu-Sa 9am-5pm. Closed Feb. Reservation deposit $10, seniors 65+ $8, students and children under 18 $5.

Once the mansion of General Foods heiress Marjorie Meriweather Post, Hillwood is now a museum displaying her collection of Russian art and French antique furnishings. She and her ambassador husband lived in Russia for a year in the late 1930s, just when the Communists were selling most of the treasures seized from the aristocracy during the Revolution. Inspired, Post amassed a collection, claimed to be the largest outside of Russia, featuring decorative arts and coins, as well as a number of Fabergé eggs (extremely ornate and bejeweled "eggs" exchanged as Easter presents among the Russian imperial family). Outside, 25 acres of gardens replicate the landscaping of England, Japan, and 19th-century Russia.

US HOLOCAUST MEMORIAL MUSEUM

🏠 *Location:* 14th St. between C St. and Independence Ave. SW. *Metro:* Smithsonian. *Contact:* ☎ 488-0400; www.ushmm.org. *Hours:* Daily 10am-5:30pm, arrive early to obtain timed tickets to permanent exhibits at the front desk. *Note:* Due to the graphic content of the permanent exhibitions, the museum recommends that parents not bring children under 11. Younger children can tour the exhibition "Daniel's Story," an account of Nazi occupation from a child's perspective.

Opened in 1993, this privately-funded museum reflects the atrocities of the Holocaust even in its architecture: a twisted skylight—symbolic of the chaos of ghettos, rail cars, and concentration camps—distorts the layout of the atrium (named **The Hall of Witness**), while exposed barriers represent the deception of the Nazis.

Special exhibitions, which can be viewed without passes, include **The Wall of Remembrance,** a touching collection of tiles painted by American schoolchildren in memory of the 1.5 million children killed during the Holocaust, and the orientation film shown daily at 15 and 45min. past the hour from 10:15am to 4:15pm. The permanent gallery is divided into three floors beginning with the Nazi occupation of Poland, continuing with the Holocaust, and ending with the aftermath of the war and moving videotaped recollections of Holocaust survivors. Exhibits include photographs, Nazi propaganda, personal effects of Jewish victims, and tapes of Hitler's speeches. The glass bridges connecting the gallery rooms are etched with the names of perished Jewish communities. Highlights include a cobblestone pathway from a Warsaw ghetto and actual bunks from the Birkenau concentration camp.

INTERNATIONAL SPY MUSEUM

🏠 *Location:* 800 F St. NW, at 9th St. *Metro:* 1 block from Gallery Place-Chinatown. *Contact:* ☎ 393-7798; www.spymuseum.org. *Hours:* Apr.-Oct. open daily 10am-8pm (last admission at 7pm), Nov.-Mar. 10am-6pm (last admission at 5pm). *Tours:* Call to arrange a group tour at a discount. *Admission:* $13; seniors and military $12, children $10, under 5 free.

Opened in 2002, Washington's newest museum is the culmination of more than seven years of work and planning by some of the nation's foremost experts and practitioners in the intelligence community. The museum is housed in a block of five buildings, of which the Atlas Building served as headquarters for the D.C. division of the US Communist Party during the 1940s. From the glowing neon lighting in the elevators to the movie-set like backdrops in some of the historical exhibits, the museum

oh!' amour

First Lady Love

I wasn't expecting to find romance when I came to DC some many weeks ago, but alas, I found her impossible to resist. Being in a big city, I was sure I would never see her again after the first time our eyes met. But there she was at the museum, again at the art gallery, and yet again at the Kennedy Center. So beautiful, so graceful, so sophisticated. That is how my love for Jackie Kennedy Onasis blossomed.

I was in luck, because the summer of 2002 turned out to be "Celebrate Jackie O. Season." She was everywhere, from the Corcoran Gallery of Art where her clothes were on display, to the Farragut McDonald's where they decorated the upstairs dining area with Mrs. Kennedy posters. I was even living a minute from the Jacquelyn Kennedy Onasis dorm on GWU's campus.

Oh, Jackie. What I wouldn't give to have known you in your college days at GWU. I went to the Museum of American History just so I could see you, the foxiest of the First Ladies.

My infatuation, I suppose, showed me just how much D.C. loves Jackie. No matter how many years pass since Camelot, she still has the city under her spell.

- Hollin Kretzmann

can feel a bit campy, but it offers unparalleled insight into the world of espionage.

The first exhibit area, **School for Spies,** explains the various skills required in a top spy, detailing the training and recruiting process. This is where visitors will find high-tech spy gadgets like the lipstick pistol (used by KGB agents during the Cold War era) and tiny hidden cameras. The following three exhibits deal with the history of the field. **The Secret History of History** traces the history of spying back to its earliest known origins in Biblical times and addresses women in the field as well (among them, Mata Hari, the infamous exotic dancer turned spy in World War I). In **Spies Among Us,** the backdrop shifts to World War II; one of the more fascinating parts of this exhibit is a hallway describing various blunders that led to the Pearl Harbor attack. But perhaps the most compelling segment is **War of the Spies,** which places visitors in divided Berlin to explore the use of espionage during the Cold War. The last exhibit addresses the challenges of 21st-century espionage.

KREEGER MUSEUM OF ART

🖪 *Location:* 2401 Foxhall Rd. NW, in Upper Northwest. *Minimally accessible by public transportation. The D6 bus from Dupont Circle runs to the corner of Reservoir and Foxhall Rd.; walk uphill ½ mi. on Foxhall.* *Contact:* ☎ 337-3050; www.kreegermuseum.com. *Hours:* Admission by pre-booked tour only Tu-F 10:30am and 1:30pm, Sa 10:30am. No reservations required for "Open Hours" Sa 1-4pm, which includes a 2pm tour. For reservations call ☎ 338-3552 or email visitorservices@kreegermuseum.com with your name, phone number, number in your party, and desired date and time. *Admission:* Suggested donation $8, students and seniors (65+) $5. Children under 12 only allowed during "Open Hours."

The late great violinist Isaac Stern claimed that David Lloyd Kreeger single-handedly transformed Washington into the cultural center it is today. Through their magnanimous gifts and tireless efforts, Kreeger and his wife, Carmen, were instrumental in promoting the arts in D.C., and the Kreeger name is prominently displayed on buildings around the city as witness to their philanthropy. Throughout his lifetime, the GEICO insurance magnate amassed one of the most impressive private art collections in the world, including nearly 180 works by the most crucial figures in Western art (including Monet, Cézanne, and Miró). The Picassos on display span the Spaniard's entire career and include one painting from Gertrude Stein's personal collection. The African art collection is small but impressive, as is their sculpture garden which also features modern works by local artists.

The museum, which was Kreeger's personal residence until his death, also holds architectural significance. Philip Johnson, well known for his work with MoMA and the Lincoln Center, both in New York City, completed the building in 1967. In addition to his passion for the visual arts, Kreeger was also an avid amateur violinist and pianist, and acoustic factors were taken into design of the Great Hall, which has been graced by such performing greats as Isaac Stern, Pablo Casals, and the Cleveland Quartet for various charitable events. Music today is an integral part of the Kreeger Museum's identity, and it holds an annual concert series featuring world-renowned string quartets, as well as master classes for local musicians.

MARINE CORPS HISTORICAL MUSEUM

Location: Navy Yard, in SE Capitol Hill. **Metro:** Eastern Market or Navy Yard. **Contact:** ☎ 433-3534; www.history.usmc.mil. **Hours:** M, W-Th, and Sa 10am-4pm; F 10am-8pm. **Admission:** Free.

The Marine Corps Historical Museum, in **Building 58** at the Navy Yard (see p. 91), marches through Marine Corps history from the American Revolution to the present. Twenty exhibit cases arranged in a circular exhibition space offer a startling surreal summation of the actions, guns, uniforms, and swords of Marines. Highlights of the museum include the actual flags (complete with bullet holes) that were raised atop Mt. Suribachi in **Iwo Jima,** inspiring the memorial in Arlington. The austerity of the diorama-like displays of uniforms and artillery is shattered by an amazingly loud, interactive video kiosk with two short films.

NATIONAL BUILDING MUSEUM

Location: 401 F St. NW, in Old Downtown. Across the street from the National Law Enforcement Memorial. **Metro:** Judiciary Sq. **Contact:** ☎ 272-2448; www.nbm.org. **Hours:** M-Sa 10am-5pm, Su 11am-5pm. **Tours:** 45min. M-W 12:30pm; Th-Sa 11:30am, 12:30, 1:30pm; Su 12:30, 1:30pm. **Admission:** Suggested donation $5. **Events:** Lectures, films, and concerts; call or see website for details. **Accessibility:** Excellent disabled access, including assistance for the visually impaired.

Architect Montgomery Meigs's National Building Museum is an ode to enormity. Its **Great Hall** is 316 ft. long, 116 ft. wide, and 159 ft. high—big enough to swallow a 15-story building. Its 75 ft. Corinthian columns are among the world's largest (and cheapest). They're made of brick painted with 4000 gallons of rose paint, giving the columns a marble appearance without marble's cost. The museum's exhibits, tucked below office space around the Great Hall, honor American achievements in urban planning, construction, and design. **2004** Exhibitions include *Up, Down, Across: Elevators, Escalators, and Moving Sidewalks* (Sept. 12, 2003-Apr. 18, 2004) and *Liquid Stone: New Architecture in Concrete* (June 19, 2004-Jan. 23, 2005).

NATIONAL MUSEUM OF WOMEN IN THE ARTS

Location: 1250 New York Ave. NW. **Metro:** Metro Center. **Contact:** ☎ 783-5000; www.nmwa.org. **Hours:** M-Sa 10am-5pm, Su noon-5pm. **Admission:** $5-8, 60+ and students $3-6, members and 18 and under free. Free admission on 1st W and Su of each month.

Located in the former Masonic Grand Lodge, this museum is the only one in the world dedicated solely to the celebration of achievements of women in the visual, performing, and literary arts from the 16th century to the present. Founded by art collectors Wilhelmina and Wallace Holladay, the museum displays paintings, illustrations, and sculptures done by women artists such as Mary Cassatt, Georgia O'Keeffe, and Frida Kahlo. Look for Ana Mendieta's *Volcanic Series no. 2,* six prints detailing the various stages of a small volcanic eruption, and candid photographs of famous figures like architect Isamu Noguchi, actress Lauren Bacall, and author Carson McCullers. For further information access the Library and Research

Very Hush Hush

There's an agency run by the Federal Government that's even more secret than the infamous Central Intelligence Agency (CIA)—the National Security Agency (NSA). The agency is so obsessed with keeping its activities unknown that it refuses to release staffing and budget needs to anyone except a select few in the government's intelligence branches.

The only way outsiders can learn about the NSA, other than obscure government pamphlets, is through a visit to the **National Cryptologic Museum.** This museum is one of D.C.'s least-known sights, and despite its being maintained with federal funding and its place among the Smithsonian Institute's holdings, the home of the US's secret history lies behind a gas station near Fort George G. Meade in Maryland (☎ 301-688-5849; www.nsa.gov/museum.).

The museum opened in 1993. Curator Jack E. Ingram was once an NSA official. When named curator, he had the dubious honor of being the first NSA employee to have his face on national TV.

This home of the unknown itself remains largely unknown but is well worth the drive required. Close to the museum is the National Vigilance Park and the Aerial Reconnaissance Memorial, created in 1997 to honor spies who have died in service to the US. The park is flanked by a hemisphere of trees intended to represent US aircraft downed during reconnaissance missions.

Center (LRC), a repository holding thousands of books, files, and exhibitions, from museum workstations and the website.

NATIONAL POSTAL MUSEUM

◪ Location: *N. Capital St. and Massachusetts Ave. NE in Capitol Hill. Located on the lower level of the City Post Office.* **Metro:** *Union Station.* **Contact:** *Information ☎ 357-2991, TDD 633-9849; www.si.edu/postal.* **Hours:** *Daily 10am-5:30pm.* **Tours:** *30min. tours subject to volunteer docent availability; call ahead.* **Admission:** *Free.* **Accessibility:** *call ahead for visual or hearing impaired tours.*

Established in 1993, the National Postal Museum is the latest addition to the Smithsonian. Displays detail the history of the postal system and showcase vehicles used to transport mail. In exchange for a photo and some personal information, a high-tech exhibit on mass mailings shows visitors why they get certain kinds of junk mail. Of particular interest to philatelists is the stamp gallery displaying nearly 65,000 stamps from around the world in pull-out frames. The stamps in this room are but a sampling of museum's collection, which numbers 13 million.

NAVY MUSEUM

◪ Location: *Building 76, Navy Yard, in Southeast Capitol Hill.* **Metro:** *Eastern Market or Navy Yard.* **Contact:** *☎ 433-4882; www.history.navy.mil.* **Hours:** *Apr.-Labor Day M-F 9am-5pm; Early Sept.-Mar. M-F 9am-4pm.* **Tours:** *Call ahead for docent-led tours.* **Admission:** *Free. The navy base is top security, so American visitors must call 24hr. in advance and bring proper ID; foreign visitors must show a passport.* **Events:** *Free lectures and book signings. Call ☎ 433-6897.*

Visitors man and rotate huge ship guns (three-inch, 50-caliber), squeeze into a bathysphere used to explore the sea floor, or roam the gun deck of a mock-up of the **USS Constitution,** the world's oldest commissioned warship (now in Boston's Charlestown Navy Yard). Children will enjoy looking through periscopes sticking out of the top of the building toward the river. Exhibits focus on the Navy's role in US wars, exploration across the globe, and Commodore Perry's landing in Japan. Next door is the **Museum Annex,** with a collection of old submarines. Also stop by the **Navy Art Gallery** and the *USS Barry,* along the waterfront; the *Barry* is open M-F 9am-5pm.

PHILLIPS COLLECTION

◪ Location: *1600 21st St., at Q St. NW, near Dupont Circle.* **Metro:** *Dupont Circle.* **Contact:** *☎ 387-2151; www.phillipscollection.org.* **Hours:** *Tu-Sa 10am-5pm, Th until 8:30pm, Su noon-5pm (summer only).* **Admission:** *Permanent collection $8, students and seniors $6, under 19 free. Audio tours free with admission. Additional for special exhibits.* **Tours:** *W and Sa 2pm (free).* **Events:** *"Artful Evenings," with music, gallery talks, and cash bar Th 5-8:30pm ($8).*

The Phillips Collection houses the first and one of the finest modern art collections in the United States. This fantastic museum is less crowded and more intimate than the Smithsonian and houses a brand-name selection of relatively recent artistic legends. Its founder, **Duncan Phillips,** was heir to the family steel company and had impeccable taste in art. Opened in 1921 in the family mansion, the museum is now home to 2500 pieces of art, only a fraction of which are shown at any given time.

The most famous work in the museum is **Renoir's** *Luncheon of the Boating Party*, a salon-size painting of bourgeois urbanites out for some daytime drinking along the river. This pastel-colored marvel contrasts vividly with the surrounding darker images of Francisco de Goya and El Greco. One whole room is dedicated to **Van Gogh,** whose harrowing descent into madness can be seen in the increasingly frenetic paintings. The stroll up the annex and through the original mansion is worth the sight of the originally furnished rooms, including the stunning Oak Room, each with a distinctive decor.

Due to construction of the new **Center for Studies in Modern Art,** portions of the Collection will be closed or on tour through 2005. The **Goh Annex** is scheduled to reopen in summer 2004, and 55 of Phillips' greatest European masterworks (including Renoir's *Luncheon*) are expected to be touring nationally until January 2005.

RENWICK GALLERY

Location: Across from the White House at 17th St. and Pennsylvania Ave. NW, in Farragut. **Metro:** Farragut West or Farragut North. **Contact:** ☎ 357-2700, TTY 357-1729, recorded info 275-1500; www.nmaa.si.edu. **Hours:** Daily 10am-5:30pm; information desk daily 10am-4pm. **Tours:** Permanent collection tours F 1pm. To arrange a group tour (M-F), call ☎ 275-1693. **Admission.** Free. **Events:** Workshops, lectures, and receptions. **Accessibility:** Wheelchair accessible via ramp at 17th St. **Note:** The Renwick Gallery is currently hosting exhibits from the National Museum of American Art and the National Portrait Gallery, which are undergoing extensive renovations until 2006.

William Corcoran originally commissioned James Renwick to design the Renwick Gallery in order to display Corcoran's mostly Renaissance art collection. The red-brick mansion is a beauty itself, and the interior's high archways, red velvet staircase, and eccentric design are equally intriguing. The little-known sister-museum of the Smithsonians is one of the finest collections of American craft. Exhibits show woodwork, glass-blowing, pottery, and sculpture techniques developed by Americans in the later 1900s. The gallery houses **Thomas Moran**'s gigantic, panoramic painting of Yellowstone that is said to have inspired Congress to declare it a national park. The focus on three-dimensional objects is a nice break from the painting galleries on the Mall. Temporary exhibitions into early **2004** include "Jewelry of Robert Ebendorf: A Retrospective of Forty Years" (through Jan.) and "Jewels and Gems" (through Feb.).

WASHINGTON DOLL'S HOUSE & TOY MUSEUM

Location: 5236 44th St. NW, 1 block west of Wisconsin Ave. between Harrison and Jenifer St., in Upper Northwest. **Metro:** Friendship Heights; from the Metro, walk away from the Maryland-D.C. border along Wisconsin Ave., making a right onto Jenifer St. and a left onto 44th St. **Contact:** ☎ 244-0024; www.dollshousemuseum.com. **Hours:** Tu-Sa 10am-5pm, Su noon-5pm. **Tours:** Group tours available by reservation only for groups of 10 or more. **Admission:** $4; students, seniors, and AAA $3; under 12 $2.

This museum, founded in 1975, is home to six rooms of antique dolls, doll houses, toys, and games, all from the collection of **Flora Gill Jacobs.** Some of the "doll houses" on display are probably construction models; others are documented Christmas gifts to little girls a century ago. One church model has stained glass windows, while the "Mexican House," found in Puebla, Mexico in 1977 and shipped the 3000 mi. here by van, is a mini-mansion. Amazingly, it includes rooms ranging from a detailed kitchen to a Christian shrine, complete with tiny crucifixes. Also of note is the 1903 "Six Story Hotel" from New Jersey; the house's details include tiny lights for each of the hotel bedrooms. Amazingly, only half of Jacobs's collection is on display at one time. **131**

INSIDE

by cuisine **133**
by neighborhood **136**

adams morgan **136** alexandria **138**
arlington **139** bethesda **141**
capitol hill **143** chinatown **145**
dupont circle **146** farragut **149**
federal triangle **150** foggy bottom **152**
georgetown **153** shaw/u district **156**
south of the mall **157** upper northwest **158**

Food & Drink

How does one feast like a senator on an intern's slim budget? Savvy natives go grubbing at Happy Hour (see **Nightlife,** p. 163). Frugal do-it-yourselfers can also pack a lunch to go and head to the choice picnic spots at Rock Creek Park, the Tidal Basin, and the Mall.

The index on the following two pages lists eateries by cuisine, followed by full reviews, organized by neighborhood. The numerical symbol after a listing indicates its price bracket. The cream of the District crop gets the *Let's Go* thumbs-up (). Major credit cards are accepted everywhere, unless otherwise noted.

BY CUISINE

NEIGHBORHOOD ABBREVIATIONS		
AM Adams Morgan	**CT** Chinatown	**FT** Federal Triangle
AL Alexandria	**DC** Dupont Circle	**SH** Shaw/U
AR Arlington	**G** Georgetown	**SM** South of the Mall
B Bethesda	**F** Farragut	**UN** Upper Northwest
CH Capitol Hill	**FB** Foggy Bottom	

AFRICAN
Addis Ababa (138) — AM ❷
Casablanca (139) — AL ❹
Medaterra (158) — UN ❸
Meskerem (137) — AM ❷
Zed's Ethiopian Cuisine (154) — G ❸

AMERICAN
a.k.a. Frisco's (161) — UN ❶
Boulevard Woodgrill (140) — AR ❸
Cafe Amadeus (152) — FT ❸
🦪 Cafe Deluxe (141) — B ❸
Florida Avenue Grill (157) — SH ❷
Gadsby's Tavern (139) — AL ❸
King Street Blues (138) — AL ❷
Market Lunch (144) — CH ❶

BAKED GOODS
Bread and Chocolate (144) — CH ❶
CakeLove (157) — SH ❷
Firehook (148) — DC ❶
Patisserie Poupon (154) — G ❶
Reeves (151) — FT ❶

BAR & GRILL
🦪 Clyde's of Georgetown (153) — G ❸
Dubliner (144) — CH ❷
Gordon Biersch (151) — FT ❸
Harry's (151) — FT ❶
Hawk 'n' Dove (144) — CH ❷
J. Paul's (153) — G ❸
Mr. Henry's Victorian Pub (145) — CH ❷
Polly's Cafe (157) — SH ❷
Rocklands (141) — AR ❶

BRAZILIAN & CARIBBEAN
Grill From Ipanema (137) — AM ❸
🦪 Red Ginger (153) — G ❸
The Islander (157) — SH ❷
🦪 Tropicana (157) — SH ❶
Zanzibar (158) — SM ❹

CAFES
🦪 Afterwords (148) — DC ❷
🦪 British Collection (138) — AL ❶
Ching Ching Cha (154) — G ❶
Cosi, (149) — DC ❶
Cup A' Cupa A' (153) — FB ❶
Cyberstop Cafe (149) — DC ❶
Dean & Deluca (155) — G ❶
Furin's (154) — G ❶
Java Shack (140) — AR ❶
Jolt 'n' Bolt (149) — DC ❶
La Madeleine (139) — AL ❶
Le Bon Cafe (145) — CH ❶
🦪 Teaism (148) — DC ❶
Tryst (136) — AM ❶

CHILI
🦪 Ben's Chili Bowl (156) — SH ❶
🦪 Hard Times Cafe (140) — AR ❷

CHINESE
China Doll (145) — CT ❷
City Lights of China (148) — DC ❷
🦪 Hunan Chinatown (145) — CT ❸
Lei Garden Restaurant (145) — CT ❹
🦪 Mei Wah Restaurant (152) — FB ❸
Tai Shan Restaurant (145) — CT ❶
Yenching Palace (160) — UN ❷

CONTINENTAL
Cafe Saint-Ex (157) — SH ❹
Local 16 (157) — SH ❸
Nathan's (155) — G ❹
Old Europe (159) — UN ❸
🦪 Tabard Inn (146) — DC ❹
The Monocle (144) — CH ❹
Two Quail Restaurant (143) — CH ❹
Zola (151) — FT ❹

CREOLE & CAJUN
🦪 New Orleans Cafe (136) — AM ❷
Louisiana Express (142) — B ❷

DELIS
Georgetown Cafe (156) — G ❷
Marvelous Market (156) — G ❶
Philadelphia Mike's (142) — B ❶
So's Your Mom (136) — AM ❶
Wisemiller's Deli (156) — G ❶

DINERS
Art Gallery Grille (136) — F ❷
Bob & Edith's Diner (140) — AR ❶
Capitol Hill Jimmy T's (145) — CH ❶
🦪 The Diner (136) — AM ❷
Five Guys Famous Burgers (138) — AL ❶
Lindy's Bon Apetit (153) — FB ❶
Luna Grill & Diner (148) — DC ❸
Royal Restaurant (139) — AL ❶
Stoney's Restaurant (151) — FT ❶
Trio Restaurant (147) — DC ❷
Wilson's (157) — SH ❷

FRENCH
Cafe La Ruche (154) — G ❷
🦪 Grapeseed (141) — B ❹
Montmartre (143) — CH ❸
Patisserie Poupon (154) — G ❶
Saveur Restaurant (159) — UN ❹

GREEK
Crystal Pallas Cafe & Grill (141) — AR ❷
Taverna the Greek Islands (145) — CH ❷
🦪 Yanni's (160) — UN ❷
Zorba's Cafe (148) — DC ❷

HEALTH FOOD & VEGETARIAN

Amma Vegetarian Kitchen (156) — G ❷
🍽 Cafe Luna (146) — DC ❶
High Noon (151) — FT ❷
Juice Joint Cafe (149) — F ❶
🍽 Thyme Square Cafe (141) — B ❷

ICE CREAM

Bob's Famous Homemade (142) — B ❶
Cone E. Island (152) — FB ❶
Lazy Sundae (140) — AR ❶
Pop's Old Fashioned Ice Cream (138) — AL ❶
Thomas Sweet (155) — G ❶

INDIAN

Aditi (154) — G ❸
Bombay Palace (149) — F ❹
Delhi Dhaba (140) — AR ❷

ITALIAN

Dupont Italian Kitchen (147) — DC ❷
🍽 Famous Luigi's (149) — F ❷
🍽 Fresco (152) — FB ❶
Il Radicchio (144) — CH ❷
🍽 La Panetteria (142) — B ❸
🍽 La Tomate (146) — DC ❹
Luigino's (152) — FT ❺
🍽 Mama Maria's and Enzlo's (159) — UN ❷
Paolo's (154) — G ❸
🍽 Pasta Mia Trattoria (136) — AM ❷
Savino's (147) — DC ❹
Tragara (142) — B ❺
Trattoria Italiana (158) — UN ❹

JAPANESE

Also see Pan-Asian & Asian Fusion
Asahi Japanese Restaurant (140) — AR ❸
Raku (146) — DC ❷
Sakana (148) — DC ❷
Spices Asian Restaurant
& Sushi Bar (160) — UN ❸
Tako Grill (143) — B ❸
Yosaku (161) — UN ❸

MEXICAN

Alero (160) — UN ❷
🍽 Burrito Brothers (143) — CH ❶
🍽 Cactus Cantina (161) — UN ❸
Casa Blanca (150) — F ❶
Chipotle Mexican Grill (158) — UN ❶
El Tamarindo (137) — AM ❷
La Frontera Bar and Grill (138) — AM ❷
🍽 Lauriol Plaza (146) — DC ❷
Rio Grande Cafe (142) — B ❷

MICROBREW

Capitol City Brewing Co. (151) — FT ❷
🍽 John Harvard's Brew House (150) — FT ❷

MIDDLE EASTERN

🍽 Bacchus (141) — B ❸
Bistro Med (156) — G ❸
Cafe Ole (161) — UN ❶
Food Factory (141) — AR ❶
Lebanese Taverna (158) — UN ❸
Mama Ayesha's Restaurant (136) — AM ❷
🍽 Marrakesh (150) — FT ❺
Moby Dick House of Kabob (155) — G ❷
Paradise Restaurant (143) — B ❸
Skewers (147) — DC ❸

PAN-ASIAN & ASIAN FUSION

bd's Mongolian BBQ (142) — B ❸
🍽 Burma Restaurant (145) — CT ❷
Cafe Asia (141) — AR ❷
Pan Asian Noodles & Grill (148) — DC ❷
Peppers (147) — DC ❷

PIZZA

🍽 2 Amys (161) — UN ❷
🍽 Armand's Chicago (143) — CH ❶
Faccia Luna (159) — UN ❷
Pizzeria Paradiso (147) — DC ❷

SEAFOOD

Bethesda Crab House (143) — B ❷
Fish Market (139) — AL ❸
🍽 Legal Sea Foods (152) — FB ❹
Lite 'n' Fair (139) — AL ❶
Phillips Flagship (157) — SM ❹
RT's Seafood Kitchen (140) — AR ❸
Steamer's Seafood House (142) — B ❸
Tony and Joe's Seafood Place (156) — G ❹
Tony Cheng's Seafood (146) — CT ❸
Wharf Street Seafood Market (158) — SM ❷

SPANISH

Jaleo (151) — FT ❹
Julia's Empanadas (149) — F ❶
Las Tapas (139) — AL ❹

THAI

49 Twelve Thai Cuisine (161) — UN ❷
Bua (147) — DC ❷
🍽 Haad Thai (150) — FT ❷
Jandara (158) — UN ❷
Sala Thai (147) — DC ❸
Thai Kingdom (150) — F ❷
Thai Kitchen (152) — FB ❷

VIETNAMESE

Miss Saigon (155) — G ❷
Nam-Viet Pho 79 (160) — UN ❷
Saigon Gourmet Restaurant (159) — UN ❸
Saigon Inn (154) — G ❷
Saigonnais (137) — AM ❷

FOOD & DRINK BY CUISINE

135

BY NEIGHBORHOOD

ADAMS MORGAN

SEE MAP P. 360 — YOU ARE HERE
U.S. Capitol Building

Adams Morgan's cultural melting pot dishes up ethnic cuisine to a young, international crowd into ungodly hours. With one of the largest Ethiopian populations in the world (well, outside Ethiopia, at any rate), Adams Morgan is famous for its Ethiopian cuisine but also offers everything from Brazilian to Vietnamese food. Establishments cluster along 18th St. and Columbia Rd. NW. Although the area is generally safe, **areas off the main streets become unsafe at night.** Adams Morgan is a 15min. walk or short cab ride from the Woodley Park-Zoo/Adams Morgan or Dupont Circle Metro.

The Diner, 2453 18th St. NW (☎232-8800). This diner's hours and quintessential American food have earned it high esteem among local college students and other late-night revelers. Lacks the dirt, grit, and shiny chrome of most chain diners. Enjoy omelettes ($5.75-7.45) and pancakes (3 for $4.50) or feast on favorites like mac and cheese ($8) and burgers ($6-7.25). Big selection of desserts like rich turtle cheesecake ($3.25). Kosher hot dogs offered. Vegetarian options available, including some vegan soups. Tu nights feature film screenings (beginning at 4pm with a kids' movie); each month typically has a different theme. No reservations; customers may expect a 30min. wait F-Sa nights. Open 24hr. MC/V. ❷

New Orleans Cafe, 2412 18th St. NW (☎234-0420). With Dixieland playing over its speakers, wall paintings of jazz bands and street musicians, and an owner whose friendliness epitomizes Southern hospitality, the New Orleans Cafe floods its customers with all things (desirable) from N'awlins. Jambalaya and cajun linguine ($8-14.25) draw big crowds, while spicy gumbo soups ($4-8) make them glad they came. The Po' Boy sandwiches ($5-9) have names like The Plantation, The Bourbon Street, and Bayou. The River Catch (cajun-spiced fried catfish with lettuce, tomato, remoulade sauce and cajun fries, $7) is served piping-hot. Try the hot bread pudding with whiskey sauce ($4); Come early on weekends because the place gets packed. Open Tu-F 11am-10pm, Sa-Su 10am-10pm. AmEx/DC/D/MC/V. ❷

Pasta Mia Trattoria, 1790 Columbia Rd. NW (☎328-9114), near 18th St. Red-and-white checked tablecloths in an airy room complete dusky evenings devoted to Disney-worthy romance. Offers standard Italian fare; *pièce de résistance* is a large selection of huge pasta entrees ($9-10). Appetizers ($7-9), salads ($4), and a few desserts. No reservations; line to get in forms quickly after opening. Open M-Sa from 6:30pm. MC/V. ❷

Tryst, 2459 18th St. NW (☎232-5500; www.trystdc.com). Deluxe coffeehouse with an atmosphere that combines an art gallery and rec room, with 6 huge sofas, pastiche paintings, board games, books, and caffeine addicts. Best for nightlife (see **Nightlife,** p. 165), but Tryst's food won't disappoint. Menu includes sandwiches named after regular customers; try Mary (oven-roasted turkey breast, avocado spread, white cheddar with rustico; $6). Order waffles ($4-6) and other breakfast items all day. Vegetarian options available, including veggie sandwiches ($5.45-6). Live jazz every other M, W, Th. 21+ F-Sa after 8:30pm. Open M-Th 6:30am-2am, F-Sa 6:30am-3am, Su 8am-12:30am. MC/V. ❷

So's Your Mom, 1831 Columbia Rd. NW (☎462-3666). This busy sandwich shop offers first-rate sandwich ingredients (such as imported meats and cheeses), portions as big as your mom, and unexpected sandwich choices, which include everything from "No Nonsense NY corned beef" ($4.45-5.50) to Nova Scotia salmon ($5). Fresh pasta and salads also available. Sandwiches $3.50-6.45. Freshly baked goods include cinnamon rolls, muffins, and other pastries ($1.45-2.25). Gourmet oils, olives, pastas, jellies, and crackers line the wall, next to the barrels upon sweet-smelling barrels of gourmet whole coffee beans. Takeout only. Open M-F 7am-8pm, Sa 8am-7pm, Su 8am-3pm. Cash only. ❶

Mama Ayesha's Restaurant, 1967 Calvert St. NW (☎232-5431; www.mamaayeshas.com), next to the Calvert St. bridge. 2003 marked 50 years of Mama Ayesha's delectable Middle Eastern cuisine. Prices make this place a bargain, but this earthy-colored restaurant has enough class to claim Capitol Hill big shots like George Stephanopoulos among its patrons. Veteran news reporter Helen

Thomas stops by at least once a week and has her own table. Mama is no longer around, but the recipes are the same ones she used in 1953. Options range from stuffed grape leaves ($10) to *shish taouk* (marinated chicken breast kebab with tomatoes and onions; $10.50). Cap it off with sweet *baklava*, a pastry with walnut filling and honey ($2.50). Large selection of appetizers $4-6; entrees $9.50-14.50. Reservations recommended for groups of 4 or more F-Sa. Open Su-Th noon-11pm, F-Sa noon-11:30pm. AmEx/D/MC/V. ❷

Meskerem, 2434 18th St. NW (☎462-4100; www.meskeremonline.com), near Columbia Rd. Bright decor and plenty of windows light up this 3 fl. restaurant named after the Ethiopian month marking spring. Appetizers include *sambussas* (vegetable, shrimp, or meat-filled dough shells; $3-5.25). For an intro to Ethiopian cuisine, split the *Meskerem Messob* ($12 for 1 person, $23 for 2), a popular combination platter with meats and vegetables served over thin *injera* bread. Vegans have plenty to choose from on the menu. Diners sit over traditional *messob* basket-tables. Lunch entrees $6-11.25; dinner entrees $8.50-13. Free delivery available. Open Su-Th noon-midnight, F-Sa noon-1am. AmEx/DC/MC/V. ❷

The Grill from Ipanema, 1858 Columbia Rd. NW (☎986-0757; www.thegrillfromipanema.com). Perennially chosen as one of the best places to eat by local newspapers, this Brazilian restaurant is well worth the extra dollars. The famous *feijoada* ($18), a black bean stew, was so special the chef only made it on certain days. Now the dish is served daily due to its popularity. Whet your appetite with *Mexilhão à Carioca*: green mussels served in a sauce of leek, watercress, garlic, and butter ($10.50). Entrees, including chicken, beef, and seafood dishes, range $13-25. Vegetarian options available. Brazilian drinks $5-6.50. Reservations taken F-Sa until 7pm, Su-Th anytime. Open M-Th 5-10:30pm, F 5-11:30pm, Sa noon-11:30pm, Su noon-10pm. AmEx/DC/D/MC/V. ❸

El Tamarindo, 1785 Florida Ave. NW (☎328-3660), just off 18th St. Offers a large number of Salvadorean entrees ($7-13), including seafood, egg dishes, burritos, *chimichangas*, and enchiladas; all come with fresh complimentary chips and salsa. For an appetizer, split the house combo plate, which includes cheese quesadillas, nachos, chicken wings, a *taquito*, and guacamole and sour cream ($8). Vegetarian options available. *Sangría* $3.75, pitchers $17; margaritas $3.75, pitchers $19. If you like any of the paintings or photography on the walls, you can probably take it home with you—most of it is for sale. Open M-Th 11am-3am, F 11am-5am, Sa 10am-5am, Su 10am-3am. 15% Student Advantage discount. AmEx/D/MC/V. **Be careful in this area at night.** ❷

Saigonnais, 2307 18th St. NW (☎232-5300; www.dcnet.com/saigonnais). Vietnamese straw hats dangle from this intimate restaurant's ceiling

Ben's Chili Bowl

Chinese Lanterns

Wharf Seafood Market

while cheery framed photos of famous past visitors line the wall. Start by rolling your own savory sugarcane spring rolls using fresh shrimp ($7.75), and then move on to try other Saigon specialties like Five Spice Chicken (served with coconut-flavored sweet rice; $9) or the grilled pork with handmade rice crepes ($9.75). Lunch specials $6-7.25; entrees (lunch and dinner) $9-15. Desserts ($3.50-5) include the banana or pineapple flambé ($4.25-5). Reservations recommended F-Sa. Open for lunch M-Sa 11:30am-3pm, for dinner daily 5-11pm. AmEx/MC/V. ❷

La Frontera Grill and Bar, 1832 Columbia Rd. NW (☎518-8848). Charming family restaurant offers classic Tex-Mex. Enchiladas, fajitas, and other entrees $7-14. Fully stocked bar carries a large variety of tequilas ($5-7). Upstairs seating converts to a dance fl. to accommodate a DJ playing Brazilian music (F-Sa 11pm-3am). Margaritas $4.50, $13-23 by pitcher; *sangría* $3.50, $11-18 by pitcher. Happy Hour deals (M-Th 4-7pm) often include $2 tecate or $2 margaritas. Vegetarian options and outdoor seating available. Su brunch 10am-3pm. Open Su-Th 11:30am-11pm, F-Sa 11:30am-midnight. AmEx/DC/D/MC/V. ❷

Addis Ababa, 2106 18th St. (☎232-6092; www.addisababarestaurant.com). A contender among Ethiopian restaurant heavyweights. Boasts 2 fl. of seating with live music and dancing on the weekends (F-Sa mixed music, Su traditional). Downstairs doubles as a sports bar. Weekend buffet (Sa-Su 11am-3pm) includes vegetarian options. Entrees $6.50-10. The Addis Ababa combo specials for one ($11-12.50) or up to 4 people (starting at $32) come with a variety of meats and vegetables served on *injera* bread. Happy Hour M-F 4-8pm means 2-for-1 drinks. Free delivery after 5pm. Open Su-Th 11am-2am, F-Sa 11am-3am. AmEx/DC/MC/V. ❷

ALEXANDRIA

SEE MAP P.367

U.S. Capitol Building

YOU ARE HERE

The dining scene in Old Town caters to an older and more sedate crowd than Georgetown, but food options here are not just for the rich. True bargains are hidden behind the colonial facades and flickering gas lamps. Bargain cuisine runs the gamut of ethnicities, but the city's specialties remain seafood and cheap barbecue. Use Metro: King St. unless otherwise noted.

The British Collection, 119 S. Royal St. (☎836-8181). Amid images of Great Britain, the British Collection offers pots of English tea for individuals ($2), 2 people ($3.65), or 4 ($5.90). Pastries ($2.15-4.15), including authentic scones ($3.25-4.25) and assorted shortbreads and fruit crumbles ($3.25). British afternoon tea includes tea sandwiches, scones with jam and Devonshire cream, cake, and a pot of tea ($12.50, $14.50 with an additional glass of sherry). Open Tu noon-6pm, W-Su 10am-6pm. Tea room closes 5pm. D/MC/V. ❶

Five Guys Famous Burgers and Fries, 107 N. Fayette St. (☎703-549-7991). Mouth-watering ingredients make for fantastic burgers. Basic burger $3.69, bacon cheeseburger $4.69; you pick all the toppings as they prepare the burger in front of you. All burgers are well done. Fries (boardwalk or Cajun) $1.19-3.49. Munch on free peanuts while you wait. Open daily 11am-10pm; 2nd location across from The Fish Market open 11am-midnight. Cash only. ❶

Pop's Old Fashioned Ice Cream Company, 109 King St. (☎703-518-5374). A definite, if somewhat artificial, amount of old-world charm here. In addition to ice cream ($2.40 small, $3.15 medium, $4 large), you can spoil yourself with Pop's selection of fountain drinks ($3.69-4.85), milkshakes ($3.69), and banana splits ($6.40). Try the Brown Cow (chocolate syrup, half & half, root beer, and vanilla ice cream; $4.85). For 2 customers or 1 adventurous human vacuum machine, the special Pop's Banana Split ($9.40) includes 6 scoops of ice cream with lots of toppings. Open Su-Th 11am-10pm, F-Sa 10am-midnight. Cash only. ❶

King Street Blues, 112 N. St. Asaph St. (☎703-836-8800), near King St. The flamboyant decor explodes with bright neon and plaster works of blues art. Southern traditions like slow-smoked ribs (½ rack $10.25, full rack $18.50), fried catfish ($12), and pulled pork "sammiches" ($7). Blue-plate special ($7; served until 7pm) changes daily. Low-fat, low-calorie options as well. Live blues Su and Th 9pm-midnight. Reservations for large parties only. Kitchen open M-Th and Su 11:30am-10pm, F-Sa 10:30am-11pm. Bar often closes later. AmEx/DC/D/MC/V. ❷

The Fish Market, 105 King St. (☎703-836-5676; www.fishmarketoldtown.com), near Union St. Rollicking restaurant features live ragtime, show tunes, jazz piano, and audience participation (F-Sa 8pm). 3 bars, maritime decor, and fresh seafood make the ancient baby-blue building a buzzing hangout. Clam chowder $3; seafood sandwiches $5-8; huge schooner glass of house beer $5.25. Fisherman's Platter (fried shrimp, scallops, fish filet, and fries; $14.50) is large and in charge. Dessert options are courtesy of **Pop's Old Fashioned Ice Cream Company** (see above) next door and include sundaes ($4.75-$6). Reservations for parties of 12 or more. Open Su-Th 11:15am-midnight, F-Sa 11:15am-2am. Kitchen closes daily at midnight. AmEx/DC/D/MC/V. ❸

Lite 'n' Fair, 1018 King St. (☎703-549-3717). Ki Choi, former executive chef of the ritzy Watergate Restaurant, runs this gem disguised by a modest entrance, a few small tables, and the convenience of takeout. Exquisite chicken and seafood sandwiches $4-6. Appetizers include smoked salmon, escargot, and calamari tempura (each $4), while main courses include seafood paella with shrimp, mussels, calamari, and saffron rice ($9). Open M 11am-3pm, Tu-Th 11am-9pm, F-Sa 11am-10pm. MC/V. ❶

Gadsby's Tavern, 138 N. Royal St. (☎703-548-1288), near King St. Costumed waiters deliver 18th-century cooking in a restaurant once frequented by George Washington. Decor retains a palpable colonial feel, with candlelighting at each table, weathered hardwood floors, and Revolution-era prints on the walls. Dinner stews, colonial pies, and other entrees $18-26. Traditional tea, bread, and English trifle for dessert ($5.50). "Colonial" entertainment (Tu-W 7pm-close) features a violinist in period costume. Vegetarian entrees include tomatoes stuffed with spinach pudding ($18); some items can be made vegan. Reservations recommended. Open daily 11:30am-3pm and 5:30-10:30pm. AmEx/DC/D/MC/V. ❸

Royal Restaurant, 734 N. St. Asaph St. (☎703-548-1616). Metro: Braddock. Celebrating its 100th anniversary in 2004, Royal Restaurant has been owned by the same family since its beginning, a tradition reflected in its homestyle cooking and decor. The king of the sandwich selection ($4-8.25) is the Charles Royal Club (wheat toast, turkey, cheese, bacon, lettuce, tomato, and mayo; $6.75 with fries). Omelettes $4-5.45 for breakfast, $5.50-5.75 for lunch or dinner. All-you-can-eat brunch buffets Sa ($6.75, 7am-1pm) and Su ($8.50, 7am-2pm). Elvis impersonators appear here twice a year, on the King's birthday and the anniversary of his death. Open M-Sa 6am-9pm, Su 7am-2pm. AmEx/D/MC/V. ❶

Las Tapas, 710 King St. (☎703-836-4000), between Washington and Columbus St. Alexandria's sole Spanish restaurant is a flamboyant affair. Wide variety of tapas ($4-7). Heftier entrees $17-23, paella $16-22.50. Flamenco performances Tu and Th at 7:45 and 9pm; gypsy music F-Sa 9pm-1am; live Spanish guitar W 8-11pm. Oil lamps at each table and colorful artistry on the walls create a romantic atmosphere. Reservations recommended. Open Su-W 11:30am-10pm, Th 11:30am-11pm, F-Sa 11:30am-1am. AmEx/DC/D/MC/V. ❹

La Madeleine, 500 King St. (☎703-739-2854; www.lamadeleine.com). Another location in Georgetown, 3000 M St. NW (☎337-6975). Cafeteria-style food, but the warm country decor and French-speaking staff eliminate institutional feel. French bakery and cafe serves great breakfast omelettes ($6.49), sandwiches, pasta, and entrees ($5-10), and an extensive selection of desserts ($2-3). *Let's Go* recommends the 🍎tomato basil soup. Open Su-Th 7am-10pm, F-Sa 7am-11pm. AmEx/D/MC/V. ❶

Casablanca, 1504 King St. (☎703-549-6464; www.moroccanrestaurant.com). Sample Moroccan cuisine during the all-you-can-eat lunch buffet ($6), but true magic is in the nightly, hours-long feast. Savor soup, salad, couscous, delicately spiced meat, pastries, mint tea, and fruit amid cushion-laden luxury (1 entree $18, 2 for $20, 3 for $22). Reservations suggested F-Sa. Section adjacent to the dining room offers take-out (salads, subs, sandwiches, and wraps $2.50-5). Open for lunch M-F 11:30am-2pm, for dinner M-Sa 5:30-11pm. AmEx/DC/D/MC/V. ❹

ARLINGTON

In terms of international cuisine, Arlington falls short of Adams Morgan, Georgetown and Bethesda when it comes to restaurant offerings. This doesn't mean that Arlington's eateries aren't superb, but the strength of D.C.'s more established ethnic restaurants overwhelm Arlington's burgeoning crop. The **Courthouse-Clarendon-Ballston corridor** is home to some reasonably priced Vietnamese restaurants, more recent culinary influences from south of the border, and timeless all-American burgers and ribs. **Lee Highway** has also earned a spot on the culinary map.

■ **The Boulevard Woodgrill,** 2901 Wilson Blvd. (☎703-875-9663; www.boulevardwood-grill.com), at Fillmore St. Metro: Clarendon. This restaurant's schizophrenic decor includes neon lighting, faux-Asian vases, and diner-style booths. Luckily, friendly service and generous portions of appetizers ($3-8) and entrees ($10-21) make up for the lack of design sense. Weekend brunch (Sa 11am-3pm, Su 10am-3pm; $7-12) is one of the best in Arlington. Open M-F 11am-11pm, Sa 10:30-midnight, Su 10am-11pm. ❸

■ **Hard Times Cafe,** 3028 Wilson Blvd. (☎703-528-2233), across from Clarendon Metro. The sign just inside the door greets customers with "Drink beer, eat chili, be happy." People have been doing just that in this restaurant for more than 20 years. Ask for a free "taster" and the waiter will bring you a sample of their 4 famous chilis. Any 1 bowl is $5.25. Burgers $6-7; chili dogs $6. The laid-back staff fits in well with the country-western decor, complete with longhorns adorning the bar and a saddle atop the jukebox. Open Su-Th 11am-11pm, F-Sa 11am-midnight. AmEx/MC/V. ❷

Delhi Dhaba, 2424 Wilson Blvd. (☎703-524-0008). Metro: Courthouse. Not easily visible from the street; enter through the parking lot behind the deli. Known in the area as one of the best bargains for dinner, the Delhi Dhaba has become a takeout staple for much of D.C. and Virginia. Delhi Dhaba provides solid Indian fare at great prices, including *Saag* lamb ($8) as well as lots of vegetarian specialties (all around $5.50-6). $10 will ensure a sumptuous meal. Open Su-Th 11am-10pm, F-Sa 11am-11pm. AmEx/DC/D/MC/V. ❷

Lazy Sundae, 2925 Wilson Blvd. (☎703-525-4960). Metro: Clarendon. The delectable homemade ice cream here comes in the traditional single ($2.50), double ($3.50), and triple scoop ($4.50), while the large selection of sundaes includes the "Lazy Sundae" itself: 4 scoops for $7. Banana split $5. Guess (or accidentally utter) the secret word of the day and get a free scoop. Ice creams come in many seasonal flavors. Open Su-Th 11am-10pm, F-Sa 11am-11pm; later hours in the summer. Cash only. ❶

Bob & Edith's Diner, 2310 Columbia Pike (☎703-920-6103; www.washingtonpost.com/yp/bobandediths). Also at 4707 Columbia Pike (☎703-920-4700). Not easily accessible by Metro, but a great place to get breakfast at 3am. Knocks the socks off the traditional pancake house—this place has grooving music and a top-notch grill. Most importantly, this diner charges truly retro prices; most dishes under or around $5. Eggs and bacon or omelettes $5; grilled cheese $2; subs around $5. Open 24hr. MC/V. ❶

RT's Seafood Kitchen, 2300 Clarendon Blvd. (☎703-841-0100; www.rtsseafood-kitchen.com). Metro: Courthouse. In the center of Courthouse Plaza, RT's has fresh seafood in an atmosphere marked by larger-than-life wall murals of beer, wine, and hot sauce bottles. Start with a cup of the she-crab soup ($4) and then try an *etouffée* (a spicy cajun dish with crab sauce; $11-15). Outdoor seating takes advantage of W night jazz, blues, or folk concerts in the plaza (June-Aug. W 6:30-8pm, weather permitting). Beers ($2.75-4) include unusual brews like Blackened Voodoo Lager. Reservations recommended for lunch and on weekends. Open daily 11am-midnight. AmEx/DC/D/MC/V. ❸

The Java Shack, 2507 N. Franklin Rd. (☎703-527-9556; www.javashack.com), off Wilson Blvd. Metro: Courthouse; from the Metro exit, follow N. Courthouse Rd. to Wilson Blvd., make a left, bearing right onto N. Franklin Rd. after 4 blocks; the Shack will be on the right. A great place to cool off or warm up over hand-painted tabletops with crazy magazine cut-outs. Pastries $1.75. Java Blizzard (coffee, espresso, chocolate, caramel, and milk blended with ice; $3.50-3.85) is delicious. Quiche selections ($3.50) are often vegetarian, while sandwiches run $5. Patrons who bring their own laptops can plug into the Java Shack's free Internet network. Open M-F 7am-10pm, Sa-Su 8am-10pm. AmEx/MC/V. ❶

Asahi Japanese Restaurant, 2250 Clarendon Blvd. (☎703-243-7007). Metro: Courthouse. Asahi is within the Courthouse Plaza. Small, clean, and efficient, this restaurant provides a bright atmosphere for a leisurely lunch or dinner. For $10, customers can get the lunch buffet, which includes noodle dishes and a selection of sushi. Dinners range from $10-15, a bit more for sushi. Open M-Th 11:30am-2:30pm and 5-10pm, F 11:30am-2:30pm and 5-11pm, Sa noon-11pm. AmEx/DC/MC/V. ❸

Cafe Asia, 1550 Wilson Blvd. (☎703-741-0870; www.cafeasia.com). Metro: Rosslyn. A lighter and low-cholesterol alternative to the predominant BBQ establishments in the area. 2 sidewalk patios and ample indoor seating provides the area's yuppie crowd with affordable Asian dishes. Entrees ($7-12) cover the range of pan-Asian cuisine. Open M-Th 11am-11pm, F-Su 11am-midnight. ❷

Crystal Pallas Cafe & Grill, 556 22nd St. (☎703-521-3870). Metro: Crystal City. Large servings and a relaxed pace make this thoroughly Greek restaurant worthy of indulgence. The chef's specialty is the slow-roasted spring lamb ($13), cooked and seasoned to perfection. Other selections include roasted red peppers mixed with feta and oregano ($4.25). The Greek salad is a feta feast on *dolma* (stuffed grape leaves) combined with a smooth homemade dressing ($6). Open M-F 11am-10pm, Sa 5-10pm. ❷

Food Factory, 4221 N. Fairfax Dr. (☎703-527-2279). Metro: Ballston. Choose from a variety of chilled kebabs in the display case waiting to be cooked upon request. The curries are also in front, ready to be slopped on your tray. The bare-bones seating area has a fast food feel, and although utensils are provided, most locals eat with their fingers. Meals are a bargain, starting at around $4. Kebabs, all made with *halal* meat, run $6-7. Open M-F 11am-10pm, Sa-Su noon-10pm. ❶

Rocklands, 4000 N. Fairfax Dr. (☎703-528-9663). Metro: Ballston. Trendy spot attached to **Carpool Bar** (p. 168). Don't let the pool tables and bar decor fool you. The chefs command a serious kitchen that can compete with the best BBQ restaurants. Great BBQ ribs ($5 half rack) and sandwiches ($7-9.50) guaranteed to be served within 8min. of your order. Whole chickens (for 4) $9. Heat seekers can sample over 120 hot sauces on the "Wall of Fire." Open Su-W 11:30am-10pm, Th-Sa 11:30am-11pm; bar menu until Carpool's last call. ❶

BETHESDA

Boasting one of the highest concentrations of restaurants in the US, Bethesda packs 150-plus eateries between **Wisconsin Avenue** to the east, **Bethesda Avenue** to the south, **Rugby Avenue** to the north, and **Arlington Road** and **Old Georgetown Road** to the west. Bethesda has dining options for almost any cuisine, ambience, or price. Use Metro: Bethesda for all of the following.

SEE MAP P. 365 *Rock Creek Park*

YOU ARE HERE

🅢 **Bacchus,** 7945 Norfolk Ave., (☎301-657-1722; www.bacchusrestaurant.com) at Del Ray Ave. Excellent Lebanese restaurant, bearing the name of the ancient Roman god of wine. Bacchus manages to create a highly elegant and authentic atmosphere without being intimidating. The menu features 50 kinds of appetizers, cold and hot, all in the vicinity of $5; the *shawarma* (grilled lamb slices served on Lebanese bread with tahini sauce, $7) is highly recommended. Entrees $13-17, but a sampling of appetizers allows for trying more items. Copious outdoor seating in a beautiful Mediterannean-style patio complete with fountains. Open M-F noon-2pm and 5:30-10pm, Sa 5:30-10:30pm. AmEx/DC/D/MC/V. ❸

🅢 **Thyme Square Cafe,** 4735 Bethesda Ave. (☎301-657-9077), at Woodmont Ave. Friendly service, colorful decorations, and healthy vegetarian salads, sandwiches, and pasta dishes radiate wholesomeness. A true vegan paradise. Start off with the complimentary multi-grain bread and sweet potato spread then savor steamed Beijing vegetable pot stickers ($9), or the avocado "PLT" (grilled portobello, lettuce, tomato, avocado, and eggless mayo on multi-grain bread; $9). Open Su-Th 11:30am-9:30pm, F-Sa 11:30am-10pm. AmEx/D/MC/V. ❷

🅢 **Grapeseed,** 4865 Cordell Ave., (☎301-986-9592; www.grapeseedbistro.com), near Norfolk Ave. Determined to make connoisseurs of us all, Grapeseed offers an unpretentious environment for experimentation in the intimidating field of wine tasting. Serves appetizers ($5-12) and entrees ($20-26) with accompanying wine recommendations. Wine can be ordered by the bottle, the glass, or the taste (a 3 oz. pour). The cornmeal fried oysters ($5.50) and white wine ($7 per glass) make a perfect combination. Hosts wine tastings twice a month (Tu 5-7pm, $15). Open M-Th 5-10pm, F-Sa 5-11pm, Su 5-9pm. AmEx/DC/D/MC/V. ❹

🅢 **Cafe Deluxe,** 4910 Elm St. (☎301-656-3131; www.cafedeluxe.com), between Woodmont Ave. and Arlington Rd. Also at 3228 Wisconsin Ave. in Cleveland Park (☎686-2233) and 1800 International Dr. in Tysons Corner (☎703-761-0600). This airy, bustling bistro offers diners low-lit booths inside and white-draped tables outside. It may be a chain, but Cafe Deluxe delivers solid American and Italian cooking at mid-range prices in a fun, neighborhood-oriented package. Wash down the ahi tuna mignon with green pepper sauce ($15) with a tartini (Stoli raspberry, Chambord, cranberry juice, and sour; $7.50) from the mahogany bar. Most entrees $9-18. Reservations recommended. Open M-Th 11:30am-10:30pm, F 11:30am-11pm, Sa 10:30am-11pm, Su 11am-10pm. AmEx/MC/V. ❸

▨ **La Panetteria,** 4921 Cordell Ave. (☎301-951-6433; www.lapanetteria.com), near Norfolk Ave. Divided into charming alcoves with skylights and hanging plants, La Panetteria offers excellent Northern Italian cuisine and unobtrusive service. Dishes like veal-stuffed tortellini in cream ($6.50) prove just as delicious as more expensive dishes such as the seafood linguine ($17). Lunch specials include salad and pasta, $7-12. Open M-Th 11:30am-10pm, F-Sa 11:30am-11pm, Su 4-10pm. AmEx/DC/D/MC/V. ❸

Steamer's Seafood House, 4820 Auburn Ave. (☎301-718-0661), near Norfolk Ave. Fresh lobster, crab, and shrimp served on picnic tables in a backyard picnic atmosphere. The main attraction: all-you-can-eat hard-shell crab (with corn, coleslaw, and fries, $30). M-F 4-7pm bar specials include $2 drafts and $2.50 rail drinks. Appetizers like Buffalo Shrimp ($10) and entrees like Alaskan King Crab ($30) also please the hungry hoards. Outdoor patio seating available. Open Su-Th noon-10pm, F-Sa until 11pm. MC/V. ❺

Louisiana Express, 4921 Bethesda Ave. (☎301-652-6945), near Arlington Rd. Serves authentic Cajun cuisine from crawfish bisque ($4.75) to chicken jambalaya ($7.75). Su brunch (9am-2:30pm) offers the "Po' Man's Breakfast" (scrambled eggs with ham, bacon, and sausage on French bread; $8.75). Delivery available M-F 11:30am-1:30pm and 5-9pm, Sa-Su 5-9pm ($15 minimum). Open M-Th 7:30am-10pm, F-Sa 7:30am-11pm, Su 9am-10pm. AmEx/DC/D/MC/V. ❷

Rio Grande Cafe, 4919 Fairmont Ave. (☎301-656-2981), near Norfolk Ave. Louder and more crowded than Mexico City, Rio packs them in for the Mexican fare, drinks, and party atmosphere. $8.50 buys 3 delicious tacos, rice, and beans. Especially brave patrons should try the *plato especial* with quail or frog legs ($18.75). Sunday brunch (11:30am-3pm) features *huevos manchados* (3 eggs scrambled with chicken or beef in a tortilla; $10). Open Su-Th 11:30am-10:30pm, F-Sa 11:30am-11:30pm. AmEx/DC/D/MC/V. ❷

Philadelphia Mike's, 7732 Wisconsin Ave. (☎301-656-0103), near Middleton Ave. Mike's successfully replicates the gooey taste of an authentic Philly cheesesteak ($4-8) served over the counter in a modest, pizza shop setting. Burgers and deli sandwiches ($3-8), breakfast subs ($2-3), and lunch sandwich specials daily ($3). Delivery minimum $10 for dinner, $12 for lunch. Open M-F 8am-9pm, Sa 9am-9pm, Su 9am-4pm. AmEx/MC/V. ❶

Tragara, 4935 Cordell Ave. (☎301-951-4935; www.tragara.com), near Old Georgetown Rd. This bistro's French chef gives Italian cuisine a creative twist. Entrees ($19-29) include the delectable lobster over asparagus risotto ($30). Choose from 13 flavors of homemade ice cream and sorbet ($7.50). Reservations recommended. Open for lunch M-F 11:30am-2:30pm, dinner M-Th 5:30-10pm, F-Sa 5:30-10:30pm, Su 5-9pm. AmEx/DC/D/MC/V. ❺

Bob's Famous Homemade Ice Cream, 4706 Bethesda Ave. (☎301-657-2963), at Wisconsin Ave. Bob's daily rotating selection of gourmet ice cream and frozen yogurt flavors ($2-3) includes orange chocolate chip, Mozambique (cinnamon, nutmeg, and clove), and rum raisin (with real, face-flushing rum). Can't choose? Get three different flavors on the banana split ($5.75). Open M-Th 7:30am-11pm, F 7:30am-midnight, Sa 11am-midnight, Su 11am-11pm; call for shorter winter hours. Cash only. ❶

BD's Mongolian Barbeque, 7201 Wisconsin Ave. (☎301-657-1080; www.bdsmongolianbarbeque.com), across Willow Ln. from the Montgomery Farm Co-op. Energy runs high at BD's, where a vibrant younger crowds come to combine a variety of meats, veggies, spices, and sauces to create their own unique stir-fry grilled before their very eyes. The faces and places of Mongolia populate the walls in photo frames, but the atmosphere is about as Mongolian as Kansas. Play Connect Four or Trivial Pursuit while you wait for your creation to be cooked. All-you-can-eat dinner $14; soup, salad bar, rice, and tortillas included. Kids under 12 $7. Lunch $10, kids $6. M-Th 11am-9:30pm, F-Sa 11am-10:30pm, Su 11:30am-9:30pm. Memorial Day to Labor Day, closes 30min. later. AmEx/D/MC/V. ❸

Bethesda Crab House, 4958 Bethesda Ave. (☎301-652-3382), a block from Arlington Rd. next to the Mercedes dealership. Following 43 years of tradition, patrons flock to long picnic tables to collect the piles of shells accumulated during the meal. All-you-can-eat crab including coleslaw and corn ($25) makes a remarkable bargain for a big eater. Crabs also available by the dozen (call ahead; medium $36, large $45). Also shrimp, crab cakes, corn on the cob, and coleslaw. Open M-Sa 9am-midnight, Su 10am-midnight. MC/V.❺

Tako Grill, 7756 Wisconsin Ave. (☎301-652-7030), near Cheltenham Dr. Modern Japanese grill ornamented with glazed wood and frequented by a young professional clientele. The $7 lunch special, including miso soup, bean sprout salad, rice, a California roll, and an entree, is impeccable. Fresh sushi appetizers $4-7, entrees with salad and rice $7-18. Try mouthwatering *nabeyaki* (udon noodle soup with chicken, egg, and seafood; lunch $7.50, dinner $11). Free delivery M-Th 5:30-9pm. Open for lunch M-F 11:30am-2pm; for dinner M-Th 5:30-10pm, F-Sa 5:30-10:30pm, Su 5-9:30pm. AmEx/MC/V. ❸

Paradise Restaurant, 7141 Wisconsin Ave. (☎301-907-7500), near Bethesda Ave. and next to the Montgomery Farm Co-op. Pictures on the menu of the various Persian and Afghan dishes make ordering less risky for the timid newcomer. Lunch (M-F $7, Sa-Su $11) and dinner (M-Th $13, F-Su $16) all-you-can-eat buffets include soup, 6 entrees, salad, and fruit (served daily 11:45am-2:30pm and 6-9pm). Try the *samosas* (deep-fried Indian pastries filled with spiced beef; 4 for $6). Entrees $9-14; baklava $2.75. Open Su-Th 11:45am-10pm, F-Sa 11:45am-11pm. AmEx/DC/D/MC/V. ❸

CAPITOL HILL

The secret to fine dining on "the Hill" is venturing away from all the white marble; peripheral areas harbor reasonably priced establishments free from congressional bigwigs dining on their lobbyists' tabs. **Pennsylvania Avenue** dominates the restaurant scene, but Massachusetts Ave. NE and the surrounding residential areas offer some attractive, unique alternatives. Over 50 eateries inhabit **Union Station.** In the glitzy food court on the lower level and on the concourse between the shops and the trains, cheap takeout counters ring the walls, offering international fast food for under $6. Outside, street vendors offer even better deals: a hot dog, chips, and soft drink run $4. Do-it-yourselfers should brave the bustle of block-long **Eastern Market,** where butchers, bakers, and farmers hawk their wares (see **Shopping,** p. 204). **At night, the areas northeast of Union Station or southeast of Seward Square warrant caution.**

🦐 **Armand's Chicago Pizzeria,** 226 Massachusetts Ave. NE (☎547-6600; www.armand-spizza.com). Metro: Union Station. The delicious Chicago-style pizzas and hearty sandwiches continue to keep Armand's a Capitol Hill hotspot. The lunch buffet (M-F 11:30am-2pm, until 3pm Sa-Su; $6) with all-you-can-eat pizza and salad. Takeout and delivery available. Pizza $7.50-16. Pasta $5.25-8. salads $3.50-6, sandwiches $4.50-5.50. Open M-Th 11:30am-10pm, F-Sa 11:30am-11pm, Su 4-10pm. ❶

🦐 **Burrito Brothers,** 205 Pennsylvania Ave. SE (☎543-6835). Metro: Capital South. This local chain is the takeout haven for busy interns and Hill staffers. The cheapest hard taco around goes for only $1.69. Nachos ($1.89), burritos ($2.50-5.75), and quesadillas ($2.65-3.50) round out the Mexican dishes. Limited counter seating only. Open M-F 10:30am-9pm, Sa 10:30am-8pm, Su 11am-7pm. MC/V. ❶

Montmartre, 327 7th St. SE, at Pennsylvania Ave. (☎544-1244). Metro: Eastern Market. French pop art and Parisian street signs welcome visitors to this pleasant bistro, but the menu seals its authenticity. Hors d'oeuvres ($5-8) include a chilled zucchini soup with poached salmon ($6) while the braised rabbit ($20) leads the creative dinner menu ($16-20). Entirely French wine list, bottles only. Reservations recommended. Open Su 11:30am-2:30pm, Tu-Th 5:30-10pm, F-Sa 5:30-10:30pm. AmEx/MC/V. ❸

Two Quail Restaurant, 320 Massachusetts Ave. NE (☎543-8030; www.twoquail.com). Metro: Union Station. Tucking its guests away in plush, private booths, Two Quail has long been heralded as Washington's most romantic restaurant. Unique entrees span multiple cuisines, like Two Quail

the BIG $plurge

TWO QUAIL

Although it's hidden away in a quiet part of Capitol Hill, **Two Quail Restaurant** is well-known by locals as the most romantic restaurant in the District. The menu offers a creative smorgasbord of continental American cuisine, and the bar serves an impressive selection of wines and *aperitifs* to toast a first date or anniversary.

What sets Two Quail apart, though, is its unparalleled ambiance for romancing. The dining room resembles a fairytale; plush seating and red velvet curtains evoke a Cinderella-type affair. The restaurant's attentive staff will even arrange for a horse-drawn carriage to pick guests up after their meal. Not a week passes at Two Quail without a marriage proposal, to which they bring out champagne and celebrate with the groom- and bride-to-be.

The restaurant also provides a few lucky couples with more private dining quarters; two booths have curtains draped around the table, one of which has a hanging locket in which patrons leave notes marking their visits. Two Quail's location in Capitol Hill proves all too convenient: several members of Congress frequent the restaurant accompanied by lady friends of the extramarital variety.

stuffed with chorizo, wild rice, and feta ($20.50). If your wallet isn't as big as your heart, bring your lover for the *prix fixe* lunch ($10). Reservations recommended. See **Big Splurge (left).** Open M-F 11:30am-2:30pm, 5-10:30pm, Sa-Su 5-11:30pm. ❹

Il Radicchio, 223 Pennsylvania Ave. SE (☎547-5114). A pleasant place to dine with an impressive painted backdrop of a small Italian farm and countryside. All-you-can-eat spaghetti starts at $6.50 per person; add 1 or more sauces ($1.50-4.50) to the huge bowls and go crazy. Sauces range from a standard *pomodoro* ($1.50) to *cozze* (mussels with tomato and basil; $3.50). 14 varieties of pizza or you can create your own ($6.50-12). Outdoor seating available. Open M-Th 11:30am-10pm, F-Sa 11:30am-11pm, Su 5-10pm. ❷

The Market Lunch, 225 7th St. SE (☎547-8444), in the Eastern Market complex. Metro: Eastern Market. The hallowed craft- and bargain-hunting halls and patios open on the weekdays for some of the freshest meals at relatively good prices. Crab cakes ($6-10) and soft-shell crab (sandwich $7, platter $12) are the local specialties, but the Blue Bucks (buckwheat blueberry pancakes; $3.50) have people lined up around the corner Sa mornings (breakfast served Sa until 11am). Open Su 11am-3:30pm, Tu-Sa 7:30am-3pm. ❶

The Dubliner, 520 N. Capitol St. (☎737-3773). Look for the Phoenix Park Hotel awning. Metro: Union Station. Relaxed professionals collect here after the working day is done for pub grub like fish and chips ($9) and Beef O'Flaherty (hot roast beef in a casserole with melted bleu cheese and fries; $9). Guinness (pint $5) flows freely. Live Irish music nightly (M-Sa 9pm, Su 7:30pm). Open Su-Th 7am-2am, F-Sa 7:30am-3am. AmEx/MC/V. ❷

Hawk 'n' Dove, 329 Pennsylvania Ave. SE (☎543-3300). Metro: Capitol South. Popular watering hole with the feel of an old English pub has served the neighborhood since 1967. Functional bar food includes sandwiches ($5.50-9), 12 bottled beers, and 13 drafts ($3.25 and up). Open M-Th 10am-2am, F 10am-3am, Sa 9:30am-3am, Su 9:30am-2am. ❷

Bread and Chocolate, 666 Pennsylvania Ave. SE, (☎547-2875). Metro: Eastern Market. This gourmet pastry and coffee shop meticulously creates and displays delicious cakes (French chocolate raspberry truffle cake or tiramisu $3.25 a slice), French pastries (raspberry tartlette $3.75, caramel triangle $3), and an assorted selection of appetizing sandwiches ($6-7). Standard breakfast menu also served. The inside seating and patio are perfect places to unwind from the hectic museum and monument crowd. Open M-Sa 7am-7pm, Su 8am-6pm. AmEx/DC/D/MC/V. ❶

The Monocle, 107 D St. SE, (☎ 546-4488) at 1st St. Metro: Union Station. Located just 2 blocks from the Capitol, this traditional steakhouse has been a congressional hangout since 1960. Lunch offerings include a steak salad over field greens with bleu cheese ($14.50) and a variety of appetizers ($5.50-9.50) and sandwiches ($8-11.50). The Colorado Lamb Chops ($28.50) and Monocle Crabcakes ($20) are excellent choices for dinner. Reservations recommended. Open M-F 11:30am-10pm. AmEx/DC/D/MC/V. ❹

Mr. Henry's Victorian Pub, 601 Pennsylvania Ave. SE (☎546-8412). Metro: Eastern Market. Victorian decor and meatloaf-heavy menu make Mr. Henry's a surefire choice for comfort food, while an outdoor patio on the 6th St. side is a popular lounge spot. A diverse crowd chows down on big burgers and sandwiches ($4-11) and entrees ($7.45-15). Live jazz on F (9pm-midnight). Open M-Th 11:15am-midnight, F-Sa 11:15am-1am; Su 10am-midnight. AmEx/D/MC/V. ❷

Le Bon Cafe, 210 2nd St. SE (☎547-7200), a stone's throw from the Capitol. Metro: Capitol South. Tastefully sparse coffeeshop makes food from scratch. Espresso ($1.25), café au lait ($1.75), and pastries ($1.25-2.75). Sandwiches ($5.25-6.25) and elegant salads ($3.75-$6.95) complete the menu. Open M-F 7:30am-4pm, Sa-Su 8:30am-3:30pm. Cash only. ❶

Taverna the Greek Islands, 305 Pennsylvania Ave. SE (☎547-8360). Metro: Capitol South. White stucco walls and shady outdoor tables host a happy clientele feasting on Moussaka a la Greek Islands (tomato and bechamel sauce over layers of eggplant, and ground beef; $10.50) and Greek sandwiches ($7-9). The Saganaki appetizer ($7) features 8 ft. flames shooting from your plate; cool off with a fresh piña colada or margarita ($5). Deli downstairs. Open M-Sa 11am-11:30pm. AmEx/DC/D/MC/V. ❷

Capitol Hill Jimmy T's, 501 E. Capitol St. (☎546-3646), at 5th St. under the brick octagonal turret. Metro: Eastern Market. Red vinyl benches and classic phone booths throw this ancient neighborhood joint back into the 50s. Friendly service and unbeatable prices: sandwiches $1.50-3.75, burgers around $3 ($5 with fries). Most items under $6. Open W-F 6:30am-3pm, Sa-Su 8am-3pm. Cash only. ❶

CHINATOWN

Most of D.C.'s best Chinese, Burmese, and Mongolian restaurants cling to tiny **H Street NW** and the adjacent blocks. Many restaurants serve dim sum (Chinese à la carte brunch), arguably the best, and undeniably most popular, meal in Chinatown. Don't be turned off by the decrepit exterior of many of these restaurants; most serve wonderful food, and have extensive takeout options. The area is fairly safe, **but exercise caution at night.** Use Metro: Gallery Place-Chinatown for all of the following.

🦑 **Burma Restaurant,** upstairs at 740 6th St. NW (☎638-1280), between G and H St. Burmese curries, unique spices, and a plethora of garnishes replace Chinese flavorings. Start with green tea salad ($7), and finish with the squid, sautéed in garlic, ginger, and scallions ($8). Vegetarians enjoy the papaya and tofu salads ($6). Entrees $6-8. Open M-F 11am-3pm and 6-10pm, Sa-Su 6-10pm. AmEx/DC/D/MC/V. ❷

🦑 **Hunan Chinatown,** 624 H St. NW (☎783-5858). Upscale restaurant serving standard Chinese food; locals maintain that the cuisine is well worth the added expense. Serves Kung Pao chicken (lunch $7), tea smoked duck (dinner $14.50), and Hunan lamb (thin slices of lamb sautéed over broccoli; dinner $14). Open Su-Th 11am-10pm, F-Sa 11am-11pm. AmEx/DC/D/MC/V. ❸

China Doll, 627 H St. NW (☎289-4755). Standard Chinese dishes and combination meals with soup, spring roll, and steamed rice (lunch $6-8; dinner $8 and up). Bakery is less predictable—Chinese and French pastries like almond cookies ($1) and fruit tarts ($2). Dim sum daily 11am-4pm. Open Su-Th 11am-10pm, F-Sa 11am-midnight. DC/D/MC/V. ❷

Lei Garden Restaurant, 629-631 H St. NW (☎216-9696). Known for lunch buffet (M-F 11:30am-2pm, Sa-Su 11:30am-3pm; $10) and dim sum. Served until 2pm weekdays and 3pm weekends. Try their specialty, Peking Duck ($26). $8 min. for credit cards. Open M-Th 11:30am-11pm, F-Sa 11:30am-midnight, Su 11:30am-10:30pm. AmEx/DC/D/MC/V. ❹

Tai Shan Restaurant, 622 H St. NW (☎639-0266). A busy lunch spot providing a quick sit-down meal, offering noodle soups ($5) and fried rice ($6). Lunch ($5) and dinner ($7) specials available. Open Su-Th 11am-midnight, F-Sa 11am-3am. AmEx/DC/D/MC/V. ❶

Tony Cheng's Seafood Restaurant, 619 H St. NW (☎371-8669), on the 2nd fl. of a garishly decorated building. The restaurant consists of a large room with enormous chandeliers and visible lobster tanks. Full dim sum brunch served daily 11am-3pm. Lunch specials $8-11. In **Tony Cheng's Mongolian Restaurant** downstairs, patrons choose from a buffet of meat and vegetables, which are then stir-fried by the ultra-coordinated cooks. One serving $9, all-you-can-eat $16. Open Su-Th 11am-11pm, F-Sa 11am-midnight. AmEx/MC/V. ❸

DUPONT CIRCLE

With crowded streets even on weeknights, dining in Dupont is as much about people-watching as finding a good meal. The restaurants on 17th St., 18th St., and Connecticut Ave. all spill out onto the street in a stream of patios which get packed daily with young professionals. Many restaurants are more upscale, and hence pricier, than those in bohemian Adams Morgan, but they are still home to delectable bargains for those willing to put down another dollar or two. The neighborhood is residentially cozy, but east of 17th St. it becomes less safe. Park as far west as possible to avoid break-ins. Use Metro: Dupont Circle for the following.

🍲 **La Tomate,** 1701 Connecticut Ave. NW (☎667-5505), at R St. This modern Italian bistro offers attentive service, a creative menu, and bread with fresh black olive spread waiting on the table. Pastas ($12.25-18) include the delectable *farfalle prosciutto e funghi*, a bowtie pasta with prosciutto, mushrooms, and a touch of cream ($12.50). Entrees $15-27. Reservations recommended. Open daily for lunch 11:30am-4pm; dinner M-W 4-10:30pm, Th 4-11pm, F-Sa 4-11:30pm, Su 4-10pm. AmEx/D/MC/V. ❹

🍲 **Tabard Inn,** 1739 N St. NW (☎785-1277; www.tabardinn.com), between 17th and 18th St. in the hotel of the same name (see p. 215). This longtime Dupont secret offers several beautiful dining rooms, a serene patio, and a menu that changes daily and features locally-grown ingredients. Appetizers ($7-11) may include lobster and mango salad in rice paper ($11). Entrees ($19-26) feature unique dishes like grilled marinated ostrich steak with horse-radish cream potato puree ($25). Although this is fine dining at its best, dress is casual and the atmosphere is entirely unpretentious. Reservations recommended, but patio seating is always first-come, first-seated. Open for breakfast M-F 7-10am; brunch Sa 11am-2pm, Su 10:30am-2pm; dinner Su-Th 6-9:30pm, F-Sa 6-10:30pm. ❹

🍲 **Lauriol Plaza,** 1865 18th St. NW (☎387-0035) at T St., between Dupont Circle and Adams Morgan. More of a complex than a restaurant, Lauriol occupies half the block with three magnificent floors of Mexican dining. Entrees, ranging $8-15, are served in copious quantities. After-work patrons can sit at tables on the sidewalk patio or the splendid rooftop deck and linger to socialize with the bar-hopping crowds. Appetizers such as fried plantains and guacamole $2.75-8. Su brunch entrees $7-12 (11am-3pm). Excellent margaritas $5, pitchers $23. Free parking. No reservations accepted, so get there early. Open Su-Th 11:30am-11pm, F-Sa and holidays 11:30am-midnight. ❷

🍲 **Cafe Luna,** 1633 P St. NW (☎387-4005; www.skewers-cafeluna.com), near 17th St. Not to be mistaken for the Luna Grill and Diner. Truly a neighborhood joint, this popular basement restaurant serves mostly vegetarian and low-fat fare for the health-conscious. Many dishes can be prepared fat-free upon request. Breakfast served all day ($2-5). Huge sandwiches satisfy almost any appetite ($4-6). Pasta $6-9. W and Su ½-price pizzas, which are only $5-7 to begin with. All pastas are ½-price M after 5pm. Brunch served Sa-Su 10am-3pm ($5-7). Local artists reserve 6 months in advance to show their work on the walls. Open M-Th 8am-11pm, F 8am-1am, Sa 10am-1am, Su 10am-11pm. AmEx/DC/D/MC/V. ❶

Raku, 1900 Q St. NW (☎265-7258, delivery ☎232-8646), off Connecticut Ave. Taking its name from the Japanese word for "pleasure," this modern Asian cafe serves a standard selection of pan-Asian noodles ($8-10), salads ($5-11), sushi ($4-6), and "pan-Asian *tapas*" (a variety of dumplings, rolls, and skewers; $4-8). Skylights illuminate the warm wooden tones of the comfortable dining room filled with picnic-table-like booths. In summer, the covered patio is an excellent place from which to sample specialty cocktails ($4.50-6). Open Su-Th 11:30am-10pm, F-Sa 11:30am-11pm. AmEx/D/MC/V. ❷

Pizzeria Paradiso, 2029 P St. NW (☎223-1245), near 21st St.; also in Georgetown at 3282 M St. NW (☎337-1245). The smell of freshly baked pizzas in their wood-burning oven will make your mouth water when you walk through the door. This refined pizza place serves fresh olives before you order. A bit pricier than the chain restaurants, but these genuine thin-crust pizzas are well worth the extra buck, and the list of toppings looks like an old Italian grocery. Wine is served in a traditional *trattoria* tumbler. 8 in. $8-10; 12 in. $13-16; toppings $1-2. Also offers an array of panini sandwiches ($6-7) and salads ($4-6). Both locations open M-Th 11:30am-11pm, F 11:30am-midnight, Sa 11am-midnight, Su noon-10pm. DC/D/MC/V. ❷

Sala Thai, 2016 P St. NW (☎872-1144). Known for both its delicious Thai cuisine and romantic, dark-blue-and-purple dining room. Enticing servings of traditional dishes like *pad thai* ($9) and harder to find *pu-nim* (2 spicy soft-shell crabs; $17), not to mention flavorful Mai Tais ($5.25). Special lunch prices draw afternoon crowds. Open M 11:30am-3pm and 4-10:30pm, Tu-F 11:30am-3pm and 5-11pm, Sa noon-11pm, Su noon-10:30pm. ❸

Skewers, 1633 P St. NW (☎387-7400; www.skewers-cafeluna.com), near 17th St. Above Cafe Luna. Middle Eastern favorites served in a stylish restaurant with mosaic surfaces, tapestries, and shimmery drapes. Lunch sandwiches include filet mignon pita ($8), grilled eggplant with yogurt ($6), and grilled vegetable ($6). The appetizer platter for 2 ($12) is a meal in itself. Appetizers $4-7. Popular dinners include kebab entrees and yogurt feta meals, a Lebanese favorite. Entrees $11-15. Open M-Th 11:30am-10:30pm, F 11:30am-midnight, Sa noon-midnight, Su 11am-10:30pm. AmEx/DC/D/MC/V. ❸

Dupont Italian Kitchen, 1637 17th St. NW (☎328-3222), at R St. Delicious, no-frills Italian food at great prices, served along excellent street-side seating. Cheese-slathered meat or vegetarian entrees served with spaghetti and tomato sauce ($6-14). Pasta $6-10. Sandwiches $5-6. Free delivery after 5pm (minimum $12). Open M noon-11pm, Tu-F noon-midnight, Sa 10:30am-midnight, Su 10:30am-11pm. Upstairs is the **DIK Bar,** a gay scene with Happy Hour deals every day 3-8pm ($2 vodka drinks, $3 domestic beer, $4 imports) and Drag Karaoke on Tu. Bar open Su-Th 4pm-2am, F-Sa 4pm-3am. ❷

Savino's, 1 Dupont Circle NW (☎872-1122; www.savinoscafe.com), southwest of the Circle at the intersection of New Hampshire Ave. New Italian cafe offers savory Northern Italian cuisine, even if the service is sometimes slow. Begin with prosciutto and fresh melon ($7.75) and continue with the *fiocchi*, pear-stuffed pasta in a light cheese and cream sauce (½ order $8.25, full order $14.50). ½ orders of pasta are small, but perfect with an entree ($17-24). Reservations recommended. Open for lunch M-F 11:30am-2:30pm; dinner M-Th 5-10pm, F-Sa 5-11pm. Bar open Su-Th until 1am, F-Sa until 2am. AmEx/DC/D/MC/V. ❹

Bua, 1635 P St. NW (☎265-0828), near 17th St. Cool, brick dining room and breezy 2nd-floor balcony specializing in spicy Thai cuisine. Nice array of vegetarian entrees (lunch $6, dinner $8). Tasty cashew chicken (lunch $6, dinner $8.25). Lunch entrees $6-8. Dinner entrees $8-15. Popular for takeout and delivery. Open for lunch M-F 11:30am-3pm, Sa-Su noon-4pm; dinner Su-Th 5-10:30pm, F-Sa 5-11pm. AmEx/DC/D/MC/V. ❷

Trio Restaurant, 1537 17th St. NW (☎232-6305), at Q St. Friendly family diner is the parent restaurant of the other two Trio offsprings, **Trio Pizza and Subs** and **Trio's Fox and Hounds.** The organizers of the 1963 March on Washington met at this historic, retro diner to strategize. Classic American meals including BLTs, turkey pot pie, steaks, and famous old-fashioned milkshakes. One of the best deals for breakfasts, served until 5pm ($2-7). Burgers and sandwiches $3-7. Entrees mostly under $10; seafood and steak under $15. Lunch specials M-F $7.50. Some vegetarian items available. Open daily 7:30am-midnight. AmEx/D/MC/V. ❷

Peppers, 1527 17th St. NW (☎328-8193; www.peppersrestaurant.com). Best for people-watching from the bustling sidewalk patio, this party-themed restaurant feels like a bar that overgrew into a restaurant. Hodgepodge menu items offers everything from fajitas and pastas to vegetarian dumplings. Specials include the "No Ordinary Calamari" (breaded squid stir-fried in soy sauce; $8). One of the few places with a late-night Happy Hour (daily 8pm-close). Deals include $1.25 drafts M after 5pm at the bar. A good place for Su dinner, which feature ½-price pizza and pasta (regularly $8-11.50) 5-10pm at the bar. Open Su-Th 11:30am-2am, F-Sa 11:30am-3am; kitchen open M-Th until 11pm, F-Su until midnight. ❷

City Lights of China, 1731 Connecticut Ave. NW (☎265-6688; www.citylightsofchina.com), between R and S St. This *Washingtonian* award-winning restaurant serves delicious Chinese food in a spacious dining room. Special steamed dishes for healthy eaters. Entrees $9-15. Reservations suggested. Open M-Th 11:30am-10:30pm, F 11am-11pm, Sa noon-11pm, Su noon-10:30pm. AmEx/D/MC/V. ❷

Luna Grill & Diner, 1301 Connecticut Ave. NW (☎835-2280; www.lunagrill.com), near N St. Friendly waitstaff serves high-quality fare in a moon-themed dining room with cosmic paintings. Salads, pastas, sandwiches ($6-9), and entrees ($10-16), all taste better, come larger, and cost more than in your typical diner. Breakfast available anytime ($4-10). The lunch crowd fills this small restaurant in a hurry, so call ahead to get on the list. No reservations otherwise. Open M-Th 8am-11pm, F-Sa 8am-1am, Su 8am-10pm. AmEx/DC/D/MC/V. ❸

Sakana, 2026 P St. NW (☎887-0900). The enticing smell of fresh Japanese food welcomes guests to this small, dimly-lit, primarily sushi restaurant. Well-prepared tempura and teriyaki dishes. Takeout available. Entrees $8.50-13, sushi rolls $2.50-10. Open M-F 11:30am-2:30pm and 5-10:30pm, Sa 5-11pm. AmEx/DC/D/MC/V. ❷

Zorba's Cafe, 1612 20th St. NW (☎387-8555; www.zorbascafe.com), at Connecticut Ave. by the Q St. entrance to the Dupont Circle Metro. Named after the title character from the novel and film *Zorba the Greek,* this family-owned restaurant offers homemade food served up quickly in a laid-back *bouzouki*-music playing atmosphere. Everything down to the bread rolls is made fresh every morning in the kitchen. Customers enjoy *spanakopita* (a spinach and feta turnover, $4.30), creamy hummus, and *baklava* ($2.85). Also popular are pizza (16 in. starting at $11.50) and pitchers of beer ($10-13). Sandwiches $5-7. Entrees $7-9. Open M-Sa 11am-11:30pm, Su 11:30am-10:30pm. AmEx/D/MC/V. ❷

Pan Asian Noodles & Grill, 2020 P St. NW (☎872-8889), at Hopkins St. Simple and affordable Asian mix-and-match restaurant offers traditional and new-age Thai, Chinese, Japanese, Filipino, and Vietnamese dishes. A favorite is the Borneo fried rice, Indonesian-style fried rice cooked with your choice of meat (lunch $6.25, dinner $8.25). Rotating lunch specials $6-8. Most entrees $8-12. Open M-Th 11:30am-2:30pm and 5-10pm, F 11:30am-2:30pm and 5-11pm, Sa noon-2:30pm and 5-11pm, Su 5-10pm. ❷

CAFES

Afterwords Cafe, 1517 Connecticut Ave. NW (☎387-1462; www.kramers.com), near Q St. Enter through Kramerbooks (see p. 198) or behind on 19th St. Overcrowded and overpriced, but one of the few places to indulge a late-night sweet tooth. Delicious cakes, pies, and mousse ($4.50-6.50), but serving size is sacrificed for presentation. Incredible selection of spiked coffee drinks ($6) and fine drafts ($4.75-5). Sandwiches and pasta also served ($10-15). 1 terminal with free Internet access at the bar. Live music W-Sa (times vary, call ahead). Open M-Th 7:30am-1am, then continuously F 7:30am-Su 1am. AmEx/MC/V. ❷

Teaism, 2009 R St. NW (☎667-3827; www.teaism.com), just west of Connecticut Ave. Also at 400 8th St. NW (☎638-6010), at D St., and 800 Connecticut Ave. NW (☎835-2233), enter on H St. between Connecticut Ave. and 17th St. Quiet teahouse offers a huge selection of teas from around the world, including Japanese Hojicha, Thai Nguyen, and Mexican Mint. Food is mostly overpriced Japanese dishes such as "Bento Boxes," lunches of salad, entree, and fruit ($8). Scrumptious ginger scones ($2). Most pots of tea $1.75-5, as high as $15 for rarer teas. Breakfast ($3.75-8.25) served M-F until 11:30am, Sa-Su until 2:30pm. Dupont location open M-Th 8am-10pm, F 8am-11pm, Sa 9am-11pm, Su 9am-10pm; 8th St. location open M-F 7:30am-10pm, Sa 9:30am-10pm, Su 9:30am-9pm; Connecticut Ave. location open M-F 7:30am-5:30pm. AmEx/D/MC/V. ❶

Firehook Coffee Shop and Bakery, 1909 Q St. NW (☎588-9296), off Connecticut Ave. Universally lauded for offering its customers one of the "best buys" in D.C., Firehook sells a variety of coffees ($1.10 a cup), cappuccinos ($2), and frozen coffee drinks ($4); however, the Firehook's unique twist on the run-of-the-mill coffee shop is that it also bakes daily a batch of organic bread (wheat, white, etc.; $4.50), massive muffins ($1.43), cookies and brownies ($1.38-1.83), and sumptuous cakes (small $23, large $34). For those who don't frequent bars until the late night, Firehook offers an excellent Happy Hour (3-5pm daily): coffee and a slice of cake is only $4. Open M-F 7am-9pm, Sa-Su 8am-9pm. AmEx/MC/V. ❶

Cosi, Dupont South: 1350 Connecticut Ave. NW (☎296-9341; www.getcosi.com), at Dupont Circle. Also at Dupont North, 1647 20th St. NW (☎332-6364), at R St. The chain coffee-house offers snacks and sandwiches ($4-7) in a cooler-than-Starbucks environment. Try the make-your-own s'mores (graham crackers or giant Oreo cookies, chocolate, marshmallows, and flame; $6.75, large $11.50). Dupont South open M-Th 6:30am-midnight, F 6:30am-1am, Sa 8am-1am, Su 8am-midnight; Dupont North open M-Th 7am-midnight, F 7am-1am, Sa 7:30am-1am, Su 7:30am-midnight. ❶

Jolt 'n' Bolt Coffee and Tea House, 1918 18th St. NW (☎232-0077), 5 blocks from the center of Adams Morgan, 6 blocks from Dupont Circle. Pleasant watering hole where mostly female students and young professionals chat it up over coffee or the latest smoothie (made with fresh fruit). Assortment of complimentary newspapers are read on the brick patio with charming fountain. Espresso drinks $1.40-3.30; 20 oz. fruit smoothies $3.65; impressive selection of desserts $1.50-3.50. Open Su-Th 6:30am-11:30pm, F-Sa 6:30am-1:30am. ❶

The Cyberstop Cafe, 1513 17th St. NW (☎234-2470; www.cyberstopcafe.com), just north of P St. 11 Internet-connected computers, 1 plug-in terminal, and free wireless Internet in this 2-story coffee-shop offering the standard selection of hot and cold drinks, sandwiches, and bagels. Take your iced mocha upstairs and surf the web on one of 6 flat-screen computers in individual carrels. $7 for 30min., $9 per hr. Coffee $1-3, cookies $1. Open M-F 7am-midnight, Sa-Su 8am-midnight. ❶

FARRAGUT

Suits and fanny pack-sporting tourists alike surge through Farragut's tasty and inexpensive lunchtime delis, quick ethnic eateries, and street vendors. Health conscious locals have also generated an array of low-fat dining options throughout the Farragut area. Cafes hawking frozen yogurt, salads, and espresso compete for attention with bars offering free Happy Hour buffets. A few remaining restaurants, however, offer fine cuisine, excellent service, and prices that are justifiably higher than the lunch take-out chains.

SEE MAP P.357 YOU ARE HERE

U.S. Capitol Building

Famous Luigi's, 1132 19th St. NW (☎331-7574; www.famousluigis.com). Metro: Farragut North, Farragut West, or Dupont Circle. Friendly service and a large selection of expertly-made pasta dishes ($10.75-17.75) have made this excellent Italian restaurant famous. Amid warm yellow walls, patrons are served favorites like the *Agnolotti di formaggio* (ravioli stuffed with ricotta, spinach, and parmesan cheese; $13). Meat and fish entrees are served with pasta and a vegetable ($14.50-18). Menu items typically $2-3 less at lunch. The *tiramisu* ($5) is not to be missed. Free delivery available. Reservations only for 10+ at lunch and 5+ at dinner. Open M-Sa 11am-midnight, Su noon-midnight. AmEx/DC/D/MC/V. ❷

Bombay Palace, 2020 K St. NW (☎331-4200; thebombaypalace@msn.com). Metro: Farragut North. *Washingtonian* calls Bombay Palace a "model of luxury Indian dining," and this restaurant more than lives up to that billing. With a sleek, mirrored interior, wonderfully attentive and unobtrusive service, and the best Chicken Tikka Masala ($13) in Washington, the Palace is the perfect downtown eatery for a power lunch or a romantic dinner. Vegetarian options available. Entrees $8-22. Open Su-F 11:30am-2:30pm and 5:30-10pm; Sa noon-2:30pm and 5:30-10:30pm. Sa-Su lunch buffet noon-2:30pm. AmEx/DC/D/MC/V. ❹

Julia's Empanadas, 1000 Vermont Ave. NW (☎789-1878). Metro: McPherson Sq. Also at 1221 Connecticut Ave. NW (☎861-8828), 1410 U St. NW (☎387-4100), and 2452 18th St. NW (☎328-6232). Julia's sells a variety of *empanadas* (dough pockets filled with various ingredients; $3) in a relaxed takeout atmosphere. Try the *saltenas* (chicken with potato, green peas, hard-boiled egg, green olives, and onion). Lunch combos $5.20. Seasonal soup menu often includes *gazpacho* ($1.85-3). Open M-F 10:30am-6:30pm. Cash only. ❶

Juice Joint Cafe, 1025 Vermont Ave. NW (☎347-6783; www.juicejointcafe.com). Metro: McPherson Sq. or Farragut North. Health nuts, vegans, and people craving cool smoothies and good food frequent this juicery. Customize your own juice ($2.75-4.25) or smoothie ($3.75-4.25) from a long list of vegetable and fruit juices, power additions, and minerals. Vegan and non-vegan (turkey burger, fresh seared yellow-fin tuna) sandwiches and wraps $3.50-7.25. Multi-grain breakfasts served until 10:30am. Open M-F 7:30am-4pm. MC/V with $5 min. ❶

Art Gallery Grille, 1712 I St. NW (☎298-6658; www.artgallerygrille.com), near 17th St. Metro: Farragut West. The Grille blends in with the other luncheon diners along I St. during the day, but unlike the other places, it stays open late and accommodates the nighttime crowd. This Art Deco flashback doesn't skimp on the neon lighting or jukebox, and a DJ spins rock hits Th-F nights. Old-style diner charm meets sophisticated, healthy, Middle Eastern cuisine (falafel tray $10). The white pizza (mozzarella, parmesan, and Havarti; $8), Caesar salad ($8.25), and specialty sandwiches ($8-11) are favorites. Happy Hour M-F 4-8pm with varied specials each night. Outdoor seating. Open M-F 6:30am onward. ❷

Thai Kingdom, 2021 K St. NW (☎835-1700), near 21st St. Metro: Farragut West or Foggy Bottom-GWU. In a bright atmosphere marked by pink wallpaper, detailed wooden lanterns, and photos of Thai celebrities and of Thailand itself, Thai Kingdom features appetizers like "Famous Wings" (chicken wings stuffed with crabmeat, mushrooms, and noodles; $6.50) and entrees like "Anna and the King" (scallops wrapped in minced chicken fried with basil sauce; $9). Vegetarian options include vegetable *pad thai* ($8). Reservations recommended, especially for lunch M-F. Open M-Th 11:30am-2:30pm and 5-10:30pm, F 11:30am-2:30pm and 5-11pm, Sa noon-11pm, Su noon-10pm. AmEx/DC/D/MC/V. ❷

Casa Blanca, 1014 Vermont Ave. NW (☎393-4430), between K and L St. Metro: McPherson Sq. or Farragut North. With its excellent Peruvian, Salvadoran, and Mexican dishes, Casa Blanca often draws a crowd. Basic tacos are 2 for $3.50. The Peruvian specialty *pollo a la braza* (roasted chicken with salad and fried potatoes or rice and beans) is a steal at $5.50. Daily specials $4-5. Menu items $0.50 less at lunch. Free delivery. Open M-F 9am-10pm, Sa 10am-11pm, Su noon-8pm. Cash only. ❶

FEDERAL TRIANGLE

YOU ARE HERE

SEE MAP P. 356

U.S. Capitol Building

Some of the best food in Federal Triangle is in **Chinatown** (see p. 145). A surprising number of good non-Chinese options also lurk among the neighborhood's delis. If food courts are your style, your best bet is the glistening new collection of 17 fast-food eateries on the lower level of the recently built **Ronald Reagan Building.** (1300 Pennsylvania Ave. NW. Metro: Federal Triangle. Open Mar.-Aug. M-F 7am-7pm, Sa 11am-6pm, Su noon-5pm; Sept.-Feb. M-F 7am-7pm, Sa 11am-6pm.) With government workers home for the weekend, this location becomes hauntingly empty, as do the **Shops at National Place and Press.** (1331 Pennsylvania Ave. NW. Metro: Metro Center or Federal Triangle. Open M-W and F-Sa 10am-7pm, Th 10am-8pm, Su noon-5pm.) Another standard food court mixed in with various memorabilia shops can be found at the **Pavilion at the Old Post Office.** (Pennsylvania Ave. and 11th St. NW. Metro: Federal Triangle. Open M-Sa 10am-7pm, Su noon-6pm.) **The area can be dangerous at night.** Use Metro: Metro Center, unless otherwise noted, for the following.

▨ **Marrakesh,** 617 New York Ave. NW (☎393-9393; www.marrakesh.us). Metro: Gallery Place-Chinatown. From the corner of 7th and H St., turn right onto 7th St. heading away from the MCI Center, go down 4 blocks, turn right onto New York Ave. The red door takes diners from the clamor of city traffic into the intoxicating milieu of Morocco. The servers begin by washing your hands in rosewater (7 course *prix-fixe* meal is eaten by hand). Reservations required. Cash or personal check only. $25 per person, not including drinks, tax, or gratuity. $5 valet parking service. M-F 6pm-11pm, Sa 5:30pm-11pm, Su 5pm-11pm. ❺

▨ **Haad Thai,** 1100 New York Ave. NW (☎682-1111), entrance on 11th St. between H and I St. The descriptive menu makes Haad Thai a good introduction for newcomers to Thai cuisine, while its extra spicy options satiate aficionados. Popular *pad thai* (lunch $7, dinner $9) and *panang gai* (chicken sautéed with fresh basil leaves in curry peanut sauce; lunch $8, dinner $10) are offered alongside their vegetarian counterparts (lunch $7, dinner $8). Open M-F 11:30am-2:30pm and 5-10:30pm, Sa noon-10:30pm, Su 5-10:30pm. AmEx/DC/MC/V. ❷

▨ **John Harvard's Brew House,** 1299 Pennsylvania Ave. NW (☎783-2739; www.johnharvards.com), below the Warner Theatre on the corner of E and 13th St. This import from Cambridge, MA bears the marquee facade of an adjoining theater, so watch carefully for it. Don't miss the rotating laundry list of beers brewed on the premises (pints $3-4, sampler of 5 beers $5) and massive grill portions. Favorites include the Brew House Burger ($7) and Chicken Pot Pie ($10). Happy Hour (M-F 4-7pm) promises $1 off pints. Takeout available. Evening reservations recommended, especially on performance nights at the Warner. Open M-Th 11am-11pm, F 11am-midnight, Sa noon-midnight, Su noon-10pm. AmEx/DC/D/MC/V. ❷

Harry's, 436 11th St. NW (☎624-0053), on the corner of E and 11th St., across from the ESPN Zone. Metro: Metro Center or Federal Triangle. Tourists spill out onto the street during the summer as they flock to try Harry's 8 oz. burgers and fries ($6.25). Come at night to cool off and watch the Orioles game with a beer ($3-5) or daiquiri ($6). Open Su-Th 11am-2am, F-Sa 11am-3am, kitchen closes at 1am Su-Th, 2am F-Sa. AmEx/D/DC/MC/V. ❶

Reeves, 1306 G St. NW (☎628-6350), between 13th and 14th St. Established in 1886, Reeves has a little bit of everything, from an all-you-can-eat breakfast and fruit bar ($6-7) and a variety of sandwiches ($3.50-6.25) to amazing cake doughnuts ($0.60), but is most famous for its mouth-watering strawberry pie (slice $2.75, whole pie $15.50). Everything on the menu is available for takeout. Open M-Sa 7am-6pm. MC/V. ❶

Jaleo, 480 7th St. NW (☎628-7949), 1 block from Metro: Gallery Place-Chinatown at 7th and E St. Cheesy Spanish decorations expose the fabricated authenticity of this commercial knock-off. Over 50 different *tapas* (appetizer-sized dishes of various meats and vegetables; $3-8). The local favorite is the *paella*, a large traditional rice dish that serves up to 4 people ($39.50). Full bar includes sangria ($16 per pitcher) and a sherry sampler ($8). *Sevillana* (similar to Flamenco) dancers on W nights at 7:50 and 8:50pm. Su brunch 11:30am-3pm. Limited reservations accepted for 5-6:30pm; expect to wait 1-2hr. after 6:30pm. Open Su-M 11:30am-10pm, Tu-Th 11:30am-11:30pm, F-Sa 11:30am-midnight. AmEx/DC/D/MC/V. ❹

Gordon Biersch, 900 F St. NW, at 9th St. (☎783-5454; www.gordonbiersch.com). The vaulted ceilings and marble columns that grace this upscale brew pub make it look like the stately bank lobby it once was. Menu includes a variety of appetizers ($5-10), pizzas ($10-11.50), sandwiches ($9), and heartier entrees ($11-21). 4 German beers brewed on site (pint $4.50-4.75). Open Su-Th 11:30am-11pm (bar until midnight), F-Sa 11:30am-midnight (bar until 2am). AmEx/DC/D/MC/V. ❸

High Noon, 1311 F St. NW (☎783-3990); 1200 19th St. NW (☎833-1326); 15th and K St. NW (☎682-2211), and 4th and F St. NW (☎393-0353) at the National Building Museum. A vegetarian's dream—offers an array of veggie soups (small $3.89, large $4.89) as well as hundreds of salad combinations. Start with a base of 3 greens (baby spinach, romaine, or spring mix; $4.29), then add your own toppings (first 2 free, each additional $0.50-1.50) and dressing. Noon specials include ½ sandwich, 8 oz. soup or side salad, and a drink ($7). Open M-F 7am-3pm. D/MC/V. ❶

Capitol City Brewing Company, 1100 New York Ave. NW (☎628-2222; www.capcity-brew.com), entrance at the corner of 11th and H St. Other locations at 2 Massachusetts Ave. NE (☎842-2337) and 2700 S. Quincy St. in Arlington (☎703-578-3888). Opened in 1992, the first brewery in D.C. since Prohibition, this faux-industrial warehouse joint is known for its home-brewed beer and hearty grub. Luckily the Filibuster Burger ($8) and "Cajun Angels" shrimp pasta ($15) taste good enough to forgive their cheesy names. Takeout available. Open Su-Th 11am-11pm, F-Sa 11am-midnight. Bar open until 2am. AmEx/DC/D/MC/V. ❷

Stoney's Restaurant, 1307 L St. NW (☎347-9163), near 13th St. Metro: McPherson Sq. Despite a recent move of headquarters, Secret Service employees still frequent this diner and bar. Longest F Happy Hour in D.C. (4pm-midnight; Corona or margarita $2.50, Bud pitchers $9) attract loyal locals; staff also recommends the "One Eye," a burger topped with a fried egg ($7). Open daily 11am-2am, kitchen closes at 1am. Cash only. ❶

Zola, 800 F St. NW, at 8th and F St. above the International Spy Museum (☎654-0999; www.zoladc.com). This chic restaurant and martini bar caters to an well-dressed middle-aged crowd. Favorites include the cheddar and pimento fondue served with sausage and sourdough ($9) and the roasted jumbo prawns served over gingered grits ($23). Appetizers $6-14, entrees $14-25. 3-course pre-event menu served daily 5-7pm ($25). Reservations recommended. Open Su-Th 11:30am-midnight, F-Sa 11:30am-1am. AmEx/DC/D/MC/V. ❹

Luigino's, 1100 New York Ave. NW (☎371-0595), enter on the corner of 12th and H St. Potted plants and certificates of award are the main decorations. Sit at the counter and watch the chefs at work. Sizable menu includes pizza ($8.50 and up), meat dishes ($15.50-$26.50), fish ($13.50-$25.50) and a variety of pastas ($12.50-$16.50). Lunch menu has lower prices. Open M-Th 11:30am-2:30pm and 5:30pm-10:30pm, F 11:30am-2:30pm and 5:30-11:30pm, Sa 5:30pm-11:30pm, Su 5:30pm-10pm. AmEx/DC/MC/V. ❺

Cafe Amadeus, 1300 I St. NW (☎962-8686), entrance on 13th St. Metro: McPherson Sq. Don't be fooled by the name—this is a hearty American grill offering healthy "hunter-style" dishes of bite-sized meat (lamb, chicken, beef, or shrimp) sautéed with vegetables and a special fat free seasoning (Lunch $11-15, Dinner $14-17). Selection of fondues for 2($15-60). Happy Hour (M-F 4-8pm) brings free appetizers with any drink. Open M-F 11:30am-9pm, Sa 11am-10pm. AmEx/D/MC/V. ❸

FOGGY BOTTOM

Foggy Bottom is by no means a food lover's paradise. However, a selection of well-hidden eateries have excellent food, low prices, or both; a walk along M St. or Pennsylvania Ave. west of the White House will reveal some enticing options. Use Metro: Foggy Bottom-GWU for all of the following.

🍴 **Mei Wah Restaurant,** 1200 New Hampshire Ave. NW (☎833-2888; www.meiwahrestaurant.com), at the corner of New Hampshire Ave. and M St. between 21st and 22nd St.. With its excellent food and classy decor, Mei Wah is a step up from the basic Chinese food. Rolling Stones lead singer Mick Jagger is supposedly a fan of the food here, such as the delicious crispy shredded beef ($15). Entrees $9-24. Wine $4, beer $3-4, cocktails $4.50-6. Takeout available. Open M-Th 11:30am-10:30pm, F 11:30am-11pm, Sa noon-11pm, Su noon-10:30pm. AmEx/DC/MC/V. ❸

🍴 **Legal Sea Foods,** 2020 K St. NW (☎496-1111; www.legalseafoods.com), between 20th and 21st St. Exceptionally fresh seafood is served in a space decorated with images of fishing boats and old sailing ships. Seafood options overall are quite extensive and come in fried ($11-21), "classic," and "specialty" varieties ($15-33), in addition to lobsters ($28-62). The Maryland cream of crab soup ($7) is exquisite. Legal Sea Foods prides itself on its wine list, and with good cause; the selection of wines by the glass ($4.50-12), by the bottle ($17-135), and by the half-bottle ($9-77) is extensive. Reservations recommended. Open M-F 11am-10pm, Sa 4pm-10:30pm. AmEx/DC/D/MC/V. ❹

🍴 **Fresco,** 2554 Virginia Ave. NW (☎337-6432), in the Watergate complex; from the Metro, walk away from Washington Circle on 23rd St., make a right onto G St. and follow it to the Watergate, going down the stairs (at the intersection of Virginia Ave. and 25th St.) and into the ground-level plaza of the complex. The chicken pesto il panini sandwich ($6.50), made right before your eyes, might be the best inexpensive lunch in D.C. Deluxe fruit and salad bar $5, frozen yogurt $1.50-3, and subs $3.50-5.50. Patrons can eat in or sit at one of the outside tables in the Watergate plaza; takeout also available. Open M-F 7:30am-7pm (breakfast served until 10am), Sa 8am-5pm (breakfast until 11am). AmEx/DC/MC/V. ❶

🍴 **Cone E. Island,** (☎822-8460), in the mall at 2000 Pennsylvania Ave. NW. GWU students flock to this modern ice-cream parlor with Ionic columns ringed in neon lights and 7 tables cramped into a small 2nd fl. space. Soft-serve frozen yogurt vies with many flavors of divinely satisfying ice cream. Turn any flavor into a smooth milkshake. Generous cones $2-4, $0.60 home-made waffle cones. Fat-free bakery treats $1-3, including delicious blondie brownies ($1.60). All ice cream is kosher, as is some frozen yogurt. Student Advantage cardholders get a free scoop for orders over $5. Open daily noon-midnight. Cash only. ❶

Thai Kitchen, 2311 M St. NW (☎452-6090), near the intersection with 23rd St. The simple yet exotic decor—complete with a fountain waterfall near the entrance, gold-colored tables, and the small, colorful ceiling lamps—matches the tasty food here. Entrees in generous portions $7.50-11 at lunch and $10-14 at dinner. Many vegetarian options. The cashew chicken ($8 lunch, $11 dinner) and coconut ice cream ($3.95) are delicious. Happy Hour (M-F 5-

7pm) $2 draft beer and ½ price soups. Wine $4.50-6.50 per glass, beer $3-7, cocktails $4-5.50. Takeout available; free delivery for orders over $15. Open M-F 11am-10:30pm, Sa noon-10pm, Su 4:30pm-10pm. Reservations recommended. AmEx/MC/V. ❷

Lindy's Bon Apetit, 2040 I St. NW (☎452-0055), near the intersection with 21st St. Lindy's is famous for its selection of over 23 humongous, creatively-titled hamburgers ($3.50-6.50), including the "Capitol Punishment," a burger with 3 different kinds of pepper. Veggie and grilled chicken substitutes are available for burgers. Lindy's location and its late hours make it ideal for hungry GWU students and interns on lunch break. Those who miss its normal business hours can still get take-out until midnight at Lindy's Red Lion (p. 176), the counterpart bar and grill one floor above. Outdoor seating. Open M-F 7:30am-10pm (breakfast until 11am), Sa-Su 11am-10pm (brunch until 1pm). ❶

Cup A' Cup A' at the Watergate, 600 New Hampshire Ave. NW (☎466-3677), at the intersection of New Hampshire and F St. in the Watergate complex. Sleek Italian interior with shiny chrome stools offers a cool venue for sipping a coffee or coffee by-product. Espressos and lattes complement sandwiches and a salad bar ($5 per lb). Reenact Nixon's infamous crimes with The "Break-In" Sandwich (turkey breast and avocado on a baguette; $6); other politically-titled specialty sandwiches ($5-6) include the "JFK," the "Hillary," and the "Moynihan." Standard wraps and sandwiches ($3.50-6.25), coffee drinks ($1.25-3.50), and great pies are also available, as are a good number of vegetarian options, including salads ($2-6.25) and veggie or blackbean burgers ($4.25-6.25). $2 bottles of beer and $1 off wine 4pm-close, so stop by on the way back from the Kennedy Center next door for a post-Mozart Bordeaux. Open M-Th 6am-8pm, F 6am-9pm, Sa 7:30am-9pm, Su 10am-6pm. AmEx/DC/D/MC/V. ❶

GEORGETOWN

Among the many quality attractions in Georgetown (shopping, shopping, and more shopping) are also fab eats. Georgetown's dining options mostly line **M St.** and **Wisconsin Ave.,** vying for the attention of college kids, tourists, and power-lunching execs. Eateries range from expensive wood-and-brass establishments to more affordable Italian, Indian, Middle Eastern, Thai, and Vietnamese restaurants. Use Metro: Foggy Bottom-GWU or Dupont Circle to access the area. It's a 20min. walk from either station to Georgetown's restaurants; take the $1 purple **Georgetown Metro Connection** shuttles from these stops to save yourself the hike. Also consider the 30-series buses, which run down M St. and Wisconsin Ave. between Downtown and Tenleytown or Friendship Heights.

YOU ARE HERE
U.S. Capitol Building
SEE MAP P. 359

Clyde's of Georgetown, 3236 M St. NW (☎333-9180; www.clydes.com), between Potomac St. and Wisconsin Ave. Even with 2 dining rooms and a bar area in the middle, this place still manages to stay packed during meal time. And rightly so—the food is delicious. Serves sandwiches ($7-12), salads ($11-13), seafood ($13-17), and pasta ($13-15). The various dining rooms each have a different theme relating to early-20th century travel or sport. 10 beers on tap ($4-5.45). Dinner prices reduced by 20% M-F 4:30-6pm. Open M-Th 11:30am-2am, F 11:30am-3am, Sa 10am-3am, Su 9am-2am. AmEx/DC/D/MC/V. ❸

Red Ginger, 1564 Wisconsin Ave. NW (☎965-7009; www.redgingerbistro.com). From M St., walk away from the C&O Canal along Wisconsin Ave.; the restaurant will be on the left-hand side at the intersection with Q St. Serves flavorful, sometimes spicy Caribbean gourmet food. The whole red snapper (with saffron rice and a mango pineapple chutney, $15) is delicious; patrons who don't want their meal literally staring back at them, however, will prefer lunch entrees ($13-16), such as the pineapple pork chop ($13). The weekend brunch offers complimentary champagne (Sa-Su 11:30am-5pm). Be sure to save room for Red Ginger's wonderful desserts, including pineapple, coconut, and orange sorbets ($7), each served in a hollowed shell of the actual fruit. Vegetarian options offered. Open Tu-F 4:30-11pm, Sa 11:30am-11:30pm, Su 11:30am-10pm. AmEx/D/MC/V. ❸

J. Paul's, 3218 M St. NW (☎333-3450; jpauls@capitalrestaurants.com), near Wisconsin Ave. More precisely a "dining saloon," J. Paul's, established in 1889, successfully maintains the turn-of-the-century feel with the dark hues of its wood-paneled and brick interior. The bar here comes from the stockyards of Chicago, where gangster Al Capone supposedly drank on its wooden surface; the rear wall of the back dining room cleverly features old elevator doors originally from New York City's Waldorf Astoria hotel. Order from a selection of burgers and sandwiches ($8-14) or from the list of favorites ($13-23). "Construction hour" Su-Th after 10pm features $3 draft beers and $5 food specials. Reservations accepted M-Th only. Open M-Th 11:30am-11:30pm, F-Sa 11:30am-midnight, Su 10:30am-11:30pm. Bar open Su-Th until 1:30am, F-Sa until 2:30am. Brunch until 4pm Sa-Su. AmEx/DC/D/MC/V. ❸

Patisserie Poupon, 1645 Wisconsin Ave. NW (☎342-3248), near the corner of Wisconsin and Q St. Start the day with a mouthwatering buttery brioche, pear danish, or croissant ($1.30-2.25). Beautifully prepared tarts and cakes in individual to party portions ($4-38). Sandwiches, quiches, and salads $4-7. Coffee bar in back. Outdoor seating features potted plants and flowers. Open Tu-Sa 8am-6:30pm, Su 8am-4pm. AmEx/D/MC/V. ❶

Furin's, 2805 M St. NW (☎965-1000; www.furins.com), at M and 28th St. The potted plants, bookshelves, old-fashioned hospitality, and good home cooking attract the masses at lunch. Businesspeople, students, and local shopkeepers flock for made-with-love sandwiches ($5-7), salads ($2.75), and sweets ($2-3). Student Advantage discount. Breakfast served M-F until 11:30am, Sa 1:30pm. Open M-F 7:30am-7pm, Sa 8am-5pm. AmEx/DC/D/MC/V. ❶

Saigon Inn, 2928 M St. NW (☎337-5588), at 30th St. The presidents of Haiti and Peru have eaten in this ornate dining room, adorned with detailed, hand-made ceiling lanterns from Vietnam. The lunch special, a generous 4-dish sampler, wins raves ($5, daily 11am-3pm). The Saigon pancake, a crispy crêpe filled with tender meat and seafood, is the house specialty ($10). Delicately spiced fresh rolls with or without the shrimp and pork ($4.75 for 2). Entrees $7-15. Free delivery ($15 minimum) available. 15% Student Advantage discount. Open M-Th 11am-10pm, F-Sa 11am-11pm, Su noon-10pm. AmEx/DC/D/MC/V. ❷

Cafe La Ruche, 1039 31st St. NW (☎965-2684; www.cafelaruche.com), 2 blocks south of M St., past the C&O Canal on the left-hand side. "La Ruche" means "the beehive," and this place gets buzzing late at night when romantics move in for dessert and coffee. La Ruche offers excellent French cuisine, including lunch offerings: soups ($4), salads and appetizers ($4-8), and quiche and sandwiches ($6.75-7); items are a few dollars higher at dinner. Enjoy the full meal or skip right to the chocolate mousse ($5.50), kiwi tart ($5), or any of the other divine desserts ($5-6). The weekend brunch offers both a fixed-price special (juice, entree, and dessert $12). Outdoor seating available. Open M-Th 11:30am-11:30pm, F 11:30am-1am, Sa 10am-1am, Su 10am-10:30pm. Brunch offered Sa-Su 10am-3pm. AmEx/MC/V. ❷

Ching Ching Cha, 1063 Wisconsin Ave. NW (☎333-8288), 1 block south of M St. If you don't want to walk all the way uphill to fancy mansion gardens for quiet contemplation, try this Chinese tea shop. The wide selection of imported teas can be purchased to take home, with prices from $1.25 to $15 per 2 oz. Sells an exquisite array of teaware; individual cups $3-6. Also serves fresh tea on-site (most teas $4-8, but some as much as $20 per pot). Open Tu-Sa 11:30am-9pm, Su 11:30am-7pm. AmEx/MC/V. ❶

Paolo's, 1303 Wisconsin Ave. NW (☎333-7353; pgt@capitalrestaurants.com), at N St. Friendly service, well-lit dining areas, and warm pastel hues set the scene for Paolo's Italian food. While munching on the free breadsticks, choose from a selection of pizzas ($8-11), salads ($6-14), and entrees ($9-21), with pasta dishes topping out at $20. A weekend brunch (served Sa-Su 11:30am-3pm) offers eggs and omelettes ($8-9). Open Su-Th 11:30am-2am, F-Sa 11:30am-3am; food ia served until 1½hr. before close. AmEx/DC/D/MC/V. ❸

Zed's Ethiopian Cuisine, 1201 28th St. NW (☎333-4710; www.zeds.net), at the corner of 28th and M St. Serves traditional Ethiopian dishes such as kitfo, steak prepared with a spiced chili powder ($14.25). Vegetarian dishes $10.25-11.75. African beer $5. Patrons might notice the series of photos of Zed with customers like Clint Eastwood, Hillary Clinton, and the elder Bushes. Reservations for parties of 5 or more. Open daily 11am-11pm. AmEx/DC/D/MC/V. ❸

Aditi, 3299 M St. NW (☎625-6825; www.image-in-asian.com/aditi), at the corner of M and 33rd St. Famous for skillfully prepared Indian food served in an elegant dining room with an ornately carved wooden ceiling. Weekday lunch specials $6. Appetizers run $2-6, while entrees (including a selection of vegetarian dishes) are $7-13 at lunch, $8-15 at dinner.

Open for lunch M-Sa 11:30am-2:30pm, Su noon-2:30pm; for dinner M-Th and Su 5:30-10pm, F-Sa 5:30-10:30pm. AmEx/DC/D/MC/V. ❸

Thomas Sweet, 3214 P St. NW (☎337-0616; www.thomassweet.com), at the intersection with Wisconsin Ave. A local ice cream parlor that serves over 130 flavors of homemade ice cream and frozen yogurt ($2.25-3.60). Smoothies and "blend-ins" are $3.63-4.09, while sundaes run $3.64-4.54. Packed pints and quarts are $4 and $7, respectively. Student Advantage cardholders get free toppings. Outside seating available. Open M-Th 8am-midnight, F-Sa 8am-1am, Su 9am-midnight. Cash only. ❶

Moby Dick House of Kabob, 1070 31st St. NW (☎333-4400; www.mobysonline.com), near the corner of M and 31st St. A popular lunch takeout spot, featuring traditional Iranian dishes with mouth-watering, lean, marinated meats. Try the Kubideh and Chenjeh combo served with rice and clay-oven pita bread ($9.70) or enjoy one of Moby's famous sandwiches ($4.15-5). Vegetarian options available ($4.75-7); the lamb dishes here are kosher. Limited seating. Open Su noon-10pm, M-Th 11am-10pm, F 11am-4am, Sa noon-4am. Cash only. ❷

Nathans, 3150 M St. NW (☎338-2000), at Wisconsin Ave. In the family tree of restaurants, Nathans is a close cousin to J. Paul's, with similar hues of dark brown in its wood paneled interior creating a turn-of-the-20th-century feel. Diners with horse and boat fetishes will enjoy gazing at the equestrian art and sailing vessels adorning the walls. Best bets are the filets ($17-20) and steak dishes ($17-27). Try the lobster fettuccini ($22). "Foggy Fridays" (F 3-6pm) feature $3 glasses of Foggy Bottom Ale. Dancing in back room F-Sa after 11pm. Dining room open daily 5:30-11pm; Sa-Su also 10am-2:30pm for brunch. AmEx/DC/MC/V. ❹

Miss Saigon, 3057 M St. NW (☎333-5545). Strings of white Christmas lights, fake straw-hut awnings, plastic palm trees, and coconuts dominate the interior—but any excess of atmosphere is pardoned by the food's excellent quality. Beef dishes ($10-13) and chicken entrees ($10), and a copious selection of vegetarian plates ($8-10). Japanese "Fuki" wines ($5). Open M-F 11:30am-10:30pm, Sa noon-11pm, Su noon-10:30pm. AmEx/DC/MC/V. ❷

Dean and Deluca, 3276 M St. NW (☎342-2500; www.deandeluca.com), next to Georgetown Park Mall, near the corner of 33rd and M St. Don't let the chi-chi atmosphere of this glitzy chain gourmet market stop you from trying out the adjacent espresso bar's offerings. Features an assortment of sandwiches, wraps, and entrees ($5.75-8), gourmet soup and sandwich combos ($8.50), coffee drinks

Got Crabs?

A long-time Maryland favorite, crab cakes are deep- or pan-fried patties of lump crabmeat and batter that together form a delectable entree. Most restaurants in the D.C. metro area serve crab cakes. The quality and size of said crab cakes vary widely among restaurants, and diners often pay up to $15 for just two crab cakes!

As such, *Let's Go* recommends this simple recipe for homemade crab cakes:

Ingredients:

1 pound backfin crab meat
1 egg, beaten
8 crumbled saltine crackers
2 tablespoons mayonnaise
1 teaspoon mustard
dash Worcestershire sauce

Preparation:

Carefully remove all cartilage from the crab meat. Put meat in a bowl and set it aside. Mix together all other ingredients. Gently mix in crab meat. Shape into 6 crab cakes. Put crab cakes on a plate, cover with wax paper, and refrigerate for an hour. In a large frying pan, heat about 1-2 tablespoons of vegetable oil. Sauté until golden brown (about 2-3 minutes per side).

Let's Go recommends serving crab cakes on a bed of field greens drizzled with Hollandaise sauce and, of course, an ice cold beer.

($1.25-4.15), and sweets ($1-5.50), as well as enticing Italian sodas (with many flavors available, $2-2.35) and *gelato* ($2.50-3.50). Tell them Javier sent you. Espresso bar open Su-Th 8am-8pm, F-Sa 8am-9pm. AmEx/D/MC/V. ●

Tony and Joe's Seafood Place, 3000 K St. NW (☎944-4545; www.tonyandjoes.com). From M. St., walk over the C&O Canal along 30th St., continuing under the Whitehurst Freeway and into the plaza area of the Washington Harbor; restaurant will be to the left. Offers a wide range of fresh fish entrees ($20-24), which can be prepared in a large number of ways to the customer's specification. Appetizers, including fried alligator ($10), are $6-13, while seafood sandwiches run $8-15. Su buffet brunch (11am-3pm) features live jazz music ($29, $32 with champagne, $16 for children). Outdoor seating offers excellent views of the Potomac from its waterfront vantage point. Open Su-Th 11am-11pm, F-Sa 11am-midnight. ●

Amma Vegetarian Kitchen, 3291 M St. NW (☎625-6625), between 33rd and Potomac St. From the M St. entrance, walk upstairs to the 2nd fl. restaurant. Amma offers traditional Indian cuisine in a white dining room with colorful wall paintings. Enjoy regional specialties like idli sambar (light, steamed rice-flour cakes in a dazzling vegetable sauce; $4). Entrees $4-8, including a selection of curry dishes ($6-8). Open M-Th 11:30am-10pm, F-Sa 11:30am-10:30pm, Su noon-10pm. AmEx/DC/D/MC/V. ●

Bistro Med, 3288 M St. NW (☎333-2333; www.bistromeddc.com), near the corner of M and 33rd St. Specializing in Levantine cuisine, Bistro Med offers *lahmaçun* (Turkish-style pizzas; $7) and pricier entrees ($10-17) like *merguez de marocaine* (lamb sausage with eggplant and couscous; $11). Open Su-F 11:30am-10:30pm, Sa 11:30am-11:30pm. ●

Georgetown Cafe, 1623 Wisconsin Ave. NW (☎333-0215), at the intersection with Q St. The perfect place for a late-night snack; it's often packed come 3am. Offers breakfast anytime ($2.25-6.75), and serves typical sandwiches ($3.75-6.75), subs ($6.50), and pizzas ($7-10), as well as Middle Eastern specialties ($5-9.50), like *baba ghanoush*, a tasty eggplant dish ($5). Lunch specials (M-F 11am-4pm) offer discounts and deals, including $2 off pizza and free fries and soda with each sandwich. An Internet station near the front entrance allows patrons to go online for $0.15-0.25 per min. Open daily 9am-6am. DC/D/MC/V. ●

Marvelous Market, 3217 P St. NW (☎333-2591; www.marvelousmarket.com), at Wisconsin Ave. Reminiscent of a neighborhood market, it sells the basics—fruits, vegetables, fresh bread, cheese, snacks, and flowers. Almost everything is made on the premises. Grab a homemade sandwich ($5-6.29), freshly baked pizza ($5-11), or coffee ($1-3) and relax at one of 10 tables in the adjacent windowed dining area. Vegetarian options available. Open M-Sa 8am-9pm, Su 8am-8pm. AmEx/DC/MC/V. ●

Wisemiller's Deli, 1236 36th St. NW (☎333-8254), between M and N St. A popular eatery among Georgetown students. Every kind of sandwich imaginable—try the Chicken Madness Sub (chicken breast with sweet peppers, hot peppers, onions, garlic, bacon, provolone, lettuce, mayo, tomato; $6). Subs and sandwiches $3.50-6.25, burgers $3-4, salads $4.25-5.75. Vegetarian options available. Open M-F 7am-11:30pm, Sa 8am-11:30pm, Su 8am-11pm. AmEx/MC/V. ●

SHAW/U DISTRICT

SEE MAP P. 361 — YOU ARE HERE — U.S. Capitol Building

Shaw's edge near the U St.-Cardozo Metro stop, in the immediate vicinity of **14th and U St. NW,** is a source for supreme soul food, chic clubs and bars, and some of the best live music in the city (see **Rock and Pop,** p. 184). Fast food options abound at 14th and U St., but nearby home-cooked options are nearly as cheap. Use Metro: U St.-Cardozo for all of the following. **This area may be dangerous at night.**

■ **Ben's Chili Bowl,** 1213 U St. NW (☎667-0909; www.benschilibowl.com), at 13th St. across from the Metro. Since 1958 passersby can't miss the yellow awning or the beckoning aromas of this neighborhood hangout. Chili dogs ($2.80), chili burgers ($3.65), chili or cheese fries ($3.10), plain chili (small $2.25, large $4), and veggie chili (small $3.10, large $4.15). Veggie subs $6.45. Photos of Bill Cosby and Denzel Washington (a scene from the movie *The Pelican Brief* was filmed here) pay homage to the diner. Open M-Th 6am-2am, F 6am-4am, Sa 7am-4am, Su noon-8pm. Breakfast M-Sa until 11am. Cash only. ●

Tropicana, 725 Florida Ave. NW (☎588-5470), between 8th and Georgia St. NW. Smoke from the chicken grill floats over the painted palm trees of this tiny Jamaican takeout. Generous portions of fried plantains ($2), jerk chicken ($6.50), fricasseed chicken ($5.50), oxtail soup ($7), and ginger beer ($1.25). Takeout only. Open M-Sa 11am-10pm. MC/V. ❶

Cafe Saint-Ex, 1847 14th St. NW (☎265-7839), at T St. New nightlife hotspot attracts a loyal crowd of late-night drinkers (see **Nightlife,** p. 178), but excellent and mostly affordable dinner menu has been under-appreciated. Owner Mike Benson says he likes a $25 steak and a $2 beer, and he serves both (New York Strip and Miller High Life, respectively). Appetizers ($5-10) like the crab and brie quesadilla ($9) please the bar crowd. Open M-F 5pm-2am, Sa-Su 11am-2am; dinner served until 11pm, late night menu until 1am. AmEx/MC/V. ❹

CakeLove, 1506 U St. NW (☎588-7100; www.cakelove.com), at 15th St. When CakeLove says it makes cakes from scratch, it means business: only imported Oaxacan cocoa beans are used for the chocolate, and 125 lb. of sugar and 300 eggs go into the batter each week. Owner Warren Brown was a federal litigator, but gave up that job to bake these now-legendary cakes—earning himself a spot as one of *People*'s Top 50 Bachelors in the process. 9" cakes $45-60. Cupcakes start at $2. Open M-F 8am-8pm, Sa 10am-6pm, Su 11am-5pm. ❷

Local 16, 1602 U St. NW (☎265-2828; www.localsixteen.com), at 16th St. Urban-chic restaurant and bar serves a New American menu to young professionals. Lamb couscous ($18) is an employee favorite. Appetizers $6-9, entrees $15-22. Three bars, including 1 on a massive roof deck, make Local 16 better known as a night hotspot (see **Nightlife,** p. 178). Reservations accepted for indoor seating. Open Su-Th 5.30pm-1:30am (dinner until 10:30pm), F-Sa 5.30pm-2:30am (dinner until 11pm, late night menu until 1am). AmEx/D/MC/V. ❸

Florida Avenue Grill, 1100 Florida Ave. NW (☎265-1586), at 11th St. The small, influential diner opened in 1944 and has since fed politicos, athletes, and entertainment celebs galore. Breakfast (served until 1pm) with salmon cakes or spicy half-smoked sausage and grits, apples, or biscuits ($2-8). Lunch specials $5.50 (Tu-F 11am-4pm). Sandwiches $3-8. Entrees (with choice of 2 veggies) $6.50-10. Open Tu-Sa 6am-9pm. AmEx/D/MC/V. ❷

Polly's Cafe, 1342 U St. NW (☎265-8385), near 14th St. Popular late-night restaurant with an jukebox-playing interior divides its menu into vegetarians and carnivores. Grilled veggie sandwich ($6) and portobello mushroom steak with bean salad ($10) are faves. Hamburger $6; grilled ham and cheese sandwich $5. Hearty American Su brunch serves mixed drinks by the pitcher ($8.25-16.50) and heaps of meat, potatoes, and eggs ($8.50-11). Live music every other Su. Open M-Th 6pm-2am, F 6pm-3am, Sa 10am-3am, Su 10am-1am. MC/V. ❷

The Islander, 1201 U St. (☎234-4971), at 12th St. Excellent cuisine from Trinidad and Tobago is served with the sweet sounds of steel drum calypso music. Favorites at this corner institution include curry goat ($12), calypso chicken ($12), and *roti* (baked bread stuffed with curried meats or vegetables and potatoes; $6-12). Ginger beer ($3) and countless varieties of rum complement your meal or your pretzels at the bar. Live jazz Su nights. Open Tu-Th noon-10pm, F-Sa noon-midnight, Su 1-11pm; kitchen closes 1hr. before bar. D/MC/V. ❷

Wilson's, 700 V St. NW (☎462-3700 or 462-2992), at Georgia Ave. Sports memorabilia deck the walls of this self-consciously local diner. Boasting the best in down-home cooking, the menu comes complete with chit'lins (a pig's large intestine, now a fairly common Southern dish) and a great selection of sandwiches (hot sandwiches $4-6.50, cold sandwiches $3), salads ($1.60), or various dinner entrees (ribs $10, pork chops $8). Open M-Th 7:30am-5pm, F-Su 7:30am-6pm. MC/V. ❷

SOUTH OF THE MALL

Water St. restaurants have steep prices in response to the high tourist demand for fresh seafood. However, find a bite of the just-caught just short of the high seas at the following tempting locales.

Phillips Flagship, 900 Water St. SW (☎488-8515 ext. 22; www.phillipsfoods.com), at 9th St. Hungry diners by the busload come to experience Phillips's all-you-can-eat seafood buffet. For $23 on evenings and weekends, and $14 for weekday lunch, customers can load up their plates again and again with crab legs, shrimp, mussels, clams, and crawfish. Buffet includes the pasta creation station, where the chef will combine any pasta with any seafood for you, as well as soups, salads, fruit, and dessert. Bar and sushi also available, but not part of the buffet. Open M-Th 11am-9pm, F-Sa 11am-10pm, Su 10am-9pm. AmEx/DC/D/MC/V. ❹

Zanzibar on the Waterfront, 700 Water St. SW (☎ 554-9100; www.zanzibar-otw.com), at 7th St. Metro: Waterfront. Self-consciously classy restaurant filled with tropical trees and large windows providing romantic waterfront vistas. Menu combines exotic African, Caribbean, and Latin American spices in dishes like mango salmon ($21). Entrees $13-26. Open for lunch (buffet only, $13) Tu-F 11am-2:30pm. Open for dinner W-Sa 5-10pm, and brunch Su 11am-4pm. Live jazz, blues, R&B for dinner hours, and free admission to club and bar upstairs (see **Nightlife,** p. 179) with meal. ❹

Wharf Street Seafood Market, between 9th and 11th St. SW and Maine Ave. NW, next to Memorial Bridge. Metro: L'Enfant Plaza. Floating booths steeped in the pungent smell of raw fish attract die-hard seafood grubbers. Specialties include seafood sandwiches ($6-10), clams ($7), and shrimp ($7) cooked while you wait. Raw seafood available for takeout. Open in summer daily 8am-9pm, in winter 8am-8pm. ❷

UPPER NORTHWEST

WOODLEY PARK

The small neighborhood has a surprising number of ethnic eateries and also houses busy local pubs, like Murphy's of D.C. (see **Nightlife,** p. 180), conveniently clustered around the Metro stop. Use Metro: Woodley Park-Zoo for all the following.

Chipotle Mexican Grill, 2600 Connecticut Ave. NW (☎ 299-9111; www.chipotle.com). Chipotle chefs prepare gigantic fresh burritos and tacos ($5-5.50) in speedy assembly-line fashion using the ingredients you select; perfect for hungry customers on the go. Patrons might notice the paper lining the burrito baskets; it includes a series of (slightly altered) movie quotes, such as "My father made them a burrito they couldn't refuse." Chipotle's $3 margaritas are likewise difficult to refuse. Open daily 11am-10pm. MC/V. ❶

Medaterra, 2614 Connecticut Ave. NW (☎ 797-0400; www.medaterra.com). The cuisine evokes the atmosphere at Medaterra. Mostly North African food served among old travel posters. Staples like hummus and *baba ghanoush* are $4-5; entrees are $10-25. Lunch is cheaper ($5-10). Vegetarian options are available, including a large number of appetizers ($4-8). "Martini Mondays" offer $5 martinis and $2 *sangría,* as well as a free appetizer with 2 drinks (M 5-7pm). Outdoor seating and take-out available. Open Su-Th 11:30am-2:30pm and 5-10pm, F-Sa 11:30am-3pm and 5-10:30pm. AmEx/DC/D/MC/V. ❸

Trattoria Italiana, 2651 Connecticut Ave. NW (☎ 332-2207; usawdc@yahoo.com). The word is still getting around about the excellent traditional Italian cuisine this restaurant offers. A low-lit interior, close quarters, and a clock (on Italy time) introduce patrons to the Mediterranean country. An attentive staff will help you navigate the overwhelming menu, including specialties such as New Zealand rack of lamb ($24). Pasta and risotto $13-20, main courses $16-29. Vegetarian options offered. Beer $4; wine by the glass $6. Takeout and outdoor seating available. Open M-Th 11am-3pm and 5-11pm, F-Su 11am-11pm. AmEx/DC/D/MC/V. ❹

Lebanese Taverna, 2641 Connecticut Ave. NW (☎ 265-8681; www.lebanesetaverna.com). Dark wood tables and the detailed textile create a romantic setting. Grilled meat plates ($13.50-19) are delectable, but sandwiches ($7.75, only available at lunch) are cheaper. Vegetarian options available, including a large number of both veggie appetizers ($4.50-7.50) and entrees ($12-13.50). Dinner entrees ($11.75-19) are cheaper at lunch. Offers a large selection of wines by glass ($4.50-12) and by bottle ($8.50 and up). Takeout, outdoor seating, and free parking available. Open for lunch M-F 11:30am-2:30pm, Sa noon-3pm. Dinner M 5:30-10pm, Tu-Th 5:30-10:30pm, F-Sa 5:30-11pm, Su 5-10pm. AmEx/DC/D/MC/V. ❸

Jandara, 2606 Connecticut Ave. NW (☎ 387-8876). Celestial decorations and heavenly blues and purples create an out-of-this-world atmosphere. Equally stunning food with Thai standards and specialty dishes ($8-15), such as *gaeng ped yang* (slices of roasted duck simmered in a red curry sauce with pineapple; $9). Enticing desserts ($3.50-4.50) include a Coconut Custard ($4). Lunch menu features reduced-price entrees ($6-10). Beer $3.50-4; wine $4.75-6.50 by glass, $6-25 by bottle; mixed drinks $5-6. Takeout and free delivery; outdoor seating available. Student Advantage cardholders save 10%. Open Su-Th 11:30am-10:30pm, F-Sa 11:30am-11pm. AmEx/DC/D/MC/V. ❷

Saigon Gourmet Restaurant, 2635 Connecticut Ave. NW (☎265-1360). Vietnamese specialties such as grilled pork and rice crêpe or beef broiled in grape leaves (both $12) are served in an atmosphere overflowing with potted plants. Appetizers ($2.50-7.50) include spring rolls and garden rolls ($4.50-5.50) and vegetarian starters (up to $4.50); meat entrees $10-15; vegetarian entrees $9-10; noodles $14. Lunch features the same items for almost half the price. Outdoor seating and free delivery available. Complimentary parking in back (enter on Woodley Rd.). Open daily 11am-3pm and 5-10:30pm. AmEx/DC/D/MC/V. ❸

GLOVER PARK

Glover Park has neither the youthful exuberance (or crowds) of nearby Georgetown nor is it in the shadow of the National Cathedral or Zoo, like more trafficked establishments in areas to the north and east. But along Wisconsin Ave. between Calvert St. and Hall Pl., lie a handful of unique restaurants with excellent, and sometimes inexpensive, offerings.

🔳 **Mama Maria and Enzio's,** 2313 Wisconsin Ave. NW (☎965-1337), near Calvert St. Amazing southern Italian cuisine served in a 9-table dining room, with a casual, family atmosphere and exceptionally warm, friendly service. Shrimp in lemon sauce ($16) is worth the wait. Begin with an appetizer like prosciutto and melon ($6.25-11.75) and move on to pastas ($9-13). Pizzas $9-12; calzones $7; cannoli $5. Lunch entrees $7-11. Entrees can be made vegetarian by request. Reservations for parties of 3 or more. Open lunch M-F 11:30am-3pm, dinner M-Sa 5-10:30pm, Su 4:30-9pm. D/MC/V. ❷

Old Europe, 2434 Wisconsin Ave. NW (☎333-7600; www.old-europe.com). Find a seat away from the view of the Wisconsin Ave. traffic and you might just convince yourself that you're in Bavaria; a series of colorful crests and shields on the ceiling and walls represent European cities and nations. Try traditional favorites such as the massive wiener schnitzel ($18) or Sauerbraten ($17). Lunch entrees $8.85-13.25. Pastries or dessert are a must ($5.45). The German theme may inspire customers to sample a frosty brew ($2.50-11) available in sizes of up to 32 oz. The restaurant observes numerous festivals throughout the year, notably Oktoberfest, featuring live music and entertainment. AAA Discount. Open M 5-9pm, Tu-Sa 11:30am-3pm and 5-10pm, Su 1-9pm (lunch until 4pm). AmEx/DC/MC/V. ❸

Saveur Restaurant, 2218 Wisconsin Ave. NW (☎333-5885; www.saveurdc.com). French gourmet cuisine is the rule at Saveur, where low lighting, candles, and a colorful decor are a perfect setting for live jazz performed every Th night. Entrees $20-30. Lunch entrees ($11-13) include "Prince Edward Island Rope Grown Mussels," mussels with pasta, herbs, parsley, and parmesan ($12). Su brunch includes appetizer, entree, dessert, and a glass of champagne for $18. Half-price on (most) wine bottles Tu. Free validated parking available, as well as free valet parking F-Sa. Open lunch M-F 11:30am-2:30pm; brunch Su 11:30am-3pm; dinner M-Th 5:30-10pm, F-Sa 5:30-11pm, Su 5:30-9:30pm. AmEx/DC/D/MC/V. ❹

Faccia Luna, 2400 Wisconsin Ave. NW (☎337-3132; www.faccialuna.com). A wood-fired oven bakes up an extensive selection of customized pizzas ($6.45-19.50). Also sandwiches ($6.25-7) and pasta dishes ($11.50-14, available after 5pm M-F and after 1pm Sa-Su); an appealing lunch special ($5-6, available M-F 11:30am-2pm) includes entree and drink. Vegetarian options available. Large selection of beers $3-4.25. Reservations not accepted. Open M-Th 11:30am-11pm, F-Sa 11:30am-midnight, Su noon-11pm. AmEx/DC/D/MC/V. ❷

CLEVELAND PARK

Just north of the Cathedral between Wisconsin and Connecticut Ave., Cleveland Park is marked by quiet, tree-lined residential streets and a handful of inviting eateries. Though not unscathed by gentrification and the occasional Starbucks, the area immediately surrounding the Metro stop has a lot to offer for discerning food lovers and budget travelers alike. Use Metro: Cleveland Park for all of the following.

the BIG $plurge

🖐 MATISSE

Behind its unassuming façade, 🖐**Matisse Restaurant** reveals a dining area of which even the French impressionist himself would approve. The food options are also artistically conceived. For $75, patrons can order a 7-course "Chef's Table" individually customized to their tastes and personally prepared and served by the chef himself. From the cozy atmosphere of the restaurant's wine cellar, customers watch each course perpared before their eyes.

Those looking for less expensive options won't be disappointed, either. Matisse's truly unique entrees generally run $10-16 at lunch and $20-26 at dinner. If you stop by for Su brunch, start with warm porridge, strawberries, and cream ($5) and proceed with an oatmeal *soufflé* with sausage and maple syrup ($14).

Matisse is a favorite with the likes of Ted Koppel, Jim Lehrer, and even First Lady Laura Bush. Henry Kissinger's birthday party was also held here.

4934 Wisconsin Ave. NW., near Fessenden St. ☎244-5322. Open for lunch Tu-F 11:30am-2:30pm; brunch Su 11am-3pm; dinner M 5-9:30pm, Tu-Th 5:30-10pm, F 5:30-10:30pm, Sa 5:30-11pm, Su 5-9pm. ❹

🖐 Yanni's, 3500 Connecticut Ave. NW (☎362-8871). Find homestyle Greek cooking in this bright, airy neighborhood restaurant, adorned with classical statues, ivy, and murals of Greek gods. Try charbroiled octopus, crunchy on the outside and delicately tender within, served with rice and vegetables ($14); the chicken *souvlaki* platter (skewers of chicken served with bread and Greek salad; $12) is also tasty. Entrees $9-18 (vegetarian options $9-12). Strong Greek coffee ($2.50) goes well with *baklava* ($5). 10% Student Advantage discount. Outdoor seating available. Open daily 11:30am-11pm. AmEx/DC/D/MC/V. ❷

Alero, 3500 Connecticut Ave. NW (☎966-2530; www.alerorestaurant.com), above Yanni's. Serves excellent Mexican food among a delightful mix of 19th-century black-and-white photos of Mexico and detailed rugs. Features staple dishes, including quesadillas ($6-8.25), fajitas ($10-15), burritos ($8-11), enchiladas ($8-12), and chimichangas ($9-11). Try the Tacos al Carbon ($11), two soft flour tortillas with chicken or beef, served with rice, guacamole, sour cream, and pico de gallo. Entrees $12-16. Margaritas $5.25-6.25; tequila $5-8. Ample outdoor seating. Open Su-Th 11:30am-11pm, F-Sa 11:30am-midnight. AmEx/MC/V. ❷

Spices Asian Restaurant & Sushi Bar, 3333-A Connecticut Ave. NW (☎686-3833; spices_dc@yahoo.com). Sleek and popular restaurant—be prepared for a wait on weekends. Pan-Asian delights include sushi (entrees $10-19), hot pots ($9-13), and a large assortment of vegetarian dishes ($7-8). Reservations for parties of 3 or more recommended F-Su. Open M-F 11:30am-3pm and 5-11pm, Sa noon-11pm, Su 5-10:30pm. AmEx/DC/MC/V. ❸

Yenching Palace, 3524 Connecticut Ave. NW (☎362-8200). The 1962 Cuban Missile Crisis was defused in this dining room, and Nixon's rapprochement with China was planned here a decade later. Decor hasn't changed much, but the circular booths still provide intimacy for late-night rendezvous. Standard Chinese fare like chicken in garlic sauce ($9, $7 at lunch). Dinner entrees $7-14, vegetarian options ($7-8). Lunch specials ($7) are a great deal (rice, egg roll, entree, and soup; M-Sa 11:30-3pm). Su buffet (noon-2:30pm) offers all-you-can-eat food for $7. Open Su-Th 11:30am-11pm, F-Sa 11:30am-11:30pm. AmEx/DC/D/MC/V. ❷

Nam-Viet Pho 79, 3419 Connecticut Ave. NW (☎237-1015; www.namviet1.com). Traditional Vietnamese entrees like curried chicken in coconut juice and special veggie dishes ($8-14). Large selection of soups ($3.25-9.25), and appetizers ($3.55-8.55) like roasted quail ($6). Known for seasonal soft shell crabs ($20), the dining room is packed on weekends. Pho 79 has catered for the Vietnamese Embassy. Reservations accepted for parties of 4 or more. Open M-Th 11am-3pm and 5-10pm, F-Sa 11am-11pm, Su 11am-10pm. AmEx/D/MC/V. ❷

TENLEY CIRCLE & FRIENDSHIP HEIGHTS

If you just can't bear to spend one more minute in chain-store hell, venture south along Wisconsin Ave. from the Friendship Heights and grab a bite to eat at one of the many cheap and unpretentious restaurants.

Cactus Cantina, 3300 Wisconsin Ave. NW (☎686-7222; www.cactuscantina.com), at Macomb St. near the Cathedral. Metro: Tenleytown-AU and any 30-series bus toward Georgetown. Entrees here could not be fresher or more delicious (even in Mexico). Try the *fajitas al carbon* (half chicken, half beef; $12) followed by the dessert *cajeta* ($5.25). A few vegetarian options available such as the veggie fajita ($9.50). Margaritas $5-9, tequila shots $5-10, *sangría* $3.75. Leads a double life as restaurant and mini-museum, with classic Native American and cowboy garb displayed in glass cases inside. Takeout available before 5pm. Reservations only accepted for large parties (and never for dinner F-Su); be prepared to wait for a table on weekends. Open Su 11am-11pm, M-Th 11:30am-11pm, F-Sa 11:30am-midnight. ❸

2 Amys Neapolitan Pizzeria, 3715 Macomb St. NW (☎885-5700), near the intersection with Wisconsin Ave. and adjacent to Cactus Cantina. Metro: Tenleytown-AU and any 30-series bus toward Georgetown. 2 Amys is named after the 2 owners' wives. Amid the pastel yellow and orange hues of the dining areas, superb, freshly cooked pizzas ($8-13) are served by a friendly waitstaff. The "Narcia" pizza (tomato, salami, roasted peppers, mozzarella, and garlic, $13) is excellent. Outdoor seating available. No reservations; expect a wait. Open Tu-Sa 11:30am-11pm, Su noon-10pm. MC/V. ❷

49 Twelve Thai Cuisine, 4912 Wisconsin Ave. NW (☎966-4696). Metro: Friendship Heights or Tenleytown-AU. Inconspicuous restaurant offers some of the best Thai food in the area. Patrons may catch a glimpse of Tom Daschle on one of his frequent visits. Delicious *pad thai* ($7 lunch, $9 dinner); other popular dishes include drunken noodles and the many varieties of curry dishes ($8-10). 10% Student Advantage discount. Free delivery 5:30-9:30pm ($15 min.). Open Su-Th 11:30am-10pm, F-Sa 11:30am-11pm. AmEx/DC/D/MC/V. ❷

Cafe Ole, 4000 Wisconsin Ave. NW (☎244-1330; www.cafeoledc.com), across from the Post Office. Metro: Tenleytown-AU. Sleek Mediterranean joint serves *mezze* dishes (small appetizers; 3 make a good-sized meal; $4.50-8 each). Try the *shankleesh,* a sharp and seasoned sheep's cheese, or the vegetable tart. Panini sandwiches ($6) and rollups ($6-7) for lunch. Open Su-Th 11am-10pm, F-Sa 11am-11pm. AmEx/DC/D/MC/V. ❶

a.k.a. Frisco's, 4115 Wisconsin Ave. NW (☎244-7847), between Van Ness and Upton St. Metro: Tenleytown-AU. A casual sandwich shop divided into small rooms imitating San Francisco with wooden floors, white walls, and light blue trim. Map of Alcatraz reminds patrons of the appeal of the "City by the Bay." Generous sandwiches ($4-4.75) and large baked potatoes ($1.25-3.75), with names like the Berkeley and the Golden Gate. Assortment of vegetarian dishes. Takeout available. Open M-Th 11am-4pm, F-Sa 11am-3pm. AmEx/D/MC/V. ❶

Yosaku, 4712 Wisconsin Ave. NW (☎353-4453; www.tonosushi.com). Metro: Tenleytown-AU. Pink tinted lights and walls adorned with snapshots of Japan provide a mellow, down-to-earth atmosphere. Dinners from the sushi bar $8-19, from the kitchen $10.50-15, soups $8-13. For the indecisive, Yosaku offers a special combination platter with soup, salad, choice of sushi or sashimi, teriyaki, and dessert ($19). Vegetarians should try the veggie sushi dinner ($11). Outdoor seating available. Free delivery over $15. Open for lunch M-F 11:30am-2:30pm, dinner M-Th 5:30-10:30pm, F-Sa 5:30-11pm, Su 5:30-10pm. AmEx/MC/V. ❸

INSIDE

by neighborhood **164**

adams morgan **164** alexandria **167**

arlington **168** bethesda **169**

capitol hill **170** dupont circle **171**

farragut **173** federal triangle **174**

foggy bottom **175** georgetown **176**

shaw/u district **178** south of the mall **179**

upper northwest **179**

gay bars and clubs **180**

Nightlife

Washington's workaholic reputation is well-deserved, but the past decade has seen a burgeoning party-hard crowd turning D.C. into a true playground after dark. If you wander out looking for a quiet wine tasting and find yourself taking bodyshots off a beautiful stranger, don't say we didn't warn you.

Here's our advice on taking on the home of all-night raves and go-go: If you ache for a pint of amber ale, swing by the Irish pub-laden **Capitol Hill.** If you dig the Polo or Abercrombie & Fitch look, hit up the raucous bars in **Georgetown** or **Arlington,** where prepsters and young professionals go to get messy. Gay and lesbian travelers traipse nightly through the glam **Dupont Circle,** as do many of the city's trendiest club and lounge-dwellers, searching for the best in house and ultra-lounge dance music. **Adams Morgan** adds mod Euro flair to a classically college and intern party scene that is anchored around live music and flirty cruise bars. To party *with* rock stars, head to **Shaw/U St.** for the best live rock 'n' roll in all of D.C., and many of the freshest see-and-be-seen lounges in downtown. To party *like* a rock star, find high times in the **Southeast** neighborhood, where all-night (and often all-day) parties unfold to the beats of the most progressive music in the area.

D.C.'s nightclub turnover rate is obscenely high. Establishments open, fold, and change hands before you can say "bottoms up." For weekly nightlife highlights, pick up the **Washington City Paper** (www.washingtoncitypaper.com) and **On Tap** (www.ontaponline.com), free newspapers available at most D.C. restaurants and bars. The following index organizes bars and clubs by neighborhood. **Let's Go Picks** (🍸) mark the coolest places to hang out until the sun comes up over Pennsylvania Ave. Establishments take all major credit cards unless otherwise noted.

HOT LIST

10. The Black Cat (p. 184). The rock-solid foundation of D.C.'s punk and hard rock scene now hosts the popular Britpop Mousetrap, Wag, and Bliss nights.

9. Whitlow's on Wilson (p. 168). 4 levels of nonstop bar action. Never a better place to flirt in Arlington.

8. Café Saint-Ex (p. 178). Sets the standard for DJ bars in the District. Patrons take in the homespun tunes from the 1st fl. bar, which came from Al Capone's speakeasy.

7. Home (p. 174). The newest addition to the F St. corridor offers a more intimate setting to groove to house and hip-hop with D.C.'s hottest.

6. 9:30 Club (p. 184). Big acts in mainstream and alternative rock always stop here to play an intimate show.

5. Nation (p. 185). The absolute finest in all-night parties in the District.

4. McFadden's (p. 175). Foggy Bottom has never seen a party like this.

3. Eighteenth Street Lounge (p. 171). The patriarch of D.C.'s ultrahip lounge scene.

2. Platinum (p. 174). With less pretense and far more style than most swank D.C. nightclubs, this converted bank is one of the best party spaces in all of Washington.

1. Adams Morgan (p. 164). No other city can boast an area with such a high concentration and wide variety of nightlife hotspots, with something for everyone.

BY NEIGHBORHOOD

ADAMS MORGAN

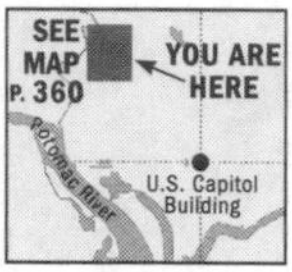

Weekends in Adams Morgan explode with a diverse crowd of 20- and 30-somethings hungry for frenzied late-night mischief and mayhem. Some of D.C.'s trendiest nightclubs, swankest lounges, and craziest drink specials can be found on the main strip near 18th and Columbia St. Although Adams Morgan is generally safe, **some areas off the main streets become dangerous at night.** It's a 10min. walk or a short cab ride from Dupont Circle or Woodley Park-Zoo Metro.

Madam's Organ, 2461 18th St. NW (☎667-5370), near Columbia Rd. A 3fl. bar with an intimate rooftop patio, Madam's Organ is one of the oldest and biggest bars in the neighborhood. A live band plays nightly on the 1st fl. (Su-Th 9:30pm, F-Sa 10pm) while pool tables entertain barflies on the 2nd fl. Famed magician Alain Nu performs on some evenings, and W's bluegrass bands have been a longtime favorite. Locals love Karen's Tijuana Hot Wings ($7), which, the menu insists, are "Hotter than Your Sister." 2-for-1 drinks during Happy Hour (M-F 5-8pm) and redheads always drink ½-price Rolling Rocks. Drafts $3.75-5.75; mixed drinks $4.75-6.75. 21+. Cover Su-Th $2-4, F-Sa $5-7. Open Su-Th 5pm-2am, F-Sa 5pm-3am. Also see **Jazz and Blues,** p. 186.

Millie & Al's, 2440 18th St. NW (☎387-8131). Jukebox bar draws an ultra-casual crowd into its booths with cheap pizza, fries, subs, and $1 jelloshooter specials when the huge bulb over the bar lights up. Nightly specials (4-7pm) feature $2 rail drinks M, ½-price pizza Tu, dollar drafts of Miller Lite and High Life W, karaoke Th, and $5 pitchers of Miller Lite F. DJs play rock and hip-hop F and S, although good music is playing here no matter what day it is. $3 burgers; $2.50 fries. Draft beers $2-3.50; bottles $3-4.25. 21+. No cover. Open M-Th 5:30pm-2am, F-Sa 4pm-3am.

The Reef, 2446 18th St. NW (☎518-3800). The newest hotspot on 18th St., The Reef provides three levels of drinking for a casual 20s crowd: jungle-themed 1st fl. (DJ on Tu, Su), aquarium-esque 2nd fl. lounge, and a massive roof deck. Rail drinks $5, 14 rotating bottled beers $3-6 each. $1 off all drinks and appetizers during Happy Hour (daily 4-7:30pm). No cover. 21+ after 9pm. Open M-Th 4pm-2am, F-Sa 4pm-3am, Su 11am-3pm (brunch) and 4pm-2am.

Brass Monkey, 2317 18th St. NW (☎667-7800). This 2nd fl. bar features a giant skylight and a patio with retractable roof to maximize partying whatever the weather. A fashionable, preppy college crowd invariably swarms the bar each night to get down to rock and hip-hop from Dylan to 50 Cent. Pool table ($1.50 per game). Happy Hour M-F 6-8pm, domestic beers $2, rail drinks $3. No cover. Open daily Su-Th 1pm-2am, F-Sa 1pm-3am.

Tryst, 2459 18th St. NW (☎232-5500). Coffee bar with an atmosphere that splendidly combines that of an art gallery and rec room: huge sofas, pastiche paintings, board games, books, and caffeine addicts. Tryst's after-hours spiked coffees ($6-7), free wireless Internet, and hyper-ambience draw a huge crowd to this smoky Bohemian hangout. Beers $3.50-5. Late night menu served until close. 21+ F-Sa after 8:30pm. Open M-Th 6:30am-2am, F-Sa 6:30am-3am, Su 8am-midnight.

Felix and The Spy Lounge, 2406 18th St. NW (☎483-3549). There's always something going on at **Felix,** whether it's Sinatra night (W), Jewish dinner (F), or the Su group viewing of *The Sopranos* ($5 Manhattans) and *Sex and the City* ($5 cosmos). At the brushed chrome, red-carpet **Spy Lounge,** local and international DJs spin house nightly, except 80s electroclash on Th. **Groove Lounge** opens F and Sa nights, spinning hip-hop and dance music upstairs and on the roof deck. Beer $4-6, cocktails $5-10. $5 cover W-Sa after 10pm. Open Su-Th 5:30pm-2am, F-Sa 5:30pm-3am.

Toledo Lounge, 2435 18th St. NW (☎986-5416). Resembling a suburban garage sale gone awry (note the shrunken head above the bar, the huge Texaco Oil sign, and the lurking jackalope), Toledo Lounge makes a chill spot for pre- or post-clubbing. Cocktails $4-6; beers $3-5. $2 drafts when it's raining M-W. Packed on weekends. The Lounge also serves burgers (with fries or onion rings $6) and sandwiches (from $4). 21+. Open Su-Th 6pm-2am, F-Sa 6pm-3am.

Kokopooli's, 2305 18th St. NW (☎234-2306; www.kokopoolis.com). This sports bar offers 8 pool tables, foosball, darts, 18 TVs, and one of the most extensive selections of tequila in the city, which can go as high as $40 a shot. ½-price drafts and pool tables daily 3-7pm. Cheap chicken wings and hot dogs ($5.50 each) will keep you occupied while you wait for the next available table. Draft beers $4, rail drinks $5. Open Su-Th 3pm-2am, F-Sa 3pm-3am. Also see **Billiards,** p. 190.

Bukom Cafe, 2442 18th St. NW (☎265-4600), near Columbia Rd. A fabulous bar and restaurant with live music by excellent West African bands, (Su-Th 9pm, F-Sa 10pm). Filled to capacity with a 30-something crowd. Also specializes in West African cuisine. Appetizers $3-4, entrees $6-10. 12oz. beer $4. F-Sa $5 cover (includes 1 drink). No cover Su-Th, but get there early if you want a place to sit. Open Su-Th 4pm-2am, F-Sa 4pm-3am.

Chief Ikes Mambo Bar

Gadsby's Tavern

D. C. at night

the insider's
CITY

Biltmore St.

19th St.

Champlain St.

4 **6**
1 **5**

Mintwood Rd.

3

Columbia Rd.

Kalorama
Park

Belmont St.

19th St.

2

Kalorama Rd.

TO **WOODLEY PARK-ZOO
ADAMS MORGAN** **M**

ADAMS MORGAN

Perhaps the oldest of D.C.'s
great nightlife standbys,
Adams Morgan seems to
anticipate enough trends to
always be in. To capitalize on
this automatic cool, hit these
bars and don't look back.

1 Begin the evening with a
microbrew and a view at
The Reef. (☎518-3800)

2 Khakis by Banana Republic, shirts by Polo, drinks by
Brass Monkey.
(☎667-7800)

3 Vamp your way past the
doorman at **Felix.**
(☎483-3549)

4 Give up the posing and let
it rip again at **Madam's
Organ,** dancing to a blues
band. (☎667-5370)

5 Jello shots at **Millie & Al's.**
Now you're feeling the buzz.
(☎387-8131)

6 Feed late night cravings
with a burger and fries from
The Diner, 2453 18th St.
(☎232-8800; open 24hr.)

Adams Mill Bar and Grill, 1813 Adams Mill Rd. NW
(☎332-9577), where Adams Mill meets Columbia St.
No sign marks this massive bar; look for the big, black
awning over the sidewalk patio where dressed-down
college grads discuss their latest game in the Adams
Morgan kickball league. A true schmoozer's paradise;
games of flip-cup are known to take place in the back.
Happy Hour M-F 4-7pm brings ½-price appetizers,
$2.50 domestic beers, and $4 rail drinks. Loud music
drowned out by even louder people on most nights.
Open M-Th 4pm-1:30am, F 4pm-2:30am, Sa 11am-
2:30am, Su 11am-1:30am.

Angry Inch, 2450 18th St. NW (☎234-3041). The
name for this new, but small, addition to 18th St. comes
not from the hit musical, *Hedwig and the Angry Inch,* but
rather from an old Irish slur that mocks men with
small...bladders. This saloon's motto, "The more you
drink, the bigger it feels!" puts all male visitors at ease.
Domestic beers $3.50, imports $4.50, and 16oz. rail
drinks $5. $1 Coors Light on Tu. DJ on Th-Sa. 21+. No
cover. M-Th 6pm-2am, F-Sa 6pm-3am.

Heaven and Hell, 2327 18th St. NW (☎332-8899;
www.80sdanceparty.com), near Columbia Rd.
Devoted partiers make pilgrimages to Club Heaven
and Club Hell, where everyone is a believer in Diony-
sian tenets. **Hell** (lower level) is a hip, smoky bar dev-
ilishly ornamented with pimpish gold tables, fire-red
chairs, and loud hip-hop or alterna-music. Happy
Hour Tu-Th until 10pm, $2 domestic beers. No cover.
Open Tu-Th 7pm-2am, F-Sa 7pm-3am. **Heaven**
(upstairs) looks more like an old townhouse with
scuffed wood, comfy couches, and 3 TVs, but the
dance floor throbs to pounding beats of underground
techno (W) or hip-hop and house (F-Sa) that spill out
onto the back patio. Th is D.C.'s longest-running and
most popular 80's dance party, starting around
10pm, with $1 shooters until then. Domestic beer
$3.50, imports $4.50, rail drinks $5. Cover W $2-3,
Th-Sa $5. 21+. Open W-Th 9pm-2am, F-Sa 9pm-3am.
Purgatory (main level) offers a less extreme option;
hip-hop and dance music Th-Sa, live band Su. Open
Su-Th 7pm-2am, F-Sa 7pm-3am.

Blue Room, 2123 18th St. NW (☎332-0800;
www.blueroomdc.com). Chic tapas restaurant by day,
alluring lounge and dance club by night. Trendy mid-
20s to early-30s clientele gravitates to this stylish,
blue world with polished chrome. Outdoor patio is a
nice place to cool off with a drink. Beers $5-9, cock-
tails $5 and up. Open turntable W, downtempo/deep-
house Th-Sa, experimental music Su. Proper attire
required (no jeans, athletic gear, or sneakers). Club
starts jumping around 11:30pm. 21+. Cover $5-10 F-
Sa. Open Su, Tu-Th 7pm-2am; F-Sa 7pm-3am.

The Common Share, 2003 18th St. NW (☎588-
7180). With rock-bottom drink prices, this is a first
stop for most 20-something weekend customers look-

ing to achieve dirt-cheap inebriation before hitting local clubs. Upstairs resembles an unfurnished version of the infamous Animal House frat with college students, plenty of alcohol, and a paint-chipped interior. The Golden Tee arcade game. Not much for ambience, but with prices this cheap, nobody's complaining. 10 draft and 7 bottled beers, $2-4 each. M-Th rail drinks $2 til 10pm. 21+. Open M-Th 6pm-2am, F 5:30pm-3am, Sa 7pm-3am.

Latin Jazz Alley, 1721 Columbia Rd. NW (☎328-6190). Live salsa music fills the dance club every Th night, and DJs play meringue, bachata, and more salsa W, F, and Sa. Beginners can enroll in a 1hr. class ($5) with the enormously popular Miguel, W 7pm, F and Sa 7:30pm. 1hr. intermediate lessons ($10) follow immediately after. $3 domestic, $4 imported beers. 21+. No cover. Open W-Th 6:30pm-midnight, F-Sa 6:30pm-3am.

La Frontera Grill and Bar, 1832 Columbia Rd. NW (☎518-8848). Upstairs seating at this top-notch Tex-Mex restaurant converts into **Azteca Bar** F and Sa to accommodate the DJ playing Latin and dance music 10pm-3am. Frozen drinks by the pitcher ($13-23). No cover. Open Su-Th 5pm-2am, F-Sa 5pm-3am.

Chief Ike's Mambo Room, Chaos, and Pandemonium, 1725 Columbia Rd. NW (☎332-2211), near Ontario Rd., 1 block from 18th St. DJ spins dance classics, hip-hop, and funk for a late 20s crowd. Live bands play rock or reggae, W-Sa. Up a red staircase are two rooms, Chaos and Pandemonium, with pseudo-Japanese decor, a pool table, and DJs at the end of the bar. $3 pints during Happy Hour, M-F, 4-8pm. Generic liquors $5. Higher drink prices and occasional cover when a DJ plays. 21+. Casual dress. Cover $3 Th, $5 F-Sa. Open M-Th 4pm-2am, F 4pm-3am, Sa 6pm-3am. Chaos and Pandemonium closed M-Tu.

ALEXANDRIA

Georgetown is only minutes away, yet Old Town has a markedly different feel than its colonial neighbor to the north. Large crowds in their late 20s and 30s carouse late into the night, but there is none of the hectic pace of M St., nor the capital prices for drinks and covers. Along with these listings, restaurants like **The Fish Market** and **King Street Blues** (see p. 138) become busy bars Thursday through Saturday. Use Metro: King St. for all of the following.

🔳 **Bullfeathers,** 112 King St. (☎ 703-836-8088; www.bullfeathersrestaurant.com). A classier take on the sports bar scene. Bullfeathers gets packed with party-goers looking for a big bar and a place to dance on the weekends. DJ Th-Su 9:30pm. Outdoor patio upstairs. Happy Hour (daily 4-7pm) features ½-price appetizers and $2 drafts and domestic bottles. Open M-F 11:30am-2am, Sa 11am-2am, Su 10am-2am.

🔳 **Pat Troy's,** 111 N. Pitt St. (☎703-549-4535; www.pattroysirishpub.com), just off King St. This Gaelic pub goes the extra mile to give guests a taste of Eire. Daily ½-price specials on entrees; ladies drink for ½-price on Th. Late night menu available 10pm-close. Guinness $5. Happy Hour 4-7pm daily offers discounted drinks. Live Irish music nightly at 8:30pm, including owner Pat Troy's spontaneous performances of "The Unicorn Song." Signs mark regulars' bar stools. Open M-Th 11am-midnight, F-Su 10:30am-2am.

Chadwicks, 203 The Strand (☎703-836-4442), between Prince and Duke St. Right off the water, Chadwicks has 2 fl. of lacquered wood and oceanic decor. Young drinkers frequent the bar for the great booze deals. Happy Hour M-F 4-7pm: generic liquors, wine, and domestics $2; most appetizers $3. M ½-price burgers 4pm-midnight. Th $2 Molson and DJ 9pm-1:30am. Open M-Su 11:30am-2am. Kitchen closes at midnight, 1am on Sa.

Tiffany Tavern, 1116 King St. (☎703-836-8844). Locals stream here to dig the live music and chat it up in the super-friendly atmosphere. Open-mike M-Th 8:30-11:30pm, live bluegrass F-Sa 9pm-1am. Happy Hour daily 5-7pm: one-third off rail drinks and domestic beers. The food is also a big draw: try the scrumptious crab cakes ($14). Open M-Tu 5pm-midnight, W-Th 11:30am-2:30pm and 5pm-midnight, F-Sa 11:30am-2:30pm and 5pm-2am.

Murphy's Grand Irish Pub, 713 King St. (☎703-548-1717), between Columbus and Washington St. Ladies in search of a few good men need look no further. Murphy's draws thirsty officers representing all branches of the military. Locals help keep the place packed during its daily 4-7pm Happy Hour ($2 pints). Open Su-Th 11am-12:30am, F-Sa 11am-1:30am.

The Bayou Room, downstairs at 219 King St. (☎ 703-549-1141; www.219restaurant.com), between Lee and Fairfax St. Below its more expensive brother, this Cajun pub offers an old-fashioned bar and delicious Creole specials, including red beans, sausage, and rice ($6), jambalaya ($6.50), and shrimp creole ($6.50). Happy Hour M-F 4-6pm offers $1.75 drafts. Open daily at 11:30am-2am, but may close earlier Su-M.

ARLINGTON

Arlington's nightlife has always been a default for its largely young professional populace. As their counterparts in the District grow tired of high prices and long lines, they, too, have begun frequenting the Arlington bars, and for good reason; the streets are safe, the happy hours are long, and the talented live music is constant.

☒ **Clarendon Grill,** 1101 N. Highland St. (☎ 703-524-7455; www.cgrill.com), between Clarendon Blvd. and 11th St. Slightly more posh, but with Arlington's unpretentious, beer-is-fun bent. Live bands and DJs Tu-Sa (cover $3-5). M is Salsa night; lessons for beginners to advanced dancers at 7pm. Happy Hour daily 4-8pm; deals 7 days a week. Specials include W $7 pitchers of Foggy Bottom, Th $8 Sam Adams pitchers, Sa $2 Yuengling pints, Su $3 Bloody Marys with brunch. $1.25 Miller Lite and Bud every day 4-8pm. Entrees and sandwiches $6-9. Open M-F 11am-2am, Sa 10:30-2am, Su 10:30-midnight.

☒ **Whitlow's on Wilson,** 2854 Wilson Blvd. (☎ 703-276-9693; www.whitlows.com). Metro: Clarendon. This huge 4-room bar has everything: live bands playing rock, jazz and blues (Su, Tu-W 9pm; Th-Sa 10pm), pool and foosball, massive TVs, and a full arsenal of alcohol and appetizers to please anyone. Try the mountain of nachos ($8.25) to go with your Happy Hour drink. M ½-price burgers; Tu $8 pitchers of PBR; W $8 pitchers of Sierra Nevada; Th $1 nachos 4-7pm. Happy Hour (M-F 4-7pm): $1 off drafts, rail drinks, and house wines. 21+ after 9:30pm. Cover Th-Sa $3-5. Open M-F 11:30am-2am, Sa-Su 9am-2am.

☒ **Arlington Cinema 'N' Drafthouse,** 2903 Columbia Pike (☎ 703-486-2345). It doesn't get any better than this: food is served and the beer flows while the movie rolls (pitchers $12-15). Non-smoking sections available. Shows the best in 2nd-run movies, making the evening even more affordable (tickets $4.50). 21+ or with a parent. Call for showtimes.

Ireland's Four Courts, 2051 Wilson Blvd. (☎ 703-525-3600; www.irelandsfourcourts.com). Metro: Courthouse. The walls are lined with personalized mugs of regulars who come for refills every week. While there's no more space on the wall, you can still buy a mug and take advantage of the cheap refills ($1 off). Enjoy Guinness ($5.25 pints) and live music, mostly traditional Irish (Tu-Sa 9pm; no cover). Su draws a young crowd with a Top-40 DJ (9pm). Serves lunch and dinner, mainly Irish food like corned beef and cabbage ($11). Happy Hour (M-F 4-7pm): $1 off all beers. 21+ after 8pm. Open M-Sa 11am-2am, Su 10am-2am.

Carpool, 4000 Fairfax Dr. (☎ 703-532-7665; www.gocarpool.com), at Quincy St. Metro: Ballston. Wash down a rack of ribs from the adjoining Rocklands (see p. 141) with a nice cold one, or 7. A thirtysomething crowd relives sauced college days through the festive atmosphere and testosterone-driven pool games. Depending on time, pool $6-10 per hr. for 1 player, $12-14 per hr. for 2. Happy Hour (M-F 4-7pm) features $2.25 Miller Lite specials. 21+ except Sa-Su afternoons. Open Su-Th 4pm-1am, F-Sa 4pm-2am.

Iota, 2832 Wilson Blvd. (☎ 703-522-8340; www.iotaclubandcafe.com). Metro: Clarendon. Famous for showcasing breakthrough bands of every musical style with performances nightly (M-Tu 8:30pm, W-Th 9pm, F-Su 9:30pm). W is open-mike. The wide, wooden-beamed bar area serves local microbrews ($4-6.25) and 35 bottled beers (from $3). Happy Hour (M-F 5-8pm): $1 off rail drinks and drafts. Cover $5-15 during shows. Call or see website for show times. Attached restaurant serves large lunches 11am-5pm, dinner Su-Th until 11pm, F-Sa midnight. M is wine night (all bottles and glasses are ½-price until 10pm). Open daily 11am-2am.

Mister Days, 3100 Clarendon Blvd. (☎ 703-527-1600). Metro: Clarendon, 1 block south of station. The premier sports bar in the D.C. area, the restaurant and bar has around 30 TVs broadcasting your favorite team—no matter your hometown. Excellent kitchen and deals during Happy

Hour (4-7pm, $1 off rail drinks and domestic beer) make it the sports fan's paradise. Beer $3.25-5.50. Open Su-M 11am-1am, Tu-Sa 11am-2am.

Galaxy Hut, 2711 Wilson Blvd. (☎703-525-8646; www.galaxyhut.com). Metro: Courthouse. The small bar seats around 25, but as many as 60 people crowd the couches and tables to hear local bands on the weekends. Acts range from good to insufferable, but all are guaranteed to be loud. The outdoor area is no more than 8 ft. across, but extends all the way to the back of the lot. Laid-back crowd takes in live acts Sa-M 9pm under the Christmas lights. No hard liquor, but plenty of exotic beers: 15 taps and over 50 bottled beers. True aficionados quaff the $16.50 Chimay Grande Reserve from Belgium. Happy Hour M-F 5-8pm: $1.30 Bud, $1 off pints, $3 off pitchers, and $1 off appetizers. Open M-F 5pm-2am, Sa-Su 7pm-2am.

BETHESDA

This land of restaurants may leave you too full to want to wander to another part of the D.C. area. Not known for nightlife, Bethesda still manages to provide some post glutton entertainment.

SEE MAP P.365 Rock Creek Park
YOU ARE HERE

Montgomery's Grille, 7200 Wisconsin Ave., at Bethesda Ave. (☎301-654-3595). This restaurant's bar and massive patio turn rowdy at night when a mixed crowd of yuppies comes by for cocktails. Happy Hour (daily 4-7pm, 10pm-close) offers $2 domestic drafts, $2.50 microbrews, and $3 rail drinks. Limited menu after 10pm (11pm on F-Sa). DJ Th-Sa 9pm. 21+ after 10pm. Open Su-Th 11:30am-12:30am, F 11:30am-1:30am, Sa 5pm-1:30am.

Rock Bottom Brewery, 7900 Norfolk Ave. (☎301-652-1311; www.rockbottom.com), near St. Elmo Ave. The only microbrew in Bethesda and the perfect place to ogle preppy guys in khakis and polos. Though you may feel silly ordering it, try the Lumpy Dog Lager ($4) with your burger (platters $8-9). 2nd fl. bar has 3 pool tables and a TV lounge with overstuffed leather sofas. Tu $1 pints, 5:30-7pm. Live rock music F-Sa 9:30pm. Open Su-Th 11am-12:30am, F-Sa 11am-2am. Kitchen closes 10pm, late-night menu available til 1hr. before close. AmEx/DC/D/MC/V.

Willie & Reed's, 4901A Fairmont Ave. (☎301-951-1100; www.willieandreeds.com), at Norfolk Ave. This upscale sports bar and restaurant features over 20 televisions, a long stainless steel bar, and of course, the Golden Tee golf arcade game. Happy Hour (M-F 4-7pm) $2 domestic drafts, $3 premium drafts, $3.50 martinis and cosmos. $5 appetizer menu. M ½-price burgers. Food served until midnight. 21+ after 8pm. Open M-Th 11am-12:30am, F-Su 11:30am-2am.

in recent news

NO IFS, NO BUTTS

On October 9, 2003, Montgomery County, MD joined the ranks of California, Delaware, Florida, and New York states by banning smoking in all restaurants and bars.

While proponents hailed the ban as a significant advance in public health, many residents of Montgomery County have decried the ban as impractical or even discriminatory. Unlike in California, where warm weather prevails year-round, establishments in colder-climate cities like New York and D.C. have fewer options for smoking patrons. In fact, since New York City's ban went into effect on March 30, 2003, smokers have been convening in droves in the streets outside popular bars and clubs, causing uproars among neighbors of these establishments.

Moreover, since none of the areas surrounding Montgomery County have enacted similar bans, restaurant and bar owners worry that they will lose business to competitors not subject to the ban.

While smoking is no longer allowed at Bethesda's eateries, smokers can still take shelter in the nation's capital...at least for the time being.
—Brad Olson

the local story

Intern Livin'

Daniel Chen's poignant interview with Erin, a college student interning at a major foreign policy think tank, sheds light on the average summer intern's experience.

Q: What specifically about Washington, D.C. have you enjoyed this summer?

A: The clubbing. And the guys. Usually poli-sci guys are a lot cuter than any others, and so you get a lot of poli-sci guys in D.C. going wild and drinking beer.

Q: How would you feel about living in D.C. in the future? Is this a city you'd live in?

A: Oh yeah, I give it a big two thumbs up. I can see myself living here because it's a really cool town, and I like all these networking functions and all the free food, they have so much free food here.

Q: Free food where?

A: If you go to these networking function things, you get on a whole bunch of list-serves and they tell you, like, oh yeah, this lobbying firm is having a reception, and you can go there and get free food. And sometimes your boss will take you out and buy you food, especially if you're cute.

Flanagan's Irish Pub, 7637 Old Georgetown Rd., at Woodmont Ave. (☎301-986-1007). The place to watch soccer or rugby while enjoying Bethesda's best beer deals M-F 3-7pm, including $2 drafts of Guinness or Bass, $1 off bottles and rail drinks, and a free appetizer buffet. Specials galore here 9:30pm-close: Su $2 pints of Bud Light, M-Th $3 pints of rotating premium beer (Harp, Guinness, etc.); F $2.50 shots of Goldschlager, Sa $3.50 pints of Grolsch. Open Su-Th 12:30pm-1am, F-Sa 12:30pm-2am. D/MC/V.

CAPITOL HILL

YOU ARE HERE
SEE MAP P. 353

While the nightlife in other parts of Washington is in constant flux, Capitol Hill stands by its steadfast neighborhood institutions. Political aides don't do much heated dancing, but visitors can capitalize on Happy Hours and bar specials all around the area.

The Dubliner, 520 N. Capitol St. NW (☎737-3773). Metro: Union Station. A more subdued crowd than Kelley's (see p. 171) enjoys Guinness and the house brew, Auld Dubliner Amber Ale ($5 a pint). Traditional live Irish music often includes familiar pop melodies injected with an Irish twist (M-Sa 9pm, Su 7:30pm). A large patio turns lounge-style for celebrators as the night ticks on. Open Su-Th 7am-2am, F-Sa 7:30am-3am. AmEx/MC/V.

Pour House/Politiki, 319 Pennsylvania Ave. SE (☎546-1001). Metro: Capitol South. 3 levels and 3 names, but young attractive interns everywhere. A dark wood paneled, subterranean bar goes Hawaiian with tiki-style drinks and food with bamboo. "Top of the Hill" martini bar open upstairs Tu-Sa. Nightly drink specials and a free buffet Su-Th 4pm-1:30am. Open M-F 4pm-1:30am, Sa-Su 10am-2:30am.

Hawk 'n' Dove, 329 Pennsylvania Ave. SE (☎543-3300). Metro: Capitol South. The 3 buildings, all over 100 years old, have served as a blacksmith shop, a saltwater taffy plant, and D.C.'s first gas station. 12 kinds of bottled beer and 13 drafts available. Sandwiches $5.50-9. Happy Hour (M-F 4-9pm) draws a sizeable Hill crowd and features changing drink specials, including $1 pints. Midnight breakfast served M-Th 9pm-1am, F-Sa 9pm-2am ($8, with steak $10). Su-Su brunch (10am-3:30pm) offers Screwdrivers, Mimosas, or Bloody Marys for $2.75. Open Su, M-Th 10am-2am, F-Sa 10am-3am.

Red River Grill, 201 Massachusetts Ave. NE (☎546-7200). Metro: Union Station. Tex-Mex bar is filled with Capitol Hill interns and staffers. Outdoor patio. Happy Hour (M-F 4-8pm) includes M $6 Miller

Lite pitchers, W $1 Bud, Th $11 margarita pitchers, and daily $2 drafts. $3 Heineken and Amstel Light F 9pm-closing. Open M-Th 11:30am-2am, F 11:30am-3am, Sa noon-3am, Su noon-2am. AmEx/MC/V.

Capitol Lounge, 224-231 Pennsylvania Ave. SE (☎547-2098). Metro: Capitol South. Despite being the closest bar to the Capitol, a sign above the bar says, "No Politics," and they mean it. This laid-back local hangout has front and back patios, a pool room, and every NFL game on Sunday. Happy Hour (M-F 4-7pm) specials include M ½-price pizza, Tu $0.10 wings, W $0.25 tacos; generic liquors $3.50, and pints of Bud Ice and House Amber $2.50. Open M-Th 3pm-2am, F 11am-3am, Sa 9am-3am, Su 9am-2am.

Cosi, 301 Pennsylvania Ave. SE (☎546-3345). Metro: Capitol South. This bakery, cafe, and coffeehouse by day morphs into a chill bar at night. Bottled beer $2.50-3.75, coffee drinks like a Mocha Kiss Cocktail $7. Don't miss their make-your-own s'mores (graham crackers or giant Oreo cookies, chocolate, marshmallows, and flame; $6.75, large $11.50). Open Su-Th 7am-11pm, F-Sa 7am-midnight.

Kelley's "The Irish Times," 14 F St. NW (☎543-5433). Metro: Union Station. Irish street signs, the *Irish Times,* and Joyce on the wall give the pub an authentic feel, but late-night disco differentiates Kelley's from most other Irish bars. Famous for its $5 20 oz. Guinness. Live music (Th-Sa 9pm) can be any genre that fits with an acoustic guitar. DJ M-W 6-11pm, F-Sa 10:30pm-closing. Open Su-Th 11am-2am, F-Sa 11am-3am. AmEx/DC/ D/MC/V.

Tune Inn, 331½ Pennsylvania Ave. SE (☎543-2725). Metro: Capitol South. Mounted fish, game heads, and sports trophies decorate the walls in this place for unpretentious fun since 1933. Laid-back, mature crowd ranges from congressional staffers to construction workers to students. Sandwiches $4.25-6.50, breakfast all day, and a well-stocked jukebox. Most drafts $1.50, bottles $2.25, mixed drinks $3.50. Open Su-Th 8am-2am, F-Sa 8am-3am.

DUPONT CIRCLE

Clubs are constantly changing owners and quality in Dupont Circle, and for the moment 18th St. is a hot spot of plush, throbbing dance clubs, while the rest of the neighborhood retains a more steady but nonetheless hopping bar scene. And of course, Dupont Circle remains the prime area for gay and lesbian nightlife (see **Gay Bars and Clubs,** p. 180). Use Metro: Dupont Circle for the following.

YOU ARE HERE
U.S. Capitol Building
SEE MAP P.355

Brickskeller, 1523 22nd St. NW (☎293-1885; www.thebrickskeller.com), between P and Q St. With over 1100 different bottled brews to choose from, the Brickskeller boasts the largest selection in the world ($3.25-19). Basement bar with tavern atmosphere welcomes both beer connoisseurs and the international crowd from nearby embassies downing their home-town beers. "Beer-tails" (mixed drinks made with beer; $3.25-6.50): try the classic Black Velvet (Guinness and champagne; $4.50). Monthly tastings Sept.-May hosted by brewers (call ahead or see website for schedule). Pub menu available: gourmet cheese board ($5-6). Be warned: you will get laughed at for ordering Miller Lite. Open M-Th 11:30am-2am, F 11:30am-3am, Sa 6pm 3am, Su 6pm-2am.

Eighteenth Street Lounge, 1212 18th St. NW (☎466-3922; www.eslmusic.com). 8 years old and still the mod-est of the mod, this progenitor of the now-swelling D.C. lounge scene draws musical tourists from around the globe to hear its top-shelf DJs and bask in this cool-ness. Outside there's a tiny brass plaque to let you know it's there, and a one-way mirror door so the fashion-police bouncers can turn away last year's Prada without looking the unworthy in the eye. Inside there are plush couches, high prices, and an outdoor patio bar. The main attraction here are the DJs, most of whom are signed to ESL's own independent record label. Dress to impress. Cover generally $10-20, but no cover Tu. Open Tu-Th 5:30pm-2am, Fr 5:30pm-3am, Sa 9:30pm-3am.

The Big Hunt, 1345 Connecticut Ave. NW (☎785-2333). Leopard-print couches adorn this jungle-themed 3 fl. bar, where the casual khaki and flip-flops crowd hunts for potential mates. Notorious pickup joint for college kids and Hill workers pretending they're still in college. 24 brews on tap ($3.75-5), including 3 house beers. Solid pub fare. Pool table. The

LGB

▼

Drag Racing

For the past 16 years, local drag queens dressed as everyone and everything from Marilyn Monroe to mermaids have flocked to the **Halloween High Heel Race** in Dupont Circle. The stilettoed sashay used to be held on the weekend of Halloween, but crowds have gotten so large recently that the race has been moved to the Tuesday prior to Halloween.

The race begins at J.R.'s, 1519 17th St. NW, the sponsors of the event, and goes to 17th and R St. Drag beauties start jockeying for prime position around 9pm, but come early to get the best possible view of Washington's loveliest ladies.

$13.50 Big Hunt Pizza is a self-proclaimed Dupont tradition. Happy Hour M-F 4-7pm: $2.50 Buds and rail drinks and $1 off all other drinks. Evening specials: M ½-price pizza (7-11pm) and free pool (4pm-2am); Tu $0.15 buffalo wings (7-11pm); W ½-price burgers (7-11pm); Th $3 pints of Redhook and house beers. Open M-Th 4pm-2am, F 4pm-3am, Sa 5pm-3am, Su 5pm-2am.

MCCXXIII, 1223 Connecticut Ave. NW (☎822-1800; www.1223.com), at 18th St. Pronounced "Twelve Twenty-three." A crowd of all ages and colors lines up to get in, but all share a cooler-than-thou attitude and love of pretentious partying. Fabric columns show off the high ceilings, while the best in house and hip-hop reverberates through the club. Tu college night hops to hip-hop and dance; W African-American night features R&B and hip-hop; Th international night; F-Sa house and dance; Su "Lizard Lounge" gay night (see p. 180). 21+. No sneakers or athletic wear. Cover usually $10. Open Tu-Th 6pm-2am, F-Sa 6pm-3am.

Timberlake's, 1726 Connecticut Ave. NW (☎483-2266; www.timberlakesrestaurant.com). Friendly neighborhood pub serves good burgers, sandwiches, and entrees. Sa-Su brunch 10:30am-3:30pm. A great place to have a brew and watch a game. Happy Hour (M-F 3-7pm) $1 off all drinks and 25% off selected appetizers. Open M-Th 11:30am-2am, F-Sa 11:30am-3am, Su 10:30am-2am.

Five, 1214-B 18th St. NW (☎331-7123; www.mthre3.com). Fashion-forward dancers take in the music on the main dance floor and 2nd fl. balcony, while more laid-back partiers retreat to the tiki-themed rooftop deck with a separate DJ. W downtempo and nu-jazz; Th "Swank" featuring hip-hop, reggae, and open bar 6-8pm; F electronica; Sa house and dance; Su reggae. 21+. Regular cover $5-10. Open Su-Th 10am-2am, F-Sa 10am-5am.

Red, 1802 Jefferson Pl. NW (☎466-3475), at Connecticut Ave. NW. This subterranean club doesn't even get hopping until 1am on weeknights and 3am on weekends, so don't bother rolling in early. Follow packs of drunken ravers, listen for thumping house music, or look for the door with the metal butterfly handle—the sign is impossible to see. Drinks $4-8. No shorts for men. Biweekly retro night on Tu; call for schedule. No cover early (usually before midnight), $5-10 once crowds start arriving. Open W-Th 10pm-3am, F-Sa 10pm-6am Su 10pm-3am.

Townhouse Tavern, 1637 R St. NW (☎234-5747), at 17th St. Young or old, gay or straight, all customers feel at home at this friendly neighborhood tavern. 3 fl. in which to hang out and get to know the locals. In summer, tables spill out onto the sidewalks. Nothing fancy, just good solid beer ($3.50-4.50). Happy Hour M-F 4-7pm, $1 off all drinks. Open M-Th 4pm-2am, F 4pm-3am, Sa noon-3am, Su noon-2am.

The Fox and Hounds, 1533 17th St. NW (☎232-6307). All ages and styles keep coming back for the strong mixed drinks and the flirty, relaxed atmosphere. Food supplied by **Trio** (see p. 147). Happy Hour M-F 4:30-6:30pm includes $2.50 rail drinks and domestic beers. Regular prices won't break any banks at $2.75-4.50 for beer. Check out the jukebox, known as one of the best in the District. Open M-Th 11:30am-2am, F 11:30am-3am, Sa 10:30am-3am, Su 10:30am-2am.

The Childe Harold, 1610 20th St. NW (☎483-6700), near Connecticut Ave. A pub-type restaurant and bar that just misses living up to its rebellious, Byronic namesake, the hero of the epic poem *Childe Harold's Pilgrimage*. The 1st fl. restaurant retains an upscale flair, with veal and steaks served for around $17 a plate, while a mixed crowd revels downstairs in the pub and on the patio, especially at Happy Hour (M-F 3-6pm), when Bud and Miller Lite are $2.25, rail drinks are $2.75, and most other drafts are $3.25. Popular for late-night munching. Open Su-Th 11:30am-2am, F-Sa 11:30am-3am. AmEx/DC/D/MC/V.

FARRAGUT

A number of bars in Farragut transform into casual quasi-clubs as the evening grows late, making Farragut a busy place to throw down and dance the night away.

🕮 **Ozio,** 1813 M St. NW (☎822-6000). Metro: Farragut North or Farragut West. The exclusive Ozio packs in a pretty crowd that poses, preens, and occasionally dances to international, house, and hip-hop while they down the club's famous high-end martinis ($8). Real and wannabe Eurotrash fill the 4 fl., 6-bar club with style and attitude until the late night. Enjoy ½-price martinis, beer, and wine during Happy Hour (M-F 5-8pm). Beer, wine $6. 21+. Nightly DJ beginning at 10pm M-W, 5pm Th-Sa. Cover F-Sa $10 after 10pm. Open M-Th 5pm-2am, F 5pm-3am, Sa 6pm-3am.

🕮 **Tequila Grill,** 1990 K St. NW (☎833-3640), entrance on 20th St. Metro: Farragut West. Southwestern food and decor most nights, but Tu and weekends (Th-Sa) bring out a Top 40, dance, and hip-hop DJ. Cheap booze and a bumping scene make the Grill a favorite with the summer intern set. Th night salsa and merengue are *mas fina* thanks to $1.50 Coronas. Inexpensive domestic beers and mixed drinks complement Happy Hour's $2.50 margaritas and ½-price appetizers (M-F 3:30-7:30pm, Sa 5-9pm). Droves of 20-somethings visit for the $5 all-you-can-drink beer night on Tu (9-11pm); some Tu nights in summer, the beer is free. Tu 18+, all other nights 21+. Open M-Th 11am-1am, F-Sa 11am-3am.

Sign of the Whale, 1825 M St. NW (☎785-1110), between 18th and 19th St. Metro: Farragut North or Dupont Circle. A comfortable bar during the week gets hopping on the weekends with a DJ (Tu-Sa from 8pm). Varnished dark wood and the usual bar decor set the scene for a casual, flirty dance party. Varied crowd ranging from mid-20s to early 40s. DJ plays Top 40 and 80s favorites. $1 off most drafts and a free buffet during Happy Hour (M-Th 4-7pm, F 4-9pm). 21+ after 11pm. No cover. Open Su-Th 11:30am-1:30am, F-Sa 11:30am-2:30am.

The Madhatter, 1831 M St. NW (☎833-1495), near 19th St. Metro: Farragut North or Farragut West. Much more arm-jostling than the Whale next door, with a younger party-hard clientele. Nightly specials, including Tu $1.50 Heineken and Amstel and free wings at 8pm, W $2 Yuengling and ½-price burgers, Th $1.50 Miller Lite and Rolling Rock and ½-price nachos. DJ spins Top 40 dance hits M-Sa from 8pm. Open Su-Th 11am-2am, F-Sa 11am-3am.

Rumors, 1900 M St. NW (☎466-7378; www.rumorsrestaurant.com), at 19th St. Metro: Farragut North or Dupont Circle. The anchor of the bar-heavy M St. block between 19th and 20th St. NW. The DJ spins Top 40 and some 80s faves for a 20-something and older crowd on a small dance floor W-Sa from 9pm. Happy Hour M-F 4-7pm: $3 domestic bottles, wines, and rail drinks. 21+ after 8pm. Cover F-Sa $3. Open Su-Th 11:30am-2am, F-Sa 11am-3am.

Ooh La La, 1800 M. St. NW (☎785-1177; www.oohlaladc.com). Metro: Farragut North. Entrance on 18th St. between L and M St. This classy martini lounge, restaurant, and bar by day turns into a pulsing international dance craze when the sun goes down. Besides looking unbearably hip, the crowd knows how to boogie, especially Sa salsa night. International, Latin, and club music F; salsa, merengue, international Sa. Happy Hour M-F 5-9pm. 21+. Cover F-Sa after 10pm $10. Open M-Th noon-10pm, F-Sa noon-3am.

Millie and Al's Bar

Club Chaos

Swingin' Summer Nights

174

FEDERAL TRIANGLE

YOU ARE HERE | SEE MAP P. 356

Clubs in Federal Triangle are concentrated in two main areas: near the McPherson Sq. Metro and along F St. between 9th and 12th St. The close proximity of many clubs makes club-hopping very tempting, despite the expense. Drinks in this area tend to be pricey, but there are a few drink specials to be found—keep your eyes open.

Home, 911 F. St. NW, at 9th St. (☎638-4663; www.homenightclub.net). Metro: Gallery Place-Chinatown. The newest addition to the F St. corridor, Home attracts a hot 20-something crowd for its thumping hip hop, house, and international music. 4 levels and a VIP room for drinking and dancing; hidden nooks and plush bed-like benches for...everything else. 21+, dress to impress. Cover $10. Open W-Sa 9pm-3am.

Platinum, 915 F St. NW (☎393-3555; www.platinumclubdc.com). Metro: Metro Center or Gallery Place-Chinatown. Snoop Dogg and Allen Iverson have been sighted at this posh club known for its top-shelf liquors (Cristal anyone?) and faux-flame chandelier. Chill in the 3rd floor VIP section (reservations required) or watch drunk couples dance badly to hip hop, house, or trance from your perch on the balcony. Beer and cocktails $5-6. Th 18+, free until midnight with college ID; F-Sa 18+, ladies free before midnight (11pm on Sa), no jeans. Su 21+, free before 11pm. Cover $10. Open Th-Su 10pm-2am, F-Sa 10pm-3am.

Fado, 808 7th St. NW (☎789-0066; www.fadoirishpub.com). Metro: Gallery Place-Chinatown. On 7th between H and I St. A self-proclaimed authentic Irish pub with a cobblestone floor, intricately carved tables, and soccer jersey decor. The bar is packed most nights with everyone from grad students to retired government workers—even the Irish Ambassador has made appearances. Most drinks $4-7. Happy Hour (M-F 7-9pm) $3.50 pints of the day's featured beer. Open Su-Th 11am-2am, F-Sa 11am-3am.

Club Insomnia, 714 6th St. NW (☎737-1003; www.insomniaclub.com). Extremely popular with the 18-26 age group. Deocrated with aluminum arrows and psychedelic murals of Indian myths. The main fl. has 40 ceilings and dance cages. Most drinks $4-8. College F hip-hop on the main fl. and Latin upstairs ($10-15, 10pm-3:30am). Sa "Glow," features nationally-known DJs spinning house, techno, and electronica ($15-20, 10pm-4am, www.clubglow.com). Schedule varies on Su; call for details. 18+.

The VIP Club, 932 F St. NW (☎347-7200, www.vipclubdc.com), across from Platinum. Draws 25+ working crowd. Stylish and classy, reminiscent of a movie set. Carpeted floors and comfortable couches. 1st fl. lounge. 2 dance floors on the second level, with music from Latin to hip hop to R+B. The place to go when lines at Platinum and Home are too long. Cover $15. F 21+, ladies free until midnight, open bar 9-11pm, no jeans, open 9pm-3am; Sa 21+, no jeans, open 9pm-3am, Su 18+ 9pm-2am.

Stoney's Restaurant, 1307 L St. NW (☎347-9163), near 13th St. Metro: McPherson Sq. Greasy spoon meets the Godfather in this neighborhood tavern with the longest F Happy Hour around (4pm-midnight; Corona or margarita $2.50, Bud pitchers $9). Kick back with law students and Secret Service agents in the homey atmosphere for cheap beer and great food. Open daily 11am-2am. Kitchen closes at 1am.

Polly Esther's, 605 12th St. NW (☎737-1970; www.pollyesthers.com), between F and G St. Metro: Metro Center. Retro club with 3 fl. spanning 3 decades—70s, 80s, and 90s—all equipped with digital video screens. Don't look twice, you *are* seeing someone wearing 13in. bell-bottoms and platform shoes. Th drink specials til midnight, 18+, cover $5 (ladies free), open 9pm-2am; F open bar all night, 21+, cover $15, open 9pm-3am; Sa bachelorettes get in free, 21+, cover $10, open 9pm-3am.

Diva, 1350 I St. NW, between 13th and 14th Sts. (☎289-7300). Metro: McPherson Sq. Face glitter and tinted sunglasses are typical accessories worn by the beautiful and young international crowd which dances the night away to hot Persian, Greek, or hip hop (music changes weekly) at this upscale bar and club. Plenty of seating and large dance area all on 1 fl. 21+. Cover $10. Open Sa 10:30pm-3am.

FOGGY BOTTOM

As home of George Washington University, the Foggy Bottom bar scene is full of students and recent grads reveling in drunken bliss. Use Metro: Foggy Bottom-GWU for the following.

YOU ARE HERE ↘   SEE MAP P. 358
U.S. Capitol Building

▨ **McFadden's,** 2401 Pennsylvania Ave. NW (☎223-2338; www.mcfaddensdc.com), at 24th St. A longtime NYC favorite, McFadden's D.C. opened on St. Patrick's Day 2003 and has been packed with attractive young partiers ever since. Over 20 TVs make this a prime sports bar. DJ (Tu-Su) draws attention away from TVs. Happy Hour (M-F 4-7pm) takes $1 off all drinks. M $5 pitchers of beers; Tu $1 Miller Lite, Coors Light, and Corona; W $1 drinks for ladies 7-10pm; Th $2 Sam Adams. 21+, men 23+ F-Sa after 9pm. Open Su-Th 11am-2am, F-Sa 11am-3am.

the hidden deal

BIBULOUS-NESS PLAN

It seems like every bar in the District has Happy Hour specials. How does one distinguish the real deals from the hype? Have no fear, dear reader. Your friends at *Let's Go* have performed night upon night of painstaking research to compile the following list (read: schedule):

Monday: Start the week off right with $5 pitchers of any draft but Guinness all night at **McFadden's** (see p. 175) in Foggy Bottom.

Tuesday: Pay just $5 and join destitute interns for a festive night of all-you-can drink beer 9-11pm at **Tequila Grill** (see p. 173) in Farragut. Occasionally in summer, beer on Tu nights is free (!).

Wednesday: Enjoy $1 Buds 4-8pm on the sprawling patio at **Red River Grill** (see p. 170) in Capitol Hill.

Thursday: Head to Cleveland Park for $1.75 domestic beers and rail drinks 4-8pm at **Nanny O'Brien's** (see p. 180).

Friday: Celebrate the beginning of the weekend with $5 pitchers of Miller Lite 4-7pm at **Millie & Al's** (see p. 164) in Adams Morgan. Want more? **Rhino** (see p. 177), in Georgetown, serves ½-price drinks 5-9pm.

Foggy Bottoms Up

D.C. can claim a native alcoholic beverage, the gourmet Foggy Bottom Family of Beer, brewed by the Olde Heurich Brewing Company. The brewery was founded in 1873, thanks to the efforts of German immigrant Christian Heurich. He lasted until the ripe old age of 102, becoming a character in the world of fine beers after 88 years in the business.

Heurich had his beer labeled with 100% purity for its ingredients by the federal government and lobbied to remove beer and wine from the 18th Amendment's prohibition on drinking, a 1918 ban on alcoholic consumption as stipulated by the Bill of Rights. Anticipating Prohibition, Heurich experimented with alcohol-free apple cider, only to produce 100,000 gallons of 6% alcohol. One of the brewer's last customers in 1933 was the White House.

The most successful products have been the Senate and Old Georgetown brands. The best-selling line, the Foggy Bottom Family of Beers was only introduced seven years ago, with Foggy Bottom Lager, Wheat, and Porter, but the brewing methods are based on a system that won the brewing company the silver medal in the 1900 Paris Exposition for purity and excellence.

Lulu's Mardi Gras Club, 1217 22nd St. NW (☎861-5858; www.lulusclub.com), at M St. Foggy Bottom's biggest bar with 8 bars on 3 floors and anywhere from 1 to 3 DJs playing hip-hop music nightly. Charming Bourbon St. decor combined with club dance floor. Draws a massive weekend crowd in their 20s and early 30s—come tipsy and prepared to be hit on. Enjoy $3.50 hurricanes and $2.50 rail drinks and domestic beers during Happy Hour (M-F 5-9pm). Outdoor seating available. Open M-Th 4pm-2am, F-Sa 4pm-3am. Bar food is served until 10pm.

Froggy Bottom Pub, 2142 Pennsylvania Ave. NW (☎388-3000). Froggy offers a popular M ½-price pizza deal, but the big attractions are Foggy Bottom Ale, the local microbrew, and the pool and foosball tables, which are usually occupied by GWU students. Standard pub menu and drink list, with rotating deals. Happy Hour, 6pm-close, features selected $2 pints and $1.25 bottles. Open M-Sa 11:30am-2am.

Lindy's Red Lion, 2040 I St. NW (☎785-2766), at 21st St. Lindy's is a neighborhood bar with reasonably priced drinks. Table service upstairs with awesome burgers and a quieter pub atmosphere. 10 beers on tap; nightly shooter specials ($2.25). Happy Hour M-F 4-8pm features appetizer specials, $2 off pitchers, and $1 off all drinks. Open Su-Th 11am-2am, F-Sa until 3am. Kitchen closes at midnight.

GEORGETOWN

Georgetown rocks at night with a variety of bars for every taste. Partygoers tend to swarm either to the bars along **Wisconsin Avenue and M Street** or the waterfront bars housed in the **Washington Harbour** complex near 31st and K St. The simplest route from the Metro to either party scene are the blue Georgetown Metro Connection shuttlebuses, which run every 10min. between the crossroads of Georgetown and the Dupont Circle, Foggy Bottom-GWU, and Rosslyn Metro stops. (Buses run M-Th 7am-midnight, F 7am-2am, Sa 8am-2am, Su 8am-midnight; $1, $0.35 with a transfer from the Metro.) To walk to Georgetown nightlife from the Metro, take the Blue/Orange line to Foggy Bottom-GWU. When you exit the station, you'll be facing 23rd St. NW and the George Washington University Hospital. Turn left down 23rd St. and walk clockwise around Washington Circle until you reach Pennsylvania Ave.; turn left onto Pennsylvania and trudge down over the bridge to M St. The Metro stays open until 3am on Friday and Saturday nights, so if you're not up for a really late night, save some bucks by taking the Metro home.

Third Edition, 1218 Wisconsin Ave. NW (☎333-3700), between Prospect and M St. Featured in the definitive Brat Pack film *St. Elmo's Fire,* this bar attracts the usual mid-20s party-hard crowd. Its 3 bars, dance floor, and summer tiki patio guarantee a good time when the place gets crowded Th-Sa nights. Sandwiches $7-10 and entrees $12-17. Domestic bottles $4.50, imports $5.50, rail drinks $5. Patio and upstairs area open W-Sa; $5 cover; enter through alley to the left of the main entrance. Open M-Th 5pm-2am, F 5pm-3am, Sa 11:30am-3am, Su 11:30am-2am.

Rhino, 3295 M St. NW (☎333 3150; www.rhinobardc.com), at the corner of M and 33rd St. The perennial favorite for Georgetown students and young professionals who wish they were still in college. A preppy crowd flirts and shoots pool ($10 per hr.) upstairs while their drunk friends grind on the downstairs dance floor. Nightly drink specials include W ½-price drinks 9pm-12:30am, Th $2 Yuengling pints, F ½-price drinks 5-9pm, Sa $2 rail drinks after 9pm, Su drinks for ladies $2 after 9pm. DJ nightly from 9pm. Open M-W 8pm-2am, Th 7pm-2am, F 5pm-3am, Sa noon-3am, Su noon-2am.

Old Glory, 3139 M St. NW (☎337-3406; www.oldglorybbq.com). Families gather at mealtime for unparalleled ribs ($15-20) featuring region-specific barbecue sauces and cooking techniques (dry vs. wet, Memphis vs. Texas). A mid-to-late-20s crowd takes over after dinner. Serious drinkers try for membership in Old Glory's Bourbon Club by sampling each of Old Glory's 80 varieties (though generally not in one sitting). Upstairs patio open Mar.-Oct. Drafts $3-4.50, bottled beer $3-4, mixed drinks $5-6. Bar open Su-Th 11:30am-2am, F-Sa 11:30am-3am; dinner served Su-Th until midnight, F-Sa until 1am. Late-night menu with fewer selections available for 1hr. after dinner ends.

The Tombs, 1226 36th St. NW (☎337-6668), at Prospect St., underneath 1789 Restaurant. Very close to Georgetown University, and a favorite with students, interns, locals, and occasionally more high-profile clients (Bill Clinton, Chris O'Donnell, and Andre Agassi, whose tennis racket hangs on the wall). Despite its ominous name, this basement restaurant is cozy, with rowing-themed decor. Drop in for burgers ($6-7), dinner ($8-11), and beer (pitchers $6-13, mugs $1.35-3). Open M-Th 11:30am-2am, F 11:30am-3am, Sa 11am-3am, Su 9:30am-2am (Su brunch til 3pm).

Tony and Joe's, 3000 K St. NW (☎944-4545; www.tonyandjoes.com), part of the Washington Harbour complex. Seafood restaurant by day, young preppy bar scene by night. Th-Sa nights, the massive patio overlooking the water is packed with young professionals checking out more than the nearby yachts. Drink prices reflect the picturesque view: beer and rail drinks $5-7. 21+ after 11pm. Open Su-Th 11am-2am, F-Sa 11am-3am.

Garrett's, 3003 M St. NW (☎333-1033; www.garrettsdc.com), near 30th St. With 1 downstairs bar and 2 bars upstairs, Garrett's is a laid-back scene known for decent prices, a railroad motif, and a crowd that spans several age ranges. The "Hemingway" rhino was supposedly shot by one of Ernest's wives, but is really a fiberglass model. Beer and mixed drinks around $3.50. ½-price domestic beer, generic liquors, and house wine during Happy Hour (M-F 5-7pm). The glass-enclosed terrace upstairs is open for lunch M-F 11:30am-2:30pm, Sa-Su noon-2:30pm; for dinner Su-Th 6-10pm, F-Sa 6-11pm. Bar open M-Th 11:30am-2am, F 11:30am-3am, Sa noon-3am, Su noon-2am.

Mr. Smith's, 3104 M St. NW (☎333-3104), near 31st St. Self-proclaimed "Friendliest Saloon in Town" tends to be a pick-up joint for Georgetown 20- and 30-somethings. Welcomes bands of all types F-Sa nights upstairs. If the bar gets too raucous, slip out to the garden seating in the enclosed greenhouse out back. $1 off draft beer, $1.50 generic liquors, and ½-price appetizers M-F 5-7pm. Mixed drinks $4.40-8. Sandwiches $6-9, entrees up to $19. Open Su-Th 11:30am-2am, F-Sa 11:30am-3am.

Nick's Riverside Grille, 3050 K St. NW (☎342-3535; www.riversidegrille.com), part of the Washington Harbour complex. A place to rock and romance. With a spacious outdoor patio offering a gorgeous view of the Potomac River and the Kennedy Center, this spot really draws the crowds on warm nights. Food is a bit pricey, with appetizers $8.50-12, sandwiches $6-12, and entrees $18-26. Beer $4-5, other drinks $5-7. Open daily 11:30am-2am.

J. Paul's, 3218 M St. NW (☎333-3450), near Wisconsin Ave. A more classy bar (too expensive for most college students) drawing a late-20s professional crowd. Known for its above-average bar food (sandwiches $9-14, entrees $11-23). Large raw bar boasts its famous

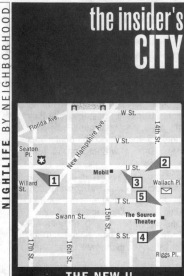

the insider's
CITY

THE NEW U

In the past four years, the U Street strip has transformed from a dangerous drug neighborhood into one of D.C.'s hottest club and lounge areas. Your search for the high life should begin and end here.

1 Start your night by sitting back and puffing on a hookah at chill **Chi Cha Lounge.** (☎234-8400)

2 The night really heats up when you dive into the throngs at **U-topia.** (☎483-7669)

3 The lounge life continues as you luxuriate at **Cada Vez.** (☎667-0785)

4 For a solid rock show, cross paths with the **Black Cat.** (☎667-7960)

5 Mingle with the rock stars after the show at **Cafe Saint-Ex.** (☎265-7839)

brand of amber ale, a recent National Beer-Tasting Award winner (pint $5). Open M-Th 11:30am-2am, F-Sa 11:30am-3am, Su 10:30am-2am. Food served until 11:30pm nightly.

Nathans, 3150 M St. NW (☎338-2000), on the corner of Wisconsin Ave. and M St. This is where the older-but-still-hip crowd goes to let their hair down Fr and Sa nights, when the restaurant clears out to make room for some booty-shaking. A well-known mating ground for Georgetown's well-educated and well-bred 30-something professionals. Draft beers $5, mixed drinks from $5. DJs play Top 40 and other dance hits at the upstairs club. Dining room open 5:30-11pm daily, and additionally Sa-Su 10am-2:30pm for brunch. Bar open Su-Th 3pm-2am, F-Sa 3pm-3am; club open F-Sa 11:30pm-3am.

SHAW/U DISTRICT

As Shaw becomes more of a nightlife destination, artsier-than-thou nightspots are giving way to more generic hangouts for the masses. Clustered around **U St.**, these bars are still neighborhood-oriented and stocked with hip regulars, making Adams Morgan seem hopelessly mainstream by comparison. For live music venues, see **Rock and Pop,** p. 184. The area can be dangerous; **exercise caution at night.** Use Metro: U St.-Cardozo for all of the following.

🖼 **Cafe Saint-Ex,** 1847 14th St. NW (☎265-7839), at T St. Shaw's newest hotspot is the brainchild of professional photographer Mike Benson, who has photographed everyone from Tony Hawk to Radiohead. Benson's connections pay off: rockers playing at the nearby clubs usually come by after their show for drinks or dinner (see **Food & Drink,** p. 157). The vintage aviation-themed bar attracts a truly mixed crowd: punk rockers and lawyers alike (really) enjoy the upstairs bar and patio and downstairs Gate 54 lounge, where DJs spin everything from downtempo to Brit pop nightly at 10pm. Beer $2-5, rail drinks $6. 21+ after 10:30pm. No cover. Open M-F 5pm-2am, Sa-Su 11am-2am.

🖼 **Local 16,** 1602 U St. NW (☎265-2828; www.local-sixteen.com), at 16th St. (go figure). The owners of Eighteenth Street Lounge (see p. 171) bring their style (and success) to Shaw with this swanky bar and restaurant (see Food & Drink, p. 178). Locals run the place Su-Tu, but swarms of young professionals (both gay and straight) take over W-Sa nights. Huge roof deck . Beer and rail drinks $5, martinis and specialty cocktails $7-9. Happy Hour daily 5:30-8pm, $1 off all drinks. 21+ after 10pm. Open Su-Th 5:30pm-1:30am, F-Sa 5:30pm-2:30am.

2:K:9, 2009 8th St. (☎667-7750; www.2k9.com), at Florida Ave. This post-industrial club rolls out reams of red carpet in its enormous dance and performance space, decorated by one of the original Studio 54 designers. A sea of black pants and dark shirts floods the martini lounge, 45 ft. bar, and 2 mega dance floors, which usually feature hip-hop and house. The glass-enclosed V.I.P. lounge offers the best view of all the action. Complimentary valet parking available. Women 18+, men 21+. Cover $5-15. Open Th-Sa 5pm-2am.

Chi Cha Lounge, 1624 U St. NW (☎234-8400; www.chicha.com). A swanky crowd dresses to impress in this mellow, 2-room lounge. Beatnik types lounge around on the ample couches sipping cocktails, enjoying Andean food, and smoking fruit-flavored tobacco from hookahs (available Su-Th). Live Latin music spices up the chill comfort Su-Th 10pm. 21+. Open Su-Th 5:30pm-2am, F-Sa 5:30pm-3am.

Bar Nun/Club 2000, 1326 U St. NW (☎667-6680), between 13th and 14th St. This smaller, older version of the clubs in Old Downtown gets frenzied faster than any other club on U St. A favorite of locals who stream to the 3 bars and get down to a mix of hip-hop, jungle, and reggae. Happy Hour Jazz F 6-11pm before the DJ arrives. 21+. Cover F-Sa $10. Open M-Th 7pm-2am, F 6pm-3am, Sa 7pm-3am, Su 7pm-2am.

Cada Vez, 1438 U St. NW (☎667-0785; www.cadavezonline.com), near 15th St. This sleek space draws a crowd of young black professionals to hear live jazz, marimba, salsa, and dance DJs. The posh seating will make you wish you had dressed nicer no matter what you're wearing. Happy Hour deals include 2-for-1 rail drinks, martinis, and beer (Tu-Sa 5-8pm) and a free hors d'oeuvres buffet (Tu-F 6-7pm). Martinis ($7-8.50). Limited menu (entrees $12-18). 21+. Cover $5-15. Open Tu-Th 5:30pm-midnight, F-Sa 5pm-3am.

U-topia, 1418 U St. NW (☎483-7669), near 14th St. This upscale bar/gallery hosts exhibits by local artists every month in the back room. With glam-townhouse decor highlighted by mood lighting, small tables, and its own permanent collection, this low-key venue satiates any jazz aficionado. Offers lunch, brunch, and dinner. Live jazz Su-W 9pm, Th-Sa 11pm (Th Brazilian jazz). Open Su-Th 11am-2am, F-Sa 11am-3am.

Cafe Nema, 1334 U St. NW (☎667-3215). Showcasing local talent, this small downstairs bar combines avant-garde art with the toe-tapping vibes of live jazz Th-Sa 10pm-1am. Internationals, who shoot the breeze with the laid back Somali owner. Happy Hour (M-F 4-8pm) 2 for $5 bottled beers and rail drinks and $1 off top shelf liquors. 21+ after 11pm. No cover but occasional 2 drink minimum. Open Su-Tu noon-1am, W-Sa noon-2:30am. Kitchen open noon-11pm.

SOUTH OF THE MALL

⧉ Zanzibar on the Waterfront, 700 Water St. SW (☎554-9100; www.zanzibar-otw.com), at 7th St. Metro: Waterfront. Shimmering water-front views, and big-name acts have made Zanzibar the premier D.C. destination for affluent black 20- and 30-somethings, including Michael Jordan, Mary J. Blige, and Allen Iverson. This entertainment center boasts

7 bars, 2 large dance floors, sweeping patios, VIP lounge, and a stage for live performances. W salsa and merengue; Th adult urban contemporary; F-Sa hip-hop and international music; open some Su for special shows. Cover $10 W-F after 7pm, Sa after 9pm; free admission with dinner (except special events). 21+. Arrive early or purchase tickets in advance for live acts (around $30). No jeans or tennis shoes. Open W-Th 5pm-1am, F 5pm-3am, Sa 9pm-4am.

UPPER NORTHWEST

With so many alternatives downtown, Upper Northwest's bars rarely draw anyone besides local residents. However, the neighborhood feel of these places can be appealing if you're looking for a change of pace from the trendy Adams Morgan or Georgetown scenes.

Ireland's Four Provinces, 3412 Connecticut Ave. NW (☎244-0860; www.irelandsfour-provinces.com). Metro: Cleveland Park. Large, open space is a refreshing break from long, narrow bars. Live Irish folk music Su-Th 8:30pm, F-Sa 9pm. Outdoor seating in summer. Happy Hour (daily 5-7pm) discounts domestics ($2.50), imports ($3.50), rail drinks ($3.50), and, of course, Guinness ($4.25). Pub Quiz W 9-11pm. Cover $5. Open Su-Th 5pm-2am, F-Sa 4pm-3am.

The Aroma Company, 3417 Connecticut Ave. NW (☎244-7995; www.thearomaco.com), between Ordway and Newark St. Metro: Cleveland Park. Under the same ownership as the eminently popular Buffalo Billiards (see p. 190), this small retro lounge features a long mosaic bar and a young, well-dressed crowd sipping on specialty drinks. Happy Hour M-F 6-8pm with $2.75 Redhooks and $4 rail drinks. 21+. Open Su-Th 6pm-2am, F-Sa 6pm-3am.

Murphy's of D.C., 2609 24th St. NW (☎462-7171), at Calvert St. Metro: Woodley Park-Zoo. An old neighborhood Irish pub with live Irish music 8pm Tu-Th, 9pm F-Sa; stay late enough in the evening and you might see the occasional impromptu jig. Caters to an older, local crowd. Guinness $5.75, microbrews $4.25, and lots more on tap. Salads, burgers, and other bar food available ($6-12), with Su brunch. Open Su-Th 11am-2am, F-Sa 11am-3am. Kitchen open daily until midnight.

Nanny O'Brien's, 3319 Connecticut Ave. NW (☎686-9189). Metro: Cleveland Park. A mix of locals, college students, and a cast of regulars cavort at this standard, dimly-lit Irish pub. Happy Hour (M-F 4-8pm) features $1.75 domestic beers and rail drinks. Nightly Irish music W-M starting around 9:30pm, both traditional and contemporary folk; Irish countryside dances in winter. Open M-Th 4pm-2am, F 4pm-3am, Sa noon-3am, Su 4pm-2am.

GAY BARS & CLUBS

J.R.'s, 1519 17th St. NW (☎328-0090; www.jrsdc.com), at Church St. Metro: Dupont Circle. D.C.'s busiest gay bar for good reasons: beautiful bartenders, fun events, and great drink deals. Packed every night with hordes of "guppies" (gay urban professionals). M offers $3 pints and Showtune Sing-a-Long at 9:30pm. Su $2 Rolling Rocks and Skyy vodka drinks all day. Happy Hour (M-W 5-8pm) brings $3 mini-pitchers, $2 rail drinks and domestic beers, and $1 sodas; the famous Power Hour follows (8-9pm), during which everything is ½-price. Open M-Th 11:30am-2am, F-Sa 11:30am-3am, Su noon-2am.

Cobalt, 1639 R St. NW (☎462-6569; www.cobaltdc.com), at 17th St. Metro: Dupont Circle. No sign marks this gay hotspot; look for the blue light and bouncer. Shirtless bartenders serve drinks ($4.75-5.75) to a young, preppy crowd who come to this 2nd fl. club for a hot dance party. Tu retro "Solid Gold", W "Girlz Night", Th "Best Package" contest with $150 first prize (12:30am), Su Gong Show Karaoke at 8:30pm. 21+. F-Sa $5 cover. Open Tu-Th 10pm-2am, F-Sa 10pm-3am, Su 8:30pm-2am. Downstairs, **30°** is a lounge offering a more relaxed atmosphere with ½-price martinis during Happy Hour (M-F 5-8pm). 21+. Open Su-Th 5pm-2am, F-Sa 5pm-3am.

Apex, 1415 22nd St. NW (☎296-0505; www.apex-dc.com), near P St. Metro: Dupont Circle. Formerly known as Badlands, this 2-story dance complex draws a young crowd for its wild dance parties. Different events Th-Sa nights, but DJs always play a mix of house, trance, and top 40 music. Th college night, $5 cover, free with student ID, $3 rail drinks. F $8 cover, drag karaoke starts at 11pm. Sa "Liquid Ladies" night (www.liquidladies.com), $7 cover, $3 Long Island iced teas. 18+. Open Th-Sa from 9pm onward.

Lizard Lounge, held at MCCXXIII, 1223 Connecticut Ave. NW (☎331-4422; www.atlasev-ents.com/lizard.html), at 18th St. Sunday can be funday, too, because the upscale MCCXXIII (see p. 172) allows D.C. boys to prolong the weekend with a gay night. $2 Absolut vodka drinks 8-10pm. 21+. No cover. Open Su 8pm-2am.

Omega, 2122 P St. NW (☎223-4917), at P St. in the alley between 21st and 22nd St. Metro: Dupont Circle. Attracts an ethnically mixed crowd of gay men who cavort under the ancient Greek prints and statues. The guy in the corner looking at his feet isn't shy; he's just watching the erotica playing on the TVs in the floor. Boasts 2 fl. of dance music, videos, arcades, and 4 bars. Happy Hour (M-F 4-9pm) features $2.25 rail drinks and $6 pitchers of beer. Specials

Worry Free Travel is Just a Click Away

Trip Cancellation
International Medical Insurance
Emergency Evacuation
All Nationalities

Personalize your travel insurance needs
with our online Policy Picker®

USA / Canada: 1 800 234 1862
International: +1 703 299 6001

ww.Letsgo.WorldTravelCenter.com   Travel Insurance Experts tell us you saw us in "Lets Go" for a **FREE** passport holder!

the ultimate
road trip

don't trip out planning your big road trip.
put contiki in the driver's seat with hassle-free vacations designed for 18 to 35 year olds. make new friends, enjoy your free time and explore the sights in a convenient vacation that gives you more bang for your buck... **from only $70/day** including accommodations, sightseeing, many meals and transportation. with contiki leading the way, you can leave the road map at home!

> **7 days eastern discovery**
  new york, washington d.c., us naval academy, kennedy space center

> **10 days canada & the rockies**
  vancouver, calgary, banff national park

> **13 days wild western**
  san francisco, grand canyon, las vegas, yosemite national park

*prices subject to change, land only.

for more info on our trips...
see your travel agent
call 1-888-CONTIKI
visit www.contiki.com

CST# 1001728-20

contiki
VACATIONS for 18-35 year olds

> europe > australia > new zealand > america > canada

every weeknight; Su, Tu, and Th $2.50 vodka drinks; M all light beers $2.50, drag show 11pm; W pool tourney, shirtless men drink free; Th Drag Karaoke 10pm. DJ nightly. 21+. No cover. Open M-Th 4pm-2am, F 4pm-3am, Sa 8pm-3am, Su 7pm-2am.

Club Chaos, 1603 17th St. NW (☎232-4141), at Q St. Metro: Dupont Circle. Lives dependably up to its name; with so many shows, deals, and games going on, it's pretty hard to have a bad time. Different nights cater to different crowds, though everynight is boisterously fun and crowded. Happy Hour Tu-F 5-8pm, ½-price rail drinks and domestic beer. Tu Drag Queen bingo and trivia at 9pm. W "G-Spot" ladies night. Th Latin night. The best drag show in town F 11pm, Sa 10pm. Su Hollywood Drag Brunch 11am-3pm. $3 cover buys a drink ticket of equal value. Open Tu-Th 5pm-2am, F-Sa 5pm-3am, Su 11am-3pm and 8pm-1am.

The Fireplace, 2161 P St. NW (☎293-1293), at 22nd St. Metro: Dupont Circle. Oddly divided 2 fl. video bar catering to older professional males and the men who love them. Mostly black crowd upstairs watches BET and plays hip-hop while the whiter scene downstairs sticks to rock and pop. Happy Hour daily 1-8pm, $2.25 domestics. M-W $2.50 rail drinks and domestics (8pm-2am); Su $2.50 vodka drinks and domestics (8pm-2am). Weekends and evenings can get pretty packed. 21+. No cover. Open Su-Th 1pm-2am, F-Sa till 3am.

Mr. P's, 2149 P St. NW (☎293-1064), near 22nd St. Metro: Dupont Circle. The oldest gay bar in the Circle attracts one of the oldest crowds, as 30-and-ups flock for $2.25 rail drinks and domestic beers during Happy Hour (M-F 3-8pm). In the evenings, patrons spill out onto the patio and head upstairs to the 2nd bar (open 9pm-closing). Karaoke W 10:30pm, drag shows Sa-Su 11pm. The Su barbecues on the back patio are a good chance to meet some of the locals. Look for their big anniversary party in Mar. 21+. No cover. Open M-Th 3pm-2am, F-Sa 3pm-3am, Su noon-2am.

INSIDE
music **183**
theater and dance **187**
comedy **189**
billiards **189**
literary life **190**
film **190**
sports & recreation **191**

Entertainment

Culturally, Washington has undergone a "Cinderella city" turnaround. From the days of city planner Pierre L'Enfant, D.C. was known as an unsophisticated country bumpkin as far as urban centers went. That all changed when the Kennedy Center (p. 186) opened in 1971. The single-minded focus of this cultural beacon, combined with the hard work of dedicated arts patrons like David Lloyd Kreeger, sparked D.C.'s transformation from provincial capital to cosmopolitan arts center. Today, the Kennedy Center proudly houses the Washington Opera, the Washington Ballet, and the National Symphony Orchestra, and dozens of professional acting troupes now perform "off Kennedy Center."

MUSIC

Symphonic strains at the Kennedy Center give way to trance, punk, and all sorts of alterna-rock around U St., where clubs like 9:30, The Black Cat, and Velvet Lounge host live shows nightly. Jazz mavens sing the blues in any number of D.C.'s smoky lounges (p. 186), as experimental plays unfold in black boxes along the 14th St. theater district (p. 187). The beauty of the D.C. arts scene is that you can enjoy much of it without forking over any precious dough. Just consult the *CityPaper* or the *Washington Post*'s Friday "Weekend" or "Style" sections for schedules of free performances and music.

Velvet Lounge

Kennedy Center for Performing Arts

Takoma Park

ROCK & POP

The D.C. punk scene is, or at least was, one of the nation's finest, but performers of every stripe frequently call on the city. The bigger, more mainstream events take place at the sports arenas: **RFK Stadium** in the summer and the **MCI Center** year-round. Tickets for many shows are available from **Protix** (☎410-481-6500, 703-218-6500, or 800-955-5566) or **TicketMaster** (☎432-7328; www.ticketmaster.com).

THE U STREET SCENE

The U District, D.C.'s ear-blasting epicenter, has sent the D.C. punk and rock scene off the Richter scale for decades. Unfortunately, the area is not the safest: **use common sense here at night.** Use Metro: U St.-Cardozo for all of the following.

🎸 **9:30 Club**, 815 V St. NW (☎393-0930, tickets 265-0930; www.930.com), at 9th St. As if to mark it as D.C.'s most established local and alternative rock venue, the 9:30 Club sports a large radio tower sticking out of its roof. Noteworthy before-they-were-big bands that played here include Nirvana, Smashing Pumpkins, and R.E.M. The club's musical tastes are broadening, though; recent headliners include the Black Eyed Peas. Tickets ($10-40) usually sell out weeks in advance, so plan ahead. 18+. Advance tickets available from Tickets.com (☎800-955-5566; www.tickets.com). Cash-only box office open M-F noon-7pm, until 11pm on show nights; Sa 6-11pm, Su 6-10:30pm on show nights only. Doors open Su-Th 7:30pm-midnight, F-Sa 9pm-2am.

🎸 **The Black Cat**, 1811 14th St. NW (☎667-7960, bar 667-4490; www.blackcatdc.com), between S and T St. One of D.C.'s most established live music venues also offers poetry and indie-movie nights (check weekly listings). Plays host to a variety of alternative rock bands, with headliners like The White Stripes, The Hives, and Foo Fighters (lead man Dave Grohl is a co-owner). The string-lit Club, where the bands perform, includes a full bar. The retro Red Room next door offers pool, pinball, booths, couches, and a rocking jukebox. F-Sa DJ on the back stage. Happy Hour (F-Sa 7-9pm) $1 off rail drinks. All ages. Some shows free, most $5-10, but no cover for the Red Room. Open Su-Th 8pm-2am, F-Sa 7pm-3am.

Velvet Lounge, 915 U St. (☎462-3213 or 462-7625 to hear samples of upcoming acts; www.velvet-loungedc.com), at 9th St. Glowing with all the intrigue of a secretive indie venue, the Velvet Lounge is actually well-known for its raucous rock acts. Live bands upstairs 7 nights a week in an intimate room that fills with loud fans and laid-back locals. Small bar downstairs. Occasional "free beer" nights with local bands announced only over their email list. 21+. Cover Su-Th $5, F-Sa $7. Open Su-Th 8pm-2am, F-Sa 8pm-3am.

OTHER VENUES

Birchmere Music Hall, 3701 Mount Vernon Ave. (☎703-549-7500; www.birchmere.com), in Alexandria. Metro: King St. This gruesomely decorated ex-factory showcases an eclectic mix of modern and Southern rock acts including Aimee Mann, Shawn Colvin, and the Bacon Brothers. Most shows start 7:30-8:30pm. Box office opens 5pm on showdates; advance tickets from TicketMaster. Tickets $15-25.

DAR Constitution Hall, (☎628-4780; www.dar.org/conthall), 18th and D St. NW. Metro: Farragut West (18th and I St. exit). 5 blocks south of Metro. The largest concert hall in the District, with a storied history that includes 4-decade tenures with both the **National Symphony** and the **National Geographic** film series. It has also hosted performances and productions such as *Jeopardy!* and Eddie Murphy HBO specials. Big bands now play at the MCI Center, along with national acts, ranging from Sonic Youth to the Isley Brothers. Tickets available through TicketMaster (www.ticketmaster.com); call the box office or visit the website for schedule info.

🏠 **Lisner Auditorium** (☎994-6800; www.lisner.org), 730 21st St. NW, at the intersection with H St. at George Washington University. Lisner hosts plays, ballets, operas, and rock concerts by alternative acts like Weird Al Yankovic and Brazilian singer Milton Nascimento. Recent acts have also included Tom Jones, Peter Frampton, Joan Baez, and an interview with actor Robert Duvall. Most shows start at 8pm. Tickets run $13-80 and can usually be ordered from TicketMaster, or from the theater itself (in person or online); the box office is open Tu-F 11am-5pm.

Merriweather Post Pavilion (☎410-730-2424; www.mppconcerts.com), in Columbia, MD, less than an hour from D.C. or Baltimore (although it takes longer with event traffic). From D.C., take I-95 North approx. 18 mi. to Rte. 32 (toward Columbia) to Rte. 29 North. Take Exit 18B (Broken Land Pkwy.); make first right into Pavilion parking lot. Hosts popular mainstream bands like Dave Matthews, No Doubt, Red Hot Chili Peppers, and their ilk. Lawn tickets run $10-40; covered seats $40-100. For tickets, call Ticketmaster (☎301-808-2405; www.ticketmaster.com).

🏠 **Nation,** 1015 Half St. SE (☎554-1500), 1 block from the Navy Yard Metro. This mega-concert hall and warehouse-style club is an inspired attempt to recreate its former glory as the Capitol Ballroom. Nation hosts themed dance parties on weekends: Th "Alchemy" spins underground 80s, goth, and industrial (doors open at 9pm; cover $7; www.alchemy-dc.com); F "Code" plays hip-hop and trance and occa-

Free Summer Lovin'

D.C.'s freebies are best savored in the summer—an intern living on the cheap can nurture urban romance on the Mall without having to spend any of that small stipend. Take these hints:

Mondays promise **"Screen on the Green,"** great American cinema classics weekly at sunset at 7th St. and Constitution Ave. For schedule check out www.screenon-thegreen.com.

Daily Kennedy Center concerts at the Millennium Stage (6pm) showcase acts from the latest hip-hop to the National Symphony Orchestra. Listen to music while basking in the fountains of the Kennedy Center—a little known trick is that you can hear the concert from outside the auditorium, providing a cooler (and more intimate) viewing experience.

Wednesdays mean a lunch-date at the **Navy Memorial** with free jazz concerts that will serenade you through lunch at nearby cafes.

Thursdays in **Fort Reno Park** near the Tenleytown-AU Metro mean moshing to one of the outdoor free concerts that feature up-and-coming **D.C. punk rock** bands.

Weekday Crossfire debates at George Washington University's **Jack Morton Auditorium,** 805 21st St. NW, provide live, nationally televised partisan debate free of charge M-F 4:30pm. Call ☎994-8266 or email cnn@gwu.edu for free tickets.

sionally becomes a foam party (doors open at 10pm; cover $10+; www.codedc.com); Sa "Velvet" caters to a mixed gay and straight crowd (doors open at 10pm; cover $8-12; www.velvetnation.com). 18+. Tickets for shows available from TicketMaster (☎301-808-2405; www.ticketmaster.com).

State Theatre, 220 N. Washington St. (☎703-237-0300; www.thestatetheatre.com), ¾ mi. from Metro: East Falls Church. Renovated 1935 movie theater brings in great emerging bands for a half-seated, half-standing crowd. Come early for dinner (call by 5pm the day before for reservations) and choice of seats (first-come, first-served), although all vantage points are fantastic. Box office (open from 6:30pm) sells tickets for same night shows only. Advance sales handled through TicketMaster. 18+. Tickets $5-50; ages 18-20 pay $3 extra.

Wolf Trap National Park for the Performing Arts, 1551 Trap Rd., Vienna, VA (☎703-255-1900; www.wolftrap.org), about 30min. from D.C. By car, take the Beltway (I-495) to Exit 45; follow Rt. 267 West to Wolf Trap exit. By Metro, take the Orange Line to West Falls Church, then hop on the Wolf Trap Shuttle (every 20min. starting 2hr. before showtime, $4 round-trip). The main performance facility, **Filene Center,** hosts acts ranging from B.B. King to Mary J. Blige. Ticket prices vary, but average $26-40 for most acts. People bring food and drinks to picnic out on the lawn, tickets for which are generally $10-20 cheaper than pavilion seats. Tickets available through box office or Tickets.com (☎703-218-6500; www.tickets.com).

CLASSICAL MUSIC

ORCHESTRA & CHAMBER MUSIC

The Folger Consort, 201 E. Capitol St. SE (box office ☎544-7077; www.folger.edu), in the Elizabethan Theatre. The resident ensemble at the Folger Shakespeare Library brings 16th- and 17th-century music to the stage. Phone box office open M-F 10am-5pm. Tickets $25-40; half-price tickets occasionally available at the door 1hr. before performances with student ID.

Kreeger Museum, 2401 Foxhall Rd. NW (☎338-3552), in Upper Northwest. Regular concerts by professionals and student performers are held in the Kreeger Museum's intimate concert hall. Ticket prices vary; call Protix to purchase tickets. See **Museums,** p. 128.

🎵 **National Symphony Orchestra** (☎467-4600 or 800-444-1324, TTY 416-8524; www.kennedy-center.org/nso). In its 73rd season, the NSO continues to delight D.C., primarily in the Kennedy Center's Concert Hall. Box office open M-Sa 10am-9pm, Su noon-9pm. See **Kennedy Center,** p. 188.

OPERA COMPANIES

🎵 **Washington Opera** (☎295-2400 and 800-876-7372, TTY 416-8534; www.dc-opera.org). Under the awesome leadership of artistic director and opera superstar Placido Domingo, performances in the Kennedy Center's Opera House (renovated in late 2003) sell out at an amazing pace. The 2004 season will bring *La Traviata, A Streetcar Named Desire, La Cenerentola,* and *Manon Lescaut;* call or check online for more info. Tickets weekday shows $41-260, weekend $42-285.

Summer Opera Theatre Company, 3801 Harewood Rd. NE (☎319-4000; www.summeropera.org), in the Hartke Theatre at Catholic University. Metro: Brookland-CUA. 2nd largest opera company in D.C. performs classics like Massenet's *Manon.* Performances June-July. Tickets $35-60; $20 cash-only rush tickets before show, based on availability. AmEx/MC/V.

JAZZ & BLUES

D.C. has a surprisingly diverse and thriving jazz and blues scene, with venues perfect for anyone's budget. The **Kennedy Center** (p. 186) and the **Smithsonian Museums** (p. 115) often sponsor free shows, especially in the summer.

Blues Alley, 1073 Wisconsin Ave. NW (☎337-4141; www.bluesalley.com), in an alley below M St. running between Wisconsin and 31st St., in Georgetown. Real jazz in an intimate, candlelit supper club. This is a listening club, not a place for conversation. Past performers include Eartha Kitt, Nicholas Payton, and Wynton Marsalis. New Orleans touches include the bread pudding ($4) and other authentic Creole dishes served 6pm-12:30am (entrees $15-20). Ticket prices $15-50. Students and congressional staff pay half-price cover for 10pm shows Su-Th, but not for advance sale shows or special events. Shows daily 8 and 10pm.

Madam's Organ, 2461 18th St. NW (☎667-5370), near Columbia Rd. in Adams Morgan. Voted one of the 25 best bars in the nation by *Playboy*. Neon signs above the door shout "Sorry, we're open" and call the party "where the beautiful people go to get ugly." A mixed, laid-back crowd mingles among the pink walls, dark red lighting, and upside down deer heads, and listens to live blues, funk, rock, or bluegrass nearly every night (Su-Th 9:30pm, F-Sa 10pm). Happy Hour (M-F 5-8pm) boasts 2-for-1 drinks. Drafts $3.75-5.75. 21+. Cover Su-Th $2-4, F-Sa $5-7. Open Su-Th 5pm-2am, F-Sa 5pm-3am. See **Nightlife,** p. 163.

Saloun, 3239 M St. (☎965-4900), between Potomac St. and Wisconsin Ave. in Georgetown. Local bar with live music nightly. Mostly local bands play jazz and R&B. Shows start at 8 or 9pm (call ahead). Extensive beer menu ($4-8). 2-drink minimum during performances. Cover Su-Th $2, F-Sa $3. Open Su-Th 5:30pm-2am, F-Sa 5:30pm-3am.

Taliano's, 7001B Carroll Ave. (☎301-270-5515; www.billtalianos.com). Metro: Takoma. Besides being a diner and bar, Taliano's provides some of the best participatory entertainment in the area. All musicians are welcome to sign up for their open blues jams on the first Su of every month (4-8pm). Other nights (particularly Su, W-Th, and every other Sa, usually 8-11pm or so) the stage is reserved for jazz, zydeco, folk, or karaoke. Cover $5-10 depending on the night and activity. Open M-Th 11:30am-9pm, F 11:30am-midnight, Sa 11:30am-10pm, Su 12:30-9pm. AmEx/MC/V.

THEATER & DANCE

D.C. enjoys a very active and experimental theater and dance scene, featuring everything from massive Broadway hits at the Kennedy Center to small, modern dance performances. Thespians particularly thrive in D.C.'s **14th Street theater district,** where tiny repertory companies explore and experiment with truly enjoyable results. However, Woolly Mammoth, Studio, Source, and the Church Street Theaters dwell in a potentially dangerous neighborhood east of Dupont Circle, near or on 14th St. NW between P and Q St., so **don't go there alone at night.**

THEATER

Arena Stage, 1101 6th St. SW (☎488-3300, TTY 484-0247; www.arenastage.org), at Maine Ave. SW. Metro: Waterfront. Often cited as the best regional theater company in America, the 51-year-old theater has its own company and 3 different stages: the **Kreeger** and **Fichandler** stages present new and classic plays, while the **Old Vat Theater** hosts more experimental productions. The 2004 season includes Tennessee Williams's *Orpheus Descending* and the world premiere of Frank Loesser's *Señor Discretion Himself.* Box office open M-Sa 10am-8pm, Su noon-8pm. Tickets $35-58, students 35% off, seniors and persons with disabilities 15% off; a limited number of ½-price tickets usually available 1½hr. before start of show. In the Old Vat, tickets $5, including a post-performance discussion with the artists.

Ford's Theatre, 511 10th St. NW, between E and F St. (☎347-4833; www.fordstheatre.org). Metro: Metro Center, 11th St. exit. The theater where President Lincoln was assassinated now occasionally hosts new American musicals and big-budget shows. *Children of Eden* will play Mar. 25, 2004-June 6, 2004. Dickens' *A Christmas Carol* plays every year Nov.-Dec. Tickets $29-45 (on sale as early as Aug.). Rush tickets sometimes available for seniors (60+) and students 1hr. before showtime. Box office open M-F 10am-5pm, and 30min. before each performance. See **Sights,** p. 72.

The Foundry Players, 1500 16th St. NW (☎332-3454; www.nbrconsulting.com/foundry), at P St. Metro: Dupont Circle. Going strong since 1946, this community theater program has renovated their stage within the elegant Foundry United Methodist Church so that the audience surrounds the actors (à la Arena Stage). Community volunteers help produce 3 performances a season, from Oscar Wilde plays to *Driving Miss Daisy*. The Players even donate part of the proceeds from each show to a different charity. Tickets available by phone or at the door ($12, seniors and students $10, under 12 $5). Call or see website for performance schedule (usually F-Sa 8pm, Su 2:30pm).

◪ **The Kennedy Center,** 2700 F St. NW, (☎467-4600 or 800-444-1324, TTY 416-8524; www.kennedy-center.org), near 25th St. and New Hampshire Ave. The Kennedy Center has 2 theaters, the **Terrace Theater** and the **Theater Lab,** and a stage for Broadway productions. *Shear Madness* still draws crowds after 16 years of production. Tickets $10-75 depending on the show, day, and time, but reduced pricing is available. Seniors and students half-price. 1 hr. of free parking is available for those buying tickets at the box office. Box office open M-Sa 10am-9pm, Su noon-9pm. AmEx/DC/MC/V. See **Sights,** p. 69.

Lincoln Theatre, 1215 U St. NW (☎328-6000; www.thelincolntheatre.org), directly across from the U St.-Cardozo Metro; take the 13th St. exit from the station. Built in 1922, the Lincoln was the first theater in the area to show movies to an integrated audience. Now the small historic venue hosts all kinds of plays, opera, jazz, movies, and comedy. Most tickets $10-50. Box office open M-F 10am-6pm and 2hr. before showtimes. Advance tickets also available through Ticketmaster (☎432-7328; www.ticketmaster.com). See **Sights,** p. 90.

◪ **National Theatre,** 1321 Pennsylvania Ave. NW (☎628-6161; www.nationaltheatre.org). Metro: Metro Center or Federal Triangle. Big-name, big-budget, big-capacity theater often hosts visitors from Broadway (like *Chicago*) at Broadway prices ($35-75, sometimes special $15 matinees). The fall-spring "M Night at the National" program puts on a free variety show in the lounge (6 and 7:30pm), and free movies play as part of the "Summer Cinema" program M at 6:30pm. "Saturday Morning at the National" is a free performance for kids (fall-spring, 9:30 and 11am). A limited number of ½-price tickets available for students, seniors, military, and the disabled for Tu-W (8pm) and Su (2pm) performances when regular tickets go on sale. Box office open M 10am-6pm, Tu-Sa 10am-9pm, Su noon-9pm.

◪ **Shakespeare Theatre** at the Lansburgh, 450 7th St. NW at Pennsylvania Ave. (☎547-1122, TTY 638-3863; www.shakespearetheatre.org). Metro: Gallery Place-Chinatown or Archives-Navy Memorial. The nation's leading Shakespeare company (*Henry IV*, Feb-May 2004) also ventures into such works as Rostand's *Cyrano de Bergerac* (June-July 2004). Call weeks in advance for reservations. Ticket prices $15-66. Discounts for students (50%) and seniors (20%). Standing-room tickets ($10) available 1hr. before sold-out performances. **"Free for All"** performance series in June (☎334-4790) presents free performances at the Carter Barron Amphitheater in Rock Creek Park. Obtain tickets in advance from the box office.

◪ **The Source Theatre,** 1835 14th St. NW (☎462-1073; www.sourcetheatre.com), between S and T St. Metro: U St.-Cardozo. 14th St.'s most renowned "alternative" theater. Produces the Washington Theater Festival (15 brand new shows plus) every summer at various D.C. locations, in addition to its regular off-Broadway shows. Shows W-Su, daily during the Festival. Tickets ($15-25) sold through Box Office Tickets (☎884-0060; open daily 9am-8pm) and on the Theatre's web site. Students and seniors, festival tickets $5 off. Source box office open 30min. prior to show.

Stanislavsky Theater Studio, 1742 Church St. NW (☎265-3748; www.sts-online.org). Metro: Dupont Circle. This medium-sized theater, set in a cozy 19th-century brick building, houses various productions of world theater. Performances Th-Sa 9pm, Su 5pm. Box office opens 1hr. before showtime. Tickets ($15-25) available online. Student and senior discounts decided on a show-by-show basis; purchase through the box office.

Studio Theatre, 1333 P St. NW (☎332-3300; www.studiotheatre.org), at 14th St. Metro: Dupont Circle. Contemporary theater on 2 stages. 2004 season includes Caryl Churchill's *Far Away* on the mainstage (opens Mar. 31, 2004) and *The Who's Tommy* on the 2nd stage (opens July 8, 2004). Mainstage plays W-Su, Second Stage Th-Su. Box office open M-Tu 10am-6pm, W-Su 10am-9pm. Tickets for Second Stage $20-25; for Mainstage $25-44.25. Students, military, and seniors $5 off Mainstage shows if purchased in advance; students can get ½-price tickets 30min. before shows, depending on availability.

Theater J, 1529 16th St. NW (☎ 777-3229; www.theaterj.org). Metro: Dupont Circle. Newly based in the auditorium of the D.C. Jewish Community Center, cutting-edge Theatre J performs the works of a wide range of contemporary Jewish playwrights, including those of its director Ari Roth. The world premiere of Wendy Wasserstein's *Psyche in Love/Welcome to my Rash* crowns the 2004 season. Tickets $15-34, available by phone, box office, or online.

Warner Theatre, 13th and E Sts. NW (☎ 783-4000; www.warnertheatre.com). Metro: Metro Center or Federal Triangle. Next to the National Theatre, the Warner Theatre hosts big names from Broadway and music and ballet acts. Box office open M-F 10am-4pm, Sa noon-3pm, and 2hr. before each performance. TicketMaster office located here as well. Tickets $18-100.

Washington Shakespeare Company, Clark St. Playhouse, 601 S. Clark St. (☎ 703-418-4808), in Arlington. Metro: Crystal City. The fluency of this local company stretches beyond the Bard to more experimental, cutting-edge dramas. Box office open M-F 10am-6pm.

▨ **Woolly Mammoth,** office at 917 M St. NW (☎ 393-3939; www.woollymammoth.net). Temporarily performing at the **Kennedy Center** (see p. 69) and the D.C. Jewish Community Center (see Theatre J, above) while they build a new theater at 7th St. and D St. NW. One of D.C.'s best-known alternative theaters not only performs popular modern plays, but also invites playwrights to send in manuscripts, which it then produces. Box office open M-F noon-6pm and 1hr. before showtime. Purchase tickets through the venue of the particular performance or online. Tickets $21-38, 25 and under $10, $5 discounts for seniors. Call for group rates.

DANCE

Dance Place, 3225 8th St. NE (☎ 269-1600; www.danceplace.org), at the intersection with Kearney St. Metro: Brookland-CUA. A dance school that focuses on modern movement and African dance. Professional or student performances every weekend. The **Dance Africa D.C. Festival** brings dance groups from the local area and Africa itself for a series of performances and master classes the first weekend in June. Tickets $16, students $12, children 17 and under $6. Call for schedule of events. Office open M-F 10am-5pm.

Washington Ballet, 3515 Wisconsin Ave. NW (☎ 362-3606; www.washingtonballet.org). Nationally recognized company performs a full season annually at the Kennedy Center (see p. 69), as well as performing *The Nutcracker* every Dec. at the Warner Theatre. The 2004 series includes Delibes's *Coppélia* and Stravinsky's *Firebird*.

COMEDY

▨ **The Capitol Steps,** 1300 Pennsylvania Ave. NW (☎ 312-1555; www.capsteps.com). Metro: Federal Triangle. This group of Congressional staffers-turned-comedians performs every F and Sa night in the Amphitheater inside the Ronald Reagan Building at 7:30pm. Their knowledge of the national government takes the form of scathing songs, skits, and parodies—a sizzling nocturnal complement to a day of museum tours and monument sightseeing. Tickets available from TicketMaster, or the D.C. Visitor Information Center (☎ 408-8736, ground level of Ronald Reagan Building). Tickets $31.50.

The Improv, 1140 Connecticut Ave. (☎ 296-7008; www.dcimprov.com), between L and M St. in Farragut. Metro: Farragut North. Cheap, wacky comedy for a young crowd. The Improv doubles as a restaurant at shows before 10pm (best seats given to dining patrons) and generally sells out on weekends; you may want to buy tickets in advance. Shows Tu-Th 8:30pm, F-Sa 8 and 10:30pm, Su 8pm. Tickets Su-Th $15, F-Sa $17.

BILLIARDS

Babe's Billiards Cafe, 4600 Wisconsin Ave. NW (☎ 966-0082), in Tenleytown. Use the west exit of the Tenleytown-AU Metro; go left on Wisconsin for two blocks. A popular pool hall and restaurant with a 20s to 40s crowd. Happy Hour (M-F 4-7pm) $1 off drafts and domestic rails. Pool $7 per person per hr. Late-night breakfast served after midnight. Draft beer $3-4.50, rail drinks $4. 21+ after 9:30pm. Open M-Th 3pm-3am, F-Su 1pm-4am. AmEx/DC/D/MC/V.

Buffalo Billiards, 1330 19th St. NW (☎331-7665; www.buffalobilliards.com), across from the 19th St. Metro exit. Metro: Dupont Circle. Wild Wild West theme in a not-so-wild saloonesque scene, but 30 pool tables, dartboards, and 2 full bars keep billiard cowboys happy. Regular rates per table average $6-16, $2-4 more Th-Sa 7pm-closing. Free lessons with Gus the Pool Shark (M and W 6-9:30pm), if you can catch him. Happy Hour M-F 4-8pm, Sa-Su 4-7pm; $2.50 domestic pints and $3 microbrews and rail drinks. Open M-Th 4pm-2am, F 4pm-3am, Sa 1pm-3am, Su 4pm-1am. AmEx/MC/V.

Georgetown Billiards, 3251 Prospect St. NW (☎965-7665), in Georgetown. Definite college hangout, with a nouveau-pub feel. 14 pool tables $7-14 per hr. Also features a ping-pong table, 4 dartboards, air hockey, and video games for the table-sport-challenged. Drinks are half off during Happy Hour (daily 6-8pm). Pub food ($4-7) served from 9pm to closing. 18+. Open Su-Th 6pm-2am, F-Sa 6pm-3am. Winter hours prone to change; call ahead.

Kokopooli's, 2305 18th St. NW (☎234-2306; www.kokopoolis.com). This pool hall-cum-sports bar attracts both players and spectators with 8 pool tables, foosball, darts, and 18 TVs. Draft beers $4 and pool tables $10 per hr., but both are half-price daily 3-7pm. Cigars ($6) available at the bar for those hoping to intimidate their opponents. Standard bar food served until midnight. Open Su-Th 3pm-2am, F-Sa 3pm-3am. Also see **Nightlife,** p. 165.

LITERARY LIFE

With one of the biggest populations of working writers in the country, D.C. has a fine appreciation for the written word. For cafe-hoppers interested in a mellow nightlife scene, there are a number of cafes and other venues around the city hosting readings and workshops for literary-charged crowds.

Iota Poetry Series, 2832 Wilson Blvd. (☎703-522-8340), in Arlington. Metro: Clarendon. At the Iota Bar and Restaurant. Poetry series occurs 2nd Su of each month at 6pm. Free.

St. Elmo's Coffee Pub, 2300 Mt. Vernon Ave. (☎703-739-9268), at the corner of Del Ray Ave., in Alexandria. Metro: King St. This laid-back neighborhood coffee bar is as close to barefoot as Alexandria gets. 2 rooms piled with old couches and community artwork attempt to recreate the Beat atmosphere. Artsy patrons contemplate verse at weekly poetry readings (weekly schedule varies; call ahead). Open M-Sa 6am-10pm, Su 7am-6pm.

The Writer's Center, 4508 Walsh St. (☎301-654-8664; www.writer.org), in Bethesda, MD. The heart of literary life in the D.C. area, The Writer's Center has workshops, a film series, calls for submissions, and readings by nationally known authors. The center's staff is eager to discuss every novel, poem, and play on sale in the very select offerings of **The Book Gallery** just inside the doors. Open Tu-F 10am-6pm, Sa 9am-5pm, Su for special events only.

FILM

For big-screen movies, try IMAX screens at the Smithsonian or The Uptown in Cleveland Park, which has a gigantic screen and booming sound systems, making them the best places to appreciate big-budget special effects. Check the *Washington Post*'s "Style" or "Weekend" sections ("Weekend" published Fridays) or the *CityPaper* for complete listings of movies showing in the District, or call ☎333-3456 and use the automated movie info line to find a film anywhere in the city. Find reviews and showtimes online at www.washingtoncitypaper.com. The **Hirshhorn Museum** (see p. 119), on the Mall at Independence Ave. and 7th St. SW, runs three separate weekly film series featuring foreign/independent films, documentaries about modern art, and animated movies for kids; call or see the front desk for a schedule. **The Museum of American History** (see p. 116) also hosts classic films, as does the **National Gallery of Art** (see p. 122). **The National Theatre** (see p. 188), 1321 Pennsylvania Ave. NW (☎783-3372; www.nationaltheatre.org/cinema/cinema.htm), runs films as part of its "Summer Cinema" series. (Films begin M 6:30pm mid-June to mid-Aug. in the Helen Hayes Gallery; limited free tickets available 30min. before shows.)

Uptown Theater, 3426 Connecticut Ave. NW (☎966-5400; www.enjoytheshow.com). Metro: Cleveland Park. First-run films in a vintage theater; even though there's only one screen, it's one of the biggest in town. $8.75, seniors and children under 11 $6.25. All shows before 6pm $6.25. Wheelchair accessible.

American Film Institute's Silver Theatre, 8633 Colesville Rd. (☎301-495-6700; www.afi.com/silver/theatre), in Silver Spring, MD. Metro: Silver Spring. Exit Metro and turn right on Colesville Rd.; theater is 2 blocks on the right. The citizens of Montgomery County and the AFI came together to save the historic Silver Theatre from destruction and, in doing so, created an incredible tribute to film. A changing repertoire of new and classic movies (from *Lawrence of Arabia* to *Chicago*) is shown in 3 auditoriums; call or visit website for showtimes. $8.50; students, seniors, and AFI members $7.50.

AMC Union Station 9, 50 Massachusetts Ave. NE (☎703-998-4262; www.amctheatres.com), on the lower level of Union Station. Shows 1st-run hits on standard-sized screens. $8.50, before 6pm $6.50. Students and seniors $6.50, ages 2-12 $5.50.

Loews Cineplex, various locations. Call ☎333-3456 and dial the extension for showtimes: 3111 K St. NW (☎342-6033), in Georgetown; 2301 M St. NW (ext. 828), in Foggy Bottom; 1350 19th St. NW (ext. 792), in Dupont Circle; 5100 Wisconsin Ave. NW (ext. 788), in Friendship Heights; 4000 Wisconsin Ave. NW (ext. 789) and 4849 Wisconsin Ave. NW (ext. 790), both near Tenleytown. Cinemas generally have identical pricing schemes: before 6pm $6, after 6pm $8.25; seniors and under 11 $5.50, students $7.

SPORTS & RECREATION
PARTICIPATORY SPORTS

The **Department of Recreation and Parks** (☎673-7660) is an excellent source of information for the athletically inclined.

HIKING, JOGGING, IN-LINE SKATING, & BIKING TRAILS AROUND D.C.	
THE MALL	Cool runnings near the museums. The Reflecting Pool, Constitution Gardens, and West Potomac Park are better suited for other recreation. See p. 53
TIDAL BASIN	D.C.'s joggers' mecca. See p. 60.
WATERFRONT	Quiet, scenic, conveniently located pedestrian pathway runs from Water St. to Fort McNair. See p. 61.
EAST POTOMAC PARK	Pleasant run to Hains Point along Ohio Dr. See p. 53.
ROCK CREEK PARK	Huge, scenic, and full of places for woodsy R&R. Beech Dr., through the heart of the park, is closed to traffic Su for rollerblading and biking. See p. 108.
GLOVER PARK	In Upper Northwest just off Tenley Circle. Very joggable park directed by the National Park Service. See p. 86.
C&O CANAL	Towpath packed on weekends. If you want, you can jog all 184 mi. from D.C. to Cumberland, VA. See p. 112.
CAPITOL CRESCENT TRAIL	A new, paved 11 mi. trail along the Potomac on an old railroad from Georgetown to Silver Spring, MD. Public parking on K St. in Georgetown (near Key Bridge), at the boat house, and in Bethesda. ☎234-4874 for info.
MOUNT VERNON TRAIL	18 mi. trail starts on Roosevelt Island and follows the Potomac to Mt. Vernon.
WASHINGTON & OLD DOMINION BIKE TRAIL (W&OD)	Starts in Arlington and runs 45 mi. west to Purcellville. To reach the W&OD heading south from D.C., take the Shirlington exit from I-395, bear right onto Shirlington Rd. (north), and go a block to South Four Mile Run Dr.
ARLINGTON NATIONAL CEMETERY	While the 1 mi. bike and walking path to Rosslyn don't go through the cemetery, the path does wind around it and goes through a pleasant neighborhood. Take the Metro to Arlington Cemetery, exit, and walk straight toward the large gray building; the dirt jogging path is on your right and the asphalt bike path is just beyond. See p. 97.

BIKING

Some of the most popular bike paths are the **C&O Canal Towpath,** the **Capital Crescent Trail,** and the **Washington & Old Dominion Bike Trail** (see p. 111). ADC's Washington Area Bike Map and the Greater Washington Area Bike Map are available at area sporting goods stores. Here are some of the many bike rental options:

Better Bikes (☎293-2080). Delivers bikes anywhere in the D.C. area. 10-speeds $25 per day, $95 per week; mountain bikes $38 per day, $135 per week. Helmet, map, backpack, locks, and breakdown service included. $25 deposit; driver's license, credit card, or passport required for collateral. Cash only. Open 24hr., although additional charges for deliveries before 8am.

Bike the Sites, Inc., 1100 Pennsylvania Ave. NW (☎842-2453; www.bikethesites.com). Metro: Federal Triangle. Offers a number of tour options, including 3hr. bicycle tours of the Capitol and 55 landmarks departing daily at 9am and 1pm ($40, under 13 $30; includes bike and helmet rental, tour guide, water, and snack). Reservations required.

BOATING

For tours, see **Once in D.C.,** p. 26. To rent your own, try:

Fletcher's Boat House, 4940 Canal Rd. NW (☎244-0461; www.fletchersboathouse.com), in C&O Canal Park. Canoes $22 per day, rowboats $20 per day. Single speed bike $8 for 2hr. No rentals after 5pm. Open M-F 9am-7pm, Sa-Su 7:30am-7pm.

Thompson Boat Center, 2900 Virginia Ave. NW (☎333-4861; www.thompsonboat-center.com) at Rock Creek Pkwy. and Virginia Ave. NW. Canoes $8 per hr., $22 per day. Single kayaks $8 per hr., $24 per day. Double kayaks $10 per hr., $30 per day. Rowing shells are $13 per hr. for single recreational or racing shells, $26 per hr. for double racing shells; shell rentals require certification through prior lessons at the Boat House. Bicycles $4 per hr., $15 per day for single-speed or children's bikes; $8 per hr. and $25 per day for all-terrain bikes. Bike and boat rentals Mar.-Oct.; rentals available daily 8am-5pm, with all boats or bikes back by 6pm.

Tidal Basin Boat House, 1501 Maine Ave. SW (☎479-2426). Metro: Smithsonian. Rents paddleboats for use in the Tidal Basin, weather permitting. 2-seaters $8 per hr., 4-seaters $16 per hr. Open mid-Mar.-early Oct. daily 10am-6pm. Boats must be returned no later than 1hr. past closing, and an ID is required as a deposit. Free parking available. MC/V.

DANCE

Joy of Motion Dance Center, 1643 Connecticut Ave. NW (☎387-0911; www.joyofmotion.org), 1 block up from Metro: Dupont Circle. Also at: 5207 Wisconsin Ave. NW (☎362-3042), 1 block south of Metro: Friendship Heights; and Bethesda at 7702 Woodmont Ave., Suite 202 (☎301-986-0016), Metro: Bethesda. A dance studio that offers everything from ballet to yoga, flamenco to swing, belly-dancing to kick-boxing. Full schedule of classes online. $12-14 for most single classes, students with ID $11.

GOLF

Langston Golf Course (☎397-8638), across from RFK Stadium. Metro: Stadium-Armory. M-F 9 holes $14, 18 holes $20. Sa-Su 9 holes $17, 18 holes $25. Club rentals $6.62 (9), $9.93 (18). Pull carts $3.07/$3.78, riding carts $12.77/$20.33. Open daily dawn-dusk.

Rock Creek Park Golf Course (☎882-7332; www.golfdc.com), in Rock Creek Park at 16th St. and Rittenhouse St. NW. M-Th 9 holes $12.50, 18 holes $18.25. F-Su 9 holes $15.50, 18 holes $23. Discounted rates of $9 for 9 holes and $12 for 18 holes given to seniors (60+) and children (17 and under), as well as general customers M-Th before 2pm. Club rentals $7 for 9 holes, $10 for 18 holes. Golf carts $13.50 (9), $21.50 (18). Open daily dawn-dusk.

HIKING

All of the following offer safe hiking adventures, but are closed at night. Within the district, the small but scenic **Roosevelt Island** (☎703-289-2500) offers about 2 mi. of trails (see p. 100). **Rock Creek Park** (☎282-1063 or 426-6829) contains a network of hiking trails, including the **Western Ridge Trail** (marked by green "blazes," or markers, on the path's trees) and the **Valley Trail** (blue blazes), both of which run approximately six miles north to south. A $6 topographical map available at the park's **Nature Center** shows the various routes in detail. Virginia's **Great Falls Park** offers 15 mi. of footpaths. (☎703-285-2965. Open year-round daily 7am to 30min. after dusk. Visitors Center open M-F 10am-5pm, Sa-Su 10am-6pm; see p. 110.) The **Sierra Club** (☎547-2326) leads guided hikes through the D.C. area. You may also want to check out *Hikes in the Western Region* published by the Potomac Appalachian Trail Club. See **Parks & Trails In & Around D.C.,** p. 108.

HORSEBACK RIDING

The **Rock Creek Park Horse Center** (☎362-0118), in Rock Creek Park, offers a slow-paced guided trail ride on one of the Center's well-cared-for horses ($30). The **Potomac Horse Center** (☎301-208-0200) in Gaithersburg, MD and **Wheaton Park Stables** (☎301-622-3311) in Wheaton, MD, also offer riding.

ICE SKATING

Pershing Park Ice Rink, Pennsylvania Ave. and 14th St. NW (☎737-6938). Open Oct.-Mar. Admission is free. Call for rental prices and opening times.

IN-LINE SKATING

Washington Area Roadskaters (☎466-5005; www.skatedc.org). This group, abbreviated "WAR," meets weekly on Pennsylvania Ave., in front of the White House, for a free city skate. Beginners F 7:15pm, intermediate Su 11am, advanced Su 11am and W 7pm. There is also a skating instructional clinic in Rock Creek Park, Sa 12:15pm; the beginner skate and skating clinic take place during daylight savings time only (Apr.-Oct.), while the intermediate and advanced skates are year-round.

Ski Center, 4300 Fordham Rd. NW (☎966-4474; www.skicenter.com), near the corner of Massachusetts Ave. and 49th St. NW. 2-day package rentals: downhill skis $32-48, snowboards $35-45, cross-country skis $25. In-line skates $15 per day, $25 for 2 days. Open May-Oct. M-F 11am-6pm, Th 11am-8pm, Sa 10am-5:30pm, Su noon-5pm; Nov.-Apr. M-F 10am-9pm, Sa 10am-5:30pm, Su noon-5pm.

PICNICS

Rock Creek Park (☎895-6000; www.nps.gov/rocr) offers dozens of designated picnic groves that can accommodate up to 150 visitors. Most areas have protected (sheltered) pavilions. Picnic groves #1, 6-10, 13-14, and 23-24 all require prior reservation with the D.C. Department of Recreation (☎673-7646); others are first-come, first-served.

STARGAZING/ASTRONOMY

Rock Creek Park (☎426-6829; www.nps.gov/rocr/planetarium) offers a monthly "Exploring the Sky" program that gives novices and experienced stargazers alike a chance to look at the heavens from the convenience of the District. The program is free; the events are held Apr.-Nov. Sa, just after sunset, in the field directly to the south of the intersection of Military and Glover Rd. NW. Telescopes provided.

SWIMMING

Call ☎673-7660 or 576-6436 to find the pool nearest you, or for a full list of information on the pools, visit www.dpr.dc.gov. Many hotels will let you use their swimming facilities for a small fee.

TENNIS

Rock Creek Park (☎722-5949), at 16th St. and Kennedy Pl. NW, and East Potomac Park, 1090 Ohio Dr. SW (☎554-5962), has indoor and outdoor courts. ($6 per hr. for hardcourt, $12 per hour for clay) **Cabin John,** 7801 Democracy Blvd. (☎301-469-7300), in Bethesda, and 11715 Orebaugh Ave. (☎301-649-4049), in Wheaton, provides indoor and outdoor courts for $12 per hr. **East Potomac Park Tennis Courts,** 1090 Ohio Dr. SW (☎554-5962) charge $6 for hard courts, $12 for clay courts. (Open M-Th 7am-10pm, F 7am-8pm, Sa-Su 8am-6pm.) Free neighborhood courts are sprinkled around D.C. Try, for example, the ones at 18th St. and Florida Ave. NW.

in recent
news

Williams at Bat

The Montreal Expos have never been a particularly successful baseball team. They have never won a pennant, and they have one of the worst attendance records in the major leagues. It's no surprise, then, that the Expos are probably packing up and leaving Montreal at the end of the 2004 season. Destinations vying for the ailing club include Portland, Oregon, Puerto Rico, Northern Virginia, and Washington, D.C.

District **Mayor Anthony Williams,** on the heels of opening of the publicly-funded new Washington Convention Center, has been aggresively pushing to bring major league baseball back to the city (the two incarnations of the Washington Senators left for Minneapolis in 1960 and Texas in 1971). Williams is proposing three potential stadium sites, the most likely of which seems near New York Ave. and North Capitol St. The stadium's cost, estimated at $436 million, is proving much harder to nail down. Williams' proposal calls for the District to foot $339 million of the cost primarily through borrowing and imposing new taxes on large businesses.

(continued on next page)

SPECTATOR SPORTS

The D.C. sports scene proves that politicians can't buy victories. In recent years, the city's pro teams have struggled to achieve mediocrity, but a number of individual players still stand out.

BASEBALL

Although D.C. packs in hard-hitters with national politics, it fouls up the national pastime. The city hasn't had a major league baseball team since 1971, when the Washington Senators left to become the Texas Rangers. Although D.C. has been content to play godparent to the **Baltimore Orioles,** there has been a recent movement to bring an expansion team to the D.C. area (see p. 194). For the time being, thousands of Washingtonians continue to commute to Baltimore's beautiful Camden Yards. (☎888-848-2473; www.orioles.mlb.com. Tickets $8-45. See **Daytripping,** p. 240.)

BASKETBALL

When it comes to the NBA, D.C. seems to delight in testing its fans' loyalty year after heartbreaking year. The **Washington Wizards,** formerly known as the Washington Bullets (1974-1997), constantly serve as the league's laughingstock for both their poor play and lame mascot (the **G-Wiz,** a half-bird, half-wizard, also available as party entertainment, ☎661-5000). Their sole championship came in 1978, when the team suffered so many injuries only seven players—one less than regulation—could suit up. A 2002 comeback fell through, even with **Michael Jordan** newly aboard as part owner; in spring 2003, Wizards management denied Jordan a position with little grace. Behold the Wizardry between November and April at the **MCI Center** (see p. 73). (☎661-5065; www.washingtonwizards.com. Tickets $10-100.)

The WNBA's **Washington Mystics** have been a disappointment since the league's inception six years ago, but star forward Chamique Holdsclaw makes the games entertaining and exciting. The Mystics play at the **MCI Center** (see p. 73) from May through August. (☎661-5050; www.wnba.com/mystics. Tickets $8-50.)

Once a perennial collegiate powerhouse, the lately mediocre **Georgetown University Hoyas** hoop it up from October to March. (☎628-3200; www.guhoyas.com. Tickets $5-22.50.) Several NBA legends got their start playing for this Catholic university: Allen Iverson, Alonzo Mourning, Dikembe Mutombo, and Patrick Ewing.

FOOTBALL

Despite its decidedly politically incorrect name, the **Washington Redskins** are a source of pride and joy for residents. With great hoopla, the franchise hired legendary University of Florida coach **Steve Spurrier** in 2002, but the team responded with its first losing season since 1998. The three-time Super Bowl champions ('82, '87, '92) still draw sellout crowds to FedEx Field, 1600 FedEx Way, Landover, MD. (☎301-276-6050; www.redskins.com. Season Sept.-Dec. Tickets $40-100. Regular season tickets always sell out, so try for pre-season ones.)

HOCKEY

The poorly supported **Washington Capitals** haven't exactly dominated American hockey, but they managed to make it to the **Stanley Cup** finals in 1998. (Games Oct.-Apr. at the MCI Center. ☎661-5065; www.washingtoncaps.com. Tickets $10-100.)

SOCCER

D.C. United had a promising beginning, drawing record crowds and winning three Major League Soccer (MLS) Championships ('96, '97, '99). Since the 2000 season, though, "the Black and Red" have failed even to make the playoffs. From mid-April to October, the United play at **RFK Stadium**, 2400 E. Capitol St. (☎547-9077; www.dcunited.com. Metro: Stadium-Armory. Tickets $16-36. Box office ☎608-1119 or Ticket-Master ☎800-551-7328.)

Not everyone in the District, however, shares Williams' pricey enthusiasm for baseball. Several of the mayor's opponents on the D.C. Council are supporting an alternative that aims to spend over $100 million on community investment before building a baseball stadium. "When it comes to choosing between baseball and neighborhoods, we want neighborhoods first," said the Rev. H. Lionel Edmonds in the *Washington Post*.

Such pressure led Williams to announce on June 24, 2003 that he will stop pushing the D.C. Council to approve his multi-million dollar stadium package until Major League Baseball announces plans to move a team to D.C.

The controversy over the stadium is sure to continue. Although Arlington has repudiated its initial claim for a potential stadium, Virginia stadium supporters say they will continue to search for an alternative location for the 42,500-seat stadium. An added complication to this already complex picture is Baltimore's fear that a home baseball team in D.C. will diminish the Orioles' fanbase. Whether, where, and when the D.C. area will have its very own baseball team still remains to be seen.

—*Brad Olson*

INSIDE

antiques **197**   arts and crafts **198** books **198**
clothing **200** comics **201** department stores **202**
erotica **202** gifts **202** malls **203** markets **204**
music **204** musical instruments **204** outdoor **205**
posters and prints **205** shoes **205** spy equipment **205**
toys & games **205**

Shopping

For guilt-free spending, try our shopping picks—they will satiate even the most prodigal spending instincts without exhausting your funds. After a day of monument-hopping, consumer therapy calls. From hole-in-the-wall vintage stores to specialty boutiques to mammoth emporiums, stumble into a shopaholic's nirvana at Adams Morgan, Alexandria, Dupont Circle, or Georgetown. Stores take all major credit cards, unless otherwise noted.

ANTIQUES

Antiques Anonymous, 2627 Connecticut Ave. NW (☎332-5555). Metro: Woodley Park. Established 23 years ago, this 2-room antique shop is filled with everything from vintage dresses to estate jewelry to furniture. Prices start around $10. Open Tu-Sa 11am-6pm. AmEx/D/MC/V.

Arise, 117 Carroll St. NW (☎291-0770; www.arisedc.com). Arise has 10 rooms big enough to host a sumo tournament, but instead, they're filled with enticing antiques and crafts from various Asian countries. Browse through shelves and racks of everything from Filipino baskets to Japanese kimonos, from "Wind-Up Sushi" toys ($3) to furniture items (some upwards of $5000). Even when they're not truly antique, the furniture, statues, and fountains could pass for artifacts. Look for deals in the sale room in the back. Some items available for sale online. Open M-Sa 10:30am-6pm, Su 11am-5pm. AmEx/D/MC/V.

Bird in the Cage Antiques, 110 King St. (☎703-549-5114; www.birdinthecage.com), in Alexandria. Metro: King St. A favorite attic of odds, ends, and everything in between. A room of vintage clothing includes pieces from the Victorian era to the 1970s (dresses $15-25), while other antiques include hats, clocks, quilts, glassware, and records. Extensive jewelry and book collection. Open Su 11am-9pm, M-Th 11am-10pm, F-Sa 11am-11pm. Hours vary by season; call ahead to confirm. AmEx/D/MC/V.

Millennium, 1528 U St. NW (☎483-1218). Metro: U St.-Cardozo. This co-op for vintage goods from the 50s, 60s, and 70s has a large collection of decor, records, clothes, and even appliances in perfect condition. Wacky accessories that you won't find elsewhere include collectible pool balls ($3 each) and *Playboy* from the 1970s ($5). Open Th-Su noon-7pm.

Takoma Underground, 7000B Carroll Ave. (☎301-270-6380). Metro: Takoma. The clutter underground hosts the best vintage action in Takoma. Rummage for sardine-packed antiques in old suitcases, baskets, and baby carriages; perfect gloves, scarves, and aprons lurk within. Underground's collection runs the gamut from $5-500, with everything from old metal signs to full wardrobes filling out the offerings. Beautiful vintage bridal wear can be found here. Open Tu-F 11am-7pm, Sa 11am-6pm, Su 10am-5pm. MC/V.

ARTS & CRAFTS

Made By You, 3413 Connecticut Ave. NW (☎363-9590; www.madebyyou.com), in Cleveland Park; 4923 Elm St. (☎301-654-3206), in Bethesda; 2319 Wilson Blvd. (☎703-841-3533), in Arlington; 209 N. Washington St. (☎301-610-5496) in Rockville. Buy unfinished ceramic pottery, mugs, and sculptures ($6-56) and paint them yourself. Use of glazes, stencils, and final firing included in price. Allow 4-7 days before picking up finished piece. If in a hurry, pick up a take-home kit ($20-25; includes paint, brushes, and sponge). Weekly discount specials; call for details. Cleveland Park: open M-Sa 10am-9pm, Su 11am-7pm; Bethesda and Rockville: M-Sa 10am-9pm, Su 10am-6pm; Arlington: M-Sa 10am-9pm, Su 11am-6pm.

Pla-za, 7825 Old Georgetown Rd. (☎301-718-8500), at the corner of Cordell Ave., in Bethesda. Metro: Bethesda. 2 floors crammed with art supplies. Expert staff. Specialties include pastel sets (from $12) and oil colors (from $7 per tube). 20% discount card available at register. Open M-F 9am-6:30pm, Sa 9am-6pm, Su noon-5pm.

BOOKS

NEW

Barnes and Noble, 3040 M St. NW (☎965-9880; www.bn.com), in Georgetown; also at 555 12th St. NW (☎347-0176), at F St., near Metro Center. 3 full fl., with a huge selection of books, as well as magazines, CDs, and DVDs. Discounts galore, with 20% off staff recommended selections and 30% off hardcover and paperback bestsellers. Georgetown location open daily 9am-11pm; Metro Center location M-F 8am-10pm, Sa 9am-10pm, Su 9am-8pm.

Borders, 5333 Wisconsin Ave. NW (☎686-8270; www.borders.com), at Chevy Chase Pavilion, but enter from Wisconsin Ave. Metro: Friendship Heights. This outlet of the national chain offers a huge assortment of books and music. Bestseller and recent release discounts. Cafe, DVDs, and music (with listening areas) upstairs. Open M-Sa 10am-10pm, Su 10am-8pm. 11 other D.C. locations.

Chapters, 1512 K St. NW (☎347-5495), in Farragut. Metro: McPherson Square. D.C.'s premier literary bookstore. Also at 445 11th St. NW (☎737-5553). The collection is thoughtfully selected, with a focus on fiction and poetry. Make yourself a cup of complimentary tea as you read the short staff-written reviews of books. Or better yet, stop by on F for free cookies and sherry all day long. Both branches open M-F 10am-6:30pm, Sa 11am-5pm.

▧ Kramerbooks, 1517 Connecticut Ave. NW (☎387-1400; www.kramers.com). Metro: Dupont Circle. This longtime local favorite is full of fiction, history, and *Let's Go* travel guides, but the organization is sometimes confusing. Adjacent cafe, **Afterwords** (see p. 148), tempts patrons away from the shelves. Live music W-Sa (times vary, call ahead). Bookstore and cafe open M-Th 7:30am-1am, open continuously F 7:30am-Su 1am.

Olsson's Books and Records, 418 7th St. (☎638-7610; www.olssons.com), in Federal Triangle; 1307 19th St. (☎785-1133), in Dupont Circle; 1200 F St. (☎347-3686), at Metro Center. Great selection of literature, travel, and history books. Staff and readers' picks up to 20%

off. Federal Triangle location open M-F 9am-8pm, Sa 10am-8pm, Su noon-7:30pm; Dupont location M-W 10am-10pm, Th-Sa 10am-10:30pm, Su noon-8pm; Metro Center location M-F 10am-7pm, Sa 10am-6pm, Su noon-6pm.

▨ **Politics and Prose,** 5015 Connecticut Ave. NW (☎364-1919; www.politics-prose.com). Metro: Van Ness; then take the L1 or L2 Metrobus, or walk 15min. north on Connecticut Ave. This celebrated bookstore attracts big-name political and literary celebrities, who often do their readings and signings in front of C-SPAN cameras. Knowledgeable staff, nightly readings and book groups, and impressive collection all keep customers coming back. Coffeehouse downstairs serves light snacks, dessert, and, yes, coffee. Open M-Th 9am-10pm, F-Sa 9am-11pm, Su 10am-8pm.

USED

Idle Time Books, 2467 18th St. NW (☎232-4774), near Columbia Rd. in Adams Morgan. A smashing selection of books ($2.50 and up) in a cramped space. Double-stacked shelves of half-price fiction and collections of non-fiction in nearly every genre. Used paperbacks are their specialty, but organization is not, so don't come looking for particular books. Also features some foreign-language titles and a charming cat. Open daily 11am-10pm.

The Lantern Bryn Mawr Bookshop, 3241 P St. NW (☎333-3222), between 33rd St. and Wisconsin Ave. in Georgetown. Great prices on used books (paperbacks from $1, hardcovers from $3). Packed but well-organized inventory. Lots of dusty LPs ($1) and some CDs (starting at $2). Open M-F 11am-4pm, Sa 11am-5pm, Su noon-4pm.

▨ **Second Story Books,** 4836 Bethesda Ave. (☎301-656-0170), in Bethesda; 2000 P St. NW (☎659-8884), in Dupont Circle; warehouse at 12160 Parklawn Dr. (☎301-770-0477, ext. 13), in Rockville. Amazing collection of used books, including rare antiquities. Also carries used prints and LPs. Dupont and Bethesda open daily 10am-10pm; Rockville open Su-Th 10am-8pm, F-Sa 10am-9pm.

SPECIALTY

Backstage, Inc., 545 8th St. SE (☎544-5744). Metro: Eastern Market. Eager to equip you with all of your theatrical needs, this store sells plays, performing art books, costumes, masks, fab wigs, and makeup. Also rents costumes, from Shakespearean outfits to poodle skirts ($30-150). Open M-Sa 11am-7pm.

Franz Bader Bookstore, 1911 I St. NW (☎337-5440; fbad@his.com), in Farragut. Metro: Farragut West. Perfect for those people who wish books had more pictures, Franz specializes in books on art and architecture. New books in the visual arts, including painting, sculpture, design, and photography. Some titles in French, German, Spanish, Japanese, and Italian. Open M-Sa 10am-6pm. AmEx.

▨ **Lambda Rising,** 1625 Connecticut Ave. NW (☎462-6969), between Q and R St. Metro: Dupont Circle. The largest selection of gay and lesbian literature in D.C., including travel guides, videos, DVDs, CDs, t-shirts, magazines, and novelty items. Serves as an info center and ticket outlet for concerts and events. Helpful, friendly staff. Frequent book signings. Wheelchair accessible. Open Su-Th 10am-10pm, F-Sa until midnight.

A Likely Story, 1555 King St. (☎703-836-2498; www.alikelystorybooks.com), in Alexandria. Metro: King St. Children's bookstore with a wide selection of fiction, non-fiction, and audio books and incredibly knowledgeable staff. Open M-Sa 10am-6pm, Su 1-5pm; readings for kids every Tu-W, Sa at 11am. MC/V.

Luna Books, 1633 P St. NW (☎332-2543; www.skewers-cafeluna.com), near 17th St., on the 3rd fl. above Skewers. Metro: Dupont Circle. A tiny bookstore devoted to liberal and radical politics and culture. Discount non-fiction and political texts. Neighborhood discussion groups and poetry readings held periodically. Open M-F 11am-3pm, Sa noon-3pm, and whenever events are held. See **Cafe Luna,** p. 146.

Newsroom, 1803 Connecticut Ave. NW (☎332-1489; www.foreignmedia.com). Metro: Dupont Circle. Thousands of American and foreign newspapers and magazines. Upstairs language room is devoted to language education books and tapes, as well as public Internet access ($5 for 30min.). Cafe downstairs serves coffee and ice cream. Open daily 7am-9pm.

---

the local story

CHANGES ON U STREET

After spending six years in consulting and publishing, Jackie Flanagan decided to open a boutique (🔲 **Nana**) in the neighborhood where she had lived for eight years. Flanagan is just one of many Shaw area residents who have left the corporate world behind to set up shop in the blossoming U Street corridor.

On the changing neighborhood: U Street has this amazing cultural history that needs to be revered. It was just this amazing place: ideas were created, things were discovered, and art was celebrated. Then it went through a really bad time for 30 years. And in the last ten years, all of a sudden, it's become this pocket of unique little shops, galleries, and great restaurants that might have been here for a really long time, but that are now being rediscovered.

On the 1500 Block: I feel really lucky to be on this block. Everyone is so interested in seeing everyone else succeed. The very first day I opened, all the other store-owners came in here, bought something, and introduced *(continued on next page)*

Sisterspace and Books, 1515 U St. NW (☎332-3433; www.sisterspace.com) at 15th St. Metro: U St.-Cardozo. This independent bookstore specializes in books by and about African-American women. On F evenings from 7-9pm, Sisterspace hosts a walking tour ($12) of the historic Shaw neighborhood, capped with culinary selections from the area. Open W-Sa 10am-7pm, Su noon-5pm.

CLOTHING

INDEPENDENT STORES

All About Jane, 2438½ 18th St. NW (☎797-9710; www.allaboutjane.net), in Adams Morgan. Hailed by *Lucky* magazine for its très-très-trendy selections, All About Jane has racks of pricey designer clothes by Laundry, Tessuto, and Juicy that might bust a limited budget ($100-200). One glance inside will explain why President Bush's daughters have been spotted shopping here. Open M-Sa 12-9pm, Su 12-7pm.

🔲 **Commander Salamander,** 1420 Wisconsin Ave. NW (☎337-2265), near O St. in Georgetown. A Georgetown original featuring alternative clothes and accessories such as wigs and Playboy paraphernalia. Handbags ($10-30), and a fantastic selection of T-shirts mom would never let you wear ($16-25) are just some of their over-the-top inventory. Open M-Th 10am-9pm, F-Sa 10am-10pm, Su 11am-7pm.

Kobos Afrikan Clothiers, 2444 18th St. NW (☎332-9580), in Adams Morgan. Although they can be a bit pricy, Kobos's beautiful traditional and contemporary clothes from West Africa are well worth at least a look. Dresses $45-85, men's shirts $35-65. Interesting selections of jewelry and CDs. Open M-Sa 11am-8pm.

🔲 **Nana,** 1534 U St. NW (☎667-6955; www.nanadc.com), near 16th St. Metro: U St.-Cardozo. Unique and affordable women's clothing; stylish fashions by regional designers in front, and "like-new" vintage clothing in the back. Sassy Jordi Labanda handbags ($38-48) are all the rage. Open Tu-Sa noon-7pm, Su noon-5pm. MC/V.

VINTAGE & CONSIGNMENT

Deja Blue, 3005 M St. NW (☎337-7100), near 30th St. in Georgetown. Jeans, jeans, jeans: flares to slim-fits, all secondhand ($30-80). Cutoffs ($10-20), Hawaiian shirts ($20-30), original Converse ($50), and more. Open M-Sa 11am-9pm, Su noon-7pm.

🔲 **Designer Resale,** 4801 St. Elmo Ave. (☎301-656-3722; www.designerresaleboutique.com) at Woodmont Ave., in Bethesda. Only designer labels (Gucci, Chanel, Burberry) make their way into this small consignment store. Furs, shoes, bags, and dresses are priced down from thousands to hun-

SHOPPING

200

dreds of dollars (and sometimes less). Owner and fashionista Tina Hayden is outgoing and incredibly helpful. Open M-Sa 10am-6pm. AmEx/D/MC/V.

Funk & Junk, 106½ N. Columbus St. (☎703-836-0749; www.funkandjunk.com), near the intersection with King St., in Alexandria. Metro: King St. Whether you're looking for an embroidered Chinese robe or a red velvet smoking jacket, chances are you'll find it here among the meticulously catalogued wealth of vintage items. Open M 1-5pm, Tu and Th-F 1-6pm, Sa 12:30pm-7pm, Su noon-4pm. May be open later some days; call ahead. AmEx/MC/V.

Gallery of Georgetown, 3223 M St. NW (☎333-3543), near Wisconsin Ave. Resembling an indoor flea market, this well-organized shop carries everything from Georgetown shirts ($10) to West African masks (starting at $20) to silver jewelry (earrings $8), charms, and beaded necklaces (3 for $5) in a room that resembles a warehouse. Open daily 10am-9pm.

Meeps Fashionette, 1520 U St. (☎265-6546), between 15th and 16th St. Metro: U St.-Cardozo. Well-stocked vintage store for men and women in a beautiful old townhouse. Clothes and accessories from the past century are marked by decade. Small section of new fashions by rotating local designers. Open Tu-Th 4-7pm, F-Sa noon-8pm, Su 1-6pm.

Rage Clothing, 1069 Wisconsin Ave. NW (☎333-1069; www.rageclothing.com), between M St. and the C&O Canal, in Georgetown. Featuring used jeans (mostly Levi's) and corduroy pants ($10-80). Bargain hunters should check out the upstairs clearance floor, where vintage shirts, shorts, and jeans can be bought for under $10. Celebs from The Who to Roseanne Barr have been spotted here picking up retro duds. Open M-Th 11am-9pm, F-Sa 11am-10pm, Su 11am-7pm.

Secondi Consignment Clothing, 1702 Connecticut Ave. NW (☎667-1122), at R St. Metro: Dupont Circle. Upstairs boutique filled with discount designer clothing, shoes, and accessories. Buy Prada on consignment and pay a fraction of the cost. Prices go down the longer the items sit on the shelf: 20% discount after 1 month, 40% after 2. Open M-Tu and Sa 11am-6pm, W-F 11am-7pm, Su 1-5pm. AmEx/MC/V.

COMICS

Aftertime Comics, Inc., 1304 King St. (☎703-548-5030), in Alexandria. Metro: King St. Tiny store unpretentiously dedicated to the art of comic book collecting. Well-aged DC and Marvel comics repose in wrapping while shelves of newer, glossier successors line the walls. Back issues of *MAD* and *Eerie* magazines. Open W 11:30am-7pm, Th-Sa 11am-7pm, Su noon-6pm. MC/V.

themselves. And we all check on each other. If something's going on at one end of the block, we all know about it. It's a great community to be a part of.

On local flavor: We don't have a Gap. We don't have a Borders. The bakery is [run by] a local person. Every person on this street is a local person who respects and loves this neighborhood.

On newcomers: I think that as long as all the people that continue to move in realize and respect the history here, and respect the people that have been here for so much longer than me, that will continue to foster a good feeling.

On outside perceptions: People come in and think that they're bringing the answer. My clothing store is not the answer to U St. I have heard people say, "this place really needs to be cleaned up." No, actually, it doesn't! It just needs to be appreciated.

Interview conducted by Brad Olson.

Big Planet Comics, 3145 Dumbarton Ave. NW (☎342-1961; www.bigplanetcomics.com), just off Wisconsin Ave. in Georgetown. No action figures here, but still a terrific selection, from graphic novels and trade paperbacks to your favorite superhero comics, fills the easily navigable shelves. Open M-Tu and Th-F 11am-7pm, W 11am-8pm, Sa 11am-6pm, Su noon-5pm.

DEPARTMENT STORES

Bloomingdale's (☎301-984-4600; www.bloomingdales.com), at the White Flint Mall, in Kensington, MD. Metro: White Flint. Home furnishings and designer garments from Polo to BCBG. Open M-Sa 10am-9:30pm, Su noon-6pm. Another location at Tysons Corner, VA (☎703-556-4600). Tysons location open M-Sa 10am-9:30pm, Su 11am-6pm.

Hecht's 1201 G St. NW, at 12th St. (☎628-6661; www.hechts.com), Metro: Metro Center. 6 other D.C. area locations. Run-of-the-mill department store with clothes, housewares, and gifts. Open M-F 10am-8pm, Sa 9am-8pm, Su noon-6pm.

Macy's, 1000 S. Hayes St. (☎703-418-4488), in Arlington. Metro: Pentagon City. 3 fl. of the latest fashions at department store prices. Sign up for a Macy's card to get special discounts. Open M-Sa 10am-9:30pm, Su 11am-7pm.

Nordstrom, 1400 S. Hayes St. (☎703-415-1121), in Arlington. Metro: Pentagon City. Also at Bethesda's Montgomery Mall and Tysons Corner, VA. Known for its excellent customer service, Nordstrom's typically upscale offerings include men's and women's clothing and shoes, as well as a variety of unique gifts. All locations open M-Sa 10am-9:30pm, Su 11am-6pm.

EROTICA

Dream Dresser Boutique, 1042 Wisconsin Ave. NW (☎625-0373), at South St. in Georgetown. Serious erotic clothing boutique, with leather, lace, and latex. Fantasy-wear French maid's uniform $150. If "healthcare" is a turn-on, the naughty nurse outfits come in vinyl ($135) or rubber ($400). Some S&M, a few sex toys. Open M-Sa 11am-8pm.

Night Dreams, 4866 Cordell Ave. (☎301-986-4711; www.nightdreams.com), in Bethesda. Amidst all of Bethesda's restaurants stands this superstore to satisfy *other* hungers. Impressive selection of erotic aids ($20-130). Adult videos and DVDs available ($15-50), as well as penis pinatas ($30). 18+ to enter store. 20% discount for exotic dancers. Open M-Th 10am-10pm, F-Sa 10am-11pm, Su noon-6pm. AmEx/MC/V.

Pleasure Place, 1063 Wisconsin Ave. NW (☎333-8570; www.pleasureplace.com), between M St. and the C&O Canal in Georgetown; 1710 Connecticut Ave. NW (☎483-3297), in Dupont Circle. Mostly sex toys, instructional books, and videos. Some sex clothing including thongs, leather, and boots. Wide array of penis-shaped novelty items. 18+. Both locations open M-Tu 10am-10pm, W-Sa 10am-midnight, Su noon-7pm.

GIFTS

Al's Magic Shop, 1012 Vermont Ave. NW (☎789-2800; www.alsmagic.com). Metro: McPherson Square. Real magic tricks for serious magic junkies. Don't expect to have all your sleight-of-hand befuddlement magically cleared, however; store policy reads, "to learn the secret you have to buy the trick." Open M-W and F 10am-5:30pm, Th 10:30am-6:30pm, Sa 10am-4pm. AmEx/DC/D/MC/V.

Chocolate Moose, 1800 M St. NW (☎463-0992). Metro: Farragut North. Bizarre boutique and sweet shop has a crazy fetish for moose: t-shirts, cards, stuffed animals, and a wall papered with news clippings about the shy, reclusive animals. Also sells weird practical jokes, toys, jewelry, clothing, and of course, chocolate. Open M-Sa 10am-6pm. AmEx/MC/V.

Fashion Gallery, Wisconsin Ave. NW (☎338-0133), near N St. in Georgetown. This tiny storefront, along with street vendors on Wisconsin Ave. between M and O St., sell handbags "inspired" by Louis Vuitton, Gucci, Prada, Burberry, Kate Spade, and others. Also features cigar box handbags and a variety of sunglasses. Open daily 9am-9pm.

Leatherrack, 1723 Connecticut Ave. NW (☎797-7401; www.theleatherrack.com), between R and S St. Dupont Circle. Primarily gay clientele shop at this leather boutique for its extensive selection of harnesses ($30-150), jocks ($20-90), gay erotica ($10-90), and sex toys. Open daily 10am-11pm.

Paula's Imports, 2405 18th St. NW (☎328-2176), in Adams Morgan. A bargain basement of new and used clothes, jewelry, bedspreads, and gifts imported from India, Pakistan, and Africa. Open M-F 12:30-7:30pm, Sa 12:30-9pm, Su 12:30-6pm.

Rockville Arts Place, 100 East Middle Ln. (☎301-309-6900; www.rockvilleartsplace.org), in Rockville. Metro: Rockville. Alternative arts space showing works of local artists whom you probably won't find in mainstream galleries downtown. A place to see and purchase works by up-and-coming artists before they make it big. Open M-Sa 10am-5pm, Th until 9pm.

The Scottish Merchant & John Crouch Tobacconist, 215 King St. (☎703-739-2302; www.scottishmerchant.com), in Alexandria. A Scottish pipe-smoker's dream, this 2-in-1 shop contains a selection of books, CDs, neckties, maps, tapes, and videos (all relating to Scotland) on display on the shelves near the front entrance; a large number of kilts and Scottish family crests also available for sale. The back rooms contain an exceptional selection of pipes, various types of loose tobacco, and a room full of cigars (many under $10). Pipes typically $30-40 and up. Open Su 11am-10pm, M-Sa 10am-10pm. AmEx/D/MC/V.

The Virginia Shop, 104 S. Union St. (☎703-836-3160; www.virginiashop.com), in Alexandria. Metro: King St. The finest selection of gifts and mementos from the Old Dominion. Pick up a "Virginia is for Lovers" T-shirt ($15) and a few bottles of Virginia wine ($15-30) for a night on the town. Open M-Th 10am-8pm, F-Sa 10am-9pm, Su 11am-7pm. AmEx/D/MC/V.

Unique, 213 King St. (☎703-836-6686), in Alexandria. Metro: King St. The offerings at Unique are indeed just that: an unusual mix of everything from greeting cards and scented candles to humorous pins and tongue-in-cheek gift items (many around $5-25). Unique has been a presence on King St. for over 30 years, and its resident orange cat, Chester, has become a mascot for the store, as well as its owners' beneficiary; Chester was the first cat to be rescued by **King Street Cats** (www.kingstreetcats.org), the all-volunteer cat shelter one floor above Unique and under the same ownership. Open daily 10am-10pm. AmEx/D/MC/V.

MALLS

Fashion Centre at Pentagon City, 1100 S. Hayes St. (☎703-415-2400), in Arlington. Metro: Pentagon City. Walk to the escalator and you're there. This bright, expansive mall is one of the area's most accessible and popular. Thanks to its clever layout and pleasant ambience, shopping at its 160 stores won't wear you out. Open M-Sa 10am-9:30pm, Su 11am-6pm.

The Shops at Georgetown Park, 3222 M St. NW (☎298-5577; www.shopsatgeorgetown-park.com), near Wisconsin Ave. Metro: Foggy Bottom, then take the Georgetown Metro Connection shuttle (see p. 78). Palatial Victorian architecture shines even underground with brass galore and 150 stores, including J.Crew, H&M, and Polo Ralph Lauren. Open M-Sa 10am-9pm, Su noon-6pm.

Mazza Gallerie, 5300 Wisconsin Ave. NW (☎966-6114; www.mazzagallerie.net). Metro: Friendship Heights. The Chevy Chase Pavilion's kid brother across the street, the slightly-smaller Mazza offers the upscale (Neiman Marcus, Saks Fifth Avenue Men's Store) and the not-so-upscale (Filene's Basement, McDonalds). 7-screen AMC movie theatre on site. Open M-F 10am-8pm, Sa 10am-7pm, Su noon-5pm.

Tysons Corner Center, 1961 Chain Bridge Rd. (☎703-893-9400; www.shoptysons.com), off the Beltway at Exit 47A in McLean, VA. The largest shopping complex in northern Virginia includes Bloomingdale's, Lord and Taylor, Nordstrom, and over 200 other shops and restaurants. Open M-Sa 10am-9:30pm, Su 11am-6pm. Its more pretentious cousin, **Tysons Galleria** (☎703-827-7730; www.tysonsgalleria.com), is just across the street, but is best accessed by Exit 46A off the Beltway. Features Neiman Marcus, Saks, Versace, and a Ritz Carlton Hotel. Open M-Sa 10am-9pm, Su noon-6pm. For both, take Metro Orange Line to West Falls Church and then take bus #28A.

203

Westfield Shoppingtown Montgomery, 7101 Democracy Blvd. (☎301-469-6000), in Bethesda. Metro: Medical Center. Take the J2 Metrobus (approx. 15min. ride from Medical Center Station). One of the more distant malls in the D.C. area, Montgomery Mall offers quality shopping from Coach to Nordstrom for those willing to make the trek. Open M-Sa 10am-9:30pm, Su 11am-6pm.

MARKETS

■ Eastern Market, 225 7th St. SE, on 7th St. SE between C St. and North Carolina Ave. From Metro: Eastern Market, walk up Pennsylvania Ave. toward the Capitol; it's on the right. Butchers and bakers hawk their wares all week. Sa-Su they are joined by farmers who line the walk outside with flowers and produce—even in Dec. Sa is the best day for produce; Su tends to be more of a flea market. Open Tu-Sa 7am-6pm, Su 9am-4pm.

Georgetown Flea Market, (☎296-4989; www.georgetownfleamarket.com), in a parking lot where 34th St. and Wisconsin Ave. NW meet in northern Georgetown. Lots of cool, pre-owned stuff including faux jewelry, vintage clothing, china, and furniture. Vendors ready to wheel and deal. Fresh fruit and vegetables, along with vendors selling sweets and focaccia. Open Su 9am-5pm year-round, weather permitting.

Montgomery Farm Women's Cooperative, on the corner of Willow Ln. and Wisconsin Ave. (www.bethesdafleamarket.com) Metro: Bethesda. Fresh veggies, baked goods, and a wide selection of meats. Outside, find wares ranging from used CDs to spectacular Chinese wood-carvings. Open W and Sa 7am-3pm. Flea market open Su 9am-5pm.

MUSIC

NEW

DJ Hut, 2010 P St. NW (☎659-2010; www.djhut.com), at 20th St. Metro: Dupont Circle. Impressive selection of hip-hop, R&B, go-go, and reggae music mostly on vinyl ($6-18) for amateur and professional DJs alike. 6 turntable listening stations allow customers to listen before they buy. Also carries a few DVDs and CDs. Open M-Th noon-9pm, F noon-10pm, Sa noon-8pm, Su 1-6pm. AmEx/D/MC/V.

Willies, 2301 Georgia Ave. NW (☎518-2400; www.turtles-music.com), along the Howard U. campus. Metro: Shaw-Howard U. Music spills out of this local shop, a favorite of Howard students for its wide selection of homegrown gospel and go-go. DJs and dub artists faint at the sight of racks of 12in. dance vinyl. Open M-Th 10am-9pm, F-Sa 10am-10pm, Su noon-6pm.

USED

CD Warehouse, 3001 M St. NW (☎625-7101; www.thinkinground.com), at 30th St. in Georgetown. Specializing in electronic dance music, this store also sells pop, rock, jazz, some classical, and movie soundtracks. Sells both new ($13 and up) and used ($6-10) CDs. Listen to about 85% of the store's music before making a purchase. Open M-Th 11am-9pm, F-Sa 11am-10pm, Su noon-7pm.

DC CD, 2423 18th St. NW (☎588-1810), near Belmont St. in Adams Morgan. Specializes in cutting-edge alterna-punk and indie bands, with a standard smattering of jazz, classical, and world music. New ($13-17) and used ($8-10) CDs and even a few LPs. Listening stations by the front window offer a selection of what's hot in non-top-40 music. Open M-Th noon-11pm, F noon-midnight, Sa 11am-midnight, Su noon-10pm.

Smash!, 3285½ M St. NW (☎337-6274), near Potomac St. in Georgetown. New and used CDs, some LPs. Specializing in punk, hardcore, goth, and alternative music and clothing. Buy, sell, or trade LPs and CDs. Open M-Th 11am-9pm, F-Sa 11am-11pm, Su noon-6pm.

MUSICAL INSTRUMENTS

■ The House of Musical Traditions, 7040 Carroll Ave. (☎301-270-9090). Metro: Takoma. A folk music enterprise with a passport: beautifully carved wooden instruments from all over the world are on display, as well as a sizeable collection of international music. Among the instrument offerings are a *saz* (stringed, guitar-like instrument) from Turkistan, percussion instruments from Egypt, Cameroon, and India, drums made in Ghana specifically for this store, and gongs from China and Indonesia. To explore your talent a bit less expensively, try a hand at the $1 nose flutes. Open Tu-Sa 11am-7pm, Su-M 11am-5pm. AmEx/D/MC/V.

OUTDOOR

Sunny's Affordable Outdoor Store, 917 F St. (☎737-2032), between 9th and 10th St. in Old Downtown. Metro: McPherson Sq. Camping gear, outdoor clothing, and sports supplies (wet suits to in-line skates) at unnervingly low prices. Open daily 9am-6:30pm.

POSTERS & PRINTS

Beyond the Wall, 3279 M St. NW (☎333-7790), in Georgetown. Sells a wide range of film, music, and art posters ($7-10). Also carries frames ($11 and up). Open M-Th 10am-9pm, F-Sa 11am-10pm, Su 11am-7pm.

Movie Madness, 1083 Thomas Jefferson St. NW (☎337-7064), in Georgetown off M St. between 30th and 31st. Small but good selection of movie posters, including classics, foreign, children's, cult, and new releases. Black and white still photographs ($3.50) and posters ($6 and up). Open W-Sa 11am-9pm, Su 11am-6pm.

SHOES

Shake Your Booty, 2439 18th St. NW (☎518-8205), in Adams Morgan. Metro: Woodley Park-Zoo. Trendy Steve Madden heels, Me Too flip flops, and simple thong sandals sold for reasonable prices (most shoes $30-80) at this shoe retreat. Also sells accessories (handbags, jewelry, t-shirts). Refreshments and special promotions every Sa 7-9pm. Open M-F noon-8pm, Sa noon-9pm, Su noon-6pm. Another location in Georgetown (☎333-6524).

Wild Women Wear Red, 1512 U St. NW (☎387-5700; www.wildwomenwearred.com), near 15th St. Metro: U St.-Cardozo. Funky, comfortable footwear for women. Co-owner Toddré Monier stocks Lisa Nading, Cydwoq, Aufley, and Camper, as well as accessories by local designers; she makes the crochet hats ($35) and bags ($29-159) herself. Open M-Sa noon-8pm, Su noon-6pm. AmEx/D/MC/V.

SPY EQUIPMENT

Security Intelligence, 1001 Connecticut Ave. NW (☎887-1717; www.spyzone.com), in Farragut. Metro: Farragut North. Soda cans that are safes, watches that are cameras, etc. Highlights include a pager that goes off when someone in the room is using a wireless microphone; cameras with lenses the size of the tip of a pen; and the "truth phone," which picks up nervous tremors in liar's voices. This place is so classified that access to the store itself is by appointment only. Open M-F 9am-6pm. AmEx/DC/D/MC/V.

TOYS & GAMES

Sullivan's Toy Store, 3412 Wisconsin Ave. NW (☎362-1343), between Newark St. and Idaho Ave. Metro: Tenleytown-AU. A nice mix of mass-produced Pokémon dolls and more unique carved toys. The perfect place to bring the kids and browse. Open M-Tu and Sa 10am-6pm, W-F 10am-7pm, Su noon-5pm.

hostels **207**
guest houses & hotels **208**

adams morgan **209** alexandria **211**
arlington **213** bethesda **213**
capitol hill **215** dupont circle **215**
farragut **216** federal triangle **217**
foggy bottom **217** georgetown **218**
south of the mall **218** upper northwest **218**
campgrounds **219**
long-term housing **219**

Accommodations

In D.C., inexpensive lodgings are harder to come by than straight-talking politicians. Using this guide and some common sense, however, visitors can track down suitable accommodations, for the short term and long term, at reasonable rates. (Note: these prices are accurate as of August 2003, when this edition was updated.)

SYMBOL	❶	❷	❸	❹	❺
Lowest price for a single	under $50	$51-75	$76-100	$101-125	$126 and over

HOSTELS

If you plan to stay in D.C. for less than a month, you might consider the time-honored institution of budget travel: the hostel. Hostelling International-American Youth Hosteling (HI-AYH) membership is $28 yearly, $18 for those 55+, and free for those under 18. Nonmembers who stay at an HI-AYH hostel pay approximately $5-10 per night extra, which may be applied toward membership. Contact HI-AYH, 8401 Colesville Rd., Suite 600, Silver Spring, MD 20910 (☎301-495-1240; www.hiayh.org), or inquire at any HI hostel.

▩ **Hostelling International-Washington DC (HI-AYH),** 1009 11 St. NW (☎737-2333; www.hiwashingtondc.org), 3 blocks north of Metro on 11th St. Metro: Metro Center. The prime location (5 blocks from the White House, 15min. walk from the National Mall), friendly staff, and reasonable rates make the hostel an appealing choice for D.C. visitors. Clean, A/C rooms with 4-12 beds. Free continental breakfast. Common room with TV, kitchen, laundry facilities, lockers, and luggage and bicycle storage ($1 per piece per day). Internet access ($1 for 8 min-

SINGLE UNDER $20 PER NIGHT		UNDER $80 (CONTINUED)	
India House Too (208) Tacoma Park, MD		Jury's Normandy Inn (210)	AM
		Swiss Inn (217)	FT
UNDER $40		Tabard Inn (215)	DC
Hostelling International (207)	FT	Windsor Inn (216)	DC
International Guest House (211)	AM		
International Student House (221)	DC	**UNDER $100**	
Thompson-Markward Hall (221)	CH	Best Western Old Colony Inn (211)	AL
		Farragut Lincoln Suites (217)	F
UNDER $60		Maison Orelans (215)	CH
Alexandria Travelodge (211)	AL	Quality Inn Iwo Jima (213)	AR
Allen Lee Hotel (217)	FB	Red Roof Inn (217)	FT
Braxton Hotel (216)	F	Waterfront Channel Inn Hotel (218)	SM
Days Inn (218)	UN		
Hereford House (215)	CH	**OVER $100**	
Kalorama Guest House (210)	AM	American Inn of Bethesda (213)	B
Kalorama G.H. at Woodley Park (218)	UN	Holiday Inn Hotel & Suites (211)	AL
Taft Bridge Inn (210)	AM	Holiday Inn Rosslyn at Key Bridge (213)	AR
Woodley Park Guest House (218)	UN	Holiday Inn Select (213)	B
		Sheraton Four Points (213)	B
UNDER $80		Topaz Hotel (216)	DC
Adams Inn (209)	AM	Windsor Park Hotel (211)	AM
Brickseller Inn (216)	DC		
Embassy Inn (215)	DC	**CAMPGROUNDS**	
Highlander Motor Inn (213)	AR	Cherry Hill Park (219)	
Hotel Harrington (217)	FT	Greenbelt Park (219)	
Inn at Rosslyn (213)	AR	Capitol KOA (219)	

AM Adams Morgan	**B** Bethesda	**F** Farragut	**SM** South of the Mall
AL Alexandria	**CH** Capitol Hill	**FB** Foggy Bottom	**UN** Upper Northwest
AR Arlington	**DC** Dupont Circle	**FT** Federal Triangle	

utes). Information desk (open M-F 10am-6pm). Elevator. Alcohol, smoking, and sleeping bags prohibited. After 6 nights' stay, non-US citizens automatically become HI-AYH members. Reception 24hr. Check-in 2pm. Check-out 11am. Credit card required for reservation. Wheelchair accessible. $29-32, non-HI-AYH members $32-35. **Be careful in this area at night.** ❶

India House Too, 300 Carroll St. (☎291-1195; www.dchostel.com), on the border of D.C. and Takoma Park. Metro: Takoma. Walk straight from the Metro stop on Carroll St. toward the hill on the right. A bit removed from the hustle and bustle of D.C., but at $20 per night, there's no complaining. Guests are encouraged to make the house their own: they can come and go as they please, smoke and drink (in certain areas of the house), or fire up a BBQ in the backyard. Quiet suburban neighborhood. After a few drinks, the gregarious innkeeper will tell you the true story of how the hostel got its name. Many of the backpackers decide to stay in and party in the basement, which has foosball, ping-pong, and pool; die-hard campers can pitch a tent in the backyard instead of sleeping in a room. Free linens and use of kitchen; lockers available. Satellite TV, laundry facilities, and free Internet access. Reservations preferred. Reception daily 8am-midnight. Maximum stay 7 nights. Guests must be 18+. Dorms with 6-8 bunk beds $20 per person; private rooms $40 (no private bath). Cash only. ❶

GUEST HOUSES & HOTELS

Downtown hotels and guest houses range from moderately to crazily expensive. D.C. also automatically adds a whopping **14.5% hotel tax** to your bill. Hotels usually charge a flat fee per room and then a fee for each additional guest, so the more people per room, the more reasonable the rates become. Some hotels will even give a third or fifth occupant a free cot.

ADAMS MORGAN

Adams Morgan's charming guest houses and small hotels lie in safe, peaceful neighborhoods. Walk the short distance to the neighborhood from the Woodley Park Metro (via either the William H. Taft or Duke Ellington bridges), or take bus #42 through the heart of Adams Morgan to stops on Columbia Rd.

SEE MAP P. 360 ← YOU ARE HERE

U.S. Capitol Building

Adams Inn, 1744 Lanier Pl. NW (☎800-578-6807 or 745-3600; www.adamsinn.com), 2 blocks north of the center of Adams Morgan. Though just a stone's throw from the animated goings-on of Adams Morgan, Adams Inn's 3 newly renovated Victorian houses have the feel of a rural country house. Guests can lounge on the benches on the front porch or admire the small garden in the back. Continental breakfast (8-9:30am), coffee and tea, and lots of apples and cookies are all complimentary. Cable TV (in common area), coin laundry facilities. Rooms vary in size and style, but all have A/C and private sinks (some with private bath). Friendly, helpful staff. Limited parking $10 per night. Free Internet access in computer room. Reception M-Sa 8am-9pm, Su 1-9pm. Credit card needed to secure reservation. Check-in 3-9pm; check-out noon. Min. stay of 2 nights if staying Sa night. Singles $75, with private bath $85; additional person $10. Weekly rates $370, $420 with private bath; additional person $70. ISIC, seniors, members of Backpackers International, employees of non-profit groups all get a 10% discount. AmEx/DC/D/MC/V. ❷

ESSENTIAL INFORMATION

RESERVATION SERVICES

For a luxury hotel experience that won't crack your credit card, try one of the following reservations services (a.k.a. "hotel brokers"). Even during full vacancy periods, these services can find rooms in high-end hotels at discounted, mid-range prices (averaging around $100-200 per night, double occupancy).

Citywide Reservation Services (☎800-468-3593; www.cityres.com)

Hotels.com (☎800-246-8357; www.hotels.com)

Hotel Reservations Network (☎800-715-7666; www.hoteldiscount.com)

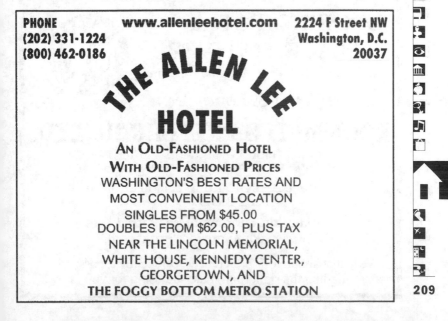

PHONE
(202) 331-1224
(800) 462-0186

www.allenleehotel.com

2224 F Street NW
Washington, D.C.
20037

THE ALLEN LEE HOTEL

AN OLD-FASHIONED HOTEL
WITH OLD-FASHIONED PRICES
WASHINGTON'S BEST RATES AND
MOST CONVENIENT LOCATION
SINGLES FROM $45.00
DOUBLES FROM $62.00, PLUS TAX
NEAR THE LINCOLN MEMORIAL,
WHITE HOUSE, KENNEDY CENTER,
GEORGETOWN, AND
THE FOGGY BOTTOM METRO STATION

Jury's Normandy Inn, 2118 Wyoming Ave. NW (☎800-424-3729 or 483-1350; www.jurysdoyle.com), 2 blocks off Columbia Rd., near the corner of Connecticut and Wyoming Ave. From Woodley Park Metro, proceed down Connecticut Ave. to the Taft Memorial Bridge, continuing across into Adams Morgan; bear left and follow Conn. Ave., making a right onto Wyoming Ave.; the hotel will be immediately on the left. Jury's offers stylish, spacious rooms with refrigerators, coffeemakers, hair dryers, safes, irons and boards, phones, and cable TV. Free wine and cheese reception Tu (5:30-7pm), complimentary coffee and cookies in the lobby every evening; a daily continental breakfast (7-10am) available for $5.50. Exquisitely furnished lobby and lounge area and an outdoor patio add a touch of charm. The nearby fitness room and seasonal pool at the Washington Courtyard available for free use by Jury's guests. 1 smoking floor. Limited underground parking $12 per night. 2 handicapped-accessible rooms. 24hr. cancellation policy. Check-in 3pm; check-out noon. Rooms $79-155; each additional person $15. AAA members typically save 10%. AmEx/DC/D/MC/V. ❸

Kalorama Guest House at Kalorama Park, 1854 Mintwood Pl. NW (☎667-6369), off Columbia Rd. a block south of 18th St. Actually 3 separate townhouses on the same street, 2 of which have rooms straight out of the late 19th century (the 3rd is more modern). The complimentary sherry kept next to the crackling fireplace should make any stay worthwhile; guests have been known to take samples at all hours of the day. Free lemonade in summer, hot apple cider in winter, and cookies year-round. Continental breakfast included. Some suites with TV and phone. Internet hookup available in certain rooms. 2 suites with kitchens for long-term visitors. Limited parking behind guest house by reservation only ($7 per night). Free laundry facilities available 5-9pm. Reception M-Tu 8am-8pm, W-Su 8am-10pm. Reservations require credit card, payment due upon arrival. Reservations recommended Mar.-May and Sept.-Nov. 2-week cancellation policy. Minimum stay 2 nights on weekends; max. stay typically 2 weeks. Check-in 1pm; guests must arrive during reception hours. Check-out 11am. Rooms with shared bath $55-70 for 1 person, $60-75 for 2; with private bath $70-95/$75-100. 2-room suites $100-125. AAA, STA members, and seniors save 10%. AmEx/DC/D/MC/V. ❷

Taft Bridge Inn, 2007 Wyoming Ave. (☎387-2007; www.taftbridgeinn.com), between 20th St. and Connecticut Ave. A short walk from Dupont Circle and Woodley Park Metro stops. Quiet B&B with beautiful antique-filled rooms in a stately 19th-century Georgian building.

LOOKING FOR A PLACE TO LIVE?

Washington DC, Virginia, and Maryland

Short Term & Long Term

ROOMMATES PREFERRED, LTD.

Professionals ~ Students ~ Interns
International Travelers ~ Language Learners

Contact Betsy Egan in person or online
202.234.5789

e-mail: info@roommatespreferred.com
www.roommatespreferred.com

We'll chat about your preferences, offer choices, assist in finding the right roommate/s/housing for you

ROOMMATES PREFERRED, LTD.

Varying rooms have claw-legged bathtubs, fancy marble floors, canopy wood or big brass beds, window seats, and fireplaces. All rooms have modem hookups, phones, voicemail, cable TV, and A/C. Most rooms accommodate 2-3 guests. Laundry facilities available. Full breakfast included. Warm fireplace for winters; relaxing porch and garden for summers. Parking $11 per day. 48hr. cancellation policy. Check-in 3-7pm; notify in advance if a late check-in is needed. Check-out 11am. Reception M-F 7am-10pm, Sa-Su 8am-10pm. Handicapped accessible. Rooms with shared bath $59-84, with private bath $119-139; additional person $15. Prices reduced 20-30% July-Aug. and Dec.-Feb. MC/V. ❷

Windsor Park Hotel, 2116 Kalorama Rd. NW (☎800-247-3064 or 483-7700; www.windsorparkhotel.com), 3 blocks west of Columbia Rd. on Kalorama. Clean, plain rooms have cable TV, phone, refrigerator, private bath, hair dryer, phone jack for modem access, and A/C. Choice of twin, double, or queen beds when available. Wheelchair accessible. Continental breakfast included. Check-in 2pm. Check-out noon. 24hr. reception. 24hr. cancellation policy. Singles $110; doubles $122. Suites (can accommodate up to 6) $165. ISIC and seniors 10% discount. AmEx/DC/D/MC/V. ❹

International Guest House, 1441 Kennedy St. NW (☎726-5808; igh-dc@juno.com), between 14th and 16th St. From Friendship Heights Metro, take the E2, E3, or E4 bus to the intersection of 14th and Kennedy streets; make a right onto Kennedy and the guest house will be on your right. This intimate 12-person lodging is in an old house; the shared double and triple rooms all have A/C and are well-kept. Basement lounge area has TV, ping-pong table, and kitchen. Continental breakfast and 9pm tea with cookies included. No alcohol allowed. 1 week max. stay for US citizens; 2 week max. for international. Reception M-Sa 7am-11pm, Su 7-10am and 3-11pm; house lock-out period Su 10am-3pm. 11pm curfew daily. 48hr. cancellation policy. Check-in anytime during reception hours; check out 10am. Christian owners create a moderate religious atmosphere, including Sunday lockout hours during which the whole staff attends church. Rooms (for ages 16+) $30 per person per night; $190 per week. Children under 6 free, ages 6-15 ½-price.❶

ALEXANDRIA

While most reasonably priced hotels in Alexandria are a 10- to 20-minute walk from King St., most provide shuttles to nearby Metro stations, Old Town, and National Airport. The **Alexandria Hotel Association** (☎800-296-1000) can help you find a room and make a reservation. Use Metro: Braddock or King St. for all of the following.

Best Western Old Colony Inn, 1101 N. Washington St. (☎800-528-1234 or 703-739-2222; www.bestwestern.com), at 2nd St. (about 10 blocks from King St. in Old Town). Large, pleasant rooms await visitors in this recently-built hotel. Nearby Holiday Inn allows Western guests to use sauna, indoor/outdoor pool, and large fitness center for free. Coffeemakers, A/C, cable TV, and complimentary hot breakfast; free Internet access in each room (or through on-site business center). Free parking. Free shuttle to National Airport and Metro every 30min. 6am-9pm. Check-in 3pm; check-out noon. 24hr. reception. Reservations recommended. Rooms $129-139 for up to 4 people; some weekend specials $89-99; additional person $10. AAA and AARP members $109. AmEx/DC/D/MC/V. ❸

The Alexandria Travelodge, 700 N. Washington St. (☎800-237-2243 or 703-836-5100; www.travelodge.com), at Wythe St. Neat, standard motel rooms with cable TV, A/C, and no-frills service. Convenient to bus stop and Metro; close to King St. Free shuttle to National Airport (M-F 7-11am and 6-11pm, Sa 9-11am and 6-11pm, Su no service). Free parking. Singles $60-75, doubles $75-90; in winter singles $45-55, doubles $49-59; additional person $5. Weekly and monthly rates available. ❷

Holiday Inn Hotel and Suites, 625 1st St. (☎703-548-6300). Elegant and spacious rooms come with coffeemakers, irons and boards, dataports for Internet access, cable TV, and A/C. Heated indoor/outdoor pool. Excellent fitness center. Free shuttle to Metro and National Airport with occasional service to the center of Old Town (every 30min. 6:30am-10:30pm). 24hr. cancellation policy. Check-in 3pm; check-out noon. Singles $129; doubles $149. AAA and AARP discounts available. AmEx/DC/D/MC/V. ❺

WASHINGTON
INTERNATIONAL

STUDENT
CENTER

2451 18th Street, N.W.
Washington D.C. 20009

(202) 667-7681

ARLINGTON

Although they may lack some of the character of accommodations within the city, Arlington's hotels are functional, less expensive, and often only a short walk from Georgetown or a quick Metro ride from the heart of the District.

Holiday Inn Rosslyn at Key Bridge, 1900 N. Fort Myer Dr. (☎800-465-4329, 800-368-3408, or 703-807-2000; www.holiday-inn.com/rosslynk-bridge). Take the N. Fort Myer Dr. exit of the Rosslyn Metro, make a right, and walk 1½ blocks. Great location: 1 block from Rosslyn Metro, 3 mi. from National Airport. Comfortable, spacious rooms with small balconies (some overlooking the Potomac and Georgetown), cable, A/C, dataports, irons and boards, safes, and coffeemakers. Heated indoor pool and fitness center. Free parking. Wheelchair accessible. 24hr. reception. Check-in 3pm, check-out noon. Weekends start at $99, weekdays at $139. AAA, AARP members 10% discount. AmEx/DC/D/MC/V. ❺

Highlander Motor Inn, 3336 Wilson Blvd. (☎800-786-4301 or 703-524-4300; www.high-landermotel.com). Metro: Virginia Square-GMU; from the Metro exit, turn left onto Wilson Blvd. and walk several blocks down; the motel is on the right. Although the outside looks a little run down and the parking lot is often littered with small debris, this classic motel has clean, spacious rooms, each with 2 double beds. Refrigerators available for free upon request. Free coffee and doughnuts every morning. A/C and cable TV with HBO. Parking included. 24hr. reception. Check-in anytime; check-out 11am. Long-term rates available (weekly $410 plus tax). Singles and doubles $77; additional adult $5, children free. *Let's Go* readers $5 off. AmEx/D/MC/V. ❷

Inn at Rosslyn, 1601 Arlington Blvd. (☎703-524-3400 or 800-504-4888; www.motelfifty.com). Metro: Rosslyn. The ultimate in budget Arlington accommodations. The modest and clean rooms include basic cable TV, free parking, continental breakfast, and A/C. Free shuttles (read: car ride) to the Metro and airport whenever you need one. Far from luxurious, but Motel Fifty's rates are hard to beat. Single $74; double $80. ❷

Quality Inn Iwo Jima, 1501 Arlington Blvd. (☎800 522 5151 or 703 524 5000). Take the N. Fort Myer Dr. exit from Metro: Rosslyn and turn left onto N. Fort Myer Dr., then turn right on Fairfax Dr. Dependable hotel with modern rooms, laundry, hair dryers, coffeemakers, cable TV, dataports, and free parking. Enclosed heated pool open all year. Bus tours leave from the hotel 3 times per day. Wheelchair accessible. Singles $89-99, depending on the season; doubles $10 extra. Additional adult $5, children free. AAA/AARP members 10% discount. ❸

BETHESDA

Bethesda offers large chain hotels where you can digest after dining in town.

Holiday Inn Select, 8120 Wisconsin Ave. (☎301-652-2000; www.holiday-inn.com/bethesdamd). Metro: Medical Center. Equipped with an outdoor pool and exercise room, restaurant, and piano bar in the lobby. Free shuttle service to Metro: Medical Center. Parking $12 per day. Reception 24hr. Weekday rates $109-229, weekends $69-109. 10% AAA discount. ❷

Sheraton Four Points, 8400 Wisconsin Ave. (☎301-654-1000 or 800-325-3535; www.four-points.com). Metro: Medical Center. Offers guests a pool, fitness room, sports bar/restaurant and Budget rent-a-car on site. Complimentary hourly shuttle Metro: Medical Center. Reception open 24hr.; Italian, German, Russian, and Spanish spoken. Rooms $169-240. ❺

American Inn of Bethesda, 8130 Wisconsin Ave. (☎800-323-7081 or 301-656-9300; www.american-inn.com). Metro: Bethesda. Pricey but elegant hotel in the middle of Bethesda is perfect for tourists. Outdoor pool and limited free parking. Continental breakfast included, coffee/tea offered in the afternoon. Reception 24hr.; Spanish and Hindi spoken. Phone reservations required. Singles $160, doubles $190. 10% discount for AAA, AARP, and students; 40% for government employees. Children under 18 stay free in same room with parents. ❺

Find (Our Student Airfares are cheap, flexible & exclusive)
great Student Airfares everywhere
at StudentUniverse.com and **Get lost.**

 StudentUniverse.com   **Student Airfares everywhere**

CAPITOL HILL

Capitol Hill's B&Bs are in great locations near the center of D.C., but the expense may not always be worth the attractive location. **Be careful in the area at night.**

YOU ARE HERE

SEE MAP P. 353

Maison Orleans, 414 5th St. SE (☎544-3694; www.bbonline.com/dc/maisonorleans). Metro: Eastern Market. 3 comfortable rooms and a furnished studio apartment with 1930s-style furniture, all with private bath. Rooms have the feel of a French Quarter home. TV, A/C, and complimentary continental breakfast. Small patio has plants and small fountains stocked with large Japanese goldfish. No smoking. Check-out 11am. 50% deposit due at reservation, remainder due on arrival. Singles and doubles $95-125. Cot $10. Cash only. ❹

Hereford House, 604 S. Carolina Ave. SE (☎543-0102; www.bbonline.com/dc/hereford), at 6th St., 1 block from Metro: Eastern Market. Only a Union Jack marks this 4-room, 6-bed, British-style B&B in a townhouse run by a friendly English hostess. 2 shared baths, laundry facilities, A/C, refrigerator, living room, and garden patio. No smoking. 50% due for reservation, balance due on arrival. Children under 12 not allowed. Singles $58-72, doubles $74-82. Intern rate $26 with one month minimum stay. Cash only. ❷

DUPONT CIRCLE

The good news: Dupont has a wide choice of lovely bed and breakfasts, all near the Dupont Circle Metro. The bad news: Dupont's prime location equals big bucks. The accommodations listed below are the best deals. Beware: parking can only be found in one of the Circle's expensive garages or on its crowded streets.

YOU ARE HERE

U.S. Capitol Building

SEE MAP P.355

Tabard Inn, 1739 N St. NW (☎785-1277; www.tabardinn.com), between 17th and 18th St. 40 individually decorated rooms in 3 townhouses connected by a maze of passages, stairways, and lounges. Offers a patio, bar, and lounges, all with quirky decor and pleasantly mismatched furniture. Rooms have hardwood floors and stone-tile bathrooms as well as A/C, phone, and data port (but no TV). Breakfast and passes to the YMCA included. Dinner at the Tabard Inn restaurant is also highly recommended (see p. 146). Reception 24hr. Singles $80-110, with private bath $110-190. $15 per additional person. AmEx/DC/D/MC/V. ❹

Embassy Inn, 1627 16th St. NW (☎800-423-9111 or 234-7800; www.windsorembassyinns.com), near R St. 38 small Victorian rooms in flowery paisley. Tea and coffee, evening sherry, daily newspaper, and continental breakfast included. Rooms have private bath, cable TV, hair dryers,

---

the BIG $plurge

Happy Aroma-Versary, Darling

For a little extra money, you can turn your weekend in Washington into an aromatic, psychedelic experience. The new-age **Topaz Hotel** in Dupont Circle offers the Anniversary Special, in which couples get a weekend stay in one of the posh hotel's most luxurious rooms.

Also included in the package are massages, energy drinks, tarot cards, a psychic reading, aromatherapy, relaxation CDs, and other unusual, indulgent perks.

If you're not married or are not celebrating an anniversary, the Topaz still offers European linens, CD stereos with remotes, and plush terry cloth robes. Each room has an automatic teapot with a selection of exotic teas and a fully-stocked minibar. Energy rooms ($40 extra) come with your choice of custom exercise equipment, while yoga rooms include yoga videos, mats, and relaxation CDs.

Evening *sangría* (M-F 5:30-6:30pm) and fruity "energy elixirs" (Sa-Su mornings) are free, as are the "energy stones" left on the pillow instead of mints.

Rooms $109-169.

(1733 N St. NW. ☎800-424-2950 or 393-3000; www.topazhotel.com). ❺

phones, and A/C, although the sinks are in the bedroom. Not wheelchair accessible. Singles $79-119; doubles $79-139. Additional adults $10, children free. AAA and AARP 10% discount. AmEx/MC/V. ❸

The Windsor Inn, 1842 16th St. NW (☎800-423-9111 or 667-0300), between Swann and T St. Same management and amenities as the Embassy Inn, including the complimentary continental breakfast and evening sherry. More personal service than most hotels, but also spares travelers the shared baths and lounges of B&Bs. Decorated with bona fide antiques and 19th-century prints. Rooms vary from small singles to expansive suites, most with sinks in the main room rather than in the bathroom. Reception 24hr. Singles $79-119; doubles $79-139; suites $119-179. AAA and AARP 10% discount. AmEx/MC/V. ❸

Brickskeller Inn, 1523 22nd St. NW (☎293-1885; www.thebrickskeller.com), between P and Q St. This 40-room inn is also a restaurant and pub with hundreds of imported beer bottles lining the wall. The restaurant serves burgers and buffalo wings (see p. 171), though the raucous downstairs may impede a restful stay. Rooms with private baths have a TV, but no cable. 24hr. reception. Singles with private bath $73; doubles with shared bath $73, doubles with private bath $92. AmEx/D/MC/V. ❷

FARRAGUT

Hotel accommodations in Farragut are generally pricey; however, they offer high quality rooms in a typically safe neighborhood. Toward the end of the summer, ostensibly upscale hotels may actually offer reasonable discount rates.

The Braxton Hotel, 1440 Rhode Island Ave. NW (☎800-350-5759; www.braxtonhotel.com), between 14th and 15th St. Metro: Farragut North, Dupont Circle, or McPherson Sq. Clean rooms, private bath, and friendly service for a great price. Its 62 rooms come with cable TV, A/C, and direct-dial phones. Refrigerator, microwave, and fax and copier services available. Free continental

Why pay full price for a hotel room?

Save up to 70% on the places you want to stay!

Washington, DC from $49.95!

hotels.com

BEST PRICES. BEST PLACES. GUARANTEED.

Save on thousands of hotels in hundreds of cities worldwide.

800-2-HOTELS

hotels.com lowest price guarantee does not apply to all dates or properties. See www.hotels.com for further details.

breakfast (6:30-9am). Limited parking ($7 per night). 24hr. reception. Check-in 2pm; check-out 11am. Reservations recommended 3 days in advance. 72hr. cancellation policy. Rooms with twin bed $50; double-sized bed $70; 2 double beds $80; $6 each additional adult, under 15 free. Discounts for *Let's Go* readers. AmEx/DC/D/MC/V. ❷

Farragut Lincoln Suites, 1823 L St. NW (☎800-424-2970 or 223-4320; www.lincolnhotels.com), near 18th St. Metro: Farragut North or Farragut West. Mostly caters to businessmen, but has decent room rates. 99 spacious suites, most with bars or kitchens, all with A/C, refrigerators, modem jacks, and coffeemakers. Free passes to nearby Bally's Holiday Spa, self-serve laundry, same-day dry cleaning. Continental breakfast M-F 7-9am, Sa-Su 7-10am. Milk and cookies daily 6-9pm. On-site parking $20. 24hr. reception. Check-in 3pm; check-out noon. Reservations recommended. 24hr. cancellation policy. All suites around $140. $10 per additional person after first 2, max. 5 per room. Discounts for extended stays, AAA, AARP, and government employees. AmEx/DC/D/MC/V. ❹

FEDERAL TRIANGLE

Federal Triangle is loaded with expensive hotels. Call one or two months in advance for reservations at one of these rare budget steals.

🏨 **Hotel Harrington,** 11th and E St. NW (☎800-424-8532 or 628-8140; www.hotel-harrington.com). Metro: Metro Center or Federal Triangle. On the verge of turning 90, this hotel offers clean rooms and a great location. 3 blocks from the Smithsonian, it features a deluxe family room (2 adjoining rooms, $145). Parking $8.50 per day. Cable TV, A/C, and laundry. Singles $89; doubles $99. Save $10 if you call from the airport, train, or bus station; 10% off on stays of 5+ days. 10% discount for students and AAA members. Kids under 16 stay free. Special group rates available. AmEx/D/MC/V. ❸

Swiss Inn, 1204 Massachusetts Ave. NW, at 12th St. (☎800-955-7947 or 371-1816; www.theswissinn.com), 4 blocks from Metro Center. More like a guest house than a hotel. 7 clean studio apartments with private baths, high ceilings, kitchenettes, A/C, and cable TV. International crowd welcomed by French- and German-speaking managers. Complimentary parking on weekends, $8.50 weekdays. Laundry service $5 per load. Credit card required to reserve. 72hr. cancellation policy. All rooms $69-119. 10-40% seasonal discounts (Nov.-Feb.) for seniors and students. ❸

Red Roof Inn, 500 H St. NW (☎289-5959; www.redroof.com), 2 blocks from Gallery Place-Chinatown Metro. Moderately priced hotel in Chinatown, 1 block from the MCI Center. Clean, comfortable rooms with A/C, cable TV, in-room video games. Small fitness center. Parking $11 per day. 24hr. check-in with reservation. Singles $90-110; doubles $100-139; additional adult $10. 10% discount for AAA members and Internet reservations. Children under 18 stay free. **Use caution in surrounding area at night.** ❹

FOGGY BOTTOM

Expensive hotels in the Foggy Bottom area cater to a business community. With a few exceptions, there's not much here for the budget traveler, as the prices reflect the area's prime location right next to the White House and federal office buildings.

Allen Lee Hotel, 2224 F St. NW. (☎331-1224 or 800-462-0186, www.allenleehotel.com). Metro: Foggy Bottom-GWU. The Allen Lee is a basic hotel (read: old, worn rooms) with exceptionally low prices. No cable TV, relatively bare walls, and occasional maintenance problems. All rooms have an individual A/C unit, telephone, and sink. Same-day laundry service available ($15 for 1 load, $20 for 2); leave bags of laundry at front desk by 7am. Check-in and check-out at noon. Singles $45 with common bath, $58 with private bath; doubles $62/74; triples $71/85; quads $85/98. Extra beds $10. AmEx/DC/D/MC/V. ❷

GEORGETOWN

Georgetown is by far the priciest place to stay in D.C. Don't even look here if you are trying to practice the art of budget travel. You aren't missing much in terms of convenience; with no Metro stop, Georgetown is less accessible from the rest of the city.

SOUTH OF THE MALL

The waterfront suffers from a lack of hotels, but the subdued atmosphere is worlds away from nearby crowded tourist areas.

Waterfront Channel Inn Hotel, 650 Water St. (☎554-2400; www.channelinn.com). Metro: L'Enfant Plaza or Waterfront. Essentially the only hotel in the Waterfront area, the Channel Inn has spacious rooms with queen beds or 2 double beds, a small sitting area, desks, A/C, cable TV, modem hookups, and balconies. Free underground parking and passes to fitness center with indoor pool. Dry-cleaning and laundry services available M-Sa. 24hr. reception. No student groups. Reservations recommended. Check-in 2pm; check-out noon. F-Sa singles and doubles $105 for up to 4 people, Su-Th $150. 10% AAA discounts available. AmEx/DC/D/MC/V. ❹

UPPER NORTHWEST

This area promises some good deals on rooms in a safe and quiet residential area.

🏠 **Woodley Park Guest House,** 2647 Woodley Rd. NW (☎667-0218 or 866-667-0218; www.woodleyparkguesthouse.com). Metro: Woodley Park-Zoo; walk 1 block up Connecticut Ave. toward the zoo. Take a left on Woodley Rd. Renovated in 2001, the Woodley Park is a gorgeous facility offering exceptional comfort at low rates. Rooms are small but charming and impeccably maintained; all rooms have A/C and restored antique furniture. Staff is friendly and welcoming. Parking $10 per night. Breakfast included (M-F 7:30-10:30am, Sa-Su 8-11am). Young children discouraged; no pets or smoking. Credit card required for reservations. Cancellations 5 days in advance of the scheduled arrival. Reception M-F 7am-9pm, Sa-Su 8am-8pm. Check-in 3pm; customers checking in past 11pm M-F or 10pm Sa-Su are subject to a $25 fee. Minimum stay typically 2 nights. Singles with shared bath $65, doubles $75-90; singles or doubles with private bath $100-150. AmEx/MC/V. ❷

Kalorama Guest House at Woodley Park, 2700 Cathedral Ave. NW (☎328-0860; www.washingtonpost.com/yp/kgh). Metro: Woodley Park-Zoo. Walk 2 blocks up Connecticut Ave. toward the zoo and take a left on Cathedral Ave.; it's 1 block up on the left. A bare guest house with aspirations toward Victorian charm. Rooms are clean, quiet, and have A/C. Laundry facilities (4-9pm), refrigerator, and microwave available. Telephone and TV, though not in guest rooms, are available in the 1st fl. parlor. Breakfast included (M-F 7:30-10:30am and Sa-Su 8-11am). No children under 6. No pets. No smoking. Limited parking (by reservation only) $7. Reception M-F 8am-8pm, Sa-Su 8am-7pm; guests cannot check in when reception is closed. Credit card required for reservations; cancellations 1 week in advance for full refund. 2-night minimum stay on weekends. Rooms with shared bath $50-75, with private bath $70-115. Free night with 7-night stay. 10% AAA discount. AmEx/DC/D/MC/V. ❷

Days Inn, 4400 Connecticut Ave. NW (☎244-5600; www.daysinn.com). Metro: Van Ness-UDC. Spacious, clean rooms with a prime on-street location just a few blocks from the Metro. A standard mid-range hotel with 24hr. reception, A/C, cable TV, and Internet access in every room. Avis car rental on-site. Check-in 3pm; check-out noon. Reservations recommended; cancel up to 4pm on the scheduled day of arrival. Wheelchair accessible. Basic singles and doubles $59-149, depending on season. AAA members 10% off. AmEx/DC/D/MC/V. ❷

CAMPGROUNDS

Cherry Hill Park, 9800 Cherry Hill Rd. (☎800-801-6449 or 301-937-7116; www.cherryhillpark.com), in Cherry Hill, MD. From D.C., follow I-95N or 495E toward Baltimore for 30min.; take Exit 25 (Rte. 1S, College Park); make the first right onto Cherry Hill Rd. and go 1 mi. to park entrance on left. Park entrance 1 mi. on right. This Las Vegas of campgrounds operates with an agenda described by owner Norman as "traditional values and modern luxuries." Most of the 400 sites are for RVs and include utilities. Cable hookup and wireless Internet available. 2 outdoor swimming pools (1 heated with whirlpool), sauna, playground, mini golf, and café. Metrobus stop on the grounds (buses leave for Metro stations every 30min.). Tent site for 2 $32; RV site with electricity and water $42; additional person $4. Coin-operated laundry. $25 deposit with reservation. AAA, military, AARP, and KOA 10% discount. ❶

Greenbelt Park, 6565 Greenbelt Rd. (☎800-365-2267 or 301-344-3948 for reservations Apr.-Nov.; www.nps.gov/gree), 12 mi. from D.C. Take I-95N to Exit 23 Kenilworth Ave. (Rte. 201S); after the exit, take the left lane to Greenbelt Rd. (Rte. 193E); the park entrance is on the right farther down the road. A short drive from Metro: College Park/UMD or Greenbelt. The cheapest and nicest place to camp year-round in the D.C. area, courtesy of the National Park Service. 174 very quiet, wooded sites for tents, trailers, and campers. Nature walking trails. No electricity, except in case of emergency. Bathrooms and showers. Leashed pets permitted. Alcoholic beverages prohibited. Max. stay 2 weeks; max. 2 tents, 2 vehicles, and 6 people per site. Check-out noon. Sites $14. 50% discount for seniors with Golden Age Pass. ❶

Capitol KOA, 768 Cecil Ave. (☎800-562-0248 or 410-923-2771; www.koakampgrounds.com), in Millersville, MD. From D.C., take Rte. 50E (John Hanson Hwy.) to Rte. 3N (Robert Crain Hwy.); bear right after 8 mi. onto Veterans Hwy. Turn left under the highway onto Hog Farm Rd.; follow blue camping signs. Mostly RVs, some cabins, and a small wooded area for tents. Pool, volleyball courts, and centrally located bathroom/shower facilities. Movies and crafts for kids nightly; occasional evening events for adults. Free weekday shuttle to MARC commuter train ($7.25 round-trip to Union Station, ages 65+ $4, up to 2 children 6 and under travel free with each adult). Weekend shuttle to Metro: New Carrollton. Max. stay 2 weeks. Open Mar. 25-Nov. 1. Tent site for 2 $33; RV complete hookup $44, water and electricity $41; 1-room cabin $58, 2 rooms $67. Additional adult $5, child $3. ❶

LONG-TERM HOUSING

DORMS

Interns and similar summer guests tend to stay in **university dorms,** where rates are cheap and students abound. Most university housing programs won't admit self-declared tourists, and even students must have a job or an official excuse to stay in the dorms. Most dorms are completely full by early spring; all require applications.

Georgetown University Summer Housing, GU Office of Housing and Conference Services, 103 Harbin Hall, Washington, D.C. 20057 (☎687-4560; http://housing.georgetown.edu/summer), on the Georgetown University campus in Georgetown. Metro: Rosslyn, Dupont Circle, or Foggy Bottom. Much of Georgetown's residential charm lies in its unique hilltop location and the hot happenings of nearby M St. The terraced campus welcomes student interns and those involved in summer programs or other educational pursuits (housing is available for non-students with the additional 14.5% D.C. hotel tax). The apartment-style rooms fill up quickly, usually before mid-May, so mail in the application early. Most apartments have 2-3 bedrooms, with carpet, kitchens, and bathrooms, and can accommodate 4-7. $35-36 per person per night. Housing offered for full summer (late May to early Aug.) only. ❶

George Washington University Summer Housing, Columbia Plaza B100, 500 23rd St. NW, Washington, D.C. 20037. (☎496-6305, http://gwired.gwu.edu/cllc/summer). Metro: Foggy Bottom-GWU. For conference groups, individual interns, intern groups, or students in academic programs only. Conveniently located campus near the Mall. Average dorm rooms with hardwood floors, A/C, and clean bathrooms. Laundry in dorms. Some dorms have kitchens,

219

carpeting, free cable hookup, and exercise facilities. Available late May to early/mid-Aug. 5-week minimum stay. 50% deposit due with application. Weekly prices vary by room type and whether the resident is a summer student at GWU; singles $178-252; doubles, triples, and quads $178-238. Townhouses for 4-16 people also available for $178 for GW summer students, $273 for others. Nightly intern group prices singles $31-36, doubles and triples $28-36, quads $28-33. 14.5% tax for non-GW summer school students. ●

Georgetown Law School Summer Housing, in the Gewirz Student Center, 120 F St. NW, on Capitol Hill. Write to: Office of Residence Life, 600 New Jersey Ave. NW, Washington, D.C. 20001-2075 (☎202-662-9290; www.law.georgetown.edu/reslife). Metro: Union Station or Judiciary Sq. Excellent apartments for students and interns in a not-so-excellent neighborhood. Carpeted 1-3 bedroom apartments with living rooms are spacious, well-furnished, and come equipped with kitchens, A/C, private phone lines, and bathrooms. Free shuttle service for nearby grocery shopping. Fitness center $45 for the summer or $25 per month (rates will likely increase after new fitness center opens in spring 2004). $50 non-refundable application fee; rent payment due in full at least 30 days prior to arrival. 3-, 5-, 7-, and 10-week rentals available June-Aug. $23-45 per person per day. Those not studying at Georgetown Law during their stay pay the 14.5% D.C. hotel tax. ●

Catholic University Housing, Student Programs and Events, 204 Pryzbyla University Center, Catholic U., Washington, D.C. 20064 (☎319-5200; http://conferences.cua.edu). Metro: Brookland-CUA. CU's quiet campus houses many American and international interns, but is open to all visitors. A variety of rooms issued on a first-come, first-served basis. Housing available mid-May to early Aug. Wheelchair accessible. Application must be received 4-5 business days prior to arrival; arrangements can be made online or by phone. $50 refundable key deposit, $100 refundable credit card deposit to reserve room. 1-week minimum stay. Non-CU student rates (for 7-30 days) are singles $25 per day, with A/C $27; doubles $46/50. Rent due in full upon arrival. D/MC/V. **Use caution in this area at night.** ●

Boston University Washington Center, 2807 Connecticut Ave NW, Suite 114 (☎756-7800; www.bu.edu/abroad/cities/washington_jp/admin.html). Metro: Woodley Park-Zoo. Located in the safe Woodley Park district, this elegant brick building opens its excellent facilities each summer to interns. The building includes laundry facilities, a library/study lounge, and a well-equipped computer center. Housing consists of 3-bedroom apartments with A/C, cable TV, 2

The
KALORAMA
GUEST HOUSE

"Prices are an unbelievable bargain...
all [rooms] are lovingly decorated with antique furniture
and homey little touches..." The Philadelphia Inquirer.

Victorian townhomes located downtown, complimentary continental
breakfast & aperitif. Walk to metro. Ask about our winter specials.

THE KALORAMA GUEST HOUSE

at Kalorama Park
1854 Mintwood Place, NW
Washington, DC 20009
(202) 667-6369

at Woodley Park
2700 Cathedral Avenue
Washington, DC 20008
(202) 328-0860

bathrooms, common area, and a kitchen. Apartments house 6 residents. Minimum stay of 8 weeks required. $300 deposit (by cashier's check only) required to secure housing, but deposit is returned at end of summer. Available late May-early Aug. $198 per week; limited number of singles available with an additional fee of $53 per week. D/MC/V. ●

Howard University Housing. To request an application, write to 2401 4th St. NW, Room 19, Washington, D.C. 20059, Attn: Summer Conference Housing. Metro: Shaw-Howard U. Housing office located at 4th and Bryant St. NW. Summer housing for interns, students, tourist groups, and youth groups. Double-occupancy dorm rooms or 3-5 person suites, which include small study area and full bath. Internet access. Not the best neighborhood. Applications accepted beginning Apr. 1; fax to 265-3152. Full payment required 1 week before arrival. Rooms available June-July. Rooms $20 per person per night, with A/C $30. ●

COMMUNAL LIVING

Community living is a quirky—and considerably more expensive—alternative to regular housing options. However, these arrangements often provide both room and board (2 daily meals), which account for some of their higher cost.

International Student House, 1825 R St. NW, Washington, D.C. 20009 (☎202-387-6445 or 202-232-4007; www.ishdc.org), near 18th St. Metro: Dupont Circle. Contact ISH for an application. Primarily long-term international students in a romantic Tudor townhouse with a mammoth dining hall, library, patio, and garden. All dorm style rooms in the townhouse and adjoining annex are fully furnished, single-sex, and have A/C. Parking (when you can get it) $100 per month, 21+ preferred. Office open M-Tu and Th-F 9am-5pm, W 9am-8pm, Sa 11am-1pm. 10% additional fee for first 2 months if stay is under 3½ months. First month's rent due upon arrival. Inclusion of daily breakfast and dinner mitigates hefty prices. Singles $935-980 per month; doubles, triples, and quads $685-835 per person per month. ●

Thompson-Markward Hall, 235 2nd St. NE (☎546-3255; www.ywch.org), 4 blocks from Union Station near C St., across from the Hart Senate office building. Metro: Union Station or Capitol South. Women ages 18-34 only. 112 dorm-style singles and 4 doubles line the clean hallways. Small bedrooms have A/C and phones; communal baths are large and clean. Laundry room. Weekly maid service provided. Bring your own sheets. Breakfast and dinner included. Elegant 1st fl. common areas with piano, library, and garden; basement TV lounge with cable, VCR, and couches. Men are not allowed beyond the lobby. No alcohol, cooking appliances, or smoking. Make summer reservations 6 months in advance. Non-refundable $60 fee required with reservation. 2-week min. stay. $154 per week, $650 per month. ●

RENTING

Unless you're planning on permanently relocating to D.C., **subletting** an apartment in the District is a smart idea. Check the **Washington Post** (esp. F-Su) and the **CityPaper** (Th). Although the *CityPaper* is available in print on Thursday, the online version (www.washingtoncitypaper.com) is published by 3pm on Tuesday—and everyone knows it, so act fast. *CityPaper* apartments often vanish before the print version of the paper hits the streets. For apartments on Capitol Hill, check out **The Hill** (www.hillnews.com). Online, try www.apartments-in-washington-dc.net, http://washington-dc-apartments.com, or www.thesublet.com. D.C.'s budding version of **Craigslist** (washingtondc.craigslist.org) also has listings. Roommate services and flyer-laden kiosks may also prove helpful.

INSIDE

baltimore **223**
annapolis **246**
eastern shore & on the atlantic **253**
virginia beach **267**
norfolk **272**
williamsburg **277**
richmond **284**
charlottesville **291**
wine & hunt country **295**

Daytripping

Washington, D.C.'s central location affords visitors the opportunity to embark on a panoply of rich and rewarding daytrips. From the islands off the coast of Virigina and Maryland to the scintillating mid-Atlantic resort beaches, to preserved colonial towns and a trove of historical trails and national parks, to college towns and upscale wining and dining in Virginia's Wine & Hunt country, visitors are never without nearby adventures and the potential for some fun in the sun. For more daytripping ideas, check out the last page of the *Washington Post's* new "Sunday Source" section for a detailed daytrip itinerary every Sunday. The following destinations are organized in an approximate geographic loop around D.C. Price information is designated by the ❶❷❸❹❺ signs; for reference scales for pricing, see **Food and Drink** (p. 133) or **Accommodations** (p. 207).

BALTIMORE   ☎ 410

City of charm, city of crime, maritine city of seafood, Baltimore is a blend of the beauteous and the decrepit, the modern and the archaic. "Charm city," though, is not for everyone, and it can sometimes be more dispiriting than charming. Inevitably, some will appreciate America's 12th largest city's unusual melange of big-city, small-town, northern-sensibilities-mixed-with southern-hospitality character. Luckily, this is an ideal time to witness Baltimore's renaissance. Traditionally a blue collar, working-class town, today Baltimore is changing faster than ever.

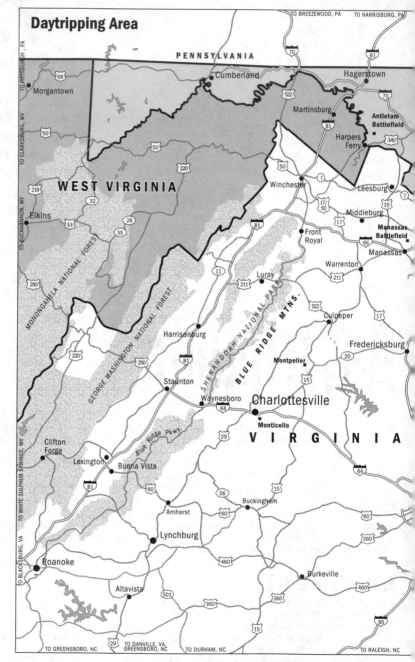

Daytripping Area

TO BREEZEWOOD, PA   TO HARRISBURG, PA

PENNSYLVANIA

TO PITTSBURGH, PA

68

Morgantown

TO CLARKSBURG, WV

Cumberland

522

Hagerstown

70

81

Martinsburg

Antietam
Battlefield

81

Harpers
Ferry

340

50

50

220

50

Winchester

7

Leesburg

219

WEST VIRGINIA

7

15

32

17
50

Middleburg

Elkins

28

17

**Manassas
Battlefield**

33

55

81

Front
Royal

66

Manassas

MONONGAHELA NATIONAL FOREST

250

11

Luray

211

Warrenton

211

522

Culpeper

17

220

GEORGE WASHINGTON NATIONAL FOREST

250

Harrisonburg

SHENANDOAH NATIONAL PARK

Montpelier

Fredericksburg

20

81

B L U E   R I D G E   M T N S.

15

TO WHITE SULPHUR SPRINGS, WV

Staunton

Waynesboro

64

Charlottesville

Clifton
Forge

Blue Ridge Pkwy.

Monticello

V I R G I N I A

29

Lexington

Buena Vista

64

TO BLACKSBURG, VA

81

60

56

15

Buckingham

60

Amherst

60

Lynchburg

460

360

Roanoke

460

Burkeville

Altavista

501

360

360

85

TO GREENSBORO, NC

29

TO DANVILLE, VA,
GREENSBORO, NC

TO DURHAM, NC

TO RALEIGH, NC

15

DAYTRIPPING BALTIMORE

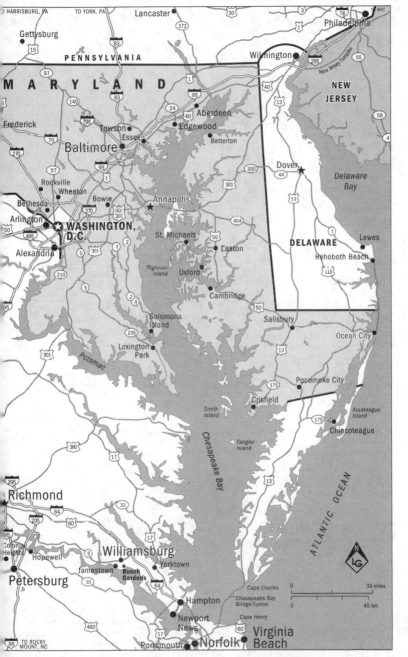

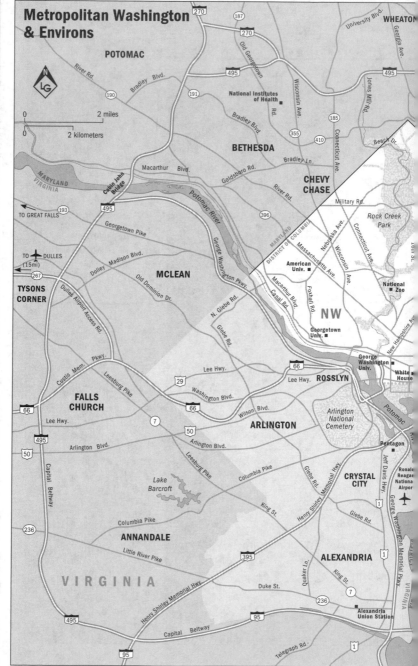

Metropolitan Washington & Environs

POTOMAC

0 2 miles
0 2 kilometers

River Rd.

Bradley Blvd.

Old Georgetown

National Institutes
of Health

Wisconsin Ave.

BETHESDA

Macarthur   Blvd.

Goldsboro Rd.

Bradley Ln.

CHEVY
CHASE

River Rd.

Military Rd.

Rock Creek
Park

MARYLAND
VIRGINIA

Cabin John Bridge

TO GREAT FALLS

Georgetown Pike

Potomac River

DISTRICT OF COLUMBIA
MARYLAND

American
Univ.

Massachusetts Ave.

Nebraska Ave.

Wisconsin Ave.

Connecticut Ave.

National
Zoo

TO DULLES
(15mi)

Dolley Madison Blvd.

MCLEAN

Old Dominion Dr.

George Washington Pkwy.

Macarthur Blvd.

Canal Rd.

Foxhall Rd.

NW

TYSONS
CORNER

Dulles Airport Access Rd.

N. Glebe Rd.

Georgetown
Univ.

New Hampshire Av.

George
Washington
Univ.

Curtis Mem. Pkwy.

Glebe Rd.

Lee Hwy.

66

Lee Hwy.

ROSSLYN

White
House

FALLS
CHURCH

Leesburg Pike

29

Washington Blvd.

66

Wilson Blvd.

Arlington
National
Cemetery

Potomac

Lee Hwy.

7

50

ARLINGTON

Pentagon

Arlington Blvd.

Arlington Blvd.

Leesburg Pike

Columbia Pike

Glebe Rd.

Henry Shirley Memorial Hwy.

CRYSTAL
CITY

Ronald
Reagan
National
Airport

Lake
Barcroft

Jeff Davis Hwy.

Glebe Rd.

George Washington Memorial Pkwy.

Capital Beltway

Columbia Pike

King St.

ANNANDALE

Little River Pike

395

ALEXANDRIA

King St.

Quaker Ln.

236

7

VIRGINIA

Duke St.

236

Alexandria
Union Station

Henry Shirley Memorial Hwy.

495

Capital   Beltway

95

Telegraph Rd.

1

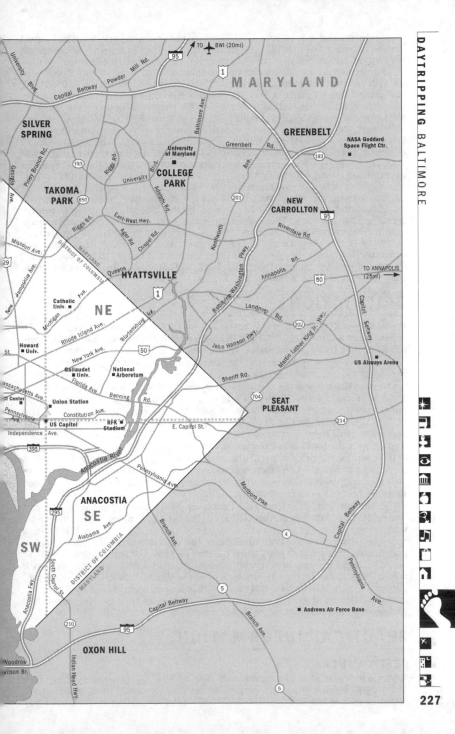

Founded on August 8, 1729, by 1768 Baltimore had grown so large that it had earned the seat of Baltimore County, a position held until 1851, when it became independent of county affiliation. Following the American Revolution, when Baltimoreans did their share in fending off the Brits, the city population doubled twice in the final quarter of the 18th century. Baltimore's rapid growth was threatened during the War of 1812; after annihilating Washington, D.C., the British turned their guns on Baltimore. It was this attack, as well as Baltimore's successful defense at Point North and Fort McHenry, that in 1814 inspired Francis Sott Key to write the "Star Spangled Banner," which was later adopted as America's national anthem. While New York focused its postwar energies on the Erie Canal and Philadelphia invested in the construction of the Pennsylvania Railroad, Baltimoreans worked on the Baltimore & Ohio (B&O) Railroad. Long considered a southern town, Baltimore suffered during the Civil War, but later demonstrated a comeback. In 1904, however, a great fire swept through the city, wiping out most of downtown and forever changing the city's skyline. Although the city was subsequently rebuilt, post-World War II "suburban flight" induced Baltimore's worst economy since the Great Depression. By the 1960s, Baltimore's downtown region had become particularly dilapidated, and the fate of the city was open to question. Investment in the Inner Harbor during the 1970s, however, led to the replacement of old warehouses along the waterfront with sparkling new buildings, a national aquarium, museums, and a shopping promenade, the heart of today's tourist attractions. Past and present Baltimoreans have included Edgar Allen Poe, John Waters, Frederick Douglass, Anne Tyler, and Babe Ruth.

ORIENTATION

Baltimore lies 35 mi. north of D.C. and about 150 mi. west of the Atlantic Ocean. To get to Baltimore from D.C., take the **Baltimore-Washington Parkway. Exit 53** for **Route 395** leads right into the **Inner Harbor.** Without traffic, the trip takes less than an hour.

The city is divided by **Baltimore St.** (east-west) and **Charles St.** (north-south). Directional prefixes indicate every other street's relation to these main streets.

The **Inner Harbor,** near the corner of Pratt and Charles St., is a scenic tourist trap home to historic ships, Baltimore's only shopping mall, and an aquarium. The museum-laden, artistic **Mount Vernon** neighborhood—served by city buses #3 and 11—occupies **North Charles St.,** north of **Baltimore St.,** around **Monument St.** and **Centre Ave. Little Italy**—served by city bus #10—sits a few blocks east of the Inner Harbor, past the **Jones Falls Expressway.** Continuing past Little Italy, a short walk to the southeast brings you past Broadway to bar-happy historic **Fells Point**—also served by city bus #10. Old-fashioned and gentrified **Federal Hill**—accessed by city buses #1 and 64—preserves Baltimore history, while the area east of **Camden Yards** has recently been re-urbanized.

The southern end of the **Jones Falls Expressway (I-83)** halves the city near the Inner Harbor, and the **Baltimore Beltway (I-695)** circles the city. **I-95** cuts across the southwest corner of the city as a shortcut to the wide arc of the Beltway. During rush hour, these roads slow to a crawl. Baltimore, like any other major US city, lacks free parking, so either come bearing shiny quarters or expect to pay garages at least $9 per day. Look for "early bird" parking specials that charge $7 or less if you park before 9am and exit by 6pm. If you don't mind the 10min. walk to the Inner Harbor, the parking garage in Federal Hill on West St. between Light St. and S. Charles St. offers all-day parking without restrictions for a reasonable $6. In general, meters and garages away from the harbor are less expensive.

PRACTICAL INFORMATION

GETTING THERE

Airport: Baltimore-Washington International (BWI; ☎859-7111; www.bwiairport.com), on I-195 off the Baltimore-Washington Parkway (I-295), about 10 mi. south of the city center, located between Baltimore and Washington, D.C. Take MTA bus (www.metroopensdoors.com) #17

($1.60) to the Nursery Rd. Light Rail station. Airport shuttles to hotels (www.supershuttle.com) run daily every 30min. 5:45am-11:30pm ($11 to downtown Baltimore, $17 round-trip). For D.C., shuttles leave every hr. 5:45am-11:30pm ($26-34). Amtrak trains from BWI run to Baltimore ($5) and D.C. ($12). MARC commuter trains are cheaper but slower, and run only M-F (Baltimore $3.25, D.C. $5).

Trains: Penn Station, 1500 N. Charles St. (☎800-872-7245; www.amtrak.com), at Mt. Royal Ave. Easily accessible by bus #3 or 11 from Charles Station downtown. Amtrak trains run every 30min.-1hr. to: **New York** ($70+); **Washington, D.C.** ($14+); and **Philadelphia** ($43+). On weekdays, 2 **MARC commuter lines** (☎800-325-7245 in MD; www.mtamaryland.com) connect Baltimore to D.C.'s Union Station (☎859-7400 or 291-4268) via Penn Station (with stops at BWI) or **Camden Station,** at the corner of Howard and Camden St. Both are $7, round-trip $14. Open daily 5:30am-9:30pm; self-serve open 24hr.

Buses: Greyhound (☎800-231-2222; www.greyhound.com) has 2 locations: downtown at 210 W. Fayette St. (☎752-7682), near N. Howard St.; and 5625 O'Donnell St. (☎752-0908), 3 mi. east of downtown near I-95. Connections to **New York** ($38, round-trip $69); **Washington, D.C.** ($11, round-trip $22); and **Philadelphia** ($20, round-trip $37.50).

GETTING AROUND

Public Transport: Mass Transit Administration (MTA), 300 W. Lexington St. (Bus and Metro schedule info ☎800-543-9809 or 539-5000, operator available M-F 6am-7pm; www.mtamaryland.com), near N. Howard St. Bus, Metro, and Light Rail service to most major sights in the city. Some buses run 24hr. Metro operates M-F 5am-midnight, Sa 6am-midnight. Light Rail operates M-F 6am-11pm, Sa 8am-11pm, Su 11am-7pm. One-way fare for all is $1.60, but higher on commuter trains that service the outer suburbs. Bus #17 runs from the Nursery Rd. Light Rail stop to BWI Airport.

Water Taxi: Harbor Boating, Inc., 1732 Thames St. Main stop at Inner Harbor (☎800-658-8947 or 563-3901; www.thewatertaxi.com). Apr.-Oct. stops every 15-18min., Nov.-Mar. every 40min. at the harbor museums, Harborplace, Fells Point, Little Italy, and more. Service May-Aug. M-Th 10am-11pm, Su 10am-9pm, F-Sa 10am-midnight; Apr. and Sept.-Oct. M-Th 10am-8pm, F-Sa 10am-midnight, Su 10am-8pm; Nov.-Mar. daily 11am-6pm. One-day unlimited rides $6, ages 10 and under $3. Ticket includes coupons for Baltimore attractions.

Taxis: American Cab, (☎636-8300). **Arrow Cab,** (☎261-0000). **Baltimore Cab,** (☎732-1600). **Checker Cab,** (☎685-1213). City fares start at $1.50 and accrue $1.20 every mi., $0.30 every cross-county mi.

The Local LEGEND

Ballad of "Hon" Man

As *The Baltimore Sun* puts it, **hon** is a "provincial term of affection" in Baltimore. Got that, hon? If you stay in the city long enough, someone is likely to call you by this appellation.

In 1994, the **"Hon Man,"** a mysterious vandal whose real name has never been revealed, led a campaign to add "Hon" to the "Welcome to Baltimore" sign on the Baltimore-Washington Parkway. For two years, he repeatedly stuck placards saying "Hon" to the sign only to have highway workers remove them.

His antics inspired state senators to add an amendment to the state budget that would have withheld $1 million in highway funds until "Hon" was permanently added to the sign. The mayor, fascinated by his pranks, even invited him to City Hall.

But the Hon Man's campaign ended in shame when state troopers caught him in the act and extracted a promise never to hang a "Hon" sign again. Except for one relapse (troopers found one of the distinctive signs up again in January of 1998), he's kept his word ever since.

TO PENN STATION, JOHNS HOPKINS, BALTIMORE MUSEUM OF ART (2mi), ZOO (5mi), E. CHASE ST., N. EAGER ST.

Read St.

MOUNT VERNON

Madison St.

Monument St.

Maryland Historical Society

Greyhound

Washington Monument

Walters Art Gallery

Mt. Vernon United Methodist

Centre St.

St. Paul St.

Calvert St.

83

Hamilton St.

Franklin St.

Enoch Pratt Free Library

Basilica of the Assumption

Pleasant St.

40

Mulberry St.

Tyson St.

Pleasant St.

Saratoga St.

Josephine St.

Kinko's

LEXINGTON MARKET

Lexington St.

Josephine St.

TO EDGAR ALLAN POE HOUSE (0.5mi.)

Marion St.

Lexington St.

City Hall

Fayette St.

Westminster Churchyard/ Edgar Allan Poe Grave

Hippodrome Performing Arts Center

CHARLES CENTER

Baltimore St.

CHARLES ST. M

CHARLES CENTER

Jewish Historical Society

Redwood St.

1st Mariner Arena

National Museum of Dentistry

Bank of America

Water St.

Lombard St.

TO B&O RAILROAD MUSEUM (0.3mi.)

Convention Center

Pratt St.

Babe Ruth Birthplace/ Baltimore Orioles Museum

Camden St.

Camden Station

World Trade Center, Top of the World

Oriole Park at Camden Yards

Conway St.

Light St. Pavilion

Clipper City

Barre St.

Welcome St.

Lee St.

FEDERAL HILL

Inner Harbor

York St.

Hill St.

Rash Field

Ravens Stadium

Hughes St.

Maryland Science Center

Key Hwy.

395

Montgomery St.

Henrietta St. Churchill St.

Warren Ave.

Wheeling St

TO 295, BWI

Cross St. Market

Cross St.

West St.

Downtown Baltimore

🏠 ACCOMMODATIONS

Admiral Fell Inn, **30**	F5
Capital KOA, **33**	A6
Radisson Plaza Lord Baltimore, **10**	B3

🍴 FOOD

Akbar, **1**	C1
Amicci's, **18**	E4
Babalu Grill, **13**	D3
Bertha's Dining Room, **28**	F5
Broadway Market, **26**	F5
Caffe Brio, **34**	B6
Corks, **35**	B6
Cross St. Market, **37**	C6
Donna's, **6**	B1
The Fudgery, **22**	C4
Harborplace, **21**	C4
The Helmand, **2**	B1
Ixia, **7**	B2
La Tavola, **20**	D4
Lexington Market, **9**	A3
Liquid Earth, **25**	F5
Matsuri, **38**	B6

Mugavero's Confectionery, **19**	E4
Phillip's Restaurant, **23**	C4
Purple Orchid, **16**	D4
Sobo Cafe, **36**	B6
Tio Pepe, **8**	C2
Vacarro's, **17**	D4
Vespa, **39**	B6

⭐ NIGHTLIFE

Allegro, **3**	B1
Baltimore Brewing Co., **15**	D4
Bar Baltimore, **11**	D3
Bohager's, **24**	E5
Cat's Eye Pub, **31**	F5
Central Station, **4**	B1
Club Orpheus, **14**	E4
Greene Turtle, **27**	F5
Hippo, **5**	B1
Howl at the Moon, **12**	D3
John Steven's, **32**	F5
Max's on Broadway, **29**	F5

Madison St.

Monument St.

Front St.

Orleans St.

Gay St.

Low St.

High Flyer

Port Discovery Museum **13**

Market Pl.

Jones Falls Expwy

Front St.

Baltimore St.

Jewish Museum of Maryland

Lombard St.

Granby St.

City Life Museums

Pratt St.

Exeter St.

Central Ave.

Eden St.

Caroline St.

Bethel St.

Broadway

Prester St.

Ann St.

Gough St.

Star Spangled Banner Museum **16**

Stiles St.

High St.

Albemarle St.

LITTLE ITALY

Bank St.

TO PULASKI HWY.

Fawn St.

Trinity St.

Eastern Ave.

Museum of Public Works

President St.

Civil War Museum

Fleet St.

Spring St.

Dallas St.

Bond St.

FELL'S POINT

Pier Six Concert Pavilion

Aliceanna St.

Register St.

Ann St.

Lancaster St.

Visionary Art Museum

Shakespeare St.

Fell's Point Maritime Museum

Patapsco R.

Dock St.

Thames St.

Wiles St.

Philpot St.

N

BALTIMORE MUSEUM
USTRY (½mi.),
cHENRY (2mi.)

0   200 yards
0   200 meters

231

Car Rental: Thrifty, BWI Airport (☎859-0280 or 800-847-4389) and 2042 N. Howard St. (☎783-0302), 9 blocks from Penn Station. Economy cars from $30 per day and $185 per week. Unlimited miles in MD and bordering states. Under 25 $15 extra per day. 21+. Credit card and $350 security deposit via credit card required. Open daily 6am-11pm. **Budget,** BWI Airport (☎800-527-0700 or 859-5395). Economy cars and trucks start at $40 per day. Under 25 $25 extra per day. Unlimited miles. Open 24hr. **Hertz,** BWI Airport (☎800-654-3131 or 850-7400). Mileage requirements and fares change daily. Call to inquire. 25+. Open 24hr. AmEx/MC/V.

Bicycle Rental: Light Street Cycles, 1015 Light Street (☎685-2234, www.lightstreetcycles.com) offers bikes for rent and sale. 1-day rental (bikes due back by closing the following day) $25, each additional day $10 per day, weekly $50, monthly $100 for older bikes only. Lock, helmet, and choice of pedals included at no extra charge. Friendly and knowledgeable staff. Tours available. Check out the *Greater Washington Area Bicycle Atlas* ($17) for an encyclopedia of local trails. Open M-F 10am-7pm, Sa 10am-6pm, Su by appointment only (ask for Penny). AmEx/D/MC/V.

PRACTICAL INFORMATION

Visitor Information: Baltimore Area Visitors Center, 451 Light St. (☎837-7024). Located in a brand-new building, the user-friendly center provides dozens of maps, brochures offering discounts for sights and restaurants, and the helpful *Quickguide*. Open M-Sa 9am-5pm, Su 10am-5pm.

Traveler's Aid: Two desks at BWI Airport. Open M-F 9am-9pm, Sa-Su 1-9pm. Direct-line telephones at Penn Station and Greyhound terminal.

Bank: Bank of America, 100 S. Charles St. (☎800-333-6262; www.bankofamerica.com), at Lomard St., **ATM**.

Library and Internet: Enoch Pratt Free Library, 400 Cathedral St. (☎396-5430; www.epfl.net). With your back toward the Inner Harbor, walk uphill on Charles St., which becomes N. Charles St.; the library will be on the left-hand side of the street after you cross Saratoga St. Free Internet access. Open M-W 10am-8pm, Th 10am-5:30pm, F-Sa 10am-5pm, Sept.-May Su 1-5pm.

Emergency: ☎911.

Help Lines: Suicide: ☎531-6677. Open 24hr. **Sexual Assault and Domestic Violence:** ☎828-6390. Open 24hr. **Gay and Lesbian:** ☎837-8888. Operators daily 7pm-midnight, recording all other times.

24hr. Pharmacy: Rite Aid, 300 Martin Luther King Blvd. (☎539-2532 or 800-748-3243; www.riteaid.com), at Howard St.

Kinkos, 300 N. Charles St. (☎625-5862; www.kinkos.com), at Saratoga St. Internet rates $0.20-$0.40 per min. depending on computer type. Open daily 6am-11pm. AmEx/D/MC/V.

Post Office: 900 E. Fayette St. (☎800-275-8777; www.usps.com). Open M-F 7:30am-10pm, Sa 8:30am-5pm. **Postal Code:** 21233.

ACCOMMODATIONS

Expensive hotels dominate the Inner Harbor, and reputable inexpensive hotels elsewhere are hard to find. For a convenient way to reserve bed and breakfasts, call **Amanda's Bed and Breakfast Reservation Service,** 1428 Park Ave. (☎800-899-7533; www.bedandbreakfast-maryland.com. From $65 per night. Open M-F 10am-5pm.)

Radisson Plaza Lord Baltimore, 20 W. Baltimore St. (☎539-8400 or 800-333-3333; www.radisson.com/lordbaltimore) between Liberty St. and Charles St. A national historic landmark built in 1928, this is the oldest functioning hotel in Baltimore. The hotel's highlights are undoubtledly its elegant lobby, mezzanine, and ballroom. Check out the hand-painted, hand-carved flower ceiling in the lobby. Be forewarned: while the entrance is breathtaking, rooms can be slightly shabby for a four-star hotel, and guests shell out $25 per night for hotel parking. On the flipside, rooms are larger than average, and the location—just six blocks from the Inner Harbor—and its historic flavor in a town filled with generic, modern accommodations proves an unbeatable combination. Reservations recommended. New fitness center, full service restaurant and bar, Starbucks and gift shop on premises. Rooms $129-209. Prices vary based on availability. 10% AAA discount. ❺

The Admiral Fell Inn, 888 S. Broadway (☎522-7377 or 866-583-4162; www.harbormagic.com), at Thames St. A veritable portal to the past with themed rooms that include canopied beds and armoirs. Two ghosts—a Miss Rebecca Milowe and a Mr. Edgar Allen Poe—haunt the premises on a regular basis, though guests attest that their presence is felt the most Th-Su. Formerly a retreat where sailors used to rest after long sojourns at sea, today the 80-room hotel consists of 8 connected buildings, a bar, and a restaurant. An entertaining place to stay, though the slightly uneven floors, oddly-shaped spaces, and small windows make for darker rooms. Unlimited Internet access, copying, faxing, local and toll free calls are included with the mandatory Internet charge ($4 per day). Valet parking $15 per night. Rooms $169-259. 10% AAA and AARP discount. ❺

Capitol KOA, 768 Cecil Ave. North (☎800-562-0248 or 923-2771, from Baltimore 987-7477; www.capitolkoa.com), in Millersville, between D.C. and Baltimore. From D.C., take Rte. 50E (John Hanson Hwy.) to Rte. 3N (Robert Crain Hwy.). Bear right after 8 mi. onto Veterans Hwy.; after a short distance turn left under the highway onto Hog Farm Rd. Follow blue camping signs. Mostly RVs, some cabins, and a small wooded area for tents. Pool, volleyball courts, and centrally located bathroom/shower facilities. Movies and crafts for kids nightly; occasional evening events for adults like slide shows and wine and cheese parties. Free shuttle to MARC commuter train Odenton Station M-F, and to New Carrollton Metro on Sa-Su. Shuttle leaves daily at 8am, and returns for pick-up at 5pm. Open Mar. 25-Nov. 1. Tent site for 2 $33; water and electricity $39; RV complete hookup $44; 1-room cabin $58; 2-room cabin $67. Additional adult $5, additional child $3. 10% discount with KOA card. ❶

FOOD

Baltimore will always be known for its Maryland **blue crab,** fresh from the Chesapeake Bay and ubiquitous in kitchens across the city. Yet there are other culinary jewels in Baltimore's crown, available to those willing to leave the tourist sanctum of the **Inner Harbor** and explore afield. The city's succulent seafood is joined by a growing number of ethnic menus and first-class wine lists.

INNER HARBOR

The neon lights of the Hard Rock Cafe and Planet Hollywood brand Inner Harbor as a fat-walleted tourist's haven. The **Pavilions at Harborplace,** 200 E. Pratt St. (☎332-4191), at Light St., have enough food stalls and restaurants to please any palate, though growing prices reflect tourism's influence. **Power Plant Live** (www.powerplantlive.com) is Baltimore's newest restaurant and entertainment district. Attracting a young, J. Crew-clad urban crowd, the district's food and bars can be expensive, but they are also a refreshing break from the more traditional eateries and nightlife scene that Baltimore typically offers. Power Plant Live is located at the intersection of Market Place and Water St., immediately off the Jones Falls Expressway.

Babalu Grill, 32 Market Pl. (☎234-9898), in Power Plant Live. This new Cuban restaurant brims with authenticity. The open kitchen shows chefs hard at work and chickens roasting rotisserie-style in hot brick ovens. Popular appetizers include Cuban-style turnovers with seasoned beef and avocado salsa ($6). Select a side of rice and beans ($4) or fried plantains ($5) to accompany boiled lobster, served hot on a bed of coconut rice ($29). The spacious dining rooms and bar turn into a hot salsa club at night ($5 cover from 9:30-11pm, $10 cover after 11pm). Open for lunch Tu-F 11:30am-2:30pm; dinner M-Th 5-10pm, F-Sa 5-11pm, Su 4-9pm. Club hours Th-Sa 10pm-2am. ❸

The Fudgery, 301 Light St. (☎539-5260), on the 1st fl. of the Light St. Pavilion. Nirvana for chocolate lovers. Singing employees turn their fudge-making into a musical performance. The woman behind the counters belts out "Hot fudge, free samples. You can try, and you can also buy." Products are pricey ($6.49 per ½ lb. slice) but worth the sacrifice for a delectable (and entertaining) treat that comes in 16 flavors. Try the chocolate walnut or the sugar-free version. Buy 3, get the 4th free. Open M-Th 10am-9pm, F-Sa 10am-10pm, Su 11am-7pm. MC/V. ❷

Phillip's Restaurant, 301 Light St. (☎685-6600), on the 1st fl. of the Light St. Pavilion. Loyal fans and families flock to the Inner Harbor's long-time seafood hot spot for a variety of marine dishes from fried scallops ($12) to soft-shell crabs ($14). Indoor and outdoor seating. Sandwiches ($6-13) are just as delicious as the expensive entrees. Open daily for lunch 11am-4pm and dinner 5-9pm. Or try **Phillip's Seafood Market,** next door, for inexpensive takeout (crab cake minis $8, deep-fried fish sandwich $6). Open M-Th 9am-9pm, Sa 10am-10pm, Su 11am-7pm. Ages 4 and under eat for free at **Phillip's Buffet,** down the pathway from the market. ❷

Purple Orchid, 729 E. Pratt St. (☎837-0080), at the corner of Pratt and I-83. An example of fusion cuisine done right, this unique bar/lounge features Asian dishes with French accents. The vegetable stir-fry sits in wine sauce ($8), the creme brulée is mixed with mango fruit salad ($6), and the taste is remarkable. Traditional Asian dishes also offered, such as pan-seared tuna in sesame sauce ($15). Extensive sushi menu ($4-8). W nights 20% off at the sushi bar. Open Tu-F 11:30am-2:30pm and 5-10:30pm, Sa-Su 4-10:30pm. AmEx/D/MC/V. ❸

FEDERAL HILL

As Baltimore's most historic district, Federal Hill is known for both its wealthy residential neighborhood and its array of quaint restaurants and cafes. Those who choose (and can afford) to sacrifice the suburban backyard for a stunning, Federal Hill-top view of the harbor are often seen enjoying picnics and parties atop their historic four-story town homes. Pricey restaurants are spread throughout S. Charles St. and Light St., but the cafes provide affordable meals. For great-tasting grab-and-go meals, check out the chaotically fun **Cross Street Market,** (see p. 236).

🦞 **Corks,** 1026 S. Charles St. (☎752-3810; www.corksrestaurant.com). A hidden retreat that specializes in a vast array of strictly American wines and fine contemporary American cuisine made with classic French techniques and Asian influences. Behind its unremarkable façade, enter into a surprisingly expansive, elegant, and sensual cavern. With a more formal appeal, the front room is ideal for dining with friends; dimly-lit, the larger back "cellar" is for sheer romance. Semi-formal attire. Open M-Th 5-10pm, F-Sa 5-11pm, Su 5-9:30pm. AmEx/DC/D/MC/V. ❺

Sobo Cafe, 6-8 W. Cross St. (☎752-1518; www.sobocafe.com). Quiet cafe distinguishes itself by changing its dinner and dessert menus daily. The turkey melt ($5), a fixture on the lunch menu, brings stability to a constantly varying array of wild choices, including the "Big-Assed Bourbon BBQ Chop" with sweet corn, cabbage, spuds, and slaw ($13). The flavorful gazpacho ($3) is highly recommended for less adventurous eaters. Local modern artists display their work on the pastel-colored walls, giving the cafe a cheery neighborhood feel. Open daily 11am-10pm. AmEx/MC/V. ❷

Vespa, 1117-21 S. Charles St. (☎385-0355). Quiet and relaxing, Vespa is a fine candle-lit Italian eatery. The owner travels to Italy on a regular basis to hand-pick the best Italian wines for his customers. The wall art changes monthly to showcase a variety of talents. Weekend visitors can expect a livelier (and louder) scene. Business casual attire. Open M-Th 5:30-10pm, F-Sa 5:30-11pm. AmEx/MC/V. ❹

Caffe Brio, 904 S. Charles St. (☎234-0235; www.caffe-brio.com). The appeal of sitting streetside, amongst flowers out back on the patio, or surrounded by colorful wall paintings on the 2nd fl. makes this cafe a good find for any caffeine fiend or chocoholic. Choose from a variety of creative coffee blends ($3 per cup) or spoil yourself with a slice of chunky monkey cake, a banana and creme filled pastry with chocolate ($5). This hip-but-not-too-trendy Federal Hill hot-spot is a vegetarian's delight; the portobello pizza ($7) is a favorite. Pool table for casual play. Open M-F 7am-10pm, Sa 8am-11pm, Su 8am-9pm. AmEx/MC/V. ❶

Matsuri, 1105 S. Charles St. (☎752-8561; www.matsurida.com). The combination of an outgoing staff, tight quarters, and a well-stocked bar creates a friendly environment for patrons to eat healthy while sake-bombing away at this popular Japanese restaurant. Locals favor Bento box lunches ($9) and sushi dinners ($12-16). Open M-Th 11:30am-2:30pm and 5-10pm, F 11:30am-2:30pm and 5-11pm, Sa 5-11pm, Su 4:30-9:30pm. AmEx/D/MC/V. ❸

MOUNT VERNON

Mount Vernon manages to squeeze a tremendous number of restaurants in between its art galleries and conservatories. Virtually all are on **North Charles Street,** within the blocks on either side of the Washington Monument. **Use caution in the areas around Cathedral Street, Saratoga Street, and Mulberry Street at night.**

Ixia, 518 N. Charles St. (☎727-1800; www.ixia-online.com). This trendy, romantic new Baltimore hot-spot doesn't fool around: it follows the formula for flashy, pricey New American establishments to a tee. The service is friendly and the atmosphere unpretentious, but elegant casual attire is preferred in this classy establishment. Those who can afford it enjoy delicious lychee honey glazed salmon filet mignon ($20) and caramelized garlic lacquered veal chop ($27). For starters, try the spinach gnocchi al gorgonzola ($8). Open Tu-Th from 5pm, F-Sa 5pm-2am, Su call for seasonal hours. AmEx/D/MC/V. ❺

Tio Pepe, 10 E. Franklin St. (☎539-4675). Known for its fresh fish and tender meats, this old-world Baltimore favorite commands high prices (entrees $15-30) for its top-drawer Spanish cooking. Dim lights, thick crimson carpet, and a staff well-versed in the vernacular of anything-you-wish service complete the plush picture. Feel free to wax cosmopolitan and order in Spanish—the waiters are fluent. Request the *Langostinos Frescos Españoles Esconal* ($15), or just call it fresh prawns in romenscu sauce—either way, it's delicious. Serious carnivores love the *Pepito de Lamo a la Parrilla* ($15), a broiled sirloin steak sandwich. Open for lunch M-F 11:30am-3pm; dinner M-F 5-10pm, Sa-Su 5-11:30pm. ❹

Akbar, 823 N. Charles St. (☎539-0944; www.akbar-restaurant.com). Excellent Indian food served with care in a small basement room (entrees $10-15). All-you-can-eat lunch buffet includes 12 different items ($7), all-you-can-eat weekend brunch buffet ($9), and the large appetizers ($2.50-5.50) are the steals. Try the tasty Chicken Malai Kabab ($12), served hot out of the oven. Lunch buffet M-F 11:30am-2:30pm. Brunch buffet Sa-Su noon-3pm. Open for lunch M-F 11am-2:30pm, Sa-Su noon-3pm; dinner Su-Th 5-11pm, F-Sa 5-11:30pm. ❸

Donna's, 2 W. Madison St. (☎385-0180; www.donnas.com), at N. Charles St. From the Walters Gallery main entrance, exit to the left; turn left at the corner and stay on the left side of the street, then walk uphill past the Washington Monument 3 blocks to Madison St. Baltimore goes for ultra-chic with this health-food cafe. If a mixed green salad topped with tasty tuna and walnuts ($8) doesn't satisfy you, try the veggie rotolo ($6.25) and add some new potatoes ($1.75) for good measure. Beer (from Donna's stock of microbrews) $4.50. Open M-Th 7:30am-11pm, F 7:30am-midnight, Sa 9am-midnight, Su 9am-10pm. ❶

The Helmand, 806 N. Charles St. (☎752-0311). This unassuming Afghan restaurant is actually the best in the area with dishes like *kaddo borani* (pan-fried and baked baby pumpkin appetizer in a yogurt-garlic sauce; $3). Entrees rarely exceed $10. Vegetarians will find a variety of options, and desserts will satisfy even the most jaded sweet tooths. Wheelchair accessible. Open Su-Th 5-10pm, F-Sa 5-11pm. AmEx/MC/V. ❷

LITTLE ITALY & FELLS POINT

Little Italy hosts an incredible number of (surprise, surprise) Italian restaurants among its row houses. Residents sit out on their stoops on summer evenings, gossiping and watching diners stroll past. If the timing is right, you'll even walk into a frenzied bocce tournament, a lawn bowling game that dates back to 5200 BC, pitting two local families in a traditional Italian contest. In contrast to Little Italy's quiet neighborhood atmosphere, the cobblestoned streets of nearby **Fells Point** swarm with visitors wandering in and out of restaurants, bars, and shops. In Fells Point, **Broadway Market** (see p. 236) sits squarely in the middle of S. Broadway St., about three blocks from the dock. To reach Little Italy from central Baltimore, take bus #7 or 10 from Pratt St. to Albemarle St. Continue on bus #7 or 10 to Broadway, and walk four blocks to Fells Point. For free help finding a great place to eat, or to learn about local lore and history, look for humorous and poetic local expert Lonnie Harris (nutcase21223@yahoo.com), Th-Su around 6pm in front of Rodos Bar, 719. S. Broadway. Tips appreciated.

Amicci's, 231 S. High St. (☎528-1096; www.amiccis.com). Mediterranean flair is everywhere at this *ristorante:* from the menu to the Italian movie decor. Live large with the renowned antipasto for two ($9), and then try the veggie gnocchi ($12). Stretch your stomach to accommodate one of the 11 immense pasta dishes under $15. Family atmosphere is warm and friendly, and with a brand new 2nd fl., Amicci's is cooking faster than you can say *prego.* Open Su-Th 11:30am-10pm, F-Sa 11:30am-11pm. AmEx/D/MC/V. ❷

Bertha's Dining Room, 734 S. Broadway (☎327-5795; www.berthas.com), at Lancaster St. The "Yar!" sign out front invites mates into this nautical-themed pub. Dig in to the black-shelled mussels ($9-11) and the vegetable mussel chowder ($3). Scottish afternoon tea offers Scotch eggs and pastries (reservations recommended; call to make a 3, 3:30, 4, or 4:30pm tea reservation). Big Bertha's Rhythm Kings plays Dixieland jazz first W of each month, all other W there's live piano jazz; Tu Paul Wingo performs guitar jazz; F Blue Flames Blues. Live music performances start around 9pm; no cover, but $0.25 extra charge for all drinks. 20 beers on tap (½-pint $3). Kitchen open daily 11:30am-11pm; bar open daily until 2am. D/MC/V. ❷

La Tavola, 248 Albemarle St. (☎685-1859; www.la-tavola.com). For the best in romantic Italian dining, visit La Tavola. Though often empty for lunch on weekdays, business picks up at night and on weekends, so be sure to call ahead for immediate seating. All pasta is made fresh. For a filling meal order the *gnocchi di patate* (potato pasta with garlic and basil in pesto; $13). To save room for dessert, go for the *petti di pollo alla florentine* (chicken breast topped with fresh spinach and mozzarella in white wine sauce; $16.50). Business casual attire. Open daily 11:30am-10pm. AmEx/D/MC/V. ❸

Liquid Earth, 1626 Aliceanna St. (☎276-6606), between Broadway and Bond St. Cleanse your spirit at this vegetarian cafe and juice/coffee bar. Unlike most other inexpensive Fells Point eateries—where the food is heavy and the scene that of a port town—both the menu and atmosphere of this new-age cafe are light and hip. The *tartine* (half baguette) with honey mustard, melted brie, walnuts, and apples with a side salad ($6) is delightful. Fresh squeezed juice blends include the "Facelifter," a smooth mix of orange, grapefruit, melon, mint, and ginger ($5). Open M-F 7am-7pm, Sa 9am-7pm, Su 10am-3pm. Cash only. ❶

Vaccaro's, 222 Albemarle St. (☎685-4905; vaccarospastry.com). Specializing in traditional Italian desserts and coffees since 1956, this pastry shop rises above the rest. Whether you crave a freshly made cannoli ($1-3), a scoop of peanut and fudge gelato ($3), or hot mochaccino ($4), your taste buds will appreciate this family owned and run *patisserie* in the heart of Little Italy. Take your pastry and espresso for a stroll to the water's edge or enjoy sit-down service. Open M 9am-10pm, Tu-Th and Su 9am-11pm, F-Sa 9am-1am. AmEx/MC/V. ❶

Mugavero's Confectionery, 300 S. Exeter St. (☎539-9798). This menu-less deli has been a fixture at the cozy corner of Fawn St. for 55 years thanks to the unwavering service of the friendly proprietor. Patrons can invent their own sandwiches or entrust their sandwich to the owner-operator's creative imagination ($5-6). Limited seating; best for takeout. Open daily 10am-9pm. Cash only. ❶

MARKETS

Office workers on lunch break, residents doing dinner shopping, wide-eyed tourists, and gregarious vendors make Baltimore's markets a scene to behold. First licensed in 1763, several of these markets are still hawking their wares today.

Cross St. Market, 1065 S. Charles St., at the intersection of S. Charles and Cross St., in Federal Hill, has been a public market site since 1846. Offers a much smaller, less chaotic, and more convenient version of the Lexington Market without losing the exciting market feel. Lunch hour brings locals and business professionals for the extravagant and inexpensive sushi bars and fish fries. Many of the businesses are family owned; some have been around for over a century. Great place to grab sandwiches ($4-6) and fruit salad ($2) for a picnic atop Federal Hill. Open M-Sa 7am-7pm.

Broadway Market, at the intersection of Fleet St. and Broadway, near Fells Point. Smaller and more subdued than other markets in town; mainly attracts senior citizens. Offers few ready-to-eat options, selling primarily uncooked prepared foods, fresh fruit, and raw fish. The fishy smell could wake the dead, but all food is extremely fresh, clean, and delicious. Open M-Th 7am-6pm, F-Sa 6am-6pm. Pizzerias remain open as late as 2am to serve the bar-hopping Fells Point crowd. **Use caution north of the market at night.**

Lexington Market, 400 W. Lexington St. (www.lexingtonmarket.com), spanning Eutaw through Greene St. Take the subway to Lexington Station or the #5, 7, 15, 19, or 23 bus. Established in 1782, Lexington is the largest market in Baltimore and the oldest operating market in the United States. The locals flock here during lunch and dinner hours for all manner of hearty, mostly greasy food. Crab cakes at **Adell's,** directly across from the main entrance to the right, are particularly good at $4. Not for the faint of heart: the stench in this enclosed market is decidely worse than at either Broadway or Cross St. Open M-Sa 8:30am-6pm. **Use caution in the market and surrounding neighborhoods at all times.**

Robert E. Lee's Boyhood Home

SIGHTS

INNER HARBOR

Baltimore's generally gray and functional harbor ends with a colorful bang in the **Inner Harbor,** a five-square-block body of water surrounded by a bevy of eateries, museums, and boardable ships.

THE NATIONAL AQUARIUM

🚩 **Location:** Pier 3, 501 E. Pratt St. **Contact:** ☎576-3800; www.aqua.org. **Hours:** M-Th 9am-5pm, F-Sa 9am-8pm, Su 9am-7pm. Remains open 2hr. after last entrance time. Tickets can be purchased from Ticket-Master (☎481-7328 before 3pm in Baltimore, 202-432-7328 in Washington, D.C.). Budget 3hr. **Admission:** $17.50, seniors $14.50, ages 3-11 $9.50, under 3 free. $5 discount on winter F after 5pm. AmEx/D/MC/V. **Accessibility:** Excellent disabled access. **Events:** Lobby displays list slide shows and feeding times.

Maryland Crabs

The National Aquarium is perhaps that one magical attraction, besides its murder rate, that sets Baltimore apart from all other major American cities. Visitors are unfailingly impressed by the awesome layout—which includes not only a gigantic deep sea tank, but also a lively tropical rainforest. Though a visit to the outdoor sea pool to watch slaphappy seals play is free to the general public, it is certainly worth the time and money to venture inside. The eerie **Wings in the Water** exhibit at the bottom of the spiral showcases 50 species of stingrays in an immense backlit pool. The **Children's Cove** was recently moved to Pier 4 and has a newly-expanded **Touching Pool.** At the top of the spiral is the steamy **Tropical Rainforest,** where piranhas, parrots, and a pair of two-toed sloths peer through

Mount Vernon

the dense foliage in a 157 ft. glass pyramid. From the rainforest, visitors descend a remarkable four-story ramp around a cylindrical tank containing a mock coral reef. Back on ground level, an enclosed bridge leads to the **Marine Mammal Pavilion,** which contains dolphins and whales, and an amphitheater featuring dolphin performances every hr. on the ½hr.

PORT DISCOVERY

⚐ Location: *35 Market Pl., in Power Plant Live.* **Contact:** ☎ *727-8120; www.portdiscovery.org.* **Hours:** *Labor Day-Memorial Day Tu-Sa 10am-5pm, Su noon-5pm; Memorial Day-June daily 10am-5pm; July and Aug. daily 10am-6pm, F Fun Nights 10am-8pm.* **Admission:** *$11, children $8.50, 3 and under free. Combination museum admission and helium balloon ride tickets $19, children 3-12 $15, under 3 free. Tickets can be purchased from TicketMaster (☎ 481-7328). AmEx/MC/V.* **Accessibility:** *Excellent disabled access.* **Events:** *Often, call for more information.*

Baltimore's children's museum, **Port Discovery,** provides children with the ultimate educational playhouse and was recently nationally ranked in the top five in its category. The creativity and imagination displayed in the museum's various programs and exhibits is remarkable. In **Miss Perception's Mystery House,** kids collect evidence and piece together clues in order to solve what is presented to them as the "world's greatest unsolved mystery." In the **Dream Lab,** kids use computers to create art that reflects their goals for the future. And, over in **Adventure Expeditions,** a lost Pharoah's tomb sits waiting to be discovered by kids on a mission to explore the land of the Pyramids. **Port Discovery** is affiliated with Baltimore's own Enoch Pratt Free Library and thus houses many children's books in the museum's **Exploration Center.**

BALTIMORE MARITIME MUSEUM

⚐ Location: *Piers 3 and 5.* **Contact:** ☎ *396-3453; baltomaritimemuseum.org.* **Hours:** *Spring-fall Su-Th 10am-5pm, F-Sa 10am-6pm; in winter F-Su 10:30am-5pm. Boats stay open 1hr. later than ticket stand.* **Admission:** *$6, seniors $5, ages 5-13 $3. For Seaport Day Pass, call ☎ 783-1490; $16, seniors $13.50, children $9.* **Accessibility:** *All boats are wheelchair accessible.*

Several ships grace the harbor by the aquarium, most of which belong to the Baltimore Maritime Museum. Visitors may clamber through the interior of the USS *Torsk,* the intricately-painted submarine that sank the last WWII Japanese combat ship. Covered under the same entrance fee are the lightship *Chesapeake* and one of the survivors of the Pearl Harbor attack, the Coast Guard cutter *Roger B. Taney.* The fee also allows access to the octagonal lighthouse on Pier 5. Other historic boats moored behind the lighthouse include the *Lady Maryland,* a replica 18th-century schooner, and the *Mildred Belle,* a 20th-century motorboat. For all this and more, purchase the **Seaport Day Pass,** which grants access to the Maritime Museum, the Museum of Industry, the view of the city from high inside Baltimore's World Trade Center, and time aboard the USS *Constellation*—the last all-sail warship built by the US Navy. Water taxi service to and from these various attractions is also included in the ticket price.

OTHER SHIPS

The Clipper City, a beautiful 19th-century topsail schooner, provides a scenic, 2hr. jaunt around the Inner Harbor. Sunset cruises offer breathtaking views and depart Su-Th at 6pm from just outside the Baltimore Visitors Center on Light St. (☎ 539-6277; www.sailingship.com. Cruises depart daily noon and 3pm. $12, children $2. F-Sa 8-11pm calypso and reggae ($20) and Su brunch ($30) sails also offered.) On weekends, the **Minnie V.,** a replica of the skipjacks used to harvest oysters from the Chesapeake, offers 2hr. history sails. ($12, children $3.) Harbor Boating rents paddle boats during the summer. (1615 Thames St., next to the World Trade Ctr. Open daily 10:30am-4:30pm. 2-person boats $8 per 30min.)

NEAR FEDERAL HILL

MARYLAND SCIENCE CENTER

🏛 Location: 601 Light St. **Contact:** ☎ 685-5225; www.mdsci.org. **Hours:** June-Aug. M-F 10am-5pm, Sa 10am-6pm, Su noon-5pm; Sept.-May M-F 10am-5pm, Sa-Su 10am-6pm. **Admission:** $15.50, seniors $14.50, 12 and under $10.50. Price includes admission to the IMAX theater and the planetarium.

This interactive museum lies south of Harborplace at Inner Harbor's far edge. Look for the waving astronaut balloon on the roof. Museum highlights include an electric shock-dispensing Van de Graph generator, a five-story IMAX, and the enormous Davis Planetarium. Those interested in astronomy can attend both nighttime and daytime observing sessions on the restored 1927 observatory telescope (stargazing every Th 5:30-10:30pm, sungazing every Su 11am-4pm; call ahead for events). The two IMAX films that provide simulated experiences, such as climbs up Mt. Everest, are discounted when viewed as a double-feature on F ($12.50, $9 regular; call ahead for times). Behind the Science Center rises **Federal Hill Park** (open daily 8am-dusk), offering unparalleled views of Baltimore Harbor. A stately Star Spangled Banner flies atop the hill, where children can run about on the playground by day and couples can delight in the romantic scenery of the city skyline by night. A statue of **Major General Satin Smith,** who thwarted a British land and sea attack on Baltimore in the War of 1812, also tops the hill.

BALTIMORE MUSEUM OF INDUSTRY

🏛 Location: 1415 Key Hwy., ¾ mi. from Light St. in the Inner Harbor. Take bus #1 or the Water Taxi. **Contact:** ☎ 727-4808. **Hours:** M-Sa 10am-4pm. **Admission:** $10; students, children, and seniors (60+) $5; families $20; under 4 free. **Accessibility:** Fully wheelchair accessible.

A former oyster cannery is an appropriate home for the Baltimore Museum of Industry. After paying at a late 19th-century replica bank teller, guests explore different stores and learn about the history of each industry through captivating paraphernalia and an innovative design. Guides lead guests through a hands-on tour of a functional belt-driven assembly line, giving their audience a chance to print a handbill on an 1880 press or pass around a weighty pair of shears once used in Baltimore's flourishing clothing trade. Recently revamped, the museum houses numerous new exhibits, including a communications theater in which actors—playing the roles of important historical figures—give interactive performances (shows every M and on the first Sa of every month; call for times). The museum sits on the harbor and houses the only operative steam tugboat on the East Coast.

FORT McHENRY NATIONAL MONUMENT

🏛 Location: At the foot of E. Fort Ave., off Rte. 2 (Hanover St.) and Lawrence Ave. **Contact:** ☎ 962-4290 or for cruise 685-4288; www.nps.gov/fomc. **Hours:** June-Aug. daily 8am-8pm, Sept.-May daily 8am-5pm. **Admission:** $5, seniors and under 16 free. 15min. film shown every 20min. from 9am-7pm. **Tours:** Take bus #1 or a narrated cruise from Finger Pier in the Inner Harbor. Cruises depart every 30min. 11am-5:30pm. Round-trip $5, ages 2-11 $3.75. AmEx/D/MC/V. **Accessibility:** Wheelchair accessible.

The fort McHenry National Monument marks the site of the union victory against British forces in the war of 1812. The British attack was, in fact, the only action taken against the fort in its 100 years of protecting water approaches to Baltimore. After firing for more than 25hr. straight, the British stared in amazement at a fort left standing, and an american flag still flying high. Visitors can see the ruins of fort McHenry—the barracks, the hideaways, the gunnery—and the site where Francis Scott Key wrote **"The Star-spangled Banner."** On weekends, the fort McHenry guard performs a living history question and answer program, recounts details of 1812 garrison life, and answers questions about the history of the fort (Sa-Su noon-4pm, weather permitting).

Roses and Cognac for Edgar Allan Poe

When Poe died in 1849, the *Baltimore Tribune* said:

"Edgar Allan Poe is dead. He died in Baltimore on Sunday, October 7th. This announcement will startle many, but few will be grieved by it. The poet was known, personally or by reputation, in all this country; he had readers in England and in several of the states of Continental Europe; but he had few or no friends; and the regrets for his death will be suggested principally by the consideration that in him literary art has lost one of its most brilliant but erratic stars."

Since 1949, on the eve of Edgar Allan Poe's birthday a dark stranger creeps to Poe's grave and performs a silent memorial service, leaving three roses and a half-empty bottle of cognac for the master of horror's spirit. In 1993, a note accompanied the eerie gifts with only the words "The torch will be passed" scrawled on the paper. Since then, three different visitors have taken up that torch. The Poe House hand-picks a group of onlookers from masses of requests to observe the mysterious man in action, never daring to question the identity of Poe's earthly friend.

VISIONARY ART MUSEUM

Location: 800 Key Hwy. **Contact:** ☎ 244-1900; www.avam.org. **Hours:** Tu-Su 10am-6pm. **Admission:** $9, students and seniors $6, under 4 free. MC/V.

On the east side of Federal Hill, the Visionary Art Museum specializes in 20th-century works by self-taught, independent artists. The museum itself is a work of modern urban renewal, with blue and white mirrored stained glass work in progress lining the entrance into what initially looks like a typical Baltimore industrial building. The art is colorful, captivating, and often troubling. The three-story museum changes its collection frequently, with exhibits revolving around themes ranging from "Love" to "Apocalypse." The museum store sells much of its impressive folk art on consignment.

WEST BALTIMORE

EDGAR ALLAN POE HOUSE

Location: 203 N. Amity St., near Saratoga St. Take bus #15 or 23. From Lexington Market, walk on N. Lexington St. with your back toward downtown and the market, turn right on Amity St., and Poe's duplex is the second house on the right. **Contact:** ☎ 396-7932; www.eapoe.org. **Hours:** Apr.-July and Oct.-Dec. W-Sa noon-3:45pm; Aug.-Sept. Sa noon-3:45pm. **Admission:** $3, under 13 $1.

Horror pioneer Edgar Allan Poe was born in 1809 in what is now a preserved historical landmark in the heart of a rundown neighborhood. In between doses of opium, Poe penned famous stories such as *The Tell-Tale Heart* and *The Pit and the Pendulum*, as well as macabre, rhyming poems like *The Raven* and *Annabelle Lee*. He wrote for money and considered his stories trash, never imagining they would be lauded as innovative or captivating. The house contains period furniture and exhibits relating to Poe, all impeccably maintained by a staff eager to regale visitors with all sorts of Poe stories. Almost as spooky as echoes of "Quoth the Raven, Nevermore" is this neighborhood at night, **so visit only in the daytime. Use caution at all times.**

ORIOLE PARK AT CAMDEN YARDS

Location: Just west of the Inner Harbor at Eutaw and Camden St. Take Light Rail to Camden Yards station. **Contact:** ☎ 547-6234, for game tickets 685-9800; www.theorioles.com. **Hours:** Apr.-Sept. 1hr. tours every hr. M-Sa 11am-2pm, Su 12:30, 1, 2, 3pm. **Admission:** $5, seniors and under 12 $4.

In response to the 1970s trend of building large, impersonal stadiums on the outskirts of cities, in 1992 Baltimore constructed an intimate, vintage-style stadium on an old industrial yard in the heart of downtown. The result: an absolute jewel of a ballpark that the Babe would have been proud to call home. Camden Yards, as it is known, proved to be a pioneer, triggering the recent Major League trend of retro ballparks. If the Orioles aren't playing in the afternoon, visitors can take a behind-the-scenes tour of the stadium that visits the clubhouses, dugouts, press box, and scoreboard.

BABE RUTH BIRTHPLACE & BALTIMORE ORIOLES MUSEUM

Location: 216 Emory St., off the 600 block of W. Pratt. Take bus #31. **Contact:** ☎ 727-1539; www.baberuthmuseum.com. **Hours:** Apr.-Oct. daily 10am-5pm, on game nights until 7pm; Nov.-Mar. 10am-4pm. **Admission:** $6, seniors $4, ages 5-16 $3, under 5 free. 20% AAA discount.

This shrine to the "Sultan of Swat" offers an in-depth look into the life of baseball's greatest star. A collection of rare artifacts, photographs, and video and audio recordings make a visit to this museum more than just a look through an old picture book. The museum chronicles Ruth's illustrious career, beginning with his brief stint with the Orioles, alongside a series of exhibits on The Ironman, Cal Ripken Jr. The museum also features exhibits on local and national ballparks, the Negro Leagues in Maryland, ballpark architecture, and sports journalism.

WESTMINSTER CHURCHYARD

Location: Fayette and Greene St. **Contact:** ☎ 706-7228. **Tours:** Apr. Nov. 1st and 3rd F of each month at 6:30pm, Sa 10am. Reservations required. **Admission:** $4, seniors and under 12 $2. Parking available at Paca St. between Fayette St. and Baltimore St.

After dying of alcoholism (or rabies or syphilis, as many argue) in 1849, Edgar Allan Poe was buried in someone else's clothes at the tiny Westminster Churchyard, where he lies alongside other notable local citizens. For over 100 years, his grave has remained a destination for horror fans. Be persistent in your search; Poe's grave can be found in the back left portion of the yard. Halloween tours are especially popular (call for info). **Use caution in this area at night.** (See **Roses and Cognac for Edgar Allan Poe,** p. 240.)

EAST BALTIMORE

CIVIL WAR MUSEUM

Location: 601 President St. at Fleet St. **Contact:** ☎ 385-5188. **Hours:** Daily 10am-5pm. **Admission:** $4, seniors $3, under 12 free.

Beyond Pier 6 at the edge of Little Italy, the Civil War Museum offers exhibits explaining the role of Baltimore railroads in the Civil War. Highlights include a display on the first blood of the Civil War, which occurred on Pratt St. in 1861 when pro-South mobs attacked federal troops, and a look at Baltimore's role in the Underground Railroad.

JEWISH MUSEUM OF MARYLAND

Location: 15 Lloyd St. **Contact:** ☎ 732-6400; www.jewishmuseummd.org. **Hours:** Su and Tu-Th noon-4pm, and by appointment. **Admission:** $5, students $3, under 12 free. **Parking:** Free parking for visitors at Lloyd and Lombard St.

In the historically Jewish heart of East Baltimore, the Jewish Museum of Maryland occupies a large, three-building complex. The left-hand building, the **Lloyd Street Synagogue,** built in 1845, was Maryland's first synagogue and the third in America. The **B'nai Israel Synagogue,** the building on the far right, was founded in 1876 to preserve Orthodox religious practices. Between the two synagogues, the **Jewish Historical Society of Maryland** houses documents and photographs reflecting on the history of Maryland's Jewish community.

HOLOCAUST MEMORIAL

↗ Location: *Hillside at Gay and Water St.*

Back toward Inner Harbor, the concrete Holocaust Memorial powerfully and graphically remembers the six million Jews who died in concentration camps during World War II. Facing Lombard St., a statue depicts the anguished faces of the Nazis' victims engulfed in flames. In the background, six columns of Venetian blinds represent the endless train tracks used to deport Jews from their European homelands and into Nazi concentration camps.

MOUNT VERNON

WALTERS ART GALLERY

↗ Location: *600 N. Charles St. Take bus #3 or 11.* **Contact:** *☎ 547-9000; www.thewalters.org.* **Hours:** *Tu-Su 10am-5pm, 1st Th every month until 8pm.* **Tours:** *W noon and Su 1:30pm.* **Admission:** *$8, students with ID $5, seniors $6, under 18 free. Admission to collection free Sa 10am-1pm and all day on the 1st Th of every month.* **Accessibility:** *Wheelchair access through the Hackerman House.*

Spanning 50 centuries through three buildings, the Walters Art Gallery, Baltimore's premier art museum, houses one of the largest private art collections in the world. The Ancient Art collection on the second level, featuring sculpture, jewelry, and metalwork from Egypt, Greece, and Rome, is the museum's pride and joy. The medieval art on the third floor from the Byzantine, Romanesque, and Gothic periods displays primarily jewelry and metalwork. Paintings on the third and fourth floors reflect every European style between the 12th and 19th centuries, highlighting the later periods. At the **Hackerman House,** an exquisite townhouse/mansion attached to the Walters, rooms filled with dark wooden furniture, patterned rugs, and plush velvet curtains display art from China, Korea, Japan, and India.

NORTH BALTIMORE

BALTIMORE MUSEUM OF ART

↗ Location: *10 Art Museum Dr., at N. Charles and 31st St.* **Contact:** *☎ 396-7100; www.art-bma.org.* **Hours:** *W-F 11am-5pm, Sa-Su 11am-6pm.* **Admission:** *$7, students and seniors $5, under 18 and Johns Hopkins students free; first Th of every month free 11am-8pm.* **Accessibility:** *Handicapped accessible. Wheelchairs available.* **Events:** *Live jazz on select summer Sa in the sculpture garden. $15, 12 and under free (call ☎ 396-6001 for tickets).*

To the west of Johns Hopkins University, the Baltimore Museum of Art houses several collections of Americana and modern art, such as pieces by Warhol and Lichtenstein. The museum is internationally renowned for its Cone Collection, which includes a wonderful variety of Picassos, Renoirs, and Van Goghs, and one of the world's largest collections of works by Matisse.

BALTIMORE ZOO

↗ Location: *Off I-83 at Exit 7; bear right off ramp onto Druid Hill Park. Shuttle bus from Woodberry Light Rail stop runs Memorial Day-Labor Day Sa-Su.* **Contact:** *☎ 366-5466; www.baltimorezoo.org.* **Hours:** *M-F 10am-4pm, Sa-Su 10am-6pm; in winter daily 10am-4pm.* **Admission:** *$10, seniors $8, under 16 $6.* **Accessibility:** *Handicapped accessible. Wheelchairs available at Raven's Roost kiosk.* **Events:** *Live jazz, country, and oldies June-Aug. Sa 4-8pm.*

The Baltimore Zoo occupies a corner of the rolling hills of **Druid Hill Park,** the nation's second largest city park after New York's Central Park. The park features a spectacular palm tree **Conservatory** (Th-Su 10am-4pm; free) housed in a soaring Victorian greenhouse, and a lake surrounded by lush greenery. In the zoo, small enclosures bring visitors almost within touching distance of some of the animals. Signs in front of the Siberian tigers warn all to avoid being sprayed when Frasier (the mascot of nearby Towson University) moves to mark the boundaries of his territory. Kids can ride a carousel and a "zoo choo" train ($1.25) or mount a camel ($2.50).

JOHNS HOPKINS UNIVERSITY

🏠 *Location:* 3400 N. Charles St. Take bus #3 or 11. *Contact:* ☎ 516-8171; www.jhu.edu. *Tours:* Sept.-May M-F 10am, noon, and 3pm; call for summer hours. *Office of Admissions:* ☎ 516-5589. Open Tu-Sa 11am-4pm, Su noon-4pm. Tours every hr. 11am-3pm. *Homewood:* ☎ 516-5589. Open Tu-Sa 11am-4pm, Su noon-4pm. $6, seniors $5, students $3. Tours every hr. 11am-3pm. *Evergreen House:* 4545 N. Charles St. ☎ 516-0341. Take bus #11. Open M-F 10am-4pm, Sa-Su 1-4pm. $6, students $3, seniors $5. Tours hourly 10am-3pm. *Lacrosse Foundation:* 113 W. University Pkwy. ☎ 235-6882. Open June-Jan. M-F 10am-3pm; Feb.-May Tu-Sa 10am-3pm. $3, students $2.

Approximately 3 mi. north of the harbor, prestigious Johns Hopkins University (JHU) spreads out from 33rd St. JHU was the first research university in the country and is currently a world leader in developments in medicine, public health, and engineering. The beautiful campus lies on a 140-acre wooded lot that was originally the Homewood estate of Charles Carroll, Jr., the son of the longest-lived signer of the Declaration of Independence. One-third of students declare pre-med as a major. Although not an athletic powerhouse, the "Johnnies" do perennially field one of the nation's premier college lacrosse teams. 1hr. campus tours begin at the **Office of Admissions** in Garland Hall.

Homewood, Carroll's Georgian mansion, displays a fine collection of 18th- and 19th-century furnishings, some original to the house. Next to Loyola College and 1 mi. north of the main campus, **Evergreen House** is an exercise in excess. Even the bathroom of this elegant mansion is plated in 23-carat gold. The 1hr. tour visits the mansion, private theater, carriage house, and gardens. Purchased in 1878 by B&O Railroad tycoon John W. Garret, the house, along with its gracefully displayed collections of fine porcelain, impressive artwork, Tiffany silver, and rare books, was bequeathed to JHU in 1942. Features in the collection include Chinese pottery, an early Picasso, two full folios of Audubon's bird sketches, and a 16th-century treatise on the New World.

FELLS POINT MARITIME MUSEUM

🏠 *Location:* 1724 Thames St. *Contact:* ☎ 685-3750; www.mdhs.org. *Hours:* Open Th-M 10am-5pm. *Admission:* $4; students, children, and seniors $3; children under 12 free.

Opened in June 2003, the Fells Point Maritime Museum showcases various artifacts, models, and paintings depicting the maritime history in and around Fells Point. The museum is housed in a 19th-century building originally used as a barn for a horse-drawn trolley service.

NIGHTLIFE & ENTERTAINMENT

MUSIC, DANCE & THEATER

Vacationing in the city can be expensive, but fortunately for the budget traveler, much of Baltimore's finest entertainment can be enjoyed free of charge. At **Harborplace,** street performers are constantly entertaining tourists with magic acts, juggling, and clowning around during the day. At night, dance, dip, and dream to the sounds of anything from country to calypso to oldies at the Harborplace (occasional Th-Sa nights). The **Baltimore Museum of Art** offers free summer jazz concerts in its sculpture garden (see p. 242). **Jazzline** (☎ 466-0600) lists jazz shows Sept.-May; call for schedules and information.

Big-name musicians, however, usually come with a price. They can be found performing several times a week May-Oct. at the canvas-topped **Pier 6 Concert Pavilion** (☎ 625-3100; open noon-6pm). Tickets ($15-30) are available at the pavilion or through TicketMaster (☎ 625-1400 or 481-7328). For a more private performance with local artists and some big names, **Fletcher's** (see **Bars and Clubs,** below) features

in the know

The Camp Industry

While Baltimore proudly claims a history of fine music, dance, and theater, the undisputed king of Charm City arts is director **John Waters,** master of the high-camp cult movie.

Born in 1946 in Baltimore, Waters grew up fascinated with sex, violence, and every other topic his Catholic-school education warned him against. By his teens he was making 8mm films and drawing fervent audiences to midnight showings. He rocketed to national prominence in 1973 with *Pink Flamingos,* his masterwork in bad taste, in which the lead actress consumes dog feces on screen.

Waters, who claims to pride himself on his works' lack of common decency and over-the-top visual appeal, has since made several toned-down mainstream comedies, like 1988's *Hairspray* and 1998's *Pecker.* Vestiges of his trademark obsessions remain, though, and as commercial as he may have become, he still shoots all his films in Baltimore.

everything from rock to rap to blues. Purchase tickets ($6-15) through the box office (☎880-8124) or TicketMaster. All shows 18+. Zydeco enthusiasts gather at **Harry's,** 1200 N. Charles St., a Las Vegas-style bar and performance space. (☎685-2828. Shows F-Sa. Cover $3-10. Open F 11am-2am, Sa 2pm-2am.)

The **Baltimore Symphony Orchestra** plays at Meyerhoff Symphony Hall, 1212 Cathedral St., from Sept.-May and during their month-long Summerfest. (☎783-8000. Tickets $15-52. Groups of 20 or more receive 20% off; discounts also available for tickets purchased 1hr. before concerts. Box office open M-F 10am-6pm, Sa-Su noon-5pm, and 1hr. before performances. Call for Summerfest dates.) The **Lyric Opera House,** at 110 W. Mt. Royal Ave., near Maryland Ave., hosts the **Baltimore Opera Company** from Oct.-Apr. (☎727-6000. Tickets $24-109. Box office open M-F 10am-5pm.)

Broadway shows are performed year-round at the **Mechanic Theater,** 25 Hopkins Plaza at Baltimore and N. Charles St. (☎800-638-2444. Tickets $27-60 through TicketMaster or at the box office. Open 9am-5pm.) The **Theater Project,** 45 W. Preston St., near Maryland St., experiments with theater, poetry, music, and dance. (☎752-8558. Shows Th-Sa 8pm, Su 3pm. $15, seniors $10. Box office open 1hr. before shows; call to charge tickets.)

The **Arena Players,** the first black theater group in the country, performs comedies, drama, and dance. (801 McCullough St., at Martin Luther King, Jr. Blvd. ☎728-6500. Tickets start at $15. Box office open M-F 10am-2pm.) The **Showcase of Nations Ethnic Festivals** celebrate Baltimore's ethnic neighborhoods with a different culture featured each week (June-Sept.). The festivals take place all over the city; call the Baltimore Area Visitors Center (☎837-7024) for info.

BARS & CLUBS

Nightlife in Mount Vernon tends more toward the classic bar populated by an older and more sophisticated set, while Fells Point and Power Plant Live are home to the college and 20-something scene. Other venues revolve around Baltimore's two major sports teams. Either way, Charm City does provide plenty of opportunities to party, but be aware of the 1:30am last call.

Bohager's, 701 S. Eden St. (☎563-7220), between Spring and Eden St. in Fells Point. Bohager's has transformed from an average bar into a tropical paradise for college students and folks who drink like they're still in college. Patrons jive to the sounds of live DJs' island and house mixes under a retractable dome. Without a doubt, the most dependably debauched club in Baltimore. Tickets available on-site or through TicketMaster (☎481-7328). Soak in gargantuan soap bubbles pumped out by cleaning machines on Th soap sud night 9pm-2am. F-Sa $15 open bar 8pm-1:45am. Occasional summer crab frenzy (all-you-can-eat crabs, drafts, corn on the cob, and fries). Open M-F 11:30am-2am, Sa-Su 3pm-2am.

Cat's Eye Pub, 1730 Thames St. (☎276-9866; www.catseyepub.com), between Broadway and Ann St., in Fells Point. An older crowd of regulars packs in one of the city's oldest buildings every weeknight for live blues, jazz, folk, or traditional Irish music (M-Th 9pm, F-Sa 4pm). Live blues Su 4-8pm. Cover for national musical acts. Over 25 different drafts and 60 bottled beers ($3.25-4.50). Most drinks $3-6. Flags drape the walls, lending this Irish bar an odd international flair. Happy Hour (M-F 4-7pm) means $2 off pints. Open daily noon-2am.

Howl At The Moon, 34 Market Pl., Power Plant Live (☎783-5111; www.howlatthemoon.com/Balthowl.html). An amusing dueling-piano bar where the crowd runs the show. All songs are by request and sing- (or perhaps "howl") -alongs are frequent. Cover $7. Beers ($3-5) and mixed drinks ($4-8). Open Tu-Th and Sa 7pm-2am, F 5pm-2am.

Max's on Broadway, 737 S. Broadway (☎675-6297; www.maxs.com), at Lancaster St. in Fells Point. Max's offers a trendy haven for those into the latest in microbrews, cigars, cocktails, and even Internet. Tu night beer socials offer connoisseurs an opportunity to discuss the quality of their beloved brew. 62 taps and over 200 different bottled brews. Happy Hour (M-F noon-8pm) offers $1 off on drafts. Downstairs open Th-Su 11am-2am; upstairs open Th-Su 6pm-2am.

Baltimore Brewing Co., 104 Albermarle St. (☎837-5000), just west of the Inner Harbor on the outskirts of Little Italy. Use back entrance at Granby St. Brewmaster Theo de Groen has captured the hearts and livers of Baltimore residents with his original lagers brewed in the landmark still out front. Pitchers of microbrews under $9. Call in advance for tours. Happy Hour (daily 4-7pm) offers $2.50 ½-liters. Open M-Th 3:30pm-midnight, F-Su 11:30am-2am.

Greene Turtle, 720 Broadway (☎342-4222). With foosball, pool ($1), and an extensive CD jukebox, this relaxed bar is popular with the Baltimore college crowd, the Ravens, and anyone else interested in tanking up for next to nothing. $2.50 drafts are $1 cheaper during Happy Hour (M-F 4-7pm), which also offers ½-price appetizers (M 7pm-2am, Tu-F 4-7pm). Nightly specials until closing, including $2 Jagermeister shots on Tu. Sa spicy steamed shrimp for $5. Domestic pitchers $3.50. Sandwiches $5-7.50. Open daily 11:30am-2am.

John Steven's, 1800 Thames St. (☎327-5561; www.johnstevenslimited.com), near the Water Taxi stop on the corner of Ann St. in Fells Point. Acclaimed wood and brass restaurant and bar caters to a quieter, more mature crowd. 20 taps priced around $3-3.50 per pint. Serves standard Baltimore sea-fare, but also has sushi bar with offerings like the "Bawlmer roll" (crab with avocado and scallions; $8). Key lime pie $3.50. Shaded patio in back. Open daily 11am-2am; kitchen closes at 11pm Su-Th, midnight F-Sa.

Bar Baltimore, 4 Market Pl. (☎385-2992; www.barbaltimore.com). Attracts a dancing-on-the-table type crowd. Always packed with energetic party-goers whose entertainment value stems from their predilection for drinking heavily. 18+ college night Th and Sa. Open Th and Sa 8pm-2am, F 7pm-2am.

Club Orpheus, 1003 E. Pratt St. (☎276-5599), in Little Italy. Don't come here without dancing shoes. Goth pervades this Art Deco establishment, a serious dance club attracting a diverse crowd. Bar offers Evian, margaritas, and Jolt ($3 each). Each night has a different theme; call ahead. Sa always **fetish industrial dance** ($5 before 11:30pm, $7 after, $10 if not in fetish attire). Open M-Sa 9pm-2am.

GAY & LESBIAN NIGHTLIFE

Baltimore's gay population concentrates its social scene in the northern portion of Mt. Vernon in an area known as the "gayborhood." Snag a free copy of *Baltimore Alternative* for complete club listings. *Baltimore Gaypaper* contains news and club advertisements for the gay and lesbian population. The *Citypaper*, Baltimore's best indie paper, lists other weekly happenings.

Central Station, 1001 N. Charles St. (☎752-7133; www.centralstationpub.com), at Eager St., across from Hippo. The hottest dance scene around. Chill under lights bought off the set of *A Few Good Men* or play some pre-partying pool with a mixed gay/straight crowd. Newly constructed disco club next door with wall-to-wall gay pride flag is the scene for bumping and grinding W-Su. Club hours F-Sa 8pm-close ($10 cover), Su 5pm-close ($3 cover), Tu-Th 8pm-close ($3 cover). Karaoke M 10pm-2am. Open mike Tu 11pm-2am. Tu Men's night, Th Ladies' night. $1 off beer Happy Hour (4-8pm daily). $2 Smirnoff Su 4pm-close. Open daily 3pm-2am.

Allegro, 1101 Cathedral St. (☎837-3906). A bright pink door marks the entrance on a dead-end block off Chase St. This popular and friendly gay nightspot welcomes everyone to join in crazy partying. Drag show 1st M of each month; Men's Night Tu; "alternative" music W; "Bay-watch" F; various themed nights Sa. Cover F-Su $3. Half-price domestics and generic liquors at Happy Hour (daily 7-10pm). Open Th-M 8pm-2am, Tu-W closed except for private parties.

Hippo, 1 W. Eager St. (☎547-0069), across the street from Central Station. Baltimore's largest gay bar provides pool tables, videos, and a packed dance floor in an industrial setting. Popular piano bar in the evenings. Interior overflows with rainbows, the color pink, and gay pride. 1st Su of every month is Ladies' Tea, one of the largest lesbian events this side of the Mississippi (6-10pm). $1 off all drinks 4-8pm daily. Tu $1 domestic drafts. Happy Hour daily 3-8:30pm. Men's Night Th, when cover includes "drink chips" redeemable for $3 of booze. Cover Th-F $3, Sa $6. Saloon open daily 4pm-2am; dance bar open Th-Sa 10pm-2am.

SPECTATOR SPORTS

The beloved **Baltimore Orioles** play ball at **Camden Yards** (see p. 240), just a few blocks from the Inner Harbor at the corner of Russell and Camden St. Tickets for Orioles games range from $7 (standing in outfield promenade) to upward of $50 for field-level boxes. The expansion-team Baltimore **Ravens,** successors to the defunct Baltimore Colts, matured fast enough to win the 2001 Super Bowl. They play in **Ravens Stadium,** adjacent to Camden Yards. To order individual game tickets, call ☎481-7328 or visit www.ravenszone.net.

ANNAPOLIS ☎410

Annapolis walks the tightrope between a residential port town and a dockside cliché. With its brick-paved sidewalks and narrow streets, the historic waterfront district retains its 18th-century appeal despite the presence of ritzy boutiques and pricey retail stores. Crew-cut "middies" (a nickname for Naval Academy students, or "midshipmen") mingle with longer-haired students from St. John's and couples on weekend getaways amid the highest concentration of historical homes in America.

Settled in 1649, Annapolis became the capital of Maryland in 1694. The fine Georgian houses once packed in colonial aristocrats and their slaves. Annapolis made history when the Continental Congress ratified the Treaty of Paris here in 1784, marking the official end of the American Revolution. After its 1783 stint as temporary capital of the US (hot on the heels of Philadelphia, New York, and Trenton, NJ), Annapolis relinquished the national limelight in favor of a more tranquil existence. Now, guests are treated to a surprisingly accurate taste of what coastal America once was: squished, pastel row houses with gorgeous gardens, friendly strollers, and an endless array of boats. Unlike Williamsburg, Annapolis is a living colonial town where most of the old homes and government buildings are still in use.

ORIENTATION

Annapolis lies southeast of U.S. 50 (also known as US 301), 30 mi. east of D.C. and 30 mi. south of Baltimore. From D.C., take U.S. 50 East, which begins at New York Ave. U.S. 50 East can also be accessed from the Capital Beltway, I-495. From Baltimore, take Rte. 695 South to Rte. 97 South to Rte. 50 East, cross the Severn River Bridge, and then take Rowe Blvd. into the city.

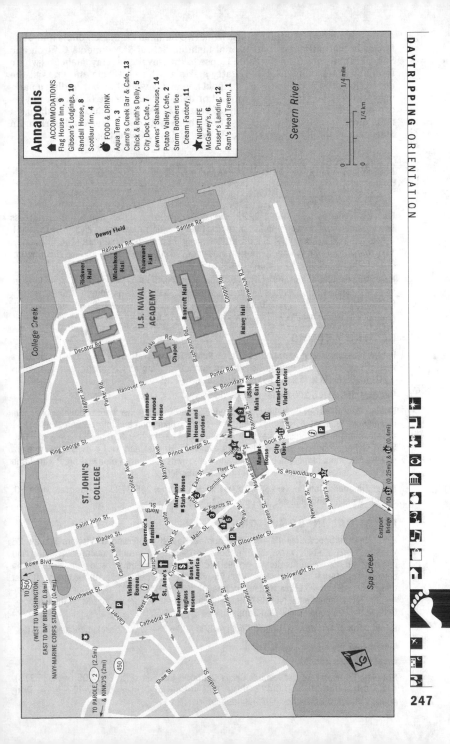

Annapolis

ACCOMMODATIONS
Flag House Inn, **9**
Gibson's Lodgings, **10**
Randall House, **8**
Scotlaur Inn, **4**

FOOD & DRINK
Aqua Terra, **3**
Carrol's Creek Bar & Cafe, **13**
Chick & Ruth's Delly, **5**
City Dock Cafe, **7**
Lewnes' Steakhouse, **14**
Potato Valley Cafe, **2**
Storm Brothers Ice
Cream Factory, **11**

NIGHTLIFE
McGarvey's, **6**
Pusser's Landing, **12**
Ram's Head Tavern, **1**

Severn River

Dewey Field
Halloway Rd.
Santee Rd.

Rickover Hall
Michelson Hall
Chauvenet Hall

U.S. NAVAL ACADEMY

Bancroft Hall

Cooper Rd.

Decatur Rd.

Buchanan Rd.
Brownson Rd.

Reiser Hall

Chapel
Blake Rd.

Porter Rd.
S. Boundary Rd.

USNA Main Gate

Armel-Leftwich Visitor Center

Wagner St.
Parker Rd.

Hanover St.

Hammond-Harwood House

William Paca House and Gardens

King George St.

ST. JOHN'S COLLEGE

College Ave.
Maryland Ave.

Prince George St.

Net Pedlers

Randall St.

Saint John St.

Bladen St.

Maryland State House

East St.
Fleet St.
Cornhill St.

Pinkney St.

Market House
Market Space

Randall St.

City Dock

Dock St.
Craig St.

Governor's Mansion

School St.
State St.
North St.

Francis St.

Main St.
Gorman St.
Green St.

Compromise St.

Carroll Ln. Walk

St. Anne's

Church Circle

Bank of America

Banneker-Douglass Museum

Duke of Gloucester St.

Newman St.
St. Mary's St.

Eastport Bridge

Spa Creek

Rowe Blvd.
TO 50

(WEST TO BAY BRIDGE, 0.8mi),
EAST TO WASHINGTON,
NAVY-MARINE CORPS STADIUM (0.4mi)

Northwest St.
West St.
Calvert St.

Visitors Bureau

Cathedral St.
South St.
Charles St.

Conduit St.
Market St.
Shipwright St.

Shaw St.
Franklin St.

TO PAROLE: 2 (2.5mi)
& KINKO'S (2mi)
450

TO 13 (0.25mi) & 14 (0.4mi)

College Creek

1/4 mile
1/4 km
0

247

The city extends south and east from two landmarks: **Church Circle** and **State Circle**. In blatantly unconstitutional fashion, **School St.** connects Church and State. **East St.** runs from the State House to the Naval Academy. **Main St.** (where food and entertainment congregate) starts at Church Circle and ends at the docks.Downtown Annapolis is compact and easily walkable, but finding a parking space—unless in an expensive lot or in the public garage ($7-11 per day)—can be tricky. Parking at the **Visitors Center** ($1 per hr., $8 max. weekdays, $4 max. on the weekend) is the best bet. There is also free weekend parking in State Lots A and B at the corner of Rowe Blvd. and Calvert St.

PRACTICAL INFORMATION

GETTING THERE

Buses: Greyhound (☎800-231-2222; www.greyhound.com) buses stop at the local Mass Transit Administration bus stop in the football field parking lot at Rowe Blvd. and Taylor St. Tickets are available from the bus driver; cash only. To and from **Baltimore** (1hr.; 5 per day; $10, round-trip $18); **Philadelphia** (4hr.; 2 per day; $20, round-trip $33); and **Washington, D.C.** (1-2hr.; 4 per day, $14, round-trip $28).

Mass Transit Administration: (☎800-543-9809 or 539-5000). Express #210 runs to Baltimore M-F (1hr., $2.85); local #14 runs daily (1½hr., $1.35). M-Sa you must take the Light Rail downtown once you reach Baltimore; Su the bus goes downtown. Buses leave from St. John's and College Ave. as well as from St. John's and Calvert St.

GETTING AROUND

Public Transportation: Annapolis Dept. of Public Transportation (☎263-7964) operates a web of city buses connecting the historic district with the rest of town. Buses run daily 5:30am-10pm. Base fare $0.75, 60+ or disabled $0.35.

Car Rental: Budget, 2001 West St. (☎266-5030).

Bicycle Rental: ⬛**Net Ped@llers,** 42 Randall St (☎263-2344; www.netpedallers.com). Run by an Australian couple, Net Ped@llers is a fantastic bike shop and Internet cafe. Internet $1 access, then $1 per 15min. Bike rates $7 per 1hr., $12 per 2hr., $16 per 3hr., $18 per 4hr., $30 per 8hr.; monthly and weekly rates available. Helmet and lock provided at no extra charge. Ask about numerous bike tours and trails; owners will even drop you off at a trail and pick you at the end of the day. Call for hours. AmEx/MC/V.

Taxis: Annapolis Cab Co. (☎268-0022). **Checker Cab** (☎268-3737). Rates start at $1.80, $1.60 for each additional mi. 3rd person $1 extra.

PRACTICAL INFORMATION

Visitor Information: Annapolis and Anne Arundel County Conference & Visitors Bureau, 26 West St. (☎280-0445; www.visit-annapolis.org). Free maps and brochures. Walking and minibus tours of Naval Academy and historic districts have enthusiastic guides dressed in colonial garb (Apr.-Oct. daily, Nov.-Mar. Sa only; $10, students $5; call for times). Center open daily 9am-5pm. **State House** information desk ☎841-3810. Desk open daily 10am-4pm. A 2nd Visitors Center (☎268-0581) is located at the bottom of Dock St. at the city dock. Dock St. location open daily 9am-5pm.

Bank: Bank of America, 10 Church Circle (☎800-333-6262; www.bankofamerica.com), **ATM.**

Emergency: ☎911.

Local Police: ☎268-9000.

Hotlines: Rape and Sexual Assault Crisis Center: 1419 Forest Dr. Ste. 100 (☎222-7273). **Youth Crisis Hotline:** ☎800-422-0009. **Poison Control Center:** ☎800-492-2414. **Drug Abuse Hotline:** ☎800-492-8477. All lines 24hr.

Internet: Kinkos, 2341 Forest Dr. Ste. A (☎573-5600). 2 mi. from center of town. Head down West St. with your back to city dock and the water, make a left on Riva St., and Kinkos will be on the left at the intersection of Riva St. and Forest Dr., in a shopping center. Internet access ($0.20 per min.) at 10 computers 24hr. daily. AmEx/MC/V.

ACCOMMODATIONS

The heart of Annapolis lacks cheap motels in favor of elegant and pricey bed and breakfasts. However, these B&Bs prove a better choice than the hotels scattered about western Annapolis, which aren't actually cheaper and are far from central attractions. Rooms should be reserved in advance, especially for weekends, spring graduations, and the busy summer months, when accommodations frequently sell out. **Bed and Breakfasts of Maryland** aids in arranging accommodations in Annapolis (☎800-736-4667, ext. 15; open M-F 9am-5pm, Sa 10am-3pm). **Amanda's** offers a similar service (☎800-899-7533; open M-F 8:30am-5:30pm). All lodgings listed are near the dock and within walking distance of major attractions.

🏠 **Flag House Inn,** 26 Randall St. (☎800-437-4825 or 280-2721; www.flaghouseinn.com). A prime location next to the Naval Academy. True to its name, six flags wave from the porch of this breezy Victorian B&B. TV, A/C, and free off-street parking. King-sized or twin beds and private baths in each of the 5 rooms, comfortable library, large front porch downstairs. Complimentary full cooked breakfast includes house specialities such as blueberry french toast and baked orange croissants. Try to reserve 2-4 weeks in advance. Most affordable rooms begin at $110, while the largest 3-person suite ranges from $225-250. MC/V. ❺

Randall House, 30 Randall St. (☎800-808-3323; http://randallhousebandb.com), next door to the Flags House Inn. A B&B run by friendly Jerry and Sandra consists of 3 adorable, smaller rooms. Just 2 years old and completely renovated, this 1880 Victorian house is within walking distance of downtown and the Naval Academy. Free on-site parking and inviting hot breakfast dishes (the egg casserole with pepperjack cheese and stuffed french toast are particularly popular) accompanied by fresh fruit and pastries. Children under 10 not permitted. Rates $130-160. 2-night minimum stay. Bonus rates for longer stays. Cash only. ❺

Gibson's Lodgings, 110 Prince George St. (☎268-5555; www.gibsonslodgings.com). One block from City Dock on Randall St. Gibson's offers a patio and spacious common parlors among its three ivy-covered brick buildings and 21 rooms. 2 night minimum stay on weekends. Some mid-week specials. Free continental breakfast and courtyard parking. One wheelchair-accessible room available. Single and double rooms range $109-189 (all with A/C). Check-in 2pm. Check-out 11am. Cot $25 extra. $10 discount in off-season. AmEx/MC/V/check. ❹

Scotlaur Inn, 165 Main St. (☎268-5665; www.scotlaurinn.com), atop Chick & Ruth's Delly. Ten tiny guest rooms with queen, double, or twin beds, A/C, TVs, and private baths grace this homey "bed & bagel." Not as fancy as the other B&Bs, but far more affordable. Most rooms include huge complimentary breakfast, including a stack of pancakes or eggs, from Chick & Ruth's (see **Food,** below), which more than compensate for any lack of luxury. Check-in 2pm. Check-out 11am. Rooms $80-150. ❸

FOOD

Most restaurants in the area cluster around **City Dock,** an area packed with people in summertime, especially Wednesday nights at 7:30pm, when the spinnaker races finish at the dock. Luckily, the brisk business has yet to drive up prices. The best place to find cheap eats is the **Market House** food court at the center of City Dock, where a hearty meal costs under $5.

🍴 **Potato Valley Cafe,** 47 State Circle (☎267-0902), across from the State House. Swedish coffeehouse with an Idaho twist. Specializes in oven-roasted baked potatoes ($5-7); one makes a filling meal. Choose from a wide variety of sour cream, cheese, bacon, or vegetable toppings. With over 15 vegetables, the Vegetarian Combo is delicious with the homebrewed iced tea. Also serves sandwiches ($5-7) and large salads ($4-7). Open M-F 10am-5pm, Sa 11:30am-5pm. MC/V. ❶

Aqua Terra, 164 Main St. (☎263-1985; www.aquaterra.com). An acclaimed menu and simple-chic design make this high-end establishment, serving contemporary American cuisine in a NYC/SF bistro-style atmosphere, a worthwhile splurge. Less expensive items include Vietnamese noodles with jumbo shrimp and bok choy ($19). Spring lamb loin with summer squash, eggplant, and goat cheese ($24) is among the pricier selections. Extensive wine list. Open M 5:30-11pm, Tu-Th 5:30-10pm, F-Sa 5:30-11pm, Su 5-9pm. AmEx/MC/V. ❹

Carrol's Creek Bar & Cafe, 410 Severn Ave. (☎263-8102; www.carrolscreek.com), in the Annapolis City Marina Complex, across the Eastport Bridge. Locals flock here for the home-cooked food and cheap drinks overlooking the Annapolis waterfront. Texas BBQ shrimp ($8) and Maryland crab soup ($5.25) are local favorites. Happy Hour (M-F 4-7pm) features $2.50 domestic drafts and $2.50 rail drinks. Open M-Sa 11:30am-4pm and 5pm-10pm; Su all-you-can-eat brunch ($19, 50% off for children under 10) 10am-1:30pm, dinner 3-9pm (10pm in summer). AmEx/DC/D/MC/V. ❷

Lewnes' Steakhouse, 401 4th St. (☎263-1617; www.lewnessteakhouse.com), across from Carrol's Creek Bar and Cafe. A local favorite, this family-owned and -run steak house is worlds better than Ruth's Chris next door. Delectable prime-center cuts and fresh seafood make the 10min. walk from Annapolis' City Dock well worth it. Start with clams casino ($7.50) but save room for the unfathomably tender filet mignon ($25). Sides of sauteed asparagus ($5) and crispy hash browns ($3.50) balance out the red-meat deluge. Fine dining atmosphere that welcomes families. Open M-Th 5-10pm, F-Sa 5-10:30pm, Su 4-10pm. ❹

Storm Brothers Ice Cream Factory, 130 Dock St. (☎263-3376). Smiley and enthusiastic teenage staff scoops up tasty and creatively named homemade ice cream like tin roof (fudge ribbon ice cream with chocolate covered peanuts) while enjoying a commanding view of the harbor. 45 ice cream flavors, 3 sherbet flavors, 8 unique sundae sauces including maple walnut and brandied peach. $1.65 for one scoop, $2.60 for two, $3.20 for three. Hand-packed pints, quarts, and half-gallons ($3.25-8.50) also available. Open M-F 10:30am-11pm, Sa-Su 10:30am-midnight. Cash only. ❶

City Dock Cafe, 18 Market Space (☎269-0961; www.citydockcafe.com), at Pinkney St. Cool coffeehouse with view of dock concerts exudes sophistication with its Frank Lloyd Wright-esque design and great espresso drinks ($1-3). Rotating art exhibits enliven an otherwise generic interior. Scrabble, dominoes, and checker boards available. The quiche ($6) and fresh fruit salads ($4) are perfectly light. Open Su-Th 6:30am-10pm, F-Sa 6:30am-midnight. MC/V. ❶

Chick & Ruth's Delly, 165 Main St. (☎269-6737; www.chickandruths.com), a block from City Dock toward the State House. Numerous newspaper clippings adorn the walls, paying homage to this pre-war Annapolis institution. Dishes named for local and national politicians like the George Bush smoked turkey sandwich. Omelettes ($3-7), freshly cooked corned beef sandwiches ($5), and malted milkshakes ($2.75) highlight an inexpensive menu. Delivery available. Buy-1-get-1-½-price ice cream. Happy Hour M-F 2-5:30pm. Open M-Tu 6:30am-4pm, W-Th and Su 6:30am-10pm, F-Sa 6:30am-11pm. ❶

SIGHTS

BANNEKER-DOUGLASS MUSEUM

🔲 *Location:* 84 Franklin St., adjacent to Church Circle. *Contact:* ☎216-6180. *Hours:* Tu-F 10am-3pm, Sa noon-4pm. *Tours:* 1hr. tour; reservations required, call ahead to schedule. $3. *Admission:* Free.

Preserving Maryland's African-American heritage, the Banneker-Douglass Museum is named after two eminent black Marylanders: Benjamin Banneker and Frederick Douglass. The stained glass windows remind visitors that the museum is housed in the Victorian-Gothic Mt. Moriah African Methodist Episcopal Church. The museum is an easy visit that highlights the history of African-Americans in Annapolis from slavery to the present, including an extensive exhibit on the life and works of Frederick Douglass.

CITY DOCK

🔲 *Contact:* ☎268-7600; www.watermarkcruises.com. *Hours:* May 17-Sept. 1, boats depart for Annapolis Harbor and Naval Academy tour M-F every hr. 11am-4pm, Sa-Su every hr. 11am-7pm. Call for additional tour information and schedules during off season. *Admission:* $7, under 12 $4, 2 and under free.

It's difficult to escape the eats and greets at Annapolis's spirited City Dock, which is easily accessed by following Main St. to its aquatic dead-end. The city's main hub of activity, restaurants, and touristy shops line the waterfront, and Naval Academy ships (skippered by fresh-faced "plebes" in the summertime) ply the waters. Civilian yachtsmen and weekend warriors congregate at bars to flex their alcohol tolerance and biceps simultaneously, earning the street its nickname, **"Ego Alley."** Smaller cruise boats leave on tours from Apr.-Oct.

STATE HOUSE

⛴ Location: *90 State Circle.* **Contact:** ☎ *974-3400.* **Hours:** *Daily 9am-5pm. Grounds open daily 6am-11pm.* **Tours:** *11am and 3pm.* **Admission:** *Free.*

Built from 1772 to 1779, the Corinthian-columned State House, in the center of State Circle, is the oldest working capitol building in the nation. It was the US Capitol building from 1783 to 1784, and the Treaty of Paris was signed inside on January 14, 1784. The State House is perfect for a romp through Maryland's history. Visitors can explore the historical exhibits and silver collection or watch the state legislature bicker in two exquisite marble halls from the second Wednesday in Jan. until mid-April. The cordial State House guide, clad in authentic colonial garb, gladly fields questions.

COLONIAL HOUSES

⛴ Location: Hammond-Harwood: *19 Maryland Ave., at King George St.* **William Paca:** *186 Prince George St.* **Contact:** ☎ *263-4683 or 263-5553; www.hammondharwoodhouse.org.* **Hours:** *Mar.-Dec. M-Sa 10am-4pm, Su noon-4pm; Jan.-Feb. T-Sa 10am-4pm, Su noon 4pm.* **Tours:** *On the hr.; last tour (45min. long) 1hr. before closing.* **Admission:** *For Hammond-Harwood $6, students $5, under 12 $3; for Paca $5 garden, $8 house and garden; uniformed armed service personnel get in free for both houses. $10 joint tickets available for both houses. MC/V.* **Accessibility:** *Houses not handicapped accessible; video available for handicapped visitors. The garden and the Shiplap building are handicapped accessible.*

The historic **Hammond-Harwood House,** an elegant 1774 building designed by Colonial architect William Buckland, retains period decor right down to the candlesticks. The house is most renowned for its impeccably preserved colonial doorway. The **William Paca House** was the first Georgian-style home built in Annapolis. Paca, an early governor of Maryland, was one of the original signers of the Declaration of Independence. The elegant house overlooks two acres of lush vegetation, and the garden hides shaded benches that gaze upon trellises, water lilies, and gazebos. Both houses feature historical exhibits on life in the late 1700s, stocked by archaeological digs on the grounds.

US NAVAL ACADEMY

⛴ Location: *52 King George St.* **Contact:** ☎ *263-6933; www.usna.edu.* **Tours:** *Every 30min. Apr.-Nov. M-F 10am-3pm, Sa 9:30am-3pm, Su 12:30-3pm; Dec.-Mar. M-Sa 10am-2:30pm, Su 12:30-2:30pm.* **Admission:** *$6.50, seniors (62+) $5.50, and K-12 students $4.50, preschoolers free. Flag Day, a 1¾hr. tour celebrating American flags, is June 14th every year; admission $12, seniors $11, K-12 students $10, preschoolers free.*

The US Naval Academy, in many senses, is Annapolis, and Annapolis is the Academy. The legendary military school, known in many circles simply as "Navy," turns harried, short-haired "plebes" (first-year students) into Naval-officer "middies" (midshipmen) through rigorous drilling and hazing. By graduation rite, each outgoing class leaps into the placid waters of the Severn River. President Jimmy Carter and billionaire H. Ross Perot number among the academy's celebrity alumni, and more recently, the school produced NBA superstar David Robinson. The first stop should be the **Armel-Leftwich Visitors Center,** in the Halsey Field House, which doubles and triples as a food court and hockey rink. Tours include historic Bancroft Hall, the crypt, a dorm room, and the athletic facilities where the middies test their seafaring prowess on land. Visitors also view the original **Tecumseh,** a shiphead carving on the third ship in the United States Navy named after an Indian chief by joking midshipmen. The name stuck, and the icon is now one of the Academy's mascots.

oh l' amour

Freudian Slipping

Like a pubescent rite of passage, first-year "plebes" at the Naval Academy must shimmy on up **Herndon Monument,** a large, imposing obelisk in front of the chapel. At the starting gun's shot, the mob of plebes sprints toward the shaft. The hilariously humiliating event ends only when a hat is snatched off the top of the structure.

Sounds easy, right? But it's not just wham, bam, thank you ma'am: the midshipmen lubricate the massive shaft with over 200 lb. of lard to prolong the event and frustrate the participants. Grunting, sweating plebes attempt to scale the slippery obelisk again and again, growing more passionately intent on their goal with each try. The climactic grasping of the hat is never a quickie: one year, the spectacle lasted over three hours.

Named for George Bancroft, founder of the first Naval school, the **Bancroft Hall** dormitory houses the entire brigade of 4000 midshipmen in an imposing stone structure about three blocks long. In the yard outside Bancroft Hall, visitors can witness the middies' noon lineup and formations. A statue of Tecumseh stands out front; Navy legend has it that landing a penny into his slightly recessed quiver garners good luck. The rest of Bancroft Hall is closed to tourists.

King Hall, the world's largest dining facility, turns into a madhouse at lunchtime, serving the entire student populace in under 20 frenzied minutes. On summer Saturdays, alumni weddings (sometimes 1 per hr.) take place in the Academy's .chapel. Underneath the chapel is the final resting place of **John Paul Jones,** father of the United States Navy, who uttered the famous words, "I have not yet begun to fight!" as he rammed his sinking ship into a British vessel. *(Chapel open to visitors M-Sa 9am-4pm, Su 1-4pm. Often closed Sa in summer for weddings.)* The **Naval Museum** in Preble Hall houses two rooms of naval artifacts, including antique swords, model ships, and the personal belongings of American prisoners of war. *(Open M-Sa 9am-5pm, Su 11am-5pm. Free.)* Throughout the summer, the academy provides entertainment for the public, from parades and sporting events to movies and concerts. A schedule is published in the **Trident,** the academy's newspaper, obtainable at the Visitors Center.

NIGHTLIFE & ENTERTAINMENT

Locals and tourists generally engage in one of two activities: wandering along City Dock or schmoozing 'n' boozing at upscale pubs. Bars and taverns line downtown Annapolis, drawing crowds every night. If you want a little more culture than drink can provide, Annapolis also has a few performance options. For an up-to-date calendar of events, visit www.capitalonline.com/cal_lively.html.

MUSIC & THEATER

Theater-goers can check out **The Colonial Players, Inc.,** 108 East St., for rare and innovative works as well as family-oriented theater festivals. (☎268-7373. Performances and ticket prices vary; call ahead for details.) During the summer, the **Annapolis Summer Garden Theater** offers musical "theater under the stars" Th-Su at 8:30pm. Seating is free on the terraced lawn overlooking an open courtyard theater near the City Dock. (143

Compromise St. ☎268-9212; www.summergarden.com.) The **Naval Academy Band** performs on the City Dock every Tu night at 7:30pm (free). **Ram's Head Tavern** (see below), 33 West St., is the city's big name performance venue, drawing strictly sit-down crowds for acts like Pat McGee Band and comedy performances. (☎268-4545 or call Ticketmaster for tickets. Prices vary.) A looser, more lively time can be had at **Acme Bar and Grill**, 163 Main St., at Church Circle, which hosts smaller bands M-Sa at 9pm and draws a younger crowd. (☎280-6486. Open daily 11:30am-2am.)

BARS & CLUBS

Pusser's Landing, 80 Compromise St. (☎626-0004; www.pussers.com), facing City Dock. As close as you can get to the water without falling in, Pusser's Landing is a working pier with seats practically leaning over the water. Crowds are mixed during the day, but it attracts a more mature clientele at night. Make sure to look up at the impressive British-style tin ceiling while waiting for your food. Pusser's Rum served in magnificent mixes, along with $2-4 beers. Open daily 7am-2am. AmEx/DC/D/MC/V.

Ram's Head Tavern, 33 West St. (☎268-4545; www.ramsheadtavern.com). Beer connoisseurs, midshipmen, and tourists enjoy 135 different ales, lagers, and stouts, including international microbrews, among the beer-history decor. Happy Hour (M-F 4-7pm and after midnight daily) provides free food and reduced prices on drafts ($2). Thick steaks ($16-22) are a popular form of sustenance. Free live music out back on patio many evenings. For bigger-name bands, a dinner and show combination ticket gets you a 10% discount on your meal and a complimentary drink. Open M-Sa 11am-2am, Su 10am-2am.

McGarvey's, 8 Market Space (☎263-5700; www.mcgarveyssaloon.com). A variety of locals and officers pack in under naval pilot-donated helmets and a 2-story Ficus tree growing through this Irish bar. Saddle up to the bar for Aviator Lager, the manliest-sounding beer in town. Parties in the summer invite patrons to dress tropical and enjoy frozen Zombies ($4) with their fish tacos ($5). Happy Hour (M and W 10pm-2am) features buffalo wings for $3-10, 32 oz. drafts for $3, and 10 oz. mugs for $1. Th 6pm-1am house beer $1.50. Open M-Sa 11:30am-2am, Su 10am-2am. AmEx/MC/V.

THE EASTERN SHORE

ST. MICHAELS, MD   ☎410

A former colonial town and maritime center, lovely St. Michaels is ideal for a quiet weekend retreat. St. Michaels was named for its 1677 Episcopal Parish, but is also known as the "town that fooled the British," for its role in the War of 1812. On August 10, 1813, the residents saved the town from a British attack by hanging lanterns in trees and ship masts to trick the Brits as to the town's whereabouts. The subterfuge proved a success, and the only house that was hit is still standing today.

St. Mary's Square, formerly the site of an open-air market established in 1805, now houses the historic St. Mary's Museum. Small boutiques, bed and breakfasts, antique stores, and restaurants saturate the heart of town, which is easily walkable by foot. Neighboring Tilghman's Island and nearby Oxford provide additional destinations to explore while you're in town.

PRACTICAL INFORMATION

Tourist Office: St. Michael's Information Center, Talbot St. at Mill St., is a self-service booth with brochures and information.

Bank: Bank of America, 305 S. Talbot St. (☎800-299-2265 or 745-5066; www.bankofamerica.com). Open M-Th 9am-3pm, F 9am-6pm, Sa 9am-noon.

Internet: Free and easy at **St. Michael's Public Library,** 106 N. Freemont St. (☎745-5877; www.talb.lib.md.us). 1hr. intervals. Hours vary.

the hidden deal

❧ I Dream of Peaches

In high-priced St. Michaels, finding affordable accommodations is nothing less than daunting. ❧ **Peaches and Dreams Bed & Breakfast,** a 19th century mansion in the heart of a 700-tree peach farm, is the light at the end of the tunnel for travelers on a budget. For those willing to travel off the beaten path 15 minutes beyond the periphery of St. Michaels, Peaches and Dreams offers first-class service for a mere $75 per night, with jacuzzi, heated towel racks, white terry bathrobes for two, fridge, large-screen Direct TV, multi-windowed, larger than average rooms with country views, and a forget-lunch breakfast served in the elegant dining room. Find yourself pampered in a quiet retreat after a day of activities in town. Just remember to bring your bug spray—this is, after all, nature in all its glory.

12824 Peach Ln. (☎820-5644; mmpeaches@goeaston.net). Check-in M-F 6pm, Sa-Su 3pm; check-out daily 11am. $75 per night. Open Jan. 3-Dec. 19. ❷

Grocery Store: Acme Markets, 114-116 S. Talbot St. (☎745-9819; www.acmemarkets.com) is the local grocery store chain. Open in summer daily 7am-9pm; off season M-Th and Su 7am-8pm, F-Sa 7am-9pm. AmEx/D/MC/V.

Bicycle Rental: Wheel Doctor Cycle & Sport Inc, 1013 S. Talbot St. (☎800-586-6645 or 745-6676) in St. Michael's Village shopping center, offers sports comfort ($20 per day) and hybrid bikes ($25 per day). Helmet, lock, and 15-40 mi. mapped local routes included. Open Apr. 1-Nov. 30 Th-Tu 9am-5pm. AmEx/MC/V.

Pharmacy: Reeser's Pharmacy, 1013F Talbot St. (☎745-2207), in St. Michael's Village shopping center. Open M-F 8am-6pm, Sa 9am-1pm. MC/V.

Marina: St. Michaels Marina, 305 Mulberry St. (☎800-678-8980 or 745-2400; www.stmichaelsmarina.com), caters to large and small vessels with 50+ slips, fuel, pump-out services, and shower and restroom facilities. Slip reservations highly recommended. Open daily 8am to dusk. AmEx/MC/V.

Emergency: ☎911.

Local Police: St. Michaels Police, 106 S. Talbot St. (☎745-9500, www.stmichaelspd.org), has a 24hr. emergency phone in the lobby. **County Sheriff** ☎822-1020. **Domestic Violence** ☎800-927-4673. **Crime Victims** and their legal rights ☎877-927-4632.

ACCOMMODATIONS

❧ **Hambleton Inn Bed & Breakfast,** 202 Cherry St. (☎866-745-3350 or 745-3350; www.hambletoninn.com), opposite the Patriot Cruise ticket booth. With great prices for a hard-to-come-by harborfront location, the Hambleton Inn has 5 cheery rooms all facing the waterfront. The laid-back couple who own the place are happy to provide advice to tourists. Hot breakfast specialties include peach french toast with walnuts and 4-cheese quiche accompanied by baked peaches and topped with yogurt and granola. M-F $125-175, Sa-Su $185-265. MC/V. ❹

The Old Brick Inn, 401 S. Talbot St. (☎745-3323; www.oldbrickinn.com), near the Post Office. Built in 1816, this inn was recently redone by a couple from North Carolina. Plain and rusty red on the outside leads to fairy-tale splendor on the inside. Go to Aix-en-Provence in the "French Country" room, or travel to Camelot in "Guinevere," complete with a knight in shining armor. 14 rooms. Children 12+ only. Daily wine and cheese social 5-6:30pm. Continental breakfast. Apr.-Nov. M-F $99-250, Sa-Su $125-350. Closed Jan. AmEx/MC/V. ❸

Wades Point Inn On the Bay, end of Wades Point Rd. (☎888-923-3466 or 745-2500; www.wadespoint.com), on the Waterfront. From Rte. 33, drive past downtown St. Michaels towards Tilghman

Island, turn right on Wades Point Rd. and follow it to the end. The pinnacle of shore-front accommodation. Rooms are simple but the indescribable views make up for any imperfections. This family-run inn includes a 1 mi. nature trail on a 120-acre, bayshore lot. Continental breakfast on weekends and full breakfast on weekdays with fresh eggs from the working organic farm. Children 1+ permitted. 3-day cancellation policy. Sa night reservations require a 2-night stay. Check-in 2-8pm; check-out 11am. Rooms $155-245. 10% discount on stays of 3 nights or more, and for seniors 60+ years old. MC/V. ❺

FOOD

Gourmet by the Bay, 415 S. Talbot St. (☎ 745-6260), a carry-out that specializes in gourmet cheese, wine, homemade ice cream, fudge, and sandwiches. This unique and elegant Zabar's-like business is renowned for its picnic baskets for 2 (starting at $20), which must be ordered 2 days in advance. Outside porch seating. Open Th-F and Su-M 9am-7pm, Sa 9am-8pm. Closed Mar. AmEx/MC/V. ❸

The Crab Claw, Navy Point (☎ 745-2900 or 745-9366; www.thecrabclaw.com), is the quintessential fish and chips harbor-hugging restaurant done right. Originally a shucking house in the mid-1940s, today this spotless joint is still run by the same local family. Open 1st fl. deck with serene water views. 2 fl. upstairs, one affording a view of the water through wall-to-wall windows. Casual dress. Free docking for customers. Cash only. ❸

Bistro St. Michaels, 403 S. Talbot St. (☎ 745-9111; www.bistrostmichaels.com), offers continental cuisine in a Gallic inspired decor with French posters, mirrors, and tables. For starters, steamed mussels in garlic broth and spicy wine ($10) are a customer favorite. Fried soft crabs with red bliss potato salad with fennel and a chili, lime, and mint sauce ($26) also comes highly recommended. Dinner entrees $25-30. Seasonal menu and full international wine bar available. Open Th-M 5:30pm-close. Closed Feb. AmEx/DC/D/MC/V. ❺

The Bridge Restaurant, 6136 Tilghman Island Road (☎886-2330). This cozy place along the waterfront is the only restaurant in the area that serves soft shell crabs year-round. Open Apr.-Nov. daily 11am-9pm; hours vary Dec.-Mar. AmEx/DC/D/MC/V. ❸❹

Taste Gourmet Deli, 105 N. Talbot St. (☎745-4100), is ideal for takeout or casual dining, offering burgers ($3.50), sandwiches ($3-6), salads ($4-6), and more. Open daily 7am-7pm. AmEx/MC/V with $10 min. ❶

SIGHTS

The **Chesapeake Bay Maritime Museum** is at Navy Point. Allot roughly 2 hr. to visit this outdoor museum. Highlights include a lighthouse with great aerial views of St. Michaels and its waterfront, an ongoing skipjack restoration project, and an oystering building that highlights the history of oystering in the Bay. (Navy Point. From Talbot St., turn toward the water on Mill St. and take first right on Mill St.; the lane is unnamed. Look for museum sign and drive under the drawbridge. ☎745-2916; www.cbmm.org. Open June 1-Sept. 1 daily 9am-6pm, Oct. 1-Nov. 30 and Mar. 1-Apr. 31 daily 9am-5pm, Dec. 1-Feb. 28 daily 9am-4pm. Adults $9; seniors 62+, AAA members, and college students $8; ages 6-17. $4; under 6 free. AmEx/D/MC/V.)

The Lady Patty, at Tilghman Island, is a restored 1935 45 ft. Bay Ketch yacht that has been to Hawaii, Cuba, and the British Virgin Islands. They offer romantic Champagne Sunset Sails ($40), a two-hour Day Sail ($30), or a narrated Lighthouse Sail (half day $60, full day $120). (From St. Michaels, take Rte. 33 to Knapp's Narrows Marina. The Lady Patty is located in front of the Bay Hundred Restaurant. ☎800-690-5080 or 886-2215; www.sailladypatty.com. Reservations required for special sail trips. AmEx/MC/V.)

Patriot Cruises, berthed at the Chesapeake Bay Maritime Museum, next door to The Crab Claw, offers 1hr. narrative tours of the Mile River daily at 11am, 12:30pm (extra-long 1½hr. tour), 2:30pm, and 4pm. Beer and wine are available at the snack bar on board. (☎745-3100; www.patriotcruises.com. Ticket booth open daily 10am-4pm. $10, children $5. Cash only.)

in recent news

Metro Unfaires

On July 1, 2003, metro fares in Maryland, Washington, D.C., and Virginia went up for the first time in eight years. At least ten transit systems joined the metro fare hike bandwagon, including Baltimore County, furthering the recent national wave of metro fare increases. The metro board committee's plan increased everything from rail and bus fares ($3, or 75 cents extra) to door-to-door service for disabled riders ($2.40, or 20 cents more).

Metro board members argue that the plan is a necessary move to prevent future budget deficit, citing that while costs rise each year, usage is actually decreasing. Supporters address the benefits of the new plan, including longer weekend service, keeping the metro open until 3am instead of 2am.

However, mostly suburban opponents of the plan believe the extra perk of later service will primarily benefit D.C. In addition, the increased parking fees will almost solely affect them, since the majority of Metro's 57,000 spaces are located in the MD and VA suburbs. Opponents are particularly annoyed in the wake of recent revelations that Metro has nearly $8 million in reserves. Despite this opposition, Baltimore residents are grudgingly adjusting to the new higher fares.

—Jennifer Jue-Steuck

SHOPPING

The Mind's Eye Craft Collection, 201 S. Talbot St. (☎745-2023). Art lovers and those who appreciate one-of-a-kind goods will adore this funky, flamboyant store filled with works in every medium, all by independent American and Canadian artists. "Story People" prints ($30) and books ($20) by Iowan Brian Andreas are best-sellers, as are unique 3-dimensional leaf collages ($125-195) by Californian artist Booker Morey. Open Apr.-Dec. Su-M and F 10am-6pm, Sa 10am-7pm; Jan.-Mar. F-Sa 10am-6pm, Su-M 11am-5pm. D/MC/V.

Annabelle, 411 Talbot St. (☎745-0811; www.annabelleshop.com), is a cute new boutique with flair in a cheerful yellow house offering imports from France. An assortment of bags, scarves, wallets, purses, prints, children's clothing, kitchenware, and jewelry. Open W-M 10:30am-5:30pm. MC/V.

Better Days Antiques, 402 S. Talbot St. (☎745-3805). A 2 fl. establishment that stands a head above the antique competition with its large selection of Haviland China oyster plates from 1890 to 1960 ($275-1000) from the UK, France, Austria, Germany, and the US, among other countries. Shoppers beware: although great items can be found, they are on the pricey side. Mar.-Dec. open daily 11am-5pm, Jan.-Feb. W-Su 11am-5pm. MC/V.

ON THE ATLANTIC

LEWES, DE   ☎302

Explored by Henry Hudson and founded in 1613 by the Dutch, Lewes was the first town in the first state and has attracted colonists, pirates, hardy fishermen, and now summer renters. Nevertheless, Lewes (pronounced Lewis) hasn't changed much with the times. Featuring untouched Victorian houses, quiet streets, and a genuine lack of tourist culture, this ferry town has remained old-fashioned for ages. The town has plotted out a walking tour of its colonial attractions, but the main draw remains Lewes's beautiful beach, which draws an older and wealthier vacationing set away from the bustling boardwalk of nearby Rehoboth Beach.

ORIENTATION

Unless you own a private chopper, automobile is the most sensible way to reach Lewes. From points north, Rte. 1 South brings you directly to Lewes and Savannah Rd., which bisects the town. From the west, begin traveling east on Rte. 404, then take Rte. 9 East at Georgetown. This will land you at Rte. 1, where you continue south until Savannah Rd.

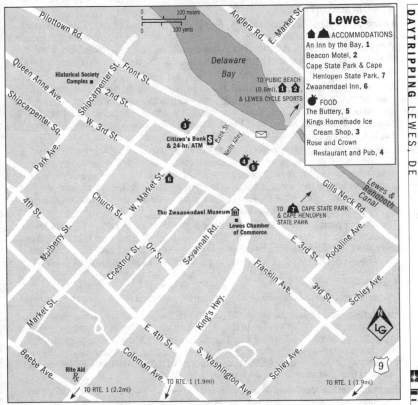

Lewes

🏕 🏕 ACCOMMODATIONS
An Inn by the Bay, **1**
Beacon Motel, **2**
Cape State Park & Cape
  Henlopen State Park, **7**
Zwaanendael Inn, **6**

🍎 FOOD
The Buttery, **5**
Kings Homemade Ice
  Cream Shop, **3**
Rose and Crown
  Restaurant and Pub, **4**

The best public transport option is the **Delaware Resort Transit** (☎800-553-3278) shuttle bus, which runs from the ferry terminal through Lewes to Rehoboth and Dewey Beach (every 30min.; operates late May-early Sept. daily 7am-3am; $1 per ride, seniors and disabled $0.40, day pass $2). **Seaport Taxis** (☎645-6800) will take you door to door anywhere in Lewes for a small fee. Note that the beach is not in town—a bridge separates the two, and it's a long walk to the beach without a car. Thankfully, abundant parking is available at the beach.

PRACTICAL INFORMATION

Tourist Office: Fisher-Martin House Information Center, 120 Kings Hwy. (☎877-465-3937 or 645-8073; www.leweschamber.com), offers everything a tourist would want to know, and then some, in a welcoming wood-shingled house. Ask about their annual garden tours, a crowd-pleaser that draws visitors from around the country. Open M-F 10am-4pm, Sa 9am-3pm, Su 10am-2pm.

Bank: Citizens Bank, 131 2nd St. (☎645-2024, www.citizensbank.com), at Bank St. **ATM.** Open M-Th 9am-4pm, F 9am-6pm, Sa 9am-noon.

Bicycle Rental: Lewes Cycle Sports, 526 Savannah Rd. (☎645-4544; www.oceancy-cles.com), on the ground fl. of the Beacon Motel, provides an ideal method of meandering about town and in nearby **Cape Henlopen State Park.** 1hr. rental $4, 4hr. rental $10, 1 day rental $14, 1 week rental $32. Complimentary helmets and locks. Boogie boards ($8 per day), beach umbrellas ($8 per day), and beach chairs ($6 per day) also available. D/MC/V.

Pharmacy: Rite Aid, 444 Savannah Rd. (☎645-6243). Open M-Sa 9am-9pm, Su 9am-5pm.

ACCOMMODATIONS

An Inn by the Bay, 205 Savannah Rd., (☎866-833-2565 or 644-8878; www.aninnbythe-bay.com), ensures a delightful stay in a Victorian-style home. Those who can afford the master suite have an entire wing of the upstairs to themselves. TV, VCR, A/C, refrigerators, and breakfast buffet. Private and shared baths. Rooms $140-240 during the summer, less expensive during the off season. AmEx/MC/V. ❺

Zwaanendael Inn, 142 2nd St. (☎800-824-8754 or 645-6466; www.zwaanendaelinn.com). From the bustle of Lewes's main thoroughfare, enter this secluded, calm, and classy inn. Be forewarned: location could not be more central, but rooms tend to be on the tighter side. In-house cafe. Check-in 2pm; check-out 11am. Standard twin rooms a reasonable $85-145 (May-Aug.), less during off season. AmEx/MC/V. ❸

Cape State Park, off Rte. 1 (☎877-987-2757 or 645-2103; www.destateparks.com). From the north, bypass Savannah Rd. and continue on Rte. 1 until signs direct you to take a left, which leads to the park. These popular sites feature new restrooms and visitors' facilities and are a short hike to the beach. Campground open Apr.-Nov. Park open all year daily 7am-11pm. Sites $22, with water hookup $24, for out-of-state visitors $2 extra. 8 people max. Parties over 4 require $2 extra per person. Cash only. ❶

The Beacon Motel, 514 E. Savannah Rd. (☎800-735-4888 or 645-4888; www.lewesto-day.com/beacon). This family-friendly, entirely nonsmoking playhouse with tropical motif takes itself less seriously than its neighbors, and proves the best budget establishment in town. Rooms Apr.-Oct. $60-175. Check-in 3pm; check-out 11am. AmEx/D/MC/V. ❷

FOOD

The few restaurants in Lewes cluster primarily on 2nd St. Check out the following:

The Buttery, 2nd St. and Savannah St. (☎645-7755; www.butteryrestaurant.com). Once a sea captain's house (c. 1895), The Buttery is the best spot for fine dining and people-watching on 2nd St. Lunch $7-15, dinner $18-$32. Su brunch (10:30am-2:30pm) includes entree, homemade bread, fruit, and choice of champagne, mimosa, or bloody mary ($18). Items range from standard burgers ($8.50) to rare Rack of Wild Boar with Island Spice Rub ($26). Seasonal menu. Reservations recommended. D/MC/V. ❹❺

Kings Homemade Ice Cream Shops, 201 2nd St. (☎645-9425), is the toast (or should we say "topping") of the town. Voted "Best Ice Cream" in 2003 by *Delaware Today*. 1 scoop $2.25, 2 scoops $3.25. Open May-Oct. daily 11am-11pm. Cash only. ❶

Rose and Crown Restaurant and Pub, 108 2nd St. (☎645-2373, www.roseandcrown.com). Locals come to the Rose and Crown to eat great burgers ($5-7) and jam to live blues and rock every F-Sa 10pm-1am. Happy Hour daily 4-6pm promises $1 discounts on all drinks. Open daily 11am-1am. AmEx/MC/V. ❶

SIGHTS

While the towns on the Eastern Shore pride themselves on their independence from the tourism industry, Lewes is struggling to turn itself into a vacationer's historical playground. Unfortunately, it has few notable historical sites—the real draw of the city is the beach. The modest hub of Lewes lies along 2nd St.

Secluded among sand dunes and scrub pines 1 mi. east of Lewes on the Atlantic Ocean is the 4000-acre **Cape Henlopen State Park.** The family-oriented beach caters to youngsters frolicking in the waves under the watchful eyes of lifeguards, while parents and young couples can soak up the rays from their lawnchairs. First-come, first-serve free bike rentals (2hr. limit; available 9am-3pm) with helmets are available at **Seaside Nature Center,** the park's museum on beach and ocean life, which holds weekly talks on local animals and leads hikes. (☎645-6852. Open daily July-Aug. 9am-5pm, Sept.-June 9am-4pm.) The park is home to sparkling white "walking dunes," a 2mi. paved trail ideal for biking or skating; a tall, well-preserved WWII observation tower; and an expansive, beautiful beach with a bathhouse. (www.destateparks.com. Path open daily 8am-sunset. $5 per car; bikes and walkers free.) The **Zwaanendael Museum,** 102 Kings Hwy., is a bright two-floor space filled with relics of maritime history, including the 1631 Dutch Settlement of Delaware, local light houses, shipwrecks, and the 1812 British attack on Lewes. The museum building itself is, appropriately, a replica of the old town hall in Hoorn, Holland. (☎645-1148; www.destatemuseums.org. Open Tu-Sa 10am-4:30pm, Su 1:30-4:30pm. Free.) The town has gathered some historic buildings into the **Historical Society Complex,** located on Shipcarpenter St. near 2nd St. Among these preserved relics stands the town's oldest surviving home, the Bunton House, built in 1690. (☎645-7670. Open June-Labor Day M-F 10am-4pm, Sa 10am-1pm. $6.)

REHOBOTH BEACH, DE ☎302

Rehoboth Beach lies between Lewes and Ocean City, both geographically and culturally. While Lewes tends to be quiet and family-oriented and Ocean City attracts rowdy underage high-schoolers, Rehoboth manages to balance its discount-board-walk fun with an antique beach cottage ambience. Well-heeled Washington families and a burgeoning gay population constitute the summer crowd, supplemented by daytrippers seeking relaxation away from their more touristy stops. The rambling patios of Rehoboth's bed and breakfasts still outnumber those of its strip motels.

ORIENTATION

Rehoboth lies about six miles south of Lewes. To reach the town from Rte. 1, take Rte. 1B to Rehoboth Ave. and follow it to the water. Don't become discouraged too quickly; you'll drive through some pasture off the exit before reaching the main strip. The vibrant section of town is very concentrated within the beachside boardwalk, so walking is the preferred mode of transportation. If using metered parking, don't press your luck—Rehoboth metermaids are on the prowl, penalizing those who return to their cars just minutes after time has expired.

GETTING THERE & GETTING AROUND

Bus: Greyhound/Trailways, 251 Rehoboth Ave. (☎800-231-2222 or 227-7223), stops next to the Rehoboth Beach Chamber of Commerce. **Buses** go to and from **Baltimore** (5½hr., 1 per day, $32 one-way), **Philadelphia** (4hr., 2 per day, $32 one-way), and **Washington, D.C.** (3½hr., 3 per day, $36 one-way).

Ferry: Cape May-Lewes Ferry (☎800-643-3779 or 644-6030; www.capemaylewes-ferry.com). This ferry to Cape May is the best option for island-hopping. 8 per day. $25 per vehicle, $8 per passenger. Office open daily 8:30am-4:30pm. AmEx/D/MC/V.

Bicycle Rentals: Bob's Bikes, 30 Maryland Ave. (☎227-7966). Single-speed bikes $3 per hr., $9 per day, $30 per week. Multispeed bikes $3.50 per hr., $10 per day, $32 per week. Tandems $6 per hr., $15 per day, $45 per week. Surries available as well. Complimentary helmets, locks, and baskets provided. Open daily 6:30am-5pm May-Sept. Cash only. **Atlantic Cycles,** 18 Wilmington Ave. (☎226-2543). Bike rentals $5 per hr. with complimentary helmets, bags, baskets, childseats, and locks. AmEx/MC/V.

PRACTICAL INFORMATION

Tourist Office: Rehoboth Beach Chamber of Commerce, 501 Rehoboth Ave. (☎800-441-1329 or 227-2233; www.beach-fun.com), a former railroad depot next to an imitation lighthouse, doles out Delaware info, maps, and coupons. Open M-F 9am-5pm, Sa-Su 9am-1pm.

Bank: Wilmington Trust, 70 Rehoboth Ave, near 1st St. **ATM.**

Pharmacy: Rehoboth Pharmacy, 107 Rehoboth Ave. (☎227-8592). Open M-F 9am-5pm, Sa 9am-1pm. AmEx/D/MC/V.

Internet: Java Beach, 56 Baltimore Ave. (☎226-3377 or 227-8418), offers first-come, first-served Internet access at 2 terminals for 30min. ($5, $3.50 with any food purchase) intervals. Open May-Sept. daily 7am-9pm; off-season hours vary. MC/V.

ACCOMMODATIONS

Inexpensive lodgings, mostly charming bed and breakfasts, abound in Rehoboth.

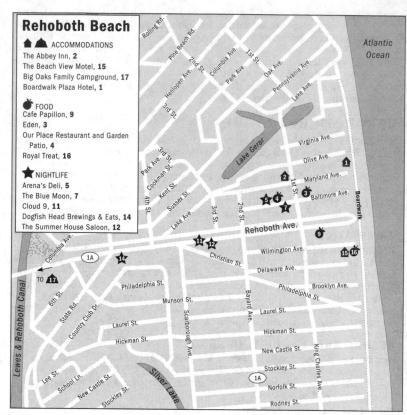

Rehoboth Beach

🏠🏔 ACCOMMODATIONS
The Abbey Inn, **2**
The Beach View Motel, **15**
Big Oaks Family Campground, **17**
Boardwalk Plaza Hotel, **1**

🍎 FOOD
Cafe Papillon, **9**
Eden, **3**
Our Place Restaurant and Garden
Patio, **4**
Royal Treat, **16**

⭐ NIGHTLIFE
Arena's Deli, **5**
The Blue Moon, **7**
Cloud 9, **11**
Dogfish Head Brewings & Eats, **14**
The Summer House Saloon, **12**

Atlantic Ocean

Boardwalk Plaza Hotel, Lewes Boardwalk (☎227-7169; www.boardwalkplaza.com), at Olive Ave. A synthesis of traditonal beach culture and East Coast sensibilities, the Boardwalk Plaza offers one-of-a-kind upscale lodging complete with lobby parrots, Victorian decor, in-house dining, and rooftop and oceanside pool. Most rooms are average-sized. Check-in 3pm; check-out 11am. Complimentary parking. Rooms $59-519 (varies by season). AAA, military, and AARP 10% discount in off-season. AmEx/D/MC/V. ❷

The Abbey Inn, 31 Maryland Ave. (☎227-7023). The Inn is just a street away from the noise of Rehoboth Ave. and always has a conversation waiting on the porch. 2-night minimum stay. Open late May-early Sept. Singles and doubles from $48 with shared bath; triples and quads $61 with shared bath; suite with private bath $105; 15% surcharge on weekends. ❶

The Beach View Motel, 6 Wilmington Ave. (☎800-288-5962 or 227-2999; www.beachview-motel.com). 50 yd. from the boardwalk, the Beach View has the feel of a hotel but the structure of a motel. Clean, nicely decorated rooms with refrigerator, telephone, microwave, continental breakfast, and helpful desk attendants. Rooms facing the pool are less expensive than those facing the ocean. Summer season $139-194; off-season $45-139. Prices change week to week. AmEx/D/MC/V. ❺

Big Oaks Family Campground (☎645-6838), 1 mi. off Rte. 1 on Rd. 270, offers a rugged alternative to town lodging. There's never a dull moment on the grounds, with game rooms, a playground, and planned activities like art contests to pass the time. Shaded sites, a bath-house, and a pool are all available. Sites $32 with or without hook-up. ❶

FOOD

Rehoboth is known for its bargain, high-quality beach cuisine and its bars. If you're in the mood for boardwalk food, stop for **Thrasher's** french fries, **Candy Kitchen's** chocolate, **Fisher's** caramel corn or **Grotto's** pizza simply because they can be found on every block—these DelMarVa traditions are the best junk food around. For more substantial fare, Rehoboth's gentrification has provided other options.

Eden, 23 Baltimore Ave. (☎227-3330; www.edenrestaurant.com), is the haute cuisine destination in Rehoboth. Pastel interior with wall paintings as beautiful as the beach. No jacket-and-tie formality here, but be ready to spend more than you did on all meals combined since coming to town. Baked brie with seasonal fruit and berries $9. "Nearly famous" wasabi and sesame-crusted yellowfin tuna, seaweed salad, and pickled calamari $28. Open daily from 6pm. AmEx/D/MC/V. ❺

Cafe Papillon, 42 Rehoboth Ave. (☎227-7568), in the Penny Lane Mall, offers an authentic European twist to a very American town. French cooks speaking the international language of good food serve fresh crêpes ($2.75-7), croissants ($2-3.50), and stuffed baguette sandwiches ($5-8). Open Apr.-June Sa-Su 8am-11pm, July-Oct. daily 8am-11pm, closed Nov.-Mar. Cash only. ❶

Our Place Restaurant and Garden Patio, 37 Baltimore Ave. (☎227-4143; ourplacergp@aol.com). The warm and inviting atmosphere will make both your stomach and wallet happy. Su brunch 9am-2pm ($9). Su $10 combo platter special. M $10 special entrees. Th $10 Asian noodle night. Open Apr.-June Th-M from 5pm, July-Labor Day Th-Tu from 5pm, Oct.-Dec. and mid-Mar.-Apr Sa-Su from 5pm. AmEx/D/MC/V. ❷

Royal Treat, 4 Wilmington Ave. (☎227-6277). A stack of pancakes and bacon is just $5.90. The line is out the door on most summer mornings, but the food is worth the wait. Royal Treat doubles as an ice cream parlor in the afternoon and evening, catering to traditionalists with an old-fashioned ice cream soda ($4) and genuine Hershey's syrup on hot fudge sundaes ($4). Breakfast served 8-11:30am; ice cream 1-11:30pm. Closed Sept.-May. Cash only. ❶

ENTERTAINMENT & NIGHTLIFE

The congestion on the sparkling **beach** thins to the north of the boardwalk. Early risers will find even the boardwalk beach deserted and may witness the daily southward commute of the dolphins. Party-goers head out early as well, given the 1am last calls. The bar with the best drink special on any given night draws the largest crowd; various locales on Baltimore Ave. are routinely busy during Happy Hour.

The Blue Moon, 35 Baltimore Ave. (☎227-6515). An established hotspot; rocks to the sounds of techno music for a gay-friendly crowd until 1am. Happy Hour M-F 4-6pm offers beer ($0.50) and mixed drink ($1) specials. Su brunch with Bloody Mary bar $17, with mimosa $19. Open daily 4pm-1am. AmEx/DC/D/MC/V.

Cloud 9, 234 Rehoboth Ave. (☎226-1999; www.cloud9restaurant.com). The gay-friendly scene in Rehoboth begins and ends here. DJs spin club rock in its celestial interior. Happy Hour offers $1 off drinks daily 4-7pm, half-price pasta M, buy-one-get-one-free entrees Th. DJ F-M. Open Apr.-Oct. daily 4pm-1am, Nov.-Mar. Th-M 4pm-1am. AmEx/DC/D/MC/V.

The Summer House Saloon, 228 Rehoboth Ave. (☎227-3895; www.summerhousesaloon.com), across from City Hall, is one of Rehoboth's favorite spots to flirt. Young twenty-something crowds take advantage of nightly drink specials and island and hip-hop music. Tropical-prep is the dress of choice. Su 4-8pm ½-priced daiquiris, M 4-11pm half-price 8 oz. burger and reduced-price bucket o' beer night, Th 9:30pm-1:30am live blues rock band, F 9pm-1am live DJ and dancing. Open May 1-Sept. 30 Tu-F 5pm-1am, Sa-M 4pm-1am. AmEx/DC/D/MC/V.

Arena's Deli, 52 Baltimore Ave. (☎227-1272; www.arenasdeli.com), offers drinks and relaxation on a newly installed deck for its predominantly local crowd. Indoors or out, the beer ($3) and create-your-own sandwiches ($5-7) attract a following. Mainly day-drinking venue; not a particularly happening scene late at night. Tu $6 crab cake special. W ½-priced sandwiches and $2 Yuengling drafts. Th Mexican night (¼-priced nachos, tacos $0.75, Mexican beers $2). Happy Hour (M-F 4-8pm) beers $1.50, ¼ lb. steamed shrimp $1.50. W, F, and Sa live music 10pm-close. Su karaoke 8pm-close. Open daily 11am-1am. MC/V.

Dogfish Head Brewings & Eats, 320 Rehoboth Ave. (☎226-2739; www.dogfish.com). Pours inventive house brews like the luscious Buxom Blond Barleywine. Original live music F and Sa 10pm-1am whips up the partying crowds. When music isn't offered, the crowd is less diverse; more tie-dye-style and laid-back. Happy Hour (M-F 4-6pm) means $2 homemade rum and gin drinks. Open May-Aug. M-Th 4pm-midnight, F 4pm-1am, Sa noon-1am, Su noon-11pm; Sept.-Apr. M and Th 4pm-midnight, F 4pm-1am, Sa noon-1am, Su noon-11pm.

OCEAN CITY, MD   ☎410, 443

Ocean City is a lot like a kiddie pool—it's shallow and plastic, but can be a lot of fun if you're the right age, or just in the right mood. This ten-mile strip of prime Atlantic beach packs endless bars, all-you-can-eat buffets, hotels, mini-golf courses, boardwalks, flashing neon, and sun-seeking tourists into a thin region between the ocean and the Assawoman Bay. Tourism is the town's only industry, and Ocean City is not afraid to shake its money-maker. The siren call of senior week beckons droves of recent high school and college graduates to alcohol and hormone-driven fun, turning O.C. into a city-wide block party in June. During this time, there is almost as much of a "balcony scene" as there is a bar scene. Those walking below are bound to be rated—naturally, the fewer the clothes, the better the rating. July and August cater more to families and professional singles looking for easily available and inexpensive fun in the sun.

ORIENTATION

Driving is the most sensible mode of transportation to reach the ocean resort. From the north, simply follow Rte. 1, which becomes Coastal Highway (also known as Philadelphia Ave.). From the west, Rte. 50 also leads directly to Ocean City. If you're trekking to Ocean City from points south, take Rte. 113 to Rte. 50 and follow that to town. Ocean City runs north-south, with numbered streets linking the ocean to the bay. Most hotels are in the lower numbered streets toward the ocean; most clubs and bars are uptown toward the bay.

GETTING THERE & GETTING AROUND

Bus: Trailways (☎800-231-2222 or 289-9307; www.greyhound.com), at 2nd St. and Philadelphia Ave., sends **buses** to **Baltimore** (3½ hr., 3 per day, $32) and **Washington, D.C.** (5hr., 3 per day, $42.50). In town, **public buses** (☎723-1607; www.ococean.com) run the length of the strip and are the best way to get around town 24hr. a day ($2 per day for unlimited rides).

PRACTICAL INFORMATION

Tourist Office: Ocean City Visitors Center, 4001 Coastal Hwy. (☎800-626-2326 or 723-8610; www.ococean.com), at 40th St. in the Convention Center, gives out discount coupons. Open June-Aug. M-F 8:30am-5pm, Sa-Su 9am-5pm; Sept.-May daily 8:30am-5pm.

24hr. Pharmacy: CVS, 1611 N. Philadelphia Ave. (☎289-6512; www.cvs.com), at 17th St. AmEx/DC/D/MC/V.

Internet: E-Point Internet Cafe, 1513 Philadelphia Ave. (☎289-9844; www.epoint-cafe.com), in the 15th St. Shopping Center complex. $2 for 15min. ($1 for students), $3 for 30min. ($2.50 for students), $6 for 1hr. ($4 for students). Cash only. **Ocean City International Student Services,** 304 Baltimore Ave. (☎289-0350), is a boarding house with Internet access available to the public. $2 for 30min., $3 for 1hr. Open Apr.-Oct.

ACCOMMODATIONS

Atlantic House Bed and Breakfast, 501 N. Baltimore Ave. (☎289-2333; www.atlantic-house.com), offers free bike rentals, full breakfast buffet, great location, and a wholesome change of pace from the Ocean City motel trend. A/C, cable TV, hot tub, parking. Compli-

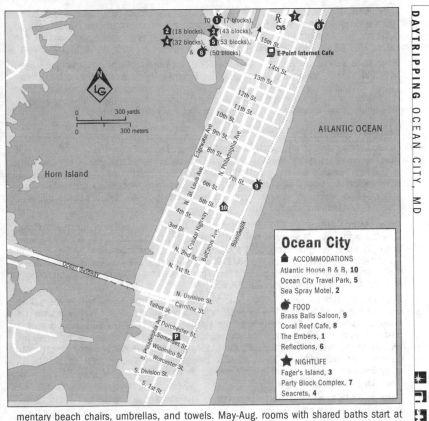

Ocean City

🛏 ACCOMMODATIONS

Atlantic House B & B, **10**
Ocean City Travel Park, **5**
Sea Spray Motel, **2**

🍴 FOOD

Brass Balls Saloon, **9**
Coral Reef Cafe, **8**
The Embers, **1**
Reflections, **6**

⭐ NIGHTLIFE

Fager's Island, **3**
Party Block Complex, **7**
Seacrets, **4**

mentary beach chairs, umbrellas, and towels. May-Aug. rooms with shared baths start at $80, with private bath $110-185. Rates drop in the off-season. Closed Dec.-Mar. except for Valentine's Day. D/MC/V. ❸

Sea Spray Motel, 12 35th St. (☎800-678-5702 or 289-6648; www.seaspraymotel.com), sports a dark wood interior and copious amenities just a half block from the beach. Some rooms have kitchens and porches; all rooms offer cable TV and A/C. Gas grill access, laundry facilities. Rooms June-Sept. $80-175. D/MC/V. ❸

Ocean City Travel Park, 105 70th St. (☎524-7601; www.occamping.com), runs the only in-town campground. Tents $27-54; RVs $32-69. AmEx/MC/V. ❶

FOOD

Ocean City's cuisine is plentiful and cheap. Don't expect gourmet quality, because you won't find any food meeting such high standards.

Reflections, 6600 Coastal Hwy. (☎524-5252), at 67th St., on the ground fl. of the Holiday Inn. Try Reflections for tableside cooking and fine dining, classic Las Vegas style. Dinner 5-10:30pm daily. Reservations recommended. Early Bird dinner entrees $10-19 (must be seated by 6pm); regular entrees start at $20. AmEx/D/MC/V. ❹

Coral Reef Cafe, 1701 Atlantic Ave. (☎289-6388; www.ocsuites.com), on the boardwalk at 17th St. For a little something that can't be found at 2am and isn't listed on a take-out menu glued to the back of a magnet, try the healthier and trendier food at Coral Reef. Crab dip with toasted focaccia ($10) and the New Orleans chicken wrap with mozzarella and homemade spicy cream cheese ($9) are just a couple of specialities worth the extra money. June-Sept. open daily 7am-10pm, Oct.-May daily 7am-9pm. AmEx/D/MC/V. ❷

The Embers, 24th St. and Coastal Hwy. (☎888-436-2377 or 289-3322; www.embers.com). With freshly caught food and a friendly atmosphere, the Embers boasts the biggest seafood buffet in town. All the clams, oysters, Alaskan crablegs, prime rib, steak, and more you can eat are $26, $2 off before 5pm (with coupon only). Open daily 3-10pm. AmEx/D/MC/V. ❺

Brass Balls Saloon, The Boardwalk (☎289-0069; www.brassballssaloon.com.on), between 11th and 12th St. Saunter up to this seaside saloon known for its $1.25 jello shots (after 10pm). The motto here is "Drink Hearty, Eat Healthy." Breakfast specials like the Oreo waffles ($5.25) or the $7 pizzas seem to defy the latter imperative, though the college crowds can't get enough of the "drink hearty" part. Open Mar.-Oct. daily 8:30am-2am. ❶

ENTERTAINMENT

Ocean City's star attraction is its beautiful **beach.** The wide stretch of surf and sand runs the entire ten miles worth of town and can be accessed by taking a left onto any of the numerous side streets off Philadelphia and Baltimore Ave. The breaking waves know no time constraints, but beach-goers are technically limited to 6am-10pm. When the sun goes down, hard-earned tans glow under the glaring lights of Ocean City's bars and nightclubs.

Fager's Island, 60th St. (☎524-5500), in the bay. The elder statesman of the bayside clubs, Fager's Island attracts hordes to walk the plank to its island location. Live rock, R&B, jazz, and reggae play nightly to accompany the 100+ beers. No one seems to know the source of the classical music tradition, but the *1812 Overture* booms at every sunset. Start the week at the M night deck party til 2am (6pm $5, after 7pm $10). Happy Hour Tu-F with ½-price drinks and appetizers. Open daily 11am-2am. AmEx/D/MC/V.

Seacrets, on 49th St. (☎524-4900; www.seacrets.com). Professional party-goers will no doubt be impressed by this virtual entertainment mecca and amusement park for adults. This island oasis, located, oddly enough, on the Maryland Shore, features 10 bars, including 2 floating bars on the bay. Barefoot partyers wander from bar to bar, sipping the signature frozen rum runner mixed with piña colada ($6) to the strains of live bands nightly. 9pm reggae band at the beach daily May-Sept., followed by alternating live rock and DJ after 10pm. A magnificent sunset view ushers in early revelers for cocktails in the raft pool. Cover $5-20. Open daily 11am-2am. AmEx/D/MC/V.

Party Block Complex, 17th St. and Coastal Hwy. A new addition to the Ocean City scene. Party Block's patrons pay one cover to flirt between 4 different clubs, from the laid-back Oasis Bar to the flashy Rush Club.

CHINCOTEAGUE, VA ☎757

In the 1600s, Chincoteague and neighboring Assateague Island were inhabited by the Chincoteague people, a subgroup of the larger, multitudinous Assateague Native American tribe. By the mid-1700s, however, most had left the area due to treaties gone sour and resulting conflict between the tribes and European settlers. By the 1800s, the population consisted of roughly 200 inhabitants, and in the first quarter of the 1900s, most had left Assateague for its more lively counterpart, Chincoteague, in part because one stubborn Assateague resident hired a cowboy to shoot any audacious neighbor who dared to cross his land to fish.

Chincoteague and Assateague attract over a million visitors every year. The rugged landscape, large assortment of wildlife and birds, outdoor activities and sports in a rural setting are enough to entice most. But what really sets the two apart from other islands in the area are the more than 150 wild ponies who parade freely around Assateague, grazing lazily in the meadows and meandering along the shore. When you cross the bridge from Chincoteague to Assateague, don't expect the ponies to magically appear when you want them to; you're not in a zoo. But just about when you're sure the island is a farce, and the ponies nothing more than a fiction promulgated by *Let's Go*, you will see the pastoral image of a quietly assembled herd on the horizon. The ponies swim from Assateague to Chincoteague during pony penning, held every year on the last Wednesday in July.

ORIENTATION

Unless you come by boat, the easiest way to reach Chincoteague is by car. From D.C., take Rte. 50 East to Salisbury, MD, then take Rte. 13 South and turn left onto Rte. 175 East. After you cross a small bridge, turn left at the light and you'll be on **Main St.** in the heart of Chincoteague. Chincoteague's main thoroughfares are Main St. and Maddox Blvd. As you enter town, turn left on Main St. to reach **Maddox Blvd.**, which will take you to **Assateague** and the Wildlife Refuge. While the town is easily explored by car, many prefer to bike both in town and in the area around Assateague.

GETTING AROUND

Taxi: Yellow Cab (☎460-0605), $1.75 plus $1.60 per mi. 24hr. service. **Action Taxi & Sedan Service** ☎460-2034. **Beach Taxi** ☎486-4304. **James Taxi Service** ☎437-2123.

Car Rental: Rent-A-Ride, 5007 Lankford Hwy., New Church, VA (☎824-4888). Daily, weekly, and weekend rates. Open M-F 8am-5pm, Sa 8am-noon.

Bicycle and Boat Rental: Bike Depot & Beach Outfitters, 7058 Maddox Blvd. (☎336-5511). Single speed bikes $3 per hr., $10 per day. **Oyster Bay Outfitters,** 6332 Maddox Blvd. (☎336-0070; www.OysterBayOutfitters.com), provides kayak rental ($10 per hr., $25 per 4hr., $40 per 24hr., $150 per week) and bike rental ($3 per hr., $10 per day). Guided kayak tours include sunrise/sunset tours ($40), moonlight tours ($40), and half-day ($60) and full-day ($80) tours. Discounts for groups of 8+. Open May-Oct. daily 10am-5pm. AmEx/D/MC/V.

PRACTICAL INFORMATION

Tourist Office: Chincoteague Chamber of Commerce, 6733 Maddox Blvd. (☎336-6161; www.chincoteague.com). Open M-Sa 9am-4:30pm.

Bank: Shore Bank, 6350 Maddox Blvd. (☎336-3144; www.shorebank.com). Open M-Th 9am-4pm, F 9am-6pm. **ATM.**

Internet: Chincoteague Island Library, 4077 Main St. (☎336-3460). Free Internet access permitted for 30min. intervals. Bring ID to use Internet. Printing $0.20 per page. Open Apr.-Nov. M, W, and F 1-5pm; Tu 10am-5pm; Th 4-8pm.

Grocery Store: Family Pride, 6277 Cleveland St. (☎336-5829), at Main St. Open Memorial Day-Labor Day daily 6am-midnight. AmEx/D/MC/V. **Wine, Cheese & More,** 4103 Main St. (☎336-2610). For gifts, unique wines, imported cheese, pastas, olives, and a new Chincoteague Wild Pony Wine in red, blush, and white ($18 per bottle). Open Mar.-Dec. daily 10am-8pm. D/MC/V.

the hidden deal

Poplar Corner & Watson House

The connected ⬛ **Inn at Poplar Corner & The Watson House Bed & Breakfast** are without doubt the best deal in town. Though Chincoteague establishments charge more reasonable rates than nearby tourist destinations, these two sister B&Bs are ahead of the competition when it comes to value. *Anne of Green Gables*-like Victorian decor, spotless rooms, dining and living quarters, and inviting, cozy bedrooms engender peaceful stays that complement the enjoy-this-moment spirit of the island. Full, hot breakfast on winding porches with water views, free bicycle rentals with baskets, beach towels and chairs, binoculars, and umbrellas are the icing on the cake.

4240 Main St. (☎800-336-6787 or 336-1564; www.poplarcorner.com; www.watsonhouse.com). Check-in 2-10pm; check-out 11am. Rates start in summer at $79 per night. 5% AAA discount. MC/V. ❸

Emergency: ☎911.

Pharmacy: H&H Pharmacy, 6300 Maddox Blvd. (☎336-3115; www.hhpharmacy.com). Open June-Aug. M-Sa 9am-9pm, Su 9am-6pm; Sept.-May M-Sa 9am-8pm. D/MC/V.

ACCOMMODATIONS

Hampton Inn & Suites, 4179 Main St. (☎336-1616; www.hamptoninnchincoteague.com), the newest lodging establishment in town and sure to razzle and dazzle jaded souls. The Hilton inn has an added bonus: reasonable rates for luxury accommodations starting at $139 June-Aug., and free breakfast 6-10am in a sun-flooded, open lounge on the waterfront. 10% AAA, AARP discount. AmEx/D/MC/V. ❺

Island Motor Inn, 4391 Main St. (☎336-3141; www.islandmotorinn.com). A waterfront establishment with great attention to detail, including a lovingly decorated lobby. Breathtaking views. Suites and rooms available in 2 adjacent buildings. Check-in 4pm; check-out 11am. Rates start at $125 in June, higher in July and Aug. 10% AAA and senior (62+) discount off-season. AmEx/D/MC/V. ❹

Maddox Family Campground, 6742 Maddox Blvd. (☎336-3111 or 336-6648). Large and sprawling campsite just across from the Visitor Center and down the road from Assateague. Ideal, convenient location. Check-in 8am-11pm only; check-out 4pm. For full hookups, reserve at least 3 months in advance. $27.13 for tent per night. For water and electric, reserve at least 1 month in advance. D/MC/V. ❶

FOOD

Main St. Shop & Coffee House, 4288 Main St. (☎336-6782; www.mainstreet-shop.com). From Main St., drive away from the mainland, turn right on Maddox Blvd., then make an immediate right into the parking lot. Offers coffee, light fare, books, original paintings, and more in a hip SoHo-esque atmostphere transplanted to rural Chincoteague. Open Easter-Labor Day daily 8:30am-5pm, Labor Day-Thanksgiving Sa-Su 8:30am-5pm. D/MC/V. ❶

AJ's On the Creek, 6585 Maddox Blvd. (☎336-5888; www.chincoteague.com/restaurants/ajs), specializes in handcut steaks and grilled fish. Dinner entrees $15-25. Happy Hour (5-7pm) offers $0.25 off domestic beer and rail drinks. Open in summer M-Sa 11am-10pm; in winter M-F 4-9pm, Sa 4-9:30pm. Lounge open daily 4pm-2am. AmEx/DC/D/MC/V. ❸

SIGHTS

CHINCOTEAGUE NATIONAL WILDLIFE REFUGE. This is the central attraction here. Go to the Visitor Center, located just inside the refuge, to learn about biking, hiking, walking, and bird and nature tours. Guided wildlife bus tours are also available ($12, kids $8; Memorial Day-Labor Day daily 10am, 1, 4pm). Trails include a 3.2 mi. Wildlife Loop (open 3pm to dusk for cars, all day for pedestrians and bicyclists), a 1.6 mi. Woodland Trail (cars not permitted), and a ¼-mi. Lighthouse Trail (pedestrians only). Follow Beach Rd. to its end to find the endless beach and sand dunes. Park rangers request that visitors resist the urge to feed the ponies, who, if overfed by guests, could potentially starve in the winter months when visitors have left the islands. *(8231 Beach Rd. ☎800-828-1140, 800-828-1120, or 336-6122; www.fws.gov. Absolutely no pets permitted ("not even in your car") due to previous pet tragedies. Open June-Aug. daily 9am-5pm.)*

OYSTER & MARITIME MUSEUM. This museum is the only non-profit museum in Chincoteague, a small but quaint musuem containing numerous samples of sea creatures and shells. Don't miss the 1865 *Barbier & Fenestre* first order Fresnel lens from the old Assateague Lighthouse, one of only 21 in the US; retired in 1961, its light could be seen from 23 mi. away. Beside it lies a much smaller sixth order lens from Ft. Washington, on the Potomac. *(7125 Maddox Blvd. ☎336-6117. Open May-Sept. M-Sa 10am-5pm, Su noon-4pm; off-season hours vary. $3, children 12 and under $1.50. Cash only.)*

CHINCOTEAGUE PONY CENTRE. The Pony Centre offers pony rides (M-Sa 9am-1pm and 3:30-6pm, Su 1-4pm) and showcases veterans of the pony swim. *(6417 Carriage Dr. ☎336-2776; www.chincoteague.com/ponycentre. After you drive over the bridge to the enter Chincoteague, turn left on Main St., followed by a right on Church St.; make a left onto Chicken City Rd., followed by a right onto Carriage Dr. Open in the summer M-Sa 9am-10pm, Su 1-9pm.)*

VIRGINIA BEACH

Virginia's largest city, once the capital of the cruising collegiate crowd, is now gradually shedding its playground image and maturing into a family-oriented vacation spot. As with its nearby neighbors Norfolk, Newport News, and Hampton, the streets of this former Spring Break mecca now welcome parents and their baby carriages alongside tipsy 20-somethings. Fast-food joints, motels, and cheap discount stores (hallmarks of every beach town) still abound, but culture now penetrates this plastic veneer. For nearly 50 years, the Virginia Beach Boardwalk Arts Festival has been a summer highlight for two weeks each June. The festival features artists, musicians, and food vendors from all across the country. Virginia Beach is distinguished from its East Coast counterparts by beautiful ocean sunrises, a substantial dolphin population, and frequent military jet flyovers.

ORIENTATION

Virginia Beach is easy to get to and easy to get around. The shortest route from D.C. follows I-64 east from Richmond through the perpetually congested Hampton Roads Bridge-Tunnel into Norfolk. At Norfolk, turn onto I-264 (the Virginia Beach-Norfolk Expwy.), which leads straight to 22nd St. and the beach. Alternatively, avoid the Hampton Roads Bridge-Tunnel by getting off I-64 East at I-664. Take I-664 to I-64 West via the Monitor-Merrimac Bridge-Tunnel. From I-64W, get off on Rte. 264 and follow it to the beach. From the northern coast (near Ocean City, MD), take Rte. 13 South across the scenic 20-mile Chesapeake Bay Bridge Tunnel (toll $10). Follow Rte. 60 East into the Virginia Beach resort community.

In Virginia Beach's busy beachfront neighborhoods, east-west streets are numbered and the north-south avenues, running parallel to the beach, have ocean names. Prepare to feel like a thimble on a Monopoly board: **Atlantic** and **Pacific Ave.** comprise the main drag. **Arctic, Baltic,** and **Mediterranean Ave.** are farther inland. Virginia Beach uses a 10-digit phone number, so be sure to dial 757 before every local number.

GETTING THERE

Trains: Amtrak (☎ 800-872-7245 or 245-3589; www.amtrak.com). The nearest train station, in Newport News, runs 45min. bus service to and from the corner of 19th and Pacific St. Call ahead to reserve your train ticket. To Newport News from: **Baltimore,** (7hr., $58); **New York City,** (9hr., $83-115); **Philadelphia,** (8hr., $68-90); **Richmond,** (2hr., $30-33); **Washington, D.C.,** (6hr., $53-62); and **Williamsburg** (2hr., $26-28).

Buses: Greyhound, 1017 Laskin Rd. (☎ 800-231-2222 or 422-2998; www.greyhound.com), station open M-Sa 7am-11am and 12:30-7pm. Connects with Maryland via the Bridge-Tunnel. ½mi. from the oceanfront area. From: **Richmond** (3¼hr., $18); **Washington, D.C.** (5½hr., $31.50); and **Williamsburg** (2¼hr., $17.50). **Hampton Roads Regional Transit (HRT)** (☎ 800-700-7433 or 222-6100; www.hrttransit.com), in the Silverleaf Commuter Center at Holland Rd. and Independence Blvd., runs buses that connect Virginia Beach with Norfolk, Portsmouth, and Newport News ($1.50, under 18 $1, seniors and disabled with ID $0.75, children under 38 in. free).

GETTING AROUND

Public Transportation: Virginia Beach Transit/Trolley Information Center (☎ 437-4768; www.vbwave.com), Atlantic Ave. and 24th St. Info on area transportation and tours, including trolleys, buses, and ferries. Trolleys transport riders to most major points in Virginia Beach. The Atlantic Avenue Trolley runs from Rudee Inlet to 42nd St. Open May-Sept. daily 8am-2am. Fare $1, seniors and disabled $0.25, kids under 38 in. free; passes 3-day $5, 5-day $8. Other trolleys run along the boardwalk, the North Seashore, and to Lynnhaven Mall.

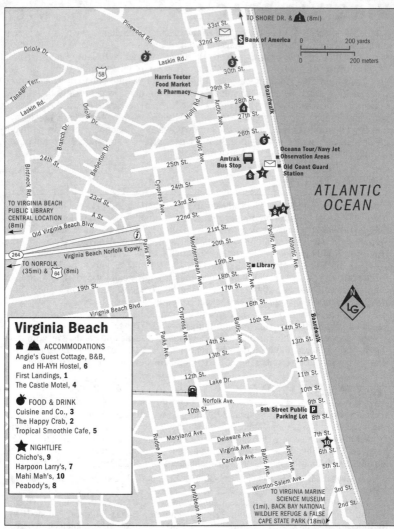

Virginia Beach

🏠 🏕 ACCOMMODATIONS

Angie's Guest Cottage, B&B, and HI-AYH Hostel, **6**
First Landings, **1**
The Castle Motel, **4**

🍴 FOOD & DRINK

Cuisine and Co., **3**
The Happy Crab, **2**
Tropical Smoothie Cafe, **5**

⭐ NIGHTLIFE

Chicho's, **9**
Harpoon Larry's, **7**
Mahi Mah's, **10**
Peabody's, **8**

Car Rental: All national companies have offices in Virginia Beach, and some, like **Enterprise Rent-A-Car,** 3269 Virginia Beach Blvd. (☎800-325-8007 or 486-7700; www.enterprise.com), will make hotel pickups within a 10 mi. radius. 30min. notice required. Open M-F 8am-6pm, Sa 9am-1pm, Su noon-4pm.

Bike Rental: RK's Surf Shop, 305 16th St. (☎428-7363), in addition to aquatic equipment, rents bikes for $4 per hr. or $16 per day. Open June-Sept. daily 9am-10pm, Oct.-May 11am-6pm; bikes must be returned 2hr. before closing. **Sandbridge Eco Sports,** 577 Sandbridge Rd. (☎800-695-4212 or 721-6210, www.OceanRentalsLtd.com). Coming from the boardwalk headed to the Back Bay Refuge and False Cape State Park, you'll see it on the right side of the Sandbridge Rd. Open May-Dec. daily, closed Jan.-Feb., hours vary Mar.-May. MC/V.

Taxi: Yellow Cab (☎460-0605). Base fare $1.75, plus $1.84 per mi. Open 24hr. **Beach Taxi** (☎486-4304). **James Taxi Service** (☎437-2123; www.jamestaxiservice.com).

PRACTICAL INFORMATION

Tourist Office: Virginia Beach Visitors Center, 2100 Parks Ave. (☎800-822-3224 or 491-7866; www.vbfunc.om), at 22nd St. Info on budget accommodations and area sights. Helpful, knowledgeable staff. Open daily 9am-8pm; Sept.-May 9am-5pm.

Bank: Bank of America, 210 Laskin Rd. (☎491-6010; www.bankofamerica.com). Open M-Th 9am-5pm, F 9am-6pm.

Library and Internet: Virginia Beach Public Library, 4100 Virginia Beach Blvd. (☎431-3000; http://vbgov.com/libraries). Free Internet access. Printing $0.15 per page. Open M-Th 10am-9pm, F-Sa 10am-5pm; Oct.-May also Su 1-5pm. Cash only. **WebCity Cybercafe,** 116 S. Independence Blvd. (☎490-8690; www.webcitycybercafe.com), exit 17B off I-264. $5 for 30min. Open M-Th 11am-10pm, F-Sa 11am-11pm, Su 1-9pm. MC/V.

Emergency: ☎911.

Pharmacy: Harris Teeter Food Market and Pharmacy, 2800 Artic Ave. (☎422-4595; www.harristecter.com). Store open 24hr. Pharmacy open M-Sa 9am-7pm and Su 12-6pm.

ACCOMMODATIONS

As might be expected with any ocean resort, a string of endless motels lines the waterfront in Virginia Beach. Oceanside, Atlantic, and Pacific Ave. buzz with activity during the summer and boast the most desirable hotels. If you reserve in advance, rates are as low as $45 in winter and $65 in summer. However, be prepared to pay 12.5% sales tax—watch your room total jump $10 at the touch of a button.

▧ **Angie's Guest Cottage, Bed and Breakfast, and HI-AYH Hostel,** 302 24th St. (☎428-4690; www.angiescottage.com). Filled with friendly staff, numerous bunk beds, and plenty of boogie boards in a prime area of town—only one block from the oceanfront. Barbara "Angie" Yates and her personable staff welcome predominantly young international and American guests with exceptional warmth, discounted trolley tokens, and great advice about the beach scene. Kitchen, lockers available. Linen $2. No A/C. Open Apr. 1-Sept. 30. Reservations recommended. 2-day min. stay for private rooms. Check-in 9am-9pm; check-out 9:30-10am. 4-9 person dorms $19.80, HI-AYH members $16.45; off-season $15, members $12. Private rooms $36, 2 people $24 per person, substantially less in off-season. MC/V. ❶

First Landings, 2500 Shore Dr. (☎800-933-7275 or 412-2300 for reservations; www.dcr.state.va.us), about 8 mi. north of town on Rte. 60. Travel north on Atlantic, bear left at the fork, at which point Atlantic becomes Shore Dr.; follow signs and turn right into the campsite section of the park. In the State Park bearing the same name, beachfront sites thrive on the natural beauty of Virginia's shore. Because of its desirable location amid sand dunes and cypress trees, the park is very popular; call at least 11 months ahead (during business hours) for reservations. The park features picnic areas, a private swimming area on a sprawling beach, a bathhouse, and boat launching areas. Cabin rates Apr.-May and Sept.-Nov. $65-75 per night, June-Aug. $85-95 per night. AmEx/MC/V. ❸

The Castle Motel, 2700 Pacific Ave. (☎425-9330), is quite possibly the best bang for your buck as far as motels go. Spacious, clean rooms come with cable TV, refrigerator, shower and bath, desk, and two full beds. The beach is just 2 blocks away. Check-out 11am. 21+. Rates start at $69 on weekdays, $99 weekends. Open May-Oct. D/MC/V. ❷

FOOD

Prepare for the greatest preponderance of greasy $6 all-you-can-eat breakfast specials outside Las Vegas. Alternatively, fish for a restaurant on **Atlantic Ave.,** where each block is a virtual buffet of fried, fatty, sweet, or creamy dining options.

Tropical Smoothie Cafe, 211 25th St. (☎422-3970; www.tropicalsmoothie.com). This new location is part of the burgeoning chain's recent growth. Smooth and silky smoothies ($3-5), medium-sized, healthy wraps ($5), and fresh salads ($4-5) served in a nondescript setting one block from the oceanfront. Open daily 9am-11pm. MC/V. ❶

Cuisine and Co., 3004 Pacific Ave. (☎428-6700; www.cuisineandcompany.com). This sophisticated escape serves gourmet lunches and rich desserts. Treats include creamy tuna melts ($5), a chunky chicken salad ($5.50), and decadent cookies ($8 per lb.). Open M-Sa 9am-7pm, Su 9am-6pm between Labor Day-Memorial Day. AmEx/D/MC/V. ❶

The Happy Crab, 550 Laskin Rd. (☎437-9200). Don't be intimidated by the massive crab carving on the wall or get entangled in the hanging fishing nets. Dine on the screened porch overlooking a small harbor. Early-bird specials (daily 5-6:30pm) offer unbeatable seafood platters ($25) or huge 1-person servings big enough to split, like sumptuous ribs ($15). Deal for 2: 2 house salads, steamed bucket of clams, oysters, crablegs, shrimp, mussels, with either blue crabs ($36) or 2 whole lobsters ($51). Open Mar.-Sept. M-Th 11am-10pm, F-Su 11am-11pm; winter hours vary. AmEx/D/MC/V. ❸

SIGHTS

The **beach and boardwalk,** jam-packed with college revelers, bikini-clad sunbathers, and an increasing number of families, is the raison d'être at Virginia Beach. Unlike similar surf-wise coastal destinations in Maryland, however, Virginia Beach provides more than a commercial, splashy boardwalk. If you're willing to drive, the environs surrounding the oceanfront offer an enticing diversion.

BACK BAY NATIONAL WILDLIFE REFUGE

🚩 *Location: Take General Booth Blvd. to Princess Anne Dr.; turn left, then turn left onto Sandbridge Rd. and continue approximately 6 mi. Turn right onto Sandpiper Rd., which leads directly to the Visitors Center.* **Be careful driving** *as Sandbridge and Sandpiper Rd. are narrow.* **Contact:** *☎721-2412; www.backbay.fws.gov.* **Hours:** *Visitors Center open M-F 8am-4pm, Sa-Su 9am-4pm. Closed Sa Dec.-Mar.* **Admission:** *$5 per car, $2 per family on foot or bike.* **Transportation:** *Tram daily 9am, return at 12:45pm; trams run by volunteers (☎721-7666 or 498-2473, www.bbrf.org); $6, seniors and under 12 $4; disabled visitors must reserve 48hr. in advance; cash only.*

Bathing suits are swapped for hiking boots at the Back Bay National Wildlife Refuge, which is bordered by the saltwater of the Atlantic Ocean on one side and the freshwater of the Back Bay on the other. Composed of islands, dunes, forests, marsh, ponds, and beaches, this remote but pristine national refuge is a sanctuary for an array of endangered species and other wildlife. With nesting bald eagles and peregrine falcons, the natural wonderland is open to the public for camping, hiking, fishing, and photography, and features a four-hour tram tour departing daily at 9am from **Little Island City Park** up the road. The Visitors Center offers a taste of the wild with captivating stuffed bird exhibits.

FALSE CAPE STATE PARK

🚩 *Location: 4001 Sandpiper Rd.* **Contact:** *☎426-7128 or 800-933-7275, 888-669-8368 or 480-1999 for tours; www.dcr.state.va.us/parks.* **Admission:** *Campsites $9; reservations necessary.*

False Cape State Park got its name because back in the day (around the 17th century or so) ships used to touch shore there, mistakenly thinking that they had landed at the nearby Cape Henry (where America's first English settlers landed in 1607). This happened so often, in fact, that the shores of False Cape eventually become a common docking place for large ships that had lost their way.

The Back Bay tram stops at False Cape State Park, where walkers trek one mile to the beach. Because there is no vehicular access to the park, a visit to False Cape gives you the opportunity to explore some of the most well-preserved natural habitats on the Atlantic coast. If you tarry and miss the 9am daily tram, prepare for an adventurous four-mile hike or canoe ride, as foot and water are the only ways to get where you want to go. Primitive campsites are available. **Kayak Eco Tours** offers kayak excursions to these areas (see **Sandbridge Eco Sports,** above).

VIRGINIA MARINE SCIENCE MUSEUM

▶ Location: *717 General Booth Blvd.* **Contact:** ☎ *425-6010, excursions 437-2628; www.vmsm.com.* **Hours:** *Daily 9am-7pm; off-season 9am-5pm.* **Admission:** *$11, seniors $10, ages 4-11 $7. IMAX tickets $7.25, seniors $6.75, ages 4-11 $6.25. Combined museum and IMAX admission $16, seniors $13, ages 4-11 $10. Excursion trips $12, ages 4-11 $10.* **Accessibility:** *Handicapped accessible.*

Located a one-mile drive or 30min. walk south down Pacific Ave. (which becomes General Booth Blvd.), the **Virginia Marine Science Museum** houses Virginia's largest aquarium and is home to hundreds of species of fish, including crowd-pleasing sharks and stingrays. Kids can get friendly with harbor seals right outside the entrance or at the museum's two touch pools. Brush up on salt marsh life at the **Owls Creek Marsh Pavilion** or during a pontoon boat ride (40min., $3, June-Aug. only). The museum also houses a six-story IMAX theater (8 screenings daily) and offers excursion trips for dolphin observation in summer and whale watching in winter.

NAVY JET OBSERVATION AREAS

▶ Contact: ☎ *433-3131; www.hrtransit.org.* **Tours:** *2hr. tours leave June-Sept. M-F 9:30, 11:30am.* **Admission:** *$10, under 12 and 62+ $8. Photo ID required to enter base.*

The frequent roar of F-14 and Tomcat engines will remind you of the navy bases nearby. For those who want a closer view of the air dynamics, the city maintains two observation areas of the base, both of which are about ten miles from town. One is off Oceana Blvd., south of Southern Blvd. and right before the turn-off to the base, and the other, a better view—300 ft. from a runway—is off London Bridge Rd.

NIGHTLIFE

On summer nights, the Virginia Beach boardwalk becomes a haunt for lovers and teenagers, and **Atlantic Ave.**, a.k.a. "Beach Street, USA," burgeons with street performers. Rousing jazz and classic rock can be heard every other block. Larger outdoor venues at 7th, 17th, and 24th St. draw bigger names and bigger crowds. (☎ 440-6628 for more info. Free. Schedules for the main events are posted along the street.)

Mahi Mah's, 615 Atlantic Ave. (☎ 437-8030; www.mahimahs.com), at 7th St. inside the Ramada Hotel. Sushi, live music, tiki parties, and oceanfront views. Wine "flights" offered W 5-9pm: choose 4 tastes ($2 each) from a selection of whites and reds. Mouth-watering sushi ($6 rolls 11am-5pm, bigger menu after 5pm; fall and winter only). Well-dressed crowd. Outdoor band nightly. Open daily 7am-1am. AmEx/D/MC/V.

Chicho's, 2112 Atlantic Ave. (☎ 422-6011; www.chichos.com), on "The Block" of closet-sized college bars clustered between 21st and 22nd St. One of the hottest spots on the hot spot strip features gooey pizza dished out from the front window ($2.25-3.25 per slice), tropical mixed drinks ($5-7), and live rock 'n' roll music M. Open May-Sept. W-Su noon-2am, M-Tu 6pm-2am May-Sept; Oct.-Apr. M-F 6pm-2am and Sa-Su noon-2am. AmEx/D/MC/V.

Harpoon Larry's, 216 24th St. (☎ 422-6000; www.harpoonlarrys.com), at Pacific Ave., 1 block from the HI-AYH hostel, serves tasty fish in an everyone-knows-your-name atmosphere. The amicable bartender and manager welcome 20- and 30-somethings to escape the sweat and raging hormones of "The Block." Nightly drink specials make it easy to drink lots and spend little. Specials include crab cakes ($7) and rum runners (Tu $2). W $1.50 Coronas with $0.25 jalapeño poppers. Happy Hour (M-F 7-9pm) offers $1 domestic drafts and $2 rail drinks. Open May-Sept. daily noon-2am; off-season hours vary. AmEx/MC/V.

Peabody's, 209 21st St. (☎ 422-6212; www.peabodysvirginiabeach.com). A young, scantily-clad crowd bops to Top 40 hits, especially during Peabody's "Hammertime" when drinks are only $1.50 (daily 7-9pm). All-you-can-eat fresh crab legs and shrimp ($13). Aside from the intense dance scene, Peabody's scores big with the fresh-faced crowd on its themed nights: Ladies Night Th, when women drink for almost nothing, College Night F (free admission with college ID during Happy Hour 7-9pm), and Bash at the Beach Sa featuring karaoke and a laser light dance party. Cover $5; pool $1. Open Th-Sa 7pm-2am. MC/V.

NORFOLK ☎757

Just west of the popular summer resort of Virginia Beach lies its less glamorous cousin, Norfolk. This city has a history of being the underdog: it was so mercilessly bombarded by cannon fire during the Revolutionary War that locals called it "Chimney Town." The infamous Monitor-Merrimac Civil War battle was also fought on its waters, and FDR deemed the city unsightly enough to make it the first in the nation to receive urban renewal funding. Today, after extensive renovations beginning in 1974, "Nawfuk" still looks like a work in progress, but gentrification is quickly spilling into areas other than downtown. Well-cared for historical buildings clash with old industrial buildings that need more than just another coat of paint. And though the waterfront and surrounding few blocks provide a beautiful setting for a long walk on a nice day, the farther away from the water you go, the less you feel like walking anywhere but back to your hotel. Perhaps most notably, Norfolk houses the United States' largest naval base and the mammoth anchor of the city's waterfront, the National Maritime Center.

ORIENTATION

Norfolk is easily accessible from points north. From the Maryland Eastern Shore area, take the scenic Chesapeake Bay Bridge Tunnel (Rte.13) to I-64 East. After entering Norfolk, connect to I-264 West. Take the Waterside Dr. Exit and follow to the waterfront. From northern Virginia, follow I-64 East over the Hampton Roads Bridge-Tunnel, which leads to I-264 West and the Waterside Dr. Exit. From Virginia Beach, use 22nd St., which becomes I-264 West. I-264 leads to the Waterside Dr. Exit. From points east and west, use I-64 and I-264, respectively, to reach the Waterside Dr. Exit.

Within the downtown area, **Waterside Dr.** runs along the waterfront and the Elizabeth River. Flanked by Monticello Ave. to the west and St. Paul's Blvd. to the east, the enormous **MacArthur Center** marks the middle of the city. Running from east to west and completing the square around the MacArthur Center are **Freemason St.** to the north and **City Hall Ave.** to the south.

GETTING THERE & GETTING AROUND

Flights: Norfolk International Airport (☎857-3351).

Buses: Greyhound, 201 Monticello Ave. (☎800-231-2222 or 625-7500; www.greyhound.com), serves downtown Norfolk from **Philadelphia** (7-8 hr., weekdays $50-105) and **Washington, D.C.** (4½-5hr., $32.50).

Public Transportation: Hampton Roads Transit System (☎222-6000; www.hrtransit.org). $1.50, 18 and under $1; 10-ride farecard $10, 7-day unlimited ride card $13 (good on ferries). Operator open M-F 7:30am-5pm.

Taxi: Norfolk Checker Taxi (☎855-3333; www.norfolkcheckertaxi.com). $1.75 per mi. **Yellow Cab** (☎622-3232, www.landcars.com), $1.75 per mi.

PRACTICAL INFORMATION

Visitors Center: Norfolk Visitors Bureau, 232 E. Main St. (☎664-6620; www.norfolkcvb.com), offers maps, dining and shopping guides, and a dose of Southern charm. Look for their walking counterparts (Public Safety Ambassadors) in the streets, wearing white safari hats, for any questions, advice, or directions. Open M-F 8:30am-5pm.

Bank: Bank of America, 821 Hampton Blvd. (☎800-299-2265 or 451-2377; www.bankofamerica.com), at International Blvd. Open M-F 9am-4pm. **ATM,** 8594 Tidewater Dr.

Library and Internet: Norfolk Public Library, Larchmont Branch, 6525 Hampton Blvd. (☎664-7323, www.npl.lib.va.us). Open M and W 10am-8pm, Tu and Th-F 10am-5:30pm, Sa 10am-5pm.

Emergency: ☎911.

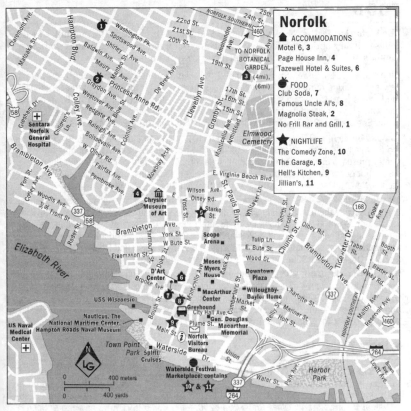

Norfolk

🏠 ACCOMMODATIONS
Motel 6, **3**
Page House Inn, **4**
Tazewell Hotel & Suites, **6**

🍴 FOOD
Club Soda, **7**
Famous Uncle Al's, **8**
Magnolia Steak, **2**
No Frill Bar and Grill, **1**

⭐ NIGHTLIFE
The Comedy Zone, **10**
The Garage, **5**
Hell's Kitchen, **9**
Jillian's, **11**

State Police: ☎ 424-6820. **Coast Guard:** ☎ 484-8192. **Physicians Referral Service:** ☎ 800-736-8272. **Traveler's Aid:** ☎ 622-7017.

24hr. Pharmacy: Rite Aid, 525 W. 21st St. (☎ 625-6073; www.riteaid.com).

ACCOMMODATIONS

Norfolk offers a number of inviting bed and breakfasts, although cheaper accommodations are available in nearby Virginia Beach.

🛏 **Page House Inn,** 323 Fairfax Ave. (800-599-7659 or 625-5033; www.pagehouseinn.com), in the historic and picture-perfect Ghent district. Gargantuan and memorable living, dining, and parlor areas, but some rooms in the only 4 diamond establishment in town will probably fail to produce the same awe. The marvelous location with views of Smith Creek sits literally across the street from the renowned Chrysler Museum of Art. Breakfast consists of omelette, strawberry-banana smoothies, yogurt parfaits, meat of the day, and bread. Homemade cookies 2-9pm daily. Free parking on premises. Check-in 2-9pm, check-out 11am. Rooms $130-250. AmEx/MC/V. ❺

Tazewell Hotel & Suites, 245 Granby St. (☎ 623-6200; www.thetazewell.com), a recently renovated, centrally located hotel from 1906. Spotless, medium-sized rooms and a modern earth-toned lobby with sedans, cathedral ceilings, and gold-painted ionic columns. Check-in 3pm, check-out noon. Rooms $99-160. AmEx/DC/D/MC/V. ❸

Motel 6, 853 Military Hwy. (☎ 800-466-8356 or 461-2380; www.motel6.com). From I-95 South, take Exit 281, "Military Highway" and it's on the right. Standard and clean (but impersonal) rooms with A/C and cable TV. Check-out noon. Rates $51-60. AmEx/D/MC/V. ❷

FOOD

The **Waterside Festival Marketplace,** 333 Waterside Dr., is home to the bulk of Norfolk's culinary options. Infiltrated by businessmen on lunch break and vacationing families, the Marketplace offers an eclectic array of choices.

Club Soda, 111 Tazewell St. (☎200-7632; www.liquidassetsrestaurants.com), provides a new and relaxing retreat in an elegant, *feng-shui* mixed with minimalism atmosphere with food locals love. Curvaceous and multidimensional design, dim lighting from floor, ceiling, and walls, white cresent moon-shaped booths, green suede bar chairs, brick walls, and wine cellar. Entrees $15-24. Dinner M-Th 5-10pm, F-Sa 5-11pm, Su 5-9pm. AmEx/D/MC/V. ❹

Famous Uncle Al's, 216 Granby St. (☎625-8319), has been a downtown Norfolk lunch staple for nearly 20 years. Everyone feels like family amid the classic sports photography and homey presence of owner Brian "Uncle Al" Calabrito. Cheap eats include the daily lunch special: 2 hot dogs, fries, and a drink ($5.15). Not quite as famous but equally mouth-watering are the New York sausages ($2.39). Open M-Sa 8am-3pm. MC/V. ❶

Magnolia Steak, 749 W. Princess Anne Rd. (☎625-0400; www.magnoliasteak.com), prides itself on serving the finest quality steaks, seafood, pastas, and salads in the area. Providing its customers with a taste of high society Southern living, the exquisite dining room features a fireplace, matching rich wood tables and armchairs, hand-carved banisters, and stunning flower arrangements. Outdoor patio, extensive wine and beer list, and full service bar. Entrees $15-28. Open M-F 11:30am-2am, Sa-Su 5pm-2am. AmEx/MC/V. ❹

No Frill Bar and Grill, 806 Spotswood Ave. (☎627-4262; www.nofrillgrill.com), serves dependably good Americana at reasonable prices. The large menu includes grilled pitas ($6-8), hearty soups ($3-6), and rich desserts, allowing customers a full scope of health foods and indulgences. In the front, the heated patio is a perfect place for Su brunch, no matter the season. Open M-Th 10am-10pm, F-Sa 10am-11pm, Su 11am-3pm. AmEx/MC/V. ❷

SIGHTS

CHRYSLER MUSEUM OF ART. This museum showcases Tiffany lamps, Warhol, and Matisse. Be sure to see the priceless Japanese screens and samurai clothing, in addition to the stunning white marble sculptures of figures from Abe Lincoln to Zeus in the Neoclassical Room. *(245 W. Olney Rd. ☎664-6200, tours 664-6269; www.chrysler.org. Open W 10am-9pm, Th-Sa 10am-5pm, Su 1-5pm. $7; AAA $6; students, seniors, teachers, military $5; children under 12 free. Free W. Handicapped accessible; Combo tickets for the Museum and Houses $10, 65+, students, and teachers $6, 12 and under free. AmEx/D/MC/V.)*

CHRYSLER MUSEUM OF ART'S HISTORIC HOUSES. This relatively unknown trove of gorgeous Georgian architecture is conveniently located adjacent to the Macarthur Center. In "Norfolk's Secret Garden," programs teach children about the medicinal powers of herbs and flowers at the **Willoughby-Baylor House,** 601 E. Freemason St., an excellent example of an upper-middle class family dwelling from the 1800s. The **Moses Myers House,** 331 Bank St., built c.1792-1797, was originally the home of an aspiring Jewish couple who moved from New York City to Norfolk in the late 1700s in search of greater religious tolerance. The house remained in the family until it was sold to a colonial housing corporation in 1931, and thus remains magnificently preserved. The federal-style home contains about 70% of the family furnishings, and includes original cornice moldings, a London triple box lock, family portraits by Gilbert Stuart (the artist whose portrait of George Washington is on the dollar bill), an original piano, cradle, and kitchen. *(☎333-1085. Both houses open W-Sa 10am-5pm, Su 1-5pm. Tours every hour; last tour 4pm. $5; AAA $4; students, seniors, teachers, and military $3; children under 12 free. Free W.)*

D'ART CENTER. A mecca for art lovers interested in unconventional museums, this working studio center houses two floors of painters, jewelers, glass workers, potters, and even calligraphers who create, display, and sell their work. The center will soon move to the Selden Arcade; please call or check the website for new location info. *(Selden Arcade. ☎625-4211; www.d-artcenter.org. Open Tu-Sa 10am-6pm, Su 1-5pm. Free.)*

NORFOLK'S BOTANICAL GARDEN. Grows artwork of the natural kind and boasts 155 acres of Virginia's most beauteous blooms. Twelve miles of pedestrian pathways allow visitors to weave their way through gardens of all types including colonial, Japanese, butterfly, Renaissance, and rose. Boat ($3) and trackless train tours are free with admission. *(6700 Azalea Garden Rd.* ☎*441-5830; www.norfolkbotanicalgarden.org. Open daily Apr. 15-Oct. 15 9am-7pm, Oct 16-Apr. 14 9am-5pm. $6, seniors $5, 16 and under $4, 5 and under free.)*

NAUTICUS. Located on the second and third floors of the National Maritime Center, Nauticus promotes itself as a maritime science center with an educational twist. Visitors may feel overwhelmed by the museum's 150 exhibits, which range from virtual-reality shark petting to playing simulated underwater video games. *The Living Sea,* the museum's permanent movie, airs periodically throughout the day, explaining the link between science, technology, and the power of the sea. The *Top Gun* "Hornet's Nest" simulator lets its users pilot a jet in a secret reconnaissance mission. After catching the daily shark feeding (10:30am), climb aboard **USS Wisconsin,** the largest and last battleship ever built by the US Navy, which saw combat in WWII, the Korean War, and Desert Storm. *(1 Waterside Dr.* ☎*800-664-1080 or 664-1000; www.nauticus.org. Open May-Sept. daily 10am-6pm; Sept.-May Tu-Sa 10am-5pm, Su noon-5pm. $10; military, AAA, seniors $9; children $7.50. USS Wisconsin audio tours $5, $3 with purchase of Nauticus ticket. Handicapped accessible.)*

NIGHTLIFE & ENTERTAINMENT

Norfolk's flourishing waterfront rules the city's bar scene. Night owls flock to the **Waterside Festival Marketplace,** which houses several bars all within convenient range of each other. Aside from this concentration of nightlife, party-seekers can opt for less scenic revelry a few blocks inland at a Granby St. bar.

🦀 **Hell's Kitchen,** 124 Granby St. (☎624-1906; www.hknorfolk.com). Inspired by the Manhattan neighborhood, this gangster-themed joint sports *Reservoir Dogs* and *Smokin' Blues* paraphernalia, movie clips on a flat-screen TV, and rock 'n' roll music. The brick walls, high ceiling, and dark atmosphere make for a nearly convincing Big Apple aura. Crab cakes $19, handcut steaks $17, veggie burgers $7. Entrees ($6-21) come with choice of 2 sides. Happy Hour (M-F 5-8pm) offers $2 domestic brews. Open daily 11am-2pm. AmEx/MC/V.

Jillian's, 333 Waterside Dr. (☎624-9100), on the 2nd fl. of the Marketplace, excites adults who revisit their childhood while simultaneously testing their hand-eye coordination in the enormous game room. The entire complex is so big that you need a map to make your way around. Pretend it's the big high school dance (but with beer $3-4.25) at Mojo, where the best 70s, 80s, and 90s dance music thumps all night long F-Sa. Live Bait, the new, outside raw bar has live bands May-Aug., weather permitting; call for schedule. *Sake* bar, hibachi grill, 40 ft. cocktail area overlooking the water, 6 pool tables, pinball machines, and live jazz. Cover $5. W night free-for-all special: 21+ $10 (under 21 $15) gets you unlimited game card and access to every club. Open M-Th 11am-1am, F-Sa 11am-2am, Su 11am-midnight. AmEx/D/MC/V.

The Garage, 731 Granby St. (☎623-0303; www.thegarage.com), an immensely popular Leather and Levi's cruise bar welcomes a gay crowd to rock to Top 40 dance hits (Tu, Th-Sa). Happy Hour daily 3-8pm. M turn out your pockets for loose change to feast on $0.20 shrimp and 3-for-$1 oysters. Tu tacos, W spaghetti, and Th prime rib. Open daily 2pm-2am. MC/V.

The Comedy Zone, 333 Waterside Dr. (☎627-4242; norfolkcomedyzone.com), provides an inexpensive way to kick back, relax, and take in a few laughs while visiting this strict military town. The club hosts national and local acts, including spotlight performances by well-known comedians like Jay Mohr. Shows Th, Su 8pm ($5), F-Sa 8 and 10pm ($10). AmEx/MC/V.

YORKTOWN

British troops led by General Charles Lord Cornwallis seized Yorktown for use as a port during the Revolutionary War in 1781. The British were left stranded, however, when 17,000 American and French infantry surrounded them while the French fleet blocked the British Navy's rescue attempt. The British surrender at Yorktown was a shock to the world and marked the end of the Revolutionary War.

YORKTOWN VICTORY CENTER

71 Location: *1 block from Rte. 17 on Rte. 238. Follow the Colonial Parkway east; the Victory Center is right off the parkway and very well marked.* **Contact:** ☎ *888-593-4682 or 887-1776; www.historyisfun.org.* **Hours:** *June 15-Aug. 15 daily 9am-6pm; other times daily 9am-5pm.* **Admission:** *$8.25, ages 6-12 $4.75. 10% AAA, seniors discount.* **Accessibility:** *Fully handicapped accessible.*

Brush up on your high school history at this paean to the 1781 Battle of Yorktown, in which George Washington defeated Charles Cornwallis, forcing a British surrender. The gripping 18-minute orientation film, shown at 15 and 45 minutes past every hour, depicts battle scenes that may be too graphic for children. Audio narratives scattered around the indoor exhibition focus on the often overlooked perspectives of women, slaves, and Native Americans. Fascinating artifacts abound, many of which were recovered from sunken ships. Upon exiting the museum, journey through the **Continental Encampment** like those that housed General George Washington's army on the eve of victory. Witness demonstrations by colonial doctors, artillery handlers, and army musicians. Moving ahead on the time line, the **1780s Farm Site** shows how many Virginians lived during the years immediately following the Revolution. Watch as a housewife preserves her family's food by pickling the vegetables and salting the meat. Learn how onion skin, pumpkin, and even the remains of mashed prickly pear cactus beetles were once used to dye fabrics. There is a daily cannon firing at approximately 2:35pm, weather permitting; ask for details.

JAMES RIVER PLANTATIONS

Built along the James River, America's first Main St., the James River Plantations housed Virginia's slaveholding aristocracy. Exhibits focus on plantation life, tobacco farming, and slavery, and include beautiful, expansive grounds perfect for picnicking. The majority are widely dispersed off Rte. 5, so plan your day accordingly.

BERKELEY PLANTATION. Touted as the most historical plantation on the James River, Berkeley Plantation witnessed the birth of short-term president William Henry Harrison, whose father, Benjamin, had refounded the plantation after it was abandoned in 1669. Historians trace the first "official" Thanksgiving dinner in 1619 and the first distilling of Bourbon whiskey in 1726 back to the gorgeous grounds of the still-occupied plantation, where the first ten presidents enjoyed Harrison's hospitality. When Union soldiers camped on the premises in 1862, a somber Yankee composed the bugle tune "Taps," now a military mourning mainstay. Today, the plantation memorializes the Civil War with an 1862 cannonball permanently embedded in a brick outbuilding. With the James River winding behind it, springing flowers in the ladies' Winter Garden, and a well-preserved 17th-century house, Berkeley Plantation exudes a historical aura aesthetically superior to its James River counterparts. Yet, like the Shirley Plantation, the house is still occupied, and public access is restricted to the first floor. *(Halfway between Richmond and Williamsburg on Rte. 5. From Colonial Williamsburg, take Jamestown Rd. and follow signs west to Rte. 5 for approximately 40 mi. ☎ 804-829-6018; www.berkeleyplantation.com. Open daily 9am-5pm. $10, ages 13-16 $7.50, ages 6-12 $5, under 6 free. Grounds only $6, ages 6-16 $3.50, under 6 free. 10% senior, AAA, and military discount.)*

SHIRLEY PLANTATION. Surviving war after war in colonial times, this 1613 plantation encompasses 800 acres and a gorgeous Queen Anne-style mansion unrivaled in beauty by other area estates. Unless you feel comfortable imposing on aristocrats, don't plan on penetrating the lavish walls of the brick mansion occupied by the 10th and 11th generations of the Hill-Carter family. One notable family member, born and raised at Shirley, was Ann Hill-Carter, the mother of General Robert E. Lee. Over 50% of the furniture is original to the family. The house survived the Civil War due to the kindness of a family member who supported wounded Union troops discovered one morning in front of the house. After hearing news of this deed, General McClellan sent an official order to his troops to protect the house from harm. Highlights include running water facilities installed in the dining room in the late 1700s. The only one of its kind in America, a three-story "floating" staircase spirals up from the ground floor, seemingly devoid of any support. The staircase is unfortunately off-limits: public access is restricted to the first floor. *(West of Berkeley on Rte. 5.* ☎ *800-232-1613; www.shirleyplantation.com. House open daily 9am-5pm, grounds 9am-6pm; closed Jan.-Feb. M-F. $10.50, ages 13-21 $7, under 6 free. Seniors, AAA, and military discount.)*

WILLIAMSBURG   ☎ 757

After its colonial prosperity, Williamsburg fell upon hard economic times until philanthropist John D. Rockefeller, Jr., restored a large chunk of the historic district, now known as **Colonial Williamsburg,** in the 1920s. Nowadays a fife-and-drum corps marches down the streets, and costumed wheelwrights, bookbinders, and blacksmiths go about their tasks using 200-year-old methods on old gas station sites. Travelers who visit in late fall or early spring will avoid the crowds, heat, and humidity of summer. However, they will also miss the extensive array of special summer programs, such as the July 4th artillery demonstration and outdoor colonial dancing. December visitors will find an array of charming colonial Christmas activities.

ORIENTATION

Williamsburg lies some 50 mi. southeast of Richmond between Jamestown (10 mi. away) and Yorktown (14 mi. away). The **Colonial Parkway,** which connects the three towns, has no commercial buildings and is a beautiful route between historic destinations. Take I-64 and the Colonial Parkway exit to reach Colonial Williamsburg.

PRACTICAL INFORMATION

GETTING THERE

Flights: Newport News and Williamsburg International Airport, 20min. away in Newport News with frequent connections to Dulles Airport by United Express and U.S. Airways. Take state road 199 West to I-64 South.

Trains: Amtrak (☎ 800-872-7245 or 229-8750; www.amtrak.com). From: **Baltimore** (5hr., 1 per day, $48-57); **Philadelphia** (6hr., 1 per day, $64); **New York** (7½-8hr., 1 per day, $81); **Richmond** (1hr., 1 per day, $22-23); and **Washington, D.C.** (3½hr., 2 per day, $41-48). Open daily 7:30am-10pm.

Buses: Greyhound (☎ 800-231-2222 or 229-1460; www.greyhound.com). From: **Baltimore** (via D.C.; 6-7hr., 3 per day, $52); **Norfolk** (1-2hr., 8 per day, $14.75); **Richmond** (1hr., 8 per day, $9.50); **Virginia Beach** (2½hr., 7 per day, $18.75); and **Washington, D.C.** (3-4hr., 8 per day, $45.50). Ticket office open M-F 8am-noon and 1-5pm, Sa 8am-noon and 1-2pm.

Transportation Center, 408 N. Boundary St., behind the fire station, houses offices for Amtrak, Greyhound, and taxi service.

GETTING AROUND

Public Transportation: James City County Transit (JCCT; ☎ 259-4093; www.williamsburgtransport.com). Bus service along Rte. 60, from Merchants Sq. west to Williamsburg Pottery or east past Busch Gardens. Operates M-Sa 6:30am-6:20pm. $1 plus $0.25 per zone change. **Williamsburg Shuttle** (R&R) provides service between Colonial Williamsburg, **Water Country USA,** and **Busch Gardens** every 30min. May 25-Sept. 3 daily 9am-10pm. All-day pass $2.

Taxi: Yellow Cab (☎ 245-7777). 24hr. $3.25 for the 1st mi., $1.50 each additional mi. AmEx/D/MC/V. **Williamsburg Limousine Service** (☎ 877-0279). Shuttle service to airports only. $22.50 to Newport News; $65 to Norfolk. Cash only.

the hidden deal

Bryant Guest House

In a town filled with sights and activities, a stay at Williamsburg's ✂ **Bryant Guest House** will help you go home with without empty pockets. In a lovely neighborhood at the edge of the College of William and Mary, this stately, exquisitely landscaped brick home offers four clean rooms with private bath. Perks include a casual sitting room with full-sized refrigerator for guests, on-street parking, and a friendly owner.

From Scotland Rd., turn right onto Richmond Rd.; turn left onto Dillard St. and you'll come face to face with the door. *702 College Terr.* ☎ *229-3320. Reservations recommended. Singles $35; doubles $45; 5-person suite $75. Cash only.* ❶

Car Rental: Colonial (☎220-3399; www.colonialrentacar.com), in the Transportation Center. $32-95 per day. 21+. Open M-F 8am-5pm, Sa 8am-2pm, Su 8am-noon. Credit card with $250 min. available balance required. AmEx/D/MC/V.

Bike Rental: Bikes Unlimited, 759 Scotland St. (☎229-4620), rents 21-speed bikes for $7.50 per hr. or $15 per day (includes lock). Open Tu-F 9:30am-6:30pm, Sa 10am-5pm, Su noon-4pm (Su Apr.-Oct. only). AmEx/D/MC/V.

PRACTICAL INFORMATION

Visitor Information: Williamsburg Area Convention And Visitors Bureau, 201 Penniman Rd. (☎253-0192; www.visitwilliamsburg.com), ½ mi. northwest of the Transportation Center. Provides the free *Visitor's Guide to Virginia's Historic Triangle.* Open M-F 8:30am-5pm. **Colonial Williamsburg Visitors Center,** 100 Visitors Center Dr. (☎800-447-8679 or 229-1000; www.colonialwilliamsburg.com), 1 mi. northeast of the Transport Center. Tickets and transportation to Colonial Williamsburg. Maps and guides to historic district, including a guide for the disabled. Info on discounts for Virginia sights. Open daily 8:30am-7pm; winter hours vary.

Emergency: ☎911.

ACCOMMODATIONS

The hotels operated by the **Colonial Williamsburg Foundation** are generally more expensive than other lodgings in the area. **Rte. 60 West** and **Rte. 31 South** are packed with budget motels, which grow cheaper the farther they are from the historic district. At the various bed and breakfasts around William and Mary, guests pay more for gorgeous colonial decor. Guest houses don't serve breakfast, but still offer a bed, a reasonable price, abounding warmth, and "like-home" feelings.

Liberty Rose, 1022 Jamestown Rd. (☎253-1260). For those who can afford it, this B&B will invite your romantic side to indulge. Victorian fancies in a colonial town—with red chairs, carpets, a working fireplace, an elegant staircase filled with paintings and portraits, intimate, plant-filled breakfast sun room, circular driveway, and attention to every detail—have collectively earned this establishment a 4 diamond AAA rating for 10 consecutive years, and accolades such as being designated one of the top 10 most romantic B&Bs in America by *America's Historic Inns.* The major street it dwells on is the only drawback; luckily, the house sits back from the road, loft-like, and protected by forest on 3 sides. Check-in 3pm; check-out 11am. Rates start at $185 per night. AmEx/D/MC/V. ❺

Colonial Gardens B&B, 1109 Jamestown Rd. (☎800-886-9715 or 220-8087; www.colonial-gardens.com), tucked in the woods just 5min. from Colo-

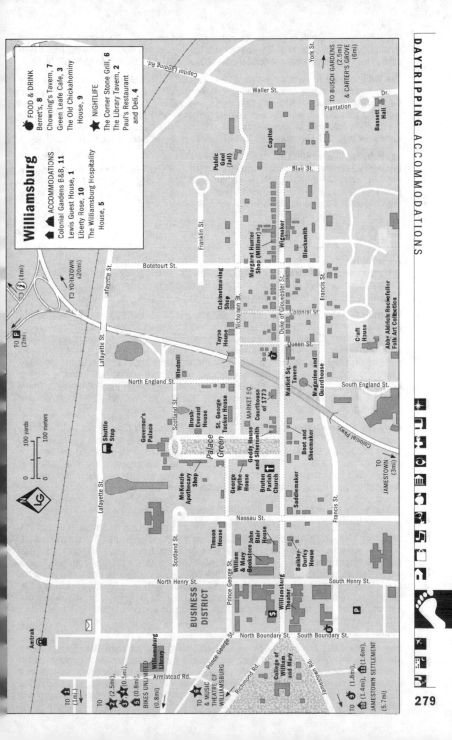

Williamsburg

ACCOMMODATIONS
Colonial Gardens B&B, 11
Lewis Guest House, 1
Liberty Rose, 10
The Williamsburg Hospitality House, 5

🍴 **FOOD & DRINK**
Berret's, 8
Chowning's Tavern, 7
Green Leafe Cafe, 3
The Old Chickahominy House, 9

★ **NIGHTLIFE**
The Corner Stone Grill, 6
The Library Tavern, 2
Paul's Restaurant and Deli, 4

nial Williamsburg. Exquisite gardens, astounding artwork created by the owners, full breakfast, gourmet pillow treats, private parking, and a warm and inviting atmosphere make this B&B a relaxing and luxurious stay. Check-in 4-6pm; check-out 11am. Rates $125-165. AmEx/D/MC/V. ●

The Williamsburg Hospitality House, 415 Richmond Rd. (☎229-4020; www.williamsburg-hosphouse.com), across from the College of William and Mary and within walking distance of Colonial Williamsburg, features elegant rooms and suites for affordable prices. The building looks like an old brick mansion with colorful gardens and a lovely seating area surrounding the pool; the rooms are lavishly decorated and include all necessary amenities as well as gym access. Rooms $79-180; suites $275-475, rates vary by season. AmEx/DC/D/MC/V. ❸

Lewis Guest House, 809 Lafayette St. (☎229-6116), a 10min. walk from the historic district, rents 2 comfortable rooms, including an upstairs unit with private entrance, kitchen, partial A/C, and shared bath. Undoubtedly the most homey lodging in the area. The ageless proprietor, Mrs. Lewis, reminisces about 1930s Williamsburg while her adorable dog, Brandy, clips at your heels. Rooms $25-35. Cash only. ●

FOOD

As steeply priced as admission to Colonial Williamsburg, the loosely scattered "taverns" are tourist traps to be avoided by the savvy budget traveler. Save your wallet some trouble and head to these local eateries for some mouth-watering Virginia ham and international cuisine.

The Old Chickahominy House, 1211 Jamestown Rd. (☎229-4689), 1½ mi. from the historic district on the Williamsburg-Jamestown border. 2 fl. of antiques, dried-flower decor, and pewter-haired locals dine amid colonial splendor. The affordable menu belies the elegant 18th-century dining room, lined with original colonial portraits. For breakfast, enjoy a plate of Miss Melinda's pancakes with a side of smoked bacon ($8). Later on in the day, Becky's "complete luncheon" includes Virginia ham, hot biscuits, fruit salad, a slice of homemade pie, and iced tea or coffee ($7). Vegetarians might have difficulty finding a meal here. Open M-F 8:30-10:30am and 11:30am-2:30pm, Sa-Su 8:30-10am and 11:45am-2pm. MC/V. ●

Chowning's Tavern, Duke of Gloucester St. (☎220-7012; http://intranetcwf.org), within the grounds of Colonial Williamsburg. Quasi-historical dishes like "Ploughman's Pastie" (roasted turkey and melted cheddar cheese in a flaky pastry with tavern slaw, $7.25) will have you chowing down like George Washington (probably even better, assuming you don't have wooden teeth). For dessert, the Cider Cake is worth the caloric overload. After 9pm, peanuts are at stake as patrons roll the dice against their servers. The merriment continues as costumed waiters sing 18th-century ballads and challenge guests to card games over light meals ($3.50-5.50). Cover $3. Open daily 11am-10pm. MC/V. ❷

Berret's, 199 S. Boundary St. (☎253-1847), located at Merchant's Square (Colonial Williamsburg's shopping district). This popular establishment combines 2 restaurants in 1: the less expensive and more casual **Tap House Grill,** and the pricey and more formal **Berret's Restaurant and Bar.** During the school year, both places are popular choices among visiting parents looking to provide their college-aged kids with one less meal in the dining hall. Start off a spending binge at the Restaurant with baked escargot ($8), then try the Virginia ham and crabmeat combination ($24). 2 light and airy, nicely decorated dining rooms, both with terrace seating options. Live music on terrace Su 6-9pm in summer. Tap House open daily from 4pm. Restaurant and bar open daily 11:30am-3pm and 5:30-10pm. AmEx/MC/V. ❹

Green Leafe Cafe, 765 Scotland St. (☎220-3405; www.greenleafe.com). Resembling a church with its wooden interior and stained glass windows, this classy restaurant gives a modern twist to pub food and great beer. William and Mary students and locals attest that the substantial sandwiches ($6-7) make a great light supper. 30 brews on tap ($2.50-4.25), including coveted Virginia microbrews. Nightly drink specials include Tu $1 drafts and Th $4 cocktails (5pm-2am). Open daily 11am-2am. AmEx/D/MC/V. ●

SIGHTS

COLONIAL WILLIAMSBURG

▶ Contact: ☎ 800-447-8679; www.colonialwilliams-
burg.org. **Hours:** Visitors Center open daily 8:30am-9pm.
Most sights open 9:30am-5pm; for complete hours see
the Visitor's Companion newsletter. **Admission:** Basic
admission ticket includes all exhibition buildings and
trade sites plus the Orientation Walk and 2 museums;
day pass $33, ages 6-12 $16.50, under 6 free; 2 consecutive days $39, ages 6-12 $19.50, under 6 free. Individual museums $10. Disability discount 50%. Tickets
available at any of the Visitors Centers. **Accessibility:**
Grounds are handicapped accessible. **Events:** A free
"Grand Illumination" festival in early Dec. signals the
start of the holiday season and draws thousands. The
4th of July festival is a salute to the 13 colonies and
includes fireworks, parades, and special programs.

Every day is a historical reenactment at Colonial
Williamsburg, often cloyingly so. Though the site
prides itself on its authenticity, the pristine paint
on the houses and dirtless garb on the "natives"
gives the place more of an amusement park feel.
The sneaky but hardly revolutionary way to
immerse yourself in the colonists' world doesn't
require a ticket—visitors can enjoy the gorgeous
gardens, march behind the fife-and-drum corps,
lock themselves in the stocks, interact with the
locals, and use the rest room without ever doling
out a dollar. Two of the historic buildings—the
Wren Building and the **Bruton Parish Church**—are
free. The Visitor's Companion newsletter, printed
on Mondays, lists free events and evening programs, and provides a highly detailed map. The
Governor's Palace 30min. tour is a must for those
short on time. Home to seven royal governors
appointed by the King, the Governor's Palace was
completed by 1722 and opened as a museum in
1934. The entryway's gaudy display of sword and
gun decorations is fascinating. The gardens,
rooms, "lusters" (chandeliers), and "glasses" (mirrors) are also worth the visit.

The real fun of Colonial Williamsburg is interacting hands-on with history. Trade shops
afford a wonderful opportunity to learn from
skilled artisans such as the carpenter, and
slightly less-skilled workmen like the brickmas-
ter, who may invite you to take off your shoes
and join him in stomping on wet clay. Though
only paying guests can enter the shops, passersby are welcome to watch from outside.

COLLEGE OF WILLIAM AND MARY

▶ Contact: ☎ 221-4423; www.wm.edu. **Tours:** M-F 10am
and 2:30pm, most Sa 10am. **Admission:** Free.

Spreading west from the corner of Richmond
and Jamestown Rd., the College of William and
Mary, founded in 1693, is the second-oldest col-

The Local LEGEND

The Bonds of Holy Bridge-Crossing

A jaunt across the **Crim Dell
Bridge** at William and Mary
College is risky business. If
student lore holds true, then
the fate of many a love-life
has been sealed in a single
crossing or, rather, in crossing singly. Superstition says
that those who take the
bridge alone will never marry.

At the opposite extreme, if
passions lead a couple to
engage in a kiss with the
bridge underfoot, destiny has
eternally bound them
together. Scared of commitment? Don't panic. Simply
break the bind by throwing
your fellow kisser over the
side. Maybe this chance to
escape "I do" has something
to do with *Playboy* naming
the bridge the "second most
romantic spot on a college
campus."

lege in the US (after Harvard) and has educated luminaries such as presidents Jefferson, Monroe, and Tyler. The **Office of Admissions,** in Blow Hall, offers free tours throughout the year, but take the free self-guided walking tour for a bit more history. **Old Campus** starts behind the concrete roads surrounding the campus as the lawn opens up and beckons romance with a delicate picket fence. The "Ancient Campus" consists of a dining hall, chapel, and library at the **Wren Building** (constructed 1695-1699), which scholars speculate was built according to the design of Sir Christopher Wren, the renowned architect of London's St. Paul's Cathedral. Amazingly, its walls have survived three fires, and its reconstructed interiors are based on engravings discovered in Oxford, England. Hard to miss in **Wren Yard** is the **Lord Botetourt Statue** (1993), a commemoration of Virginia's former colonial governor; a major contributor and supporter of the college in its early years, he is appropriately buried in the **Wren Building Chapel.** Most visitors will, if anything, remember Thomas Jefferson's sprawling, ancient-looking **Sunken Garden,** in the heart of campus. During the 1760s, Jefferson and other intellectual students formed a society to gather at pubs and chat about politics. Disbanded in 1762 and then reinstituted in 1776, Jefferson's brainchild became America's first fraternity, **Phi Beta Kappa.** Old "TJ" would be proud to know that his original conception has stood the test of time: over 200 years later, Phi Beta Kappa students still gather in pubs, or at least at the library.

ENTERTAINMENT

Following true colonial tradition, most activity in Williamsburg comes to a halt when the sun goes down. Shell out more than a few shillings to be treated to one of Colonial Williamsburg's early evening programs, like **"Spellbound,"** a storytelling program where wide-eyed young audiences listen to the recounted legends of Colonial Williamsburg ($12, under 6 $7; daily 7 and 8:30pm). The **"Ghosts of Williamsburg" Candlelight Tours** reveal stories of the lost souls of the town and the bizarre phenomena that still occur today. (☎ 229-7193; www.theghosttour.com. Tours daily 8pm; $9, under 6 free; call before 5pm for reservations). Away from the city, the **Music Theatre of Williamsburg,** 7575 Richmond Rd. offers summer performances of folksy music in the Southern "Opry" style. Call for performance schedules. (☎ 888-687-4220 or 564-0200; www.musictheatre.com. Box office open M-Sa 9am-10pm. Closed Jan.-Mar. except for occassional weekend performances. D/MC/V.)

NIGHTLIFE

Corner Stone Grill, 1203 Richmond Rd. (☎ 259-7300; www.cornerstonegrill.com). Without doubt, the Corner Stone Grill has the liveliest after hours scene in town. A DJ spins rap, classic rock, and R&B nightly as customers of all ages enjoy $1.50 brews and gigantic mixed drinks ($2.50-7). Happy Hour (daily 5-7pm) welcomes an energetic crowd to watch sporting events while munching on first-rate appetizers ($8-$9), including fried calamari and oven-roasted potato skins. Open daily 4:30-10pm. Bar open 10pm-close (latest 2am). MC/V.

Library Tavern, 1330 Richmond Rd. (☎ 229-1012), turns literary greats into great sub sandwiches ($6.50). Ambitious eaters (and readers) will want to tackle the Hemingway, while others cite the Thesaurus. The main attractions at the Library, ironically enough, are the rowdy DJ-fueled dance (F-Sa) and "European Night," where visiting European students can bring in any CDs from home (W). Open daily 11am-2am. AmEx/MC/V.

Paul's Restaurant and Deli, 761 Scotland St. (☎ 229-8976; www.paulsdelirestaurant.com). No longer the "in" spot for nightlife, it still draws crowds who rock to an ancient jukebox playing the hits of hometown hero Bruce Hornsby, among other classic rockers (busiest on W; $1 Coronas). Open daily 10:30am-2am. MC/V.

NEAR WILLIAMSBURG

The "Historic Triangle" is bursting with U.S. history. More authentic and less crowded than the Colonial Williamsburg empire, Jamestown and Yorktown show visitors where the start of British colonization began. Jamestown, founded in 1607 as the first permanent English settlement in the New World, eventually failed as a settlement, but set American democracy in motion by electing the first representative legislature. Twenty miles to the east lies Yorktown, which witnessed the end of British rule in America when George Washington and his persistent rebels forced the Redcoats to surrender, assuring American independence. Williamsburg's central location allows easy access to its counterparts on the James River by way of the shaded, rock-paved, and richly green Colonial Parkway, which runs from Williamsburg to both Jamestown and Yorktown. Farther down the James River, southern culture dominates at 19th-century plantations. (Unless otherwise noted, all of the attractions have area code 757.)

JAMESTOWN

In 1607, the crew of 104 prosperous Englishmen carrying a charter drawn by the Virginia Company established the first permanent English settlement in the American colonies at Jamestown. The town's natural defensive position could not guarantee a stable economy—industries like silk farming and glass-blowing failed to yield profits. Luckily, John Rolfe pioneered tobacco cultivation, and Jamestown became a thriving business center as well as Virginia's capital and home to the first representative assembly. Less than a century later, however, the town was severely weakened by Native American attacks and soil exhaustion, and the capital moved to Williamsburg. Today, you must push aside the settlement's swampy, deserted appearance to imagine Jamestown's crucial importance in jumpstarting the American nation.

JAMESTOWN SETTLEMENT

Location: Off Rte. 31, outside Colonial National Park. From Williamsburg, follow Jamestown Rd., which becomes Rte. 31 South. The settlement is approximately 3 mi. down on the left. *Contact:* ☎ 888-593-4682 or 229-1607; www.historyisfun.org. *Hours:* June 15-Aug. 15 open daily 9am-6pm, rest of the year daily 9am-5pm. *Tours:* 1hr. tours 10am-3:30pm. *Admission:* $10.75, ages 6-12 $5.25. Combination ticket including Yorktown Victory Center $16, ages 6-12 $7.75, under 6 free. 10% senior or AAA discount. AmEx/MC/V. *Accessibility:* Ships not handicapped accessible.

Let the 50 proudly flying flags of each US state escort you into the Visitors Center, which springboards guests into a fascinating museum and numerous demonstrations of "living" history. With an emphasis on daily life and a chronology leading from prehistoric times to today, the museum is an ideal starting point before venturing to Yorktown or Colonial Williamsburg. The 10min. film, the most current of the colonial attractions' videos, focuses on Native American lives. Dance in the **Sacred Circle** within the **Powhatan Indian Village** and find out little-known information, like the secret to keeping animal skins soft (rubbing them with brains). By the dock, clamber aboard three **ships**, replicas of the first vessels to land at Jamestown. In **James Fort**, visitors try on armor and marvel at the fort's minimalist lodging. Jamestown is captivating for kids and adults, primarily because the settlement is more authentic than Colonial National Park or the Yorktown attractions.

COLONIAL NATIONAL PARK

Location: Southwest of Williamsburg on Rte. 31. Follow Jamestown Rd. and take a left at the Jamestown Settlement. The National Park is a mile beyond the settlement on the right. *Contact:* ☎ 229-1733 or 898-2410; www.nps.gov/colo/home.htm. *Hours:* Park entrance open year-round daily 9am-5pm; once you enter you are allowed to remain until dusk. Visitors Center closes 30min. before park entrance. Glasshouse open daily 9am-5pm. *Tours:* 35min. walking tour. 10:15am and 2:45pm (free with site admission). *Admission:* $5 (Yorktown), $6 (Jamestown), under 17 free; $9 joint pass includes either Jamestown and Yorktown sites.

Containing a few of the country's most historically significant sites, Colonial National Park takes its visitors on a journey from the beginning (Jamestown Settlement, 1607) to the end (Yorktown Battlefield, 1781) of the American colonial period. While waiting for a tour, pass the time by browsing through the Visitors Center's colonial artifacts, including armored suits and housewares. The movie, narrated

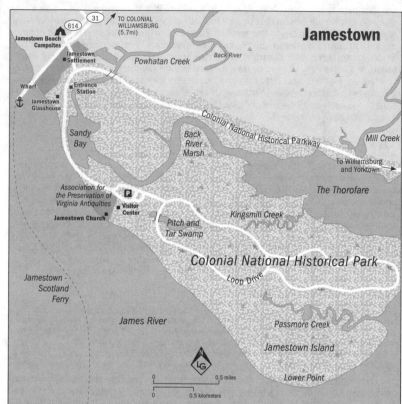

from the island's point of view, is melodramatic but informative. For healthy portions of natural and historical beauty, recreational activities include hiking, biking, fishing, and bird-watching. For a more guided understanding of the park, take a 45min. audio tape tour ($2) that narrates the three- or five-mile **Island Loop Route** through woodlands and marsh (loop may be closed due to preparation for the 2007 celebration). Be sure to catch **Jamestown Church** (which once doled out unfathomably cruel punishments for swearing), watch artisans plying their craft at the **Glasshouse,** and visit the **archaeological dig site,** where workers have unearthed the skeleton of an original settler who died of a gunshot wound to the leg. Every September, the park stages a reenactment of the 1676 Bacon's Rebellion, a colonial uprising against the royally appointed Governor Berkeley, which marked the first stirrings of revolutionary ire against England.

RICHMOND   ☎ 804

Once known as the "Cradle of the Confederacy," Richmond has a survivor's history of conflicts, disasters, and triumphs. William Mayo created the blueprint for what would become Richmond, officially charted in 1742. Between 1607 and 1780, the capital of the British royal colony, originally settled in Jamestown in 1607, moved twice: first to Williamsburg in 1698, then to Richmond in 1780. Unfortunately, fire struck in 1781, and Richmond burned to the ground as a result of a British attack led by Benedict Arnold. Unlike Jamestown and Williamsburg, Richmond remained Virginia's capital through fire and catastrophes in later times, such as the "Year of Disasters" (1870) when a great flood washed through the city, a major fire struck a hotel, and Robert E. Lee died. By the 1940s, postwar Richmond made herculean efforts to thrive, and it paid off: by 1946, Richmond's economy and industrial strength outpaced every other city's growth in the nation.

Richmond introduced an electric streetcar system to the United States in 1888; and in 1903, St. Luke Penny Savings Bank became the first bank founded and run by an African American woman—Maggie L. Walker. Well-known Richmonders, past and present, include L. Douglas Wilder, the country's first African American governor (1990), tennis star Arthur Ashe, actor Warren Beatty, actress Shirley MacLaine, dancer Bill Bojangles Robinson, and journalist Tom Wolfe.

ORIENTATION

Broad St. is the city's central artery, and the streets that cross it are numbered from west to east. Most parallel streets to Broad St., including **Main St.** and **Cary St.**, run one-way. Both I-95, leading north to Washington, D.C., and I-295 encircle the urban section of the city. The **Court End** and **Church Hill** districts, on Richmond's eastern edges, comprise the city's historic center. Further southeast, **Shockoe Slip** and **Shockoe Bottom** overflow with after-dark partiers. **Jackson Ward**, in the heart of downtown (bounded by Belvedere, Leigh, Broad, and 5th St.), recently underwent major construction to revamp its City Center and revitalize the surrounding community. The **Fan,** named for its geographical shape, is bounded by the Boulevard, I-95, the walk of statues along **Monument Ave.**, and **Virginia Commonwealth University.** The pleasant bistros and boutiques of **Carytown,** past the Fan on Cary St., and the tightly knit working community of **Oregon Hill** add texture to the cityscape.

PRACTICAL INFORMATION

GETTING THERE

Trains: Amtrak, 7519 Staple Mills Rd. (☎800-872-7245 or 264-9194; www.amtrak.com). To: **Washington, D.C.** (2¼hr., 8 per day, $32-37); **Williamsburg** (1¼hr., 2 per day, $22-23); **Virginia Beach** (3¼hr., 2 per day, $30-33); **New York City, NY** (6hr., 8 per day, $81-115); **Baltimore, MD** (3½hr., 8 per day, $43-51); and **Philadelphia, PA** (4¾hr., 8 per day, $60-74). Station open 24hr. **Taxi** fare to downtown $17-18.

Buses: Greyhound, 2910 N. Blvd. (☎800-231-2222 or 254-5910; www.greyhound.com). 2 blocks from downtown. Take GRTC bus #24 north. To: **Washington, D.C.** (2-3hr., 14 per day, $18.50-21.25); **Charlottesville** (1½hr., 2 per day, $20); **Norfolk** (2½hr., 8 per day, $17); **New York City, NY** (7-8hr., 20 per day, $60-64); **Baltimore, MD** (3-5hrs., 21 per day, $22-24); **Philadelphia, PA** (7-8hr., 12 per day, $40-43); **Williamsburg** (1hr., 11 per day, $8-9).

GETTING AROUND

Public Transportation: Greater Richmond Transit Co., 101 S. Davis Ave. (☎358-4782). Maps available in the basement of City Hall (900 E. Broad St.), the 6th St. Marketplace Commuter Station, and in the Yellow Pages. Most buses leave from stops along Broad St. downtown. Bus #24 goes to the Greyhound station. $1.25, $0.15 with transfer. Seniors $0.50. Supersaver tickets $10 for book of 10 tickets (must show Medicare or GRTC ID card).

Taxi: $2.50 plus $0.30 per one-fifth mi. **Veterans Cab** (☎276-8990); **Yellow Cab** (☎222-7300); **Star Cab** (☎754-8556).

PRACTICAL INFORMATION

Visitor Information: Richmond Metropolitan Visitor's Bureau, 405 N. 3rd St. (☎783-7450; www.richmondva.org). In the Richmond Convention Center; exit off 95 South onto I-64 East/Third St. (Exit 75) and stay to the right as you exit. The Greater Richmond Center Parking is straight ahead on the left. Helpful 9min. video introduces the city's attractions. Bus/van tours available, as well as

Downtown Richmond

▲ ACCOMMODATIONS
Be My Guest B & B, **3**
Comfort Inn Executive Center, **1**
Massad House Hotel, **5**
Pocahontas State Park, **19**

✦ FOOD
Bev's Homemade Ice Cream, **17**

Bottoms Up, **10**
Ma-Masu's, **2**
Mrs. Marshall's Carytown Cake, **14**
The Rivah Bistro, **8**
Strawberry St. Cafe and Market, **4**

★ NIGHTLIFE
Matt's Pub and Comedy Club, **6**

Medley's, **9**
The Tobacco Company Club, **7**

🛍 SHOPPING
Bygones, **13**
Clementine, **12**
The Phoenix, **18**
Pink, **11**
Posh Boutique, **15**
St. Tropez, **16**

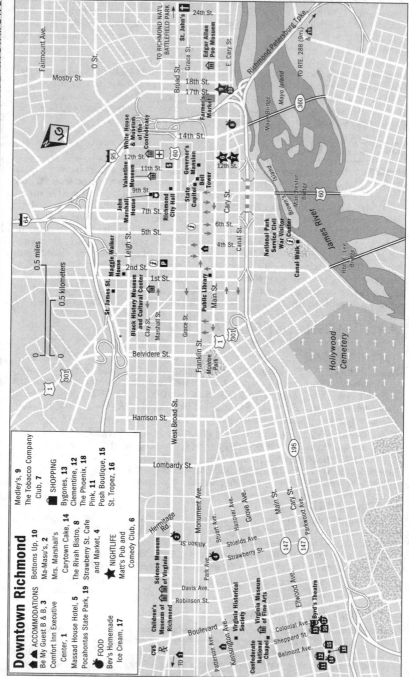

maps of downtown and the metro region. Offers same-day discounted accommodations. Open daily 9am-6pm. AmEx/MC/V.

Library and Internet: Richmond Public Library, 101 E. Franklin St. (☎646-4867; www.richmondpublicli-brary.org/branches/main/main.htm). Open M-Th 9am-9pm, F 9am-6pm, Sa 10am-5pm.

Emergency: ☎911.

Crisis Hotlines: Rape Crisis (☎643-0888). **AIDS/HIV** (☎800-533-4148). Open M-F 8am-5pm. **Crisis Pregnancy Center** (☎353-2320). **Women's Health Clinic** (☎800-254-4479). Open M-F 8am-5pm, Sa 7am-noon. **Richmond Organization for Sexual Minority Youth (ROSMY;** ☎353-2077).

24hr. Pharmacy: CVS, 2738 W. Broad St. (☎355-9122; www.cvs.com). **Rite Aid,** 520 W. Broad St. (☎225-1340; www.riteaid.com).

ACCOMMODATIONS

Budget motels in Richmond cluster on **Williamsburg Road,** at the edge of town, and along **Midlothian Turnpike,** south of the James River; however, public transport to these areas is unreliable. As usual, the farther you stay from downtown, the less you pay. The Visitors Center can reserve accommodations, often at $20-35 discounts (see above).

Comfort Inn Executive Center, 7201 W. Broad St. (☎800-221-2222 or 672-1108; www.choicehotels.com/hotel/va419). Take 64W to 95N, Exit 78, merge left, turn right on Robinhood Rd. Then left on North Blvd. and right on Broad—it's on the left side of the road 6 mi. from downtown beside a convenient, upscale shopping center. Recently renovated, this hotel strikes the city's best balance between desirable accommodation and affordable prices. Provides cable TV, A/C, coffeemakers, high-speed Internet hookup, free, unlimited 24hr. high-speed Internet, fitness center, and pool. Free deluxe continental breakfast includes waffles. Singles $69 ($49 with Visitors Center discount); 2-room suites $139. AmEx/DC/D/MC/V. ❷

Massad House Hotel, 11 N. 4th St. (☎648-2893). Surround yourself with antique furnishings, oil paintings, and a European atmosphere 5 blocks from downtown. A/C and cable TV. Recently renovated rooms. Free parking across the street. Singles start at $70, doubles start at $75. Student and seniors 10% off. MC/V. ❸

Pocahontas State Park, 10301 State Park Rd. (☎796-4255, 800-933-7275 or 255-3867 for reservations; www.dcr.state.va.us/parks/pocahontas). From Richmond, take I-95 south to Rte. 288; after 5 mi., connect to Rte. 10, exit on Ironbridge Rd. East,

the hidden deal

Be My Guest B&B

For those looking for a good time in Richmond on a budget, ▨ **Be My Guest Bed and Breakfast** is quite literally a hidden deal. Located in the heart of Richmond, across the street from the prestigious Virginia Historical Society, neither a sign nor a Yellow Pages listing marks this establishment. In fact, business is the almost solely the result of word of mouth.

The excellent location—just steps from Monument Blvd.—upscale neighborhood, and other nearby attractions preview the perks inside. A pleasing decor—artistic, classy, and modern feel with mosaic tiles, elegant dining room, and brand new bathrooms—not to mention a full hot breakfast, and room rates from $60-125 year round make this a truly auspicious place to stay.

More modest $60 rooms have a trundle bed capable of a max. of 2 people; pricier rooms, ideal for couples or good friends, are inviting and worth the extra cash. 2 rooms share a spacious, elegantly decorated bathroom.

Check-in, check-out times are flexible; call ahead to arrange.

2926 Kensington (☎358-9901). Open year-round. Reservations highly recommended. Cash only. ❷

turn right on Beach Rd.; the Park is 4 mi. down on the right. Showers, biking, boating, picnic areas, and the 2nd largest pool in Virginia. Rent a canoe, rowboat, kayak, or paddleboat ($6 per hr. or $22 per day). Open year-round. $20; all sites include water and electricity. MC/V.❶

FOOD

College students strapped for cash dominate the downtown Richmond cuisine scene—which ranges from greasy spoons to inexpensive Southern and ethnic foods. The outdoor **Farmer's Market,** N. 17th and E. Main St., brims with farm fruits, veggies, and homemade delicacies. Surrounding the market in **Shockoe Bottom,** pizza and deli food top the menu. A self-segregating hipster crowd from Virginia Commonwealth University convenes in hip coffeehouses in the area.

The Rivah Bistro, 1417 E. Cary St. (☎344-8222; www.rivahbistro.com), is where the stars dine when they come to town. Serving some of the best bistro food in a city full of bistros, this classy establishment has a cosmopolitan flair thanks to its French-Moroccan chef. Delicacies include lobster ravioli ($20). Regulars never pass up dessert. The vanilla crème brûlée ($6) is enticing. Open for lunch M-Sa 10:30am-4pm, dinner M-Th 4-10pm, F-Sa 4-11pm, Su 3-9pm. Su brunch 10:30am-3pm. Bar open until 2am. AmEx/D/MC/V. ❹

Strawberry Street Cafe and Market, 421 and 415 N. Strawberry St. (cafe ☎353-6860, market 353-4100; www.strawberrystreetcafe.com), is surprisingly not filled with strawberries at all. A Fan district favorite for casual dining, Strawberry Street offers an unlimited salad bar ($8), a brunch bar (unlimited baked ham, salad, homeade muffins, pastries, yogurt, fruits, and breakfast foods for $10; available Sa-Su until 3pm), and an array of what can only be called Americana classics like chicken quesadillas ($7), vegetarian bean burgers ($6), and chicken parmigiana ($11) in a dark and intimate atmosphere. Lunch M-F from 11:30am, dinner daily from 5pm, brunch Sa-Su until 3pm. AmEx/D/MC/V. ❷

Ma-Masu's, 2043 W. Broad St. (☎355-8063; www.menus.com/mamusus). Ma-Masu, "Spiritual Mother" extraordinaire, introduces her guests to Liberian culture with a mural that reads, "It's okay to lick your fingers here." *Keli-willy* (fried plantains with spices and onions) and *toywah beans* $6, collard greens $2.50, coconut juice $2. Delivery available. Open Tu-Th noon-9pm, F noon-10pm, Sa 2-10pm. AmEx/D/MC/V. ❶

Bottoms Up, 1700 Dock St. (☎644-4400; www.bottomsuppizza.com), at 17th and Cary St. Named "Richmond's Best Pizza" 5 years in a row. Take a choose-your-own-pizza adventure, or go with signatures like the Jo-Jo (tomatoes, feta, and shrimp) or the Chesapeake (spicy crab meat). Pizza $4-6.30 per slice. Drafts $5, bottles $3.50-4.50. Eat in and hope your meal doesn't coincide with the passing of a train overhead, or call for delivery. Open M-Tu 11am-10pm, Th 11am-midnight, F-Sa 11am-2am, Su 11am-11pm. AmEx/D/MC/V. ❶

SIGHTS

ST. JOHN'S CHURCH & ENVIRONS

St. John's Church, opened in 1741, was formerly nicknamed "the church on the hill" and the "Henrico Parish Church" until it received its official appellation in 1828. St. John's location has saved it from the fate of most of Richmond's prominent old buildings, burned or destroyed in warfare. When Benedict Arnold attacked Richmond in the Revolutionary War, the church was left untouched since it stood high above the burning town. Perhaps best known as the site of **Patrick Henry's** famed 1775 "Give me liberty or give me death" speech, it is less known for its connection to **Edgar Allen Poe,** whose mother is buried close to the periphery of the church wall to keep her as far away as possible from the church since she had dared to be, of all dreaded professions, an actress. Today the church still serves as an active house of worship (services Su 8:30am and 11am). Actors recreate the Patrick Henry speech on summer Sundays at 2pm (Memorial Day-Labor Day), which is proceeded by an organ recital at 1:30pm. (2401 E. Broad St. ☎648-5015; www.historicstjohnschurch.org. 25min. tours M-Sa 10am-3:30pm, Su 1-3:30pm. Church gates locked at 4pm. $5, seniors

62+ $4, ages 7-18 $3. MC/V.) With one's back to the original church wall parallel to, and across from, 24th St., one faces the **Elmira Shelton House,** 2407 E. Grace St., home to Poe's lifelong love. Nearby is the **Edgar Allan Poe Museum,** where visitors try to unravel the mysterious death of the enigmatic and morbid author in Richmond's oldest standing house (c. 1737). Inspect a coffin fragment and a lock of hair to draw your own conclusions, then bristle with fear as Poe's bust glares at you from a spooky archway in the garden. (1914 E. Main St. ☎ 888-648-5523 or 648-5523; www.poe-museum.org. Open Tu-Sa 10am-5pm, Su 11am-5pm. Tours on the hr., last one at 4pm. $6, seniors, students, and AAA $5; under 9 free. MC/V.)

CONFEDERATE SOUTH

The Civil War South is celebrated at the **Museum of the Confederacy.** To feel most welcome, wear hometown gray while wandering through the first floor's memorial to the "Great War of Northern Aggression." Of interest are the poignant painting *Last Meeting of Lee and Jackson* and the collection of artifacts and documents detailing gruesome Confederate medical treatments. The museum also runs 45min. tours through **The White House of the Confederacy** next door, where a South-shall-rise-again attitude is still in the air. After having served as Richmond's first public school for 20 years, the building was meticulously restored—items auctioned off after the Civil War were hunted down and repurchased—and officially became a museum in 1896. Make sure to catch the easily overlooked water dispenser in the living room (1st fl.) with the engraving *Colonel Barker's Civil War Loot from Jefferson Davis' House 1865,* and the working miniature cannon in the children's quarters upstairs that Jefferson Davis, Jr. used to shoot at targets for play. The portrait of Jefferson Davis, president of the Confederacy during the Civil War, hanging in the 1st floor parlor was his only live sitting portrait taken during the conflict. Abraham Lincoln arrived at the library adjacent to the parlors just two days after Davis left Richmond and only one day after Richmond was sacked by the Union army. (1201 E. Clay St. ☎ 649-1861; www.moc.org. Open M-Sa 10am-5pm, Su noon-5pm. $9.50, seniors (62+) $9, ages 7-18 $5, under 7 free. Tours every 30min. M, W, F-Sa 10:30am-4:30pm; Tu and Th 11:30am-4:30pm.)

There are no cupids or candy hearts in **The Valentine Museum,** just the South's largest collection of costumes. Here, ruffles abound—and that's just the men's clothing. Old playbills, diaries, photographs, and letters fascinate. Admission price includes a guided tour through the **Wickham House,** an architectural masterpiece by Alexander Parris—the architect of both the Virginia Governor's Mansion and Boston's Faneuil Hall. (1015 E. Clay St. ☎ 649-0711; www.richmondhistorycenter.com. Open Tu-Sa 10am-5pm, Su noon-5pm. House tours every hr. Tu-Sa 11am-4pm, Su 1-4pm. $7, students and seniors $6, ages 7-12 $4, ages 3-6 $1, under 3 free.)

INTERACTIVE MUSEUMS

Play with laser beams, motors, magnetic fields, and electric toys at the **Science Museum of Virginia,** where adults have as much fun defying gravity as kids. The large domed museum was once the city's main railroad station, designed by architect John Russell Pope, designer of the National Gallery Art, Jefferson Memorial in D.C., and the National Archives. Now the museum houses numerous play stations such as the **Very Small Gallery,** which explores life on a cellular level, the **My Size Gallery,** which teaches about humans and their health, and the **Really Big Gallery,** which provides a history of the Earth from evolution to extinction. (2500 W. Broad St. ☎ 800-659-1727 or 864-1400; www.smv.org. Open Memorial Day-Labor Day M-Th 9:30am-5pm, F-Sa 9:30am-7pm, Su 11:30am-5pm. $7, seniors $6.50, ages 4-12 $6. IMAX $7. Combo tickets $12.50, seniors $12, ages 4-12 $11.50.) Equally as entertaining but geared more toward a younger crowd is the **Children's Museum of Richmond,** adjacent to the science museum, where biology, chemistry, and physics are presented as fun. Ranked as one of the best children's museums in America, this educational playhouse focuses on the hows and whys of everyday life—things which we should all know, but probably don't. (2626 W. Broad St. ☎877-295-2667 or 474-2667; www.c-mor.org. Open Tu-Sa 9:30am-5pm, Su noon-5pm, Memorial Day-Labor Day only M 9:30am-5pm. $6.50, seniors $5.50.)

FAN DISTRICT

This old-world section of Richmond is home to the country's largest and best-preserved Victorian neighborhood. Stroll down Monument Ave., a boulevard lined with gracious old houses and towering statues of Virginia heroes—a true Richmond memory lane. The statue of Robert E. Lee faces south toward his beloved Dixie; Stonewall Jackson faces north so that the general can perpetually scowl at the Yankees. The statue of African-American tennis hero Arthur Ashe, who died of AIDS, created a storm of controversy when built at the end of the avenue. **The Fan is notoriously dangerous at night, so exercise caution.**

VIRGINIA HISTORICAL SOCIETY

The Virginia Historical Society proves that historical societies can be worthwhile. Two floors of elaborate and gorgeous exhibits make Virginia's history visceral, palpable, and exciting. For those short on time, "The Story of Virginia, an American Experience," a permanent collection, is a must: first watch the flashy-Hollywood-style documentary for a roadmap of the exhibit, then dive into the multidimensional experience that includes a streetcar, a handsome restored carriage, a Conestoga wagon, numerous artifacts, high-tech interactive computer games, learning centers, and more. The research library, Virginia House (part of a reassembled, 12th-century English house), and gardens are open to visitors. (428 North Blvd. ☎358-4901; www.vahistorical.org. Open M-Sa 10am-5pm, Su 1-5pm. $5, seniors (55+) $4, children and students $3. MC/V.)

VIRGINIA MUSEUM OF FINE ARTS

The Virginia Museum of Fine Arts—the South's largest art museum—features a masterful collection of art by some of the world's most renowned painters: Monet, Renoir, Picasso, and Warhol, as well as treasures from ancient Rome, Egypt, and Asia. (2800 Grove Ave. ☎340-1400; www.vmfa.state.va.us. Open W-Su 11am-5pm. Free highlight tour 2:30, 6, and 7pm. Suggested donation $5.) Check out the anomalous mosaic stained-glass windows at **The Confederate Memorial Chapel** (c.1887), across from the main entrance to the museum. (2900 Grove Ave. ☎674-7022. Open W-Su 11am-3pm. Free admission and tours.)

ENTERTAINMENT

One of Richmond's most entertaining and delightful diversions is the marvelous old **Byrd Theatre,** 2908 W. Cary St. Movie buffs buy tickets from a tuxedoed agent and are treated on weekends to a pre-movie Wurlitzer organ concert. (☎353-9911; www.byrdtheatre.com. All shows $2; Sa balcony open for $1 extra.) Free concerts abound downtown and at the **Nina Abody Festival Park,** near the bottom of 17th St. *Style Weekly,* a free magazine available at the Visitors Center, and its younger counterpart, *Punchline,* found in most hangouts, both list concert lineups. Cheer on the **Richmond Braves,** Richmond's AAA minor-league baseball team, on Boulevard St. for a fraction of major-league prices. (☎359-4444; www.rbraves.com. Boxes $9, general $6, youth and seniors $3.)

NIGHTLIFE

Student-driven nightlife enlivens **Shockoe Slip** and sprinkles itself throughout the Fan. After dark, **Shockoe Bottom** turns into college-party central, with transient bars pumping bass-heavy music early into the morning.

The **Tobacco Company Club,** 1201 E. Cary St. (☎ 782-9555; www.thetobaccocompany.com). From the north, take 95S, follow 64E when it splits from 95S, then exit immediately at 3rd St. Coliseum, turn left on Cary St., and it's on the right side at the corner of 12th St. After enjoying a savory meal at the adjacent **Tobacco Company Restaurant** (Dinner M-Th 5:30-10pm, F-Sa 5:30-10:30pm, Su 5:30-9:30pm; lunch M-Sa 11:30am-2:30pm; Su brunch 11am-2:30pm, venture into this high society bar where an older crowd—and some young'uns trying to act older—drinks martinis, smokes cigars, and discusses the joys of oppressing the underclass. Drink specials 8-9pm. Ladies Night Th. No bikini contests here (or tennis shoes, jeans, or boots): signs warn customers to maintain a "neat and tidy appearance." Cover $3 (dinner guests free). 21+. Open Th-Sa 8pm-2am. AmEx/D/MC/V.

Matt's Pub and Comedy Club, 109 S. 12th St. (☎ 643-5653), pours out a bit of Brit wit within dark wooden walls. Tex-Mex and pub cuisine $3-7; microbrews and drafts $2.75-$3.60; cocktails $3.25. Stand-up comedy F 8 and 10:30pm (winter) and at 9pm only in summer, Sa 8 and 11pm; reservations recommended. Cover cash or $9.75 charge. Open F-Sa 11:30am-2am. MC/V.

Medley's, 1701 E. Main (☎ 648-2313; www.medleys.com). A place where your level of coolness increases as soon as you step through the door. Live blues and French-Cajun food. Po' boy sandwiches $9.25; gumbo $8. Cover F-Sa $5. Open Tu-Sa 6pm-2am. AmEx/D/MC/V.

AFTERNOON SHOPPING IN CARYTOWN

Carytown, a nine-block area past the Fan near the VCU campus, exudes a vivacious, not-quite-upscale-but-not-completely-gritty college-town feel and caters to the wealthy and starving students at the same time. The area's real gems are, without doubt, its elegant boutiques. Shoppers, beware: you've stumbled upon Richmond's version of SoHo, a wanna-be Rodeo Drive.

Find young and hip contemporary dresses, pants, and tops at **Posh Boutique,** 3105 W. Cary St. (☎ 257-4333) and **St. Tropez,** 2933 W. Cary St. (☎ 342-1115). Then put together the perfect vintage outfit or costume at **Bygones,** 2916 W. Cary St. (☎ 353-1919. AmEx/D/MC/V), and head down to the new and darling ♦**Clementine,** 3118 W. Cary St., for nearly-new designer steals: tops ($4-25), pants ($10-30), and dresses ($15-50), as well as shoes and bags (☎ 358-2357. AmEx/D/MC/V). Trendier upscale **Pink,** 3158 W. Cary St., features NYC-themed chic ($50-400) and more affordable casual pants, tops, and dresses ($9-200) (☎ 353-0884, AmEx/MC/V). A slightly more mature crowd may appreciate **The Phoenix,** 3039 W. Cary St., where clothing is saturated with sagacity and an international flair (☎ 354-0711).

Shopping is hard work, so make sure to reward yourself by grabbing a quality sandwich ($4-7) at **Mrs. Marshall's Carytown Cafe,** 3125 W. Cary St. (☎ 355-1305: www.MrsMarshalls.com. AmEx/D/MC/V), followed by the you-don't-even-have-to-like-coffee-to-appreciate-it "Espresso Oreo" ice cream at **Bev's Homeade Ice Cream Shops,** 2911 W. Cary St. (☎ 204-2387; kiddie $1.90, reg. $2.70, large $3.60; cash only). **Use caution in this area at night.**

CHARLOTTESVILLE   ☎ 434

Thomas Jefferson, composer of the Declaration of Independence and colonial Renaissance man, built his dream house, Monticello, high atop his "little mountain" just southeast of Charlottesville. Around his personal paradise, Jefferson endeavored to create the ideal community. In an effort to breed further intellect and keep him busy in his old age, Jefferson humbly created the University of Virginia (UVA). Jefferson would be proud to know that his time was not wasted—today the college sustains Charlottesville, geographically and culturally. UVA forms the core of a vibrant college town that still pays homage to its founder at almost every turn.

ORIENTATION

Charlottesville's streets are numbered from east to west, using compass directions; 5th St. NW is 10 blocks from (and parallel to) 5th St. NE. There are two downtowns: **The Corner,** on the west side across from the university, is home to student-run delis and coffeeshops. Historic **downtown,** about a mile east, is a tad higher on the price scale. The two are connected by east-west **University Avenue,** which starts as Ivy Rd. and becomes Main St. after the end of the bridge in The Corner district.

PRACTICAL INFORMATION

GETTING THERE & GETTING AROUND

Trains: Amtrak, 810 W. Main St. (☎800-872-7245 or 296-4559; www.amtrak.com). Trains run once daily on the line to New Orleans. From **Washington, D.C.** (2hr., $20+). Ticket office open daily 6am-9:30pm.

Bus: Greyhound/Trailways, 310 W. Main St. (☎800-231-2222 or 295-5131; www.greyhound.com). Buses from: **Baltimore** (5hr., $40+); **Richmond** (1¼hr., $15+); and **Washington, D.C.** (3hr., $20+).

Taxis: Carter's Airport Taxi (☎981-0170). **AAA Cab Co.** (☎975-5555).

PRACTICAL INFORMATION

Visitor Information: Chamber of Commerce, 415 E. Market St. (☎295-3141), at 5th St. Within walking distance of Amtrak, Greyhound, and downtown. Maps, guides, and info about special events available. Open M-F 9am-5pm. **Charlottesville-Albemarle County Convention and Visitors Bureau** (☎977-1783), off I-64 on Rte. 20. Arranges discount lodgings and travel packages to Jeffersonian sights and shows a free 30min. film about Jefferson's life, *The Pursuit of Liberty.* Also features a free exhibit with 400 original Jeffersonian objects. Open daily Mar.-Oct. 9am-5:30pm; Nov.-Feb. 9am-5pm. **University of Virginia Information Center** (☎924-7969), at the Rotunda in the center of campus, offers brochures, a university map, and tour information. Open daily 9am-4:45pm. Film in summer every hr.; off-season 11am and 2pm.

Emergency: ☎911.

Local Police: ☎970-3280. **UVA Campus Police** (☎924-7166, 4-7166 on a UVA campus phone). Exit 120A off U.S. 250W.

Hotlines: Region 10 Community Services (☎972-1800). Open 24hr. **Sexual Assault Crisis Center** (☎977-7273). Open 24hr. **Mental Health** (☎977-4673). Open M-F 9am-6pm. For emergencies, call Region 10. **Women's Health Clinic** (☎800-254-4479), in Richmond, VA. Open M-Sa 8am-5pm.

24hr. Pharmacy: CVS Pharmacy, 1137 Emmet St. (☎293-5346; www.cvs.com).

Bank: Bank of America, 300 E. Main St. (☎800-880-5454; www.bankofamerica.com).

Internet: Jefferson Madison Regional Library, 201 E. Market St. (☎979-7151; http://jmrl.org). Free. Open M-Th 9am-9pm, F-Sa 9am-5pm, Su 1-5pm. **Mud House,** 318 W. Main St. (☎984-6833; www.mudhouse.com) offers 1 free Internet terminal.

ACCOMMODATIONS

Boar's Head Inn, 200 Ednam Dr. (☎800-476-1988 or 296-2181; www.boarsheadinn.com), is by far one of the classiest, most convenient, and costly places you can stay in town. Some B&B rates are more affordable starting at $118 per night. Packages include on-site golfing, wine tours, and "girl's getaway" with spa treatments. AmEx/D/MC/V. ❹

The Inn at Monticello, 1188 Scottsville Rd. (☎979-3593; www.innatmonticello.com), boasts the most auspicious location for those who want to mold their trip around visits to Jefferson's home. This 1850 manor-turned-B&B is within a 5min. drive of Monticello. Lovely antiques, elegant rooms, full breakfasts. Rates $125-175. AmEx/MC/V. ❺

High Meadows Vineyard Inn and Restaurant, 55 High Meadows Ln. (☎800-232-1832 or 286-2218; www.highmeadows.com), a 25min. drive from downtown Charlottesville. Surround yourself with antiques and *fin-de-siècle* charm in this unusual B&B with local vineyard and restaurant. Specials include a 6-course candlelit dinner ($45) and dinner for 2 ($50). Su brunch 11am-3pm ($13). Rooms $99-290 per night. MC/V. ❸

The Budget Inn, 140 Emmet St. (☎800-293-5144; www.budgetinn-charlottesville.com), is the closest motel to the university. 36 big rooms with lots of sunlight and cable TV. Rooms $40-90; each additional person $5. AmEx/D/MC/V. ❷

FOOD

🦀 **Littlejohn's,** 1427 University Ave. (☎977-0588). During lunch hours, this deli becomes as overstuffed as its sandwiches. In the wee, wee hours of the morning, barflies trickle into littlejohn's to kick back and relax with the Easy Rider (baked ham, mozzarella, and cole slaw; $3.75). Many, many beers ($2-3). Open 24hr. ❶

Blue Light Grill and Raw Bar, 120 E. Main St. (☎295-1223; www.bluelightgrill.com), on the mall. Ideal for seafood lovers, this grill has a modern, uncluttered atmosphere with red walls and high ceilings. The grilled scallops with *haricots verts* ($19) and the lobster, scallops, mussels, and shrimp in a saffron cream sauce over *radiatore* ($20) are both excellent. Open M 5:30-10pm, Tu-Sa 11:30am-2:30pm and 5:30-10pm. AmEx/D/MC/V. ❹

Chaps, 223 E. Main St. (☎977-4139), is a local favorite for homemade ice cream. With limited bar seating, light green booths, and a diner-that's-been-here-forever feel, the joint also serves simple grub such as grilled cheese ($2), hamburgers ($3), and veggie burgers ($3.30). Ice cream $2-4. Open M-F 7am-10pm, Sa-Su 7am-11pm. Cash only. ❶

Rapture, 303 E. Main St. (☎293-9526). Savor creative dishes such as falafel with pecan crusted chevre, hummus, pita triangles, and Greek salad ($12), lamb and curry over rice with *pappadum* chips ($11), or grilled salmon with scallion sushi rice cakes, potato haystacks, and carrot lemongrass-ginger broth ($14). Outside seating available. 21+ after 11pm. Open 5:30pm-2am (kitchen open until 11pm). ❸

SIGHTS

UNIVERSITY OF VIRGINIA & ENVIRONS

UNIVERSITY OF VIRGINIA. Most activity on the grounds of the University of Virginia (UVA) clusters around the **Lawn** and fraternity-lined **Rugby Rd. Montincello** (see below) is visible from the lawn, a terraced green carpet and one of the prettiest spots in American academia. Professors inhabit the Lawn's pavillons, each of which Jefferson designed in a different architectural style. Privileged Fourth Years (never called seniors) are chosen each year for the small Lawn singles. Room 13 is dedicated to ne'er-do-well Edgar Allen Poe, who was kicked out of the university for gambling. The early morning clanging of the bell that used to hang in the Rotunda provoked one incensed student to shoot at the building. (☎924-7969. *Tours meet at Rotunda entrance facing the Lawn. Tours daily 10, 11am, 2, 3, 4pm; no tours on Thanksgiving, mid-Dec.-mid-Jan., and early-mid-May.*)

MICHIE TAVERN. This partially reconstructed tavern was established in 1784 by William Michie, a Jacobian rebel and Scotsman who was banished forever to the New World. In 1927, the tavern was carefully dismantled and rebuilt from original materials at its present site over a period of two years. Tours lead guests through the ladies' parlor (where Michie's rule was no more than five to a full-sized bed) the gentlemen's quarters, and an upstairs assembly room. The clock in the lobby, which has ticked and chimed since 1790, was shipped from Scotland. On the tour you'll also learn the origins of expressions like "mind your beeswax," "sleep tight," "toast," and "pop goes the weasel." Today the tavern houses an operating grist mill and a general store. *(Just west of Monticello on the Thomas Jefferson Pkwy. ☎ 977-1234; www.michietavern.com. Open daily 9am-5pm; last tour 4:20pm. $8, seniors and AAA $7, ages 6-11 $3.)*

MANSIONS IN & AROUND CHARLOTTESVILLE

MONTICELLO. Thomas Jefferson oversaw every stage of development of his beloved home between 1769-1809, a house that truly reflects the personality of its brilliant creator. Monticello is a quasi-Palladian jewel filled with fascinating innovations, such as a fireplace dumbwaiter to the wine cellar and a mechanical copier (all compiled or conceived by Jefferson). The grounds include orchards and gardens that afford magnificent views. *(1184 Monticello Loop. ☎ 984-9822; www.monticello.org. Open Mar.-Oct. daily 8am-5pm, Nov.-Feb. daily 9am-4:30pm. $13, ages 6-11 $6. AmEx/MC/V.)*

MONTPELIER. James Madison supported his more than 100 slaves and property with tobacco, wheat, and corn crops. Find inner walls exposed from an architectural investigation in 2001-2002 (www.montpeliersearch.org). Dolly Madison, a celebrated host, has been recalled fondly for her feasts, parties, and social events at the house. In 1832, due to staggering debts amounting to roughly $40,000 (equivalent to $500,000 today) accumulated by Dolly's son, James Madison mortgaged half the house for cash. In 1836, Madison died, leaving Dolly to pay off the remaining debts. Forced to sell her beloved home, Dolly departed and Montepelier fell into disrepair. Montpelier was not restored to its former glory until 1901, when William Du Pont, Sr. (1855-1928) purchased the home. The first floor and lovely gardens are open for self-guided exploration; the second floor is only accessible by "Behind the Scenes" tours (included in the price of admission; every 30min. 10:30am-4pm; arrange a reservation when you arrive at the house). *(Rte. 20. ☎ 540-672-2728; www.montperlier.org. Open Apr.-Oct. daily 9:30am-4:30pm. AmEx/MC/V. $11, seniors and AAA $10, ages 6-14 $6.)*

ASH-LAWN HIGHLAND. This 535-acre plantation and former home of President James Monroe is less distinctive and regal than Monticello, but reveals more about early 19th-century family life, hosting living history exhibitions. Kids are mesmerized by the colorful peacocks in the backyard. *(1000 James Monroe Pkwy., off Rte. 792, 2½ mi. east of Monticello. ☎ 293-9539; www.ashlawnhighland.org. Open Mar.-Oct. daily 9am-6pm; Nov.-Feb. daily 10am-5pm. Tour $9, seniors and AAA $8, ages 6-11 $5. MC/V. Wheelchair accessible.)*

NIGHTLIFE

Buddhist Biker Bar and Grille, 20 Elliewood Ave. (☎971-9181). UVA students and local twenty-somethings flock to this bar for its huge lawn and drink specials. The food ain't bad either—try the spinach dip ($5) or stuffed mushrooms ($3.75). Beer $2.50-4. M $1 beers, W $2 cocktails, Th live bluegrass. Open M-Sa 3:30pm-2am.

Baja Bean, 1327 W. Main St. (☎ 293-4507). Cheap burritos, tamales, and *chimichangas* go down smooth for under $8 at this Mexican bar and restaurant. Every 5th of the month is the Cinco Celebration, a fiesta with $3 Coronas. W 9pm-midnight dance parties with lasers and DJ-fueled music. Dollar Night (Tu and Th 8pm): bottle of the day, Baja Gold, and Mudslide Shooters $1 each; margaritas and strawberry daiquiris $3. Happy Hour (M-F 3-7pm) with $1.50 mudslide shooters, $1.75 Baja Gold drafts $2 rail highballs, and $3 Rox Rum Ritas. Open daily 11am-2am (kitchen until midnight). AmEx/D/MC/V.

Orbit, 102 14 St. NW (☎984-5707). A hot new bar and restaurant popular with C-ville locals. The recently opened downstairs has a *2001: A Space Odyssey* theme, and the garage-door windows open on hot summer nights. Upstairs has 8 pool tables and another bar with extensive beers on tap, including numerous imports ($2.50-4.50). Tu after 5pm ladies shoot pool for free. Th $2 drafts. Occasional Su live acoustic music. Open daily 5pm-2am. MC/V.

WINE & HUNT COUNTRY

LEESBURG, VA   ☎703, 571

Originally known as "George Town," an homage to King George II, Leesburg was officially founded in 1758 and renamed after the prominent Lee family. During the Civil War, the town became the planning site for the Battle of Balls Bluff (1861). Today, Leesburg is known for its plentiful selection of shops, antique stores, restaurants, a picturesque downtown, and nearby wineries.

ORIENTATION

Leesburg is 35 mi. northwest of Washington, D.C., in Loudon County, VA. Without a doubt, the best way to reach town is by car. From D.C., take Rte. 66 W to the Dulles Toll Rd. (Rte. 267). Follow the Toll Rd. local lanes until it turns into the Dulles Greenway (Rte. 267). At the end of the Greenway, after 13 mi., take the left-hand exit. Stay in the right lane and take the first right exit, Leesburg Business. Follow King St., then make a left onto Loudon St., and you will see the Leesburg Town Public Parking Garage on the right. While the town is best explored by foot, cars offer the possibility of visiting nearby vineyards, historic mansions, and trails.

   Leesburg consists of one main thoroughfare with some small cross streets. **King St.** is the heart of town, bounded by **Market St.** on one side and **Loudoun St.** on the other.

GETTING THERE & GETTING AROUND

Bus: Greyhound/Trailways, 502 S. King St. (☎800-231-2222 or 777-3730; www.greyhound.com). Buses from: **Baltimore** (3hr., $21); **Richmond** (4hr., $30); and **Washington, D.C.** (1½hr., $15+). No ticket office; order tickets online or by phone. Open 24hr.

Public Transportation: Loudoun Transit (☎877-777-2708). Operator M-F 7am-6pm.

Taxi: Leesburg Taxicab (☎777-7773). **Loudoun Taxi** (☎430-8300).

Bicycle Rental: Plum Grove Cyclery, 26 W. Market St. (☎777-1868; http://plumgrovecyclery.com). Comfort and mountain bikes (2hr. $20, 1 day $25). MC/V.

PRACTICAL INFORMATION

Visitor Information: Loudoun County Visitor Information Center, 222 Catoctin Circle SE, #100 (☎800-752-6118, ext. 11 or 771-2617, ext. 11; www.visitloudoun.org or www.leesburgva.org), a few minutes outside downtown. Offers extensive info on Historic Leesburg, including brochures, advice, local maps, and useful listings. Open daily 9am-5pm.

Bank: Middleburg Bank, 4 S. King St. (☎777-6327; www.middleburgbank.com). Open M-F 10am-2pm. 24hr. **ATM.**

Emergency: ☎911.

Local Police: ☎771-4500. **Loudoun Country Sheriff** (☎777-0445).

Pharmacy: Rite Aid, 448 S. King St. (☎777-3111). Open M-Sa 9am-9pm, Su 10am-6pm.

Internet: Loudoun County Libraries, 908 Trailview Blvd. SE, #A (☎777-0368). Free Internet. Open M-F 9am-5pm.

ACCOMMODATIONS

The Norris House Inn, 108 Loudoun St. (☎800-644-1406 or 777-1806; www.norrishouse.com). An alluring atmosphere with elegant rooms, full breakfast, and amicable service makes this inn a memorable stay. Excellent location. Open year-round. Rooms $85-150. AmEx/D/MC/V. ❸

Bears Den Hostel, 18393 Blue Ridge Mt. Rd. (☎554-8708; info@bearsdencenter.org). From D.C., take VA Rte. 7 to VA 601 and then turn left onto Blue Ridge Mt. Rd. The hostel is on the right side without a sign. Look for an open gate, dirt road, and mailbox #18393. In a lush mountain forest 19 mi. west of Leesburg on an affluent, mansion-filled road, this

the BIG $plurge

Wine & Dine B&B

Just 10mi. outside downtown Leesburg is a hidden haven where up to eight lucky guests can retreat after a day on the town. With just four rooms, **Tarara Winery and Bed & Breakfast** graciously sits on 475 acres of vineyards and forest, offering guests unparalled perks for just marginally more than a stay in town. The modern, minimalist, uncluttered feel of the lobby welcomes guests with cathedral ceilings and sleek floors in a one-of-a-kind stone home designed by its owners. Rooms are larger than average, cozy, romantic, and comfortable.

But what really sets this B&B apart are the grounds. Guests have free, unlimited access to an onsite tennis court, a lake, a pond, a 6000 sq. ft. wine cave, 6 mi. of winding jogging paths, picnic spots in the forest, complimentary use of the golf carts and bicycles to explore the vineyard, and access to local events held on the premises such as summer concerts. A light continental breakfast is also included.

13648 Tarara Ln. ☎771-710; www.tarara.com. Winery open daily 11am-5pm. Rooms $120-165. MC/V. ●

former summer house for a doctor and his opera singer wife welcomes students, families, and Appalachian trail hikers year-round. Hiking paths. Check-in 5-9pm; check-out 9:30am. Entrance gate locked at 10pm. Dorms with bunk beds $18 per night ($13 per night for hikers). Private double room with bath $42 per night. Large, rustic, camp-like cottage in the woods $55 (sleeps max of 9). Camp sites $6 per person per night (kids under 12 free). MC/V. ●

FOOD

Leesburg Restaurant, 9 S. King St. (☎777-3292), has been serving customers since 1865, and is the local hot spot for juicy gossip and town news served over breakfast. Savor "our breakfast special" (2 eggs any style, juice, bacon/sausage, home fries, toast, and coffee/tea), a short stack with butter and syrup ($2.65), french toast ($4), or eggs benedict with home fries ($5.65) in faded wooded booths or at the bar. Gregarious staff and central location. Open Su-Th 7am-8pm, F-Sa 7am-9pm. AmEx/D/MC/V. ●

The Coffee Bean of Leesburg, 110 S. King St. (☎800-2326-872; www.beanusa.com), roasts their imported coffee beans on the premises in a 1930s antique roaster. Coffee lovers can explore a panoply of flavors including maple walnut, praline, chocolate raspberry, macadamia nut, or Irish cream, while those who want the taste without the caffeine can sample chocolate mint, seville orange, and chocolate almond, among others (8 oz. $6, 1 lb. $12; decaf $6.45/$13). Open M-F 8:30am-6pm, Sa-Su 8:30am-5pm. AmEx/MC/V. ●

Lightfoot, 11 N. King St. (☎771-2233; www.lightfootrestaurant.com). This bank-turned-upscale-restaurant is sure to entertain and charm. For dinner, try the seared jumbo lump crab cake with corn-Holland pepper relish and dijon honey crème fraiche ($10.50), followed by sauteed salmon topped with an artichoke gratin and colossal crab over sauteed California baby spinach and currant-pinenut couscous with mandarin beurre blanc ($23). Open M-Th 11:30am-11pm, F-Sa 11:30am-midnight, Su 11:30am-10pm (brunch 11:30am-3pm). AmEx/DC/MC/V. ●

SIGHTS

OATLANDS PLANTATION. Explore this 1804 Greek revival mansion and grounds just outside downtown, where families lived with carefree insouciance for generations. Guided garden tours, house self-guided tours with detailed descriptions of each stunning room, and a self-guided plantation walking tour.

(20850 Oatlands Plantation Ln. ☎777-3174; www.oatlands.org. $8, ages 12-17 and 60+ $7, ages 5-11 $1. MC/V.)

ENTERTAINMENT

Art fans will enjoy the **First Friday Gallery Walk**, which graces the town with a wine and cheese gallery open house. (Feb.-Dec. 1st F of every month 6-9pm. Info and map available at Loudoun Visitor and Convention Association, 222 Catoctin Circle, Ste. 100. ☎888-478-1758; www.loudouncounty.com/art/walk.htm.) On Sundays at 7pm, visitors can take advantage of the free **Bluemont Concert Series.** (Courthouse Lawn. ☎703-777-6306. June-Aug.) Alternatively, catch a flick at Leesburg's **Tally Hoe Theatre.** (19 W. Market St. ☎669-8444; www.tallyhotheatre.com. $8, seniors and under 13 $5. Matinees $5.)

Light Reading

SHOPPING

Those with a car and a flair for outlet shopping will want to head to the **Leesburg Corner Premium Outlets** to find name-brand outlet stores such as J. Crew, Levi's, Banana Republic, Burberry, BCBG, and Off 5th-Saks Fifth Avenue Outlet. From D.C., take I-495 to Rt. 267 West; take Exit 1B to Rte. 15 North, follow the signs to the exit for Fort Evans Rd., and stay in the far right lane. *(241 Fort Evans Rd., NE. ☎737-3071; www.premiumoutlets.com/leesburg. Open M-Sa 10am-9pm, Su 11am-6pm. Call for seasonal hours.)*

The Carriage House, 24 S. King St. (☎443-0721). This former carriage house offers fine soaps, sleepwear, custom jewelry, and French, English, and Italian imports. Open M-Sa 10:30am-6pm. MC/V.

Crème de la Crème, 101 S. King St. (☎737-7702). Find your enamel *chat lunatique, chat fort, mechant, et peu nourri,* and *le chef a toujours raison* signs here for $15. Imports from Provence, Italy, and Portugal include linens, pottery, and other colorful goodies for home and creature comforts in an elegant and colorful display. Open M and W-F 10am-6pm, Tu and Sa 10am-5pm, Su 1-5pm. AmEx/MC/V.

Fine Dining in the Suburbs

MIDDLEBURG, VA   ☎540

Founded in 1787 by Levin Powell, a Revolutionary War hero and Virginia politician, Middlesburg is home to just 600 today. Levin chose the name "Middleburg" based on its auspicious location along the Ashby Gap trading route, today's Rte. 50, halfway between Alexandria and Winchester. Discreet and protected, Middleburg is sheltered from the hubbub of aesthetically atavistic American chain chaos and consumption. Not one Starbucks or McDonalds can be found

Mount Vernon

here, and residents and visitors prefer the status quo. Middleburg is horse country, nicknamed the "nation's horse and hunt capital," marked by endless lines of brown fences.

GETTING THERE & GETTING AROUND

Neither Amtrak nor Greyhound stop in Middleburg, so unless you own a plane, car is the most reliable form of transportation. From DC, drive west on I-66 to Rte. 50 West for about an hour. Rte. 50 becomes **Washington St.**, Middleburg's heart.

Public Transportation: Loudoun Transit, ☎877-777-2708, operator M-F 7am-6pm.

Taxi: Purcellville Cab (☎338-8995), **Loudoun Taxi** (☎430-8300).

PRACTICAL INFORMATION

Visitor Information: The Pink Box Information Center of Historic Middleburg, 12 North Madison St. (687-8888; www.middleburgonline.com). Pamphlets, advice, and local information about places to stay, eat, and visit. Open M-F 11am-3pm and Sa-Su 11am-4pm.

Emergency: ☎911. **Local Police:** ☎687-6633.

Internet: Loudoun County Library, Middleburg Branch, 101 Reed St. (☎687-5730; www.lcpl.lib.va.us), offers free Internet. Open M-Th 10am-9pm, F-Sa 10am-5pm.

ACCOMMODATIONS

The Red Fox Inn, 2 East Washington St. (☎687-6301; www.redfox.com). Floors with wooden beams, elegant rooms, first-class service, and breakfast served in a rustic 18th-century tavern make for an unforgettable stay. Stellar location. Check-in 3pm. Check-out noon. Full service tavern restaurant on premises. Rooms are located in 3 separate houses, so be sure to ask which house you'll be staying in. Rates from $150 per night. AmEx/DC/D/MC/V. ❺

Briar Patch Bed & Breakfast, 23130 Briar Patch Ln. (☎866-327-5911 or 703-327-5911; www.briarpatchbandb.com). Just a few miles down Rte. 50 from the heart of town, this B&B provides a more affordable stay for those who want charming rooms without sacrificing an arm and a leg. 7 rooms, 1 private cottage. Rates start at $95 in off-season. AmEx/MC/V. ❸

FOOD

Dank's Deli, 2 N. Liberty St. (☎687-3456). The hot spot for classic sandwiches ($5) with locals. Reminiscent of a Manhattan deli, it is hardly spacious, but does offer some seating indoors and out. Order at the counter and take a seat. Daily 10am-6pm. Cash only. ❶

Black Coffee Bistro, 3 W. Washington St (☎687-3632; www.blackcoffeebistro.com), proves more than its unassuming appellation implies. Locals attest to its excellent food in a simply elegant atmosphere in the center of town. Feast on Moroccan-spiced game hens with grilled broccoli, dried fruit, and black olive couscous with a citrus balsamic glaze ($16) or a cornmeal-crusted rockfish ($20). Open Tu-Th 11:30am-2:30pm and 6-9pm, F-Sa 11:30am-2:30pm and 6-10pm, Su 11:30am-2:30pm. AmEx/DC/D/MC/V. ❹

Hunter's Head, 9048 John Mosby Hwy. (Rte. 50; ☎592-9020). A mid-18th century British-themed log cabin and farm with original walls and fireplaces makes for an enchanting experience for meat lovers and vegetarians alike. Order your 100% organic 12 oz. Grilled Steak ($22) or Boca Burger & Cheese ($7) at the bar, then take a seat and soak up the sumptious atmosphere. Open M 5-10pm, Tu-Su 11:30am-10pm. AmEx/D/MC/V. ❸

The Upper Crust, (☎687-5666; www.countrycookies.com), a one-of-a-kind shop frequently visited by both locals and tourists. Try their raspberry linzer hearts ($1.50), homemade Pork Barbeque ($4.25), or the Mutton Buttons (shortbread with chocolate filling; $0.65). Open M-Sa 7:30am-4pm. Cash only. ❶

SHOPPING

Those who stop and explore horse country's central cluster of shops and restaurants will be rewarded with unique and high end products. From French and Italian imported ceramics, dishware, bags, furniture, and textiles to stuffy prep clothes and NYC boutique dresses and skirts, come prepared with both paper and plastic because you need *mucho dinero* to shop *très chic* Middleburg.

Beyond the Pale, 22 E. Washington St. (☎687-8050). Explore palettes, hues, textures, creams, glosses, powders, and perfumed products—for girls who just want to have fun *and* be gorgeous. Australian line Bloom, NYC-based Joey, Mario Badescu, and Tocca are just a handful of the melange of products available here ($15-35). Open M-F 10am-5pm, Su noon-5pm. AmEx/DC/D/MC/V.

INSIDE

when to go **301**

embassies & consulates **301**

money **304**

health **307**

insurance **308**

packing **308**

accommodations **309**

getting to d.c. **311**

specific concerns **314**

other resources **316**

Planning Your Trip

WHEN TO GO

D.C. grows extremely hot and humid between June and August; try to avoid the muggy summer along with the busloads of tourists who make the city their destination at precisely this time. D.C. is pleasant in the fall and spring—particularly during March and April when gorgeous **cherry blossoms** cover the city. Although winter is relatively mild, even the slightest snowstorms regularly incapacitate the city—leading to unplowed streets, shop closings, and general dismay. Average high and low temperatures (in degrees Fahrenheit) and the average monthly rainfall (in inches):

January		April		July		October	
Temp	**Rain**	**Temp**	**Rain**	**Temp**	**Rain**	**Temp**	**Rain**
43°F/22°F	3.0 in.	67°F/42°F	3.5 in.	88°F/66°F	3.9 in.	69°F/45°F	3.5 in.

EMBASSIES & CONSULATES

US EMBASSIES & CONSULATES ABROAD

For a list of embassies that can provide consular services in D.C., see **Once In**, p. 27. Contact the nearest embassy or consulate to obtain information regarding visas and permits to the United States. Offices are only open limited hours, so call well before you depart. The US **State Department** provides contact information for US diplomatic missions on the Internet at http://foia.state.gov/keyofficers.asp. For a more extensive list of embassies and consulates in the US, consult the web site **www.embassy.org.**

AUSTRALIA. Embassy and Consulate: Moonah Pl., Yarralumla **(Canberra)**, ACT 2600 (☎02 6214 5600; http://usembassy-australia.state.gov/consular). **Other Consulates:** MLC Centre, Level 59, 19-29 Martin Pl., **Sydney,** NSW 2000 (☎02 9373 9200; fax 9373 9184); 553 St. Kilda Rd., **Melbourne,** VIC 3004 (☎03 9526 5900; fax 9510 4646); 16 St. George's Terr., 13th fl., **Perth,** WA 6000 (☎08 9202 1224; fax 9231 9444).

CANADA. Embassy and Consulate: Consular Section, 490 Sussex Dr., **Ottawa,** P.O. Box 866, Station B, Ottowa, Ontario K1P 5T1(☎613-238-5335; www.usembassycanada.gov). **Other Consulates** (☎900-451-2778; www.amcits.com): 615 Macleod Trail SE, Room 1000, **Calgary,** AB T2G 4T8 (☎403-266-8962; fax 264-6630); 1969 Upper Water St., Purdy's Wharf Tower II, suite 904, **Halifax,** NS B3J 3R7 (☎902-429-2480; fax 423-6861); 1155 St. Alexandre, **Montréal,** QC H3B 1Z1 (mailing address: P.O. Box 65, Postal Station Desjardins, Montréal, QC H5B 1G1; ☎514-398-9695; fax 981-5059); 2 Place Terrasse Dufferin, behind Château Frontenac, B.P. 939, **Québec City,** QC G1R 4T9; 360 University Ave., **Toronto,** ON M5G 1S4 (☎418-692-2095; fax 692-2096); 1075 W. Pender St., Mezzanine (mailing address: 1095 W. Pender St., 21st fl., **Vancouver,** BC V6E 2M6; ☎604-685-4311; fax 685-7175).

IRELAND. Embassy and Consulate: 42 Elgin Rd., Ballsbridge, **Dublin** 4 (☎01 668 8777 or 668 7122; www.usembassy.ie).

NEW ZEALAND. Embassy and Consulate: 29 Fitzherbert Terr. (or P.O. Box 1190), Thorndon, **Wellington** (☎04 462 6000; fax 478 0490; usembassy.org.nz). **Other Consulate:** 23 Customs St., Citibank Building, 3rd fl., **Auckland** (☎09 303-2724; fax 366-0870.

SOUTH AFRICA. Embassy and Consulate: 877 Pretorius St., **Pretoria,** P.O. Box 9536, Pretoria 0001 (☎012 342 1048; http://usembassy.state.gov/pretoria). **Other Consulates:** Broadway Industries Center, Heerengracht, Foreshore, **Cape Town** (mailing address: P.O. Box 6773, Roggebaai, 8012; ☎021 342 1048; fax 342 2244); 303 West St., Old Mutual Building, 31st fl., **Durban** (☎031 305-7600; fax 305-7691); No. 1 River St., Killarney, **Johannesburg,** P.O. Box 1762, Houghton, 2041 (☎011 644-8000; fax 646-6916).

UK. Embassy and Consulate: 24 Grosvenor Sq., **London** W1A 1AE (☎020 7499 9000; www.usembassy.org.uk). **Other Consulates**: Queen's House, 14 Queen St., Belfast, **N. Ireland** BT1 6EQ (☎028 9032 8239; fax 9024 8482); 3 Regent Terr., Edinburgh, **Scotland** EH7 5BW (☎0131 556 8315; fax 557 6023).

DOCUMENTS & FORMALITIES

PASSPORTS

REQUIREMENTS. Citizens of Australia, Canada, Ireland, New Zealand, South Africa, and the UK need valid passports to enter the US and to re-enter their home countries. The US does not allow entrance with a passport that expires in under six months after one's departure; returning home with an expired passport is illegal.

NEW PASSPORTS. Citizens of Australia, Canada, Ireland, New Zealand, and the UK can apply for a passport at any post office, passport office, or court of law. Citizens of South Africa can apply for a passport at any Home Affairs Office. Any new passport or renewal applications must be filed well in advance of the departure date, although most passport offices offer rush services for a very steep fee. Citizens living abroad who need a passport or renewal services should contact the nearest consular service of their home country.

PASSPORT MAINTENANCE. Be sure to photocopy the page of your passport with your photo, passport number, and other identifying information, as well as any visas, travel insurance policies, plane tickets, or traveler's check serial numbers. Carry one set of copies in a safe place, apart from the originals, and leave another set at home.

LOST PASSPORTS. If you lose your passport, notify the local police and the nearest embassy or consulate of your home government. To expedite its replacement, you will need to show ID and proof of citizenship. In some cases, a replacement may take weeks to process, and it may be valid only for a limited time. Any visas stamped in your old passport will be irretrievably lost. In an emergency, ask for immediate temporary traveling papers that will permit you to re-enter your home country. Your passport is a public document belonging to your nation's government. You may have to surrender it to a foreign government official, but if you don't get it back in a reasonable amount of time, inform the nearest mission of your home country.

VISAS, INVITATIONS & WORK PERMITS

Canadian citizens do not need to obtain a visa for admission to the US. Citizens of Australia, New Zealand, and most European countries can waive US visas through the **Visa Waiver Program.** Visitors qualify if they are traveling only for business or pleasure (*not* work or study), are staying for fewer than **90 days,** demonstrate intent to leave (e.g. a return plane ticket), possess an I-94W form, are traveling on particular air or sea carriers, and have a machine-readable passport from their country of citizenship. See http://travel.state.gov/vwp.html for more info.

Citizens of South Africa and most other countries need a visa—a stamp, sticker, or insert in your passport specifying the purpose of your travel and the permitted duration of your stay—in addition to a valid passport for entrance to the US. See http://travel.state.gov/visa_services.html and www.unitedstatesvisas.gov for more information. To obtain a visa, contact a US embassy or consulate. Recent security measures have made the visa application process more rigorous, and therefore lengthy; apply well in advance of your travel date.

Admission as a visitor does not include the right to work, which is authorized only by a **work permit.** Entering the US to study requires a special visa. For more information, see **Alternatives to Tourism,** p. 319.

IDENTIFICATION

When you travel, always carry two or more forms of ID , including at least one with your photo. A passport along with a driver's license or birth certificate usually serves as adequate proof of your identity and citizenship. Never carry all your IDs together; split them up in case of theft or loss, and keep photocopies of them in your luggage or at home.

DRIVER'S LICENSE. A foreign driver's license is usually acceptable for driving in the United States and Canada for a temporary period. To rent a car, purchase an **International Driving Permit** from a certified agent, such as the AA in the UK (☎0990 600 0371; www.theaa.com). A photo-less driver's license is unlikely to be accepted.

TEACHER, STUDENT & YOUTH IDENTIFICATION. While more widely used in Europe, the **International Student Identity Card (ISIC)** is still the most-accepted form of student identification. Flashing this card can often procure you discounts for sights, theaters, museums, transportation, and other services. You must present an ISIC card to purchase reduced-rate student fare airplane tickets. Cardholders have access to a toll-free 24hr. ISIC helpline whose multilingual staff can provide assistance in medical, legal, and financial emergencies overseas (☎877-370-4742 in the US and Canada; elsewhere call US collect ☎+1 715-345-0505). US cardholders can also receive certain insurance benefits (see **Insurance,** p. 308). Applicants must be enrolled students at a secondary or post-secondary school and must be at least 12 years old. Because of the proliferation of fake ISICs, some services (particularly airlines) require additional proof of student identity. Many student travel agencies around the world issue ISICs, including STA Travel (www.statravel.com) in Australia and New Zealand; Travel Cuts (www.travelcuts.com) in Canada; USIT (www.usitnow.ie/countries/ire-

Get to D.C. by Trolley

By Boat

By Horse

land) in Ireland and Northern Ireland; SASTS in South Africa; Campus Travel and STA Travel in the UK; Council and STA in the US.

The **International Teacher Identity Card (ITIC)** offers teachers the same insurance coverage as well as similar but limited discounts. For travelers who are 25 or under but are not students, the **International Youth Travel Card (IYTC)** also offers many of the same benefits as the ISIC. Similarly, the **International Student Exchange ID Card (ISE)** provides discounts, medical benefits, and the ability to purchase student airfares.

Each of these identity cards costs $22 or equivalent. ISIC and ITIC cards are valid for roughly 1½ academic years; IYTC cards are valid for one year from the date of issue. Many student travel agencies issue the cards; for a list of issuing agencies, or for more information, contact the **International Student Travel Confederation (ISTC),** Herengracht 479, 1017 BS Amsterdam, The Netherlands (☎ +31 20 421 28 00; www.istc.org).

CUSTOMS

Upon entering the United States, you must declare items acquired abroad and pay a duty on the value of those articles if it exceeds the amount allowed by the US Customs Service. Note that goods and gifts purchased at **duty-free** shops abroad are not exempt from duty or sales tax at your point of return and thus must be declared; "duty-free" means that you don't pay a tax in the country of purchase. Upon returning home, you must similarly declare all articles acquired abroad and pay a duty on the value of articles in excess of your home country's allowance. In order to expedite your return, make a list of any valuables brought from home, register them with customs before traveling abroad, and keep receipts for all goods acquired abroad.

MONEY

CURRENCY & EXCHANGE

The currency chart below is based on August 2003 exchange rates between local currency and Australian dollars (AUS$), Canadian dollars (CDN$), Irish pounds (IR£), New Zealand dollars (NZ$), South African Rand (ZAR), British pounds (UK£), European Union euros (EUR€), and US dollars (US$). Check the currency converter on financial websites such as www.bloomberg.com and www.xe.com, or a large newspaper for the latest exchange rates.

US DOLLAR ($)	
AUS$1 = US$0.64	US$1 = AUS$1.55
CDN$1 = US$0.71	US$1 = CDN$1.40
NZ$1 = US$0.58	US$1 = NZ$1.72
ZAR1 = US$0.13	US$1 = ZAR7.43
UK£1 = US$1.60	US$1 = UK£0.62
€1 = US$0.88	US$1 = €1.13

As a general rule, it's cheaper to convert money in the US than at home. While currency exchange and ATMs are available at Reagan National, Dulles, and BWI airports, it's still wise to bring enough US dollars to last for the first 24hr. of your trip.

When changing money, try to go only to banks that have at most a 5% margin between their buy and sell prices. Banks, ATMs, and credit cards will offer the best rates. Since you lose money with every transaction, **convert large sums** (unless the currency is depreciating rapidly), **but no more than you'll need.**

If you use traveler's checks or bills, carry some in small denominations (the equivalent of $50 or less) for times when you are forced to exchange money at disadvantageous rates, but bring a range of denominations since charges may be levied per check cashed. Store your money in a variety of forms—cash, traveler's checks, and ATM and/or credit cards.

TRAVELER'S CHECKS

Traveler's checks are one of the safest and least troublesome means of carrying funds. American Express and Visa are the most widely recognized brands. Check issuers provide refunds if the checks are lost or stolen, and many provide additional services, such as toll-free refund hotlines abroad, emergency message services, and stolen credit card assistance. Traveler's checks are readily accepted in D.C. Never countersign your checks until you are ready to cash them, and always bring your passport with you when you plan to use the checks.

American Express: Checks available with commission at select banks and all AmEx offices. US residents can also purchase checks by phone (☎888-269-6669) or online (www.aexp.com). AAA offers commission-free checks to its members. Checks available in US, Australian, British, Canadian, Japanese, and Euro currencies. *Cheques for Two* can be signed by either of two people traveling together. For purchase locations or more information contact AmEx's service centers: In the US and Canada ☎800-221-7282; in the UK 0800 521 313; in Australia 800 25 19 02; in New Zealand 0800 441 068; elsewhere US collect +1 801-964-6665. **In D.C.**, American Express offices are located downtown at 1150 Connecticut Ave. NW (☎457-1300). **In Virginia**, offices at Pentagon Row, 1101 S. Joyce St., Suite B2, in Arlington (☎703-415-5400) and at Tyson's Galleria, 1801 International Dr., in McLean (☎703-893-3550). AmEx offices cash checks commission-free, but often at worse rates than banks.

Travelex/Thomas Cook: In the US and Canada ☎800-287-7362; in the UK 0800 62 21 01; elsewhere UK collect +44 1733 31 89 50; online at www.travelex.com. Checks available in 13 currencies. Offices cash checks commission-free. **In D.C.**, Travelex offices at Union Station, 50 Massachusetts Ave. NE (☎371-9220), and at 1800 K Street, Ste. 103 (☎872-1428).

Visa: Checks available (generally with commission) at banks worldwide. For the location of the nearest office, call Visa's service centers: In the US ☎800-227-6811; in the UK 0800 89 50 78; elsewhere UK collect +44 020 7937 8091; or visit www.visa.com. Checks available in US, British, Canadian, Japanese, and Euro currencies.

CREDIT, DEBIT, AND ATM CARDS

Credit cards are generally accepted in all but the smallest businesses in D.C. and are sometimes required to reserve hotel rooms or rental cars. Credit cards often offer superior exchange rates—up to 5% better than the retail rate used by banks and other currency exchange establishments. Credit cards may also offer services such as insurance or emergency help. **MasterCard** and **Visa** are the most welcomed and can

Find (Our Student Airfares are cheap, flexible & exclusive)
great Student Airfares everywhere
at StudentUniverse.com and Get lost.

 StudentUniverse.com   Student Airfares everywhere

be used to extract cash advances in dollars from associated banks and teller machines throughout D.C.; **American Express** cards work at some ATMs and at AmEx offices and major airports.

ATM cards are widespread in D.C. Depending on the system that your home bank uses, you can most likely access your personal bank account from the U.S. ATMs get the same wholesale exchange rate as credit cards, but there is often a limit on the amount of money you can withdraw per day (around $500), and computer networks sometimes fail. There is typically also a surcharge of $1-3 per withdrawal.

The two major international money networks are **Cirrus** (☎800-424-7787; www.mastercard.com) and **Visa/PLUS** (☎800-843-7587; www.visa.com). Allfirst (☎800-842-2265 or www.allfirst.com), Riggs (☎800-368-5800 or www.riggsbank.com), and SunTrust (☎800-786-8787 or www.suntrust.com) banks are widespread in the D.C. area.

COSTS

To give you a general idea, a bare-bones day in D.C. (camping or sleeping in hostels/guest houses, buying food at supermarkets) would cost about $35; a slightly more comfortable day (sleeping in hostels/guesthouses and the occasional budget hotel, eating one meal per day at a restaurant, going out at night) would run $65; for a luxurious day, the sky's the limit.

TAXES

The prices quoted throughout *Let's Go: Washington, D.C.* are the amounts before sales tax has been added. Sales tax is 5.75% in D.C., 5% in Maryland, and 4.5% in Virginia. D.C. hotel tax is 14.5%; restaurant, car rental, and liquor taxes are all 10%. Parking in commercial lots (as opposed to Metro lots) incurs a 12% tax. The D.C. government often grants sales-tax free holiday weeks at the end of the summer.

HEALTH

BEFORE YOU GO

In your passport, write the names of any people you wish to be contacted in case of a medical emergency, and list any allergies or medical conditions. Matching a prescription to a foreign equivalent is not always easy, safe, or possible, so carry up-to-date, legible prescriptions or a statement from your doctor stating the medication's trade name, manufacturer, chemical name, and dosage.

USEFUL ORGANIZATIONS & PUBLICATIONS

The US **Centers for Disease Control and Prevention** (**CDC**; ☎877-394-8747; www.cdc.gov/travel) maintains an international travelers' hotline and an informative website. The CDC's comprehensive booklet *Health Information for International Travel*, an annual rundown of disease, immunization, and general health advice, is free online or available for $30 via the Public Health Foundation (☎877-252-1200). Consult the appropriate government agency of your home country for consular information sheets on health, entry requirements, and other issues for various countries. For information on medical evacuation services and travel insurance firms, see the US government's website at http://travel.state.gov/medical.html or the **British Foreign and Commonwealth Office** (www.fco.gov.uk).

HIV & AIDS

Among U.S. cities, D.C. has one of the highest HIV infection rates annually. In D.C., the **Whitman-Walker Clinic,** 1407 S St., NW (☎202-797-3500; www.wwc.org) is synonymous with AIDS treatment. Whitman offers a variety of resources, such as counseling, medical care, legal service, housing, and HIV/AIDS education. If you are **HIV-**

positive, contact the **Bureau of Consular Affairs,** Department of State, 2201 C St. NW, Washington, D.C. 20520 (☎202-647-9577; http://travel.state.gov). According to US law, HIV-positive persons are not permitted to enter the US. However, HIV testing is conducted for permanent immigration.

For more information on **Acquired Immune Deficiency Syndrome (AIDS),** contact the **US Center for Disease Control's** 24hr. hotline at ☎800-342-2437, or contact the **Joint United Nations Programme on HIV/AIDS (UNAIDS),** 20 Ave. Appia, CH-1211 Geneva 27, Switzerland (☎+41 22 791 3666; fax 22 791 4187) for statistical material on AIDS internationally.

WOMEN'S HEALTH

Women using birth control pills should bring enough to allow for possible loss or extended stays. Bring a prescription, since forms of the pill vary. Abortions are legal in the US. In D.C., the **National Abortion Federation Hotline,** 1755 Massachusetts Ave. NW, Suite 600 (☎800-772-9100) provides referrals to area physicians. **Planned Parenthood,** 1108 16th St. NW (☎202-347-8500; www.ppmw.org) provides birth control, emergency contraception, and abortions.

INSURANCE

Travel insurance generally covers four basic areas: medical/health problems, property loss, trip cancellation/interruption, and emergency evacuation. Although your regular insurance policies may extend to travel-related accidents, you might still consider purchasing travel insurance if the cost of potential trip cancellation/interruption is greater than you can absorb. Prices for travel insurance purchased separately generally run about $50 per week for full coverage, while trip cancellation/interruption may be purchased separately at a rate of about $5.50 per $100 of coverage.

Medical insurance (especially university policies) often covers costs incurred abroad; check with your provider. **Canadians** are protected by their home province's health insurance plan for up to 90 days after leaving the country; check with the provincial Ministry of Health or Health Plan Headquarters for details. **Homeowners' insurance** (or your family's coverage) often covers theft during travel and loss of travel documents (passport, plane ticket, railpass, etc.) up to $500.

ISIC and **ITIC** (see p. 303) provide basic insurance benefits, including $100 per day of in-hospital sickness for up to 60 days, $3000 of accident-related medical reimbursement, and $25,000 for emergency medical transport. Cardholders have access to a toll-free 24hr. helpline (run by the insurance provider **TravelGuard**) for medical, legal, and financial emergencies overseas (US and Canada ☎877-370-4742, elsewhere call US collect ☎+1 715-345-0505). **American Express** (☎800-528-4800) grants most cardholders automatic car rental insurance (collision and theft, but not liability) and travel accident coverage of $100,000 on flight purchases made with the card.

Council and **STA** (see p. 311) offer plans that can supplement your basic coverage. Other private insurance providers in the US and Canada include: **Access America** (☎800-284-8300; www.accessamerica.com); **Berkely Group/Carefree Travel Insurance** (☎800-323-3149; www.berkely.com); **Globalcare Travel Insurance** (☎800-821-2488; www.globalcare-cocco.com); and **Travel Assistance International** (☎800-821-2828; www.europ-assistance.com). Providers in the **UK** include **Columbus Direct** (☎020 7375 0011). In **Australia,** try **AFTA** (☎02 9264 3299).

PACKING

Pack lightly: Lay out only what you absolutely need, then take half the clothes and twice the money. Most necessities and supplies can easily be purchased in D.C.

CONVERTERS, ADAPTERS & TRANSFORMERS. In the U.S., electrical appliances are designed for 120V current. Canadians, who also use 120V at home, will be able to use electical appliances in the U.S. with no problem. Visitors from the U.K., Ireland, Australia, New Zealand (who use 230V) as well as South Africa (who use 220-250V) often won't need a converter, but will need an adapter. In addition, you may need to purchase a transformer to convert the lower American voltage to the higher voltage required for most appliances; certain electrical devices may accept both 230V and 120V. For further details, check out http://kropla.com/electric.htm.

ACCOMMODATIONS

HOTELS

The cheapest **hotel singles** in D.C. start around $50-60 per night, **doubles** around $70 per night, although most hotels are more expensive, usually $100 or more per night for a single. It is easiest to make reservations over the phone with a credit card. Hotels are a reasonable option for short stays or fat budgets. For a more complete price range of hotels in D.C., see the **Accommodations Price Chart**, p. 207.

OTHER TYPES OF ACCOMMODATIONS

BED & BREAKFASTS AND GUESTHOUSES

For a cozy alternative to impersonal hotel rooms, **Bed & Breakfasts (B&Bs)**, private homes with rooms available to travelers, range from the acceptable to the sublime. Prices range depending on the B&Bs location as well as the season. For more info on B&Bs, see **Bed & Breakfast Inns Online**, P.O. Box 829, Madison, TN 37116 (☎615-868-1946; www.bbonline.com/dc/washington.html), **InnFinder,** 6200 Gisholt Dr. #105, Madison, WI 53713 (☎608-285-6600; www.inncrawler.com), or **InnSite** (www.innsite.com/browse-DC.html). In D.C., there is often little difference between B&Bs and other **guesthouses**. Like B&Bs, guesthouses regularly include breakfast and often cost less than hotels. For a sense of the cost of B&Bs and guest-houses in D.C., see the **Accommodations chart**, p. 207.

HOSTELS

Hostels are generally laid out dorm-style, often with large single-sex or mixed rooms and bunk beds, although some offer private rooms for families and couples. They often have kitchens and utensils for your use, bike or moped rentals, storage areas, transportation to airports, breakfast, Internet access, and laundry facilities. In D.C., a dorm bed in a hostel will average around $20-32 and a private room around $40. For more info on hostels in Washington, see **Accommodations,** p. 207.

UNIVERSITY DORMS

Many **colleges and universities** open their residence halls to travelers during the summer. Getting a room may take a couple of phone calls and require advanced planning, but rates tend to be low, and many offer free local calls and Internet access. Usually, residents of university dorms who are not also students of the university must pay the 14.5% D.C. hotel tax. See **Dorms**, p. 219.

HOME EXCHANGES

Home exchange offers the traveler various types of homes (houses, apartments, condominiums, villas, yachts), plus the opportunity to live like a native and to cut down on accommodation fees. For more information, contact **HomeExchange.Com** (☎800-877-8723; www.homeexchange.com), or **Intervac International Home Exchange** (☎800-756-4663; www.intervacUS.com).

Find (Our Student Airfares are cheap, flexible & exclusive)
great Student Airfares everywhere
at StudentUniverse.com and **Get lost.**

 StudentUniverse.com

Student Airfares everywhere

GETTING TO D.C.

BY PLANE

When it comes to airfare, a little effort can save you a bundle. If your plans are flexible enough to deal with the restrictions, courier fares are the cheapest. Tickets bought from consolidators and standby seating are also good deals, but last-minute specials, airfare wars, and charter flights often beat these fares. Students, seniors, and those under 26 should never pay full price for a ticket.

AIRFARES

Airfares to D.C. peak between mid-June and early September, and holidays are also expensive periods to travel. Midweek (M-Th) round-trip flights run $40-50 cheaper than weekend flights. However, bargain weekend fares to D.C. can be found from many US cities. Not fixing a return date ("open return") or arriving in and departing from different cities ("open-jaw") can be pricier than round-trip flights.

Round-trip **fares** from Western Europe to D.C. range from $150-450 during the off-season to $250-650 during the summer; from Australia and New Zealand the cost ranges from $800-1100; from South Africa the cost ranges from $1100-1500. If you are flying to Washington's **Reagan National Airport** from New York, the **Delta Shuttle** (☎800-221-1212; www.delta.com) and the **US Airways Shuttle** (also flies from Boston; ☎800-428-4322; www.usairways.com) are usually quicker and cheaper than by train. Be prepared to shell out $200-500 from the US or Canadian West Coast.

WASHINGTON AIRPORTS

From within the US, it's most convenient (and scenic) to fly into **Ronald Reagan National Airport** (☎703-417-8000; www.mwaa.com/national/), known as National, located in Arlington County, VA. National is on the Metro's Blue and Yellow lines and is a short cab ride to downtown. Though National is more convenient, **Dulles International Airport** (☎703-572-2700; www.metwashairports.com/dulles/), in rural Dulles, Virginia, is Washington's major international airport; many domestic flights touch down here, too. The drive from downtown takes about 40min. (but more during rush hour). Dirt-cheap flights come into **Baltimore-Washington International (BWI) Airport** (☎800-435-9294; www.bwiairport.com), which is 10 mi. south of Baltimore.

BUDGET & STUDENT TRAVEL AGENCIES

usit world (www.usitworld.com). Over 50 **usit campus** branches in the UK, including 52 Grosvenor Gardens, **London** SW1W 0AG (☎0870 240 10 10); **Manchester** (☎0161 273 1880); and **Edinburgh** (☎0131 668 3303). Nearly 20 **usit NOW** offices in Ireland, including 19-21 Aston Quay, O'Connell Bridge, **Dublin** 2 (☎01 602 1600; www.usit-now.ie). Other offices throughout Europe.

CTS Travel, 44 Goodge St., **London** W1T 2AD, UK (☎0207 636 0031; www.ctstravel.co.uk).

STA Travel, 7890 S. Hardy Dr., Ste. 110, Tempe, AZ 85284, USA (24hr. reservations and info ☎800-781-4040; www.sta-travel.com). A student and youth travel organization with over 150 offices worldwide (check their website for a listing of all their offices). Ticket booking, travel insurance, railpasses, and more.

Travel CUTS (Canadian Universities Travel Services Limited), 187 College St., **Toronto,** ON M5T 1P7 (☎416-979-2406; www.travelcuts.com). Offices across Canada and the United States in Seattle, San Francisco, Los Angeles, New York and elsewhere. Also in the UK, 295-A Regent St., **London** W1R 7YA (☎0207 255 1944).

✈ **FLIGHT PLANNING ON THE INTERNET.**
Many airline sites offer last-minute deals on the Web. Other sites compile the deals for you—try www.bestfares.com, www.flights.com, www.hotdeals.com, www.lowestfare.com, www.onetravel.com, and www.travelzoo.com.

■ **StudentUniverse** (www.studentuniverse.com), **STA** (www.sta-travel.com), and **Orbitz** (www.orbitz.com) provide quotes on student tickets, while **Expedia** (www.expedia.com) and **Travelocity** (www.travelocity.com) offer full travel services. **Priceline** (www.priceline.com) allows you to specify a price, and obligates you to buy any ticket that meets or beats it; be prepared for antisocial hours and odd routes. **Skyauction** (www.skyauction.com) allows you to bid on both last-minute and advance-purchase tickets.

COMMERCIAL AIRLINES

The commercial airlines' lowest regular offer is the **APEX** (Advance Purchase Excursion) fare, which provides confirmed reservations and allows "open-jaw" tickets. Generally, reservations must be made seven to 21 days ahead of departure, with seven- to 14-day minimum-stay and up to 90-day maximum-stay restrictions. These fares carry hefty cancellation penalties (fees rise in summer). Off-season fares should be cheaper than the **high-season** (mid-Jun to early Sept.) ones listed here.

AIR COURIER FLIGHTS

Those who travel light should consider courier flights. Couriers help transport cargo on international flights by using their checked luggage space for freight. Most flights are round-trip only, with short fixed-length stays (usually one week). Most of these flights also operate only out of major gateway cities, mostly in North America. Generally, you must be over 21 (in some cases 18). In summer, the most popular destinations usually require an advance reservation of about two weeks (you can usually book up to two months ahead). Super-discounted fares are common for "last-minute" flights (three to 14 days ahead). Groups such as the **Air Courier Association** (☎ 800-282-1202; www.aircourier.org) and the **International Association of Air Travel Couriers** (☎ 308-632-3273; www.courier.org) provide their members with lists of opportunities worldwide for an annual fee. Check out www.couriertravel.org, and www.aircourier.co/uk/ for more information.

STANDBY FLIGHTS

Traveling standby requires considerable flexibility in arrival and departure dates and cities. Companies dealing in standby flights sell vouchers rather than tickets, along with the promise to get to your destination (or near your destination) within a certain window of time (typically 1-5 days). You may receive a monetary refund only if every available flight within your date range is full; if you opt not to take an available flight, you can only get credit toward future travel. To check on a company's service record in the US, call the Better Business Bureau (☎ 212-533-6200). Check out www.airhitch.org and www.airtech.com for some standby deals.

TICKET CONSOLIDATORS

Ticket consolidators, or **"bucket shops,"** buy unsold tickets in bulk from commercial airlines and sell them at discounted rates. The best place to look is in the Sunday travel section of any major newspaper, where many bucket shops place tiny ads. Availability is often very limited. Not all bucket shops are reliable, so insist on a receipt that gives full detail of restrictions, refunds, and tickets, and pay by credit card (in spite of the 2-5% fee) so you can stop payment if you never receive your tickets. For more info, see www.travel-library.com/air-travel/consolidators.html.

Within the US and Canada, consolidators worth trying are **Interworld** (☎ 305-443-4929; fax 443-0351); **Rebel** (☎ 800-227-3235; www.rebeltours.com); **Cheap Tickets** (☎ 800-377-1000; www.cheaptickets.com). Yet more consolidators on the web include the **Internet Travel Network** (www.itn.com); **Flights.com** (www.flights.com); **TravelHUB** (www.travelhub.com); and **The Travel Site** (www.thetravelsite.com). Keep in mind that these are just suggestions to get you started in your research; *Let's Go* does not endorse any of these agencies.

BY TRAIN

Amtrak (☎ 800-872-7245; www.amtrak.com) is the only provider of intercity passenger train service in the US. Its web page lists up-to-date schedules, fares, and arrival and departure info. Amtrak's Acela Express speedily connects D.C., New York, and Boston, but costs the equivalent of a shuttle flight. You can reserve tickets on the web page. Many travelers qualify for discounts: senior citizens (10% off); students (15% off with a Student Advantage Card; call ☎ 800-962-6872 to purchase the $20 card); travelers with disabilities (15% off); children ages 2-15 accompanied by a parent (50% off); children under two (free); members of the US armed forces, active-duty veterans, and their dependents (25% off).

Amtrak's trains connect D.C. to most other parts of the country through **Union Station,** 50 Massachusetts Ave. NE (☎ 202-371-9441; www.unionstationdc.com). Amtrak leaves for D.C. from **Baltimore** (40min., 5per day, $14; Metroliner and Acela Express 35 min., 5 per day, $39); **Boston** (8½hr., 4 per day, $81; Acela Express 6½hr., 6 per day, $165); **New York** (3½hr.; 4 per day; $72; Metroliner and Acela Express 3hr.; 6 per day; $128-147); and **Philadelphia** (2hr., 5 per day, $45; Metroliner and Acela Express 1hr. 40min., 5 per day, $97-108). Additional routes to D.C. start in **Richmond** (2½hr., 7 per day, $32-37); **Virginia Beach** (6hr., 2 per day, $53); **Williamsburg** (3½hr. 2 per day, $41). Maryland's commuter train, **MARC** (☎ 410-539-5000 or toll-free ☎ 866-743-3682; www.mtamaryland.com), also departs from Union Station. It offers weekday service to **Baltimore** ($7, round-trip $14) and elsewhere.

BY BUS

If you're coming from outside the East Coast or have a tight budget, you might want to consider traveling to D.C. by bus. **Greyhound** (☎ 800-231-2222; www.greyhound.com) operates the largest number of lines, departing for D.C. daily from **Baltimore** (1-1½hr., 32 per day, $11); **New York City** (4½-5½hr., 23 per day, $42); **Philadelphia** (3¼-4¼hr., 10 per day, $22); **Richmond** (2-3hr., 17 per day, $16.65). Washington's Greyhound station, 1005 1st St. NE (☎ 202-289-5154) at L St., is rather decrepit. A number of **discounts** are available on Greyhound's standard-fare tickets: 15% off with a Student Advantage Card; 10% off for senior citizens 62+ who pay a one-time $5 fee; 50% off for children ages 2-11; travelers with special needs and their companions ride for the price of one. Active and retired US military personnel and National Guard Reserves receive 10% off and their spouses and dependents may take a round-trip between any two points in the US for $169. If you purchase your ticket 3 days in advance in the off-season or 7 days in advance in the summer, a 2nd ticket is ½-price.

BY CAR

Most drivers reach D.C. from the north or south, on or parallel to I-95. **From the north**: To go downtown from the **Baltimore-Washington Parkway**, follow signs for **New York Avenue**. From **I-95**, get onto the **Capital Beltway (I-495)** and get off the merry-go-round at whichever exit you choose. Three of the easiest and most useful exits are **Wisconsin Avenue** (to Upper NW and Georgetown), **Connecticut Avenue** (Chevy Chase, Upper NW, Adams Morgan, Dupont Circle, and downtown), and **New Hampshire Avenue** (through Takoma to downtown). **From the south**: Take I-95 to I-395 to the 14th St. Bridge or Memorial Bridge (both lead downtown). **From the west**: Take I-66E over the Roosevelt

Bridge and follow signs for Constitution Ave. I-66 is more direct than I-495 when heading downtown. Due to congested rush hours, the stretch of I-66 inside the Beltway (between the Beltway and the Theodore Roosevelt Bridge) is restricted to vehicles with at least two passengers ("High Occupancy Vehicles" or HOV-2; in effect on I-66E M-F 6:30-9am and on I-66W M-F 4-6:30pm). Outside the Beltway (between the Beltway and Route 234 in Manassas), I-66 reserves the left-hand lane for HOV-2 vehicles during the morning and evening rush hours (in effect on I-66E M-F 5:30-9:30am and on I-66W M-F 3-7pm). Try to steer clear of I-66, I-495, I-270, and I-95 during these hours. The **speed limit** in most of D.C. is 25 m.p.h., or about 40km per hr.

SPECIFIC CONCERNS

WOMEN TRAVELERS

If women travelers encounter unwanted advances, a polite, "No, I'm sorry," almost invariably results in gracious good-byes and being left alone. For rude or frightening propositions, the best answer is no answer—stare straight ahead and make a swift retreat to a safe, populated area. Youth hostels, university housing, bed and breakfasts, and organizations offering rooms to women only may give an opportunity to meet people with whom you can explore at night.

The National Organization for Women (NOW), 733 15th St. NW, Fl. 2, Washington, D.C. 20005 (☎202-628-8669; www.now.org), has branches across the US that can refer women travelers to rape crisis centers and counseling services.

TRAVELING ALONE

Visiting a cosmopolitian city like D.C. by yourself is not at all uncommon. However, any solo traveler is a more vulnerable target of harassment and street theft. As a lone traveler, try not to stand out as a tourist, look confident, and be especially careful in deserted or very crowded areas. If questioned, never admit that you are traveling alone. Maintain regular contact with someone at home who knows your itinerary. For more tips, pick up *Traveling Solo* by Eleanor Berman (Globe Pequot Press, $17) or subscribe to **Connecting: Solo Travel Network,** 689 Park Road, Unit 6, Gibsons, BC V0N 1V7, Canada (☎604-886-9099; www.cstn.org; membership $35). **Travel Companion Exchange,** P.O. Box 833, Amityville, NY 11701 (☎631-454-0880, in the US 800-392-1256; www.whytravelalone.com; $48), will link solo travelers with companions with similar travel habits and interests.

OLDER TRAVELERS

Discounts abound for travelers over 62 (and sometimes, over 60). All you need is ID proving your age. Pick up the free **Golden Washingtonian Club Gold Mine** directory, which lists establishments offering 10-20% discounts to seniors on goods and services, at local hotel desks or at the **D.C. Office on Aging,** 441 4th St. NW, Ste. 900S (☎202-724-5626). The Office on Aging also offers an info and referral service for those 60 and over. (Open M-F 8:30am-5pm.) The books *No Problem! Worldwise Tips for Mature Adventurers,* by Janice Kenyon (Orca Book Publishers; $16) and *Unbelievably Good Deals and Great Adventures That You Absolutely Can't Get Unless You're Over 50,* by Joan Rattner Heilman (NTC/Contemporary Publishing; $13) are both excellent resources. Also useful are the following websites:

Elderhostel, 11 Ave. de Lafayette, Boston, MA 02111 (☎877-426-8056; www.elderhostel.org). Organizes 3- to 7-day educational adventures in D.C. for those 55+.

The Mature Traveler, P.O. Box 15791, Sacramento, CA 95852 (☎800-460-6676; www.thematuretraveler.com). Deals and travel packages for the 50+ traveler. Subscription $30.

BISEXUAL, GAY & LESBIAN TRAVELERS

Washington's bisexual, gay, and lesbian communities are exceptional for their diversity and visibility, and for the comfortable geographic and legal positions they occupy within the city. **Dupont Circle** is the hub of gay activity in D.C. Easily accessible by Metro, the neighborhood offers whole blocks of gay and gay-friendly establishments. Most bars and restaurants cluster around 17th and P St. between 21st and 22nd St. **Southeast** Washington also contains 10 or so gay and gay-friendly bars and clubs, but exercise caution if you choose to explore Southeast.

There are a handful of gay publications in D.C. **The Washington Blade** (www.washblade.com) is an indispensable source of news, reviews, and club listings. Published every Friday, it's available in virtually every storefront and many restaurants in Dupont Circle. **MetroWeekly** (www.metroweekly.com), a newer arts and entertainment weekly published on Thursdays, contains brief public interest items, short fiction, and extensive nightlife coverage, and is almost as easy to find as *The Blade*. **The Lambda Rising Bookstore** (see p. 199) is a source for these periodicals. For the most comprehensive listing of businesses serving Washington's gay community, try **The Other Pages,** a free gay and lesbian telephone directory available at Dupont Circle restaurants or online at www.otherpages.com. For gay and lesbian nightlife, see **Gay Bars and Clubs,** p. 180.

> **FURTHER READING: BISEXUAL, GAY, & LESBIAN.** *Spartacus International Gay Guide 2001-2002.* Bruno Gmunder Verlag ($33).
> *Damron Men's Guide, Damron Road Atlas, Damron's Accommodations,* and *The Women's Traveller.* Damron Travel Guides ($14-19). For more info, call ☎800-462-6654 or visit www.damron.com.
> *Ferrari Guides' Gay Travel A to Z, Ferrari Guides' Men's Travel in Your Pocket,* and *Ferrari Guides' Inn Places.* Ferrari Publications ($16-20). Purchase the guides online at www.ferrariguides.com.
> *The Gay Vacation Guide: The Best Trips and How to Plan Them,* Mark Chesnut. Citadel Press ($15).

TRAVELERS WITH DISABILITIES

Parts of D.C., especially those administered by the federal government, do their best to accommodate disabled travelers. At any Smithsonian information desk, visitors can pick up a free copy of **Smithsonian Access,** which gives details regarding the accessibility of each Smithsonian museum (access online at www.si.edu/opa/accessibility). The **Metro System Guide** (☎202-637-7000; www.wmata.com) provides information on public transit for the disabled. **The Washington Convention and Visitor's Association** (☎202-789-7000; www.washington.org) publishes a fact sheet that gives details on the accessibility of area hotels, restaurants, malls, and attractions. Guide dogs are allowed almost everywhere in Washington, but call ahead to be sure. Both **Amtrak** and major airlines will accommodate disabled passengers if notified at least 72 hours in advance. Hearing-impaired travelers may contact Amtrak using teletype printers (☎800-872-7245). **Greyhound** (☎800-752-4841) buses will provide free travel for a companion. For more info on getting to or around D.C., see p. 331.

USEFUL ORGANIZATIONS

Mobility International USA (MIUSA), P.O. Box 10767, Eugene, OR 97440 (voice and TDD ☎541-343-1284; www.miusa.org). Provides a variety of books and other publications containing information for travelers with disabilities.

Society for the Advancement of Travel for the Handicapped (SATH), 347 Fifth Ave., #610, New York, NY 10016 (☎212-447-7284; www.sath.org). An advocacy group that publishes free online travel information and the travel magazine *OPEN WORLD* ($18, free for members). Annual membership $45, students and seniors $30.

TOUR AGENCIES

Directions Unlimited, 123 Green Ln., Bedford Hills, NY 10507 (☎800-533-5343). Books individual and group vacations for the physically disabled; not an info service.

The Guided Tour Inc., 7900 Old York Rd., #114B, Elkins Park, PA 19027 (☎800-783-5841; www.guidedtour.com). Organizes travel programs for persons with developmental and physical challenges in the US, as well as other destinations.

TRAVELERS WITH CHILDREN

Washington is a great place for kids. Just about everything that fascinates children—animals, dinosaurs, railroad trains, crime fighters, presidents—is represented in the D.C. area. Consult the list of kid-friendly upcoming events which appears every Friday in the *Post*'s Weekend section for great ideas on what to do with children in D.C.

DIETARY CONCERNS

Travelers who keep kosher should call the **Jewish Information and Referral Service** (☎301-770-4848; www.jirs.org), which provides listings for kosher restaurants in D.C. Also check www.kosherdelight.com/kosherestaurantsDC.htm and www.ekosherstore.com. Vegetarian and vegan eaters will have little trouble finding suitable meals in D.C. *Let's Go* lists many establishments that serve vegetarian options.

OTHER RESOURCES

Let's Go tries to cover all aspects of budget travel, but we can't put *everything* in our guides. Listed below are some tourism bureaus, books, and websites that can serve as jumping off points for your own research.

TOURISM BUREAUS

IN D.C.

Washington, D.C. Convention and Tourism Corporation (WCTC), 1212 New York Ave., NW, Ste. 600 (☎202-789-7000 or toll-free info line 800-422-8644; www.washington.org). Call for a visitor's guide and calendar. Open M-F 9am-5pm; toll-free info line M-F 9am-8pm.

DC Visitor Information Center, on the ground floor of the Ronald Reagan Int'l Trade Center Building, 1300 Pennsylvania Ave., NW (☎866-324-7386; www.dcvisit.com).

OUTSIDE D.C.

Conference and Visitors Bureau of Montgomery Country, MD 11820 Parklawn Dr., Ste. 380, Rockville, MD 20852 (☎800-925-0880 or 301-428-9702; www.cvbmontco.com).

Delaware Tourism Office, 99 Kings Highway, Dover, DE 19901 (866-284-7483; www.visitdelaware.net).

Fairfax County Convention & Visitors Bureau, 8300 Boone Blvd., Vienna, VA 22182 (☎703-790-3329; www.visitfairfax.org).

Maryland Division of Tourism, 217 E. Redwood St., 9th fl., Baltimore, MD 21202 (☎800-634-7386; www.mdisfun.org).

Virginia Department of Tourism, 901 E. Byrd St., Richmond, VA 23219 (☎800-847-4882; www.virginia.org), which also offers a **Virginia Bed and Breakfast Information and Reservation Service** (☎800-934-9184).

USEFUL PUBLICATIONS

To get acquainted with the Washington area in advance, check out **The Washington Post**, particularly the *Metro* section. **Washingtonian Magazine** is a fabulous resource for visitors to and residents of the D.C. area alike. The **CityPaper** lists numerous daytime and night-time activities, geared toward a younger, hipper readership. All these publications can be accessed online (see below).

TRAVEL PUBLISHERS & BOOKSTORES

Travel Books & Language Center, Inc., 4437 Wisconsin Ave. NW, Washington, D.C. 20016 (☎202-237-1322 or 800-220-2665; www.bookweb.org/bookstore/travelbks). Over 60,000 titles from around the world.

WORLD WIDE WEB

Our website, www.letsgo.com, now includes introductory chapters from all our guides and a wealth of information on a monthly featured destination. As always, our website also has info about our books, a travel forum buzzing with stories and tips, and additional links that will help you make the most of a trip to D.C. In addition, all nine Let's Go City Guides are available for a download on Palm OS PDAs.

THE ART OF BUDGET TRAVEL

How to See the World (www.artoftravel.com). A compendium of great travel tips, from cheap flights to self defense to interacting with local culture.

Rec. Travel Library (www.travel-library.com). A fantastic set of links for general information and personal travelogues.

Lycos (http://cityguide.lycos.com). General introductions to cities and regions throughout, accompanied by links to applicable histories, news, and local tourism sites.

INFORMATION ON D.C.

Cultural Tourism D.C. (www.culturaltourismdc.org). Excellent information about neighborhood history, museums, educational talks, and walking tours throughout the city.

Washingtonian (www.washingtonian.com). Every imaginable "best" and "worst" list, plus gossip-a-go-go and the best food critics around.

Washington Post (www.washingtonpost.com). A fantastic amount of information on everything D.C., from news and reviews to daytrips and dancin' gear.

CityPaper (www.washingtoncitypaper.com). The CityPaper online posts news as well as cool events around the city.

D.C. Pages (http://dcpages.com). A great list of links to hot D.C. web sites.

MusicDC (www.musicdc.com). Check out the D.C. scene and keep up on D.C. concerts.

Smithsonian (www.si.edu). Everything about the museums.

TravelApe (http://washington-dc.travelape.com). Lively site packed with helpful D.C. info.

Washington, D.C. Convention and Tourism Corporation (www.washington.org). The "official tourism web site of Washington D.C." Info on attractions, special events, accommodations, dining, and nightlife.

White House (www.whitehouse.gov). Info on presidents, current political information, press releases, links to federal services, and pictures of the building.

INSIDE

volunteering **320**

studying **324**

working **325**

Alternatives to Tourism

When *Let's Go* started out in 1961, about 1.7 million people in the world were traveling internationally each year; in 2002, nearly 700 million such trips were made, and this figure is projected to rise to a billion by 2010. This dramatic increase in tourism underscores the interdependence between the economy, environment, and culture of destinations and the tourists they host. Each year, Washington, D.C. alone welcomes over 20 million visitors.

Those who wish to **volunteer** and get involved with local community service programs have many options. You can participate in projects from observing animals at the National Zoo to serving meals to the hungry, either on an infrequent basis or as the main component of your trip. Later in this section, we recommend organizations that can help you find the opportunities that best suit your interests, whether you're looking to pitch in for a day or a year.

There are any number of other ways that you can integrate yourself in the communities you visit. Studying at a college or language program is one option. D.C. is filled with college students both during the academic year and in the summer, making it a very exciting and rewarding place to learn. Many travelers also structure their trips by the work that they can do along the way—either odd jobs as they go, or full-time stints in cities where they plan to stay for some time. With so many government agencies, political organizations, activist groups, and museums, Washington is teeming with internship opportunities. Keep in mind, however, that positions with high-ranking government officials may be highly selective. Short-term job opportunities are probably most easily found by working with a temp agency.

For those who seek more active involvement, Earthwatch International, Operation Crossroads Africa, and Habitat for Humanity offer fulfilling volunteer opportunities all over the world. For more on volunteering, studying, and working in D.C. and beyond, consult Let's Go's alternatives to tourism site, **www.beyondtourism.com.**

HISTORICAL CONTEXT TO SOCIAL PROBLEMS IN D.C.

Although parts of the city, particularly Northwest, are wealthy and prosperous, poverty is a serious problem in the rest of the city—most notably Southeast and Anacostia. In order to get involved in these needy communities with compassion, it's important to first understand the historical context behind the city's social ills.

> Before handing your money over to any volunteer or study abroad program, make sure you know exactly what you're getting into. It's a good idea to get the name of **previous participants** and ask them about their experience, as some programs sound much better on paper than in reality. The **questions** below are a good place to start:
>
> Will you be the only person in the program? If not, what are the other participants like? How old are they? How much will you be expected to interact with them?
>
> Is room and board included? If so, what is the arrangement? Will you be expected to share a room? A bathroom? What are the meals like? Do they fit any dietary restrictions?
>
> Is transportation included? Are there any additional expenses?
>
> How much free time will you have? Will you be able to travel around the island?
>
> What kind of safety network is set up? Will you still be covered by your home insurance? Does the program have an emergency plan?

In the years after the Civil War, during the Great Migration of the 1920s, and during the population shifts caused by labor shortages in the WWII era, many poor Southern blacks migrated north, settling in northern cities including Baltimore and Washington. These years were a time of *de jure* segregation in D.C., but perhaps segregation became even more dramatic after it was legally abolished by the Civil Rights Act of 1964. In the mid-to-late 1960s, urban riots in D.C., as well as many other US cities, destroyed whole neighborhoods with arson and violence. Perhaps more importantly, they led to increasing white flight to the suburbs, taking much-needed tax dollars out of the neighborhoods that stood to benefit the most from them.

Today, *de facto* segregation is an entrenched and troubling fact of life in D.C. Not only is segregation suspect in a social and moral sense, but it also hurts struggling communities economically. Because of the shortage of tax dollars in impoverished neighborhoods, D.C. public schools are some of the worst in the country—ironically located just a few miles from some of the country's most prestigious private schools. Teachers suffer from a lack of basic school supplies. School facilities are themselves inadequate: in 1997, a number of D.C. public schools had to be shut down for several weeks because they failed to meet fire safety standards. Children enrolled in these schools often receive little educational support at home, making the job of overworked and under-paid teachers even more daunting. Expectations of failure often lead these teachers to promote students with inadequate reading skills from grade to grade. Improving these troubled schools is the key to ending the vicious cycle of poverty, ignorance, and drugs. Volunteers who become involved in mentoring inner-city kids can truly make a personal difference in the lives of children desperate for an education. Read on to find out how you can get involved in aiding inner-city schools, as well as other ways to contribute to the city's needy communities.

VOLUNTEERING

Though D.C. is considered wealthy in worldwide terms, there is no shortage of aid organizations to benefit the very real issues the region faces. Despite the city's affluence, many struggle to find food and shelter on a daily basis. With such pressing needs being left unfulfilled, visitors to D.C. have the opportunity to help improve lives in addition to being tourists. Volunteering can be a highly fulfilling experience, especially when combined with the thrill of traveling in a new place.

A NEW PHILOSOPHY OF TRAVEL

We at *Let's Go* have watched the growth of the 'ignorant tourist' stereotype with dismay, knowing that the majority of travelers care passionately about the state of the communities and environments they explore—but also knowing that even conscientious tourists can inadvertently damage natural wonders, rich cultures, and impoverished communities. We believe the philosophy of **sustainable travel** is among the most important travel tips we could impart to our readers, to help guide fellow backpackers and on-the-road philanthropists. By staying aware of the needs and troubles of local communities, today's travelers can be a powerful force in preserving and restoring this fragile world.

Working against the negative consequences of irresponsible tourism is much simpler than it might seem; it is often self-awareness, rather than self-sacrifice, that makes the biggest difference. Simply by trying to spend responsibly and conserve local resources, all travelers can positively impact the places they visit. Let's Go has partnered with **BEST (Business Enterprises for Sustainable Travel,** an affiliate of the Conference Board; see www.sustainabletravel.org), which recognizes businesses that operate based on the principles of sustainable travel. Below, they provide advice on how ordinary visitors can practice this philosophy in their daily travels, no matter where they are.

TIPS FOR CIVIC TRAVEL: HOW TO MAKE A DIFFERENCE

Travel by train when feasible. Rail travel requires only half the energy per passenger mile that planes do. On average, each of the 40,000 daily domestic air flights releases more than 1700 pounds of greenhouse gas emissions.

Use public mass transportation whenever possible; outside of cities, take advantage of group taxis or vans. Bicycles are an attractive way of seeing a community firsthand. And enjoy walking—purchase good maps of your destination and ask about on-foot touring opportunities.

When renting a car, ask whether fuel-efficient vehicles are available. Honda and Toyota produce cars that use hybrid engines powered by electricity and gasoline, thus reducing emissions of carbon dioxide. Ford Motor Company plans to introduce a hybrid fuel model by the end of 2004.

Reduce, reuse, recycle—use electronic tickets, recycle papers and bottles wherever possible, and avoid using containers made of styrofoam. Refillable water bottles and rechargable batteries both efficiently conserve expendable resources.

Be thoughtful in your purchases. Take care not to buy souvenir objects made from trees in old-growth or endangered forests, such as teak, or items made from endangered species, like ivory or tortoise jewelry. Ask whether products are made from renewable resources.

Buy from local enterprises, such as casual street vendors. In developing countries and low-income neighborhoods, many people depend on the "informal economy" to make a living.

Be on-the-road-philanthropists. If you are inspired by the natural environment of a destination or enriched by its culture, join in preserving their integrity by making a charitable contribution to a local organization.

Spread the word. Upon your return home, tell friends and colleagues about places to visit that will benefit greatly from their tourist dollars, and reward sustainable enterprises by recommending their services. Travelers can not only introduce friends to particular vendors but also to local causes and charities that they might choose to support when they travel.

Most people who volunteer in D.C. do so on a short-term basis, at organizations that make use of drop-in or once-a-week volunteers. The best way to find opportunities that match up with your interests and schedule may be to check with local D.C. organizations and seach the internet. **Greater D.C. Cares** provides listings for hundreds of Washington public service organizations and helps prospective volunteers find positions that meet their needs. Internet sites such as **Idealist** (www.idealist.org) or **VolunteerMatch** (www.volunteermatch.com) are also good resources for volunteer placements. The most common volunteer placements include working in homeless shelters, soup kitchens, or in one of D.C.'s many museums.

HUNGER

Nearly 40% of Washington D.C.'s population lives below the poverty line. With so many poor people it is not surprising that many go hungry. Soup kitchens and food banks play an important role in combatting the hunger problem by providing hot meals to hundreds of people a day who might otherwise go hungry. With so many people to serve, volunteers are essential to serving the large numbers of the needy.

Bread for the City, 1525 7th St. NW, Washington D.C., 20001 (☎202-265-2400; www.breadforthecity.org). Also at 1640 Good Hope Rd. SE, Washington D.C., 20020 (☎202-561-8587). Provides at-risk D.C. residents with food, clothing, medical care, and legal services in an atmosphere of dignity and respect. Its activities are made possible largely by the contributions of a large number of volunteers.

Capital Area Food Bank, 645 Taylor St. NE, Washington D.C., 20017 (☎202-526-5344; www.capitalareafoodbank.org). As the largest public, non-profit food bank and nutrition education center in the D.C. metropolitan area, the this Bank has many volunteer opportunities.

Martha's Table, 2114 14th St. NW, Washington D.C., 20009 (☎202-328-6608; www.marthastable.org). Martha's Table is a non-profit organization that provides assistance to low-income and homeless children, individuals, and families. Thousands of volunteers tutor, mentor, serve food, and offer support to those in need.

HOMELESSNESS

Homelessness continues to be a subtantial problem in Washington, D.C. Each year in D.C., around 15,000 people find themselves without a home. Recent economic declines have only made matters worse for the less fortunate. D.C.'s homeless shelters provide the support and resources the impoverished need to have a chance to improve their lives. Volunteers play an integral role in providing the homeless the opportunity to live, not just to survive.

Community Council for Homelessness at Friendship Place (CCH/FP), 4713 Wisconsin Ave. NW, Washington D.C., 20016 (☎202-364-1419; www.cchfp.org). Volunteers work as mentors, financial advisors, and outreach assistants, as well as prepare and deliver meals to D.C.'s homeless.

Community for Creative Non-Violence (CCNV), 425 2nd St. NW, Washington, D.C., 20001 (☎202-393-1909; users.erols.com/ccnv/). A non-profit organization that provides 1350 beds, food, clothing, medical and mental care, drug and alcohol rehabilitation services, and educational and cultural programs. Volunteer and intern opportunities always available.

Covenant House Washington, 2001 Mississippi Ave. SE, Washington D.C., 20020 (☎202-610-9600; www.covenanthousedc.org). Also has Community Outreach Centers in SE and NE D.C. Provides food, shelter, 24hr. support, medical care, counseling, training, as well as emotional support to homeless, abused, or neglected youth in the D.C. area. Has a wide range of volunteer opportunities.

D.C. Habitat for Humanity, Office Address: 843 Upshur St. NW, Washington, D.C., 20011, Mailing address: P.O. Box 43565, Washington D.C., 20010 (☎202-882-4600; www.dchabitat.org). Volunteers help build homes for low-income families in an effort to combat poverty and homelessness. No building or construction experience is required. For those not interested in assisting in construction, volunteer opportunities are available in public relations, resource development, family selection, and office support.

MUSEUMS

Washington D.C is known for its many exceptional museums. Each day hundreds of toursists and locals alike flock to the Smithsonian museums that line the Mall, the National Zoo, and numerous other museums throughout the city. With so many visitors and so much information to offer, many museums rely on volunteers to assist with exhbibits and museum operations. Volunteering at one of D.C.'s many museums can be a great way to combine learning with public service.

Hirshhorn Museum and Sculpture Garden, 7th St. and Independence Ave. NW, Washington D.C., 20560 (☎202-633-4674, www.hirshhorn.si.edu). Volunteer opportunities are available in several areas, including education, public relations, exhibitions, and the library. Volunteers can also assist with art programs for children and adults.

Smithsonian National Air and Space Museum, 7th and Independence Ave. SW, Washington D.C., 20560 (☎202-357-2700; www.nasm.si.edu). Has regular volunteer opportunities ranging from information desk positions to assisting with discovery station presentations, in addition to various seasonal positions.

National Museum of Natural History, 10th St. and Constitution Ave. NW, Washington D.C., 20560 (Smithsonian visitor information ☎202-357-2700; www.mnh.si.edu). Students can volunteer to work in a variety of areas, including paleobotany, fossil collection, and evolutionary biology.

OTHER OPPORTUNITIES

American Red Cross, 2131 K St. NW, Washington D.C. 20037 (☎202-728-6400; www.redcrossdc.org). The National Capital Area chapter provides volunteer opportunities in a variety of fields including youth services, blood donation, disaster response, health and safety, development and human resources as part of the American Red Cross's commitment to preparing for and responding to emergencies.

Big Brothers, Big Sisters of the National Capital Area, The Aerospace Building, 10210 Greenbelt Rd., Suite 900, Lanham, Maryland, 20706 (Volunteer Hotline ☎800-NEED-BIG, Otherwise 301-794-9170; www.bbbsnca.org). Volunteers make a more long-term commitment to become mentors and friends to children in the D.C. area in an effort to support children growing up in single-parent households.

Columbia Lighthouse for the Blind, 1120 20th St. NW, Suite 750 South, Washington D.C., 20036 (toll-free ☎877-324-5252 or 202-454-6400; www.clb.org). The Lighthouse runs a variety of programs for the blind and visually impaired, including reading, job search assistance, children's summer camps, and special event coordination.

FLEXIBLE PROGRAMS

Capital Action, (www.capitalaction.org). Capital Action is a volunteer organization of 20- to 30-somethings dedicated to making a positive contribution to the D.C. community. Volunteers create and implement their own community projects and events. Projects range from clothing drives, read-a-thons, and book giveaways to fundraisers and neighborhood cleanups.

City Year, 140 Q St. NE, Washington D.C., 20002 (☎202-776-7780; www.cityyear.org/sites/dc). City Year places volunteers in a variety of service programs in D.C., lasting from one day to a full ten-month tour. Volunteers who serve the term receive weekly stipends, health insurance, and, upon completion, a $4725 education allowance. City Year is a division of **AmeriCorps,** (www.americorps.org), which runs similar programs in D.C.

Greater DC Cares, 1725 I St. NW, Suite 200, Washington D.C., 20006 (202-777-4440; www.dc-cares.org). Connects volunteers with community service organizations throughout the D.C. area. Includes listings and contact information for hundreds of local service organizations seeking volunteers.

InterAction, 1717 Massachusetts Ave. NW (☎202-667-8227; www.interaction.org). This broad-based international agency connects volunteers with Non-Governmental Organizations (NGOs) in Washington and worldwide.

STUDYING

There are many opportunties to study in D.C. Washington has no shortage of colleges, universities, and graduate schools. Many colleges in other parts of the U.S. offer term-time exchange programs, during which students spend a semester learning or interning in D.C. Check with your college to see if such programs exist. Considering the high concentration of foreign embassies, immigrants, and residents in D.C., it is no wonder that language study is also readily available at one of the city's several language schools.

STUDY VISAS

Two types of study visas are available: the **F-1,** for academic studies (including language school) and the **M-1,** for non-academic and vocational studies. In order to secure a study visa, you must already have been accepted to a full course of study by an educational institution approved by the Immigration and Naturalization Services (INS). F-1 applicants must also prove that they have enough readily available funds to meet all expenses for the first year of study. M-1 applicants must have evidence that sufficient funds are immediately available to pay all tuition and living costs for the entire period of intended stay. Applications should be processed through the American embassy or consulate in your home country (see **Planning Your Trip,** p. 301).

EXCHANGE PROGRAMS

International Association for the Exchange of Students for Technical Experience (IAESTE), 10400 Little Patuxent Pkwy. Ste. 250, Columbia, MD 21044-3519, USA (☎410-997-2200; www.aipt.org). 8- to 12-week programs in D.C. and throughout the U.S. for college students who have completed 2 years of technical study. $25 application fee.

LANGUAGE SCHOOLS

D.C.'s large crop of language education centers serves its burgeoning international student population, the many Washington natives interested in learning English as a second language (ESL), and American diplomats in need of a new tongue. For general info on language study in the U.S. consult *English Language and Orientation Programs in the U.S.* (IIE Books, $43), *Funding for U.S. Study* (IEE Books, $40), or *Study Abroad* (Peterson's, $27). The following institutions may be helpful for fulfilling your language needs:

Lado International College, 2233 Wisconsin Ave. NW (☎337-1118; www.lado.com). Specializes in preparing non-English speakers for university study or professional careers in the English-speaking world. Intensive 4-week program $680.

Language Learning Enterprises, 1627 K Street NW, Suite 610 (☎888-464-8553 or 775-0444; www.lle-inc.com). From Afrikaans to Zulu, a wide range of services—instruction, translation, interpretation, and proficiency testing. Prices and schedules vary, call for details.

Language One, 2305 Calvert Street NW (☎800-849-5695 or 328-0099; www.languageone.com). Full array of foreign language courses, ESL, translation and interpretation services, accent reduction, and TOEFL preparation. Call for details.

COLLEGES AND UNIVERSITIES

While not known as a college town, Washington prides itself on the top-notch colleges within its confines. Georgetown, Howard, George Washington, American, Catholic, and Gallaudet Universities rank among the best colleges in the country. Georgetown's undergraduate and graduate programs at the School of Foreign Service are world-renowned, and Gallaudet is the nation's premier university for the hearing-impaired. Historically black Howard has produced African-American leaders for generations. In the heart of Foggy Bottom, George Washington has expanded at a rapid rate over the past decade, amassing space and faculty. The unique political climate of the city promises D.C. students an educational experience unlike any other. See the chart below for contact information.

SCHOOL	LOCATION	CONTACT	AFFILIATION/SPECIALTY
American University	4400 Massachusetts Ave., in Tenleytown in Upper NW	☎202-885-6000 www.american.edu	Private. National and international student body.
The Catholic University of America	Main entrance at Michigan Ave. and 4th St. in NE	☎800-673-2772 www.cua.edu	Private, Catholic. Liberal arts, theology, and philosophy.
Gallaudet University	800 Florida Ave. and 8th St. in NE	☎202-651-5000 TDD 202-651-5050 www.gallaudet.edu	Private university for the deaf, with a renowned drama department.
George Mason University	4400 University Drive in Fairfax, VA	☎703-993-1000 www.gmu.edu	Private liberal arts college.
Georgetown University	Main gate at 37th and O St. in Georgetown	☎202-687-1457 www.georgetown.edu	Private, Catholic and Jesuit. Hosts many international programs.
George Washington University	North of F St. in Foggy Bottom; Visitors Center at 801 22nd St. NW	☎202-994-4949 www.gwu.edu	Private liberal arts college.
Howard University	2400 6th St. NW in Shaw	☎202-806-6100 www.howard.edu	Top historically black university.
Marymount University	2807 Glebe Rd. in Arlington, VA	☎800-548-7638 www.marymount.edu	Private, Catholic.
Southeastern University	501 I Street in SW	☎202-265-5343 www.seu.edu	Private, coed. Has international campuses.
Trinity College	125 Michigan Ave. in NE	☎202-884-9000 www.trinitydc.edu	Private, Catholic, women's college. Has a weekend college program.
University of the District of Columbia	4200 Connecticut Ave. NW in Cleveland Park	☎202-274-5000 www.udc.edu	Public, with open admissions for District residents.

WORKING

As with volunteering, work opportunities tend to fall into two categories. Some travelers seek long-term jobs that allow them to get to know another part of the world as a member of the community, while other travelers seek out short-term jobs to finance the next leg of their travels. As Washington is one of the most tech-savvy cities in the world, the Internet is a priceless resource when looking for a job here. But for technophobes and neo-Luddites, highlighting listings in D.C.'s newspapers and old-fashioned legwork will prove fruitful as well. Be sure to check out the classifieds in *The Washington Post* and *The Washington Times*. In addition, many of D.C.'s colleges and universities have **career and employment offices;** even if you can't get into the office itself (some may require a school ID to enter), most have bulletin boards outside for you to peruse (for a list of colleges and universities in D.C., see above). For the most up-to-date listings, don't bother waiting around for the morning *Post*. Those in the know hunt for jobs the cyber way. The sites below are D.C.-specific; see the Service Directory (**Internet Job Search Resources,** p. 333) for general sites.

WORK PERMITS

In typical bureaucratic style, there are dozens of employment visas, most of which are nearly impossible to get. There are three general categories of work visas/permits: **employment-based visas,** generally issued to skilled or highly educated workers

A Quick Guide to Think Tanks

Want to feel like a true Belt-way insider? Then you've got to know your tanks. In a 1964 interview on the occasion of his 80th birthday, ex-President Harry Truman said he hoped to live another decade, "but only if the old think tank is working." He meant his brain, but the belt-way crowd soon sucked up the phrase. By 1967, think tank had supplanted "task force" as a label for a group of experts tackling a problem. The experts are typically former government policy wonks in search of employment. Often they are academics with strong ideological slants. While most think tanks are non-profits, they are flush with cash. Some occupy the swankiest buildings in D.C.

American Enterprise Institute (www.aei.org): What do Reaganophiles do now that the Soviet Union no longer exists? Find a new target! In July 2002, this think tank's online magazine blamed France "for just about every recent war" and called the French "cheese-eating surrender monkeys."

Brookings Institution (www.brook.edu): The dean of the think tanks: their web site has a .edu suffix and the members call themselves "scholars."

Carnegie Endowment for International Peace (www.ceip.org): For issues concerning Russia, Eurasia, or China, CEIP is your best bet.

who already have a job offer in the US; **temporary worker visas,** which have fixed time limits and very specific classifications; and **cultural exchange visas,** which allow for employment by participants in either fellowships or reciprocal work programs. For more on the requirements for each type of visa, visit (http://travel.state.gov/visa_services.html.) While the chances of getting a work visa may seem next to impossible, there is hope: the **Council on International Educational Exchange (CIEE)** facilitates a **work/study/intern exchange** program between the US and citizens of Australia, China, France, Germany, Italy, Japan, Spain, Taiwan, and the UK. For a fee, CIEE guides university students and recent graduates through the visa application process; once in the US, they can help you find employment (see **Getting A Job,** below). For more information, visit the CIEE web site (www.ciee.org).

LONG-TERM WORK

If you're planning on spending more than three months working in D.C. search for a job well in advance. **Internships,** usually for college students, are a good way to segue into working abroad, although they are often unpaid or poorly paid (although many former interns say the experience is well worth it).

INTERNSHIPS

Every summer, when sensible year-round Washington politicos escape the sweltering city, their ranks are fortified by an influx of collegiate go-getters with bigshot dreams. Internships give students a glimpse of the Washington lifestyle, countless connections to build on, and perhaps even a chance to have their say in the machinations of political power. **Congress** employs the most summer interns: Senators stuff their office with anywhere from five to 15 interns, and the typical representative's office snags two or three. House interns usually hail from their boss's own district, whereas Senate internships are less geographically correlated. Many interns work for a committee or a subcommittee, meaning that they work for the committee chair. Other prime intern-havens are **think tanks,** the **White House** and other executive branch agencies, and **lobbying groups.**

If you're interested in an internship, start looking early—by January, it may be too late. Connections help, of course—this is politics. To inquire about interning for a congressman, contact his or her office (Senate ☎ 224-3121, House 225-3121). Send many, many, many cover letters and resumes to congressional offices, the White House, government departments, museums, lobbying groups, and any other organizations that interest you. If you're lucky, you'll get an invitation to intern for a summer amid a pile of curt rejection letters.

The vast majority of summer opportunities for college students are non-paying. Fortunately, there are ways to finagle some cash out of the deal. Some universities and foundations award grants to students to cover the summer expenses of working at an unpaid public-sector job. Some government branches might have intern funds at their disposal. The House of Representatives, for instance, retains an endowment known as **The Lyndon Baines Johnson (LBJ) Fund,** which gives each member $2000 to split among any number of interns from his home district.

GOVERNMENT

The White House Internship Program, 1600 Pennsylvania Ave. NW, Washington D.C., 20500 (www.whitehouse.gov/government/wh-intern.html). A highly competitive, unpaid program allowing interns to observe the nation's highest public officials and participate in the functions of the federal governement. Applicants must be at least 18 years old and U.S. citizens. Internships are available in the fall, spring, and summer and last up to 90 days.

U.S. Department of Commerce, 14th and Constitution Ave. NW, Washington D.C., 20230 (☎202-482-4883; www.osec.doc.gov/oebam/internwebsite.htm). The Department's Postsecondary Internship Program offers college students the opportunity to work at the Department of Commerce in the fall, spring, or summer. Interns receive stipends, as well as assistance making temporary housing arrangements. U.S. citizenship is required.

U.S. Department of Justice, 950 Pennsylvania Ave. NW, Washington D.C., 20530 (☎202-353-1555; www.usdoj.gov). Each year nearly 1800 law students work in unpaid positions as part of the Legal Intern Program. Work-study compensation is available in some instances and there are a limited number of part-time paid positions.

U.S. Department of Housing and Urban Development, 451 7th St. SW, Washington D.C., 20410 (☎202-708-1112; www.hud.gov/offices/adm/jobs/internship.cfm). Five different internship programs are available to students. All students are eligible for some programs while others require more advanced degrees. Time commitments range from summer to two year commitments. Four of the five programs are paid internships.

The Cato Institute (www.cato.org): The number-one libertarian stronghold. Once produced an album of anti-big-government rap.

Center for Strategic and International Studies (www.csis.org): Ex-CIA types and defense specialists migrate here.

Common Cause (www.commoncause.org): Founded by John Gardner in 1970, it established its liberal credentials with pro-civil rights stances and opposition to the Vietnam War.

Democracy 21 (www.democracy21.org): The McCain-Feingold Campaign Finance Reform Act of 2002 began right here.

Family Research Council (www.frc.org): This socially conservative tank frequently allies itself with Christian conservatives.

Heritage Foundation (www.heritage.org): If it's right-wing, it's right here.

Institute for International Economics (www.iie.com): Across from Brookings in Dupont, IIE reopened its doors at its new location in 2001 at a gala featuring Alan Greenspan.

New America Foundation (www.newamerica.net): The new kid on the block. Run by 30-somethings, it looks to shake up the think tank industry.

Washington Institute for Near East Policy (www.washingtoninstitute.org): Its experts spin opinion on Middle East strategy, with an eye to American and Israeli interests.

THINK TANKS AND POLICY ORGANIZATIONS

Cato Institute, 1000 Massachusetts Ave. NW, Washington D.C., 20001 (☎202-842-0200; www.cato.org). The Cato Institute is a non-profit public policy research foundation that supports the principles of limited government, individual liberty, free markets, and peace. Interns work in a variety of policy areas such as health care reform, constitutional law, and foreign policy. While interns are responsible for doing some clerical work, they also attend forums and debates, and are actively involved in weekly seminars and writing workshops.

National Republican Senatorial Committee, 425 2nd St. NE, Washington D.C., 20002, (☎202-675-6000, internship coordinator 202-675-6095; www.nrsc.org). Offers internships to college student in the fall, spring, and summer. Interns are placed in one of several departments, including the finance, legal, corporate affairs, poltical, and press divisions. Interns also learn the intricacies of campaign strategy and finance.

Democratic National Committee, 430 S. Capitol St. SE, Washington D.C., 20003 (☎ 2020-863-8000; www.democrats.org). Unpaid internships are available in the fall, spring, and summer to those who want to learn more about Democratic campaigns and help elect Democratic officials.

Amnesty International, 600 Pennsylvania Ave. SE, Washington D.C., 20003 (Intern coordinator ☎202-675 8573; www.amnestyusa.org). Amnesty International's Washington office hires interns througout the year to work in its government, communications, death penalty, human rights, refugees, women's rights, and other departments. Internships are unpaid, except daily commuting costs are reimbursed. All are welcome to apply.

MUSEUMS

Corcoran Gallery of Art, 500 17th St. NW, Washington D.C. 20006 (☎202-639-1700; www.corcoran.org). Offers both academic year and summer unpaid internship programs to college and graduate students. Interns assist with departmental duties, as well as attend exhibitions and events in Washington-area arts and humanities institutions.

Hirshhorn Museum and Sculpture Garden, 7th St. and Independence Ave. NW, Washington D.C., 20560 (☎202-633-4674; www.hirshhorn.si.edu). Fall, spring, and summer unpaid internships are available to undergraduates and graduates in the curatorial division, and the education, exhibiton, design, conservation, and public affairs departments.

Historical Society of Washington D.C., 801 K St. NW, Washington D.C. 20001 (☎202-383-1800; www.citymuseumdc.org). Internship positions are available in library research and special collections. Those interested should contact Gail Redmann (☎202-785-2068, ext. 111).

National Museum of American History, 14th St. and Constitution Ave. NW, Washington D.C., 20560 (Smithsonian visitor information ☎202-357-2700; www.americanhistory.si.edu). Internships are available in a wide variety of areas, such as photographic services, museum management, conservation, exhibit planning, and education.

National Museum of Natural History, 10th St. and Constitution Ave. NW, Washington D.C., 20560 (Smithsonian visitor information ☎202-357-2700; www.mnh.si.edu). Offers a long list of internships to undergraduates, along with a summer research program for minority high school students.

Smithsonian National Air and Space Museum, 7th and Independence Ave. SW, Washington D.C., 20560 (☎202-357-2700; www.nasm.si.edu). Undergraduates can take advantage of the museum's 10-week summer internship program with placements in departments ranging from aircraft restoration, aviation history, and planetary science to education and public relations. The program offers a $3,500 stipend.

OTHER RESOURCES

The Fund for American Studies, 1706 New Jersey Ave., NW, Washington D.C., 20009 (☎800-741-6964; www.dcinternships.org) Offers semester and summer programs arranging internships with a long list of organizations in government, public policy, journalism, and corporate affairs.

The Politix Group, (☎202-478-0456; www.politixgroup.com/dcintern.htm). Offers an extensive listing of internships available in D.C. government, political organizations, and policy groups.

The Internship Bible, by Mark Oldman and Samer Hamadeh. Princeton Review. (☎800-733-3000; www.review.com/tools/books).

Peterson's Internships, Peterson's (☎800-338-3282; www.petersons.com).

http://dc.preferredjobs.com features lists of job fairs and a directory of current openings.

www.dc.localopenings.com has "smartmail," automatic email notification of new openings.

www.eih.com/dc.jobs presents a search-by-category database with message boards.

www.fedjobs.com is a database of currently available federal jobs.

www.washingtonpost.com offers a searchable directory of job listings by category.

SHORT-TERM WORK

Traveling for long periods of time can get expensive; therefore, many travelers try their hand at odd jobs for a few weeks at a time to make some extra cash to carry them through another month or two of touring around. Visitors to D.C. will have trouble finding jobs that allow them to exchange work for room and board. These sort of arrangements are generally illegal, and in a law-oriented city like D.C., almost all employers insist on payment above the table. The best bet for a short term job in D.C. is to work for a temp agency. Most jobs are secretarial in nature: data entry, filing, answering phones, etc. Agencies may be able to place you in full-time work after only a few weeks; if they do, health insurance is often included. The list below includes some temp agencies serving the D.C. area:

Career Blazers, 1025 Connecticut Ave. NW, #210, Washington D.C., 20036 (☎202-467-4222; www.careerblazers.com). Provides job listings for both temporary and long-term employment in D.C. and throughout the Northeast.

NRI Staffing Resources, 1889 L St. NW, Washington D.C., 20036 (☎202-466-4670; www.nri-staffing.com). Offers listing and temporary and permanent job placement assistance for postions throughout the D.C. metropolitan area.

www.state.gov/m/dghr/flo/rsrcs/pubs/7248.htm. A State Department site offering listings of many temp agencies in D.C., with listings for searching for in specific fields.

Service Directory

ACCOMMODATIONS SERVICES
Bed & Breakfast Accommodations, Ltd., P.O. Box 12011, Washington, D.C. 20005 (☎413-582-9888 or toll-free 877-893-3233; www.bedandbreakfastdc.com).

APARTMENT HUNTING
Apartment Solutions (www.apartmentsolutions.com) provides assistance with apartment searches.

The Registry (☎800-999-0350; www.dcregistry.com) lists apartments online for D.C., Maryland, and Virginia.

BEAUTY & HAIRDRESSERS
Casa Del Sol Tanning Club, 4906 Wisconsin Ave. NW (☎363-2401).

Headlines, 326 Massachusetts Ave. NE (☎546-5151).

Styles International Incorporated Hairstylists, 611 K St. NW (☎638-1751).

Supercuts, 3416 Connecticut Ave. NW (☎244-6800).

BUDGET TRAVEL AGENCIES
AAA Travel Services, 701 15th St. NW (☎331-3000). Members only. Open M-F 9am-5:30pm.

Cheap Tickets (☎800-377-1000; www.cheaptickets.com).

STA Travel, 3301 M St. NW (☎337-6464 or 887-0912; www.statravel.com). Open M-Sa 10am-6pm, Su 11am-5pm.

Travel Avenue (☎800-333-3335; www.travelavenue.com).

CAR RENTAL
Also see ***Once in D.C.: Getting Around by Car,*** p. 25.

Alamo (☎800-462-5266; www.alamo.com), branches at Union Station, and both National and Dulles Airports.

Avis (☎800-230-4898; www.avis.com), branches at National and Dulles Airports, 1722 M St. NW, and 4400 Connecticut Ave. NW.

Bargain Buggies Rent-a-Car, 3140 N. Washington Blvd. (☎703-841-0000), in Arlington, VA. Open M-F 8am-7pm, Sa 9am-3pm, Su 9am-noon.

Budget (☎800-527-0700; www.budget.com), branches at Union Station and downtown.

Dollar (☎800-800-4000; www.dollar.com), branches at National and Dulles Airports.

Hertz (☎800-654-3131; www.hertz.com), branches at National, Dulles, and downtown.

Rent-A-Wreck, 910 M St. NW (☎408-9828; www.rentawreck.com). Bethesda, MD branch, 5455 Butler Rd. (☎301-654-2252). Open M-F 8am-6pm, Sa 9am-noon, Su 8am-9pm.

Thrifty (☎800-847-4389; www.thrifty.com), branches at National and Dulles Airports and downtown.

COMPUTER SERVICES

*Also see **Internet Access.***

Advanced Computer Center, 4709 Wisconsin Ave. NW (☎237-8827).

CompUSA, 5901 Stevenson Ave. (☎703-212-6610), Alexandria, VA.

Novell Computer Clinic Center, 4433 Wisconsin Ave. NW (☎362-9702).

CURRENCY EXCHANGE

Thomas Cook Currency Services, (☎800-287-7362; www.travelex.com), branches at National and Dulles airports, and 2 locations downtown.

DRY CLEANING

Dry Clean Express, 6450 Georgia Ave. NW (☎829-8578).

Esteem Cleaners, 2100 Pennsylvania Ave. NW (☎429-0591).

Lee's Custom Tailoring and Dry Cleaning, 529 14th St. NW (☎639-8590).

Snow White Dry Cleaning, 333 Hawaii Ave. NE (☎636-3700).

Tony's One Hour Martinizing, 6143 Georgia Ave. NW (☎882-7725).

EMERGENCY

Emergency Assistance (☎911).

Park Police (☎619-7300). Emergencies in Rock Creek Park or on federal parklands.

Poison Center (24hr. ☎800-222-1222 or 625-3333).

GYMS

Bally's Total Fitness, 200 L St. NW (☎331-7788).

City Fitness, 3525 Connecticut Ave. NW (☎537-0539).

Gold's Gym & Aerobics Center, 4310 Connecticut Ave. NW (☎364-4653).

HOSPITALS

*Also see **Dentists and Doctors; Emergency; Pharmacies.***

Children's National Medical Center, 111 Michigan Ave. NW (☎884-5000).

Elizabeth Taylor Medical Center, 1701 14th St. NW (☎745-700).

Georgetown University Medical Center, 3800 Reservoir Rd. NW (☎687-2000).

George Washington University Medical Center, 901 23rd St. NW (☎994-1000).

Howard University Hospital, 2041 Georgia Ave. NW (☎865-6100).

Planned Parenthood, 1108 16th St. NW (☎347-8500).

Sibley Memorial Hospital, 5255 Loughboro Rd. NW (☎537-4000).

HOTLINES & SUPPORT CENTERS

AIDS Hotline (☎800-342-AIDS/2437 or TDD 800-243-7889). Open 24hr.

Crisislink Suicide Hotline (☎800-784-2433). Open 24hr.

Mental Health Crisis Line (☎561-7000). Open 24hr.

Domestic Violence SOS Hotline (☎783-3003). Open 24hr.

Gay and Lesbian National Hotline (☎888-843-4564). Open M-F 4pm-midnight, Sa noon-5pm.

Abortion Federation Hotline (☎800-772-9100). Open M-F 8am-10pm, Sa-Su 9am-5pm.

National Organization for Victim Assistance (☎232-6682). Open 24hr.

Planned Parenthood, 1108 16th St. NW (☎347-8500).

Rape Crisis Hotline (☎333-7273). Open 24hr.

Traveler's Aid Society, desks at Union Station (☎ 371-1937; open M-F 9:30am-5pm), National Airport (☎ 703-417-3972; open daily 6am-10pm), and Dulles Airport (☎ 703-572-8296; open daily 10am-9pm).

INFORMATION LINES
Dial-a-Museum (☎ 357-2020).

Dial-a-Park (☎ 619-7275).

News (☎ 334-9000).

Time (☎ 844-1212).

Weather (☎ 936-1212).

INTERNET ACCESS
Also see Computer Services.

Atomic Grounds, 1555 Wilson Blvd. (☎ 703-524-2157), in Arlington, VA. Open M-F 6:30am-6:30pm, Sa 8:30am-5pm, Su 10am-6pm.

The Cyberstop Cafe, 1513 17th St. NW (☎ 234-2470), near P St. Open M-F 7am-midnight, Sa-Su 8am-midnight.

INTERNET JOB SEARCH RESOURCES
See Job Hunting On the Internet (p. 328) for D.C.-specific job search websites.

About.com (jobsearch.about.com). Links to hundreds of job-searching resources, from sample cover letters to actual job databases.

Careerbuilder.com (www.careerbuilder.com). A searchable job database.

Craigslist (washingtondc.craigslist.org). An invaluable resource. Post your resume, search available jobs and apartment listings in your city, and learn about community resources.

Employment Guide (www.employmentguide.com). Instead of posting your resume, you answer a series of questions that form an interview in the industry of your choice. You can build a resume at the completion of your interview. Also has extensive job database and job fair information.

Foreignborn.com (www.foreignborn.com/career_ctr.htm). Foreignborn.com's career center lets you submit your resume for viewing by US-based companies looking specifically for foreign-born employees. Also offers visa information.

HotJobs (www.hotjobs.yahoo.com). Allows potential employees to post resumes and search a huge job database.

Monster.com (www.monster.com). Search the database and post your resume on this highly acclaimed site (also known for its catchy Super Bowl commercials).

Recruiters Online Network (www.recruitersonline.com). Find thousands of current job listings. Post your resume; locate recruiters and employers in your industry and location.

JOBS, TEMPORARY
See also Internet Job Search Resources, p. 333 and Alternatives to Tourism, p. 329

Career Blazers, 1025 Connecticut Ave. NW, Ste. 210 (☎ 467-4222; www.careerblazers.com).

Manpower Temporary Services, 1130 Connecticut Ave., Ste. 530 (☎ 331-8300; www.manpower.com).

NRI Staffing Resources, 1899 L St. NW, Ste. 300 (☎ 659-8282; www.nri-staffing.com).

Randstad, 1100 New York Ave. NW, Ste. 175 (☎ 289-6566; www.randstad.com).

LANGUAGE SCHOOLS
International Language Institute, 4301 Connecticut Ave. NW, #147 (☎ 362-2505).

Lado International College, 2233 Wisconsin Ave. NW (☎ 223-0023; www.lado.com).

Language Learning Enterprises, 1627 K St. NW, Suite 610 (☎ 888-464-8553 or 775-0444; www.lle-inc.com).

Language One, 2305 Calvert St. NW (☎ 328-0099; www.languageone.com).

LAUNDROMATS
Capitol Hill Cleaners & Laundry, 661 C St. SE (☎ 544-7934).

Global Cleaners, 3700 Martin Luther King, Jr. Ave. SE (☎ 561-3500).

Hamilton Laundromat, 5201 Georgia Ave. NW (☎ 829-2262).

The Laundry Basket, 5007 New Hampshire Ave. NW (☎ 291-3450), 317 Kennedy St. NW (☎ 726-7688), and 5567 South Dakota Ave. NE (☎ 529-1511).

Quality Wash, 5926 Georgia Ave. NW (☎ 722-0834), 3210 14th St. NW (☎ 234-3226), and 1535 7th St. NW (☎ 232-4391).

Spinners, Inc., 3915 S. Capitol St. SW (☎ 562-1338).

LIBRARIES

Arthur R. Ashe, Jr. Foreign Policy Library, 1744 R St. NW (☎797-2301; www.transafricaforum.org).

Folger Shakespeare Library, 201 E. Capitol St. (☎544-4600; www.folger.edu).

Georgetown Branch Public Library, 3260 R St. (☎282-0220; www.dclibrary.org), at Wisconsin Ave.

Library of Congress, 100 1st St. NE (☎707-5000; www.loc.gov).

Martin Luther King, Jr. Memorial Library, 901 G St. NW (☎727-1111; www.dclibrary.org). Central library of the DC public library system.

PHARMACIES

Berkshire Food & Drug, 4201 Massachusetts Ave. NW (☎363-6546).

Cathedral Pharmacy, 3000 Connecticut Ave. NW (☎265-1300).

CVS (☎800-746-7287; www.cvs.com). 46 locations in DC, including 1199 Vermont Ave. NW (☎628-0720), 67 Dupont Circle NW (☎785-1466), and 4555 Wisconsin Ave. NW (☎537-1587). Open 24hr.

POST OFFICES

Main Office, 900 Brentwood Rd. NE, 20066 (☎635-5300; www.usps.com). Mail sent "General Delivery" always comes here. Open M-F 8am-8pm, Sa 8am-6pm, Su noon-6pm.

Farragut Station, 1800 M St. NW, 20033 (☎523-2024). Open M-F 9am-5pm.

Friendship Station, 4005 Wisconsin Ave. NW, 20016 (☎842-3332). Open M-Sa 8am-6pm, Su 10am-2pm.

Georgetown Station, 1215 31st St. NW, 20007 (☎842-2487). Open M-F 8am-6pm, Sa 8am-2pm.

Martin Luther King, Jr. Station, 1400 L St. NW, 20043 (☎842-1350). Open M-F 8am-7pm, Sa 10am-2pm.

National Capitol Station, 2 Massachusetts Ave. NW, 20013 (☎523-2368), at Metro: Union Station. Open M-F 7am-midnight, Sa-Su 7am-8pm.

Temple Heights Station, 1921 Florida Ave. NW, 20009 (☎234-4253), near Connecticut Ave. between Dupont Circle and Adams Morgan. Open M-F 9am-5pm.

RELIGIOUS SERVICES

Islamic Center, 2551 Massachusetts Ave. NW (☎332-8343), North of Dupont Circle, on the L2 and L4 bus routes. Prayers 5 times per day.

Kesher Israel, 2801 N St. NW (☎333-4808), in Georgetown. Orthodox. Time of services depends on the season; call to find out weekly schedules.

St. Matthew's Cathedral, 1725 Rhode Island Ave. NW (☎347-3215; www.stmatthewscathedral.org). Metro: Farragut North. Catholic. Mass M-F 7, 8am, 12:10, 5:30pm; Sa 8am, 12:10, 5:30pm; and Su 7, 8:30, 10 (in Latin), 11:30am (ASL), 1 (in Spanish), 5:30pm.

St. Nicholas Cathedral, 3500 Massachusetts Ave. NW (☎333-5060; www.stnicholasdc.org), on L2 and L4 bus lines. Russian Orthodox. Liturgies are Sa (English and Slavonic), Su at 9 (English) and 10:45am (Slavonic).

St. Sophia (☎333-4730; www.saintsophiawashington.org), at the corner of 36th St. and Massachusetts Ave. NW, on the N6 bus lines. Greek Orthodox. Liturgy is Su at 10am.

Temple Micah, 2829 Wisconsin Ave. NW (☎342-9175; www.templemicah.org), near Garfield St. on the 30-series bus route. Reform. Services F 6:30pm, in summer Sa 10:15am.

SHOE REPAIR

Cobbler's Bench Shoe Repair, 1050 Connecticut Ave. NW (☎776-0515).

SUPERMARKETS

Giant Food Supermarkets, locations at 3460 14th St. NW (☎202-387-4010; open daily 7am-10pm); 1414 8th St. NW (☎234-0215; open M-Sa 24hr., Su 6am-11pm); 3406 Wisconsin Ave. NW (☎363-3809; open M-Sa 7am-10pm, Su 8am-9pm).

Safeway, 1855 Wisconsin Ave. NW (☎333-3223); 1747 Columbia Rd. NW (☎667-0774); 1800 20th St. NW (☎483-3908). Most open M-Sa 7am-10pm and Su 8am-7pm, but call to verify hours at location.

TAXIS

Diamond Cab D.C., 110 Q St. NW (☎387-6200).

Empire Cab, 1625 S. Capitol St. SW (☎488-4844).

Lincoln Cab, 129 Q St. SW (☎484-2222).

Mayflower Cab, 920 1st St. SE (☎783-1111).

Yellow Cab, 1636 Bladensburg Rd. NE (☎544-1212).

TICKET SERVICES

TicketMaster (☎432-7328; www.ticketmaster.com).

TICKETplace (☎842-5387 for recorded information), in the Pavilion at the Old Post Office, 1100 Pennsylvania Ave. NW. Sells same-day tickets at half price. Open Tu-Sa 11am-6pm.

TOURIST OFFICES

Washington, D.C. Convention and Tourism Corporation (WCTC), 1212 New York Ave. NW, Ste. 600 (☎789-7000; www.washington.org). Open M-F 9am-5pm.

D.C. Visitor Information Center, in the Ronald Reagan International Trade Center, 1300 Pennsylvania Ave. NW (☎866-324-7386; www.dcvisit.com). Open M-F 8:30am-5:30pm, Sa 9am-4pm.

TOURS

Also see Once in D.C.: By Tour, p. 26.

D.C. Ducks (☎832-9800; www.dcducks.com). 1½hr. amphibious tours. Mar.-Oct. daily every hr. 10am-3pm. $26, children 4-12 $13.

Grayline (☎289-1995 or 800-862-1400). Bus and trolley tours. Rates vary depending on route ($28-80), children 3-11 ½-price.

Old Town Trolley, 2640 Reed St. NE (☎832-9800; www.trolleytours.com). Ticket sales June-Aug. daily 9am-9pm, last reboarding at 5pm; Sept.-May 9am-3:30pm, last reboarding at 4pm. $26, children 4-12 $13.

Scandal Tours (☎800-758-8687). Tours Apr.-Sept. Sa at 1pm. Reservations required.

Tour D.C. (☎301-588-8999; www.tourdc.com). Walking tours of Dupont Circle and Georgetown. Call or visit website for schedule. $15, under 18 free, group rates available.

Tourmobile Sight-Seeing, 1000 Ohio Dr. SW (☎554-5100 or 888-868-7707; www.tourmobile.com). Daily 9:30am-4:30pm. $20, children 3-11 $10.

TRANSPORTATION

See Car Rental, p. 331, and Taxis, p. 334.

Amtrak (☎800-872-7245; www.amtrak.com).

Baltimore-Washington International (BWI) Airport (☎800-435-9294; www.bwiairport.com).

Dulles International Airport (☎703-572-2700; www.metwashairports.com/dulles).

Greyhound (☎800-229-9424; www.greyhound.com).

MARC train (☎800-543-9809; www.mtamaryland.com).

Metro (☎637-7000; www.wmata.com).

Ronald Reagan National Airport (☎703-417-8000; www.metwashairports.com/national).

Union Station (☎484-7540; www.unionstationdc.com).

TRAVELERS WITH DISABILITIES

Mobility International USA (MIUSA), P.O. Box 10767, Eugene, OR 97440 (☎541-343-1284 voice and TDD; www.miusa.org). Sells *A World of Options: A Guide to International Educational Exchange, Community Service, and Travel for Persons with Disabilities* ($35).

Moss Rehab Hospital Travel Information Service (☎215-456-9600; www.mossresourcenet.org). A telephone and Internet information resource center on international travel accessibility and other travel-related concerns for those with disabilities.

Washington Ear, Inc., 35 University Blvd. E., Silver Spring, MD 20901 (☎301-681-6636; www.washear.org). For visually impaired travelers. Sells large-print and tactile atlases of the D.C. area. The organization also offers dial-in daily readings of the *Washington Post*, *Washingtonian* magazine, and other publications for the blind; call or visit website for details.

WOMEN'S RESOURCES

D.C. Rape Crisis Center (☎333-7273).

National Women's Health Information Center (☎800-994-9662).

Planned Parenthood Emergency (☎703-847-4368; www.ppmw.org). Open 24hr.

Planned Parenthood Marjorie Schumacher Center, 1108 16th St. NW (☎347-8512; www.ppmw.org), by appointment. Metro: Farragut North.

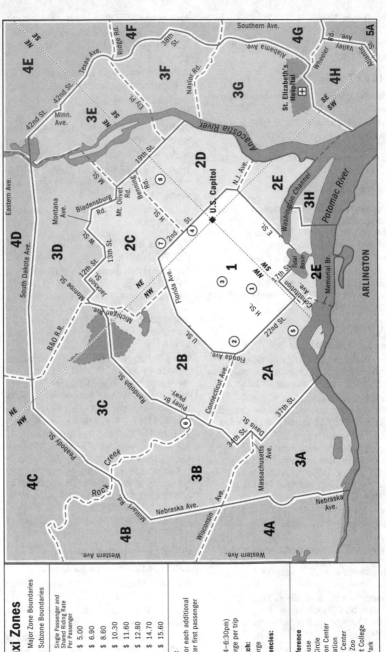

D.C. Taxi Zones

— — — Major Zone Boundaries
- - - - Subzone Boundaries

Zone and Fares	Single Passenger and Shared Riding Rate Per Passenger
1 Zone	$ 5.00
2 Zones	$ 6.90
3 Zones	$ 8.60
4 Zones	$ 10.30
5 Zones	$ 11.60
6 Zones	$ 12.80
7 Zones	$ 14.70
8 Zones	$ 15.60

Group Rates:
$1.50 extra for each additional passenger after first passenger in group

Rush Hour:
(7–9:30am; 4–6:30pm)
$1.00 surcharge per trip

Radio Dispatch:
$1.50 surcharge

Snow Emergencies:
Double fare

Points of Reference
1. White House
2. Dupont Circle
3. Convention Center
4. Union Station
5. Kennedy Center
6. National Zoo
7. Gallaudet College
8. Lincoln Park

Index

1 208
14th Street theater district 187
2K9 179
2 Amy's Neapolitan Pizzeria 161
49 Twelve Thai Cuisine 161
9:30 Club 42

A

a.k.a Frisco's 161
Abbey Inn 260
abortion 308
About.com 333
accommodations 207
Acme Bar and Grill 253
Adams Inn 209
Adams Memorial 41
Adams Mill Bar and Grill 166
Adams Morgan
  accommodations 209–211
  food & drink 136–138
  nightlife 164–167
  sights 85–86
Adams Morgan Day 18
Adams, John 63
adapters 308
Addiction Prevention Hotline 332
Addis Ababa 138
Adelle's 237
Aditi 154
Admiral Fell Inn, The 233
Affrica 83
African American History Tour 26
African Art and Sackler Gallery Complex 120
African-American Civil War Memorial 90
African-American history 90, 103
African-American literature 43
Aftertime Comics, Inc. 201
Afterwords 198
Afterwords Cafe 148
AIDS 307
  TDD hotline 332
Air Courier Association 312

airfares 311
airplane travel 311
  courier 312
  standby 312
airports 311
  Baltimore-Washington International 23, 228, 311
  Dulles International 21, 311
  Ronald Reagan National 21, 311
  Williamsburg International Airport 277
AJ's On the Creek 266
Akbar 235
Al's Magic Shop 202
alcohol 30
Alero 160
Alexandria
  accommodations 211
  food & drink 138–139
  nightlife 167–168
  sights 104–107
Alexandria African-American Heritage Park 106
Alexandria Antiques Show 18
Alexandria Archaeology Museum 107
Alexandria Ballet 107
Alexandria Lodge, The 211
All About Jane 200
Allegro 246
Allen Lee Hotel 217
alternatives to tourism 319–329
Amanda's Bed and Breakfast Reservation Service 232, 249
AMC Union Station 9 191
American College Theater Festival 16
American Express 305, 307
American Film Institute's Silver Theatre, 191
American Inn of Bethesda 213
American Red Cross 62, 66, 323
American University 86, 325
AmeriCorps 323
Amicci's 236
Amma Vegetarian Kitchen 156
Amnesty International 328
Amtrak 313, 335

Anacostia
  sights 92–94
Angie's Guest Cottage-Bed and Breakfast and HI-AYH Hostel 269
Angry Inch 166
Annabelle 256
Annapolis and Anne Arundel County Conference & Visitors Bureau 248
Annapolis Cab Co. 248
Annapolis Summer Garden Theater 252
Annapolis, MD 246–253
  accommodations 249
  food 249–250
  nightlife and entertainment 252–253
  sights 250–252
Anthony S. Pitch (tours) 26
antiques 197
  D.C. Spring Antiques Fair 16
Antiques Anonymous 197
Anton Gallery 83
Apex 180
Aqua Terra 250
architecture 41
area codes 28
Arena Players 244
Arena Stage 43, 187
Arena's Deli 261
Arise 197
Arlington
  accommodations 213
  Food & Drink 139–141
  nightlife 168–169
  sights 96–101
Arlington Cinema 'N' Drafthouse 168
Arlington National Cemetery 10, 97, 191
Arlington Visitors Center 97
Armand's Chicago Pizzeria 143
Armel-Leftwich Visitors Center 251
art
  outdoor 42
art galleries
  Dupont Circle 82
Art Gallery Grille 150

Art Museum of the Americas 67
Arthur M. Sackler Gallery 120
arts
  visual 41
Arts & Industries Building 120
arts and crafts 198
Asahi Japanese Restaurant 140
Ash-Lawn Highlan 294
astronomy 193
Athenaeum 107
Atlantic House Bed and Breakfast 262
ATM cards 307
Australia Embassy and Consulate 302
Australian Embassy 27
Avis 332
Aztec Garden 67
Azteca Bar 167

B

B'nai Israel Synagogue 241
Babalu Grill 233
Babe Ruth Birthplace 241
Babe's Billiards Cafe 189
Bacchus 141
Back Bay National Wildlife Refuge 270
Backstage, Inc. 199
Bacon, Henry 58
Baja Bean 294
Baltimore Brewing Co. 245
Baltimore Maritime Museum 238
Baltimore Museum of Art 242, 243
Baltimore Museum of Industry 239
Baltimore National Aquarium 237
Baltimore Opera Company 244
Baltimore Orioles 194
Baltimore Orioles Museum 241
Baltimore Ravens 246
Baltimore Symphony Orchestra 244
Baltimore Zoo 242
Baltimore, MD 223–246
  accommodations 232–233
  food 233–237
  nightlife and entertainment 243–246
  sights 237–243
Baltimore-Washington

International Airport 23, 228, 311
Bancroft Hall 252
Banneker-Douglass Museum 250
Bar Baltimore 245
Bar Nun/Club 2000 179
Bargain Buggies Rent-a-Car 332
bargaining 30
Barnes and Noble 198
Barracks Row 91
Bartholdi Park 51
baseball 194
Basilica of the National Shrine of the Immaculate Conception 94
basketball 194
Bastille Day 17
Bayou Room, The 168
bd's Mongolian Barbeque 142
Beach View Motel, The 260
beaches
  Ocean City, MD 264
  Rehoboth, DE 259
  Virginia Beach 267
Beacon Motel, The 258
Bears Den Hostel 295
beauty salons 331
Bed & Breakfast Accommodations, Ltd. 331
Bed & Breakfast Inns Online 309
Bed & Breakfasts (B&Bs) 309
Bed and Breakfasts of Maryland 249
Ben's Chili Bowl 156
Berkeley Plantation 276
Berret's 280
Bertha's Dining Room 236
Best Western Key Bridge 213
Best Western Old Colony Inn 211
Bethesda
  accommodations 213
  food & drink 141–143
  nightlife 169–170
Bethesda Crab House 213
Bethune, Mary McLeod 124
Better Bikes 192
Better Days Antiques 256
Bev's Homeade Ice Cream Shops 291
Beyond the Pale 299
Beyond the Wall 205
bicycle trails 108
Big Brothers, Big Sisters of the

National Capital Area 323
Big Hunt, The 171
Big Oaks Family Campground 260
Big Planet comics 202
Bike the Sites, Inc 192
Bike the Sites, Inc. 27
biking 191
biking tours 26
Bill of Rights 71
billiards 189
Birchmere Music Hall, 185
Bird in the Cage Antiques 197
Bistro Med 156
Bistro St. Michaels 255
Black Cat, The 42, 184
Black Coffee Bistro 298
Black History Resource Center 106
Black History Tour 26
Bloomingdale's 202
blue crab 233
Blue Light Grill and Raw Bar 293
Blue Moon 261
Blue Room 166
Bluemont Concert Series 297
blues 186
Blues Alley 186
B'nai B'rith Klutznick National Jewish Museum 125
Boar's Head Inn 292
Boardwalk Plaza Hotel 260
boating 192, 238
Bob & Edith's Diner 140
Bob's Famous Homemade Ice Cream 142
Bohager's 244
Bombay Palace 149
Booeymonger 156
Book Gallery, The 190
bookstores 198
Boston University Washington Center 220
Bottoms Up 288
Boulevard Woodgrill, The 140
Brass Balls Saloon 264
Brass Monkey 164
Braxton Hotel, The 216
Brazilian Embassy 84
Bread and Chocolate 144
Bread for the City 322
Briar Patch Bed & Breakfast 298
Brickseller Inn 216
Brickskeller 171, 216
Bridge Restaurant, The 255

British Collection, The 138
British Embassy 27, 84, 302
British Foreign and
  Commonwealth Office 307
Broadway Market 236
Brown, Chuck 42
Bua 147
Buddhist Biker Bar and
  Grille 294
Budget (car rental) 332
Budget Inn, The 293
budget travel 317
budget travel agencies 331
Buffalo Billiards 190
Bukom Cafe 165
Bullfeathers 167
Burdick Gallery 83
Bureau of Consular Affairs 308
Bureau of Engraving and
  Printing 61
Burma Restaurant 145
Burrito Brothers 143
bus 24
Buttery, The 258
Bygones 291
Byrd Theatre 290
Byzantine Collection 126

C

C&O Canal 79, 191
  towpath 191
C&O Canal National
  Historical Park 112
Cactus Cantina 161
Cada Vez 179
Cafe Amadeus 152
Cafe Asia 141
Cafe Deluxe 141
Cafe La Ruche 154, 156
Cafe Luna 146
Cafe Nema 179
Cafe Ole 161
Cafe Papillon 261
Cafe Saint-Ex 178
Caffe Brio 234
Cakelove 157
Camden Station 229
Camden Yards 194, 240
campgrounds 219
Canadian Embassy 27, 41,
  73, 302
Candy Kitchen 261
Cape Henlopen State Park

257, 258
Cape State Park 258
Capital Action 323
Capital Area Food Bank 322
Capital Beltway (I-495) 313
Capital Children's Museum 125
Capital KOA 233
Capital Pride 17
Capitol 11
Capitol building 33
Capitol City Brewing
  Company 151
Capitol Crescent Trail 191
Capitol Entertainment
  Services 26
Capitol Hill 45
  accommodations 215
  food & drink 143-145
  nightlife 170-171
  sights 45-53
Capitol Hill Jimmy T's 145
Capitol KOA 219
Capitol Lounge 171
Capitol, The 46-49
car rental 26
Career Blazers 329
Careerbuilder.com 333
Carlyle House 107
Carnegie Institution 84
Carnival Extravaganza 17
Carpool 168
Carriage House, The 297
Carrol's Creek Bar & Cafe 250
Carter Barron Amphitheater
  110
Carytown, VA 291
Casa Blanca 150
Casablanca 139
Castle Motel, The 269
Cat's Eye Pub 245
Catholic University 220
  housing 220
Catholic University of
  America 325
Cato Institute 328
CD Warehouse 204
CDC 307
Center for Studies in Modern
  Art 131
Centers for Disease Control
  (CDC) 307
Central Station 246
Chadwicks 167
chamber music 186
changing money 304
Chaos and Pandemonium.

See Chief Ike's Mambo Room
Chaps 293
Chapters 198
Charlottesville, VA 291-294
Charlottesville-Albemarle
  County Convention and
  Visitors Bureau 292
Checker Cab 229
Cherry Blossom Festival 16, 60
Cherry Blosssom Festival 53
Cherry Hill Park 219
Chesapeake Bay Maritime
  Museum 255
Chi Cha Lounge 179
Chicho's 271
Chick & Ruth's Delly 250
Chief Ike's Mambo Room,
  Chaos, and Pandemonium 167
Childe Harold, The 173
children 316
Children's Museum of
  Richmond 289
Children's National Medical
  Center 332
China Doll 145
Chinatown 71, 145
  food & drink 145-146
Chincoteague Chamber of
  Commerce 265
Chincoteague National
  Wildlife Refuge 266
Chincoteague Pony Centre 266
Chincoteague, VA 264-266
Chinese New Year Parade 15
Ching Ching Cha 154
Chipotle Mexican Grill 158
Chocolate Moose 202
Chowning's Tavern 280
Chrysler Museum of Art 274
  historic houses 274
Cirrus 307
City Dock 249, 250
City Dock Cafe 250
City Lights of China 148
City Paper 29, 43, 183
City Year 323
Civil War
  sights 289
Civil War Living History Day 18
Civil War Museum 241
Clarendon Grill 168
classical music 186
Clementine 291
Cleveland Park 89
  food & drink 159-160
Clipper City, The 238

clothing stores 200
Cloud 9 261
Club Chaos 181
Club Insomnia 174
Club Orpheus 245
Club Soda 274
Clyde's of Georgetown 153
Cobalt 180
Coffee Bean of Leesburg, The 296
collect calls 29
College of William & Mary 281
colleges 324
Colonial Gardens B&B 278
Colonial National Park 283
Colonial Parkway 283
Colonial Players 252
Colonial Williamsburg 281
  visitors center 278
Columbia Lighthouse for the Blind 323
comedy 189
Comedy Zone, The 275
Comfort Inn Executive Center 287
comics 201
Commander Salamander 200
Common Denominator 30
Common Share, The 166
communal living 221
communication 27
Community Council for Homelessness at Friendship Place (CCH/FP) 322
Community for Creative Non-Violence (CCNV) 322
CompUSA 332
computer services 332
concerts 70
Cone E. Island 152
Congress, viewing sessions of 52
Conservatory 242
Constitution 71
Constitution Gardens 56
consulates 27, 301
converters 308
converting currency 304
Coral Reef Cafe 263
Corcoran Gallery of Art 66, 125, 328
Corks 234
Corner Stone Grill 282
Cosi 149, 171
Council on International Educational Exchange 326
Council Travel 331

courier flights 312
Covenant House Washington 322
Crab Claw, The 255
Craigslist 333
credit cards 305
Crème de la Crème 297
Cross St. Market 236
Cross Street Market 234
Crypt, The 48
Crystal Pallas Cafe & Grill 141
C-SPAN 30
Cuisine and Co. 270
Cup A' Cup A' at the Watergate 153
currency exchange 304, 332
customs 304
CVS Pharmacy 334
Cyber Cafe, The 149
Cyberstop Cafe, The 149

D

D.C. Blues Festival 18
D.C. Ducks 27
D.C. Habitat for Humanity 322
D.C. Spring Antiques Fair 16
D.C. Taxicab Commission 25
D.C. United 195
D'Art Center 274
Dali, Salvador 123
dance 43, 189, 192
Dance Africa D.C. 17
Dance Africa DC Festival 189
Dance Place 189
Dank's Deli 298
DAR Constitution Hall 185
Darth Vader 88
DASH (bus) 24
Daughters of the American Revolution 62
Daughters of the American Revolution Constitution Hall 66
Days Inn 218
Daytripping 223
daytrips 223–299
DC CD 204
DC Live 175
Dean and Deluca 155
Decatur House 41, 65
Declaration of Independence 71
Deja Blue 200
Delhi Dhaba 140

Delta Shuttle 311
Democratic National Committee 328
Department of Defense Open House 17
Department of Human Services Crisis Line 332
Department of Recreation and Parks 191
Department of State. See State Department
Department of the Interior 67
department stores 202
Designer Resale 200
dietary concerns 314, 316
DIK Bar 147
Diner, The 136
Directions Unlimited 316
directory assistance 29
disabled travelers 315
Discover Downtown DC 26
Diva 175
DJ Hut 204
Dogfish Head Brewings & Eats 262
Dollar (car rental) 332
Donna's 235
dorms 219, 309
Douglass, Frederick 94
Dream Dresser Boutique 202
driver's license 303
driving 25
drugs 30
Druid Hill Park 242
dry cleaning 332
Dubliner, The 144, 170
Duck Tours 335
Duke Ellington Mural 91
Dulles International Airport 21, 311, 335
Dumbarton House 80
Dumbarton Oaks Estate 78
Dumbarton Oaks Museum 126
Dunbar, Paul 43
Dupont Circle
  accommodations 215–216
  food & drink 146–149
  nightlife 171–173
  sights 81–85
Dupont Italian Kitchen 147, 148

E

East Potomac Park 191
Eastern Market 143, 204

Eden 261
Edgar Allan Poe House 240
Edgar Allan Poe Museum 289
Eighteenth Street Lounge 171
Einstein Planetarium 119
Eisenhower Executive Office
  Building 64
El 137
El Tamarindo 137
Ellipse 63
embassies 27, 84, 301
  Australia 27, 302
  Brazil 84
  Canada 27, 41, 302
  Finland 87
  Indonesia 84
  Ireland 27, 302
  New Zealand 27, 302
  South Africa 27, 302
  UK 27, 302
Embassy Inn 215
Embassy Row 10, 84
Embers, The 264
emergency assistance 332
employment
  internships 326
  through CIEE 326
Employment Guide 333
Enid A. Haupt Garden 120
entertainment 183–195
Environmental Film Festival 16
erotica 202
Evergreen House 243
exchange programs 324
exchange rates 304
exercise 191–193
  Mall, The 191
  Tidal Basin 191
  Waterfront 191
exercise trails 108

F

Faccia Luna 159
Fado 174
Fager's Island 264
Fairfax County
  sights 101–104
fake IDs 30
False Cape State Park 270
Famous Luigi's 149
Famous Uncle Al's 274
fares 311
Farmer's Market 96, 104
Farragut
  accommodations 216

food & drink 149–150
  nightlife 173
  sights 74–75
Farragut Lincoln Suites 217
Farragut Square 74
Fashion Centre at Pentagon
  City 203
Fashion Gallery 202
FBI 71
Federal Bureau of
  Investigation (FBI) 71
Federal Hill Park 239
Federal Triangle 37
  accommodations 217
  food & drink 150–152
  nightlife 174–175
  orientation 70
  sights 70–74
FedEx Field 195
Felix and The Spy Lounge 165
Fells Point Maritime
  Museum 243
festivals 15–19
Fettoosh Express 156
Fichandler Stage 187
Filene Center 186
film 190–191
Filmfest DC 16
financial matters 304
Finnish Embassy 87
Firehook Coffee Shop and
  Bakery 148
First Friday Gallery Walk 297
First Landings 269
Fish Market, The 139
Fisher's 261
Fisher-Martin House
  Information Center 257
fishing 100
fitness 191–193
Five 172
Five Guys Famous Burgers
  and Fries 138
Flack, Roberta 42
Flag House Inn 249
Flanagan's Irish Pub 170
Fletcher's 243
Fletcher's Boat House 192
flights
  Internet 311
Florida Ave. Grill 157
Foggy Bottom
  accommodations 217
  food & drink 152–153
  nightlife 175–176
  sights 62–70
Folger Consort 186

Folger Shakespeare Library 51
Fondo del Sol Visual Arts
  Center 83
food and drink 133–161
Food Factory 141
food shopping 334
football 195
Ford, Susan 63
Ford's Theater 72
Ford's Theatre 187
Foreignborn.com 333
Fort McHenry National
  Monument 239
Foundry Gallery 83
Foundry Players, The 187
Fountain of Neptune 50
14th Street theater district 187
Fox and Hounds, The 173
Franklin Delano Roosevelt
  Memorial 41, 59
Franz Bader Bookstore 199
Frederick Douglass Home,
  The 94
free stuff 14
Freer Gallery 121
Freer, Charles L. 121
Fresco 152
Friendship Heights 88
  food & drink 161
Froggy Bottom Pub 176
Fudgery, The 233
Fund for American Studies,
  The 328
Funk & Junk 201
Furin's 154, 156

G

Gadsby's Tavern 106, 139
Galaxy Hut 169
Gallaudet University 95, 325
Gallery 10 Ltd. 83
Gallery K 83
Gallery of Georgetown 201
Gallery Place 42
games 205
Garage, The 275
Garrett's 177
Gay and Lesbian Hotline 332
gay nightlife 180–181, 245
gay travelers 314, 315
  newspapers 315
General Delivery 28
George Mason University 325
George Washington Masonic

National Memorial 105
George Washington
 University 62, 68, 219, 325
  Medical Center 332
Georgetown 33
 accommodations 218
 food & drink 153–156
 nightlife 176–178
 orientation 78
 sights 75–81
Georgetown Billiards 190
Georgetown Cafe 156
Georgetown Flea Market 204
Georgetown Metro
 Connection 24
Georgetown Park 203
Georgetown University 79, 325
 basketball 194
 Law School 220
 Medical Center 332
 summer housing 219
Georgia Ave. Day 17
getting around D.C. 23
getting into D.C. 21
Gibson's Lodgings 249
gifts 202
Glen Echo Park 112
Glover Park 87, 191
 food & drink 159
Go 30
GO25 card 304
go-go 42
golf 192
golf courses 110
Gordon Biersch 151
Gourmet by the Bay 255
Grapeseed 141
Grayline 335
Great Falls Park 110, 192
Greater D.C. Cares 322
Greater DC Cares 323
Green Leafe Cafe 280
Greenbelt Park 219
Greene Turtle 245
Greyhound 313
Grill from Ipanema, The 137
Groove Lounge 165
Grotto's 261
guesthouses 309
Guided Tour Inc., The 316
Gunston Hall 103
Gutenberg Bible 50
gyms 332

H

Haad Thai 150
Hackerman House 242
hair salons 331
Hambleton Inn Bed &
 Breakfast 254
Hammond-Harwood House 251
Hampton Inn & Suites 266
Happy Crab, The 270
Harborplace 243
Hard Times Cafe 140
Harpoon Larry's 271
Harry's 151, 244
Hawk 'n' Dove 170
health 307
Heaven and Hell 166
Hecht's 202
Hell's Kitchen 275
Helmand 235
Hereford House 215
Herndon Monument 252
Herring Hill 81
Hertz 332
HFStival 42
High Meadows Vineyard Inn
 and Restaurant 293
High Noon 151
Highlander Motor Inn 213
hiking 110, 192, 193
Hill Rag 30
Hillwood 89
Hillwood Museum &
 Gardens 127
Hippo 246
Hirshhorn Museum and
 Sculpture Garden 119, 190,
 328
Hirshhorn Museum and
 Sculpture Garden, 323
Hirshhorn Sculpture Garden 42
Hispanic Festival 17
historic homes 65, 104, 105,
 243, 251
 Annapolis 251
Historical Society Complex 259
Historical Society of
 Washington D.C. 328
history
 cold war 37
 financial problems 35, 40
 Great Depression 35
 home rule for D.C. 37
 social problems 320
 World War II 37

HIV 307
hockey 195
Holiday Inn Hotel and Suites
 211
Holiday Inn Rosslyn at Key
 Bridge 213
Holiday Inn Select 213
Holocaust Memorial 242
Holocaust Memorial
 Museum 11, 127
Home 174
home exchange 309
HomeExchange.Com 309
homelessness 322
Homewood 243
Hope Diamond 84, 117
Horne, Shirley 42
horseback riding 193
hospitals 332
Hostelling International-
 Washington DC 207
hostels 207, 309
Hotel Harrrington 217
hotels 208, 309
HotJobs 333
House and Senate
 Chambers 48
House of Musical Traditions,
 The 204
House of Representatives 46
House Office Building 51
Howard University 91, 325
 hospital 332
 summer housing 221
Howard, Gen. Oliver Otis 91
Howl At The Moon 245
Hughes, Langston 35, 43
Hunan Chinatown 145
Hunan Dynasty 145
hunger 322
Hunter's Head 298

I

ice skating 193
ID 303
Idealist 322
identification 303
 fake 30
Idle Time Books 199
Il Radicchio 144
IMAX Theater 118
Improv, The 189
In Towner 30
Independence Day

Celebration 17
India House Too 208
Indonesian Embassy 84
info lines 333
in-line skating 108, 193
Inn at Monticello, The 292
Inn at Rosslyn 213
Inn By The Bay, An 258
InnFinder 309
insurance 31, 308
InterActIon 324
International Association of
 Air Travel Couriers 312
international calls 28
International Guest House 211
international operator 29
International Spy Museum 127
International Student
 Exchange ID Card 304
International Student House
 221
International Student
 Identity Card (ISIC) 303
International Teacher
 Identity Card (ITIC) 304
International Youth Discount
 Travel Card 304
Internet
 flight planning 311
Internet access 333
Internship Bible, The 329
internships 326
 government 327
 museums 328
 think tanks and policy
  organizations 327
Intervac International Home
 Exchange 309
Iota 168
Iota Poetry Series 190
Ireland's Four Courts 168
Ireland's Four Provinces 180
Irish Embassy 27, 302
ISE 304
ISIC card 303
Islamic Center 84, 334
Island Motor Inn 266
Islander, The 157
ITIC card 304
itineraries 11
 three days 12
 five days 12
 seven days 13
Iwo Jima Memorial 99, 100
Ixia 235

J

J. Paul's 153, 177
J.R.'s 180
Jack's Place 139
Jackson, Andrew 64
Jaleo 151
James Madison Building 50
James River Plantations 276
Jamestown Church 284
Jamestown Settlement 283
Jamestown, VA 283–284
Jandara 158
Java Shack, The 140
jazz 186
Jazzline 243
Jefferson Building 50
Jefferson Memorial 11, 59
Jefferson, Thomas 60
Jewish Film Festival 18
Jewish Historical Society of
 Maryland 241
Jewish Information and
 Referral Service 316
Jewish Museum of Maryland
 241
Jillian's 275
Joaquin Miller Cabin 110
John Adams Building 50
John Harvard's Brew House 150
John Steven's 245
Johns Hopkins University 243
Joint Services Open House 17
Joint United Nations
 Programme on HIV/AIDS
 (UNAIDS) 308
Jolt 'n' Bolt Coffee and Tea
 House 149
Joy of Motion Dance Center 192
J.R.'s 180
Juice Joint Cafe 149
Julia's Empanadas 149
July 4 Celebration 17
Jury's Normandy Inn 210

K

Kalorama Guest House at
 Kalorama Park 210
Kalorama Guest House at
 Woodley Park 218
Kalorama House and
 Embassy Tour 18

Kathleen Ewing Gallery 83
Kayak Eco Tours 270
Kelley's The Irish Times 171
Kenilworth Aquatic Gardens 95
Kennedy Center 11, 41, 43,
 69, 186, 188
Kennedy Center Holiday
 Celebration 19
Kennedy Center Open
 House 18
Kennedy Gravesites 98
Kennedy-Warren
 Apartments 89
King Hall 252
King St. 106
King Street Blues 138, 139
King Street Cats 203
Kings Homemade Ice Cream
 Shops 258
Kobos Afrikan Clothiers 200
Kokopooli's 165, 190
Korean War Veterans
 Memorial 58
Kramerbooks 198
Kreeger Museum 86, 186
Kreeger Museum of Art 128
Kreeger Theater 187
Kwanzaa Celebration 19

L

La Frontera Grill and Bar
 138, 167
La Madeleine 139
La Panetteria 142
La Tavola 236
La Tomate 146
Lado International College 324
Lady Patty, The 255
Lafayette Park 64
Lambda Rising 199, 315
Landmark Parking 25
Langley Theater 119
Langston Golf Course 192
Language Learning
 Enterprises 324
Language One 324
language schools 324, 333
Lantern Bryn Mawr
 Bookshop, The 199
Las Tapas 139
Latin Jazz Alley 167
laundromats 333
Lauriol Plaza 146

Lazy Sundae 140
Le Bon Cafe 145
Leatherrack 203
Lebanese Taverna 158
Lee-Fendall House 105
Leesburg Corner Premium Outlets 297
Leesburg Restaurant 296
Leesburg, VA 295–297
Legal Sea Foods 152
Lei Garden Restuarant 145
lesbian nightlife 245
lesbian travelers 314, 315
Lewes, DE 256–259
Lewis Guest House 280
Lewnes' Steakhouse 250
Lexington Market 237
Liberty Rose 278
libraries 334
Library of Congress 41, 43, 49
    James Madison Building 50
    Jefferson Building 50
    John Adams Building 50
Library Tavern 282
license 303
Lightfoot 296
Likely Story, A 199
Lincoln Memorial 41, 57
Lincoln Theatre 188
Lincoln Theatre, The 90
Lindy's Bon Apetit 153
Lindy's Red Lion 176
Liquid Earth 236
Lisner Auditorium 185
Lite 'n' Fair 139
literature 43, 190
    African-American 43
Little Island City Park 270
littlejohn's 293
Lizard Lounge 180
Lloyd Street Synagogue 241
Local 16 157, 178
Loews Cineplex 191
long-term housing 219–221
long-term work 326
lost passports 303
Loudoun County Visitor Information Center 295
Louisiana Express 142
Lover's Lane 79
Lowell, Robert 43
Luigino's 152
Lulu's Mardi Gras Club 176
Luna Books 199
Luna Grill & Diner 148
Lyceum 106

Lyndon Baines Johnson Fund 327
Lyric Opera House 244

M

m 181
ma 136
Macy's 202
Madam's Organ 164, 187
Maddox Family Campground 266
Made By You 198
Madhatter, The 173
Madison, Dolley 62
Magna Carta 71
Magnolia Steak 274
Mahi Mah's 271
mail 27
    general delivery 28
Mailer, Norman 43
Main St. Shop & Coffee House 266
Maison Orleans 215
Major League Baseball 246
Mall, The
    feature article 54
    sights 53–60
malls 203
Mama Ayesha's Restaurant 136
Mama Maria and Enzio's 159
Ma-Masu's 288
Manassas National Battlefield Park 111
MARC commuter lines 229
Marine Barracks 92
Marine Corps Historical Museum 129
Marine Corps Marathon 18
Marine Corps War Memorial 100
Market House 249
Market Lunch, The 144
markets 204
Marrakesh 150
Marsha Mateyka Gallery 83
Martha's Table 322
Martin Luther King, Jr. Library 73
Marvelous Market 156
Mary McLeod Bethune Council House 124
Maryland Science Center 239
Marymount University 325
Massad House Hotel 287

MasterCard 305
Matsuri 234
Matt's Pub and Comedy Club 291
Max's on Broadway 245
Mazza Gallerie 203
MCCXXIII 172
McGarvey's 253
MCI Center 10, 73, 80, 195
McPherson Square 74
Mechanic Theatre 244
Medaterra 158
media 29–30
    print 29
    television 30
media, print 43
medical assistance 307
Medical Referral Line 332
medical services 31
    health insurance 31
Medley's 291
Meeps Fashionette 201
Mei Wah Restaurant 152
Mellon, Andrew 122
Memorial Day Jazz Festival 17
Memorials 41
memorials
    African American Civil War Memorial 90
    Franklin Delano Roosevelt Memorial 90
    George Washington Masonic National 105
    Grant 46
    Holocaust 242
    Iwo Jima 99
    Jefferson 59
    Korean War Veterans 58
    Lincoln 57
    National Law Enforcement Officers Memorial 73
    National World War II Memorial 53
    Vietnam Veterans 57
    Vietnam Veterans Memorial 57
    Vietnam Women's Memorial 57
    Women in Military Service for America 99
Meridian International Center 85
Merriweather Post Pavilion 185
Meskerem 137
Metro 23–25
    Georgetown Metro Conenction 24
    one-day pass 24
    parking 23
    SmarTrip 24
Metro System Guide 315

Metrobus 24
Metrorail 23
Michie Tavern 293
Middleburg, VA 297–299
Millennium 198
Millie & Al's 164, 165
Mind's Eye Craft Collection, The 256
Minnie V. 238
Miss Saigon 155
Mister Days 168
Mixtec 137
Mobility International USA (MIUSA) 315
Moby Dick House of Kabob 155
money 31, 304
Monocle, The 144
Monster.com 333
Montgomery Farm Women's Cooperative 204
Monticello 294
Montmartre 143
Montpelier 294
Moses Myers House 274
mosques 334
Motel 6 273
Mount Moriah African Methodist Episcopal Church 250
Mount Vernon 10, 102
Mount Vernon Open House 16
Mount Vernon Trail 191
Mount Zion United Methodist Church 81
Movie Madness 205
movies 190–191
Mr. Henry's Victorian Pub 145
Mr. P's 181
Mr. Smith's 177
Mrs. Marshall's Carytown Cafe 291
Mugavero's Confectionery 236
Mullet, A.B. 41
Murphy 167
Murphy's Grand Irish Pub 167
Murphy's of D.C. 180
Museum Annex 130
Museum of American History 190
Museum of the Confederacy 289
museums 115–131
  African-American history 250
  art 240, 242
  history 241
  industry 239
  internships and jobs 328
  Jewish 241
  military 252
  off the Mall 124–131
  on the Mall 115–124
  Smithsonian 115
  volunteering 323
music 42, 183–187
  blues 186
  chamber music 186
  classical 186
  jazz 186
  orchestra 186
  pop 184
  rock 184
music stores 204
Music Theatre of Williamsburg 282
musical instruments 204
MW (newspaper) 315

N

Nam-Viet Pho 79 160
Nana 200
Nanny O'Brien's 180
Nathans 155, 178
Nation 185
National Abortion Federation Hotline 308
National Academy of Sciences 67
National Air and Space Museum 118
National Arboretum 95
National Archives 10, 70
National Army Band's 1812 Overture Performance 18
National Building Museum 41, 129
National Capital Barbecue Battle 17
National Capitol Postal Station 53
National Cherry Blossom Festival 16
National Christmas Tree 19, 63
National Frisbee Festival 18
National Gallery of Art 11, 41, 53, 122, 190
National Gallery Sculpture Garden 42
National Garden 51
National Geographic 185
National Geographic Society 75
National Law Enforcement Officers Memorial 73
National Museum of African Art 120
National Museum of American Art 129
National Museum of American History 48, 57, 116, 328
National Museum of American Jewish Military History 83
National Museum of Natural History 117, 323, 328
National Museum of Women in the Arts 129
National Organization for Victim Assistance 332
National Postal Museum 130
National Republican Senatorial Committee 328
National Symphony 185
National Symphony Orchestra 70, 186
National Theatre 188, 190
National Woman's Party 52
National World War II Memorial 53
  feature article 55
National Zoo 10, 89
Nature Center 108
Nauticus 275
Naval Academy Band 253
Naval Heritage Center 72
Naval Museum 252
Navy Jet Observation Area 271
Navy Memorial 72
Navy Museum 130
neighborhoods 5–10
Net Ped@llers 248
Netherlands Carillon 101
New Orleans Cafe 136
New York Avenue Presbyterian Church 73
New Zealand Embassy 27, 302
newspapers 29, 75
Newsroom 199
Nick's Riverside Grille 177
Night Dreams 202
Nightlife 163
nightlife
  gay 180
Nina Abody Festival Park 290
9:30 Club 42, 184
Nixon, Richard "Tricky Dick" 47
No Frill Bar and Grill 274
Nordstrom 202
Norfolk Visitors Bureau 272

Norfolk, VA 272–277
Norfolk's Botanical Garden 275
Norris House Inn, The 295
Northeast
  orientation 94
  sights 94–96
NRI Staffing Resources 329, 333

O

Oatlands Plantation 296
Observatory Circle 87
Ocean City International Student Services 262
Ocean City Travel Park 263
Ocean City Visitors Center 262
Ocean City, MD 262–264
Oktoberfest 18
Old Brick Inn, The 254
Old Chickahominy House 280
Old Ebbitt Grill 152
Old Europe 159
Old Executive Office Building 64
Old Glory 177
Old House Chamber 47
Old Post Office 41, 72
  Pavilion 150
Old Senate Chamber 48
Old Stone House 79, 110
Old Supreme Court Chamber 48
Old Town Trolley 335
Old Vat Theater 187
older travelers 314
Olsson's Books and Records 198
Omega 180
on 218
On Tap 30, 43
Once in D.C. 21–31
One-Day Pass (Metro) 24
Ooh La La 173
opera 43, 244
opera companies 186
operator 29
Orbit 294
orchestra 186
Oriole Park 240
Orioles, Baltimore 246
Other Pages 315
Our Lady of Perpetual Help Church 92
Our Place Restaurant and Garden Patio 261

outdoor art 42
outdoor gear 205
Oval Office 63
Owls Creek Marsh Pavilion 271
Oyster & Maritime Museum 266
Ozio 173

P

paddleboats 192
Page House Inn 273
Pageant of Peace 19
Pan Asian Noodles & Grill 148
Pandemonium. See Chief Ike's Mambo Room
Paolo's 154
Paradise Restaurant 143
park police 332
parking 23, 25
parks 108–113
  C&O Canal 191
  Cape Henlopen State Park 258
  Colonial National Park 283
  East Potomac 191
  False Cape State Park 270
  Glover 191
  Great Falls Park 192
  Little Island City Park 270
  Rock Creek 191
Party Block Complex 264
passports 302
  lost 303
Pasta Mia Trattoria 136
Pat Troy's 167
Patisserie Poupon 154
Patriot Cruises 255
Paul's Restaurant and Deli 282
Paula's Imports 203
Pavilions at Harborplace 233
Peabody's 271
Peirce Barn 108
Peirce Mill 108
Penn Station (Baltimore) 229
Pensler Gallery 83
Pentagon City Mall 203
Pentagon, The 101
Peppers 147
Pershing Park Ice Rink 193
Petersen House 72
Peterson's Internships 329
pharmacies 334
Philadelphia Mike's 142
Phillip's Buffet 234
Phillip's Restaurant 234
Phillip's Seafood Market 234

Phillips Collection 130
Phillips Flagship 157
Phillips, Duncan 131
Phoenix, The 291
phone operator 29
phones 28
  international access codes 28
  international calls 28
pickpockets 31
picnics 193
Pier 6 Concert Pavilion 243
Pink 291
Pinsky, Robert 43
Pinter, Harold 43
Pitch, Anthony S. (tours) 26
Pizzeria Paradiso 147
planetarium 119
Planned Parenthood 308
planning your trip 301–317
Platinum 174
Pla-za 198
Pleasure Place 202
PLUS 307
Pocahontas State Park 287
poetry readings 110, 190
poets 43
Poison Center 332
Political Washington 45
  sights 45–53
Politics and Prose 199
Politiki. See Pour House/ Politiki 170
Politix Group, The 329
Polly Esther's 175
Polly's Cafe 157
pool/billiards 189
pop 184
Pop's Old Fashioned Ice Cream Company 138
Pope, John Russell 41, 60
Pope-Leighey House 104
Port Discovery 238
Posh Boutique 291
post offices 334
posters 205
Potato Valley Cafe 249
Potomac Horse Center 193
Potomac plantations 102
Potomac Riverboat Tours 106
Pound, Ezra 43
Pour House/Politiki 170
Power Plant Live 233
Powhatan Indian Village 283
President's Own, The 92
print media 29, 43
prints 205

Protix 184, 189
public transportation 23–25
punk 42, 184
Purple Orchid 234
Pusser's Landing 253

Q

Quality Hotel & Suites 213
Quality Inn Iwo Jima 213

R

Radisson Plaza Lord
 Baltimore 232
Rage Clothing 201
Raku 146, 148
Ram's Head Tavern 253
Ramsey House Visitors
 Center 105
Randall House 249
Rape Crisis Center 332
Rapture 293
Ravens Stadium 246
Reagan National Airport 335
recreation 191–193
recreational sports 110
Recruiters Online Network 333
Red 172
Red Cross Waterfront
 Festival 17
Red Fox Inn, The 298
Red Ginger 153
Red River Grill 170
Red Roof Inn 217
Reel Affirmations 18
Reeves 151
Reflecting Pool 56
Reflections 263
Registry, The 331
Rehoboth Beach Chamber
 of Commerce 259
Rehoboth Beach, DE 259–262
religious services 334
Rent-A-Wreck 332
Renwick Gallery 131
reverse-charge calls 29
RFK Stadium 184
Rhino 177
Richmond Metropolitan
 Visitor's Bureau 285
Richmond, VA 284–291
Ride-On 24

Rio Grande Cafe 142
Rivah Bistro, The 288
Robert Brown Gallery 83
rock 184
rock 'n' roll 42
Rock Creek Park 108–110,
 191, 193
Rock Creek Park Golf Course
 110, 192
Rock Creek Park Horse
 Center 110, 193
Rock Creek Parkway 108
Rock Greek Park
 golf course 192
Rocklands 141
Rockville Arts Place 203
Ronald Reagan Building 150
Ronald Reagan National
 Airport 21, 311
Roommates Preferred 331
Roosevelt Island 100, 192
Rose and Crown Restaurant
 and Pub 258
Royal Restaurant 139
Royal Treat 261
RT's Seafood Kitchen 140
Rumors 173
running
 Mall, The 191
 Tidal Basin 191
 Waterfront 191

S

S. Dillon Ripley Center's
 International Gallery 120
Sackler Gallery 120
Sackler Library 121
safety 30
 self-defense 31
Saigon 159
Saigon Gourmet Restaurant 159
Saigon Inn 154
Saigonnais 137
Sakana 148
Sala Thai 147
Saloun 187
Saveur Restaurant 159
Savino's 147
Scandal Tours 26, 27, 335
Science Museum of Virginia 289
Scoop Grill and Homemade
 Ice Cream, The 139
Scotlaur Inn 249
Scottish Merchant & John

Crouch Tobacconist, The 203
Scottish Rite Freemasonry
 Temple 83
Sculpture Garden 119, 124
Sea Spray Motel 263
Seacrets 264
Sean Donlon Pub 253
Seaside Nature Center 258
Second Story Books 199
Secondi Consignment
 Clothing 201
Security Intelligence 205
self defense 31
Senate 46
Senate Office Building 51
senior travelers 314
services 331–335
Sewall-Belmont House 52
sexually transmitted
 diseases 307
Shake Your Booty Shoes 205
Shakespeare Theatre 188
Shaw/U District
 entertainment 184–185
 food & drink 156–157
 nightlife 178–179
 sights 90–91
Sheraton Four Points 213
Sheridan Circle 84
Shirley Plantation 276
shoe repair 334
shoe stores 205
Shopping 197–205
Shops at National Place and
 Press 150
short-term work 329
Showcase of Nations Ethnic
 Festivals 244
Sibley Memorial Hospital 332
Sierra Club 193
sights 45–113
Sign of the Whale 173
Sisterspace and Books 200
Sizzling Express 150
Skewers 148
Ski Center 193
SmarTrip 24
Smash! 204
Smithson, James 115
Smithsonian Castle Garde 42
Smithsonian Folklife Festival 17
Smithsonian Institute 53, 186
 disabled visitors 315
Smithsonian Kite Festival 16
Smithsonian Museums 11,
 115–124

Smithsonian National Air and Space Museum 323
Smithsonian National Air and Space Museum, 328
So's Your Mom 136
Sobo Cafe 234
soccer 195
social problems 320
Society for the Advancement of Travel for the Handicapped (SATH) 315
Soul Searchers 42
Source Theater, The 188
Sousa, John Philip 42
South African Embassy 27, 302
South of the Mall
  accommodations 218
  Food & Drink 157–158
  nightlife 179
  sights 61–62
Southeastern University 325
special concerns
  children 316
  dietary concerns 314
special events 15–19
specific concerns
  bisexual, gay, and lesbian travelers 314, 315
  disabled travelers 315
  senior travelers 314
  women travelers 314
spectator sports 194
speed limit 314
Spices Asian Restaurant & Sushi Bar 160
sports 191–195
  participatory 191–193
  spectator 194–195
Spy Lounge 165
Spy Museum 127
spy stores 205
Squished Penny Museum 123
St. Elmo's Coffee Pub 190
St. John's Church 41, 64, 288
St. Luke's Gallery 83
St. Michael's Information Center 253
St. Michaels, MD 253–256
  shopping 255
St. Sophia Greek Festival 18
St. Tropez 291
STA Travel 311, 331
Stabler-Leadbeater Apothecary Museum & Shop 107
standby flights 312

Stanislavsky Theater Studio 188
stargazing 193
State Department 62, 68
State House 251
State Theatre 186
Statuary Hall 47
Steamer's Seafood House 142
Stoney's Restaurant 151, 175
Storm Brothers Ice Cream Factory 250
Strawberry Street Cafe and Market 288
Street of Presidents 70
Studio Gallery 83
Studio Theatre 188
study visas 324
studying 324–325
Sullivan's Toy Store 205
Summer House Saloon, The 261
summer housing
  Boston University Washington Center 220
  Catholic University 220
  George Washington University 219
  Georgetown Law School 220
  Georgetown University 219
  Howard University 221
  sublets 221
Summer Opera Theatre Company 186
Sunny's Affordable Outdoor Store 205
supermarkets 334
SuperShuttle 21
Supreme Court 49
swimming 193
Swiss Inn 217

T

Tabard Inn 146, 215
Taft Bridge Inn 210
Tai Shan Restaurant 145
Tako Grill 143
Takoma Park 96
Takoma Underground 198
Taliano's 187
Tally Hoe Theatre 297
tanning salons 331
Tap House Grill 280
Taste Gourmet Deli 255
Taste of D.C. Festiva 18

Taverna the Greek Islands 145
taxes 30, 307
taxis 25, 334
  DC Taxicab Commission 25
  Yellow Cab 25
Tazewell Hotel & Suites 273
Teaism 148
Tecumseh 251
telephone operator 29
telephones 28
  international access codes 28
  international calls 28
television 30
Temporary Jobs 333
Temps & Co. 333
Tenley Circle 88
  food & drink 161
tennis 193
tennis courts 110
Tequila Grill 173
Terrace Theater 188
Thai Kingdom 150
Thai Kitchen 152
The Aroma Company 180
The Cyberstop Cafe 149
The Fireplace 181
The Reef 164
theater 43, 187–189
Theater J 189
Theater Lab 188
Theater Project 244
theft 31
Third Edition 177
Thomas Cook 305
Thomas Sweet 155
Thompson Boat Center 192
Thompson Boat House 110
Thompson-Markward Hall 221
Thrasher's 261
Three Servicemen 57
Thrifty Car Rental 332
Thyme Square Cafe 141
ticket consolidators 312
Ticket Services 335
TicketMaster 80, 184
Tidal Basin 11, 60
  boat house 192
Tidal Basin Boat House 192
Tiffany Tavern 167, 168
Timberlake's 172
Tio Pepe 235
tipping 30, 307
Tobacco Company Club, The 291
Tobacco Company Restaurant 291
Toledo Lounge 165

Tomb of the Unknowns 99
Tombs, The 177
Tony and Joe's 177
Tony and Joe's Seafood
  Place 156
Tony Cheng's Mongolian
  Restaurant 146
Tony Cheng's Seafood
  Restaurant 146
Torpedo Factory 107
tour agencies 316
Tour D.C. 27, 335
tourism bureaus 316
tourist information 316
tourist office 27
  D.C. Information Center 27
tourist offices 335
Tourmobile Sightseeing 26, 335
tours 26
  biking 26
  boat 62
  bus and trolley 26
  oddball 27
  scandal 27
  walking 26
towed cars 26
Townhouse Tavern 172
toys 205
traffic tickets 26
Tragara 142
trails
  Capitol Crescent 191
  Mount Vernon 191
  Valley 192
  Washington & Old
    Dominion 191
  Western Ridge 192
transformers 308
transportation 335
  bus 313
  car 313
  planes 311
  train 313
Trattoria Italiana 158
travel agencies 311
Travel Avenue 331
travel books 317
Travel CUTS 311
Traveler's Aid Society 232, 333
traveler's checks 305
travelers with disabilities 335
Travelex 305
traveling with children 316
Treasury Building 34
Trident 252
Trinity College 325
Trio Pizza and Subs 147

Trio Restuarant 147
Trio's Fox and Hounds 147
Tropical Smoothie Cafe 269
Tropicana 157
Tryst 136, 165
Tudor Place Estate 80
Tune Inn 171
Tuscana West 175
Two Quail Restuarant 143
Tysons Corner Center 203
Tysons Galleria 203

U

U 179
U Street 200–201
U.S. Department of
  Commerce 327
U.S. Department of Housing
  and Urban Development 327
U.S. Department of Justice 327
UK Embassy 27
Union Station 23, 41, 52,
  143, 313
Union Station Plaza 53
Unique 203
universities 324
university dorms 309
University of the District of
  Columbia 325
University of Virginia 293
Upper Crust, The 298
Upper Northwest
  accommodations 218
  food & drink 158–161
  nightlife 179–180
  sights 86–90
Uptown Theater 191
US Airways Shuttle 311
US Botanical Gardens 51
US Naval Academy 251
uses 208
usit world 311
U-topia 179
Utopia/The Bar 179

V

Vaccaro's 236
Valentine Museum, The 289
Valley Trail 192
valuables, protecting 31
Velvet Lounge 184
Vermeer 122

Vespa 234
Veteran's Day Ceremonies 18
Vice Presidential Mansion 87
Vie de France 150
Vienna Halloween Parade 18
Vietnam Veterans Memorial
  10, 41, 57
  Virtual Wall 57
Vietnam Women's Memorial 57
VIP Club, The 174
Virginia Beach Visitors
  Center 269
Virginia Beach, VA 267–271
  practical information 267
Virginia Gold Cup 17
Virginia Historical Society 290
Virginia Marine Science
  Museum 271
Virginia Museum of Fine Arts 290
Virginia Scottish Games 17
Virginia Shop, The 203
Virtual Wall, The 57
Visa 305
visas 303
  study 324
  through CIEE 326
Visionary Art Museum 240
visual arts 41
Voice of America 61
volunteering 320, 320–324
  homelessness 322
  hunger 322
  museums 323
VolunteerMatch 322

W

Wades Point Inn On the Bay 254
walking tours 6–8, 14
Walters Art Gallery 242
Warner Theatre 189
Washington & Old Dominion
  Trail 111
Washington Afro-American 29
Washington and Old
  Dominion Bike Trail 191
Washington Area
  Roadskaters 193
Washington Ballet 43, 189
Washington Blade 29, 43, 315
Washington Capitals 195
Washington CityPaper 29, 43
Washington Color School 42
Washington Convention and
  Visitor's Association 315

Washington Doll's House and Toy Museum 89, 131
Washington Ear, Inc. 335
Washington Flower and Garden Show 16
Washington Flyer Coach Service 23
Washington Jewish Weekly 29
Washington Monthly 29
Washington Monument 41, 53
Washington Mystics, WNBA 194
Washington National Cathedral 10, 87
Washington National Cathedral Christmas Celebration and Services 19
Washington Opera 43, 186
Washington Post 29, 43, 74, 190
Washington Printmakers Gallery 83
Washington Redskins 195
Washington Shakespeare Company 43, 189
Washington Theater Club 43
Washington Times 43
Washington Wizards 194
Washingtonian magazine 29
Waterfront
 orientation 61
 sights 61–62
Waterfront Channel Inn Hotel 218
Watergate 69, 71, 75
Waterside Festival Marketplace 274
Western Ridge Trail 192
Westfield Shoppingtown Montgomery 204
Westminster Churchyard 241
Wharf Street Seafood Market 158
Wheaton Park Stables 193
Where 30

WHFS 42
Whistler, James McNeil 121
White House 11, 34, 62
 Fall Garden Tours 18
White House Easter Egg Roll 17
White House Fall Garden Tours 18
White House Internship Program, The 327
White House of the Confederacy 289
White House Spring Garden Tours 16
Whitlow's on Wilson 168
Whitman, Walt 43
Whitman-Walker Clinic 307
Wickham House 289
Wild Women Wear Red 205
William Paca House 251
Williams, Anthony A. 40
Williamsburg Area Convention And Visitors Bureau 278
Williamsburg Hospitality House, The 280
Williamsburg International Airport 277
Williamsburg, VA 277–284
Willies 204
Willoughby-Baylor House 274
Wilson's 157
Windsor Inn, The 216
Windsor Park Hotel 211
Wisemiller's Deli 156
Wolftrap National Park for the Performing Arts 186
women
 health 308
 memorials 57
 travelers 314
 women's history 47, 52
Women in Military Service for America Memorial 99
women's health 308

Women's Resources 335
Woodley Park 89
 food & drink 158–159
Woodley Park Guest House 218
Woodrow Wilson House 85
Woolly Mammoth 189
work
 long-term 326
work permits 303
work permits. See visas 325
working 325–329
 internships 326
 museums 328
 short-term work 329
 think tanks and policy organizations 327
world wide web 317
Wrap Works 156
Writer's Center, The 190

Y

Yanni's 160
Yellow Cab 25
Yenching Palace 160
Yorktown Victory Center 276
Yorktown, VA 275–277
Yosaku 161

Z

Zanzibar on the Waterfront 158, 179
Zed's Ethiopian Cuisine 154, 156
Zola 151
zoo 89
Zorba's Cafe 148
Zwaanendael Inn 258
Zwaanendael Museum 258

Map Appendix

INSIDE:

D.C. Inner and Outer Neighborhoods 352
Capitol Hill 353
The Mall 354-5
Gallery District 354
17th & P St. 354
Dupont Circle 355
Federal Triangle & China Town 356
Farragut 357
Foggy Bottom 358
Georgetown 359

Adams Morgan 360
Shaw/U District 361
South of the Mall 362
Takoma Park 362
Northeast Overview 363
Upper Northwest Overview 364
Bethesda 365
Southeast & Anacostia 366
Arlington & Alexandria 367
Wilson & Clarendon Blvd. 368
Old Town Alexandria 369

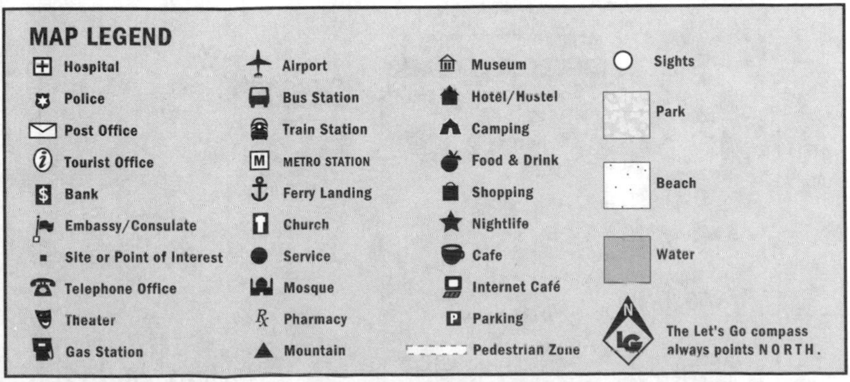

MAP LEGEND

⊞ Hospital	✈ Airport	🏛 Museum	○ Sights
✪ Police	🚌 Bus Station	Hotel/Hostel	
✉ Post Office	🚍 Train Station	⛺ Camping	Park
ⓘ Tourist Office	Ⓜ METRO STATION	Food & Drink	
$ Bank	⚓ Ferry Landing	Shopping	Beach
Embassy/Consulate	Church	★ Nightlife	
■ Site or Point of Interest	● Service	Cafe	Water
☎ Telephone Office	Mosque	Internet Café	
Theater	℞ Pharmacy	P Parking	The Let's Go compass always points NORTH.
Gas Station	▲ Mountain	----- Pedestrian Zone	

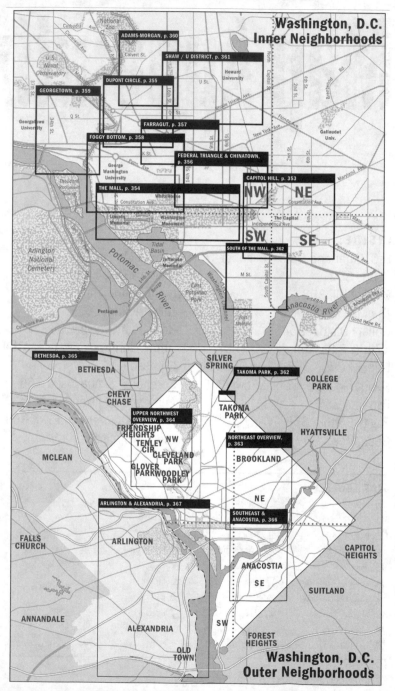

Washington, D.C. Inner Neighborhoods

ADAMS-MORGAN, p. 360

SHAW / U DISTRICT, p. 361

DUPONT CIRCLE, p. 355

GEORGETOWN, p. 359

FARRAGUT, p. 357

FOGGY BOTTOM, p. 358

FEDERAL TRIANGLE & CHINATOWN, p. 356

THE MALL, p. 354

CAPITOL HILL, p. 353

NW   NE

SW   SE

SOUTH OF THE MALL, p. 362

National Zoo
Cathedral Ave
Cleveland Ave
U.S. Naval Observatory
Calvert St.
Howard University
U St.
37th St.
Georgetown University
Q St.
34th St.
Rhode Island Ave
New York Ave
North Capitol St.
2nd St.
Brentwood Rd.
Gallaudet Univ.
George Washington University
K St.
Penn. Ave
14th St.
16th St.
9th St.
6th St.
Maryland Ave
Thodore Roosevelt Island
WhiteHouse
Constitution Ave
Constitution Ave
Arlington National Cemetery
Lincoln Memorial
Washington Monument
The Capitol
Independence Ave
Mass. Ave
Tidal Basin
Jefferson Memorial
Pennsylvania Ave
East Potomac Park
South Capitol St.
M St.
Potomac River
Washington Channel
Anacostia River
Pentagon
Fort McNair
Good Hope Rd.
Columbia Pike
Anacostia Pkwy.
14th St.

Washington, D.C. Outer Neighborhoods

BETHESDA, p. 365

SILVER SPRING

TAKOMA PARK, p. 362

COLLEGE PARK

BETHESDA

CHEVY CHASE

UPPER NORTHWEST OVERVIEW, p. 364

TAKOMA PARK

FRIENDSHIP HEIGHTS   NW

HYATTSVILLE

TENLEY CIR

NORTHEAST OVERVIEW, p. 363

MCLEAN

CLEVELAND PARK

BROOKLAND

GLOVER PARK WOODLEY PARK

NE

ARLINGTON & ALEXANDRIA, p. 367

SOUTHEAST & ANACOSTIA, p. 366

FALLS CHURCH

ARLINGTON

CAPITOL HEIGHTS

ANACOSTIA

SE

ANNANDALE

SUITLAND

ALEXANDRIA

SW

OLD TOWN

FOREST HEIGHTS

Capitol Hill

🏠 **ACCOMMODATIONS**
Hereford House, **28**
Maison Orleans, **27**

🍴 **FOOD & DRINK**
Armand's Chicago Pizzeria, **4**
Le Bon Café, **32**
Bread and Chocolate, **26**
Burrito Brothers, **29**
Capitol Hill Jimmy T's, **15**
The Dubliner, **3**
Hawk 'n' Dove, **36**
The Market Lunch, **23**
The Monocle, **5**
Montmartre, **25**
Mr. Henry's Victorian Pub, **24**
Il Radicchio, **30**
Taverna the Greek Islands, **34**
Two Quail Restaurant, **7**

⭐ **NIGHTLIFE**
Capitol Lounge, **31**
Cosi, **33**
The Dubliner, **3**
Hawk 'n' Dove, **36**
Kelley's "The Irish Times," **2**
Pour House/Politiki, **35**
Red River Grill, **6**
Tune Inn, **37**

⭕ **SIGHTS**
The Capitol, **13**
Folger Shakespeare Library, **14**
House Office Building: Cannon, **21**
House Office Building: Longworth, **20**
House Office Building: Rayburn, **19**
The Library of Congress: John Adams
 Building, **17**

The Library of Congress: Thomas
 Jefferson Building, **16**
The Library of Congress: James
 Madison Building, **22**
Senate Office Building: Dirksen/
 Hart, **10**
Senate Office Building: Russell, **9**
Sewall-Belmont House, **11**
The Supreme Court, **12**
Taft Memorial, **8**
Union Station, **1**
US Botanic Garden, **18**

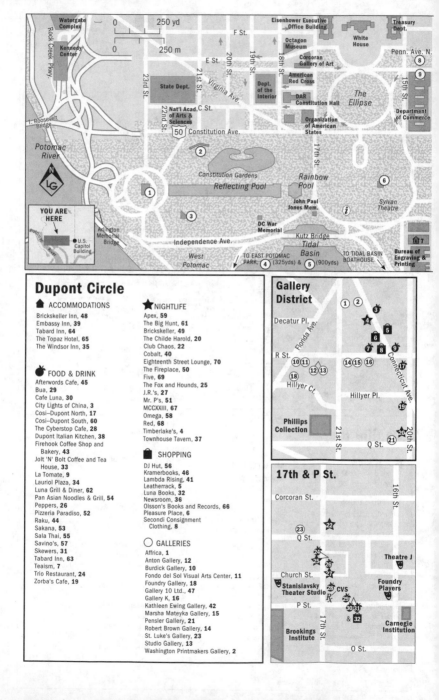

Dupont Circle

🏠 ACCOMMODATIONS

Brickskeller Inn, **48**
Embassy Inn, **39**
Tabard Inn, **64**
The Topaz Hotel, **65**
The Windsor Inn, **35**

🍎 FOOD & DRINK

Afterwords Cafe, **45**
Bua, **29**
Cafe Luna, **30**
City Lights of China, **3**
Cosi–Dupont North, **17**
Cosi–Dupont South, **60**
The Cyberstop Cafe, **28**
Dupont Italian Kitchen, **38**
Firehook Coffee Shop and
  Bakery, **43**
Jolt 'N' Bolt Coffee and Tea
  House, **33**
La Tomate, **9**
Lauriol Plaza, **34**
Luna Grill & Diner, **62**
Pan Asian Noodles & Grill, **54**
Peppers, **26**
Pizzeria Paradiso, **52**
Raku, **44**
Sakana, **53**
Sala Thai, **55**
Savino's, **57**
Skewers, **31**
Tabard Inn, **63**
Teaism, **7**
Trio Restaurant, **24**
Zorba's Cafe, **19**

⭐ NIGHTLIFE

Apex, **59**
The Big Hunt, **61**
Brickskeller, **49**
The Childe Harold, **20**
Club Chaos, **22**
Cobalt, **40**
Eighteenth Street Lounge, **70**
The Fireplace, **50**
Five, **69**
The Fox and Hounds, **25**
J.R.'s, **27**
Mr. P's, **51**
MCCXXIII, **67**
Omega, **58**
Red, **68**
Timberlake's, **4**
Townhouse Tavern, **37**

🛍 SHOPPING

DJ Hut, **56**
Kramerbooks, **46**
Lambda Rising, **41**
Leatherrack, **5**
Luna Books, **32**
Newsroom, **36**
Olsson's Books and Records, **66**
Pleasure Place, **6**
Secondi Consignment
  Clothing, **8**

⭕ GALLERIES

Africa, **1**
Anton Gallery, **12**
Burdick Gallery, **10**
Fondo del Sol Visual Arts Center, **11**
Foundry Gallery, **18**
Gallery 10 Ltd., **47**
Gallery K, **16**
Kathleen Ewing Gallery, **42**
Marsha Mateyka Gallery, **15**
Pensler Gallery, **21**
Robert Brown Gallery, **14**
St. Luke's Gallery, **23**
Studio Gallery, **13**
Washington Printmakers Gallery, **2**

Gallery District

17th & P St.

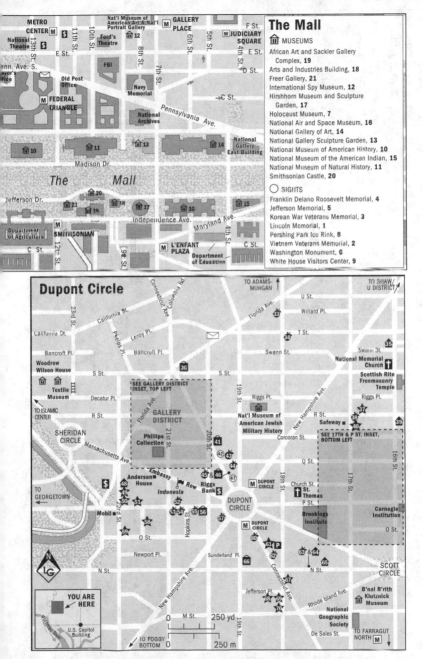

The Mall

🏛 MUSEUMS

African Art and Sackler Gallery Complex, **19**
Arts and Industries Building, **18**
Freer Gallery, **21**
International Spy Museum, **12**
Hirshhorn Museum and Sculpture Garden, **17**
Holocaust Museum, **7**
National Air and Space Museum, **16**
National Gallery of Art, **14**
National Gallery Sculpture Garden, **13**
National Museum of American History, **10**
National Museum of the American Indian, **15**
National Museum of Natural History, **11**
Smithsonian Castle, **20**

◯ SIGHTS

Franklin Delano Roosevelt Memorial, **4**
Jefferson Memorial, **5**
Korean War Veterans Memorial, **3**
Lincoln Memorial, **1**
Pershing Park Ice Rink, **8**
Vietnam Veterans Memorial, **2**
Washington Monument, **6**
White House Visitors Center, **9**

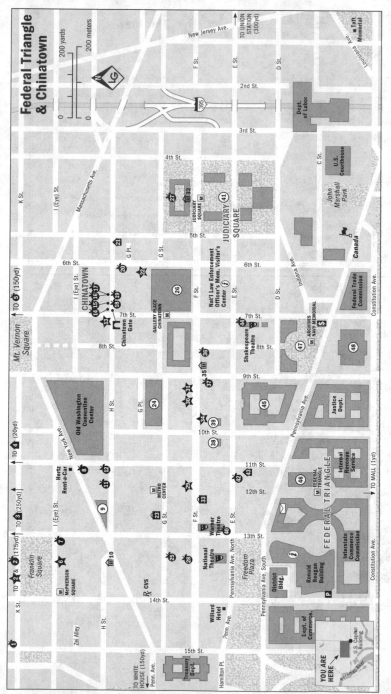

Federal Triangle & Chinatown

Federal Triangle & Chinatown

▲ ACCOMMODATIONS
Hostelling International -
 Washington D.C. (HI-AYH), 4
Hotel Harrington, 43
Red Roof Inn, 21
Swiss Inn, 3

● FOOD & DRINK
Burma Restaurant, 20
Cafe Amadeus, 7
Capitol City Brewing Co., 12
China Deli, 15
Gordon Biersch, 37
Haad Thai, 8
Harry's, 42
High Noon (1311 F St.), 28
High Noon (intersection of 15th and K), 1
High Noon (National Building Museum), 27
Hunan Chinatown, 18
Jaleo, 44
John Harvard's Brew House, 40
Le Garden Restaurant, 14
Luigino's, 11
Merriwesh, 5
Reeves, 25
Stoney's Restaurant, 2
Tai Shan Restaurant, 19
Tony Cheng's Mongolian Restaurant, 16
Tony Cheng's Seafood Restaurant, 17
Zola, 36

★ NIGHTLIFE
Club Insomnia, 22
Diva, 6
Fado, 13
Home, 31
Platinum, 30
Polly Esther's, 29
Stoney's Restaurant, 2
The VIP Club, 34

● SHOPPING
Hecht's, 23
Olsson's Books & Records, 33

○ SIGHTS
Federal Bureau of Investigation, 45
Ford's Theatre, 39
International Spy Museum, 35
Martin Luther King, Jr. Library, 24
MCI Center, 26
National Archives, 48
National Building Museum, 32
National Law Enforcement Officers
 Memorial, 41
National Museum of Women in the
 Arts, 10
Navy Memorial & Naval
 Heritage Center, 47
New York Avenue Presbyterian Church, 9
Old Post Office, 46
Petersen House, 38

Farragut

▲ ACCOMMODATIONS
The Braxton Hotel, 1
Farragut Lincoln Suites, 9
Hostelling International-
 Washington DC, 16

● FOOD & DRINK
Art Gallery Grille, 20
Bombay Palace, 17
Casa Blanca, 12
Famous Luigi's, 8
Juice Joint Cafe, 13

Julia's Empanadas, 14
Thai Kingdom, 10

★ NIGHTLIFE
The Madhatter, 2
Ooh La La, 7
Ozio, 4
Rumors, 5
Sign of the Whale, 3
Tequila Grill, 18

■ SHOPPING
Al's Magic Shop, 15
Chapters, 19
Chocolate Moose, 6
Franz Bader
 Bookstore, 19
Security Intelligence,
 11

Foggy Bottom

▲ ACCOMMODATIONS
Allen Lee Hotel, 17

● FOOD & DRINK
Cone E. Island, 9
Cup A' Cup A' at the Watergate, 15
Fresco, 13
Legal Sea Foods, 5
Lindy's Bon Apetit, 7
Mei Wah Restaurant, 3
Thai Kitchen, 1

★ NIGHTLIFE
Froggy Bottom Pub, 6
Lindy's Red Lion, 8
Lulu's Mardi Gras Club, 2
McFadden's, 4

○ 🏛 SIGHTS
American Red Cross, 22
Corcoran Gallery, 21
Daughters of the American Revolution, 24
Decatur House, 11
Department of the Interior, 23
Eisenhower Executive Office Building, 19
The Kennedy Center, 16
National Academy of Sciences, 25
The Octagon, 18
Organization of American States, 26
Pershing Park Ice Rink, 27
Renwick Gallery, 12
St. John's Church, 10
State Department, 22
The Watergate Complex, 14
The White House, 20
The White House Visitors Center, 28

Foggy Bottom

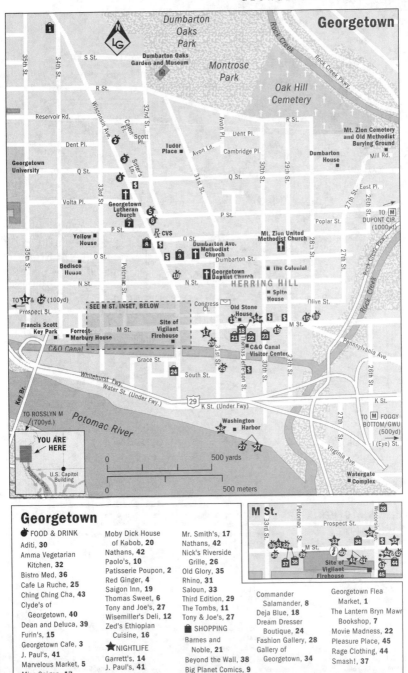

Georgetown

🍴 FOOD & DRINK

Aditi, **30**
Amma Vegetarian
 Kitchen, **32**
Bistro Med, **36**
Cafe La Ruche, **25**
Ching Ching Cha, **43**
Clyde's of
 Georgetown, **40**
Dean and Deluca, **39**
Furin's, **15**
Georgetown Cafe, **3**
J. Paul's, **41**
Marvelous Market, **5**
Miss Saigon, **13**

Moby Dick House
 of Kabob, **20**
Nathans, **42**
Paolo's, **10**
Patisserie Poupon, **2**
Red Ginger, **4**
Saigon Inn, **19**
Thomas Sweet, **6**
Tony and Joe's, **27**
Wisemiller's Deli, **12**
Zed's Ethiopian
 Cuisine, **16**

⭐ NIGHTLIFE

Garrett's, **14**
J. Paul's, **41**

Mr. Smith's, **17**
Nathans, **42**
Nick's Riverside
 Grille, **26**
Old Glory, **35**
Rhino, **31**
Saloun, **33**
Third Edition, **29**
The Tombs, **11**
Tony & Joe's, **27**

🛍 SHOPPING

Barnes and
 Noble, **21**
Beyond the Wall, **38**
Big Planet Comics, **9**
CD Warehouse, **33**

Commander
 Salamander, **8**
Deja Blue, **18**
Dream Dresser
 Boutique, **24**
Fashion Gallery, **28**
Gallery of
 Georgetown, **34**

Georgetown Flea
 Market, **1**
The Lantern Bryn Mawr
 Bookshop, **7**
Movie Madness, **22**
Pleasure Place, **45**
Rage Clothing, **44**
Smash!, **37**

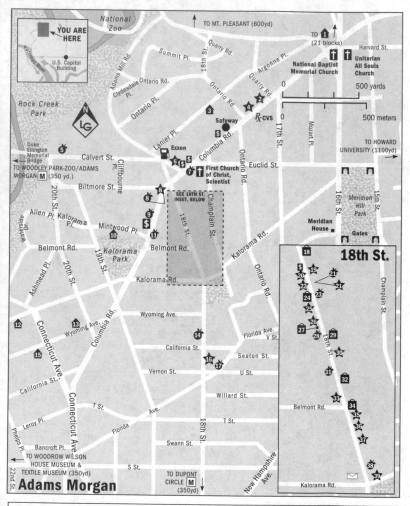

Adams Morgan

🏠 ACCOMMODATIONS
Adams Inn, **3**
International Guest House, **1**
Jury's Normandy Inn, **15**
Kalorama Guest House at Kalorama
Park, **10**
Taft Bridge Inn, **13**
Windsor Park Hotel, **12**

🍴 FOOD & DRINK
Addis Ababa, **14**
The Diner, **23**
El Tamarindo, **17**
The Grill from Ipanema, **11**
La Frontera Grill and Bar, **8**

Mama Ayesha's Restaurant, **5**
Meskerem, **28**
New Orleans Cafe, **31**
Pasta Mia Trattoria, **7**
Saigonnais, **38**
So's Your Mom, **9**
Tryst, **21**

⭐ NIGHTLIFE
Adams Mill Bar and Grill, **6**
Angry Inch, **20**
Blue Room, **36**
Brass Monkey, **37**
Bukom Cafe, **25**
Chief Ike's Mambo Room, **4**
Heaven and Hell, **35**
The Common Share, **16**

Felix and the Spy Lounge, **33**
Kokopooli's, **39**
La Frontera Grill and Bar, **8**
Latin Jazz Alley, **2**
Madam's Organ, **19**
Millie & Al's, **26**
The Reef, **22**
Toledo Lounge, **30**
Tryst, **21**

🛍 SHOPPING
All About Jane, **27**
DC CD, **32**
Idle Time Books, **18**
Kobos Afrikan Clothiers, **24**
Paula's Imports, **34**
Shake your Booty, **29**

Shaw/U District

🍴 FOOD & DRINK

Ben's Chili Bowl, **16**
Cafe Saint-Ex, **11**
CakeLove, **8**
Florida Avenue Grill, **18**
The Islander, **17**
Local 16, **2**
Polly's Cafe, **13**
Tropicana, **22**
Wilson's, **23**

⭐ NIGHTLIFE

2:K:9 **21**
9:30 Club, **20**
Bar Nun/Club 2000, **15**
The Black Cat, **12**
Cada Vez, **9**
Cafe Nema, **14**
Cafe Saint-Ex, **11**
Chi Cha Lounge, **1**
Loca 16, **2**
U-topia, **10**
Velvet Lounge, **19**

🛍 SHOPPING

Meeps Fashionette, **5**
Millennium, **4**
Nana, **3**
Sisterspace and Books, **7**
Wild Women Wear Red, **6**
Willies, **24**

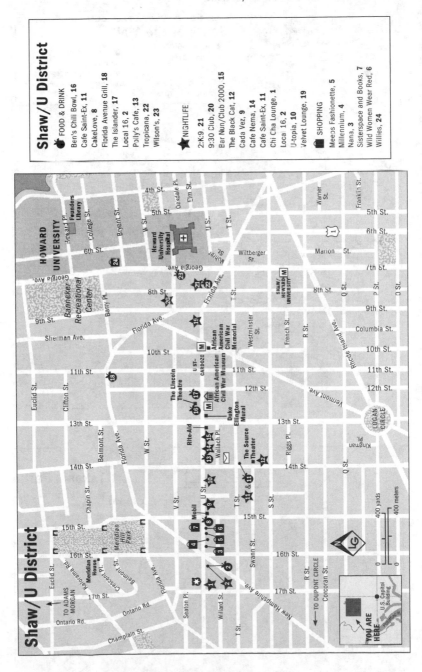

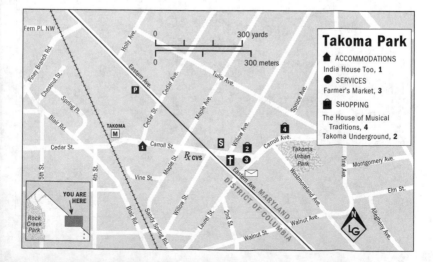

Northeast Overview

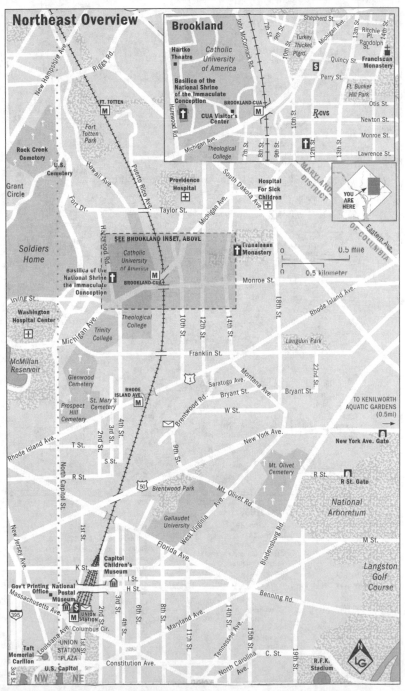

Brookland

Hartke Theatre

Catholic University of America

Basilica of the National Shrine of the Immaculate Conception

CUA Visitor's Center

Shepherd St.

Turkey Thicket Plgrd.

Franciscan Monastery

Ft. Bunker Hill Park

Quincy St.

Perry St.

BROOKLAND-CUA

Rovs

Otis St.

Newton St.

Monroe St.

Lawrence St.

Michigan Ave.

Theological College

John McCormack Rd.

7th St.

8th St.

9th St.

10th St.

12th St.

13th St.

14th St.

Ritchie Pl.

Randolph St.

Harewood Rd.

FT. TOTTEN

New Hampshire Ave.

Riggs Rd.

Fort Totten Park

Rock Creek Cemetery

U.S. Cemetery

Grant Circle

Hawaii Ave.

Fort Dr.

Puerto Rico Ave.

Soldiers Home

Providence Hospital

Hospital For Sick Children

South Dakota Ave.

Michigan Ave.

Taylor St.

MARYLAND

DISTRICT

YOU ARE HERE

OF COLUMBIA

Eastern Ave.

SEE BROOKLAND INSET, ABOVE

Catholic University of America

Basilica of the National Shrine the Immaculate Conception

BROOKLAND-CUA

Franciscan Monastery

Monroe St.

0   0.5 mile

0   0.5 kilometer

Harewood Rd.

Theological College

Washington Hospital Center

Irving St.

Michigan Ave.

Trinity College

McMillan Reservoir

Glenwood Cemetery

Prospect Hill Cemetery

St. Mary's Cemetery

RHODE ISLAND AVE.

4th St.

3rd St.

2nd St.

Rhode Island Ave.

T St.

S St.

R St.

10th St.

12th St.

14th St.

18th St.

Rhode Island Ave.

Langdon Park

22nd St.

Franklin St.

Saratoga Ave.

Montana Ave.

Bryant St.

Bryant St.

W St.

Brentwood Rd.

9th St.

New York Ave.

TO KENILWORTH AQUATIC GARDENS (0.5mi)

New York Ave. Gate

Brentwood Park

Mt. Olivet Cemetery

Mt. Olivet Rd.

R St.

R St. Gate

North Capitol St.

1st St.

Gallaudet University

West Virginia Ave.

Bladensburg Rd.

National Arboretum

New Jersey Ave.

Florida Ave.

M St.

Langston Golf Course

Capitol Children's Museum

Gov't Printing Office

National Postal Museum

Massachusetts Ave.

K St.

UNION STATION

Columbus Cir.

I St.

H St.

3rd St.

4th St.

6th St.

8th St.

Maryland Ave.

11th St.

Benning Rd.

Louisiana Ave.

UNION STATION PLAZA

Taft Memorial Carillon

U.S. Capitol

3rd St.

Constitution Ave.

Tennessee Ave.

North Carolina Ave.

C. St.

14th St.

15th St.

19th St.

R.F.K. Stadium

NW   NE

N

LG

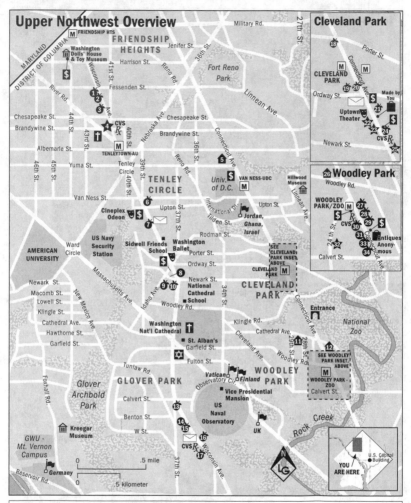

Upper Northwest Overview

🏠 ACCOMMODATIONS
Boston University Washington Center, **12**
Days Inn, **5**
Kalorama Guest House at Woodley Park, **11**
Woodley Park Guest House, **26**

🍴 FOOD & DRINK
2 Amys Neapolitan Pizzeria, **9**
49 Twelve Thai Cuisine, **2**
a.k.a. Frisco's, **6**
Alero, **19**
Cactus Cantina, **10**
Cafe Ole, **7**
Chipotle Mexican Grill, **34**

Faccia Luna, **15**
Jandara, **33**
Lebanese Taverna, **28**
Mama Maria and Enzio's, **16**
Matisse Restaurant, **1**
Medaterra, **30**
Nam-Viet Pho 79, **21**
Old Europe, **13**
Saigon Gourmet Restaurant, **29**
Saveur Restaurant, **17**
Spices Asian Restaurant & Sushi Bar, **24**
Trattoria Italiana, **27**
Yanni's, **20**
Yenching Palace, **18**
Yosaku, **3**

⭐ NIGHTLIFE
The Aroma Company, **22**
Babe's Billiards Cafe, **4**
Ireland's Four Provinces, **23**
Murphy's of D.C., **32**
Nanny O'Brien's, **25**

● SERVICES
Laundromat, **8**
Laundromat, **31**
Laundromat, **14**

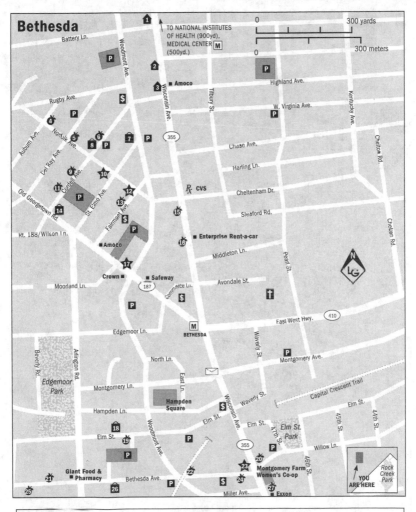

Bethesda

To National Institutes of Health (900yd), Medical Center M (500yd.)

0 — 300 yards
0 — 300 meters

Battery Ln.
Woodmont Ave.
Highland Ave.
Kentucky Ave.
■ Amoco
Tilbury St.
W. Virginia Ave.
Rugby Ave.
Wisconsin Ave.
Chelton Rd.
Chase Ave.
Norfolk Ave.
Auburn Ave.
Del Ray Ave.
Harling Ln.
Cheltenham Dr.
Old Georgetown Rd.
Cordell Ave.
St. Elmo Ave.
Fairmont Ave.
℞ CVS
Sleaford Rd.
Rt. 188/Wilson Ln.
■ Amoco
■ Enterprise Rent-a-car
Middleton Ln.
Pearl St.
Chelton Rd.
N LG
Crown ■
■ Safeway
Moorland Ln.
Avondale St.
Commerce Ln.
Edgemoor Ln.
East West Hwy.
410
M BETHESDA
North Ln.
Montgomery Ave.
Beverly Rd.
Arlington Rd.
Edgemoor Park
Montgomery Ln.
East Ln.
Waverly St.
Capital Crescent Trail
Elm St.
45th St.
44th St.
Hampden Ln.
Hampden Square
Woodmont Ave.
Elm St.
Wisconsin Ave.
Elm St.
47th St.
Elm St. Park
Willow Ln.
46th St.
Rock Creek Park
YOU ARE HERE
18
Elm St.
19
Giant Food & ■ Pharmacy
21
25
Bethesda Ave.
22
26
Montgomery Farm Women's Co-op
23
24
20
■ Exxon
Miller Ave.

Bethesda

🏠 **ACCOMMODATIONS**
American Inn of Bethesda, **2**
Holiday Inn Select, **3**
Sheraton Four Points, **1**

🍴 **FOOD & DRINK**
Bacchus, **5**
bd's Mongolian BBQ, **20**
Bethesda Crab House, **25**
Bob's Famous Homemade Ice Cream, **24**
Cafe Deluxe, **19**
Grapeseed, **6**
La Panetteria, **9**

Louisiana Express, **21**
Paradise Restaurant, **27**
Philadelphia Mike's, **16**
Rio Grande Cafe, **13**
Steamer's Seafood House, **4**
Tako Grill, **15**
Thyme Square Cafe, **22**
Tragara, **11**

⭐ **NIGHTLIFE**
Flanagan's Irish Pub, **17**
Montgomery's Grille, **23**
Rock Bottom Brewery, **10**
Willie & Reed's, **12**

🛍 SHOPPING
Designer Resale, **7**
Made by You, **18**
Night Dreams, **8**
Pla-za, **14**
Second Story Books, **26**

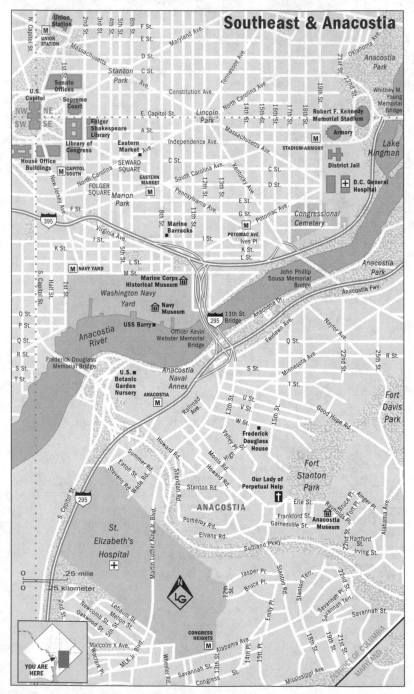

Southeast & Anacostia

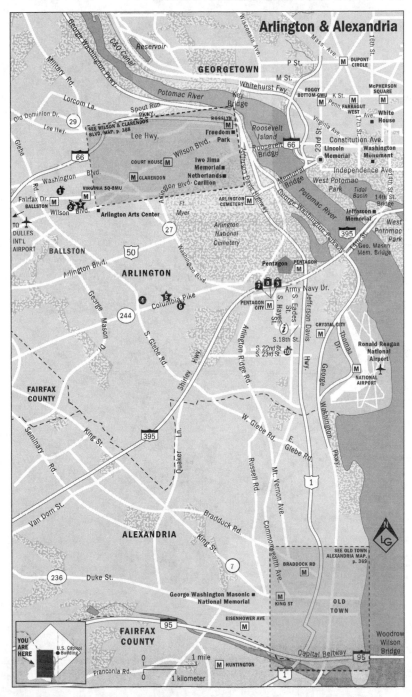

Arlington & Alexandria

Arlington & Alexandria SEE MAP ON PAGE 367

🍴 FOOD & DRINK
Bob & Edith's Diner, **6**
Crystal Pallas Cafe & Grill, **10**
Food Factory, **1**
Rocklands, **2**

⭐ NIGHTLIFE
Arlington Cinema 'N'
Drafthouse, **5**
Carpool, **3**

🛍 SHOPPING
Fashion Centre at Pentagon
City, **7**

Macy's, **8**
Nordstrom, **9**

⬤ SERVICES
Laundromat, **4**

Wilson & Clarendon Blvd.

🏠 ACCOMMODATIONS
Highlander Motor Inn, **1**
Holiday Inn Rosslyn at Key Bridge, **19**
Inn at Rosslyn, **16**
Quality Inn Iwo Jima, **17**

🍴 FOOD & DRINK
Asahi Japanese Restaurant, **14**
Boulevard Woodgrill, **5**
Cafe Asia, **18**

Delhi Dhaba, **12**
Hard Times Cafe, **4**
The Java Shack, **12**
Lazy Sundae, **6**
RT's Seafood Kitchen, **13**

⭐ NIGHTLIFE
Clarendon Grill, **3**
Galaxy Hut, **10**
Iota, **8**
Ireland's Four Courts, **15**
Mister Days, **2**
Whitlow's on Wilson, **7**

⬤ SERVICES
Whole Foods Market, **9**

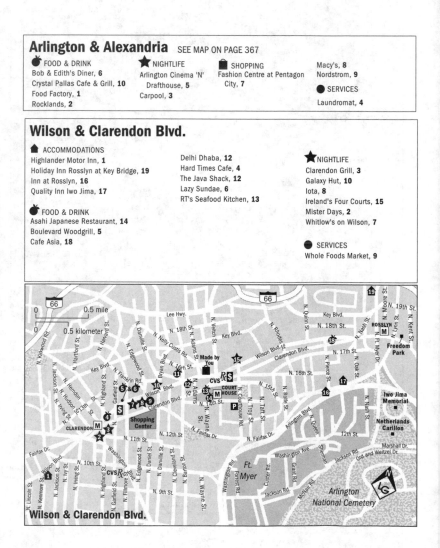

Wilson & Clarendon Blvd.

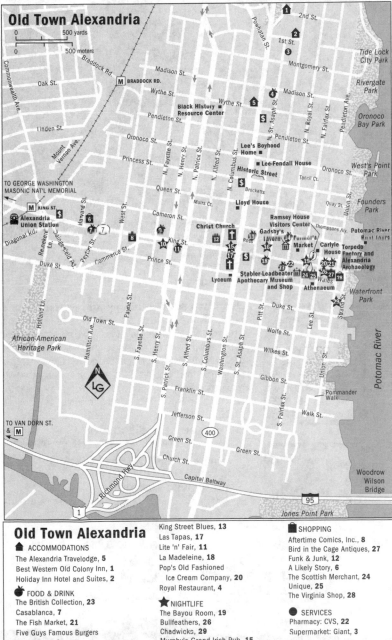

Old Town Alexandria

ACCOMMODATIONS

The Alexandria Travelodge, **5**
Best Western Old Colony Inn, **1**
Holiday Inn Hotel and Suites, **2**

FOOD & DRINK

The British Collection, **23**
Casablanca, **7**
The Fish Market, **21**
Five Guys Famous Burgers
  and Fries, **9**
Gadsby's Tavern, **14**

King Street Blues, **13**
Las Tapas, **17**
Lite 'n' Fair, **11**
La Madeleine, **18**
Pop's Old Fashioned
  Ice Cream Company, **20**
Royal Restaurant, **4**

NIGHTLIFE

The Bayou Room, **19**
Bullfeathers, **26**
Chadwicks, **29**
Murphy's Grand Irish Pub, **15**
Pat Troy's, **16**
Tiffany Tavern, **10**

SHOPPING

Aftertime Comics, Inc., **8**
Bird in the Cage Antiques, **27**
Funk & Junk, **12**
A Likely Story, **6**
The Scottish Merchant, **24**
Unique, **25**
The Virginia Shop, **28**

SERVICES

Pharmacy: CVS, **22**
Supermarket: Giant, **3**

the ultimate
road trip

don't trip out planning your big road trip.
put contiki in the driver's seat with a hassle-free vacations designed for 18 to 35 year olds. make new friends, enjoy your free time and explore the sights in a convenient vacation that gives you more bang for your buck... **from only $70/day** including accommodations, sightseeing, many meals and transportation. with contiki leading the way, you can leave the road map at home!

> **7 days eastern discovery**
new york, washington d.c., us naval academy, kennedy space center

> **10 days canada & the rockies**
vancouver, calgary, banff national park

> **13 days wild western**
san francisco, grand canyon, las vegas, yosemite national park

*prices subject to change, land only.

for more info on our trips...
see your travel agent
call 1-888-CONTIKI
visit www.contiki.com

contiki
VACATIONS for 18-35 year olds

CST# 1001728-20

> **europe** > **australia** > **new zealand** > **america** > **canada**

FOUR-STAR HOTEL PAID FOR WITH MONEY FOUND IN COUCH.

Save up to 70%
on great hotels
with OrbitzSaver rates.*

©2003 Orbitz, LLC. CST# 2063530-50 *Savings based on comparison with published rack rates.

Discover Washington
with Hostelling International

Get into the groove with Hostelling International-USA. With over 110 locations, we offer the largest network of quality hostel accommodations in America.

HI-Washington DC is centrally located to help you experience the diversity and splendor of this geat city. We're within walking distance of the White House, Capitol, Smithsonian Museums, Chinatown, as well as theatres and restaurants. All you'll need is time to explore.

Make our great rates and warm welcome your first discovery when you visit Washington, DC!

For more information about HI-Washington DC, or our hostels throughout the USA, visit: www.hiusa.org

For reservations email: reserve@hiwashingtondc.org or call (202) 737-2333